ETHEL IN THE WORDS OF THOSE WHO HAVE KNOWN HER...

'Ethel's a baby-making machine—wind her up and she becomes pregnant."
—*Jacqueline Kennedy Onassis*

'Ethel Kennedy has the mind-set of a vulture. She's the most highly competitive and insanely jealous human being I have ever met."
—*Truman Capote*

'Life at home was mayhem, a mess. My mother was always having screaming rages. She didn't know how to deal with so many kids."
—*David Kennedy*

'If somebody crossed Bobby, she gave you the kiss of death."
—*Retired Judge George Tremblay*

"I came to realize that it was a professional mistake to have gotten close to Ethel."
—*Newscaster Roger Mudd*

Ethel was formally introduced to Bobby by his sister Jean during the winter of their freshman year at Manhattanville. Jean had grown so fond of Ethel that she actually wanted her to become part of the Kennedy family—and so did Ethel, with a vengeance. The two girls, along with various friends and family members, had gone to Mont Tremblant for a ski weekend. Jean had a strong feeling that Bobby and Ethel would instantly hit it off. But she was wrong. It was actually Jean's brother Jack who made Ethel swoon.

"Ethel came back to Manhattanville from that ski trip and she was insane about Jack," recalled Margaret Geoghegan Adams. "She talked to me about him non-stop; not just me, the world! She was nuts about him and didn't think that much of Bobby. 'Jack's so handsome, so glamorous,' she said. Ethel felt Jack had much more wit and pizzazz, and that Bobby was too shy."

But a member of Ethel's circle advised: "You're definitely not Jack's type." Ethel quickly came to that realization, too. Unlike Bobby, Jack was a man of the world, pursuing glamorous women, about to embark on a triumphant political career. Ethel, a skinny college kid, made no impression on him whatsoever.

At the time of the ski weekend, Ethel knew Bobby slightly because he'd had occasional, informal dates with her sister Pat, and had been in and out of the Skakel home. Ethel had also seen him at the Kennedys' in Hyannis Port and in Palm Beach during visits with Jean. But Bobby never paid much notice to Ethel, and she harbored no secret fantasies about him.

It would take a while for the two of them to click. . . .

ALSO BY JERRY OPPENHEIMER

Barbara Walters: An Unauthorized Biography

Idol: Rock Hudson, The True Story of an American Film Hero

THE OTHER MRS. KENNEDY

JERRY OPPENHEIMER

THE OTHER MRS. KENNEDY: ETHEL SKAKEL KENNEDY: AN AMERICAN DRAMA OF POWER, PRIVILEGE, AND POLITICS

Cover photographs courtesy Black Star.

Stepback photograph credits: Ethel on horse, courtesy Georgeann Dowdle; with Bill Clinton, AP/Wide World; Bobby and Jackie, AP/Wide World; Ambassador Hotel, UPI/Bettmann; Wedding, UPI/Bettmann; Ethel with Ted and Joan, UPI/Bettmann; with Andy Williams, Archive Photos; at Bobby's funeral, Archive Photos/Archive France.

Library of Congress Catalog Card Number: 94-6279

ISBN: 0-312-95600-2

Printed in the United States of America

St. Martin's Press hardcover edition/September 1994
St. Martin's Paperbacks edition/May 1995

10 9 8 7 6 5 4 3 2

For D. L. O.

Acknowledgments

I'M INDEBTED TO literally hundreds of people who agreed, in one way or another, to help in what turned out to be a much more complex endeavor than I had initially projected. This book took four years of research, writing, and editing. It was supposed to have taken two. It could not have been accomplished without the goodwill, generosity, and dedication of relatives, friends, and colleagues of Ethel Skakel Kennedy who, instead of taking the easy way out by saying no to me, decided that the true story of this extraordinary woman should finally be told.

Many initially questioned the unauthorized nature of the book. But they also realized that their very private friend would never document her life in writing. This biography, they finally came to see, would likely be the only written record in which to dispel the myths and misconceptions, to set the record straight.

My goal was to write an objective portrait of Mrs. Kennedy, to allow the readers to make up their minds. In this effort, I was assisted by countless sources, most of whom agreed to talk on the record for the first time. I am also indebted to those who, for various reasons, asked for and were granted anonymity.

George Skakel, Sr., Ethel's father, was a brilliant but uneducated man who built from scratch one of the largest privately held corporations in America. Through the years he eschewed any form of self-promotion or publicity. "You can't quote silence," was his philosophy. This he handed down to his seven children. For Ethel, who became a public person in 1950 when she married

Bobby Kennedy, being in the public eye has always been a struggle.

Over the years, though, her relatives on the Skakel side were able to maintain their anonymity, much as George Skakel had done. However, many agreed to break their long, self-imposed silence and cooperate with me in the writing of this book.

In particular, I want to thank Ethel's brothers, Jim and Rushton Skakel, and their wives, Virginia and Anna Mae. I owe a great deal of gratitude to Ethel's niece Georgeann Dowdle; Ethel's brother-in-law George Terrien (who passed away as the book neared completion); a former brother-in-law, John McCooey, and Ethel's first cousins Bob Skakel and Betty Skakel Medaille. I thank each and every one of them for sharing candid, insightful, and perceptive anecdotes about Ethel, Bobby, the Skakel family, and the Kennedy clan. Their revelations about early Skakel family history, and Skakel family triumphs and tragedies, added so much to this story and shed greater light on Ethel's persona. I am also indebted to Jim and Virginia, and Georgeann, for permission to publish Skakel family photographs.

Others close to the Skakel family whom I thank for offering their time and information include but is not limited to: Mary Begley, Martin McKneally (who passed away near the completion of the book), and Florence Kumpfer.

Dozens of Skakel friends from the family's early days in Greenwich, Connecticut, and scores of Ethel's pals from her youth—elementary school through college—agreed to be interviewed, and their insights and anecdotes added enormously to this portrait. I thank all of you.

Ethel's marriage to Bobby brought about a drastic change in her life. For almost two decades—from Bobby's early days as a young lawyer in Washington working for the infamous Senator Joseph McCarthy, through Camelot, his Senate term, and his ill-fated 1968 Presidential campaign—Ethel was at the center of a high-powered group often referred to as the "best and the brightest."

Scores of people who were part of Ethel's life during those years—friends, journalists, celebrities—shared their reminiscences with me. I am forever grateful.

More than a quarter-century has passed since that fateful day in Los Angeles when the light of Ethel's existence was snuffed out. I interviewed dozens of eyewitnesses to Ethel's life during those tragic and sensitive years. To all of them, I owe my heartfelt thanks for their forthrightness.

For her help in conducting the research for this book, I want to express a special thanks to Caroline Walton Howe, who worked untold hours tracking down and interviewing dozens of long-lost sources. Steve Hammons was instrumental in searching out obscure documents, published articles, names and telephone numbers. In his research in Greenwich, Mike Hoffman found everything that needed to be found, and more. Numerous sources pointed me in the right direction. You know who you are. Thank you.

Throughout this project Judy Oppenheimer has been a great supporter, often taking away valuable time from her own writing projects to offer advice and counsel. Her editorial direction regarding the writing and organization could never be surpassed. Her deft touch on early drafts of the manuscript made the later stages go so much smoother.

I'd like to thank Stuart Krichevsky, my agent at Sterling Lord Literistic, who smoothed the way throughout the process.

The team at St. Martin's Press was impressive for helping guide this book to completion. In particular, I'm grateful to Tom McCormack, Sally Richardson, David Kaye, Paul Sleven, John Murphy, Meg Drislane, Karen Thompson, and Tory Foran. My editor, Charles Spicer, has won my everlasting respect for his creative talents, his enthusiasm and energy. He is a rarity in publishing.

And my love to my sons, Jesse and Toby.

Contents

SKAKEL FAMILY TREE

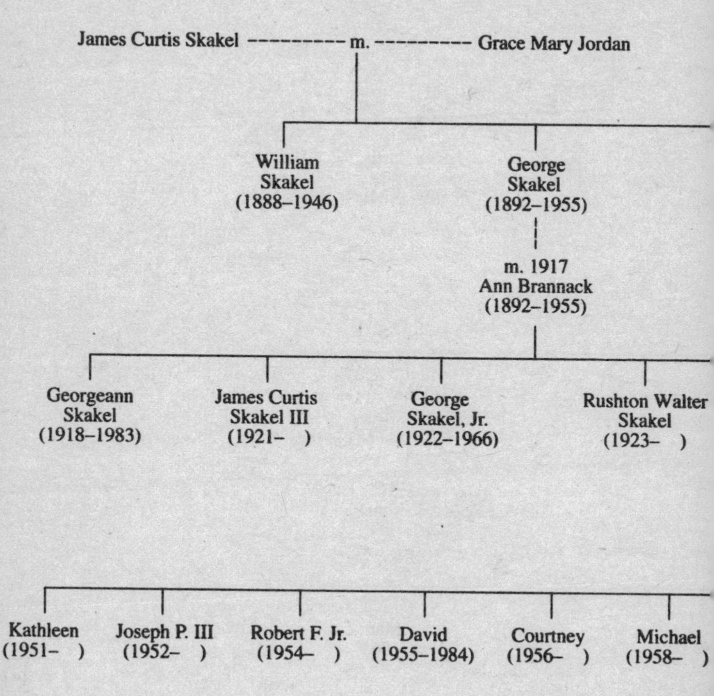

Margaret
Skakel
(1894–1983)
James Curtis
Skakel, Jr.
(1899–1984)

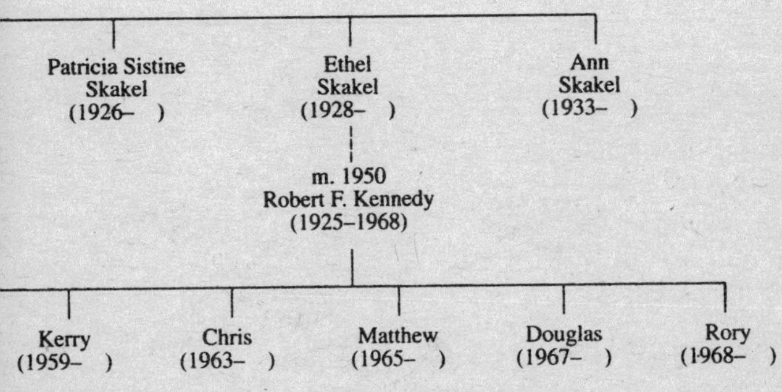
Patricia Sistine
Skakel
(1926–)
Ethel
Skakel
(1928–)
Ann
Skakel
(1933–)
m. 1950
Robert F. Kennedy
(1925–1968)
Kerry
(1959–)
Chris
(1963–)
Matthew
(1965–)
Douglas
(1967–)
Rory
(1968–)

"All history is gossip."
—PRESIDENT JOHN F. KENNEDY

PART I

Beginnings

1 ✻ *Yazoo County, Mississippi*

ETHEL SKAKEL KENNEDY'S roots are buried deep in the plantation life and cotton fields of Mississippi.

Her paternal great-grandfather, German Nicholas Jordan, was a playboy and gigolo who became a slave- and landowner by marrying wealthy young women, one of whom he practically shanghaied from a convent.

Born in Campbell County, Virginia, on August 20, 1828, German Jordan was the eighth of eleven children. The only descendant who would ever match his parents' prolific birthing record would be Ethel, some one hundred and forty years later.

Most of the Jordans and their relatives through marriage were hardworking, hellfire-and-brimstone Baptists who believed that "a little more sleep, a little more slumber; so cometh destruction upon us." German Jordan was the exception. A handsome and charming ladies' man, he had never done an honest day's work in his life and proudly displayed his uncallused hands to friends to prove it.

In 1853, at the age of twenty-five, Jordan traveled to Washington, D.C., where he met Mary Roach, a native of Natchez, Mississippi, who suited Jordan's purposes perfectly. Not only did her family own a sprawling plantation called Tallulah in Yazoo County, Mississippi, but Mary was beautiful. She liked older men and they fell for each other instantly, Jordan for pragmatic reasons—her money; Mary, for romantic ones. There were, however, a couple of hitches in their love story. The first was that Mary was only fifteen, and the second was that her parents had placed her in a convent.

But the cloistered nuns didn't have a chance. After a brief courtship, Mary crept out one night and met her lover on the nearby banks of the Potomac River, where he was waiting under a moonlit sky with a rowboat and a friend. A few days later Mary Roach became the first Mrs. German Jordan. Not long after, the young marrieds arrived to take up residence on the Roach plantation, to the extreme displeasure of Mary's parents, who considered their new son-in-law to be nothing more than a gold digger.

Located near the Mississippi, not far from the Arkansas-Louisiana border, Yazoo was a lively, social place. Political barbecues, traveling magicians, freak shows, horse racing, and numerous tippling houses kept local cotton growers entertained. Slave sales were popular weekly events. Newspapers often published lists of the runaways; those caught were either whipped or branded.

Mary was soon pregnant, but mother and twin babies died on the delivery table. German Jordan, who inherited his wife's plantation and slaves, overnight joined Mississippi's landed gentry.

His next target was pretty Sarah Virginia Hendricks, a virginal eighteen, a student at Emma Willard's Female Institute in Troy, New York. Sarah fell under Jordan's spell on a Mississippi River steamboat. The daughter of a prominent New Brunswick, New Jersey, lawyer who had settled in Yazoo, she was as wealthy as her predecessor. On July 2, 1856, Sarah became the second Mrs. German Jordan.

In six years, Sarah had two daughters and a son. Her first, Grace Mary Jordan, born November 5, 1858, was Ethel Kennedy's paternal grandmother. When Gracie was eleven, her mother died of pneumonia.

The outbreak of the Civil War in 1861, and Lincoln's Emancipation Proclamation in 1863, turned the Jordans' world upside down. During 1863–64, Yazoo County became a bloody battlefield. Fearing for their safety, the Jordans abandoned Tallulah and fled to Winchester, Virginia, where some three decades earlier an entrepreneurial member of the Jordan family, Branch Jordan, had established a fashionable health resort called Jordan White Sulphur Springs. The resort's two hotels had been converted into hospitals for whichever army had possession of the area.

Most of the Jordans moved on, but Gracie stayed with her uncle and aunt, Ed and Belle Jordan, who were now running the place. Meanwhile, Gracie's father went in search of another wealthy, attractive, and younger woman, the widowed Mrs. Mary Wootington Rodell Nolan of Baltimore, a descendant of Lord Nelson. The third Mrs. German Jordan, however, outlived her husband, who died at age sixty-one on October 30, 1888, at his home at 606 Charles Street in Baltimore. His obituary in the Winchester, Virginia, *Times* described "a gentleman of fine intelligence, polished manners and . . . excellent traits of character."

After the war, and some schooling, Gracie made her way north and west from Virginia, living off a small inheritance.

2 ✳ *Alcohol, Bigotry, and Racism*

IN CHICAGO, GRACE Mary Jordan met James Curtis Skakel. They fell in love and got married in 1885, when she was twenty-seven and he was thirty-five. Her family was furious. The Jordans could not condone the fact that Gracie's husband was a damned Yankee. As a result, she was ostracized by her people and lost all contact with them.

Curt and Gracie made an attractive couple. Gracie's oval face was framed by shiny dark brown hair parted in the middle. Her lips were full, her eyes almond in shape, her tiny nose upturned. Though taller than Gracie's four feet ten inches, Curt stood only five feet six inches. He was thin and sported a pompadour of fluffy dark brown hair and a goatee. His piercing dark brown eyes would eventually render him nearly blind because of a severe case of nearsightedness. Skakel's eyesight, however, would be the least of the couple's problems.

Curt was born on November 18, 1850, in Canada, the seventh and last child of George Skakel and Sarah Sawyer Skakel, an Englishwoman. His sisters—Dicey, Bess, Hattie, and Maggie—were housekeepers extraordinaire. They each had at least four sets of china—everyday china, Sunday china, celebration china, and china that never saw the light of day—all stacked neatly in cupboards. One of their specialties was jelly with a rose preserved in each jar. All of the early Skakels were farmers.

By the time Curt and Gracie got married, he was an alcoholic, physically and verbally abusive when he drank. Skakel's temperament was volatile, and he had a contemptuous air about him and a certain roughness of manner. These were traits, along with the drinking, that some members of Ethel's generation of Skakels would inherit.

Curt Skakel was also a strict Protestant and a bigot who denounced Catholics and Jews with equal ferocity. While Gracie, an Episcopalian, quickly grew to fear and despise Curt's drinking, she avidly shared his prejudices. Though sweet, refined, petite, and with a lovely drawl and a beautiful command of the English language, Gracie was a racist who railed against the freeing of the slaves and exuberantly supported the Ku Klux Klan.

"The Skakels were the kind of Protestants who believed that nuns and priests carried on, and that the basements of convents were full of baby bones from the illegitimate births of nuns," a descendant would say. "The Skakels were quite sure that the confessional was a sure way to hell."

For more than seven years, Curt and Gracie lived in Chicago, where he tried his hand at a variety of jobs and businesses, failing miserably at all of them. During that time Skakel fathered three children: William, born on November 30, 1888; George, who would become Ethel's father, born July 16, 1892; and Margaret Virginia Skakel, born October 18, 1894. Years later, Margaret Skakel observed that "the family fortunes were low, there are no two ways about it, because of whiskey. Dad would, but seemingly would not, shake its hold upon him. A good business that had been built up by vigorous planning and energetic and arduous effort would go to pieces."

Ethel's father and his siblings often saw their father swear and hit their mother when he was drinking. What's more, they were inculcated with their parents' religious and racial prejudices.

Ethel's first cousin Betty Skakel Medaille, daughter of Curt and Gracie's firstborn, William, asserted that her father was brought up to be "a violently anti-Catholic Protestant." She said: "It was a parody in contempt. My father knew nothing about the rituals, or the Church. He just blindly hated Catholics. An anti-Jewish attitude was also common. He wasn't overly fond of blacks, either. My father's hate was something he was raised with."

Gracie's daughter Margaret—Ethel's aunt—passionately and blindly hated blacks. In her writings, Margaret referred to a black person whom she knew as "old darky." In one letter to Ethel, Margaret used a curiously racial metaphor to underscore how her genealogical work involving the Skakel family was so complex that it felt like a ride to nowhere on a carousel. "This reminds me of the story about the darky who was crazy about riding on the merry-go-round," Margaret wrote. "His mother said to him, 'Now you spent yo-ah money, whar you bin?' "

Said Medaille: "Aunt Margaret, whose nearest experience to the South, I believe, was having once lived in Illinois, had a terrifically anti-black prejudice. Blacks revolted her. Her attitude was that they were an alien people, and by alien I mean nonearthly. The Skakel children—my father, Bill; Ethel's father, George; Aunt Margaret—were all raised with those prejudices."

Medaille's views were supported by another first cousin of Ethel's, Bob Skakel, whose father was the last of Curt and Gracie's four children. Bob Skakel often stayed with his aunt Margaret and grandmother Gracie and was his grandmother's favorite.

"She used to talk on and on about how proud she was of making hoods and sewing the sheets for the Klansmen right after the Civil War," Bob Skakel said. "There was a point in time when my own father was very prejudiced." Bob Skakel's mother, Doris, described her husband, whom she later divorced, as "a bigot." She said, "That's one of the reasons the marriage ended."

After Grace Mary Skakel's death, Margaret recounted with delight for her nieces and nephews the stories her mother told her about growing up in the South.

"White women just didn't do any work because they had colored slaves to do it for them," Margaret Skakel said. "But after the war, many of the slaves walked off. Mother used to say that many white women who hadn't so much as dressed themselves were forced to go into the fields and pick the cotton and cut the tobacco. It just goes to show that we never know what we would do if we were confronted with a certain situation."

3 * Billy "The Clock" Skakel

BECAUSE OF HIS drinking, Curt Skakel began to rely heavily on his older brother Bill for financial and moral support. Billy "The Clock" Skakel, Ethel's paternal great-uncle, was the most successful and colorful of his generation.

Skakel had fought against Gracie's South in the Civil

War. He was mustered out in Baltimore, where he had gotten a job as a bricklayer, but laying bets interested him more than laying bricks. Skakel took his savings back to Chicago and opened a gambling house of his own that became an overnight success.

He also had suspected interests in bawdy houses, and owned a monopoly in a financial scam known as "bucket shops." Each day Skakel's employees put together stock quotations supposedly based on actual trading in western mining shares. But the numbers were bogus—something the players, who bet on whether the next figures would be higher or lower, didn't know. Billy Skakel took twenty-five cents on every two dollars bet. The quarters added up because as many as a thousand bets were made daily.

Years later, when Ethel discovered that she had a penchant for politics after her marriage into the Kennedy family, her interest could be traced back directly to her great-uncle Billy, whose questionable moneymaking operations were tied to his role as a power in Chicago's Democratic machine.

Skakel ran with the likes of the legendary Michael "Bathhouse John" Coughlin and Michael "Hinky Dink" Kenna, the corrupt bosses of the Windy City's vice-saturated First Ward, who ruled from 1890 to 1940.

Skakel was a shrewd and tough politician, known for putting together political armies of toughs and saloon-keepers who'd show up at campaign appearances of opponents, staging fistfights and brawls. In 1894, Skakel ran unsuccessfully against Coughlin for the powerful job of alderman of the First Ward, despite the fact that an influential local publication, *Mixed Drinks: The Saloon Keeper's Journal*, threw its support behind him.

Billy Skakel had made numerous investments with his ill-gotten funds. He had bought large tracts of land in South Dakota from the U.S. government at homesteader prices. And by the late 1880s and early 1890s he owned three ranches there. Skakel was devoted to his brothers and sisters but gave the most assistance to the alcoholic

Curt—five years Billy's junior—who was having a hard time making a go of it with Gracie and the three children.

Billy Skakel, who would eventually have a hand in raising Ethel's father, decided that Curt would be better off away from the gin mills of Chicago, so he arranged to have a ranch house built on some of his land in South Dakota. After some coaxing, Curt agreed to move there with Gracie and the children. He promised his brother he'd run the spread and go on the wagon.

4 ✻ Ranch Life

IN FEBRUARY 1896, the family moved to the 640-acre Skakel ranch, located near a dot on the map known as Tyndall, in southeastern South Dakota, not far from the Missouri River. The seat of government of Bon Homme County, Tyndall was a grim place, with wooden sidewalks, one-story wood-frame stores, a two-block-long, unpaved Main Street, and a station for the Sioux City, Iowa–Yankton, South Dakota, branch of the Chicago, Milwaukee & St. Paul Railway. Without the railroad, there probably wouldn't have been a Tyndall, which was only seventeen years old when the Skakels arrived.

Many of the Irish who built the railroad stayed, but the biggest group of newcomers were German and Czechoslovakian immigrants. They were merchants and farmers who grew corn, oats, and barley. Like Curt and Gracie Skakel, they'd come from Chicago to find a new life. The immigrants were wide-eyed optimists who were still learning the language, newly sworn U.S. citizens with names like Vavruska and Petrik, Hanrahan and Mallory. They were attracted to South Dakota's wide, open spaces and inexpensive land.

While Gracie and the children—Bill, now eight; George, four; and Margaret, almost two—settled into life on the Skakel spread, Curt discovered the legacy of the Irish railroad workers.

"There were eleven saloons in the little town of Tyndall," Margaret Skakel wrote to her niece Ethel years later. "Dad's drinking was always a problem."

After one binge, Skakel passed out beside the railroad tracks just outside of town. He was found by a couple of his cronies, who cleaned him up as best they could and brought him back to the ranch. "Why in hell didn't you leave him there!" an irate and disgusted Gracie admonished.

About three years after the Skakels moved to the ranch, on November 18, 1899, Gracie Skakel gave birth to her fourth and last child, another son, whom she named James Curtis Skakel, Jr., after his father.

For Gracie, life was harsh on the South Dakota prairie. With little help from her alcoholic husband and having been rejected by her own family, she felt isolated, forced to care for the children and handle most of the chores herself. As her daughter Margaret put it years later, "Mother was a slave at home. But she never complained. She just pitched in and did it."

When Curt Skakel wasn't drinking he was reading, a difficult hobby because of his poor eyesight. "He'd have to hold something right up to his nose," his daughter, Margaret, remembered. "Consequently the rest of the family read to him. As a child it was my daily task to read the newspapers aloud."

In 1900, disaster struck while Curt Skakel was in town getting drunk. "The foreman, a scoundrel, drove the year's crop of sheep off and sold them and skipped with the money," Margaret Skakel recalled. "This infuriated Uncle Bill, and we departed from Tyndall in January or February 1901."

Billy Skakel owned two other spreads in Bon Homme County, and offered his brother one. Curt naturally chose the place closest to the saloons in Tyndall.

The Skakels' new home was a one-time hotel-bar

and bawdy house that had thrived in the mid-1800s. Before the railroad, the main means of transportation had been by wagon, or by the steamboats that navigated the nearby Missouri River. The boats anchored on the river, and the passengers transferred to smaller vessels that brought them up Choteau Creek to a dock within walking distance of the Skakel place.

While Billy Skakel was aware of the house's history—he may have even had a financial interest in the place during its colorful heyday—Curt and Gracie were not. To them, it was just a spacious home with a curiously large number of small bedrooms upstairs. The Skakels and their children didn't know they were sleeping in rooms where prostitutes and their clients had once frolicked. Years later, Margaret Skakel, a Victorian-like spinster, recalled that as a child she always wondered why "each bedroom was numbered."

5 * Death from Drinking

LIFE AT THE Skakels' was hellish. Curt's oldest sons, Bill and George—Ethel's father—were so traumatized that they stopped going to school; only their sister, who loved to read and write poetry, graduated from high school, and for years boasted about being crowned queen of a school spelling bee.

George Skakel despised his father, ashamed of his drinking and angry at the abuse he saw heaped upon his mother. Early on, he realized he'd have to make his own way in the world. He earned a reputation among the people in Tyndall as a mannerly, friendly, ambitious boy who always was thinking of ways to earn a dollar. When the local theater had an amateur talent show offering a five-dollar prize to the winner, George Skakel got up onstage and sang "My Name Is Joe Bowers." He knew he didn't have the talent, and he didn't win the contest, but his entry showed his entrepreneurial spirit.

Of all the Skakel children, George was most like his mother, the one who had the most determination and drive to deal with adversity.

By age fourteen, following in the footsteps of his older brother William, George ran away from home, returning to Chicago to stay for a time with his powerful uncle, Billy Skakel.

Meanwhile, Margaret Skakel spent her life denouncing liquor and resenting men. Over and over she'd tell friends and relatives about the evils of both.

"What a curse drinking is," she'd say, "not only to the person who drinks, but also to those around him. Many a time I've seen Dad put his arms around Mother and say, 'Grace, I'll never touch another drop as long as I live,' and mean it. And then he'd come home reeling that very evening, and maybe curse Mother up hill and down dale. Dad was a nice man when he was sober, but when he was drinking, he was a different man altogether."

As Margaret grew into womanhood, her mother constantly warned her of the dangers of drink and men.

"Never marry a man who drinks," Gracie would intone. "And you know how I took that?" Margaret said. "I took that to mean never marry a man."

In the end, Margaret never even went out with a man. "She had one date arranged, but when Grandmother heard about it, she threw a fit and as a result Margaret canceled the date," Bob Skakel said. "Grace held the power over Margaret."

One day, in the winter of 1916, Curt Skakel had his last drink. After an afternoon of saloon-hopping, he tripped and fell into a muddy ditch. Somehow he managed to get back on his feet and stagger home. Soon after, he came down with pneumonia, and died on January 5, 1917.

Curt Skakel's legacy was his drinking, which would

spread like a horrible plague through future generations of Skakels, Ethel's in particular. Because Ethel rarely spoke about her Skakel family roots, preferring to think of herself as a Kennedy, her son Bobby Kennedy, Jr., was forced to seek information from others. Once, at a family gathering, he approached Bob Skakel and asked whether it was true that his great-grandfather had died an alcoholic. Bobby Jr. was keenly interested because he himself had gone through a difficult period of drug abuse.

"I told Bobby that some say his great-grandfather died of alcoholism and some say he died of pneumonia. I told him the story of what happened and asked Bobby what he thought. He didn't say anything. He got the picture," Bob Skakel said.

Curt Skakel's widow, Gracie, would live for another two decades, thankful to be rid of her husband.

Gracie and her daughter returned to Chicago, where Margaret helped support her mother by working as a secretary for the U.S. Treasury Department. Margaret's brothers, George, William, and James Curtis, Jr., had gone off to seek their fortunes. As Gracie's health deteriorated, Margaret decided they should move to a warmer climate. Around 1920, they bought a two-bedroom cottage with a palm tree in the front and an avocado tree in the back on South Fifth Street, in Alhambra, a working-class suburb of Los Angeles. The spinster daughter and her mother shared the same bedroom. Later, a female friend of Margaret's moved in and the two women became business partners, earning extra money importing and selling oriental covers for grand pianos.

But over the years mother and daughter would be helped financially by Gracie's most successful offspring, George, who would make millions by, as one colleague bluntly put it years later, "turning shit into gold."

PART II

❋

The Patriarch

6 ✻ Finding a Wife

UNLIKE HIS FATHER, George Skakel had excellent eyesight. He also had keen powers of observation and a phenomenal memory for numbers. Those attributes, which would help make him a wealthy man, were displayed on his first full-time job as a lowly freight-rate clerk on the Sioux City line of the Chicago, Milwaukee & St. Paul Railway.

The year was 1913, and George was twenty-one. He'd been working for the railroad about six months, getting by on minimal wages with no future for advancement, when a notice was posted on the company bulletin board informing employees that a string of freight and coal cars had recently been stolen. Listing the cars' serial numbers, the company asked employees to be on the alert for the equipment. While his co-workers ignored the bulletin, George took it seriously. He jotted down the numbers and committed them to memory.

Several weeks later, as George was sitting in one of the switch towers beside the tracks chatting with a co-worker, a long freight train rumbled slowly by. Suddenly George recognized something familiar about the rolling stock passing below. In his mind's eye, he saw the numbers he'd memorized. He raced out the door and onto the roadbed, waving his arms and yelling at the engineer to stop.

Grabbing on to a handrail, he pulled himself aboard and made his way to the cab. Moments later, at George's behest, the railroad detectives arrived. He'd found the stolen cars.

George was soon standing in the executive offices

accepting congratulations. Two weeks later, he was made traffic manager, the youngest in the railroad's history, and given a two-dollar raise, bringing his salary to six dollars and fifty cents a week.

George stayed with the railroad for the next few years, becoming progressively bored and disenchanted, another cog in the company wheel. The final blow came when he learned that a longtime employee was about to be fired just two weeks before retirement so the company wouldn't have to pay his pension. George, who would always have strong feelings for the working man, was outraged. But his philosophy—"Never break another man's rice bowl"—met with deaf ears when he protested the dismissal to his superiors. "Mind your own business," they told him. Disgusted, George quit.

Not long after leaving the railroad, he got a job as a salesman at William Howe Co., a coal distributor. He also started dating a pretty office worker there. Ann Brannack was her name. She was a tall, "Liverpool Irish" girl with a cameo complexion and lustrous blonde hair who lived near Wabash Avenue in the blue-collar South Side.

Unlike the colorful history of the Skakels and the Jordans, Ann's roots were drab. Her mother's family, the Hughes clan, and her father's, the Brannacks, were poor and uneducated. Their forebears were among the hundreds of thousands who fled Ireland, sailing from Liverpool to the United States, in the midst of the tragic potato famine of the 1840s, when starvation from the potato-crop failure claimed 750,000 lives.

Ann was cute, funny, boisterous, bright. But George had to look up to her because, as one of their offspring would note years later, "Dad was only about three-quarters as big as mother." The size difference didn't matter, though. George liked everything about Ann—except for her religion.

Ann Brannack was a staunch Catholic. Her mother, Margaret, was an Episcopalian who'd converted to Catholicism at her husband's urging when Ann was ten. Subsequently, Margaret Brannack had become a fervent and demonstrative Catholic who raised Ann to be a crusader like herself. Margaret Brannack was as intensely Catholic as Gracie Skakel, George's mother, was anti-Catholic. Ann was required to attend early-morning Mass every day at St. James Roman Catholic Church on Wabash Avenue, trudging through deep Chicago snows if she had to, before going to classes at St. James Catholic School. And when she was old enough she taught Sunday school at St. Mary's Catholic Church. "It was a very religious environment that Ann lived in," remembered her lifelong friend, Florence Ferguson Kumpfer. "We used to go to church together every day. The nuns were very strict. Ann was a Catholic's Catholic. Her mother instilled that strong, strong religion in her." Ann would imprint the same kind of religious zeal on her own children, especially her daughter Ethel.

Ann was closest to her mother, rushing home after school every day to the family's small apartment on East Fifty-second Street. "Ann was more or less a homebody," said Kumpfer. "She and her mother did everything together. She taught Ann to be a homemaker." Life at the Brannacks' centered in the kitchen, where mother and daughter—along with Ann's younger sister, whom Ethel would be named after—had contests to see who could make the best-tasting jellies and cakes.

Ann's father, Joseph Brannack, was as big and burly as any Chicago cop, and Ann would take after him physically. A hard-drinking Irishman, he was rarely around and offered little security for the family, jumping from one menial job to another—hotel worker, night watchman—supporting his family as best he could. When he was at home he'd often get drunk and surly in front of Ann and her mother. In many ways, the Brannack household was as dysfunctional as the Skakels'. Because of Joe Brannack's drinking, he and his wife separated. Margaret Brannack would eventually spend the rest of her years living with her daughter Ann and her enormously successful son-in-law, George Skakel.

After graduation from high school, Ann enrolled in a secretarial-business school that advertised on matchbooks. She had a natural ability as an office worker and got high marks for her typing, filing, and shorthand.

At one point she suffered an unexplained health problem. With the help of the Catholic Church, she left Chicago for about a year and went out West, where she worked on an Indian reservation teaching English to the children.

"When she was growing up, she always talked about having a big family," said Florence Kumpfer. "There was a woman who lived in our neighborhood who had a lot of little ones and on Saturdays Ann would go visit the woman just to be with the children. Ann wrote me letters from the Indian reservation telling me how much she loved spending time with the children."

Ann returned to Chicago in better health and shortly thereafter met George Skakel. "She thought he was wonderful. George became her whole life," Kumpfer said.

Having grown up in a home where Catholicism was condemned, George had serious doubts about getting too deeply involved with a woman like Ann. His brother Bill had shocked and angered their mother a few years earlier when he married a Catholic girl. When George told his mother about Ann Brannack, Gracie was heartsick. She advised George to drop her.

But Ann was a determined, persuasive, and domineering young woman and refused to be shunted aside. She saw something in George that she'd never perceived in a man before. She felt his innate strength, drive, and ambition and knew for certain that he'd be a success. She was determined to win him, determined to escape Chicago's poor Irish ghetto. "Ann was a strong woman. She told George that if he wanted her, the only way he'd get her was by allowing a Catholic priest to marry them," said Florence Kumpfer. "That was the rule in those days for girls marrying a man who didn't have the same religion. Ann was a Catholic and George had no special beliefs. Ann felt there was no reason for George to object."

George, who privately questioned the validity of his

parents' prejudice toward Catholics, finally succumbed. On November 25, 1917, the two were joined in holy matrimony by Father Edward Mallon, a Paulist priest, at St. Mary's.

"It was a very simple, very small wedding," recalled Kumpfer, one of the few guests. "After the ceremony they had a breakfast or a lunch and that was it. I can't even remember if there was a honeymoon. All I know is that George gave Ann a ring and he would give her a good life. He adored her. He was a good man."

Before George could say the word *rosary*, he found himself living in one of Chicago's densest Catholic neighborhoods—two blocks from the parish church and school—with a live-in Irish-Catholic mother-in-law and a controlling and calculating wife who would bring seven ardent Catholics into the world during their first ten years of marriage.

7 * *Off to War*

WHILE GEORGE AND Ann were still courting, fighting had broken out in Europe. Just seven months before their wedding, President Wilson brought the United States into the First World War. A few days later the Selective Draft Act was signed into law requiring all men between the ages of twenty-one and thirty to register for possible service. Somehow George escaped the draft. It wasn't until February 26, 1918, three months after he married Ann, that he enlisted in the Naval Reserve Force, reporting for boot camp at the Great Lakes Naval Training Center.

It was a tumultuous time for the newlyweds because Ann had just learned she was pregnant. Naturally, Ann and George were scared. With George in training, Ann went back to her job at the coal company and lived with her mother. Luckily, she'd be able to see George on weekends because the Great Lakes base was just north of Chicago.

With Ann to support and a baby on the way, George decided to become an officer for the additional salary. Despite the fact that he didn't have a high school diploma, he took the officers' candidate test, scoring impressively in the top 3 percent.

Everywhere he went, George seemed to make his presence felt at the top, even at boot camp, where he was one serial number among thousands.

One bitter night, while walking guard, George spotted a civilian car speeding toward the main gate. As it entered the base, George raised his rifle, but the car raced past him. George hurled his rifle, with a scabbarded bayonet attached, through the rear window. The car stopped. With the captain of the guard at his side, George yanked open the door and discovered that the driver was none other than the commanding officer of the entire training center. His actions caused a scandal and resulted in the disciplinary transfer of the CO, George boasted later.

After boot camp, George was shipped to a naval reserve training facility in Cleveland to study tackle, lines, and towing. A few weeks later, he was transferred to a base in New York City, where he became proficient at docking tugboats. On October 7, 1918, he received his commission as an ensign. George's salary increased just in time. A week later, on October 15, Ann gave birth to a girl whom the proud parents had decided to name Georgeann, after themselves. They chose that name because at the time they thought they would have just one child. A month after the baby's birth, Germany signed the armistice. George was released from active duty and was home in time to celebrate Christmas 1918. He had served only eight months.

George returned to his job at the coal company where he'd first met Ann. He was virtually penniless, so broke that the only suit he owned was his Navy uniform.

Knowing that railroads often cheated their clients, George took it upon himself to analyze the coal company's freight bills covering the years of the war that had just ended. His suspicions were well-founded. George's unofficial audit revealed that the coal company had been overcharged by some fifty thousand dollars. He told his bosses about his discovery, promising them he could get the railroads to reimburse. George wrote a series of letters threatening legal action and, in short order, was able to recoup the money. His bosses congratulated him, but when George asked for a raise they refused. Furious, he demanded a 10 percent commission—five thousand dollars—for the money he recovered, but the bosses laughed in his face. George quit, determined that he'd never work for anyone again.

• • •

At the coal company he had forged a close friendship with two young men, Walter Gramm and Rushton L. Fordyce, both of whom had come from somewhat better backgrounds than George had. The Gramm family, dating back three or four generations, had been in the retail business and construction in Chicago. Fordyce's wife was the daughter of one of the senior executives of the Standard Oil Company. All three men shared an entrepreneurial spirit.

The day after George quit he telephoned Gramm and Fordyce and they decided to start their own coal brokerage. Fordyce guaranteed a formidable first customer: Standard Oil.

On May 20, 1919, with each of them putting up a thousand dollars, Skakel, Gramm, and Fordyce formally signed a simple copartnership agreement renewable on a year-to-year basis establishing Great Lakes Coal & Coke Co., a catchy name with a nice ring. Their first office, which consisted of a long desk with multiple telephones and a couple of filing cabinets, cost them nothing because of Fordyce's connection. His father-in-law had put in a good word for the boys at Standard Oil, and they were given some spare space. The new partners had an impressive letterhead printed with the company's name and first address in a thick, black typeface:

GREAT LAKES COAL & COKE CO.
General Offices, Standard Oil Co. Building
910 South Michigan Ave.
Phone—Wabash 9490, Chicago.

They were on their way.

Skakel, Gramm, and Fordyce complemented one another nicely, at least in the beginning.

"George Skakel was a man of vision," observed Walter Gramm's son Patrick. "He was a man of inexhaustible energy and smarts. He was good with figures. He was a leader with savvy who wouldn't let anything stand in his way. Most important, he could smell a profit when he saw it.

"My father," Gramm continued, "was a super salesman. He was able to sell himself as well as the idea of what they were doing at the time.

"Rushton Fordyce was the partner whose wife had the initial contact. It gave them *entrée*. Otherwise, they had no reputation.

"They started out as have-nots who were driven. They felt in their own peer group they could do as well as the next guy, given an even playing field. They were very competitive. Every day they enjoyed what they were doing because, from the start, they were successful at it."

Above all George Skakel was a clever, enterprising, and creative entrepreneur. And he had a lot of luck.

From the beginning, Skakel decided Great Lakes Coal & Coke would only sell large quantities of high-quality coal, a marketing approach most competitors weren't taking because of the risk of getting stuck if the sales didn't pan out. But George was a born risk-taker. "When my father got into the coal business he said there's no use selling ten tons of coal or a carload of coal. Sell freight-rates and that's it. That was his mentality—just go for the big orders," George's eldest son, Jim Skakel, said later.

There were thousands of mines in the United States, and the coal they produced had different characteristics. George quickly learned the differences, focused on the coal that was most salable, and made deals with the mine owners to buy large quantities at lower-than-market prices. As a result they started selling better-quality coal at cheaper prices and the customers, like Standard Oil, eagerly lined up.

But the money really started rolling in because of George's uncanny ability to buy and sell what everyone else considered waste. The mines had tons of an unmarketable sandlike residue known as "fines" sitting around in huge piles. When the surplus became too much, the mine owners often dumped it in rivers. George, however, realized that when coal was in short supply, the fines could be sold. He called delighted mine owners across the country, offering five cents a ton for what they had been throwing out. In short order, Great Lakes Coal owned thousands of tons of fines. "He had the foresight and the nerve to buy it when nothing was going on," said Jim Skakel. "If there was no strike, he'd be stuck with it." When the coal strikes came, and they did, Great Lakes Coal, which had cornered the market on fines, was virtually minting money—selling what had cost pennies for six or more dollars a ton.

Although he had never gone beyond grade school, George was a voracious reader. He consumed books on chemistry, metallurgy, and geology, and business journals. An article about carbon in *Fortune* magazine caught his interest. It talked about the growing use of aluminum in the booming aviation industry. Aluminum required a pure form of carbon. George could smell profits. He knew enough about coke to realize that if you put it in a cement kiln and burned off the gases and impurities, you'd get a pure form of carbon, precisely what the aluminum companies required.

George then learned from Fordyce's father-in-law that the big oil-refining companies generated enormous quantities of coke during the process of manufacturing gasoline. Like fines in the coal business, the stuff was just sitting around, or being dumped into rivers. As he had in the past, George saw an opening.

With Fordyce's help, he quickly signed lengthy contracts, some for as long as ninety-nine years, with Standard and other major oil companies, to buy their coke at pennies a ton.

One of the contracts was with the Texas Co., which had a refinery in Port Arthur, Texas. George and his partners decided this was where they'd build their first calcining plant to refine coke. The Aluminum Company of America (Alcoa) had expressed interest in seeing Great Lakes Coal's finished product. But Skakel and his partners had to raise the money to build the plant. They began making the rounds of banks, finally finding a receptive ear at Continental of Chicago. "They were persuasive in the extreme," said Patrick Gramm, "and the market for aluminum was growing rapidly, so the bank felt they were a good risk." With a fifty-thousand-dollar loan in hand, George went down to Port Arthur, bought a secondhand kiln and conveyors, and began running the coke through the refining process. He sent samples of the finished product to Alcoa. The carbon met their standards, and they were the first to sign a long-term contract.

George also convinced Alcoa's competitors—Reynolds Aluminum and Kaiser Aluminum, among others—to commit to similar deals.

"My father and his partners bragged between themselves that they used to pay out that Port Arthur plant every six weeks," said Jim Skakel. "The plant cost fifty thousand dollars and every six weeks they *made* fifty thousand dollars. After the first six weeks they paid off their loan and it was all pure profit from there on in. In theory, there was no reason for their company to exist. The oil companies and the aluminum companies could have easily dealt directly with one another. They didn't need Great Lakes. But they didn't want to bother. They had bigger fish to fry. Anybody could have done what George Skakel and his partners did. They were very lucky. The money started rolling in."

8 ❊ Mining Money

"GEORGE SKAKEL MADE money and Ann Skakel showed him how to spend it," declared Florence Kumpfer. "Ann felt that if anybody suddenly got a lot of money handed to them, it would be stupid if they didn't know how to spend it. Ann wasn't stupid."

It was the Roaring Twenties. The Jazz Age and Prohibition were upon the land. Chicago's speakeasies were booming. Hemlines and stocks were soaring, and Great Lakes Coal & Coke was literally mining money.

Ann Skakel began celebrating like the rest of the country. She felt as if she'd won the Irish Sweepstakes, and friends watched in awe as Ann transformed herself overnight from a humble secretary into a young matron on the way up.

Ann would jump behind the wheel of the shiny gray Packard with leather seats that George had given her and drive downtown every day to shop. She hired a full-time nurse named Alice to take care of little Georgeann. With a retinue that consisted of her proud Irish mother, Margaret, delighted sister Ethel, and awed friend Florence Kumpfer, Ann cruised the fashionable stores, spending wildly on herself and generously on the others. "She could buy whatever she wanted because George was very generous," recalled Kumpfer. Ann suddenly developed a taste for fine antiques, becoming a regular at the shows, salons, and private sales. "She aspired to have beautiful things," said Kumpfer, "and, if you had enough money like Ann did, you could have *everything* beautiful."

While Ann bought some things without thinking twice about price, she was also a legendary haggler. The big

Chicago department store Marshall Field had a division that was open only to large institutions such as hospitals and orphanages that bought in quantity and received steep discounts. Somehow Ann got her hands on a card identifying her as a representative of the Catholic Archdiocese and began shopping at Marshall Field's wholesale store. "She always bought everything in large quantities—two dozen sheets, two dozen towels," said Kumpfer.

Ann took on the bearing of a woman of means, joining various charity organizations whose membership rolls were filled with the wives of other businessmen, most of them Catholic, unlike George. Ann was one of the early members of the Miserecordia Board, founded by Chicago's Cardinal Mundelein to run a fancy ball to raise money for an unwed mothers' home run by the Sisters of Mercy on Chicago's South Side. "It became an annual event and everyone looked forward to going," recalled Liz Henebry, whose parents, the McGuires, were close friends and neighbors of the Skakels. Ann also became active with the Big Sisters, another organization to help poor and unmarried mothers. "They'd meet once a week and fold bandages," recalled Florence Kumpfer. "Ann became active in everything. She was a churchwoman, joining church boards and frequently running church functions such as bridge and sewing parties. Anyone who needed a leader or help, they'd call on Ann. She also got involved in political organizations for the socializing."

Despite all of Ann's early efforts to reinvent herself, she still "wasn't very sophisticated or cosmopolitan," recalled Patrick Gramm, whose mother was a member of Chicago's WASP society. "Ann Skakel was part of the Irish enclave on the South Side, a very fine lace-curtain group. She was a woman who found her greatest satisfaction within the confines of her church as a devout Catholic. There were always a few priests around the Skakel house."

As part of doing business, George upgraded his image by joining the fancy Chicago Athletic Club and the predominantly Catholic South Shore Country Club, where he took up golf to entertain customers. "It was a big step up for Dad in those days," recalled Jim Skakel. George was rightfully proud of his rise in the business world, boasting in letters to his mother, Gracie, about playing golf with the general manager of the Illinois Central Railroad and the Lieutenant Governor of Iowa.

Besides entertaining customers and VIPs on the links, he lured them with expensive hunting trips, supplying the gear, the weapons, and eventually several beautiful lodges he'd purchased in Canada. "There weren't any limits on the number of birds you could shoot in those days," recalled Ethel's brother Rushton Skakel. "Dad had been out hunting with his customers and he brought home three hundred dead ducks and Mommy had to prepare them so Dad could give them to his customers as gifts. Isn't that amazing? Dad was a fabulously great outdoorsman."

George's love affair with guns had begun on the South Dakota prairie. He now always kept a loaded revolver in a nightstand next to the bed, and he amassed an outstanding collection of expensive pistols, rifles, and shotguns. He also taught his sons to shoot when they were just out of diapers, and instilled in his daughters a rare ease and confidence around firearms. Many years later, it took the assassinations of her brother-in-law and then her husband to change Ethel Skakel Kennedy's lifelong positive feelings about guns.

George and Ann Skakel had addictive personalities, which were manifested by her obsessive desire to spend, and his compulsive need to drive himself from dawn to dusk. But neither of those pursuits was outwardly injurious. The dark side of their personalities was their drinking. Alcohol was an accepted part of their world: at the clubs; after golf or a day in the woods stalking deer; at George's business luncheons and at Ann's dinner parties. Florence Kumpfer observed, "Neither of them knew how to drink. They couldn't hold their liquor." As the years passed, George became an alcoholic, and Ann was borderline. While George went on the wagon for lengthy periods, he'd eventually fall off. His drinking was hereditary, a problem most of his children would inherit.

9 ✻ Baby Ethel

SHE HAD BROWN eyes and a slight wisp of brown hair. She was exceedingly short and appeared terribly scrawny. Cradled in her mother's strong arms, nuzzled against her enormous breasts, the baby whom Ann and George named Ethel was barely visible. But she had a strong cry that pierced the corridor at Chicago's Lying-In Hospital, her voice louder and her lungs stronger than any of the other babies born at the maternity hospital on April 11, 1928.

Ann was thirty-six years old when she had Ethel, her sixth and next-to-last child. With each pregnancy, she had put on weight, which she never lost. By the time Ethel was born, the matriarch tipped the scales at close to two hundred pounds, and still counting. She was now referred to by friends and family as "Big Ann."

Seeing Ethel for the first time, the Skakels were concerned. Turning to Dr. Robert Delee, who delivered her, and Dr. Blanche Mayes Elfrink, the pediatrician, George asked whether the newborn was healthy, was unencumbered by any handicaps. Both George and Big Ann had good reason to worry. Their last baby, Patricia Sistine Skakel, whom the mother had named after the chapel in Rome, had been born with a club foot, a condition that caused intense anguish for the child and the whole family. "When she was born that way they didn't show her foot," recalled Florence Kumpfer. "Pat's ailment was just kept quiet. That was the way the Lord sent her and they tried to accept it." By the time Ethel was born, Pat was two and undergoing the first of more than a dozen operations. But the doctors told

George and Ann that Ethel was perfectly healthy, not to worry about her small size. They pointed out that Ethel's sisters, Georgeann, now nine, and Pat, were also petite, perhaps taking after their father.

The Skakel household had exploded into a large, boisterous, and disruptive environment with little, if any, parental control. With Ethel now part of the brood, the family needed larger quarters. They moved into a big, red-brick house with a telephone booth in the vestibule. It was a few blocks from St. Ambrose, where the Skakel boys—Jimmy, George, and Rushton—got their early education. "It was an old-fashioned Catholic grammar school," said childhood friend Dodie Dwyer. "Like a dungeon." A few years earlier, the neighborhood where the school and the Skakel home were located had been the scene of the "Crime of the Century" kidnapping of little Bobby Frank by teenage millionaire thrill-killers Nathan Leopold and Richard Loeb. "The kidnapped boy walked right down the same street that we did to get to school," Dodie Dwyer recalled.

"There were no blacks," was the way Jim Skakel remembered the neighborhood. "In those days in Chicago if blacks came over past Cottage Grove Boulevard to the Lake Michigan side where we lived, the cops stopped and searched them. A lot of people might not admit that today, but that's the way we lived."

Ann, who had always wanted lots of children and "was always happy being pregnant," according to Florence Kumpfer, now had a skewed conception of what family life really entailed. Since George had given her the wherewithal to hire help, Ann's world now revolved around her many outside social activities, and much of her energy was focused on keeping George, her successful breadwinner, happy. Increasingly, she had little time left for her children.

George's firm belief in the sanctity of the family had shifted, too. While he deeply loved his children, Great Lakes Coal & Coke, which was growing in huge leaps, was his real baby and required his constant attention. "At the core, George Skakel was a businessman," observed Patrick Gramm. "He didn't have the time for his family."

George Skakel had become a driven man. He would spend the rest of his life escaping the demon of his alcoholic father and his impoverished roots by pursuing wealth and all of its trappings. As Ethel's brother Jim observed years after their father's death, "If all of his kids had been born without legs, that would have been the luck of the draw. Dad would still be out doing business."

George was traveling extensively now, and Ann usually accompanied him. The Skakel children felt alone, isolated, and abandoned, left at home for long stretches in the care of nurses, baby-sitters, and their grandmother. "Mrs. Brannack, Ann's mother, actually helped raise those children," Florence Kumpfer said. Years later Rushton Skakel acknowledged that he and his brothers and sisters were deeply affected by their parents' long absences. "They were gone for three months at a time," he said. "We always missed them."

The oldest of the three Skakel boys, Jimmy, who was named after his alcoholic paternal grandfather, was already a problem child when his new sister Ethel joined the family. "Jim was the trial in both Mother and Daddy's life," said Rushton. Jim was a seven-year-old terror in knickers who was in desperate need of his father's guidance and discipline and his mother's love. He had already begun causing mischief and was constantly crying out for his parents' attention, behavior that would continue into adulthood.

"Jimmy was a wild one, a terror, a little villain," said Florence Kumpfer. "He was into everything, so he demanded more attention. He was the oldest boy, his mother's favorite, and Ann had the most problems with him. I remember he came to visit us one night for dinner and we all had to go to church. So we left Jimmy at home. When we returned, we discovered that he'd entered the basement of the apartment house behind us and stolen the toys of the children who lived there."

Part of the route that Jim Skakel took to St. Ambrose was along heavily traveled Cottage Grove Boulevard.

While the other children trudged through the snow and cold to get to class, Jim found a faster, more exciting route. He'd wait for a trolley car to stop at the corner and then grab on to the rear post, getting a free but dangerous ride. He'd do the same thing on his way home for lunch.

"Some of the mothers saw him do it and the principal found out about it and called Jimmy in and warned him not to do it again," Kumpfer said. "Jimmy didn't stop, so the nuns expelled him because they couldn't be responsible for his safety. Ann was very upset. She pleaded with the nuns at St. Ambrose and they finally permitted him to come back."

Ann never told George that his son had been expelled because she was afraid he'd punish him. Ann acted on the advice of her mother, who loved Jimmy intensely. "Ann's mother would do anything rather than see Jimmy get punished, even though he was always getting into trouble," recalled Florence Kumpfer.

Ann had more than she could handle dealing with Jim's behavior, Pat's handicap, and the precociousness and wildness of her three other children, ranging in age from five to nine. As a result she couldn't devote as much time as she might have to little Ethel.

Ethel would feel compelled to compete with her siblings for parental attention and approval. In the end, she would all but abandon her own flesh and blood for a new family that would accept her more fully as one of their own: the Kennedys.

Besides Jim, there were two other brothers at home when Ethel arrived. George Jr., six, the second son, the most handsome of the boys, was named after his father and great-grandfather. Almost as wild as Jim, he would one day inherit his father's mantle, but his life would be riddled with personal scandal and end tragically. The other son, Rushton Walter, was almost five, the quietest of the brothers, named in honor of his father's partners, Rushton Fordyce and Walter Gramm. Rushton was the good boy in the family, angelic-looking with rosy cheeks. Dodie Dwyer, who went to St. Ambrose with the Skakel boys, remembered him coming to her aid in third grade when a bully gave her a terrible bump. "Rushton came running over and I remember him being very kind."

The eldest child, Georgeann, was nine years old when Ethel was born and she was her mother's shining star. Bright, precocious, and responsible, Georgeann was being molded by Big Ann into her own image. "Ann taught her about antiques, entertaining, shopping, cooking, and taking care of the other children," said Florence Kumpfer. "Georgeann kind of took over for Ann when she was away. Even though she was just a girl, Georgeann referred to her sisters and brothers as 'the children.' It was as if she were the mother. Ann trusted her implicitly." Even at a young age, Georgeann was a Catholic zealot who accompanied her mother to every Mass that was offered, and was the pride of the Sisters of Mercy nuns who taught her at St. Xavier's, a convent school not far from St. Ambrose.

Ann had unilaterally decided to raise all of her children as Catholics, which disturbed George. But he was not the type of man who verbalized his feelings; introspection and communication would never be Skakel traits. When it came to their religious differences, particularly in the raising of the children, George acquiesced to Ann. But he once expressed his intense feelings during a visit with his brother Curt's second wife, Doris.

"I remember we were talking about our families and George said, 'Sometimes my children don't seem to belong to me.' My mouth dropped because I knew George loved his children," she said later. "But he gave me the strong feeling that he felt alienated from them because Ann was such a strong Catholic and raised her children that way. He never felt a part of any of that. The whole Catholic issue put a strain on their marriage."

10 ✻ The Crash

THE YEAR 1929 began happily for the Skakels. Over Easter, George and Ann, along with year-old Ethel and ten-year-old Georgeann, took a three-day train trip to New Orleans to see the Mardi Gras and visit George's older brother Bill Skakel and his family. Aside from exchanging holiday cards and gifts by mail, George and Ann had never met Bill's wife, Julia, or their children, George William, fifteen; Robert Curtis, fourteen; and Betty, who was nine.

Ever since they'd run away from the South Dakota homestead as teenagers, the brothers had been somewhat distant. When George started Great Lakes Coal, he asked his brother to join him, but Bill stubbornly refused, asserting that he would never earn a dime. Instead, Bill chose to become a manufacturer's representative for a hearing-aid company, then watched enviously as George built an empire. While he earned a decent living, he'd never come anywhere near George's league. But Bill Skakel had different values than his brother. A lively and charming man with dark good looks, he acted in little theater, enjoyed literature, classical music, and the arts, was an avid gardener, and had an eye for pretty women.

George and Big Ann arrived in New Orleans bearing gifts: an expensive momma doll for Betty; a cloisonné watch for Julia. Throughout the week, George and Big Ann entertained their poor relatives in style, taking them to expensive restaurants and attending Mardi Gras balls and parties.

Betty Skakel Medaille remembered her uncle George as "a tiny man having enough charm to impress everybody'' and her aunt Ann as a mountainous, spontaneous woman prone to capriciousness, a side of her personality that surfaced at one of the Mardi Gras parades.

''We were sitting down front in the reviewing stands when the queen of this particular parade, a little girl, stopped in front of us. It was a chilly night and she was only wearing a rhinestone tiara, gloves, and an evening dress. Ann said to my mother, 'Julia, what is that child doing out there without a coat?' My mother told her that she was probably too poor to own one. Aunt Ann, a giant of a woman in all proportions, who was wearing an ermine cape that reached to the ground, said, 'This is ridiculous,' and gave her fur to the queen to wear for the evening. This was typical of Ann. She was given to generous impulses.''

Not long after George and Big Ann returned to Chicago, Bill Skakel ran off with a pretty secretary who had become pregnant. ''Uncle George was very upset with my father,'' said Betty Medaille later. ''I don't know whether he believed that marriage was an endurance contest, but he felt it should last forever. While he wasn't a Catholic, he didn't believe in divorce.'' George felt so strongly about his brother's indiscretion that he never spoke to him again.

That summer of 1929 George was busy traveling on business while Ann vacationed with the children and the Kumpfers, renting a cabin on a lake in Merrill, Wisconsin, a five-hour drive northwest of Chicago. Ann brought her mother and the nurse to help care for the children while she idled away her days reading. George wrote to his mother that business was taking all of his time and that he missed his family. He noted that the children were healthy and that little Ethel, having celebrated her first birthday, was doing especially well.

The family reunited in late August. In September, the oldest children returned to school. Five weeks later, when Ethel was eighteen months old, the stock market crashed. It was Black Thursday, October 24, 1929. WALL ST.—the famous banner headline in *Variety* exclaimed—LAYS AN EGG.

For the Skakels, the nonstop ride on cloud nine would take a sudden, but temporary, nosedive.

• • •

George Skakel never gambled with his own money. Unlike others during the twenties, he didn't speculate; he didn't participate in the margin-buying frenzy, though he did make a sizable investment in conservative utility bonds. Taking a big hit, George was suddenly cash poor. Remembering that difficult time, Jim Skakel said, "Dad didn't go broke, but he didn't have the money that he had before. One minute we had a big house near the University of Chicago. When the bottom fell out, we were back in an apartment on Drexel Boulevard."

Industry came to a virtual standstill. As Patrick Gramm put it, "The company took a little dip when the Depression came. It was nip and tuck for a while."

By the time of the Crash, Great Lakes Coal & Coke had one less partner to feed. Rushton Fordyce, whose connections a decade before had given the company its much needed initial kick start, had been ousted because, according to Rushton Skakel, he tended to "glub, glub, glub."

Jim Skakel explained what happened: "Fordyce was a drinking man and one day he turned in an order for a couple of trainloads of coal to be shipped to Standard Oil. My father got the coal and had it delivered. A few days later the head of the refinery, Fordyce's father-in-law, called and said, 'What the hell is this?' My father said, 'It's the coal you ordered.' The head of the refinery said, 'George, I know you real well. You wouldn't do anything like this. We'll take the coal, but we didn't order it.' Fordyce was drinking and he just made up the order out of thin air."

George, who prided himself on his integrity, was furious. The original partnership agreement stated that if any of the principals "flagrantly and clearly violate" any of the terms, "the copartnership may be dissolved by any of the copartners who have not violated the terms. . . ."

A few days after George talked to Standard Oil, Fordyce was ordered to clean out his desk.

With Fordyce out of the picture, George decided to go it alone—without Gramm. But Gramm asserted his rights as one of the original partners. "Just cut me in any way you want," Gramm told Skakel. "So at that point in time," Jim Skakel explained, "my dad gave Gramm twenty percent of the company and he kept eighty percent."

At least that's one version of the events.

Another, more hotly disputed, scenario was described years later by Ethel's sister Georgeann, who would become the single largest holder of Great Lakes stock. She claimed that her father discovered that Gramm was playing the market on margin with company funds. When the Crash came, George discovered that the coffers were empty. At that point, he made Gramm an offer he couldn't refuse: George wouldn't report Gramm to the authorities if he agreed to an eighty-twenty split in favor of Skakel. Gramm readily agreed.

Whichever way it happened, Skakel and Gramm worked closely and hard to keep the company afloat in the aftermath of the Crash and the beginning of the Great Depression.

Patrick Gramm, who'd eventually become a director of the company alongside Ethel and her siblings, said his father "always felt he had enough and he was never made to feel that he was a junior partner."

Because Skakel and Gramm needed money to remain afloat, several sources offered to come to their rescue: their creditors, George's brother-in-law, and Big Ann herself.

"Aunt Ann was a resourceful woman," observed Betty Skakel Medaille. "Over the years Uncle George would ask her how much she needed to run the house and she would tell him a figure that was twice as much as she actually needed. He would fork it over and she would bank half of it. And then in the middle of the month she'd come to George again. So she had a healthy little account. When the Crash came and George found his private parts in the proverbial sling, Aunt Ann said, 'Here, dear, let me help you out.' "

Joe Solari, a shrewd Italian immigrant with a law degree who had married Big Ann's sister Ethel, had risen to the post of secretary at Peabody Coal, one of Chicago's largest coal companies. During the worst part of the Depression, Solari saw an opportunity to get a piece of his brother-in-law's action. He offered $500,000 to George for equity in Great Lakes Coal & Coke. George said thanks, but no thanks. He didn't want to give up any part of the company, confident that things would improve. "Solari was a very shrewd guy, moneywise," said Jim Skakel. "But so was my dad." Years later Joe Solari and his son would attempt to wrest control of the company away from the Skakels in a behind-the-scenes corporate power struggle that would pit brother against brother, sister against sister, cousin against cousin.

For now, though, it was mainly the oil companies that kept Great Lakes Coal & Coke's head above water when others in the business were drowning.

"Those people were willing to carry the company for a while," said Patrick Gramm. "George and my father had marvelous relationships with their suppliers, the oil companies, who had deep pockets. The oil companies saw Great Lakes Coal as doing a service for them—making a market for the petroleum coke. The oil companies didn't want to see them go under, so they said, 'Well, don't worry about paying the bills for a while.'

"I remember in the thirties, when everyone else was doing badly, we were living a very good life."

Joe Solari, a shrewd Italian immigrant with a law degree who had married Rik Audi's sister Estelle, had risen to the post of secretary-treasurer of one of Chicago's largest coal companies. During the worst part of the Depression, Solari saw an opportunity to grab a piece of his wonder-in-law's action. He offered $500,000 to George for equity in Great Lakes Coal & Coke. George said thanks, but no thanks. He didn't want to give up any piece of the company, confident that things would improve. "Solari was a very shrewd guy, moneywise," said Jim Crown. "But so was my dad." Years later, Joe Solari and his son would attempt to wrest control of the company away from the Stakels in a bitter Byzantine corporate power struggle that would pit brother against brother, sister against sister, cousin against cousin.

For now, though, it was mainly the oil companies that kept Great Lakes Coal & Coke's head above water when others in the business were floundering.

"Those people were willing to carry the company for a while," said Patrick Crown. "George and my father had marvelous relationships with their suppliers, the oil companies, who had deep pockets. The oil companies saw Great Lakes Coal as doing a service for them—making a market for the petroleum coke. The oil companies didn't want to see them go under, so they said, 'Well, don't worry about paying the bills for a while.' I remember in the thirties, when everyone else was doing badly, we were living a very good life."

PART III

❊

Bowl of Cherries

11 ❊ Depression Years

BY 1932 THE Great Depression was at its peak.

Chicago's factories and rail yards resembled ghost towns; the streets were unswept, the parks overgrown. More than fifty thousand unemployed men and women roamed the streets. The city was "shrouded in hopelessness and despair," wrote journalist and historian Cabell Phillips.

It was in Chicago that stifling June of 1932 that both national political parties met in convention. The Republicans renominated President Herbert Hoover, whom many blamed for the current mess. The Democrats chose New York Governor Franklin Delano Roosevelt, who pledged to bring back prosperity.

Songwriters sat at their keyboards in Tin Pan Alley documenting America's mood in lyrics; the song most descriptive of the unrelenting agony was Bing Crosby's "Brother, Can You Spare a Dime?"

For the Skakels, though, a popular tune by Rudy Vallee and his Connecticut Yankees seemed more apropos. It was called "Life Is Just a Bowl of Cherries."

After a brief hiatus, Great Lakes Coal & Coke was rolling in money once again, while all around the economy worsened.

The aluminum industry was one of the few that had made a quick recovery, producing the metal that was used to manufacture airplanes, and George's company had a virtual monopoly on supplying the necessary ingredient. Aluminum production soared through the Depression because the airline business was growing quickly. In its maiden flight over the Rocky Mountains, the aluminum alloy DC-1 had performed well, another step forward in convincing the public of the safety and practicality of commercial aviation. Highly publicized record-breaking flights by aviators like Wiley Post and Amelia Earhart added to the excitement.

The number of *known* millionaires in America had dropped substantially to only about two dozen. George Skakel, who kept a low profile and whose company was privately held, had become one of them.

"In judging other men," noted Jim Skakel years later, "my father's standard was *when* those men made their fortune, not how *big* it was. He was always proud he made his money in the Depression, the *worst* of the Depression."

One of the keys to George's enormous success was his obsession with secrecy and privacy. Over the years, as the company grew, business publications ranging from the *Wall Street Journal* to *Fortune* tried unsuccessfully to interview and profile him. Eventually, Great Lakes would become one of the largest, if not *the* largest, privately owned companies in America, yet the number of words written about it would fill less than a column of newsprint. Whenever a colleague would advise him to talk to a journalist to get free publicity, George would scoff. His philosophy was, "You can't quote silence."

"We always tried to keep a low profile," noted Patrick Gramm. "We never sought PR because we were one of the largest private companies and had a monopolistic position in certain areas and we just didn't want to attract attention to ourselves. We just stayed quiet and made money."

Years later, after Ethel married Bobby Kennedy, a longtime family friend noted wryly that one of the major differences between George Skakel and Ethel's father-in-law, Joe Kennedy, was that "old man Skakel paid to keep his name out of the paper and old man Kennedy paid to put his name in the paper."

Because business was so good, Ethel, just four, was seeing even less of her parents. George and Ann spent much of their time in New York City, commuting back and forth virtually on a weekly basis aboard the *Twentieth Century Limited*. George's days were filled with rounds of meetings with bankers, suppliers, and customers, while Ann shopped and prayed on Fifth Avenue, at Saks and Bergdorf's and St. Patrick's Cathedral, respectively.

Manhattan had become George's second home because that was where the company's new lead banks, Chemical and New York Trust, were located. The city was also headquarters for some of the major oil refiners that Great Lakes did business with.

Even more important, George had expanded operations over the past two years into the international market. Great Lakes Coal & Coke now had one- or two-man sales offices in most foreign and Asian countries, including Germany and Japan. Since most had representatives in New York, George's presence was required there on a regular basis. Eventually, 65 percent of the company's income would be derived from foreign sales.

Of all of the world's powers, George saw the Soviet Union as the biggest threat to Great Lakes Coal & Coke's survival. Hungry for hard currency in the worldwide Depression, the Russians had started sending tankers to the United States, selling oil for as little as fifty cents a barrel when the going rate was three times that. George's greatest fear was that the Russians, with their huge oil fields, might be tempted to dump carbon and coke on the world market, thus wreaking havoc with his company's price structure. Worse, if the aluminum companies started dealing with the cut-rate Russians, George would be left sitting on tons of unsalable coke and carbon, which would wipe him out overnight. With that threat hanging over him, he began making surreptitious trips to spy on his Russian competition.

George's other enemy was Franklin D. Roosevelt. His apprehension about the new President centered on the thicket of regulations that Roosevelt intended to impose on big business. The concept of Big Government and the New Deal sickened the boss of Great Lakes Coal & Coke. "George hated Roosevelt," said Jay Mayhew, the company's chief geologist and George's longtime confidant. "He felt that Roosevelt would run the country into the ground. He felt Roosevelt could have become a dictator."

George would be shocked years later when his daughter Ethel joined America's bastion of liberalism, the Kennedy clan, emulators of many of Roosevelt's social and political philosophies.

12 ✻ *Moving East*

BECAUSE SO MUCH business was now being conducted in New York, George decided to move East permanently to establish executive offices in Manhattan, while Walter Gramm remained in Chicago, running the research, development, engineering, and service divisions.

In the months prior to the move, scheduled for late spring of 1933, Big Ann was filled with a mixture of ebullience and melancholy.

The decision to relocate, which George had made quickly and unilaterally, had left his wife unnerved. Big Ann loved Chicago, where her friends and family lived. This venture East into uncharted territory, for which she was unprepared socially and intellectually, made her feel anxious and vulnerable.

A bigger shock came in May 1932. At the age of forty, as she was looking forward to a more leisurely life as a wife of a rising baron of industry, Big Ann discovered that she was due to have her seventh child around the time of the stressful move. Despite a full-time nurse, household help, sitters, and her mother, she felt her hands were full with the six she already had—ranging in age from Ethel, an antsy five, to Georgeann, an adolescent fifteen.

But a greater emotional blow was in store for Big Ann, one that would leave her devastated for months to come. In quick succession, her sister Ethel, and one of her best friends, Francis McGuire, died suddenly. Coming home late one night from a party, Ethel Brannack Solari suffered a massive heart attack. Only thirty-five, she left three young children, Joel, Bobby, and Celeste, and a husband who would never be the same. Her death was a shocker for another reason: it revealed a genetic heart problem that would severely impact the next generation of Skakel males.

However, on February 14, 1933, Big Ann gave birth without complication to her seventh child, her fourth daughter, a healthy, pink-cheeked blonde with blue eyes whom she named after herself. "Little Ann looked like her mother more than any of the others," said Kumpfer. "She was the only blonde child."

In June 1933, following a family visit to Chicago's spectacular Century of Progress Exposition, the Skakels piled into two chauffeur-driven Lincoln touring cars and headed for their new life on the East Coast. The trip, which took more than a week over two-lane roads, included overnight stays at the Depression-ravaged homes of farmers who charged travelers minimally for room and board as a way of bringing in some money. Because the trip would be too strenuous for the baby, Big Ann left her in the care of a nurse in Chicago. After the family reached their first destination, a small, family-style hotel in New Rochelle, New York, she returned for the four-month-old.

The family briefly stayed at the hotel, then rented an oceanfront mansion surrounded by a high wall of hedges in Monmouth Beach, New Jersey, an area populated by a number of Prohibition gangsters. Because of the Depression, the rent was minimal and there were few, if any, vacationers. Early each morning George's chauffeur drove him up the Jersey coast to a point where he boarded a ferry to Manhattan, and then took a cab to the company's offices in the recently built Empire State Building.

At home, Big Ann lolled on the beach, watching little Ethel chase her brothers. The child was generally boisterous and bouncy, tossing a beach ball and getting the boys to teach her how to throw a football. Within days of hitting the beach she got a full tan: she liked to run around without any clothes on. "She was cute and talkative and agreeable, a sweet little girl who played with the boys all the time," said Florence Kumpfer. "But there was nothing exceptional about her. She toddled along with the rest of them."

In the fall, the Skakels moved again, this time to a mansion in Larchmont, New York, a small, affluent town with a good-sized Catholic population, which appealed to Big Ann. Set on more than a dozen manicured acres, the furnished house was so enormous that the children never saw all of the rooms, and their mother only used a portion of them. "It was a fabulous place," recalled Rushton Skakel, "so big none of us could believe it, and mind-bogglingly beautiful." Again, because of the Depression, the Skakels got the house for virtually nothing, renting it from another high-rolling Catholic family who were living in Europe. The estate was a perfect setting for George to entertain his clients, which he and Big Ann did in grand style several times a week.

For Big Ann, the house was flawless for another reason: it was situated directly across the road from a Catholic church and school that specialized in teaching difficult children, of which she had her share.

The Dominican Day School, where Big Ann enrolled five-and-a-half-year-old Ethel in kindergarten and her older brothers and sisters in higher grades that September 1933, was a private academy founded and ruled over by Sister Rose Alma, a stern nun in her midthirties who had "something of a masculine nature and mentality—direct and hard," a relative said. Rose Alma had seen that the well-heeled Catholic parents of Larchmont and neighboring Rye desperately needed a private, progressive school that could give their spoiled, ill-mannered, and often troubled children special attention in the basics and social graces.

By the time the Skakels had moved in—their children perfect candidates for Rose Alma's educational philosophy—the school was going strong in an old three-story, red-brick house just across the street.

13 * *Larchmont Living*

UNFORTUNATELY, ROSE ALMA'S liberal teaching environment could not rehabilitate Big Ann's increasingly uncontrollable brood. The children's life at home had become the antithesis of everything the nun was trying to accomplish in the classroom.

The Skakel home had become the setting for one round of parties after another, beginning in the early morning when George held breakfast meetings with his business colleagues and ending long past midnight, following cocktails, dinner, and more drinks, with other associates. George, with Big Ann's full and complete support, was attempting to establish an immediate and resounding presence for himself and Great Lakes Coal & Coke in New York, and the impressive Larchmont house—staffed with servants, stocked with the best liquor and the finest foods—was his lure, delighting and overwhelming all those who were invited. He used the house as he did the hunting trips and the golf links, to generate business. The house and his home life became an extension of his business. Even the children were part of the tableau he presented to his cronies and customers. Having little Ethel, George Jr., Jimmy, Rushton, Georgeann, and Pat present during the parties, rather than hidden away upstairs, suggested to George's guests that he was just a regular family man at heart; that the Skakels were a happy family. Ann even brought down the baby so the businessmen could fawn over her. Seeing the family together like that gave George's clients a wholesome feeling about him, the kind they got looking at a Norman Rockwell family on the cover of the *Saturday Evening Post*. Realizing the public-relations benefits of the family, George even trotted out the children at business meetings in a kind of dog and pony show. So driven were they in their desire for success and wealth that George and Big Ann were oblivious to the catastrophic impact their actions were having on their children.

Years later, Ethel's brother Rushton Skakel, by then a recovering alcoholic, remembered that fateful time:

"I was ten years old when we moved to the house in Larchmont. That house, all of our houses, in fact, were used mainly for business, the way for Dad to get together with his customers. Dad was establishing his company in New York, so my parents had parties, parties, parties. I mean there were parties literally every day. There were business parties and social parties.

"That's when Dad started drinking. Dad's alcoholism hit him when we were in Larchmont because of all those parties and all of the drinking that went on. I never considered my mother an alcoholic. She drank with Dad, but I never saw her snockered.

"And that's when *we* started drinking. As little tots, my sisters and brothers and I would take the glasses with a little liquor or wine left in them into the kitchen and we'd empty [drink] them. My sister Georgeann, who was fifteen when we got to Larchmont, was an alcoholic. Alcohol ran through our family. That's how we grew up.

"When there wasn't a party, Dad would go to bed at eight o'clock in the evening because at five-thirty in the morning he was up to meet customers for breakfast. So we never saw much of him except on weekends, when we'd take long walks in the woods.

"My father practically never went to a business meeting without one of us. We'd go into major board meetings at the big companies and we'd be sitting there with all these industrialists and moguls. You'd be the only child in the meeting, and it made a difference with those people. It impressed them and made the meeting a personal, beautiful thing, in their eyes.

"And then our parents traveled a lot, so we had to go from that little nun's school to boarding school because there was nobody home."

According to a Skakel family friend, Mary Begley, Georgeann Skakel wasn't the only one of the children who suffered severe drinking problems. "Jimmy Skakel's reputation was perfectly horrible," Begley said. "You would hear about these crazy Skakels, their name would come up in conversation. You'd hear people say, 'Oh, can you imagine the Skakels, they have a son who's an alcoholic at age sixteen.' "

When George and Big Ann traveled, more and more of the responsibility was put on the shoulders of Georgeann—"the little mother," as one observer put it. While she was quite competent and mature for her age, she did have a major flaw: her drinking. As the Skakels' trips grew longer and the children got older and more undisciplined, Big Ann decided to send the boys away to school and get them out of her hair. For the time being, she permitted the little girls—Ethel, Pat, and Ann—to remain at home.

The Skakels stayed in Larchmont for two years before renting another impressive house, a large, white, frame colonial, a few miles north, in Rye.

By that time the boys—Jim, fourteen; George Jr., thirteen; and Rushton, twelve—were having serious difficulties with their studies and were considered disciplinary problems at their new school, Canterbury, a monastic Catholic boarding school located on a barren, wooded hill near New Milford, Connecticut. Canterbury was a grim institution run by a stern Roman Catholic, Dr. Nelson Hume. Most of the students, sons of affluent Catholic families, were homesick and lonely, their long days filled with English, math, and the sciences, along with regular, tedious religious lectures. The Skakel boys, who'd never faced any form of discipline, were like fish out of water. Because of the strict rules, punishments, and rigid academic standards, the drop-out rate at Canterbury was high; only a few years before the Skakel boys were admitted, one of the students who quit because of mediocre grades, ill health, and homesickness was a thirteen-year-old from another big Catholic family. John Fitzgerald Kennedy eventually transferred to Choate, but would always remember and despise his time at Canterbury.

"It was a strict school in the English tradition, with high tea, noon tea, blazers," recalled Jim Skakel. "The highest grade you could get was about a sixty-five, which was passing. They'd get you for signing your name, or the date, improperly, or if you didn't do something fast enough. There was that kind of discipline. It was tough."

Jim Skakel was expelled from Canterbury after one year following an angry confrontation with a staff member. "I caught the headmistress of the house I was living in going through my bureau drawers and my clothes and stuff," he said. "She was just one of those nosy broads, but that was my personal property and nobody goes in that. I told her off and that ended that."

When Dr. Hume summoned Big Ann in the spring of 1935 to come get Jim and to find another, more suitable school for his brothers, she was naturally upset. But her irritation was not entirely related to her sons' academic and behavioral problems. She and George had a busy schedule of travel ahead—a three-month trip to Europe was on the agenda for that summer—and Big Ann didn't want to have to stay behind to deal with her boys' difficulties. A week before the Easter vacation, she sent an SOS to Sister Rose Alma at the Dominican Day School, where Ethel, seven, and Pat, nine, were still students, seeking any help the nun could offer.

14 * The Tutor

THE ANSWER TO all of Big Ann's problems arrived in the person of Rose Alma's nephew, Martin Boswell McKneally, a tall, handsome twenty-one-year-old pre-law major at Holy Cross, whose chiseled features, patrician manner, and precise way of speaking made him look and sound more like a Shakespearean actor than the son of a Newburgh, New York, plumbing contractor.

It was a propitious meeting in Rose Alma's study a few days later; Big Ann and McKneally hit it off immediately.

She was impressed with the young man's academic credentials and demeanor, and he liked her style, too. She was, he would say later, "a woman of the greatest largesse, a woman of enormous personality, charm, and vigor. She had great style and the money to back it up."

McKneally was to become a close friend, family adviser, and confidant—a featured player in the many dramas of the Skakel family over the ensuing years. Eventually, he'd fall from grace.

The moment Big Ann met McKneally for the first time she saw success written all over him. And her perception about him was on the mark.

After graduating from Holy Cross, McKneally got his law degree. During the war, he would serve as an officer and become active in the American Legion, rising to the powerful post of national commander. A superpatriot at the height of the Communist witch-hunts of the fifties, he would denounce the United Nations, federal aid to education, and cultural exchanges with the Soviet Union. His financial backers would consist of close Skakel and Kennedy family friends, among them Senator Joe McCarthy and his cohort Roy Cohn, both of whom McKneally idolized. He would eventually enter politics, winning election to the U.S. Congress. But his political career would end in shambles after only one term when a federal grand jury indicted him on charges of failing to file income-tax returns for four years on almost eighty thousand dollars. He would eventually plead guilty to one count, receive a five-thousand-dollar fine, and be placed on probation.

Martin McKneally would remain a bachelor and, although he was once described in a *New York Times* profile as "flamboyant," his true sexual preference would never be revealed. Through the years, while he'd taken care of the Skakel boys and courted and sought the hand in marriage of one of the Skakel girls—with the family's full and complete support—he kept his homosexuality in the closet. It was this revelation, in part, which eventually caused a breach with the Skakels.

"He suddenly started coming to the Great Lakes stockholders' meetings with his live-in," Rushton Skakel said later. "And the live-in, who was older, was the male member and Martin was the female. Oh, wow, what a shocker."

In the spring of 1935, though, Big Ann saw young McKneally as her saving grace, an erudite, mature young man in whose hands she felt she could safely place the enormous responsibility of tutoring her sons and daughters and acting as their companion.

Years later, Ethel would place her own troubled sons in the hands of a man of similar demeanor. His name was Lem Billings.

Two days after his first meeting with Big Ann, McKneally arrived at the Skakel house to spend the Easter break helping the failing Skakel boys with their studies.

"From the beginning I was highly attracted to the boys, who were extraordinarily handsome and could have been in pictures," McKneally said later. "They allowed wit, humor, and laughs. I went upstairs with them to the third floor, which they occupied, and by the end of that week we became great friends.

"As for the girls, Ethel, who was a mere child at the time, was hyperkinetic like Jimmy, loved the wildness of the boys, followed them around like a puppy dog. She was always flighty, seemed lost, was never very bright, so she had to find her own identity, which was through riding horses and athletics. But she was a most charming girl who gave her father, when he was home, which was rarely, many moments of amusement and entertainment and pleasure because she clowned for him to get his attention, and she was funny, relating things to him in her special way."

Big Ann, McKneally said, was so devoted to her husband that she was willing to allow the kids to fend for themselves. "Ethel and the others were getting used to their parents going off and letting others care for them," he recalled. "Big Ann felt she had to always be with her husband, just as later Ethel felt she always had to be with Bobby, leaving her kids in the care of others. Mrs. Skakel would tell Georgeann, 'Now I have to go away, so make certain that the household runs, dear.' Of course, there was a good deal of household help—a cook, waiters, waitresses, and chambermaids."

George soon asked McKneally to be the children's paid companion for the summer while he and Big Ann were in Europe. George also indicated that if the arrangement worked out there'd be a job in the company. "He liked the cut of my jib," McKneally asserted. "He seemed desperately anxious to have someone in the company with whom he could be close, a confidant. He needed someone whose loyalty would be intense and unquestionable."

Big Ann's immediate concern before leaving for Europe was to get the boys into another school.

On Rose Alma's suggestion, she contacted Portsmouth Priory, which in many ways was like Canterbury. Established in the early 1920s, it was located on Narragansett Bay in Portsmouth, Rhode Island. The goal of the school, which was operated by monastic, Benedictine monks, was to ground the students thoroughly in Catholicism and give them a liberal academic education with a Catholic point of view. Big Ann took the boys for a visit, and while George Jr. liked the place and decided to stay, Rushton and Jim hated it. Jim felt the Gothic environment was as stultifying as Canterbury and told his mother he wouldn't go there. Rushton followed suit, but his reason for refusing admittance was quite different: the monk who took him on a tour had only one eye and the image frightened and upset the twelve-year-old.

Big Ann was able to convince Nelson Hume to readmit Rushton at Canterbury. Finding a school for Jim, on the other hand, was a bit more difficult. She finally enrolled him at an off-beat, progressive, non-Catholic boarding school, Raymond Riordon, in Highland, New York, where students learned to fly planes as an intellectual pursuit, chopped wood to supply heat for the place, and played in football games that never quite went the distance if the players got bored. Offering lots of freedom, it was Jim Skakel's kind of school.

During his senior year at Priory, George Jr. crossed paths with another rich Catholic boy who was having problems in school. Small and skinny, Robert Francis Kennedy was as mediocre a student as George was. During one visit home, George told his brothers about meeting the son of the U.S. Ambassador to Great Britain. "He's a real little dick," was the way he described him. Bobby, who entered Priory in the winter of 1939, remained there through the end of the 1941–42 school year. Like the Skakel boys, he jumped from one boarding school to another, six in ten years. His younger brother, Teddy, also spent time at Priory, which at times seemed like a halfway house where wealthy and busy Catholic parents could deposit their wayward sons.

It was still some years down the road before the two families—the Skakels and the Kennedys—would come together.

With the boys now enrolled in schools in three different states for the fall 1935 term, and with a suitable male companion in place to guard over the brood at the house in Rye for the summer, George and Big Ann felt a sense of well-being as they prepared for their trip. Big Ann left a detailed note for Martin McKneally about how to handle each of the children. Because little Ethel had had a foot-stamping fit when she found out her parents were going away again, Big Ann instructed McKneally to "keep Ethel real busy. If she's active, she'll just forget we're gone." The next day the Skakels steamed out of New York Harbor aboard the *Normandie* en route to Europe for three months of business and pleasure. Their shipboard companions were George's partner, Walter Gramm, and his wife.

Great Lakes Coal & Coke was raking in more money than ever, and George was in a celebratory mood, which was underscored by an incident that happened one stormy night in the mid-Atlantic. After an evening of toasting their good fortune with champagne, the Skakels and the Gramms ventured out on deck for some air. The sky was black, the waves high, and the wind strong, but all George felt was the bubbly he'd consumed. Suddenly, as Big Ann and the Gramms looked on in horror, George slowly climbed onto the ship's railing. As he stood up on unsteady legs, the stormy sea far below, Big Ann dropped to her knees and prayed aloud, while the Gramms begged George to come to his senses. But George ignored their pleas, walking the rail with his arms outstretched to keep his balance. Finally, George hopped back on deck with an evil grin. Big Ann, furious at the risk he'd taken, dragged him back to their cabin, screaming at him all the way.

"George Skakel was a very dynamic guy and he had great flair and great self-confidence," observed Patrick Gramm years later. "But he could be a flamboyant guy, a very free spirit who drank deeply of life. Those who came later, his sons, emulated his style somewhat. When he took it upon himself to walk the railing of that ship to the great dismay of his wife and my mother and father, he was showing his bravado, the daredevil in him."

Back at home, Martin McKneally and the Skakel children were having a grand time, too. He tutored the boys in Latin, math, and English several hours each day, but the rest of the time the Skakel brothers and sisters had fun with their companion.

"It was a great summer," recalled McKneally. "We had all the country clubs we could possibly want. We had swimming pools. We had badminton. We had outings. We had *everything*."

PART IV

❋

The Greenwich Years

15 ✻ Lake Avenue

"I WAS WONDERING, Ann, why in the world would you move to Greenwich of *all* places?" Dodo Jacob asked, standing in the driveway of Rambleside, the Skakels' enormous estate.

"*Taxes*, my dear," Big Ann responded. "That's the *only* reason. *Taxes*."

An old-line, genteel Beacon Hill Episcopalian who had attended Miss Porter's with George Bush's mother—an upbringing far removed from Big Ann's South Side Chicago roots—Mrs. Jacob was the mother of Anita ("Pan") Jacob, one of Ethel's closest friends at her new school, Greenwich Academy. The Skakels' recent move into the mansion on Lake Avenue in Greenwich, Connecticut, a white Anglo-Saxon bastion of privilege and wealth, had set the tongues of the blue bloods wagging. Who, they wondered, was this new family that seemed so out of place? Mrs. Jacob, wife of a globe-trotting International Telephone & Telegraph executive, was one of the few women in town who even acknowledged Big Ann's presence, and that only because their daughters were school chums. She seized the moment to get some answers.

Big Ann explained that George was taking home an enormous salary from his company—"Mr. Skakel just can't help making money," she said almost apologetically—and had been paying a healthy chunk of it to the state of New York. Since there was no income tax in Connecticut, and real-estate taxes were lower, their decision to move across the state line and settle in Greenwich had been based strictly on economics.

The Great Depression was still wracking the land when the Skakels moved in, but its impact was barely visible in Greenwich, though the Crash had wrought some changes. Membership in the fashionable Indian Harbor Yacht Club had dropped from 345 to 167. A few chauffeurs had been laid off and some of the wealthy families had reduced their full-time staffs. But less than a thousand of Greenwich's small working-class population were unemployed, and they were quickly put to work grading streets and landscaping school and park grounds, their salaries coming out of a forty-one-thousand-dollar fund established by the town.

"A lot of people in Greenwich, such as our family, didn't even know there was a Depression," observed Peggy Klipstein Larned, a daughter of old money, who became a friend of Ethel's. "Life seemed the same."

When Zalmon Gilbert Simmons, heir to the Simmons mattress fortune, died in 1934, his widow, Frances, couldn't bear to live alone in the thirty-room English country manor house they'd shared since the place was built in the 1920s, even though her sons, Zalmon Jr. and Grant, occupied two immense homes on either side. Once again George Skakel was in the right place at the right time with cash in his pocket. Because the Depression was at its peak, there were no interested buyers, and an extremely wealthy widow anxious to sell at any price. "Dad paid one hundred thousand dollars for the house," recalled Rushton Skakel. "In those days that was a fortune to most people, but the price was a bargain."

The Skakels, who'd moved East with only their clothing, bought the Simmons place fully furnished.

"The furniture was big and heavy and dark, great big tables and sideboards and ornate things, almost like church pieces," recalled Pat Grant Mudge, who became a friend of Ethel's. "You couldn't use those pieces in any other house because they were so monstrously large."

Rarely did anyone set foot in the formal living room on the first floor, which was filled with furniture covered in old plush velvet and had a large organ that looked like it came from the set of *The Phantom of the Opera.*

Most of the family used the more comfortable and warm second-floor living room, which was connected to a sunporch where George and Big Ann often slept.

The house in Greenwich where Ethel grew up was magnificent. The three-story stone and brick mansion with its varicolored slate roof and seamed granite trim consisted of a twenty-five-foot entrance hall with an inlaid copper and black marble floor that was part of the design of Elsie de Wolfe, the famed interior decorator, who had been a personal friend of Frances Simmons. The handsome library, which was almost sixty feet in length, had a black marble fireplace, teak floors, recessed bookcases, Corinthian columns, and immense bay windows that looked out to the spectacular grounds. Outside, there were sixty thousand irises, an eight-acre spring-fed lake, stately elm trees which cost Zalmon Simmons thousands of dollars to truck in and replant, boxwood-bordered formal gardens, a wisteria-covered pergola that led to the Adam and Eve Garden, a 150-foot reflecting pool with a fountain in its center, greenhouses, vegetable gardens, grape arbors, an apple and pear orchard, and majestic sweeping lawns. Before the Depression, the Simmonses had eighty-three gardeners working on the property every day. When George bought the place, he added an elevator near the kitchen for the use of his aging mother-in-law and Big Ann, and a seventy-five-foot swimming pool. Besides the main house—which also consisted of six double bedrooms, two single bedrooms, three staff bedrooms, six baths, a master suite with sitting room, fireplace, two dressing rooms with baths, a heated, glass-enclosed sleeping porch, billiard room, children's playroom—there was a guest house, Tea House, two servants' houses, a six-car garage, and a small stable.

Rambleside was one of the most spectacular estates in one of the most desirable areas of Greenwich, and with the colorful Skakels in residence, it would become one of the most notorious homes in town.

"They were a speck wilder than the staid group in Greenwich," observed Bobby Banks Kaufman, who would go to school in Greenwich with Ethel and whose father was the realtor who sold the Simmons house to the Skakels. "They had fancy cars, and were full of pizzazz."

Peggy Klipstein Larned noted that the Skakels were "a harum-scarum family, a high-spirited bunch. My parents were established and the Skakels were not, so they just never crossed paths."

Priscilla ("Pixie") Meek, one of Ethel's closest childhood friends, summed up the general view: "Ethel's family was a bit bizarre."

When George moved to Lake Avenue, he was under the misguided and naive impression that Greenwich would welcome him with open arms and respect, as a self-made millionaire amassing a fortune at the height of the Depression. But the Skakels' arrival was met with silence and upturned noses.

Some longtime Greenwich residents viewed them harshly. The scion of one old family, who eventually befriended the Skakel boys, said his parents thought of the newcomers as "rowdy Irish micks. A lot of it had to do with whether you'd gone to Yale, Harvard, or Princeton. George Skakel hadn't done any of those things and he didn't have anything in common with the people who had done those things."

Few, if any, of the parents of Ethel's friends would ever socialize with Big Ann and George. As the daughter of a longtime Greenwich family observed years later, "My parents and Ethel's just wouldn't have been congenial together. Their backgrounds were so different. They just didn't have *anything* in common."

Pan Jacob, looking back to those years, recalled Ethel telling her how much her family loved Larchmont because it wasn't as rigidly snobbish as Greenwich, and there were more Catholics there. "The Skakels were *not* in the *Social Register* and that was a problem for them—a very sad problem," she observed.

"I felt the Skakels were sort of pathetic, moving into Greenwich with this incredible powerhouse of people—the WASP culture of the world—and they did it only because of the taxes. They were too naive to know what they were getting into. They were totally ignored, totally shunned. I'd hear remarks about them from my mother, or my mother's friends. They viewed the Skakels as *very nouveau.*

"It was hurtful for the children, too, although Ethel wasn't terribly conscious of any of that. I know she thought about who she was, but her way of dealing with herself was to joke about herself."

Rushton Skakel, who finally decided to leave Greenwich in 1993, acknowledged, "We weren't accepted for a long time, and maybe never. We hadn't been brought up in a Greenwich type of world. We were brought up the Chicago way, where you were innocent until proven guilty. In Greenwich, you were guilty until proven innocent. You could live there for forty years and you wouldn't know your neighbor's middle name. In Chicago everybody was effusive, outgoing, talkative. There was no braggadocio. In Greenwich it was, 'What club do you belong to? Where do you vacation?' "

Worse still, the same intense prejudice toward Catholics that George Skakel's parents had nurtured on the barren plains of South Dakota in the late 1800s now affected his own family. In the mid-1930s, in the drawing rooms, private clubs, and salons of that WASP enclave, a strong anti-Catholicism—not to mention racism and anti-Semitism—flourished. (The wealthy department-store family Isaac and Bernard Gimbel had managed to move into Greenwich in the early thirties, but Bernard's wife, Alva, couldn't join the Hunt because she was a Jewess.)

Pan Jacob, who came from a highly educated family and was herself a precocious bookworm, was brought up believing that Catholics were inferior and different. Though she never said anything to Ethel, Pan would have sworn as a child that Catholics could be identified by an odor that Episcopalians didn't have. "Other than Ethel, I didn't know any Catholics except our Irish maids, and they *smelled* different," Jacob acknowledged later. "I guess it was the incense they burned in their rooms, I don't know. But that's how I identified a Catholic—by their smell."

It didn't take a lot of perception on George's part to see that the family was being snubbed. The fact that all of the Skakels were perceived as Catholics, even though George himself wasn't, added to their difficulty, so he decided to take steps he hoped would ease the family's path into Greenwich's social mainstream.

His first move was to make certain that the other residents recognized the fact that he himself wasn't Catholic. In a Greenwich directory that gave biographical data on the town's most prominent residents, George listed his church as Episcopalian, even though he had never attended a day in his adult life. He fancifully listed the Kent Preparatory School as one of the places where he was educated.

His next step was to convince Big Ann to allow the Skakel girls to go to a nondenominational school to assimilate. "He felt that their Catholic education was far too insular," Martin McKneally acknowledged later. It was the first time in nearly two decades of marriage that he interjected himself in Big Ann's role as the family's Catholic leader. Not surprisingly, his request resulted in one of their few marital battles. But in the end Big Ann conceded with a proviso: that later she be allowed to send Ethel and her sisters to Catholic boarding schools and colleges. George, having won what he felt was a major victory, readily agreed.

At that point Big Ann was willing to try anything, so unhappy was she about the family's reception in Greenwich. Once, when Pan Jacob's mother stopped by to pick up her daughter, the usually ebullient Big Ann let down her hair for a rare moment. Despite the trappings of wealth, she admitted, "I'm miserable here. I'd be willing to crawl the length of Michigan Avenue on my hands and knees if only Mr. Skakel would take me back to Chicago."

16 ✻ A WASP School

BIG ANN TOOK the girls—Ethel and Pat, who were the only ones in grammar school at the time—out of Sister Rose Alma's Dominican Day School and enrolled them in Greenwich Academy, where Ethel quickly assimilated, rising above her family's problems.

"Ethel had the best of it because she was younger, could make contacts and grow up within the community of Greenwich Academy and have friends," Pan Jacob observed later. "Ethel was so open and so honest that everybody adored her. She was successful because she was so natural about herself."

Located in a red-brick building on Maple Street, Greenwich Academy was founded as a coed institution in 1827 by Dr. Darius Mead, a Greenwich native and minister of the Second Congregational Church. At one point in the mid-1800s, the school property was controlled by New York political power William Marcy ("Boss") Tweed, and one of his sons, Charlie, had been a Greenwich Academy student.

By the time Big Ann enrolled Ethel, Greenwich Academy was considered one of the leading day schools for girls in the Northeast, "a school that instilled God and country and all the good things," said Peggy Klipstein Larned, a proud graduate. "Every morning at assembly we had to say the Pledge of Allegiance to the flag and sing an Episcopal hymn. The school was sort of based on the English system. It was strict."

Ethel was required to wear a winter uniform that consisted of a green Harris tweed skirt and jacket, a blouse with a tan necktie, lisle stockings held up by garters, and brown shoes with a big, ugly tongue. In spring, the uniform changed to cotton dresses. "Even our underpants had to match," said Larned. "We were just like cookie-cutter kids."

Ethel arrived at Greenwich Academy each day in a chauffeur-driven car, her driver armed with a loaded revolver, standard operating procedure in the wake of the Leopold and Loeb, and the Lindbergh baby, kidnappings.

She was one of the skinniest girls in class but always had a voracious appetite, coming to school each day with the same snack in a brown bag. While the other girls had cookies and milk, Ethel consumed two huge sandwiches: white bread covered with peanut butter, jelly, mayonnaise, and lettuce, which turned the stomachs of her classmates.

As part of the sports program—the only area of academia where Ethel ever excelled—the school offered a curious course to improve posture developed by a French woman named Bess Mensendieck, who asserted that "our present-day physical education cannot do away with such prevalent defects as stooped shoulders, bowed legs, crooked arms, weak ankles, and sunken arches." Greenwich Academy's impeccably erect headmistress, Ruth West Campbell, was a staunch advocate, and the Mensendieck system was eagerly adopted into the curriculum. As a result, Ethel and the other girls were required to perform their exercises in the nude, in a special studio equipped with full-length mirrors and a camera. Snapshots of the girls were then used to critique their posture. "About ten of us at a time had to get stark naked in front of these mirrors and the camera and do the forward bend and the squat," recalled one of Ethel's classmates. "I know that after Ethel married into the Kennedys she joked that one of the pictures of her might turn up in a girlie magazine and become a political bombshell." Rumors also persisted for years that the juiciest glossies were smuggled out and secretly circulated at the nearby Brunswick School for Boys.

But any photograph of Ethel wouldn't have been

very titillating. "She didn't have any bosom," recalled Pan Jacob. "Puberty didn't seem to happen to her."

Skinny and self-conscious, Ethel watched anxiously as the bodies of Pan and her other classmates blossomed while hers remained flat and straight as a board.

Anne Morningstar Huberth, one of Ethel's pals during adolescence, recalled that Ethel didn't reach puberty until the age of sixteen. "It bothered her and it bothered her mother even more. I went through that period of time with Ethel and it was worrisome and problematic for her. Then it came along finally. There was a change in her body. She never had to wear a C-cup, but everything was fine."

17 * Bearer of the Cross

ETHEL'S PAL PIXIE Meek was the daughter of one of Greenwich's most esteemed families. Her father, Samuel Meek, an executive at J. Walter Thompson, was responsible for the growth of advertising in Europe. Pixie's mother, Priscilla, also educated at Miss Porter's with Pan Jacob's mother and Dorothy Bush, was establishing herself as one of Greenwich's grande dames.

When Pixie and Pan and the other young ladies from Greenwich Academy came to visit Ethel, George would nod to Big Ann as if to say, "I was right, look at the caliber of Ethel's circle of friends now that she's out of Catholic school."

Big Ann would give big bear hugs to all the girls who visited and, over homemade cookies and cakes, she'd ask probing questions about their backgrounds. "Now, dear, who did you say your father was?"

Franny Pryor Haws's father, Sam Pryor, for one,

was aide de camp to Pan American Airlines founder Juan Trippe. Pryor was a colorful fellow who had mynah birds and gibbon apes as house pets, boasted that he met a baboon in Africa who drank martinis, and liked to shoot off guns in the middle of the night to scare Ethel and his daughter when they had sleepovers in tents on the Pryor grounds.

Franny had the kind of breeding George sought in his daughter's new friends. But, like many of the others, she was an Episcopalian, which didn't sit well with Big Ann, who frequently proselytized when Ethel's pals came to visit.

"She'd sweep me into her arms and those great big bosoms of hers and tell me about going to Catholic school," Franny said later. "She really wanted me to go."

Likewise Ethel often spoke of the virtues of her religion and eagerly took her friends to Sunday morning Mass at St. Mary's Roman Catholic Church in Greenwich.

"I used to have to go to church with her on our way to horse shows," said Haws, who, along with Ethel, had taken up riding with a passion. "To look more presentable in church, we'd wear these long raincoats that Ethel supplied to cover up our riding clothes. I remember being scared to death because I didn't know how to genuflect. I used to follow Ethel in and just do whatever she did. It was a big mystery."

Anne Morningstar Huberth also was forced to go to church with Ethel when they were on the horse-show circuit. "But I couldn't swallow the Catholic faith so she and I never discussed religion."

Like Pan Jacob, Pixie Meek never had a Catholic friend before Ethel. "Everything I knew about Catholicism at that time, she taught me," Pixie said later. "I was fascinated. If *we* missed a day of church it wasn't a sin, but for Ethel it was, so I was intrigued by that. She was very devoutly religious, extremely so. She used to tell me she'd only marry a Catholic."

Naturally, the girls would go home filled with

thoughts and questions about what they heard and saw at the Skakels': the crosses on the walls, the priests and nuns who were frequent guests of Big Ann's, the rosary beads that Ethel carried everywhere, the library shelves filled to the ceiling with books on Catholicism, the constant proselytizing.

Franny Pryor Haws said that when her mother heard about Big Ann's Catholic-school lobbying, "she was absolutely adamant that I not listen to that kind of talk. There was a point where I didn't go to the Skakel house on weekends anymore, probably because of my mother's influence."

Relatives, particularly from the Skakel side, were also put off. One summer, George Skakel's sister-in-law and young son came to visit. It was quite an eye-opener for eight-year-old Bob Skakel and his mom, who at the time were living in virtual poverty in a three-room house on the Texas-Mexico border, where James Curtis Skakel, Jr., worked as a U.S. border patrolman.

"The swimming pool. The thirty rooms. I must say I was a little green-eyed," recalled Bob Skakel years later. "My father was nothing like Uncle George. Dad couldn't sell a dollar bill for fifty cents if he tried."

But by the end of the month-long visit, Bob had lost all feelings of envy. He watched as Ethel's brothers arrived home from their various boarding schools, only to be shipped out again a few days later to go to summer camp. Upstairs, on the third floor, completely ignored by the brothers, was a room filled with electric trains that made Bob's mouth water because he had only a cheap wind-up set. He watched as Ethel sat at an elegant grand piano in the huge library confidently playing "Red Sails in the Sunset" for a small audience of her mother's matronly friends, who applauded the child's efforts politely. But there was something missing in this opulent lifestyle.

"What I saw," observed Bob Skakel later, "was too much money, too much everything, and no closeness. I felt sorry for the boys having to go away to camp when they'd just come home from school. I felt I wouldn't trade places with them for anything in the world. I've felt the same way as an adult." One afternoon Big Ann took her nephew to see Ethel compete in a swimming meet at a country club in New Rochelle. Bob was shocked to see Ethel win a bronze metal by blatantly cheating.

"The pool was perhaps a hundred feet long and the lanes were divided with a rope supported by buoys every ten feet," he remembered clearly. "There were only three girls competing. While the other two girls swam, Ethel pulled herself along on the rope. Naturally she won. I just thought that was pretty damned unfair and I was a little ticked off at her. Everyone there, like Aunt Ann, was all quite well-to-do and they thought, 'How cute.' Ethel acted as if she actually deserved winning, and so did Aunt Ann."

But the greatest impact on the boy—and his mother—came from the religious atmosphere in the Skakel house. Because his father was still spewing the anti-Catholic vitriol he'd heard from his parents, young Bob was more than a little surprised to visit relatives whose home resembled a cathedral. "On Sunday, after Mass, the sisters and the priests came for cocktails and conversation," he recalled. "It was a Sunday-afternoon ritual. I'd never seen anything like it. Aunt Ann always held forth."

Ethel's religious fervor also surfaced. A small, thin, bashful boy, Bob spent afternoons playing with Ethel and her sister Pat in Ethel's second-floor room, which paid homage to her two consuming passions: horses and Catholicism. The walls were covered with photos of Ethel on horseback. Over her bed hung a large cross and rosary beads. Books on Catholicism were stacked on the night table.

One day, out of the blue, Ethel's impish face took on a serious expression. "You're not going to heaven when you die, Bob Skakel," Ethel said with conviction. "Do you know that?" Stunned, the boy stuttered, "What? . . . Why not?" In a more mocking and teasing singsong tone, Ethel continued, "Yeah, Bob Skakel, you're not Catholic, so you're not going to go to heaven. You're going to go to hell."

His face burning with embarrassment, near tears, Bob ran from Ethel's room—the sound of her laughter ringing in his ears—and into the arms of his mother, who had been resting in a guest room. "Mom," he blurted out, his voice quivering, "I'm not going to heaven." Doris Skakel smiled gently. "Why not?" she asked. "Because I'm not Catholic. That's what Ethel said. Ethel said I'm not going to heaven because I'm not Catholic."

After a few moments, Doris Skakel managed to reassure her son that he'd go to heaven whether he was Catholic or not. "Don't worry," she said, patting his head, "your cousin Ethel was just kidding." But Doris wasn't surprised by Ethel's taunts.

One afternoon the sisters-in-law were chatting in the kitchen when Big Ann brought up her favorite subject in a manner that left Doris nonplussed.

"Doris, if you and Curt would become Catholic, there's nothing I wouldn't do for you," Big Ann said suddenly. Keenly aware that her sister-in-law "very much wanted all of the family to be Catholic," Doris attempted to change the subject, but to no avail. Big Ann said, "It would be very beneficial. Things could be much better. We could do a lot for you and Curt."

Years later, Doris Skakel said, "I viewed what she said to me as a bribe. I didn't like what she said, but I didn't answer her back, and I never told Curt because it would have made him angry."

On another occasion during the visit, Doris accompanied Big Ann and the children to Sunday Mass. Afterward, a group of friends returned to Lake Avenue for drinks on the sunporch. Doris Skakel was sitting by herself reading the newspaper when she overheard some of the others loudly discussing "damned heretics."

"Their feeling was that if you didn't believe in Catholicism you were a heretic, and I thought, 'God, that's me,' and it hurt and made me feel alienated," she recalled. "I thought, 'My goodness, is that the way they feel if we're not Catholic?' One of the men who was involved in the conversation suddenly sat down next to me and he said, 'Hello, aren't you one of the Skakels from out West?' I was so angry I said, 'Yes, I'm one of the *goddamn heretics*!' He looked shocked and embarrassed. That ended the discussion." Doris Skakel said she never mentioned the incident to Ethel's father because "I know how upset it would have made him."

Of Big Ann's seven children, Ethel was most like her mother. "From the time she was a little child Ethel helped Big Ann carry the cross," Martin McKneally observed. "There were only two things of real importance in Ethel's life—Jesus Christ was first and later came Bobby Kennedy."

Over the years, because of her incessant proselytizing, Big Ann won more than a few converts, a skill she taught Ethel, who would have her own successes later in life.

From the time the Skakels moved to Lake Avenue, Big Ann had begun filling the shelves of her immense library with books on Catholicism, some of them rare and priceless manuscripts, and first editions. Through her friendship with Daniel C. Walsh, a professor who would teach philosophy to Ethel at college, Big Ann became the first secretary to Thomas Merton, a Roman Catholic Trappist monk. Merton's best-selling autobiography, *The Seven Storey Mountain,* had been published to great critical acclaim while he was living at Our Lady of Gethsemane Abbey in Kentucky.

"The Skakels were our earliest and best benefactors," said Brother Patrick Hart of Our Lady of Gethsemane Abbey, who followed Big Ann as Merton's secretary. "By financing the monastery, the Skakels were allowing a monk to sit at a typewriter and write."

Big Ann's friends always worried that her devotion and generosity made her a sitting duck for charlatan clerics. But, in the case of Merton, it appeared as if the innocent, monastic monk was being taken for a ride by Big Ann herself.

As Merton's secretary, she was able to keep his increasingly valuable original drafts. She had at least five of them—*Sign of Jonas, Ascent to Truth, No Man Is an Island, Last of the Fathers,* and *Silence of Heaven*—and a number of his first editions that he signed for her.

"Ann was interested in authors and wanted to get their manuscripts," explained Brother Patrick. "She was a great saver, a great collector. Originally, I thought Merton was the only one, but Ann said that she got manuscripts from other writers whom she didn't identify. She'd tell them, 'I'd love to do your secretarial work.' She'd get the manuscripts that were annotated by the author and she would have her secretaries type clean copies, whatever number the author wanted. But Ann kept the original, which had all of the author's markings. As a result, she built a superb collection. She was shrewd enough to know that these could be very valuable. She'd have them bound elegantly in leather, just gorgeously, the best binding you can imagine. She realized the value in Merton, that he had a powerful voice, and that people would have to reckon with him in years to come. It's my feeling that Mrs. Skakel obviously thought she could cash in those manuscripts someday."

Big Ann never actually lifted a finger to type the manuscripts. She hired several women to do that, along with opening and answering Merton's fan mail.

But because of her efforts, Dom M. James Fox, the sixth abbot of Gethsemane, a frequent guest at Lake Avenue, christened the Skakel house *Regina Laudis*—In Praise of the Virgin. Big Ann proudly used the Latin name on her personal stationery. Years later, a chapel was dedicated in honor of the Skakels at Our Lady of Gethsemane Abbey.

For a time in the mid-forties, Big Ann Skakel became part owner of the Guild Book Shop, which specialized in religious books, at 117 East Fifty-seventh Street, in New York City. Her partners included Hilda Shriver, mother of Sargent Shriver, and Mrs. Maisie Ward Sheed, author of a popular new book at the time, *The Splendor of the Rosary*. The shop specialized in religious tracts and books aimed at laypeople considering conversion.

At first Ann Skakel spent several days a week at the

shop, checking incoming stock for first editions that she added gratis to her library. She also went to the shop to socialize with many of the other Catholic matrons who stopped in to browse. The store lasted only a few years, lost money, and was sold. One day Big Ann walked past the shop with a friend and turned red with anger and embarrassment. She'd been describing the store's virtuous and pious past when she suddenly saw the book being featured in the window. It was Polly Adler's *A House Is Not a Home*, a best-selling story about a madam and her prostitutes.

George Skakel distanced himself from his wife's religious interests, and warned friends and colleagues to do the same. When Great Lakes geologist Jay Mayhew was about to make his first visit to Lake Avenue, George warned him about his wife's library. "He told me, 'Don't you dare go into that room. You don't want to see it.' It was obvious, I concluded, that he didn't agree with her Catholicism," recalled Mayhew, a Quaker. "George said he just didn't *like* the library. He surprised me because he never indicated in any other way, at any other time, that there was some point of disagreement between him and his wife."

One afternoon, waiting until her husband was out of the house, Big Ann dragged the reluctant Mayhew into the library. "She just said, 'Come on, I'm taking you to see it.' Who was I to say no to her? She was the boss's wife. The room looked like the Mormon Tabernacle, only on a smaller scale. There were religious statues and busts and figures with wings like angels and floor-to-ceiling books."

By the time little Bob Skakel and his mother had come East, there was a well-defined schism between Big Ann and the Skakel family over the issue of her Catholicism. "There was *not* a lot of closeness with Grandmother Grace Skakel and Big Ann at that point in time," acknowledged Bob Skakel. "The division between her Catholicism and the Skakels' Protestantism was very strong."

Their differences were so great, in fact, that

George's mother never visited her son's family. In hopes of making peace, George once took his wife, Ethel, and Jim to California, the first and last time that Ethel met her paternal grandmother. "George really loved those family get-togethers," Doris Skakel, his sister-in-law, recalled. But the bad blood and hostility that existed between his wife and mother—two strong-willed, sharp-tongued, opinionated women—was so overt that George finally dropped any hope he held for a rapprochement.

"During that visit," Doris Skakel said, "Big Ann grabbed Gracie, a tiny and frail-looking woman, as she walked out of the kitchen. Ann plunked Gracie on her knee and proceeded to bounce her up and down like a little child, while Gracie tried desperately to squirm free, helpless in Big Ann's grip. Ann laughed uproariously—you could hear her a block away—and Gracie was horribly, horribly embarrassed. I was really shocked. If George had been there, he'd have been very upset."

In the end, George used the excuse of business trips to the West Coast to visit his mother, leaving Big Ann behind. He also became his mother's main source of financial support. On one visit he asked his sister, Margaret, for the keys to her car, returning to the house an hour later with a gift, a new model Ford.

On January 4, 1936, Grace Skakel died of a heart attack at the age of seventy-eight. George flew out and made the funeral arrangements, but no one in the family could remember Big Ann or any of her brood being present at the service, which was held in a small Episcopal church.

About religion, George tried to be open-minded. He once fired a Great Lakes Coal & Coke personnel manager when the man, knowing George wasn't Catholic, boasted to him that he didn't hire Catholics at his plant.

According to his son Rushton, George Skakel harbored no prejudices; every man was equal in his eyes. Associates of his father supported the son's contention. Rushton asserted that his father "got the first Jew in" as a member of the exclusive Greenwich Country Club in the 1940s. Eager to underscore his father's liberalism even more, Skakel said he himself was permitted to learn to swim at a Jewish community center when the family still lived in Chicago. "The Jews," he noted, "were the only ones who could afford a pool."

While his father wasn't a Catholic, Rushton maintained, he was "godly good." To stress that fact, he said, "During my whole life my father told me only one joke that was not nice. He said, 'I know a lady who sleeps with cats [Katz] . . . and sometimes Mr. Nussbaum, too.' "

18 * The PEP Girls

SPOILED BY HER parents, with no discipline or controls imposed on her at home, Ethel had emerged as quite a little wildcat at Greenwich Academy, where she became part of a triumvirate, along with Pixie Meek and Pan Jacob. Theirs was a bond forged through a mutual love of horses and mischief. The threesome, who had dubbed themselves the PEP girls, from the initials of their first names, were inseparable, teasing and tormenting their teachers and causing general mayhem, much to the delight of their classmates and even some of the staff.

Ethel, who had a tin ear for languages, loathed her French teacher, Madame Peiloir, a serious woman of sallow mien who wore drab clothing and tied her salt-and-pepper hair in a tight knot. During class, Ethel amused Pixie and Pan by hurling spitballs at the teacher when her back was turned. One day, in total fury, Madame Peiloir spun around after being stung. "You are nothing but a package of nerves!" she yelled at Ethel with a hard glare. *"Vous n'êtes q'un paquet de nerfs!"*

"Pixie and I thought that was the funniest thing we'd

ever heard in our lives," recalled Pan Jacob. "Ethel taunted that woman unmercifully. She hated her so."

Besides French, Ethel had trouble with her own language. Although she'd been only five when the family moved East, she'd already developed a strong Midwestern accent that deeply annoyed Headmistress Ruth West Campbell, the rigid Englishwoman who taught elocution. Every girl in Miss Campbell's class was required to choose one poem and recite it weekly, again and again as a means of measuring improvement. Ethel chose a poem called "The Great God Pan," in honor of her best buddy. But instead of the clear Shakespearean tones that Campbell sought, Ethel delivered pure South Side Chicago, culminating in a nasal *Paa-yin* that drove Campbell up the wall every time she heard it.

The headmistress became a woman obsessed. For two long years she strove to teach Ethel the proper pronunciation of the word *Pan,* never realizing that Ethel was purposefully mispronouncing the word just to bait her.

Katherine Hewitt was a Greenwich Academy graduate who'd come back to work at the school as a study-hall supervisor. Because Hewitt was an authority figure, Ethel loathed her. One day Ethel, Pan, and Pixie spotted Hewitt going into the rest room and Ethel decided it was time to take action. She got a key and locked her in. Hewitt had to pound on the door and yell at the top of her lungs until someone came and rescued her. From a vacant classroom, the PEP girls watched in hysterics.

"Ethel and I were always being sent to Miss Campbell's office," said Pan Jacob. "Being naughty was part of Ethel's whole syndrome of being noticed, of being a celebrity."

Under Ruth West Campbell, the school had a lively music, art, and dance curriculum, which Ethel enjoyed. She learned to play the piano, becoming quite proficient at the keyboard because "she had rather large hands and fingers," Pixie said.

Ethel also enjoyed drawing, and the PEP girls held the unofficial record for crayoning the biggest mural Greenwich Academy had ever seen.

"Ethel, Pixie, and I were not terribly good artists," said Pan. "But we thought that mural was the greatest picture. We called it 'The Biggest Picture in the World.' In one corner was a hockey game; in another the Army-Navy game. It was a series of small patches, each one filled with a little team sport. The art teacher had this huge roll of brown wrapping paper and she'd just roll it out and we'd continue drawing and drawing until the mural was *enormous*."

When the school's gym teacher, Jean Pethick, started teaching tap, Ethel became one of her most exuberant students, appearing in several of Pethick's productions—*A Military Review, Academy Tap-ics,* and *A Boy, a Girl and the Apple,* in which Ethel played a boy head-over-heels in love with a girl "he" couldn't have. "She was always a tomboy," recalled Pat Grant Mudge, the girl Ethel pursued in the play.

It was for dancing that Ethel received one of her very first press notices, when she appeared in a dance recital at Mamaroneck High School for the benefit of the crippled children at St. Agnes Hospital in White Plains. "Miss Ethel," said a brief item in *The Greenwich Time*, "will be a Pierrot in a dance arrangement and will also do a solo, 'Visions.' " The story included a photo of a skinny, smiling Ethel pirouetting. Mrs. Dana Clark, of Larchmont, Ethel's publicity-seeking instructor, always made certain the local papers—*The Daily Times* in Mamaroneck, *The Greenwich Time*, and the *New York Herald Tribune*—ran items about her dancers' activities. "Dainty toe dancer, Ethel Skakel of Greenwich, will appear tonight in 'Spectre de la Rose,' " was another typical mention.

At Greenwich Academy, Ethel appeared in other productions: she was the Fairy Godmother in a French version of *Cinderella;* an elf in *Rip Van Winkle;* one of the two guards outside Jesus' tomb in John Macefield's *Easter*. With the auditorium filled with parents, alumni, and school staff, Ethel gazed at Pan, who played the other guard. Seeing how ridiculous Pan looked in her helmet and armor and sporting a shield and spear, Ethel began giggling uncontrollably, causing an uproar.

Ethel actually enjoyed being on stage and liked to ham it up. At school she developed a taste for theater, and one of her favorite forms of family entertainment was going to Broadway shows. Such excursions became, for a time, a Friday night ritual in the Skakel household. The family was driven into the city by the chauffeur, had dinner at the Biltmore, and then had the best seats for popular musicals such as *Knickerbocker Holiday*.

While Ethel loved music, singing, and dancing, her tin ear for languages also applied to music, and she couldn't carry a tune. In Lowell Beveridge's chorus rehearsals, she was instructed to mouth the lyrics, but not use her actual voice. "You cannot sing. So *do* not sing," intoned Beveridge, a noted Harvard music professor who taught at Greenwich Academy twice a week. Because chorus was compulsory—the school had started participating in the Greenwich Choral Society concerts—Ethel was required to sit in the alto group and lip-synch. Ethel spent most of the time fidgeting, giggling, and mouthing innocent swear words.

It was on the playing fields at Greenwich Academy, and at horse shows, where Ethel truly excelled. "That's the way she wormed her way into everybody's heart—with her athletic ability, and her good nature," observed Pat Grant Mudge. Ethel had a natural flair for almost every athletic activity: skiing, ice skating, swinging a tennis racket, and sailing. At eleven she participated in the sailing regatta at the Larchmont Yacht Club with her sister Pat and friend Mary Russell. One of Ethel's friends, Jane O'Connor, had named her boat the *Sink or Swim*. Ethel, always the tough competitor, claimed she'd used the name first—so she renamed her craft *Sink or Swim the First*.

Ethel was considered one of the top athletes at Greenwich Academy, which was divided into two teams—the Green and Gold. For her prowess in several sports, especially as a fleet-footed wing on the field hockey team, she was named the best athlete of the Greens and was awarded a special green blazer.

19 ✻ National Velvet

DURING ADOLESCENCE RIDING became Ethel's passion. Outside of her Greenwich Academy uniform her wardrobe consisted of jodhpurs, top coat, riding hat, and crop.

"I don't know how she got through school because we were always riding in the afternoons, and showing on weekends," said Franny Pryor Haws. "I don't recall us doing a lot of homework." Ethel and Pixie Meek, though, wanted to become veterinarians so they could spend *all* of their time with horses.

On Saturday afternoons, if they weren't riding, Ethel and Franny could be found in the front row of the Pickwick Theater in town, eating popcorn and watching the latest cowboy film, Ethel's favorite genre, because of the horses and the handsome riders. For a time, she idolized Alan Ladd, and when *National Velvet* opened, Ethel was in heaven; she saw the film featuring a young Elizabeth Taylor at least a dozen times.

During those years Ethel owned several horses: Smoky Joe, who was black with white socks; a chestnut mare working hunter named Guamada; and Beau Mischief, a dark bay. "Big Ann wasn't an outdoorsy type and she especially despised horses," said Martin McKneally. "She was always bemoaning the fact that Ethel exuded the smell of horse dung."

Ethel's pal Billy Steinkraus, who went on to become a member of the U.S. Olympic riding team, said, "She took to riding the way she took to touch football with the Kennedys."

As young as eight, Ethel was already competing. In

April 1936, she took part in the spring competition of the Kenilworth Riding Club, in Rye, of which she was a member. She got a mention and her picture in *The New York Times*. An oval, sepia photograph of Ethel, her brothers George and Rushton, and sisters Pat and Georgeann—all in full riding regalia—appeared over the caption: FIVE MEMBERS OF ONE FAMILY RIDE IN THE SAME HORSE SHOW. Subsequently there would be dozens of stories about Ethel's victories, and her room would become filled with trophies and ribbons.

Ethel was taught by one of the premier horsemen in the area, Teddy Wahl, who had stables at Greenwich's exclusive Round Hill Club, where the riding trails wound around the golf course. Ironically, one of the first show horses Ethel rode under Wahl's expert tutelage was Step Aside, who had once been owned by Janet Lee Bouvier, mother of a pretty girl named Jackie. The Bouvier girl sometimes rode on hunts with Teddy Wahl's group, but she and Ethel had never met. By the time Ethel got on Step Aside, the horse had been bought by Peggy Klipstein Larned. An expert rider, six years older than Ethel, Peggy was the captain of the Greenwich Academy riding team, and had become Ethel's "horse guru."

Teddy Wahl harped constantly on safety, something Ethel cared little about, and she was constantly breaking Wahl's rules, resulting in some near serious accidents. Ethel eventually moved to another stable where there was less discipline. "She was a gutsy rider and she felt Teddy was too oppressive," Franny Pryor Haws said. "No one had the drive that Ethel had with horses."

Ethel would enter the most difficult competitions, such as bareback jumping contests. She'd ride two on a horse, performing dangerous stunts like jumping obstacles or even jumping from horse to horse.

"She'd do anything on a dare," recalled Billy Steinkraus. "She had a lot of falls because she was a go-for-broke person."

Ethel and her friend Anne Morningstar Huberth had fallen in love with two horses, Magic and Red Butler. One summer the two girls spent a week visiting them at a stable in Chester, Vermont. During their stay, the young equestriennes were enlisted to act as judges in a local horse show, but were soon pressured into performing because of a white lie they had told.

"We came back from dinner and we were in dresses," recalled Huberth. "There was a beautiful full moon and Ethel said, 'Let's get Red out and take him for a ride.' So we rode him double to the top of the hill where the ring was and we just walked around the ring with him and came back.

"No one could see us up there, so we told everyone that because the moon was so bright we had enough light to jump all of the fences. The next day at the horse show the farmers were saying, 'We want to see those two girls who rode double and jumped double in the moonlight.'

"We hadn't done anything of the kind. We were just kidding, but of course we had to jump double the day of that show. I drew the front position because I knew Red better. Ethel was sitting behind me hanging on and we went out and practiced. We did the first jump and we fell off and landed on the ground. Ethel said, 'We're going to get this right.' We did and we jumped the fences in the ring and they thought we were wonderful."

On weekends, Anne, Franny, Pixie, and some of Ethel's other friends rode over to Lake Avenue, where they could ride as they pleased without supervision. They'd jerry-rig hunt courses and ride through and over the Skakels' rose gardens with complete impunity, using rosebushes and stone walls as jumps, often riding bareback and without hunt caps.

On one occasion, Ethel's sister Ann suffered serious injuries as a result of the foolhardy riding that went on at Lake Avenue. That day the group included Ethel, her brothers, Jimmy and George, and Franny. Because there was no adult supervision, they were jumping on muddy ground, riding three abreast, and Ann was wearing clunky ski boots instead of riding boots. When her horse slipped—at the same time Jim's and George's mounts fell—one of Ann's boots became lodged in the stirrup.

"We were sort of showing off for our parents, who

were watching from the dining room," said Jim Skakel. "Ann broke the cardinal rule because ski boots do not slip out of stirrups. Her foot was crushed in the steel stirrup by the weight of the horse. My parents ran out of the house. Ann was half passed out. My father called for an ambulance and the doctor. They took her to Greenwich Hospital, where they had a hell of a time getting her foot out of the boot and the stirrup. They had to operate on her that day to get everything straightened out. She had severe damage to that foot. It took her six months to a year to recover. She was on crutches for a long time. Ann was lucky she could walk naturally after that."

Not content with the vast grounds of her family's estate, Ethel occasionally broadened her riding territory to include the interior of the big house as well. She shocked Teddy Wahl's daughter, Bobbie, one afternoon by riding straight through the front door, over the elegant Elsie de Wolfe flooring in the entrance hall, tromping over the rugs in her path, and galloping out the back door.

"Ethel told me, 'Just gallop and go!' She went right through the house yelling, 'Yoo-hoo,' " recalled Bobbie Wahl, who was following in Ethel's wake on her own horse. "Ethel was galloping like hell and shot right through the whole house."

Ethel traveled throughout the Northeast on weekends participating in shows and hunts, and usually winning. It was an expensive hobby, what with the van fees to transport the horses, stabling and grooming fees at the various shows, expensive tack, overnight accommodations at inns, and pocket money. But to Big Ann it was worth every penny. "It kept Ethel out of her mother's hair," asserted Martin McKneally. "That was the only thing Mrs. Skakel liked about Ethel's interest in horses."

20 ✻ Fast Cars and Smoking Guns

JIM AND GEORGE Skakel quickly earned a reputation in Greenwich as hooligans and vandals. They were gun-toting joyriders who tooled around the countryside in their expensive cars, leaving a wide swath of destruction in their wake. Of the Skakel girls, Ethel was considered most like her brothers: irresponsible, unruly, arrogant.

"Those Skakel kids would get it up to ninety miles an hour in nothing flat and tear all over the place, very likely shooting large-caliber pistols out of the window at the same time," said Ken McDonnell, a friend of the boys. "They were always looking for trouble."

Pan Jacob placed the blame on the lack of discipline and parental oversight at Lake Avenue:

"The Skakel kids weren't spoiled so much as they were deprived. They had money but they didn't have anything else. There was no structure. Most families have a way of doing things, a pattern of behavior. There was no pattern at Lake Avenue. It was an abstract painting as opposed to a formal painting, more surreal than Rembrandt; a Jackson Pollock world where everything was exploding, where there was no cohesiveness. The Skakel house had a sadness about it. It didn't have a core. The family had no established roots. *We* all felt secure. I don't think they did. In fact, they were a mass of insecurity."

As soon as each Skakel child was of driving age, George and Big Ann got them a new car. Their driving became so legendary that the chief of the Greenwich Police Department routinely stationed a motorcycle officer at the end of the Skakel driveway, hoping to nab any one of them for speeding or reckless driving.

"Every cop in Greenwich was waiting for a Skakel car," recalled Franny Pryor Haws. "They were all stopped at one time or another."

But for the most part, the Skakels usually received no more than a slap on the wrist for their misbehavior. The Greenwich police were looked upon by the local gentry as menial help, and they dared not invite a problem by threatening to put anyone in jail. "It was," said one longtime resident, "a servant–head of the manor relationshp with the police."

Ethel's first car was a sleek red convertible. "We'd cruise because there wasn't much else to do. She used to go racing down the Merritt Parkway with the top down and waving at everybody," said Haws. "Ethel would yell out to the driver of the car next to us, 'Hey, your right-rear jocelyn is loose!' And the guy would look and look and eventually pull over, and I can remember sitting in the backseat going, 'Oh, no, we're going to get into trouble.' I remember Ethel being stopped by the police and I was scared."

Ethel drove recklessly and at high speeds, sometimes at night with her lights off. Once, coming back from a horse show, she drove her car off the road and through the woods as a shortcut home. One year, she had a car without a reverse gear and everywhere she went she caused a traffic jam and hot tempers if she had to back up, which she found hysterical. Ethel or her passengers would push the car backward.

When the Second World War came and gasoline was rationed, neighbors and local authorities thought the highway menace posed by the young Skakels would come to an end. But the Skakels were always able to connive extra gasoline from a local garage. "They had a way of getting anything they wanted," remembered Pan Jacob.

Jim and George Skakel, Jr., both of whom almost died in separate high-speed auto accidents, were considered such dangerous drivers that Ethel's friends were grounded by their parents if they set foot in a car driven by a Skakel boy."

On one occasion, George Jr. drove to a friend's house to swim and decided to park next to the pool instead of in the driveway. As the friend and his parents watched in horror, George came down the hilly lawn, picking up speed as he went. Just before slamming into the patio he hit on the brakes, ripping up fifty feet of turf.

George Skakel, Sr., came home one evening with a new Lincoln Zephyr. "It's *my* car," he announced firmly. Late that night one of the Skakel boys and two friends sneaked into the garage, pushed the car to the top of the hill on Lake Avenue, jumped in, released the brake, and coasted into a rocky and muddy ditch.

When George gave Big Ann a new car on another occasion, it was wrecked before she ever had a chance to see it. "The car wasn't even twelve hours old," recalled Jim Skakel, laughing.

One day the brothers decided to build a bridge across a small lake near the Skakel home. Their construction material consisted of half a dozen expensive Buicks that were driven into the lake hood-to-trunk, allowing the boys to traverse the water on the roofs of the cars.

"All those cars ended up accordion-pleated in the water," recalled Pan Jacob, "and that was considered lots of fun by them. No one in the house said, 'What a horrible thing to do!' It was just 'Isn't this fun? Isn't this amusing? Those naughty boys!' There was no punishment."

Jim Skakel maintained years later that his parents tried to instill "responsibility, competitiveness, and good behavior" in their sons and daughters, "but it wasn't *Deutschland über Alles*" around the house. "We had a lot of fun. Our parents weren't strict, but we didn't do anything too ridiculous, either. There wasn't any pressure. The philosophy was 'Enjoy yourself.' "

By the time Jim and George Skakel, Jr., were in their teens, they'd become gun nuts like their father, who had a standing order with Abercrombie & Fitch for the latest rifles with the greatest range and killing power. But while George Skakel, Sr., kept his shooting confined to game, everything became targets to his sons.

"They used to shoot up mailboxes and streetlamps," asserted childhood pal Ken McDonnell. "There were some forty-five-caliber bullet holes in some of those mailboxes. They were using big stuff, and there was some retaliation. Some people went up there to the Skakel house and put a few holes in their mailbox.

"They were a crazy bunch. They were aimed for trouble. You could almost smell it. Even as a youngster you could feel it."

One of the more serious incidents, the shooting of Skakel pal Greg Reilly at Lake Avenue, was hushed up, and never investigated by authorities. One version of the story had Jim Skakel and his friends shooting squirrels. Suddenly everyone opened fire at some rocks. Ricocheting bullets flew everywhere, and one struck Reilly.

Scared and bleeding, Reilly was placed in a car by the boys and driven to the hospital in Port Chester rather than to nearby Greenwich Hospital. The reason was to protect the Skakels. Had Reilly been taken to Greenwich Hospital, the shooting would most certainly have been promptly reported to police because everyone in town knew of the Skakels' predilection for guns. Luckily, Reilly's wounds weren't serious, and he was treated and released at the Port Chester hospital, without any police involvement. His parents were furious, but no legal action was taken because no one could determine who actually fired the bullet.

The shooter in what became known as the Moab Motel Incident was clearly identified, however. He was George Skakel, Jr., and he shot his brother Jim, according to Jay Mayhew. The shooting was the culmination of a wild summer when the Skakel boys worked under Mayhew's supervision as roughnecks on the drilling rigs at the eleven-hundred-acre Skakel Ranch in Moab, Utah. George Sr. had bought the spread in hopes of finding minerals. Mayhew was aware of Jim and George's propensity for guns. Once, while on a visit to Lake Avenue, he watched, horror-stricken, as Jim and George Jr., armed with rifles, opened fire from a window inside the house at an irreplaceable Grecian marble statue that stood on the lawn near the pool. "The last one to shoot an ear off that statue was a 'Nigger baby.' That was the game," recalled Mayhew. "They destroyed the statue in the process."

When George telephoned Mayhew asking if he'd watch over the boys for the summer, the company geologist cringed. "They were wild, wacky, young broncos. How the hell could I handle them if their own father couldn't? George just said that I would be the boss and tell them what to do, and if they didn't do it, let him know and he'd get them back home."

George Jr. and Jim arrived in the small town of Moab and checked into the local motel armed for a revolution.

"They flew in on the company plane bringing automatic rifles, which were illegal for a non-Army person to have at the time," recalled Mayhew. "They had cases of ammunition and forty-five-caliber pistols, whew, boy! The purpose of all the artillery was just to have fun while they were there. They'd race around in their cars shooting out of the windows. By the time they left town, a lot of the signs around Moab were cut off at ground level. I finally got an understanding from them that they wouldn't carry guns when they were in a car with me."

Late one afternoon after a day of working on the drilling rigs, Jim, George Jr., and Mayhew returned to their room at the motel.

"Jim was laying on the bed relaxing," recalled Mayhew, who was still unsettled years later by what happened next. "George asked Jimmy something and Jimmy didn't answer and George said, 'By God, when I ask you a question I want you to answer.' With that George pulled out a loaded and cocked forty-five, aimed it at his brother, and pulled the trigger. The explosion of the gun going off in that little room was enormous, and I smelled the gunpowder and I thought that when I opened my eyes I'd see Jimmy dead on the bed.

"What happened was the bullet had put a crease just above Jim's stomach. It wasn't that bad, just enough to make a red line. Jesus! George asked Jimmy, 'Does it hurt?' And Jim said, 'I felt it.' We didn't even go to the hospital. But Jim could have been killed."

21 * *Skakels at War*

DECEMBER 7, 1941, was a typical Sunday at Lake Avenue. The family had an early breakfast and then Ethel and Big Ann went off to Mass at St. Mary's. Ethel was now midway through the ninth grade at Greenwich Academy, her last year there before heading off to a Catholic girls' boarding school. At the moment, she was anxiously awaiting the family's annual Christmas vacation at Lake Placid.

Ethel and her mother returned from church with Big Ann's usual coterie of priests, who spent the day at the house eating, drinking, and discussing Catholicism. The guest of honor for dinner that Sunday was a monsignor who had gained national prominence for his activities in the labor movement. He was one of the few of the many clerics who visited the house with whom George had anything in common.

Around five o'clock, a family friend dropped by to talk about the horrible news—the Japanese attack on Pearl Harbor—which the Skakels were unaware of. Ethel had just turned on the radio to hear one of her favorite weekend serials, but was disappointed when she heard a newscaster talking about the outbreak of war in the Pacific, so she switched it off.

"No one gathered around the radio," recalled Jim

Skakel. "Nobody got excited. Pearl Harbor just didn't ring a bell with us."

America's dramatic entry into the war would quadruple the amount of business the company, recently renamed Great Lakes Carbon Corp., was generating. On the day that would live in infamy, the company was swimming in money, with a whopping $50 million in hard cash earning interest in just one bank account alone.

Early in the war, George got inside information that the U.S. government was working on a secret weapon that would require uranium. He immediately dispatched Jay Mayhew to the Skakel Ranch to search for the radioactive material. While Mayhew didn't find uranium, the fuel needed for the atomic bomb, he did strike oil. At George's instant direction, Mayhew set up an oil and gas division for the company, which was now netting a healthy twelve hundred barrels a day. "It was big money and George rubbed his hands together and said, 'Oh, boy! Where have I been? I like this business!'" Mayhew recalled.

Meanwhile, George was always thinking of new ways to help win the war. One of his Rube Goldberg schemes involved using boats equipped with pumps, flexible pipelines, and hydraulic motors to drown heavily armed Japanese soldiers hiding in caves on South Pacific islands. The War Department wasn't interested.

On the home front, George showed his appreciation to America's fighting men on leave by giving those he knew carte blanche at fancy bars, such as the Rainbow Room in New York. The Skakels also entertained members of the armed forces at Lake Avenue. Early in the war, Big Ann and George hosted a dinner dance for more than a hundred and fifty guests to honor seventeen members of the only squadron of the Royal Air Force in the United States, which was headed by Capt. Philippe Livry, a friend of George's. Ethel and her sisters were there to receive the Australian, English, and New Zealand fliers. The Skakels' terrace, where an eight-piece orchestra provided dance music, was decorated with the flags of England and the United States. The next day, Big

Ann gave a breakfast party, took the RAF boys on a trip aboard the yacht *Duke*, and then swimming at the Larchmont Yacht Club.

Big Ann had a Victory Garden, assigning her gardeners to raise potatoes and corn. She also attended "Bundles for Britain" benefits at the Ritz-Carlton in New York, and held teas at Lake Avenue with the proceeds going to aid refugees in the United States. The guest of honor at one such function, which featured hand-sewn linens and hand-painted trays designed and fashioned by a group of French refugees, was Mrs. Wendell Willkie, wife of the Republican leader and unsuccessful Presidential candidate.

Ethel's pal Pan Jacob worked as a nurse's aide at Greenwich Hospital, as did Ethel's sister Georgeann, who also spent the first winter of the war doing volunteer hostess work at Fort Bragg, in North Carolina. Pixie Meek knitted mittens and scarves for servicemen. But none of the girls could remember Ethel giving any of her time. "She was always riding," said Bobbie Wahl. However, Ethel did participate in competitions whose proceeds went to organizations such as the British War Relief Fund and the American Red Cross.

Ethel's brothers were eventually called to arms, all of them seeing the war as a good reason to drop out of school. The Navy drafted twenty-year-old Rushton, a nervous type, who stayed in just eleven and a half days before he was discharged, suffering from duodenol ulcers, a problem that had not surfaced prior to his reporting for duty. "I had no idea why I had ulcers at such a young age, but the Navy threw me out," he acknowledged later. Rushton, who was a sophomore at Amherst when he was conscripted, was sent home, where he was treated by family doctors. Following nine months of rest, care by his mother, and a diet of milk, he was pronounced fit for service by the draft board and went into the Army Air Corps, where he served without distinction.

Jim Skakel, plagued with a number of childhood illnesses, also suffered sudden, inexplicable medical problems when Uncle Sam called him to duty in the

Army Air Corps, and he too was quickly discharged. He never bothered to return to Northwestern University, where he had already grown bored studying engineering at his father's urging.

Only George Skakel, Jr., endured the full wartime experience, dropping out of Amherst and serving in the South Pacific. After receiving his Navy flight training at the Naval Air Training Center in Pensacola, Florida, and his commission as an ensign in the Naval Reserve, Skakel was shocked to get orders assigning him to instructors' school rather than to a combat unit. With the philosophy that no one tells a Skakel what to do, he adamantly refused the assignment. Like a scene out of a zany World War II film, the truculent young flier took a Navy plane and flew home to show his displeasure. "My brother took on the whole Navy because he was determined *not* to be an instructor," said Jim Skakel. Luckily for him, George Jr.'s mutinous and macho behavior actually impressed his superiors, so they decided not to throw him in the brig. But the Navy took away his gold wings, and got him out of its hair by shipping him off to Truk, a tiny slice of land in the Caroline island chain, northeast of New Guinea, where he spent the duration overseeing the airstrip. Later, he boasted that he once flew a fighter plane under the Boardwalk in Atlantic City, and that he machine-gunned "like ducks" a bunch of Japanese soldiers taking baths on an island. Knowing George's propensities, no one questioned his stories.

Back at home, George Skakel, Sr., found another way to make money from the war. He linked up with a well-connected Army colonel, Alfred Parry, a former vice president of Lykes Brothers Shipping, who was now in a good position with the Army Transportation Corps in Washington. George financed the purchase of several tramp steamers known as Hog Islanders, which he named for his daughters. The *Ethel Skakel*, the *Patricia Skakel*, and the *Ann Skakel* were operated for the War Shipping Administration under a lucrative government contract that was secured with Parry's help and influence. Great Lakes Carbon owned 75 percent of the shipping company, while Parry, who ran the business for George, was given 25 percent. "It was good timing and they made good money," said Jim Skakel later. As soon as the war ended, George, who'd made a bundle from the ships, one of which was sunk by a German U-boat, got out of the shipping business, but not before selling off the two remaining tubs for scrap at a healthy profit.

Other than making the Skakels wealthier, the war had little impact on life at Lake Avenue. The family's screwball lifestyle continued unabated.

To many who knew them during those years, the Skakels' world was like a pilot for the "Beverly Hillbillies" TV show. Like the fictional, ingenuous Clampetts who struck oil in their backyard, the Skakels had piles of money and little sophistication.

The toilets in the two powder rooms on the main floor were constantly overflowing and, as a result, that area of the house sometimes smelled like an outhouse. "God knows what those kids threw down the johns, but Mrs. Pulaski, the Polish day worker, was always mopping up the ladies' room and the men's room, which were on opposite sides of the hall from each other," recalled Hope Larkin Johnston, a childhood pal.

While Big Ann tried to keep the number of stray dogs in the house to no more than two at a time, a pack of mutts usually had the run of the place, ruining rugs and staining floors. "Dad must have been unusual because any dog who ever saw him left their house and followed him home," said Rushton Skakel. "We had over fifteen or more dogs. In those days dogs worth five hundred dollars would follow Dad and stay with us. The owners would find out where the dog was and demand that Mother pay them the five hundred dollars. They were justifiably angry. Mother would say fine, but then she'd actually send them a dog-food bill that was higher than the price they wanted for the dog."

The Skakel dogs would come charging at visitors walking up to the front door at Lake Avenue, or they'd jump in the pool and playfully try to drown anyone swimming. Like the backyard of the Clampetts' place, the Skakels' estate also began to resemble a farm. On the grounds were a billy goat, a couple of pigs, some sheep, and dozens of mutts, chickens, and bunny rabbits. Of all the animals, the dogs were Ethel and her father's favorites. The Greenwich blue bloods often joked about running into Ethel or her father on a trail with a pack of his mixed breeds while they were out hunting with their expensive hounds. "Ethel and her family had whims with animals," Anne Morningstar Huberth remembered. "But the thrill would wear off quickly."

Big Ann was oblivious to the mess at Lake Avenue. She'd leave the clogged plumbing and the odiferous animal cleanup to the housekeeper and spend the day in Manhattan regally dressed in floor-length furs, shopping for clothes or antiques.

"One day on the train she said to me, 'Dear, do you realize I have three mink coats on?' " recalled a family friend. "I thought, 'What is she *talking* about?' She then explained that because of her size the number of pelts for her coat would make three mink coats. She didn't have a lot of finishing, but she sure was a character."

Despite the size of her mink, Big Ann earned a reputation around town for being tight-fisted. She counted the eggs to make sure the servants weren't stealing. And when it came to paying the family's bills, she held on to her household money for as long as she could, infuriating merchants and vendors who sometimes never saw a cent for the goods and services they supplied to Lake Avenue.

"The Skakels were great so long as they paid their bills," said Joe Busk, a Greenwich merchant. "When they came into the shop, there would be this big flurry of activity because they bought in quantity. But the only thing that was really exciting was whether or not we were going to get paid. Fortunately *we* never got stuck for any great amount, but other stores were not quite so lucky. The word about the Skakels around the trade was 'Watch out.' "

22 ✻ *Balls, Teas, and Spaghetti Dinners*

AS THE WAR years dragged on, Big Ann's own conflict with the WASPs of Greenwich continued unabated. Finally, she resigned herself to the fact that she would never be fully accepted as a part of town society. "She was never able to make a life for herself there," said Pixie Meek. "The kids did, but Mr. and Mrs. Skakel didn't."

While Big Ann had her own crowd of friends, most of them from Chicago and Larchmont, some of her husband's own business associates viewed her style as tacky, vulgar, and pushy.

Company geologist Jay Mayhew, for one, said, "Mrs. Skakel was overbearing. She had a lot of money and she lorded it over anyone she felt was beneath her. She constantly picked on little people like waiters and waitresses—'Take it back! Warm it up!' 'Do this, do that.'

"George, who was a gentle man, watched her and he obviously was offended and embarrassed by her actions. He never said anything, but I could tell by the look on his face. He was quite expressive and his eyes got wider and he'd look away. It was clear that Mrs. Skakel felt that her money gave her power, something she didn't have when she was growing up. So she wielded it. Otherwise her repertoire was not very broad. She was pretty narrow."

Big Ann loved to entertain and did so frequently and on a grand scale. She dolled herself up in black dresses, diamonds, and orchids of deep purple, but that still didn't satisfy the matrons of Greenwich, who thought she looked tasteless no matter what she did to herself.

"She might have been a beautiful woman if she hadn't been so heavy and disported herself as a plain, shabby woman," said the daughter of one of them. "She wore a bluish tint of liner around her eyes, wore her blonde hair cropped with no styling, and her stout figure had no contours, so she looked like a big block. Had she been smaller and thinner, she would have been pretty. Still, she would never have fitted in."

Nothwithstanding, Lake Avenue was the setting for a constant round of elaborate garden parties, dinner parties, cocktail parties, tea dances, and teas, hosted by Big Ann. There also were casual pool parties, with guests being thrown fully clothed into either the pool or the fountain. "That was part of the initiation," said Anne Morningstar Huberth. Years later, Ethel would make front-page news with her own pool dunkings.

Ethel and her siblings threw birthday parties and dances attended by as many as three hundred and fifty guests, with entertainment provided by New York nightclub orchestras and fortune-tellers with names like "Annabelle" and "Miss Esther." The Skakel girls wore beautiful gowns and carried bouquets of flowers like characters in Southern romance novels. Because her life revolved around horses, Ethel often threw hunt breakfasts for members and guests of the Fairfield and Westchester Hounds, and on the eve of the big National Horse Show at Madison Square Garden, where she competed in a variety of events, she hosted dinner parties at the Biltmore Hotel.

Big Ann surrounded herself at soirées with people whom she considered celebrities and royalty: Countess Isabelle Colicicchi of Rome; Count Lorenzo de Haven of Hungary; Lady Gainsborough of England; Count and Countess Serge Fluery; radio fashion-commentator Tharo Winslow; syndicated advice-to-the-lovelorn columnist Annette "Doris Blake" Donnelley; movie critic Kate Cameron; Manhattan nightclub vocalist Maggie McMillis. On many occasions her dinners had a religious theme and the guests of honor were prominent theologians.

When she wasn't entertaining on the sweeping terraces and verandas of Lake Avenue, Big Ann gave parties aboard the *Bavois*, the Skakels' chartered sixty-eight-foot yawl, which was anchored at the Larchmont Yacht Club. The revelers often cruised to places like Nantucket and Huntington, Long Island.

Not all of Big Ann's entertaining was fancy, though. "She'd have spaghetti parties of all things, which were unheard of in Greenwich in those days," recalled a woman who was still shocked years later by what she saw as Big Ann's gaucheness. "She'd have all the guests come in evening clothes, distribute white cotton bibs to everyone, and then serve up big plates of spaghetti and tomato sauce—all you could eat. I'd been to many places, but never to a spaghetti party. We just didn't do that sort of thing in Greenwich."

It's a wonder that Big Ann was able to entertain at all because she had an extremely difficult time keeping help. A New York agency was constantly sending out new recruits. "With all of those children, the house was completely disorganized," said a family friend. "The kids would never come to meals on time and the help couldn't deal with it."

The only long-term live-in was a French seamstress who was hired to sew and mend for the roughhousing brood. The elderly woman was often enlisted to vacuum and dust. Big Ann's gnomelike, aging mother, Margaret Brannack, also pitched in. "She was like a little specter, a little witch with a broom in her hand, her gray hair in a bun and wearing gingham dresses that looked like they came off the rack at Sears, three for ten dollars," recalled Pan Jacob. In terms of rotating cooks, there was a method to Big Ann's madness.

"What Mother would do was amazing," Rushton Skakel boasted later. "She would hire a cook, learn what she knew that Mother didn't know about cooking, and as soon as Mother knew, she'd fire the cook and hire another one so she could learn something new."

With the start of the war, everyone in Greenwich, not only the Skakels, was having a difficult time retaining or getting help because the defense plants offered better salaries and benefits. To help manage the house and entertain guests, Big Ann turned to Georgeann, who had trained at the Cordon Bleu after graduating from Marymount College, in Tarrytown, New York, in June 1939.

By the early 1940s, though, Georgeann's drinking had worsened. "She was getting into the bottle," said Anne Morningstar Huberth. "So we all covered for her. Ethel and I would make sure we got her into bed when she was drunk, that sort of thing." Big Ann was worried because Georgeann's drinking was making her reclusive, so she pushed her to become more social.

Reluctantly following her mother's lead, Georgeann began throwing lavish parties at Lake Avenue, theater parties in New York City, and she became active in various volunteer groups where she rubbed shoulders with young ladies from the cream of New York's Irish Catholic society. While Georgeann was serving on the junior committee for the annual Gotham Dance, a Catholic charities fund-raiser, she made the acquaintance of a pretty nineteen-year-old Bostonian named Eunice Kennedy. That was the earliest known social contact between the two families.

During the war, Georgeann began dating John J. Dowdle, Jr., a handsome Navy flier and hero, whom she'd known as a youngster when the Skakels lived in Chicago and the Dowdles in suburban Wilmette. The two got engaged in April 1945 and were married the following month. Georgeann was the first of the Skakel children to tie the knot.

Like Georgeann, Dowdle was a drinker. Feeling the pressures and anxieties of the wartime business boom, George Skakel, Sr., was also hitting the bottle regularly.

"It was no secret that Mr. Skakel used to get roaring drunk on the weekends," recalled Hope Larkin Johnston. "He'd get drunk on Saturday, Mrs. Skakel would try to sober him up on Sunday, and he'd go back to work on Monday. She'd always have priests in the house on the weekends and I'd see them helping her take Mr. Skakel up the stairs."

One of George's favorite luncheon spots was the Men's Bar at the Waldorf. One day, after having a few too many, he got surly, threw a glass, smashed one of the expensive mirrors behind the bar, and then reeled back to the office. His top assistant, Henry Walker, was immediately dispatched to take care of the mess by paying for the damages. "The hotel management accepted gracefully because George was a good customer and they didn't want to hurt that relationship," said Tom Hayes, who was in the office the day of the incident.

In the early 1940s, the Skakel family began vacationing in Cuba. George and Big Ann sometimes spent the whole winter season there, living like royalty in a spacious home with servants, on property owned by another wealthy American. The house was located in Varadero, about eighty miles from Havana, and not far from the hacienda of Fulgencio Batista, Cuba's dictator. "As little kids we would go up and bang on the door and say, 'Come to our party,' and Batista's guards would laugh," recalled Rushton Skakel. He said his father spent his days golfing, fishing, and quail hunting, and his nights drinking. "He became a serious alcoholic in Cuba. Mother was very concerned." At one point, George became friends with Ernest Hemingway, who had a house in Cuba, and the writer and the businessman frequently drank together. "I can remember my brother and I going to Hemingway's house because he called us and said, 'You've got to pick up your father. He's drunk,' " Rushton Skakel said.

Every so often Jim Skakel, a heavy drinker himself, accompanied his father to one of the bars in Greenwich. George would have a little too much and get into an argument and Jim, who stood six foot two, would have to bail him out. "My father would get himself in a jam, and then he'd introduce me to the other guy, so I'd have to be a quick negotiator for him. I'd usually say, 'We were just leaving.' After we left the bar, I'd tell Dad, 'Don't get into those things.' "

Drinking was part of a dark side of George's character that belied his seemingly sunny nature. "Dad was gentle and kind, but he could be very tough, too," said Rushton Skakel. "If he talked to a statue, the statue would say, 'Yes sir, no sir, no excuse, sir.' "

George sometimes exhibited a toughness, cockiness, and brusqueness that caught people who didn't know him by surprise because he was such a small man. Some people were wary, even frightened, of him. He'd sometimes swagger into shops in Greenwich, demand instant service, and pay in cash, peeling off bills from a thick roll of hundreds held together with half a dozen rubber bands. George Skakel idolized hard-boiled types like Jimmy Cagney, Pat O'Brien, and Leo Durocher, sometimes emulating their style.

Sam Robbins got to know George as a customer when he'd come into his Greenwich shop to buy rifles and ammunition. On occasion the two men went trap shooting together. Robbins said, "He was not a simple, lovable guy. He was short and abrupt, something of an introvert. He didn't like to get too cozy. He didn't say a lot but whatever he said, he meant every syllable. In that sense, he wasn't a gentle man. He was a tough guy, a ruffian, no doubt about it.

"George Skakel was the strength and he was the tower of Great Lakes Carbon. He thought big, and a lot of it worked. All of his kids inherited that same sense of thinking in awfully big terms."

23 ✻ *Ethel of the Sacred Heart*

HAVING ALLOWED ETHEL to attend a nonsectarian school, Big Ann now declared it was time to get her back into a Catholic institution. She chose the Convent of the Sacred Heart, Maplehurst, a five-day-a-week boarding school, at 174th Street and University Avenue, in a slowly deteriorating section of the Bronx, a thirty-minute train ride from Greenwich.

Girls from many of the prominent Catholic families of the day were getting Sacred Heart educations. Two of the Kennedy girls, Patricia and Jean, had gone to Maplehurst, a tradition started by their mother, Rose, a vocal advocate of the order's principles.

Because Maplehurst was located on the grounds of a Revolutionary War–era estate, with acres of plush rose gardens and stately maple trees, a visiting priest once described the school as "an oasis in the middle of the Bronx."

But the beauty of the grounds camouflaged the true bleakness of life there. Entering its gates was like landing on another planet for a rich, undisciplined fifteen-year-old like Ethel.

When she arrived in September 1943 to begin the eleventh grade, the cloistered nuns of the Society of the Sacred Heart were still living a medieval existence, acting roles of humility, penance, and deprivation. They were the descendants of an order founded during the violent anticlericalism of the French Revolution by St. Madeleine Sophie, the daughter of a winemaker. The nuns inflicted pain upon themselves using a whiplike device called the discipline, or with a spike-covered small metal ring that fit over their arms. There were iron-clad rules about everything; in certain instances, nuns could only have their spartan meals unobserved, forcing some to eat in a restroom stall. When they first entered the order, young nuns were told to bring a supply of diapers to be worn in place of sanitary pads when they had their periods.

"Maplehurst," remarked Margot Gotte MacNiven, who lived down the hall from Ethel, "was a world unto its own." But none of it came as a surprise. Ethel's sister Pat, herself a recent Maplehurst graduate, had recounted many of the horror stories.

At Maplehurst, Ethel landed on her feet running, "a self-willed, spontaneous little creature with merry brown eyes and a laughing face," recalled Mother Elizabeth

Farley, who taught Ethel English literature. "She was a good student, but certainly not what we called 'Blue Ribbon.' Her main interest seemed to be horses." "Just plain Ethel" was a roommate's description. "She was skinny with bobbed brown hair, not pretty, not even cute. She had a physical thing that embarrassed her, a bump in the middle of her chest, a chicken-breasted thing, a protuberance. It wasn't anything really noticeable, but Ethel talked about it incessantly. She also had very small breasts, so she refused to wear anything with a V neck."

Ethel's face was usually red and dripping perspiration from hard play on the hockey field, and she always seemed breathless; words came tumbling out of her mouth and suddenly in midsentence she'd pause, take a deep breath, talk some more, pause, breathe, and talk. She started greeting everyone with such endearments as "Hey, kid!" and "Hiya, babe!" whether she knew the person well or not, and she always seemed to be smiling, even at inappropriate times. "It was a strange kind of smile that made her look as if she was thinking about something that none of us were aware of," noted a classmate.

Ethel didn't waste any time establishing her reputation as the most brazen of the thirteen students in the class of 1945. "She was easily the most spirited," said Louise Wood Paul, who entered Maplehurst with Ethel.

Her first night Ethel waited until lights out, sneaked out of bed, and began rummaging through her suitcases, banging and crashing around in the dark, all the while swearing, "Dammit to hell" loudly to herself. Hearing determined footsteps approaching, roommate Eleanor Conroy McGrath warned Ethel that a nun was coming. Ethel tossed everything in the closet, raced to her bed, and pulled the covers over her face. "Just what is going on in here?" the nun demanded. "Oh, *nothing,* Mother," responded Ethel angelically. "I'll bet," said the nun. Ethel gave the sister a few minutes, then hopped out of bed, dashed to the closet, and continued the racket.

The Sacred Heart rules were rigid, but Ethel consistently flaunted them, risking the wrath of Mother Marion Duffy, the stern young director of students, who was dubbed the "mistress of discipline," or facing the enmity of Mother Helen Bourke, the formidable, didactic dean of students. Ethel's passage, though, was smoothed considerably by Big Ann, who had forged a close friendship with Mother Bourke by helping the school financially, donating funds for a small chapel. As a result, the nuns tended to be a bit more lenient when the daughter of one of the school's benefactors stepped out of line.

"We didn't think she would last two weeks because of the discipline and training," said Mother Duffy years later. "In her own home she did not have a lot of discipline, was a free spirit, an extrovert of the first order, not introspective. She didn't care about fitting in."

Ethel's long day started at six-fifteen A.M., when she came flying out of her small, austere room and lined up in the cold hallway to get a pitcher of water to wash her face and brush her teeth. "It was pretty spartan," said classmate Alice Meadows Buetow, a day student who lived across the street from Maplehurst. "For girls like Ethel, having to share a bathroom was extreme. There were no luxuries and she wasn't used to roughing it." Minutes after awakening, Ethel had to have her nightclothes folded, her bed made, and be in proper uniform: a plain navy blue skirt and jacket and white blouse for class; a jumper with silly bloomers, white blouse, and black cotton stockings for athletics; a simple aqua blue shirtwaist dress with white collar for dinner. Like drill sergeants, the nuns came by to inspect the rooms, and if Ethel's bed wasn't up to snuff, they'd tear it apart and force her to make it over. On her way to Mass and breakfast, Ethel had to curtsy to anyone in authority. Through much of the day, she was not permitted to speak, except in class, or when spoken to. French was permitted at breakfast, but Ethel's pronunciation was so poor that she pointed rather than face the consequences of getting caught whispering in English.

"No one spoke a word," said Sister Duffy. "It was a calamity if they did." In study hall, or between classes, the nun was vigilant for anyone "breaking the Silence." "You," she'd yell at Ethel, caught talking, "are a detriment to civilization." When it was time for the girls to move, Duffy slapped together two pieces of wood called "the clapper."

Nevertheless, Ethel talked when she shouldn't have, used swear words, squirted ink at classmates, cut study hall regularly, smoked, and was consistently late for Monday morning's assembly, where she usually forgot to wear the requisite white gloves.

"She'd always see if she could get caught doing something wrong," said Alice Meadows Buetow.

More often than not, Ethel was nabbed in the act and dragged off to Mother Bourke, who read her the riot act. Ethel would promise to work on improving herself, then boast about how she'd conned Bourke once again.

Because of the constant surveillance, most of Ethel's juiciest escapades took place after dinner, when the nuns retired to their rooms.

One of her signature practical jokes was to short-sheet someone's bed. But Ethel went one step farther. "She'd put stuff in the bed too, like toothpaste," recalled roommate Mary Bayo Garofoli. "She thought it was funny to destroy something for a joke, like tear bedsheets, or hide something of someone's—hide it and then lose it. To her it didn't seem to mean much."

But there also was a warm and compassionate side to Ethel. One afternoon Eleanor Conroy McGrath, shy and introverted, was required to recite something in front of the entire school, but did poorly because she was so nervous. "Afterwards, all of the others looked at me disdainfully thinking, 'Oh, God, what is *her* problem?' " McGrath remembered. "Only Ethel came up to me, knowing I was embarrassed, and quietly said, 'Don't feel bad, I couldn't have done it either.' "

Ethel's horseplay of choice was the powder fight, until she got caught. One evening, out of the cloud of talcum and face powder, appeared Mother Duffy. "Girls, I'm shocked! I'm shocked!" she sputtered. Ethel was sent to get mops and pails and ordered to clean up the mess.

Ethel's antics, frowned upon publicly by the nuns, actually amused them privately, especially the younger ones. Once a week an elderly woman by the name of Mrs. Hubble, who had Jackie Bouvier as a student at Miss Porter's, came to the school to teach dance etiquette and comportment under Mother Duffy's supervision. The girls were required to wear white gloves and dresses, and to curtsy. They'd slow dance with each other because boys weren't permitted. "Ethel always had everyone in absolute hysterics," recalled Mother Duffy. "She would come into the dance class with a straight face and act so proper. Just the *way* she did it would have everybody in such a state that they could hardly dance, laughing so hard, including me. She just had a wonderful sense of humor."

One fall weekend the girls took the train to Greenwich to watch Ethel compete in a horse show. She picked them up in one of the Skakels' station wagons, packing all of her classmates into the car. Then she proceeded to drive home on the wrong side of the road with one of her tanned, skinny legs dangling out of the window as she boasted that her brother George drank a lot and had been arrested the night before for speeding and was still in jail, which she thought was a riot. Most of the ride Ethel spent laughing raucously at her classmates' desperate pleas not to get them all killed.

The girls were awed by the immensity of the Lake Avenue house and grounds. A few thought the first beautiful home they passed driving in was Ethel's, but she pointed out that it was just one of the guest houses. During lunch, one of the girls excused herself to go to the bathroom, winding up in Big Ann's immense john, which was furnished with exercise machines, a steam box, and a toilet custom-built to look like a gold-gilded throne complete with armrests and padding of red velvet covering the back and the seat. As they left to go to the horse show, Ethel gave the girls a tour of the grounds. Pointing to the next estate over, she said that was where her father and brothers had fun stealing apples and hoped the neighbor spotted them because "the thrill is to be caught and then run." As the girls left at the end of the day, they couldn't help but notice the flock of sheep grazing on the front lawn. "We got them to keep the grass short," Ethel explained.

The day had been a big surprise because, as one classmate noted later, "Ethel was very private about her life in Greenwich." Unless a girl bragged, no one knew who had a millionaire daddy.

Every so often during her weekend visits and holidays at home, Ethel got together with her old Greenwich pals Pan and Pixie, but the PEP girls' alliance was quickly fading. Pixie Meek was now a junior at fashionable Madeira in Virginia, and Pan Jacob had been packed off to her mother's alma mater, Miss Porter's, where Jackie Bouvier had become one of her chums.

"Jackie was very boring, very solemn and close-mouthed," said Pan, who often accompanied Jackie to one of her relatives' houses for tea and an afternoon of croquet. "Jackie was not at all an outgoing, warm, loving, adorable character like Ethel. She was the antithesis."

Looking back years later, Pan felt that Big Ann had made a wise decision sending Ethel to Maplehurst. "Sacred Heart was a place where Ethel could find herself more easily than in a school like Farmington," she observed. "At Sacred Heart, Ethel would eventually meet girls like the Kennedys. That's where and how her future was determined."

With their new friendships and activities, the PEP girls began to grow apart; eventually there'd be no contact whatsoever. "For a while we kept in touch with Ethel through Christmas cards, but it didn't go on and on," Pan said later. "Pixie and I kept up because our families were close, but there was nothing to bond Ethel and us."

At Maplehurst, Ethel once again made her mark as an athlete. "Sports were more important to her than studies," said Mother Duffy. "Ethel was not considered the summa cum laude type."

On the hockey field, Ethel was a formidable opponent. "You'd have to brace yourself when she came down the field because she'd run right through you," said fellow hockey player Nancy Corcoran Harrington. "She was extremely tough, competitive, enthusiastic."

But Ethel loathed the monthly written tests and feared the oral examinations conducted before a tribunal of nuns in black habits. "The orals were horrible," recalled Alice Meadows Buetow. "You had to be composed. You had to answer whatever question was asked of you and you didn't know what it was going to be. It was tremendously scary." However, classmates recalled that Ethel handled the ordeal well. "She could think on her feet faster than many of us," said Harrington. "She had confidence, but she wasn't outstanding in any one direction."

Commented Anne Morningstar Huberth, "The Church and the school were influencing girls like Ethel to get married and have babies, and I remember that was her goal in life, her thinking—marry well and produce children. But there was never a thought of a career."

Ethel's sole interest besides sports was religion. The fire that Big Ann had ignited within her was now being stoked professionally by the nuns of the Sacred Heart. "We were encouraged to read spiritual books besides literature and other required reading and Ethel read everything that was recommended," recalled Louise Wood Paul. "She savored her religion classes, was always asking questions."

Another classmate, Margot Gotte MacNiven, said, "Ethel embraced a lot at Maplehurst that others didn't, such as 'the Silence.' It was the kind of thing that you bought or you didn't buy. Ethel bought it, in part because she'd already been indoctrinated by her sister, who'd been to Maplehurst."

Ethel was active in the school's Christopher Club, a social-action and missionary group that worked with the poor, taught catechism classes to neighborhood children, and helped patients at a nearby cancer hospital.

Every year the girls went on a weeklong retreat, returning all fired up with thoughts of becoming nuns.

"She was interested in religious life at one point as many of the girls are when they're young," recalled Mother Duffy. "But she certainly did not have a religious vocation. She had great faith and loved life. We would hear that when she had parties in Greenwich on the weekends she'd end them on the dot of midnight because in those days you had to fast after twelve o'clock. Ethel would say, 'Now that's it. No more eating. We're going to Mass in the morning.' And they would all go to Mass with Ethel."

As Mother Elizabeth Farley saw it, "Ethel was certainly not religious in the pious sense. She was too lively. But she had a lot of faith, and inherited a lot of faith, and influenced others with her faith."

Sex education was taught in biology class and, as one classmate of Ethel's recalled, "They showed us a pear-shaped uterus on the blackboard and never mentioned men. I don't think they ever used the word *sperm*. I don't think any of us knew what a penis was."

In the spring of 1945, in a quick and simple ceremony, Ethel received her high school diploma. No one remembered any of the Skakels being present. After a traditional farewell dinner, the girls stayed up all night singing songs and talking about their futures, except for Ethel. "That was our last night together," said Alice Meadows Buetow, "but right after we ate, Ethel left. Somebody called from Greenwich and suddenly she was gone."

PART V

College Girl

24 ✻ Off to College

IT WAS A time of celebration in America, that late summer of 1945. In New York, strangers danced and kissed and, in dark places, made love. Drunken, joyous sailors tore through the streets of San Diego, smashing store windows. The Andrews Sisters, on a USO tour in Italy, had just finished singing "Don't Sit Under the Apple Tree" to an audience of a thousand dogfaces when someone handed Maxine Andrews an urgent note. "The Japs have just surrendered!" she squealed to the troops, touching off a volley of airborne hats and shoes.

On Lake Avenue, the victory was being celebrated in inimitable Skakel fashion.

Just discharged from the Marines, Sylvester Larkin, scion of a prominent Greenwich family, drove to the Skakels' hoping to see his chums, George, Rushton, and Jim. The maid who answered the door said they were out. Hearing familiar voices, Larkin walked into the living room and found George Sr., Big Ann, and three uniformed Royal Canadian Air Force pilots in the midst of a bacchanal.

Standing beside Mrs. Skakel was another maid holding a silver tray piled high with water-filled balloons. The three young aviators, and the senior Skakels, were laughing and shouting as they bobbed and weaved in what was clearly a water-bomb fight fueled by alcohol. All of them were drenched; the furniture and rugs were sopping.

Larkin, who was in his freshly pressed khaki uniform, wanted no part of the absurdity he was witnessing. George and Ann Skakel were so far gone they hadn't even noticed his arrival, so he quietly left. "They're plastered," he thought as he drove home. "Nothing's changed. They're all still crazy." Meanwhile, everything in Ethel's world was *"Sensational!"* as she exclaimed over and over.

Early in September 1945, Ethel, still the prankish tomboy at eighteen, arrived at Manhattanville College of the Sacred Heart, at 133rd Street and Convent Avenue, a virginal white oasis in the heart of New York's black Harlem.

Her first gag upon arriving on campus was to tell some of the other freshmen that while her mother was of fine Irish Catholic stock, her father was a Jew. One longtime college friend believed Ethel's story for years. "She thought she'd shock us, you know—a *Jewess* at Manhattanville!"

By the time Ethel arrived, the Harlem neighborhood surrounding the campus was changing from white to black. The college was surrounded by gray stone walls topped with steel spikes. At night the metal gates were locked, and the girls were warned never to leave campus alone, never to wait for a bus or to go to the subway stop unless accompanied by someone. Apocryphal stories circulated about white slavery rings, of girls being "drugged and forced into prostitution by colored pimps," all of which struck fear in the hearts of the young virgin debutantes arriving from segregated and restricted communities like Greenwich.

There were only three black students in the entire school and not a single black nun in the entire Sacred Heart order.

The year Ethel matriculated, one of Manhattanville's leaders, Mother Grace Cowardin Dammann, died. Dammann, who had served as the school's president for fifteen years, worked hard to battle discrimination.

It was during Dammann's tenure that a group of students drafted what was known as the "Manhattanville Resolutions," which urged the girls to practice racial tolerance. Mary Byles, who later became a Sacred Heart nun teaching Western Civilization to Ethel, was a campus liberal and activist who helped draft the resolutions. "The student body adopted them and the press printed them," Sister Byles said. "The first resolution was 'I will never again use the word *nigger*,' and the second resolution was 'If I get on the Fifth Avenue bus and there's an empty place beside a Negro person, I will sit down beside that person.' " While the resolutions were hailed by liberal educators, the Manhattanville girls looked the other way for the most part.

Because she was an integrationist, Mother Dammann was despised by many Manhattanville parents, particularly those from the South and Midwest, who took their daughters out of the school after a semester or two.

"We were all pretty much unaware of social and political issues," said a member of Ethel's college circle. "Our goals were to have fun, get out of college, and get married. It was a terribly self-centered existence and a very unreal one."

For the most part, the class of 1949 consisted of wealthy girls from homes where the only blacks in evidence were kitchen help, servants, and caretakers. On Lake Avenue, the Skakels' favorite servant at the time was a butler whom the family nicknamed Happy.

"Sometimes the families that got on the best with the blacks we found were the families who had black servants, because they *knew* them," said Sister Mary Byles later. "They *understood* them and they didn't look down on them. The black Mammies were very much loved by them." Societal ills such as racism didn't concern the Skakels and certainly were not on Ethel's mind.

When Mother Eleanor O'Byrne, the college president, gave her pitch during fund-raising and recruiting efforts, she'd boast that "ninety percent of our girls are engaged before they graduate." Half jokingly, the girls often gathered around a campus statue of St. Joseph, who, legend had it, would help you find a good husband if you prayed hard enough. Part of the philosophy of the Sacred Heart education, in fact, was to train young women to be the partners of successful men, to be *ladies*, to be the mothers of tomorrow. In Ethel's era, only a handful of Manhattanville girls went on to graduate school, and only about a dozen entered the convent each year.

The other reason Ethel had decided on Manhattanville was because the nuns at Maplehurst had promoted it as the jewel in the Sacred Heart crown. Big Ann saw the college as the perfect place for Ethel to mix with Catholic society girls, which appealed to Ethel, too. Another influence was her sister Pat, who was a campus heroine, having reigned for four years as president of the class of 1946. Ethel loved the fact that the school was in New York, giving her easy access to shopping and nightlife. Moreover, Manhattanville was in close proximity to Greenwich: more than anything Ethel wanted to be near the family frolics, and her horses.

Ethel would become the most famous—and controversial—member of the class of 1949.

Ethel's eventual fame resulted from a friendship, both propitious and fateful, that she forged at Manhattanville in her first hectic week there—a bond that would last a lifetime.

Opposites are said to attract, and at first glance Ethel Skakel and Jean Kennedy could not have been more dissimilar. Ethel, the wiry, high-spirited hare; Jean, the pudgy, painfully shy, inhibited tortoise, a bit more worldly and urbane, older than Ethel by fourteen months.

But both girls had gone to Sacred Heart high schools, had privileged upbringings, were from large, idiosyncratic families. Their fathers were self-made men; their brothers were handsome rogues. Both girls grew up in strict Catholic environments, were the next-to-the-last-born in their families, and had parents who were often absent for weeks and months at a time. Jean Kennedy, born February 20, 1927, was the eighth child—the fifth daughter—of Joseph Patrick and Rose Elizabeth Fitzgerald Kennedy.

25 ❋ The Kennedy Clan

JOE KENNEDY'S STORY begins in 1849, when his Irish immigrant grandparents, Patrick, a farmer, and Bridget Kennedy, arrived in Boston. They had four children, three girls and a boy, the last being Patrick Joseph Kennedy, called P.J. Less than a year after the boy's birth, his father died of cholera, forcing Bridget to get work as a shop girl. Despite the family's financial hardships, P. J. Kennedy, an ambitious bear of a man with a beefy face, red hair, and blue eyes, was able at age twenty-two to finance the purchase of a ramshackle saloon in a shabby Boston neighborhood.

Not long after, he bought a second tavern, and he began making money. He eventually became a partner in a Boston hotel and started a liquor importing business, P. J. Kennedy and Company, supplying Haig and Haig Scotch to the city's better restaurants and hotels. While he sold liquor, he never drank; he was a teetotaler, unlike Ethel's alcoholic paternal grandfather. Besides his saloon business, Kennedy had gotten involved in Boston politics and rose quickly to ward leader. In November 1887, he married Mary Augusta Hickey, a large woman—bigger than P.J. himself, a woman much like Big Ann Skakel.

Joe Kennedy, who would become the patriarch of the Kennedy clan, was the first of P.J.'s children, born on September 6, 1888, four years before George Skakel.

P.J.'s political career continued to soar: he gave a seconding speech for Grover Cleveland at the Democratic National Convention, he served for three terms in the Massachusetts Senate, he held a number of Boston patronage positions, and he ran Ward Two like an Irish

Mafia godfather, working out of the back of one of his saloons.

At home Mary Kennedy had cooks and maids. The family wintered in Florida and had a sixty-foot yacht. Mary focused on young Joe, selecting after-school jobs that would allow her son to mix with Boston's elite; one involved delivering hats from a posh millinery shop. Catholic schools were not worldly enough, so she sent him to the prestigious Boston Latin School, and later to Harvard.

Shortly after the turn of the century, P.J. became friendly with another powerful Boston politician, John F. ("Honey Fitz") Fitzgerald, who ran Boston's North End. Despite being of slight physical stature, Fitzgerald carried himself like a heavyweight: boisterous, cocky, with tough-guy mannerisms.

Fitzgerald had spent a year at Harvard Medical School, dropping out when his father died. He worked in the insurance business for a time. He played polo to make social, business, and political contacts. Like P. J. Kennedy, Fitzgerald was a born politician. He went from local ward politics to the State Senate, and was elected to the U.S. House of Representatives. In 1905, he became Boston's first mayor of Irish heritage.

His wife, Mary Hannon Fitzgerald, a pious Catholic, gave him six children. The first was Rose Elizabeth Fitzgerald, born in 1890, two years before Big Ann.

Despite being a regular at church, Fitzgerald was a philanderer of the first order whose political career came to a sudden end when a rival threatened to publicly reveal his affair with a Boston nightclub cigarette girl named "Toodles" Ryan.

As a young woman, Rose Fitzgerald often found herself acting as a hostess for her father. A reporter at the time wrote that Rose showed "remarkable tact and poise . . . brimming with animation and charm and girlish spirits." Rose often found herself defending her father's questionable politics; years later she would similarly defend her husband and sons.

Rose Fitzgerald met Joe Kennedy because of their

fathers' association. Their courtship infuriated Fitzgerald, who felt the Kennedys were inferior, too Irish Catholic. On October 7, 1914, wearing a two-carat diamond, Rose Fitzgerald became Rose Kennedy.

Jean was the next-to-last of Rose's children, followed into the world in 1932 by her fourth brother, Edward "Ted" Moore Kennedy. At the time of Jean's birth, Joe Kennedy, who had gone into the movie business, was having a passionate affair with Hollywood sex goddess Gloria Swanson. Like Kennedy, Swanson was married. Rose knew about her husband's adultery, but she chose to suffer in silence rather than risk losing him, a trait that would become common to the next generation of women who married Kennedy men. Moreover, she would never have considered divorce. When Jean's birth was announced, Rose received hundreds of flowers and cards, including a bouquet from the brazen Swanson.

Kennedy met Swanson after he became an overnight "movie magnate" with the $1 million purchase in 1925 of the Film Booking Office of America, a financially troubled, British-owned production company. Under Kennedy, the company churned out cheap cowboy shoot-'em-ups that were popular with small-town audiences.

But Kennedy also cut lucrative production deals with RCA chief David Sarnoff; Kennedy bought the giant Keith-Albee-Orpheum chain of theaters; Kennedy was one of the architects of the RKO merger. He also took over Swanson's management, which included the establishment of her own production company. In short order, he became a Hollywood power, gaining the respect and admiration of the immigrant Jews who predominated in Hollywood. They viewed him as one of them: a shark. He called them pants pressers.

Joe Kennedy and Gloria Swanson slept together for the first time in Palm Beach, the setting for lurid Kennedy scandals years later involving the sons of Ethel and Jean; the consummation of Joe and Gloria's affair would be only the first of such scandals.

"He moved so quickly that his mouth was on mine before either of us could speak," Swanson wrote breathlessly years later of her first time in bed with Joe Kennedy. "With one hand he held the back of my head. With the other he stroked my body and pulled at my kimono. He was like a roped horse, rough, arduous, rearing to be free. After a hasty climax, he lay beside me, stroking my hair."

With Swanson's husband out of the picture—Kennedy procured a film job for him in France—the lovers began sleeping together regularly at Kennedy's Rodeo Drive home. In order to protect his family image during the affair and to avoid scandal, Kennedy assigned various employees to shuttle his mistress between her house and his. But their affair soon became widely known and a rumor even surfaced that Kennedy fathered one of Gloria's children, a son whom she named Joe.

On trips home from Hollywood, Kennedy brought back filmland mementos and souvenirs for his children. Once, he even had the gall to invite Swanson to be a houseguest along with her daughter. Pat Kennedy, about ten at the time, took the child to school with her, but nobody believed her boast that the youngster was the daughter of the famous film star. If Rose Kennedy knew about her husband's affair she remained mum. In her autobiography, which was published when she was eighty-four, Rose wrote about her friendship with the actress, her favorite Swanson films, and "the excitement and fun" of being with her husband, his sister, and Swanson in Paris in 1928. Rose ran into Swanson years later at the Ritz in Paris. "We chatted together a couple of minutes, recalling old times," Rose wrote. She protected Joe's image to the end.

Joe Kennedy had a twisted sense of loyalty. At one point during their adulterous relationship he swore to Swanson that he'd been loyal to her, meaning he'd not slept with Rose. To prove his point he invoked the name of his daughter Jean. Kennedy's proof was that while he and Gloria were involved Rose had not—since Jean's birth—become pregnant.

By the time he had fathered Ted, his affair with

Swanson had cooled, but their friendship continued for years.

Adultery wasn't Joe Kennedy's only vice. During Prohibition he was allegedly funding, and profiting from, illegal shipments of liquor. Mobster Frank Costello asserted later that Kennedy had been a partner in bootlegging and rum-running in the early 1920s.

Joe Kennedy was a major player on Wall Street for years, but having sensed the end of the bull market, he divested himself of high-flying speculative stock, gaining notoriety as a profiteer but emerging in the black from the 1929 Crash. Even his children were aware of their father's image. Coming home after a day of selling, Kennedy was greeted by little Jean exclaiming, "Daddy is a bear! Daddy is a bear!" While others were leaping from tall buildings, Kennedy was secure in the family's recently purchased $250,000 mansion in Bronxville, New York.

During the 1930s Kennedy, by then a very wealthy man, decided that public service would give him the status he wanted and felt he rightfully deserved, so he put his substantial financial and business clout behind President Franklin Delano Roosevelt, George Skakel's nemesis. In return, a grateful FDR offered Kennedy the ambassadorship to Ireland, which he rejected. Many years later, Jean Kennedy would accept that same appointment from another so-called Democratic reformer, President Bill Clinton. Joe Kennedy subsequently accepted the chairmanship in 1934 of the new Securities and Exchange Commission and, in 1937, chairmanship of the new Maritime Commission.

The next year Roosevelt gave Kennedy the payoff he sought, appointing him to the highly prestigious post of American ambassador to the Court of St. James's. Roosevelt's decision caused consternation among liberals who were aware of Kennedy's isolationist and anti-Semitic feelings. As ambassador he'd have diplomatic dealings with Nazi Germany at a sensitive and dangerous time in world history.

In early 1938, the Kennedys arrived in London. Rose

enrolled Jean and her sisters, except for Rosemary, who was mentally retarded, in the Sacred Heart Convent in Roehampton, where they were remembered as being "birds of Paradise, bringing glamour and worldliness" to the otherwise austere school. Jean, then eleven years old, "was still a little chubby and less dignified," one classmate recalled. "On the first day of school, when the teacher pointed out a mistake she'd made in her arithmetic, she coolly eyed the figures on the paper and said, 'Well, five goes into nine in America; I don't see why it doesn't in England.' "

As Hitler's threat of war intensified, Kennedy sent Rose and the children to Ireland. Shortly after Britain declared war, he decided that the family should return to the United States.

Back on U.S. soil, Rose shipped Jean off to Eden Hall, a Sacred Heart Convent school in Philadelphia. She spent two years there before transferring to Noroton in Connecticut, one of the strictest, and most austere, of the Sacred Heart schools.

A classmate at Noroton, Jeanne Cassidy Duffy, who went on to Manhattanville with Jean, remembered her as "very childlike, very naive and shy—not at all outgoing. She didn't have very many friends."

26 ❊ *Ethel and Jean*

BY THE TIME Jean Kennedy and Ethel Skakel arrived at Manhattanville together in September 1945, Jean's father's affair with Gloria Swanson was known to many of the other girls; gossip like that moved swiftly within the tight Irish Catholic social hierarchy. Moreover, Jean's sister Eunice had graduated from Manhattanville in 1943, so scuttlebutt about her father and his mistress had circulated on campus for several years.

"My mouth fell open," said Margaret Geoghegan Adams, a member of Ethel and Jean's elite circle. "That goes back to a time when morals were strong. But no one would ever dare say anything to Jean, and I was convinced she wasn't aware of the scandal."

One evening during freshman year, Joe and Rose Kennedy took Jean and Margaret to dinner at Le Pavillion and afterward to see *State of the Nation*. It was a wonderful experience for Adams, an ingenuous girl from Cincinnati society. After the show, Joe dropped off Rose at the Plaza before retiring for the night in his suite at the Waldorf. Innocently curious, Margaret asked Jean about her parents' separate sleeping arrangements. "My father loves staying at the Waldorf for business reasons and my mother can't stand the noise there, so when they're in New York they just stay separate," Jean responded naively.

"I'm not sure that Jean at that age knew the reasons why her parents had separate bedrooms," Adams felt. "The children would have been the last to know. Jean idolized both her parents, and was in awe of her father."

Ethel, recalled a friend, "was mortified" when she heard the gossip about the affair. "This may seem hard to believe but at age eighteen Ethel thought adultery was something mentioned only in the Bible, that it was not an actual practice. I remember her getting very upset when she heard us talking about Joe Kennedy and Gloria Swanson. 'That's not true. I don't want to hear talk like that.' Ethel was so innocent, so naive."

The first week at Manhattanville saw Ethel, who couldn't keep a tune, with her new friend, Jean, on their knees foolishly singing a sappy little song called "The Donkey Serenade." When they were ordered to "scramble like an egg!" Ethel and Jean dropped obediently to the floor, giggling with delight, wriggling around until they were told to get up. It was all part of the junior class's hazing of the freshmen. Ethel thrived on such high jinks, but Jean was different.

"Ethel had a very magnetic personality," said Kay Simonson Waterbury, a Park Avenue girl who was a member of Ethel and Jean's circle. Waterbury would eventually be related to Jean through marriage, and Ethel would one day become godmother to one of Waterbury's children. "Ethel loved life and having fun. But Jean was—and is—very much into herself, much more private than Ethel, and very shy. As a result she's misunderstood because people think she's snobby."

Another member of the clique, Ann Marie O'Hagan Murphy, a Charlottesville, Virginia, debutante, observed: "Ethel was totally different from Jean. Ethel was not sophisticated when she came to college. She had not traveled a lot like Jean had. Her family wasn't important in political and social circles."

Abbyann Day Lynch, a scholarship student and campus activist, said, "The two of them made an ideal combination. One of them could do the outgoing stuff, and the other could be quiet and a good friend, a good companion."

Ethel and Jean had become inseparable. They were often seen being picked up by a driver in a big black car for the drive to Greenwich. And Ethel often traveled to the Kennedy home at Hyannis Port with Jean.

Ethel became Jean's "great friend," as Rose Kennedy put it later.

Ethel's first visit to the Kennedys at Hyannis Port was just a month after freshman year started. Ethel, Jean, and a few friends went to Boston, where Rose met them with a car and driver. Ethel's memory of the "event" underscored how impressionable and innocent she was at the time.

"There were a bunch of us, so the car was crowded—very crowded—and it was raining. That gives the general picture: a pile of kids and luggage, driving for two hours in a closed car on a rainy day. Mrs. Kennedy spent practically the whole ride giving us a history lesson—and she was great. It was October thirty-first, Halloween, so there were jack-'o-lanterns on people's porches and in windows, and that's what started her off.

She said, 'Now, why do you suppose people have jack-'o-lanterns, how did that custom ever begin?' That led back to All Hallows' Eve and witchcraft and all that, and then to the Church and saints' days and then up into American history and Pilgrims and pumpkins and superstitions and autumn harvest and protect the crops and pumpkin pies and apple cider and . . . anyway, I thought she was fascinating, she knew so much, and twitted us a little if we didn't know as much as we should've, and she got us all involved and probably all of us did learn something and pretty soon the trip was over and we were at Hyannis Port.

"And I remember arriving at the Cape and going to Jean's room and thinking how everything was so well thought out for the happiness of children and guests. There were fresh flowers. There were interesting books on the bedside table. It was all so comfortable and pleasant and beautifully done—all those niceties that can make life so pleasant. She had thought of them all. Nothing showy, just very nice."

It was far different from the topsy-turvy world of Lake Avenue.

Some college chums believed that Jean sought out Ethel, intrigued by the Skakel girl's open, bold, and brash style. Others took a more cynical view, contending that Ethel pursued Jean with ulterior motives.

As Margaret Geoghegan Adams observed, "At Manhattanville, people toadied to Jean; she was pretty influential because of her family. Ethel attached herself to Jean to get access to the Kennedys, although she *genuinely* liked Jean. It worked conveniently for Ethel because being friends with Jean gave Ethel the opportunity to be around her brothers, which Ethel enjoyed."

Both theories have validity. As their friendship intensified, Jean seemed to emerge from her shell, getting into minor scrapes with school authorities: chewing gum in class; not dressing properly for dinner. "Ethel and Jean just didn't like to obey laws or rules," said a classmate, Helen Quigley Williams.

To observers, Ethel benefited more from the friendship than did Jean. While Jean became more outgoing, Ethel got the brass ring, gaining entrée to the Kennedys, fulfilling her unspoken desire to be part of their mystique. Classmates envied Ethel's touch. "A lot of girls wanted to get close to Jean but couldn't," said one. "But Ethel captivated Jean like no one else could and, believe me, many tried. Ethel had the magic elixir."

Pat Norton Mullins, a senior, vice president of her class, a close friend of Pat Skakel's, and a frequent visitor to the Skakel home, remembered Ethel and Jean as " 'Hiya, kid,' slap-on-the-back, happy-go-lucky types, but not very thoughtful. Jean was nothing like her sister Eunice, who was very cerebral at Manhattanville. Jean and Eunice were as different as Ethel and her sister Pat."

On the surface, Ethel appeared as the dominant one in the relationship, but Jean was far from submissive. Friends say she *chose* to remain in Ethel's shadow, quietly pulling the strings behind the scenes. As Jean's friend Abbyann Day Lynch observed, "She appeared to be very quiet and compliant, but underneath she had a great many of her own ideas."

"In the beginning, Ethel jumped when Jean said jump," said a close friend. "Jean was the real power behind those two. Ethel heeded her. She bided her time."

Another observer of the friendship noted, "There was a lot of manipulation, probably unconscious manipulation, but manipulation nevertheless. Those two girls came from families where manipulation was a primary trait; it was in their blood whether they realized it or not."

By her sophomore year, thanks to Jean, Ethel would have what she wanted: a Kennedy man.

Besides their personalities, differences existed between Ethel and Jean academically. "Ethel was a B-plus student and Jean, who was a C-plus student, seemed lazy," said one of the nuns, Sister Mary Byles, who taught both girls in her Western Civilization class. "Jean didn't work as hard as Ethel and maybe her mind wasn't as sharp as Ethel's, either."

Near the end of their freshman year, Ann Cooley Buckley, who had come from Noroton with Jean, asked Ethel to be her roommate in sophomore year. "I thought she was fun and neat," Buckley said. "But Ethel told me no, that she'd be rooming *alone*."

In fact, Ethel had decided to room with Jean. They'd quietly sought out Sister Mary Esther McCarthy, their house warden, and made their request. McCarthy, who also taught philosophy, had the task of making sure the dorm rooms were neat and orderly, handing out demerits if they weren't. The nun decided that Ethel and Jean "kept their rooms in sensible order," so she granted them permission. They were assigned a "suite," two small bedrooms separated by a tiny bathroom. They'd remain roommates until graduation, shortly after which they'd become sisters-in-law, remaining lifelong friends. Ethel would become closer to Jean and the other Kennedys than to her own family.

27 ✻ Rich Girls

"EACH CLASS HAS its 'in-crowd' and Ethel's was *it* in the class of 1949," observed Nancy Davis Sweeney, a Manhattanville tennis player.

In freshman year, about a dozen affluent girls were part of Ethel's circle. They set themselves apart from "the goody-goods," who did the nuns' bidding. Deciding their elite group needed a name, Ethel suggested "The Twelve Apostles," after the original disciples of Christ who were sent out to preach the Gospel.

Unlike the indigence and privation of the Apostles, Ethel's crowd had one major common denominator: money. They were the privileged daughters of wealthy bankers and lawyers; cotton kings and oil barons; ranchers and industrialists; securities brokers and inventors.

Coddled by their parents, pampered by servants, few could handle the simplest task. Ethel, for one, didn't know how to cook an egg, or how to iron a blouse. One of her closest pals once took expended flash bulbs rather than film to the drugstore to be developed.

"We were very cliquey-cliquey," said a member of the group years later. "We were more fun-loving than the other girls were—the real studious types. We thought we were the swiftest ones; we thought we were very cool."

Jeanne Cassidy Duffy, one of some thirty cadet nurses whose education at Manhattanville was funded by the U.S. government as part of the war effort, remembered the circle as snobbish. "Their group thought we were working girls, not quite up to snuff. They came from privileged backgrounds and they felt they wanted to be around privileged people. Ethel and Jean were the nucleus of that group."

Some members of Ethel's circle, looking back years later, expressed regret over the treatment accorded the sole black girl in the class of 1949. June Mulvaney Romaine was a Russian-German language major, a scholarship student, a member of the Interracial Club, who went home every day to Brooklyn, a "day-hop," as such nonboarding students were termed.

"On the whole, we girls weren't always nice to her," observed Margaret Geoghegan Adams. "She was a lovely girl, but we ignored her. We certainly didn't embrace her."

Campus activist Abbyann Day Lynch, who lived across the hall from Ethel and Jean during junior and senior years, said admission of blacks to Manhattanville was *the* burning political issue on campus during the class of '49's tenure, but that Ethel and her crowd had shown little interest in participating.

"I knew June Mulvaney pretty well," said Lynch. "It was a question of trying to make her feel comfortable in a white ocean. Ethel's group was indifferent at best. It wasn't so much a question of, 'We don't want you here,' as 'Why should we get involved in this? It's okay for the school to decide to integrate but what's it got to do with us? We'll go on with our friends anyway.' "

Lynch remembered having at least one informal meeting with Ethel and her friends to discuss the racial issue, "but I figured it wouldn't pay off, that it might even make it worse. Partially, their disinterest came from being sheltered, more sheltered than some; living within their own kind of cocoon and social circumstances. They hadn't been educated to think about it."

Years later, after her marriage to the politically liberal Bobby Kennedy, Ethel showed a marked and very public interest in civil rights and human rights causes, surprising those who were aware of her youthful apathy and insensitivity to such issues.

• • •

From her mother, Ethel learned to appreciate the finer things in life. Like Big Ann, Ethel spent George Skakel's money with abandon. George had always coddled Ethel, giving her as much spending money as she wanted. By the time Ethel got to college, she'd become a world-class shopper and clotheshorse. She fancied expensive dresses, suits, coats, and accessories and, like her mother, often made quantity purchases, getting wholesale prices when and where she could. While she dressed preciously collegiate—cashmere sweaters, Shetland wool skirts—her closets also overflowed with stunning apparel from the best shops on Fifth Avenue. She had gowns and evening dresses costing thousands of dollars alongside her muddied gabardine, leather, and suede riding garb. Few of her friends knew that Ethel, a tomboy on the surface, wore satin and lace lingerie that was sewn by the family's seamstress at Lake Avenue.

"Manhattanville girls were supposed to be well dressed," said Kay Simonson Waterbury, "but it was almost sinful to spend three thousand dollars on a dress as Ethel would do. She had beautiful Ferragamo purses and accessories. I remember arguments among the girls about Ethel's spending because we were taught by the nuns that it was very wrong to spend lots and lots of money on clothes."

Waterbury's roommate, Courtney Murphy Benoist—once described as a "*Vogue* fashion plate"—said that Ethel had "terrific taste."

Ethel went to extremes at times, fashionwise. On campus, she often wore a ratty old double-breasted camel-hair coat, belted in the back, with white pearl buttons, over her ugly blue gym suit.

The war had caused one major disappointment for Ethel—she couldn't buy expensive shoes, which she loved. Ethel had a lifelong shoe fetish. But leather was being used for combat boots, not high heels; restrictions and rationing had been in effect for the duration, so the stylish had difficulty finding fashionable footwear. But with the conflict now over, chic, extravagantly priced shoes were returning to the marketplace.

One Saturday Ethel decided to stock up, dragging Ann Marie O'Hagan Murphy to the most elegant shoe salon on Fifth Avenue. There on the shelves, just arrived, were the latest sling-back, toeless, platform alligator high heels.

"They were very, very expensive, very, very sexy," said Murphy. "Nobody would be ostentatious enough to own them, especially a girl in her sophomore year at a Catholic college. She just wouldn't. They were the kind of shoes a mother would own. But Ethel said, 'I love them!' So she giggled, took out her checkbook, and bought them in red, green, black and blue. *Four pairs!* I almost flipped."

One weekend, Ann Marie accompanied Ethel to Manhattan's Garment District to buy what she thought would be a single hat. "In those days we wore hats and gloves when we went out," she said. "Ethel's mother had told her to go to one particular millinery showroom where she'd arranged for the Skakel girls to buy at wholesale. Ethel spent an hour trying on hats before buying at least *ten!* She knew no stops, whether it be how she drove her car, or how she spent her money."

At her mother's knee, Ethel learned to haggle and

finagle. At Andre de Printemps, an exclusive hair salon on Fifth Avenue, she convinced the owner to give her a discounted "college rate," after having intimated that she was just a poor Catholic schoolgirl who couldn't afford to spend more. She then charmed him into offering the same low rate to her rich college pals.

The most extreme example of penny-pinching by this rich girl from Greenwich who thought nothing of spending hundreds on shoes was how she routinely conned the toll-taker on the Triborough Bridge out of paying the toll.

"I remember us dashing off campus on Friday afternoons in Ethel's station wagon," said Kay Simonson Waterbury. "Ethel never had any cash on her, so she'd always have some wonderful story to tell the man in the toll booth. She'd say she was going to pray for him and he was going to get anything he wanted in the world if he let her cross the bridge without paying the toll. It worked every time."

28 ✻ Chasing Boys

ETHEL OFTEN JOINED her chums in the search for eligible young men, but she wasn't terribly enthusiastic about the hunt, or making the catch.

It's not that she didn't like men: she thoroughly enjoyed their company, and would have close male friends throughout her life. She'd grown up surrounded by handsome, boisterous brothers, so she felt comfortable around men. But few young college women were sexually active in those days, especially girls from Catholic schools like Manhattanville, girls with deep religious beliefs, girls who were taught to believe that sexual thoughts, let alone acts, were immoral and sinful. Sister Mary Byles, who lectured the girls on the subject of "dating and mating," later claimed, "Ninety-nine percent of them were virgins. I don't think there's any doubt about that."

Ethel would never pursue sex just for the pleasure. Sex, Ethel would always believe, was for making babies.

Ethel tended to catch men's eyes with her daring antics and her athletic prowess. While she had crushes, they were those of a starstruck adolescent rather than á sexually mature young woman. "Ethel was always like a buddy, a pal," said a male friend who has known her throughout her life. "She was fun, but she didn't stir a man's blood."

Prior to falling for Bobby, Ethel was crazy about equestrian Billy Steinkraus. "Besides Bobby, there was never anybody in Ethel's life that I could see except maybe Billy," said Kay Simonson Waterbury. "He was the only one she had a crush on. Billy cut a nice figure on a horse and Ethel was always admiring him, saying how wonderful he was. But most of the time, when she talked about men like that, it was all jokey-jokey."

Ethel was twelve and Steinkraus was fifteen when they first met, competing against each other at horse events in Greenwich, in Fairfield County, and on Long Island. The son of the chairman of Bridgeport Brass and a one-time president of the U.S. Chamber of Commerce, Steinkraus lived in nearby Westport, but went to Greenwich Country Day, Brunswick, and rode at Round Hill, so he got to know the young Skakels well. His education at Yale was interrupted by the war. He enlisted for the horse cavalry, ending up in Burma with mules. After the war he resumed his show-riding career, gaining international prominence as a member of the 1952 U.S. Olympic equestrian team, which won a bronze medal. Refined, handsome, he could have been on the covers of magazines like *Country Life*, *The Sportsman*, or *Spur*, which he consumed with a passion. During college, Ethel and Billy saw each other often at competitions. So smitten was Ethel that she once went to Dublin to watch Steinkraus ride in a horse show, but she never made him aware of her feelings.

"*Crush* is not the word I'd use," remarked Steinkraus later. "We never even dated, but we were together a lot. Ethel wasn't a great beauty, but her eyes were always sparkling and her skin was nut brown in all seasons because she loved the outdoors and she really exuded health and naturalness, so I found her attractive in that way."

Steinkraus had also become a friend of young Jackie Bouvier, and often rode with her.

Comparing the two young women later, he said, "Ethel was a real tomboy. As a man you didn't have to make special allowances for Ethel. You could treat her like a brother. Jackie might burst into tears on some occasion if some behavior had erupted that was not exactly what she thought was appropriate."

Ethel and her crowd went looking for eligible young men on ski weekends to Stowe, Vermont, and Mont Tremblant in the Laurentian Mountains of Quebec. But she seemed so indifferent that she sometimes skied wearing the same old camel-hair coat on the slopes that she wore going to and from classes at school, not a real male attention-getter.

Every so often the handsome cadets from West Point arrived at Manhattanville for a tea dance. Often the girls took a cab downtown to chic East Side and Midtown clubs popular with the prep school and collegiate crowd: places like La Rue, for dancing on Friday or Saturday nights. They'd often hang out at the German-American, or the cocktail lounge at the Biltmore. Sometimes for an evening of slumming they'd venture into Greenwich Village.

But traditional society nightspots were Ethel's cup of tea, clubs where she could kick up her heels and have fun. "She adored the fast dancing, the jitterbugging, the Charleston, that kind of thing," said Kay Waterbury. "Ethel was one of the best dancers in the clique. She entered all of the contests and she was the only one to go on the floor in her high heels. The floors were so slippery, but she was the one who ended up excelling and staying out there after everyone else had given up."

On Sundays, Ethel's crowd went to the Stork Club,

where they'd have brunch and get balloons and door prizes and free samples of Sortilege perfume. Sometimes the girls checked into rooms at the Biltmore or the Waldorf, paying college rates. Other times they'd stay at Pat Kennedy's Manhattan apartment when she was out of town. They'd shop or go to movies in the afternoon and get dressed up to go to the clubs at night for innocent flirtations with boys from Princeton, Yale, Harvard, and Georgetown.

Most of the girls in Ethel's circle had brothers, so a lot of dates were arranged that way. For instance, Margaret Geoghegan Adams's ebullient, fun-loving brother, Bill Geoghegan, was in law school at Harvard, so she asked him to arrange dates for herself, Ethel, and Jean. They'd drive up to Boston and check into the Fitzgeralds' suite at the Copley Plaza. Then they'd get together with Geoghegan and his law school roommates, Dey Watts and Jim Kerrigan, who'd graduated from Princeton, and Ross Traphagen, from Yale, all of whom were at least five years older than Ethel and her friends. The young men had rooms on the top floor of a brownstone on Bay State Road near the Charles River. When Ethel came to visit, one of her pals whose father owned a brewery filled the trunk of Ethel's car with cases of beer, which they'd put on ice in the law students' bathtub.

Watts saw Ethel about a dozen times as part of the group—before she and Bobby Kennedy became a steady item. "I never had the feeling she and the girls were looking . . . it was something to do for the weekend . . . just a good group of guys and girls," he said. The roommates shared a 1937 seven-passenger Lasalle—the "Black Beauty"—which the crowd piled into to go to dinner in Cambridge.

While Ethel and Watts were just friends, Traphagen and Jean Kennedy were "kind of an item," said Watts. "Ross was very interested in her, but I don't think Jean was quite so interested in him. Neither Ross nor I were Catholic, so that had something to do with it." Traphagen agreed that being Catholic was a prerequisite for any serious relationship with girls like Ethel.

"Jean was a very pretty young Irish girl," he said, "but there was no romance. We certainly weren't an item." Traphagan said Ethel made little if any impression on him, noting that "the Skakels were all a little bit crazy because they had sudden wealth, which they didn't know how to handle except by spending a lot of money and having raucous times."

The dates with the girls, he recalled, were "promoted" by Geoghegan, who "was obviously interested in these recognizably important families."

(Years later, because of those college connections, Bill Geoghegan, a bright, aggressive young lawyer in his hometown of Cincinnati, wrote Presidential aspirant Jack Kennedy a long letter expressing his enthusiasm and analyzing the Ohio political situation. His eventual reward was a job as one of Attorney General Robert Kennedy's top assistants at the Justice Department. During those years he became a close friend of Ethel's.)

Traphagan went on to become a managing partner in the prestigious New York firm of Goldman, Sachs, and married a Noroton girl, a friend of Jean's. Years later, at a Washington party, his wife would be propositioned by Attorney General Bobby Kennedy as Traphagan looked on in disgust.

But back in the late 1940s, the lives of these young people were simpler, wholesome, and high-spirited, without such intrigues. One evening in New York City, after meeting under the clock at the Biltmore, the gang went to the Blue Angel, a jazz club on Fifty-second Street, where a friend hypnotized Ethel. Throughout the night the friend kept an eye on Ethel, uncertain as to whether she was susceptible to hypnosis "because she was so strong-minded." As they all were leaving, the friend whispered something in Ethel's ear.

Turning on her heel, Ethel walked slowly back to their table, which had not yet been cleared, and proceeded to knock a dozen beer bottles to the floor. Without knowing what she'd done, she walked innocently out of the club.

29 ✳ Bobby Kennedy

ROBERT FRANCIS KENNEDY was the third son and seventh child of Joe and Rose Kennedy. Bobby was born November 20, 1925, in Brookline, Massachusetts. Rose, who viewed Bobby's being number seven in her brood as a "lucky" sign and a good omen, was having a baby on the average of once every eighteen months. "We were all happy he was a boy baby after four girls," she said later. "It was wonderful for the girls, and for us."

Not long after he was born the family moved into a rented home overlooking the Hudson in the Riverdale section of Upper Manhattan, where they stayed a short time before Joe Kennedy bought a five-acre estate in Bronxville, Westchester County, a short drive from the city.

Bobby became Rose's favorite, a Mama's boy. When he once got a miserable grade in a religion course while at a boarding school, Rose wrote him a note lightly scolding him. Whenever the family traveled together, Bobby always sat next to his mother, whom he worshiped.

With four sisters born before him, he was lost in a sea of women; his brothers were away at school, his father was involved with business and with other women. And when Joe Kennedy was at home, he was tough and demanding on Bobby. Later, many felt that the adult Bobby was much like his father—not just the same pale blue eyes, but icy, tough, brutal. However, Bobby resembled his mother, having the same hawklike face, hooked nose, and deep-set eyes. When his brothers Jack, whom he would always idolize, and Joe, who showed him the most love and affection, roughhoused together, Bobby hid upstairs with his sisters, sometimes breaking into tears because of the turmoil, hiding his face in his hands. There was fear that he might be unmanly, effete. "By the time Teddy arrived in 1932," said Rose, "Bobby was already more than seven years old. So there he was, with two older brothers and one very much younger, none of whom was much use to him as boyhood pals, playmates. . . . I remember my mother said, 'He's stuck by himself with a bunch of girls. He'll be a sissy.' "

Bobby was the runt of the family, not handsome like his brothers. He needed to have his teeth straightened. He was often ill. The first time Rose sent Bobby to summer camp, when he was twelve, he came down with pneumonia.

"Bobby had a lot going against him," said longtime family friend Lem Billings. "He was small, shy, uncertain, and lost . . . had a hard time asserting himself . . . nothing came easy to him but he never stopped trying." According to Billings, Bobby felt he was the least loved of the Kennedy children, despite his mother's attention. To compensate, he battled to be the best at everything, from his behavior to his Catholicism. Like his mother, like Ethel, Bobby was a daily communicant, and would be throughout most of his life. He had his first Communion at age seven. He wanted to be an altar boy. He read the Bible. He worked hard at learning Latin. "We always had a rosary on our beds," said his sister Pat. "Mother would hear our bedtime prayers and do our catechism with us every week for Sunday school." Luella Hennessey, the family nurse, felt for years that Bobby would enter a seminary and become a priest.

Bobby once tried to mirror Joe's entrepreneurial spirit by securing a newspaper route, but couldn't take the daily grind. His mother discovered that he'd talked the family chauffeur into driving him on his route, making his deliveries in a Rolls-Royce. He then came down with what Rose described as "summer flu," which ended the short-lived venture. As a teenager he secured a clerking job in a Boston bank where his father had once worked.

As a student, he got poor grades, and hated reading. His brother Jack, on the other hand, read voraciously. Jack's favorite book as a child was *Billy Whiskers*, a story about a billy goat that featured black people drawn with large red lips, wide noses, and illustration captions such as, "Don' Shoot! Don' Shoot! I'se Neber Gwan To Steal No Mo' Yo' Melons!"

Bobby went to lower schools in Hyannis Port, Bronxville, Riverdale. When his father was ambassador, Bobby was enrolled in two different schools in London in a short span of time; schools where, at age thirteen, he wore stiff British uniforms, blazers, and flannel short pants. He hated England, refusing to join the British Boy Scouts because he'd have to swear allegiance to the King. Joe arranged for Bobby to wear an American scout uniform, get his Tenderfoot rank, and attend meetings as a "visiting" member, which placated the boy. The press reported on all of the Kennedys' doings in England, even Bobby's clumsy effort to talk to Princess Elizabeth at a party.

When the family returned home, Bobby was shipped off to an assortment of boarding schools: the very strict Portsmouth Priory in Rhode Island, where a couple of the Skakel boys had gone for a time; St. Paul's, a Protestant preparatory school in New Hampshire; then, in September 1942, to the very Protestant Milton Academy near Boston, where, as a 150-pound eighteen-year-old, he made the football team. At Milton, for the first time in his life, Bobby seemed somewhat happy, grounded. But he was still bashful, shy and awkward around girls, and remained a mediocre student. It was during this period that his brother Joe was killed in combat, and a PT-boat, designated 109, carrying his brother Jack was sliced in half by a Japanese destroyer.

After graduating from Milton, Bobby managed to get into Harvard, where his goal was to drop out and get into the war like his brothers. As a student, he joined the Naval Reserve and dreamed of becoming a flier. His father and Jack would hear none of it. The war had already claimed one son and brother. Bobby lobbied constantly. On his own he quit the officers' training program with hopes of entering the service as an enlisted man. But it wasn't until the war was officially over that Joe Kennedy decided it was time for his son to serve his country. He used his influence with Navy Secretary James Forrestal to get Bobby assigned to the newly commissioned destroyer U.S.S. *Joseph P. Kennedy, Jr.*, as a seaman's apprentice. His shipboard naval career lasted from February to May of 1946, during which time he was assigned to routine details on a short Caribbean cruise that included a trip to the U.S. Navy's base in Cuba. With his discharge papers, he was awarded two routine medals and a promotion to seaman second-class. He returned to Harvard in the fall of 1946.

It was during this time that Bobby got a taste of Kennedy-type politics, campaigning in Jack's first Massachusetts Congressional race in the Eleventh District, an Irish and Italian stronghold of Boston. Kennedy won by a landslide, a victory attributable to the financial resources and political clout of his father. Jean had recruited her friend Ethel into the fray and she, too, took to the streets, handing out Kennedy literature, helping to serve snacks at campaign headquarters.

One of Bobby's roommates at the time was George Terrien, two years older, handsome and more worldly, a veteran of the war who had flown dozens of sorties against the Japanese in Navy fighter planes from the aircraft carrier *Independence*. "Bobby and I were very close friends from the beginning," said Terrien years later. "You couldn't live with him, but we got along. He was a royal pain in the ass. He was a bulldog about certain things, but I tolerated him." Terrien, who had a lot of influence over Bobby during their college years, grew up in a modest home in New Hampshire. His father, a Harvard-trained lawyer specializing in appellate work, had lost his money in the Crash and never recovered financially. A friend remembered George Terrien in college as "very outgoing, friendly, very Irish, and very impressed by the Kennedy money and position." Bobby and George would eventually room together at the University of Virginia Law School, they'd travel through Europe together, and Terrien would eventually become a central figure in the Skakel family drama, working for George Skakel and marrying one of his daughters, just like Bobby.

Besides Terrien, Bobby's only friends at Harvard were other football players. He lacked interest in his studies, and his exam scores showed it. His goal was to make the varsity team and get his Harvard letter, despite being a mediocre player and suffering injuries. Because of his small size he was bumped to lower squads, but later in the year he made the varsity team and became a member of the Varsity Club, a decision some of the better players questioned. He was so desperate to be a football hero that he played one game with a broken leg, or so the legend goes.

It was to this brooding, insecure, highly competitive young man from a powerful and wealthy Catholic family in many ways like her own that Ethel Skakel was drawn.

30 ⁕ Man of Her Dreams

ETHEL WAS FORMALLY introduced to Bobby by his sister Jean during the winter of their freshman year at Manhattanville. Jean had grown so fond of Ethel that she actually wanted her to become part of the Kennedy family—and so did Ethel, with a vengeance. The two girls, along with various friends and family members, had gone to Mont Tremblant for a ski weekend. Jean had a strong feeling that Bobby and Ethel would instantly hit it off. But she was wrong. It was actually Jean's brother Jack who made Ethel swoon.

"Ethel came back to Manhattanville from that ski

trip and she was insane about Jack,'' recalled Margaret Geoghegan Adams. ''She talked to me about him non-stop; not just me, the world! She was nuts about him and didn't think that much of Bobby. 'Jack's so handsome, so glamorous,' she said. Ethel felt Jack had much more wit and pizzazz, and that Bobby was too shy.''

But a member of Ethel's circle advised: ''You're definitely not Jack's type.'' Ethel quickly came to that realization, too. Unlike Bobby, Jack was a man of the world, pursuing glamorous women, about to embark on a triumphant political career. Ethel, a skinny college kid, made no impression on him whatsoever.

At the time of the ski weekend, Ethel knew Bobby slightly because he'd had occasional, informal dates with her sister Pat, and had been in and out of the Skakel home. Ethel had also seen him at the Kennedys' in Hyannis Port and in Palm Beach during visits with Jean. But Bobby never paid much notice to Ethel, and she harbored no secret fantasies about him. It would take a while for the two of them to click.

The young Kennedys and Skakels had first bonded when Georgeann met Eunice some six years earlier. Later, Pat Kennedy and Pat Skakel were schoolmates and chums at Maplehurst, about the time Ethel was transferring there from Greenwich Academy. Pat Kennedy went on to Manhattanville, joining Eunice. Pat Skakel arrived at the school in 1942, and the Skakel and Kennedy girls became instant friends.

As a result, matches were constantly being made between Kennedy boys and Skakel girls and vice versa. ''At one time or another there were four Skakels going around with four Kennedys,'' said Jim Skakel. ''When you're in the same circle everybody's moving around, dating each other, and that's what was happening with the Skakels and the Kennedys.''

Jim was the first Skakel to date a Kennedy seriously. His romance with Pat lasted about a year. By the time Jim met her, she had blossomed into a chic, glamorous young woman. Jim was immensely attracted to Pat, and their romance flourished. "They fell in love," recalled Margaret Geoghegan Adams.

But Jim's drinking and flightiness made Pat wary. Later, Jim maintained it was he who finally ended the relationship. "The Kennedys were too clannish for me," he said. "If you went out with one Kennedy, you went out with all of them, so I said, 'The hell with it! We were just not suited for each other.' "

At one point, Ethel tried to play Cupid, too, arranging for Jean to date her brother Rushton. Like Jim, he said, "I couldn't have handled it. The Kennedys weren't my cup of tea."

The reality was that Jean wasn't attracted to the mild-mannered Skakel boy. She was more interested in the handsome Corroon brothers, Larry and Bob, scions of a wealthy and prominent Garden City, Long Island, Irish Catholic family in the insurance business. Their beautiful sister, Joan Patricia ("Pat") Corroon, had dated Rushton Skakel for a time, but George Jr. moved in on him, marrying her in 1948.

There were also hopes that the youngest Kennedy boy, Ted, would get together with the youngest Skakel girl, Ann, who also went to Manhattanville. But she wasn't attracted to him. "Ann was adamant," recalled Frannie Pryor Haws. "She wouldn't have anything to do with Ted." Jean Kennedy, however, was the catalyst in what became the scandalous marriage between Ted and Joan Bennett, another Manhattanville girl.

Before Ethel and Bobby became serious, he had taken out Pat Skakel on a number of occasions and found the two sisters as different as night and day. Pat was quiet while Ethel was loud. Pat garnered respect while Ethel got laughs. Pat was an academic while Ethel was a jock. Pat was also more feminine. Ethel's bedroom at home, which adjoined Pat's, was always a mess, more like a boy's room. Pat's, on the other hand, was soft and refined: French Provincial furnishings, white satin on the headboard, wall-to-wall white fur carpeting in her private bathroom.

According to some, Pat Skakel wasn't interested in

Bobby, whom she viewed as immature, tedious, and intellectually inferior. "Pat never really liked Bobby very much," said Pat Norton Mullins, her close friend at Manhattanville. "I never felt, 'Whoops! Here's Bobby Kennedy, a big romance in Pat's life.' " Bobby did take Pat to her senior prom in the spring of 1946 at *her* invitation because "there was no one else," said Mullins.

"It was only a casual thing with Pat—a friendship—and then he started seeing Ethel," agreed Ethel's friend Courtney Murphy Benoist.

Some Manhattanville girls maintained that Ethel was jealous of Pat's involvement with Bobby, no matter how uninspired it might have been; that with Jean's backing, Ethel aggressively elbowed Pat out of the picture.

Ann Marie O'Hagan Murphy felt Pat "was crazy" about Bobby and "in some way or another Ethel—I don't know if I should say stole him away—but Bobby's affections were turned toward Ethel. We felt it was awfully peculiar for the younger sister to steal the beau from the older sister, if that's what happened. It was the big talk at Manhattanville that Ethel was now dating Bobby instead of Pat. People were angry."

There had always been a simmering sibling rivalry between Ethel and Pat, a competitive spirit between two sisters who were three years apart chronologically and worlds apart in terms of their intellect and personalities. On the surface, though, they appeared devoted—it was a "neat sisterly relationship," as one classmate put it. But Ethel felt she could never live up to Pat's near perfect image at home and at school.

All Ethel would ever say on the subject of Pat and Bobby was that they "fell in love . . . and he went with her for two years." That statement, though, is an exaggeration, made a quarter of a century later, a sop of sorts to Pat, who by then had distanced herself from the Skakel family by making a permanent life for herself in Ireland.

Bobby soon became a presence around Manhattanville, coming down from Harvard to pick up Ethel for weekend dates. "We used to tease her if we happened to be around when he came to take her out," said Mamie Jenkins. "Being silly college girls, we would giggle and make fun and Ethel *pretended* to be upset, but she was *flattered* that we knew that she was going out with a Kennedy."

Said Ann Marie O'Hagan Murphy, "Ethel was head-over-heels in love with Bobby. That's all she talked about and wanted. She couldn't wait for the weekends so she could see Bobby. As soon as she started going with him, it was *Bobby, Bobby, Bobby;* it was *Kennedy, Kennedy, Kennedy*—and not much Skakel anymore."

By the beginning of Ethel's junior year and Bobby's senior year, the two were going steady. Ethel was telling friends that she intended to marry Bobby, even though their formal engagement would not be announced until six months after her graduation.

"After every weekend," giggled Kay Simonson Waterbury, "we'd all go scrambling up to Ethel's room at college to get *all* the details about what happened. Sexual activity was unheard of. We'd talk about sex, but in such a naive way. Ethel talked about kissing and holding hands and stuff like that."

Despite their infatuation, Ethel and Bobby weren't exactly models of youthful, fiery passion. Hand-holding was the closest anyone ever saw of their affection and attachment. In terms of love and romance, Bobby was puritanical, Ethel prudish. They appeared caring, but not physical, more like siblings who were extraordinarily close, rather than two young people in love.

Bobby was at the Skakels' virtually every weekend now, tutoring Ethel and her Manhattanville chums on American history, despite the fact that he was no Quiz Kid himself. "Bobby was very helpful when he came into the picture," recalled Kay Simonson Waterbury. "We'd be up there in Greenwich and he'd sit on the couch and we'd sit around him and cram for our tests and essays. It was something we looked forward to. He was a terrific help because he made the subjects so realistic and engaging."

31 * Wild Child

FOR ETHEL, COLLEGE was prison. She couldn't wait until the last class on Friday afternoon so she could be with Bobby. "She wrote and wrote and wrote, taking profuse notes in class, more than any of us, until her hands and wrists ached," a classmate recalled. "She had to work very hard to get good grades and she did that only so she could escape on weekends."

Ethel, whose major was English and minor was history, had a passing interest in philosophy and theology, was thought of as a fair essay writer, and enjoyed poetry, all in all an average student. Aside from Clark Gable and Montgomery Clift, over whom she swooned, Ethel had little, if any, interest in the arts. As her college pal Courtney Murphy Benoist said, "Ethel wasn't too keen on the cultural."

Because her main goal was to get off campus, Ethel also cared little about extracurricular acitivities, except for hockey, tennis, swimming—but only if it didn't cut into her weekends. When one of her teams lost, it was usually Ethel who wrote the funny lyrics for the traditional song the losers sang to the winners.

Next to Bobby, Ethel's riding continued to be her passion. Her reputation as a horsewoman was generating major press notices in the sports and society pages. Photographed in full riding regalia jumping a fence aboard her favorite horse, Guamada, Ethel's riding abilities were trumpeted in newspapers like the *New York World-Telegram*. One story noted that she would compete in the annual Alfred B. Maclay horsemanship championship at the National Horse Show in Madison Square Garden. "Although Ethel Skakel is above the usual seventeen-year-old limit for the Maclay Trophy, a relaxation of the rules this year will make it possible for her to enter," said the story, which also noted that thirteen-year-old Ann Skakel would also be riding in the show, aboard appropriately named Little Sister.

• • •

Despite the fact that she was a middling student, Ethel nevertheless wielded an enormous amount of personal power on campus, and possessed a certain sense of entitlement and importance, mainly because of the Skakel money and her ties to Jean and Bobby, children of what one Manhattanville nun years later reverently called "the greatest Irish Catholic family in America. Ethel knew it and took advantage of it. She just did it in such a *nice* way."

Said classmate Abbyann Day Lynch: "She knew how to do things to get people on her side. If she was going to the Tea House with two or three people she'd say, 'Come and join us.' If she knew you didn't have money, she'd pay. If you didn't have a ride, she'd say, 'Hop in.' I think just about everybody reaped the benefit of that kind of generosity."

One weekend she decided to show off Bobby—and a new jewelry box he'd given her—to some of her classmates who hadn't already met him. Bright and early on Monday morning, Ethel strode proudly into her first class on the arm of her shy and reluctant beau. The nuns were shocked and the girls were awestruck—both by Ethel's impudence and the couple's charm. "It was the first time I'd ever even seen a man—a boyfriend—on campus like *that*," recalled Helen Quigley Williams. "But Ethel could do it because she had the reputation and clout. Bobby Kennedy had *the* magic name, even then, and no one would have had the nerve to question that he was there. They walked in areas that no one else walked. They thought it was their due."

Only upperclassmen were permitted to have cars on campus, but Ethel used her influence and charm to have one whenever she needed it. Her excuse was that she had to commute to horse shows or to her stables in

Greenwich, but she mostly used the car for joyriding with pals.

One Saturday morning, in her sophomore year, she was scheduled to ride in a major horse show at Madison Square Garden. She ran into heavy southbound traffic along Central Park. Rather than risk being late, Ethel paved her own route, jumping the curb and driving across the grass, changing direction here and there, to avoid hitting trees and shrubs and an occasional pedestrian. Ann Marie O'Hagan Murphy, riding shotgun, feared for her life and reputation. "For God's sake, Ethel, quit it. Get off the grass or we're gonna land in jail and you won't get to ride at all!" she screamed. Ethel just laughed. "You worry too much," she said with finality.

Often, when it suited her purpose, Ethel ran roughshod over classmates, too, particularly those who were less fortunate. Any number of Manhattanville girls found themselves seething because of her arrogance.

Mary Adele Bernard Hill, a music major who lived across the hall from Ethel and Jean, was ironing when Ethel popped into the laundry room one afternoon, plunking herself down on a table. "Hey, kid, who taught you to do that? That's *sensational!*" Mary Adele, who came from a working-class home, said she had learned watching her mother. Ethel said she had never ironed anything in her life; she had all of her things sent home to the laundress. "But you're now going to show me how to do it!" she said. "I'll just run and get something." A few moments later Ethel returned with a wrinkled blouse and asked Bernard for a demonstration. When she was done, Ethel put it on. "Thanks a lot, kid!" she said, dashing out of the room giggling. "That," said Bernard years later, "was the last time I ever saw Ethel in the laundry room."

More often than not, Ethel's entire class would be punished for her cavalier and sophomoric high jinks, a prime example of which involved the case of the missing demerit book.

It all began on a Friday afternoon when Ethel had tried to sign out so that she could go skiing with Bobby.

Because of her numerous demerits for cutting class she was not permitted to leave. It was one of the few times the administration cracked down on her.

The demerit book was kept in the office of the class warden, Mother Kathryn Sullivan, whose door was always left open. "Ethel grabbed the book and made it disappear," said a classmate years later. "She threw it down the incinerator and went off on her weekend. Of course, the rest of us would never, never have told on her, and no one ever did. It was a big mystery, but we all knew who did it."

Some students had heard that Jean had aided and abetted Ethel, and may have even instigated the heist, since she knew that her brother desperately wanted to see her roommate that weekend. "Jean was behind Ethel in a lot of those pranks," a friend of both girls said. "They cooked up those kinds of things together."

Everyone was furious. Class president Tish Coakley O'Neil, with the backing of the student government, called a special assembly to plead for the thief to give herself up, but she was met with silence. Because the perpetrator never admitted to the theft, the students were restricted to campus as punishment.

(Many years later, when Ethel appeared headed for the White House as First Lady, Jean Kennedy Smith offered a different version of what had happened that day, one that put her now-famous sister-in-law in a better light. "Ethel entreated me to do something about the demerit book, so *I* filched it, and threw it down the incinerator.")

On another occasion, a note was found on the windshield of a new black Cadillac driven by the Right Reverend Monsignor John Hartigan, who taught a Christian marriage class. The note read: "The collections must be good, Father!" Hartigan, a close friend of New York's Cardinal Spellman, was furious and demanded that Mother Eleanor M. O'Byrne, Manhattanville's president, find and punish the offender. Ethel's friends believed she was the author. Because no one ever confessed, everyone was restricted to campus.

Ethel rarely returned the books she borrowed from the Manhattanville library. When a number of the lace mantillas the girls wore to chapel disappeared, Ethel was the suspect. Sister Mary Esther McCarthy, the house warden of Ethel's dorm, warned there would be hell to pay, unless they were returned. Not long after, the nun was headed toward the chapel when she spotted Ethel moving stealthily in the same direction, her hands behind her back. "Ethel had eight or nine veils in her possession. She put the veils in their place and as she was walking away I said, 'Young lady, I'm glad you paid attention to what I said.' "

Unprepared for an exam in Lloyd B. Holsapple's freshman Latin class, Ethel wrote a cute letter to the professor in her blue book, hoping her ingenuity would impress him and that he'd give her a passing grade. "It was just amazing that she thought she could get away with it," said Marie Haggerty Hennelley, who had the dorm room next to Ethel and Jean's. "Ethel was very innovative. She wasn't above trying *anything*."

• • •

Despite her behavior, Ethel said her rosary and went to Mass and took Communion every day, meditating for an hour afterward. Like Rose Kennedy, she had become a member of Child of Mary, which allowed Ethel to write *E. de M*. next to her name, and have her Child of Mary medal dipped in gold at Cartier's as was the fashion at the time. She was considered a leader at class retreats, which consisted of three days of prayer and silence in the Manhattanville chapel.

Ethel often put her religion to work for her. When Jim Skakel disappeared along the Amazon River during one of his adventures and the family feared the worst, Ethel asked a group of her college friends to pray for his safe return. She also pledged that if he was found alive, she'd give up smoking. After Jim turned up a few days later, Ethel never lit another cigarette.

"I really thought she might have a vocation, but then she met Robert Kennedy and we lost her," said Sister Josephine Morgan.

"The nuns gave Ethel a very good feeling of a personal relationship with God," observed Ann Cooley Buckley. But while her classmates were helping the poor and infirm at settlement houses such as Casita Maria in East Harlem, or at Knickerbocker Free Hospital, Ethel was involved in more leisurely pursuits.

As her pal Courtney Murphy Benoist recalled, "We went to a campus hangout called Doc's and had bacon, lettuce, and tomato sandwiches, and then we went to a place called La Petit Parisienne, two blocks up the street, and we'd have French pastry. I don't think we ever did anything involving Catholic Action."

Added another classmate sardonically, "Ethel was otherwise occupied."

32 ❋ Homecoming Queen

ON FRIDAYS, ETHEL made the rounds of the girls in her circle, or other acceptable young women who were far from home. "Are you goin' anywhere, kid? . . . You got anything doin'? . . . Well, come home with me!" She rarely received a rejection.

By now everyone knew that an invitation to the Skakels' meant a madcap, rollicking good time. "The Skakel family was *the* legend in the school," said Anne Heide Quigley. "You always came back to campus with another story about some outlandish incident, some absurdity."

If Big Ann wasn't on another jaunt with George, she was usually stationed at the front door of the mansion, beckoning Ethel's collegiate guests inside like the jovial fat lady at a carnival funhouse.

Ethel's clique had mixed reactions to her parents, seeing them as friendly but distant. "They seemed culturally deprived," said one frequent weekend visitor. "It was party, party, party—but there was no depth, no intellectual stimulation, no culture." Some felt overpowered by Big Ann, while Ethel's father seemed to be a milquetoast. "Mrs. Skakel ruled with sort of an iron hand and I was terrified of her," recalled Kay Simonson Waterbury. It was clear to Waterbury and the other girls that Ethel favored her father, but had her mother's personality and values.

During one visit several of the girls sat at the kitchen table giggling nervously, embarrassed as they overheard Big Ann on the telephone arguing with Macy's. It seemed she had missed a white sale and was demanding that she be given the discount price retroactively. "I was convulsed," recalled Pat Norton Mullins. "I was listening and thinking about my very reserved mother in Jersey City who thought nothing about buying at Saks, or Bergdorf's, or Lord and Taylor's and paying top dollar—and here's Mrs. Skakel, in this enormous mansion in Greenwich, haggling over the price of sheets."

As a result of Big Ann's wholesale shopping sprees, there were countless cases of seltzer water and ginger ale in the cupboard at Lake Avenue. Ethel's youthful weekend guests divided into teams and one favorite game involved grabbing a bottle of soda, shaking it, and then chasing members of the opposing team through the house, squirting each other—and everything in sight.

"I didn't enjoy having a good dress on and getting it all wet," recalled one of the players. "Everyone was drenched and so was the furniture and the walls and the draperies, and everything else in the line of fire. Mr. and Mrs. Skakel didn't care one iota about the carnage."

Ethel's friends from college couldn't help but notice the never-ending flow of alcohol in the Skakel household, and the inebriated state of some of the family members, such as Georgeann and John Dowdle, who were still living in one of the guest houses. They desperately wanted children, but Georgeann was having a difficult time conceiving. As a result, both were depressed and drowning their sorrow in alcohol.

In the midst of the turmoil on Sundays, one of the Skakels' priest friends usually held a Mass for everyone. After the prayers, the party continued, with Ethel's parents proceeding to get smashingly drunk as the young people ran rampant.

Darts was a favorite pastime during those weekends, but instead of a dart board, Ethel permitted her friends to use the beautiful wood paneling in one of the rooms. Ethel drew the circles on the wall with lipstick.

One weekend Ethel brought a group of her buddies home to celebrate yet another new convertible her parents had bought for George Jr. "He had the top down and was doing the whirlies and drove the car right into the pool—this brand-new, expensive convertible," said a houseguest. "Ethel led the applause."

Not all of those weekends ended so uproariously. One Saturday evening in the winter of 1946, while everyone was at home reveling, George Jr. and an Amherst College pal, Bob Judge, had a brush with death. "We had been playing charades and George and his friend got bored and had gone into New York to go barhopping," said one of the Manhattanville girls who was at the house that night. A state trooper had spotted the car, with George at the wheel and Judge in the passenger seat, speeding and weaving. Hearing the police siren, George floored the accelerator. At an intersection he veered left, the car fishtailed, and George lost control and slammed into an abutment, hurling both young men into the windshield. Bob Judge required dozens of stitches in his face, but recovered quickly. George's jaw was broken and had to be wired shut for months. Because of the long recuperation, he dropped out of Amherst and never earned a college degree.

"That accident was horribly scary and Ethel was devastated by the possibility that her brother might die," said a guest who was at the house that night. "Ethel and her parents rushed to the hospital and the rest of us went back to campus. It was very scary and very sad. Those Skakels lived on the edge. They courted catastrophe."

33 ✻ Bobby's Fling

BOBBY KENNEDY RECEIVED his B.A. from Harvard in March 1948, near the end of Ethel's junior year. His goal was to go to Harvard Law, where Jack had gone, but Bobby's grades were too low. He was finally accepted at the University of Virginia Law School, in Charlottesville, which noted in its consideration of him that he had a "far from outstanding record at Harvard." At the time, UVA didn't have the elite reputation it was to earn in later years. It was still a school for good ol' boys from moneyed families. Dubious about his son's future, Joe Kennedy wrote to a friend that Bobby had the difficult task of following in the footsteps of "two brilliant brothers," Joe Jr. and Jack.

Joe Kennedy felt that Bobby needed some worldly experience, so he arranged for him to have a grand tour abroad as a "news correspondent"—armed with credentials from the *Boston Post* and with letters of introduction from Cardinal Spellman, among others. His paid traveling companion was George Terrien. "Old Joe wanted me to go along to take care of Bobby," said Terrien later. "Bobby was very capable, but Joe wanted someone with a lot of seasoning to baby-sit for him."

On March 5, 1948, with Ethel to see them off, Bobby and George set sail for Europe aboard the *Queen Mary*. Their itinerary included England, Egypt, Israel, Lebanon, Turkey, Greece, Italy, Holland, Germany, Austria, and Denmark.

Two months into the trip, tragedy struck. On May 13, Kick Kennedy Hartington, twenty-eight, was killed along with her lover Peter Fitzwilliam when their small, private plane, en route to Cannes, crashed into the side of a mountain in France's Rhone Valley. Only days before, Kick had told her mother about Peter, enraging Rose, who declared she'd never allow her daughter to marry a divorced man because it would forever deny her the Sacraments. She threatened to disown Kick.

Rose was even more wrathful than she had been several years earlier when Kick married a non-Catholic, the wealthy and powerful William ("Billy") Cavendish, the Marquess of Hartington. Only Kick's brother Joe Jr. was present at the wedding, underscoring the family's outrage. Just four months after the nuptials, Hartington was killed in combat.

Bobby was in bed at the Grande Hotel in Rome recovering from a case of jaundice when he received word from Jack, calling from Hyannis Port, that his sister was dead. "Bobby broke down like a little kid," recalled Terrien, who was there when the call came. But because of his illness, Bobby missed the funeral. Still angry at her daughter, Rose refused to go.

Depressed, Bobby returned to London. In hopes of cheering him up, one of Kick's close friends, the British playwright William Douglas-Home, gave him tickets to see his long-running play, *The Chiltern Hundreds,* at London's Vaudeville Theater.

The moment the house-lights dimmed and the female lead walked on stage, Bobby's gloom began to fade. Joan Winmill was a blonde, hazel-eyed, twenty-one-year-old beauty with a soft British accent. Eerily, the character Joan was playing onstage was based on Bobby's sister. "It was strange, really, that there I was in this play and he was watching me pretend to be Kick," Joan said later.

Bobby was smitten. Joan remembered him "with his freckled face and white, toothy grin," standing there admiring her. His look made her "feel weak at the knees."

"It was," she declared, "love at first sight. When Bobby asked me out to dinner the following evening, I accepted like a shot."

For Joan Winmill, living in a modest flat and earning the equivalent of thirty-two dollars a week, the two-year clandestine romance she would have with the handsome son of the former British ambassador was like a fairy tale come true.

Bobby, meanwhile, kept his involvement with the British beauty well hidden from his girl in Greenwich. One of the few who knew of his British escapade was George Terrien, who had been sworn to secrecy. "Joan was a far different kind of gal from Ethel. She was sexy and sophisticated and I never had a doubt that Bobby was in love with her," Terrien said years later. "Shortly after Bobby met Joan, he told me, 'Ethel's fun, but she's just a girl. Joan's a real woman.' So he began seeing her steadily and on the sly while we were in England."

Bobby and Joan, sometimes with Terrien tagging along, took romantic trips into the countryside, including visits to Chatsworth, the spectacular estate in Derbyshire owned by his late sister's father-in-law. During stays at Chatsworth, Bobby and Joan took long walks, talking, holding hands, kissing. "It was quite romantic," she reflected.

It was in the Devonshire's family plot, near Chatsworth, that Kick was buried. There, accompanied by Joan, Bobby often visited his sister's grave, spending solitary moments in prayer. But there was a gay side to their country jaunts. Even though Joan didn't drive, Bobby put the terrified young woman behind the wheel of his car, scaring villagers and policemen along their routes. She was also the constant brunt of Bobby's teasing because she was Protestant, not Catholic. Bobby spent hours telling Joan about life in America, about the country's history and the Kennedys' place in it.

"We had great times," Winmill reminisced. "We went to the theater a lot. We'd go to dinner. We'd go dancing. He'd bring me flowers. After a date we'd go back to Kick Kennedy's house in Smith Square. It was very exciting."

Bobby, too, was ecstatic. Like his father, he was now having his own affair with an actress.

Despite his shy demeanor, Bobby was as hot-blooded as any young man Joan had met, and he was constantly trying to seduce her. "He was a *very* passionate Irishman. He was *very* romantic," she said. But Winmill claimed she never slept with Bobby. "I was able to reason with him," she said.

When Joe Kennedy got wind of Bobby's romance, he was furious. From his own experience, he feared that Bobby's involvement with an actress might somehow cause a scandal, embarrass the family, ultimately injure Jack's burgeoning political career. But Bobby scoffed at his father's warnings, and accused him privately of being a hypocrite. "He treated his father's feelings more as a joke," recalled Winmill. "He didn't feel there was anything for us to be worried about. He was like any son laughing at a father's foolishness."

Bobby assured Joan, "Nobody is going to break us up." He never mentioned Ethel.

But he was sufficiently concerned to keep his relationship out of the limelight. He rarely took Joan to parties or clubs where they might be spotted by the press. "If they had known, they would have written something," said Winmill. Bobby's routine was to pick up Joan after each night's performance at the theater, located on the Strand. They'd walk across the street to the Savoy Hotel and have dinner in a quiet corner of the dining room. Afterward, they went to Kick's townhouse. "For the most part, we kept our relationship very low key. As a result, there was never any publicity."

But a potential disaster was about to happen. Ethel and Jean unexpectedly arrived in London in July, ostensibly to see the summer Olympic Games at White City Stadium, and the horse show in Dublin, where Ethel's idol, Billy Steinkraus, was riding. But stories about Bobby's British escapades may have reached Ethel's ears.

Knowing he couldn't hide his relationship with Joan because his family already knew about it, Bobby played it down, taking both Jean *and* Ethel to see Joan's play. Backstage, Bobby introduced Ethel as Jean's friend, not his girlfriend.

"I vaguely was aware Ethel was looking at Bobby and me almost as if she were jealous," said Winmill. "I didn't even know they were going together. He never told me he was dating Ethel. I just thought she was with his sister."

In August, after the Olympic Games, Bobby and George Terrien returned to law school. Before he boarded the ship, Bobby put his arms around Joan. "He held me tenderly and he told me, 'Don't cry. I'll be back next summer. I can't stay away from you.' "

England was still recovering from the war, and many items were in short supply. "I was really a struggling actress," said Winmill. "Bobby was a very caring person. He never gave me any money or anything, but he would notice things that I needed and send them to me without my even asking for them." When he arrived home, Bobby quietly sent Joan "care" packages—perfumes and soaps, gourmet foods, chocolates, and elegant clothes with famous labels—Saks, Bonwit's, Bergdorf's—that he told Joan he'd snitched from the closets of his sisters, Jean and Pat.

Besides the gifts, Bobby and Joan were exchanging "piles of letters . . . I considered myself to be in love," she said. "He epitomized everything one could dream of."

The following summer, Bobby returned to London—and Joan—and their relationship resumed. The day he left he invited her aboard the ship to say good-bye. "We talked about my coming over to be with him," she said.

In early 1950, Joan was anxiously awaiting Bobby's invitation, but instead she got a "Dear Joan" letter postmarked Hyannis Port. Bobby, as Joan recalled, wrote: *I am getting married to Ethel Skakel.* Joan was devastated.

"We were boyfriend and girlfriend," she said later. "It was like an old-fashioned romance. I'd fallen in love. I was furious. I went to a drawer, pulled out Bobby's love letters, lighted a match, and burned them. I got rid of them all."

Musing about their relationship, Joan said, "Those days I spent with Bobby were some of the happiest times I had then. As time has passed, I've realized that Bobby and I were not suited at all. I'm not a very athletic person as was Ethel. I had only two children. If I was to have had eleven children as Ethel did, I would never have made it. I also know I wouldn't have fitted in with the family. Everybody in the family—except for Joan Kennedy and, of course, Jacqueline—were very competitive, athletic, and had tremendous energy, *especially* Ethel. I'm not that way. As it turned out, Ethel was *perfect* for Bobby."

34 ✻ Don't Look Back

ETHEL BEGAN HER last year at Manhattanville in the fall of 1948, spending most of her weekends visiting Bobby in Charlottesville. Because of her morals, she refused to spend the night with the man she intended to marry, instead staying with Ann Marie O'Hagan Murphy, who had already graduated from another college and was temporarily living on her family's big farm on the outskirts of Charlottesville.

It was during that period that Ethel was required to write her senior thesis. With her deadline looming, Bobby suggested the subject and helped her with the research and the writing. It was on the same subject as Jack Kennedy's Harvard senior thesis, "Appeasement at Munich: The Inevitable Result of the Slowness of the British Democracy to Change from a Disarmament Policy." Kennedy's paper—with the influence of his father—was quickly turned into a commercial, best-selling book, the title changed to *Why England Slept*. It sold close to three hundred thousand copies here and abroad and brought him a cum laude degree. Ethel's paper—uninspired—was considered merely acceptable.

At the senior prom, Ethel caused a minor scandal when Sister Mary Byles caught her and Bobby with a fifth of Old Grand-Dad, a major violation of the rules that could have resulted in her suspension or even expulsion, but no action was taken against her.

In June 1949, Ethel graduated from Manhattanville, with a bachelor's degree. Her academic standing was somewhere in the middle of the class. It would not have mattered whether she had been first or last; she'd already decided that her career would be that of wife to Bobby Kennedy and mother of his children.

The lasting memory of Ethel at Manhattanville is etched in the *Tower,* her class yearbook. The photo shows her chipmunk smile, her hair cropped short, a crucifix around her neck. The caption reads:

"An excited hoarse voice, a shriek, a peal of screaming laughter, the flash of shirt-tails, a tousled brown head—Ethel! Her face is at one moment a picture of utter guilelessness and at the next alive with mischief. Those who have spent a weekend at Skakels' have only two comments—hilarious and unique. 'Laughter holding both its sides' had nothing on us when Ethel does her rendition of 'McNamara's Band,' complete with brogue. The 49ers didn't have to search very far to find Ethel a heart of gold."

The yearbook staff's description of Ethel might have been less exuberant had it been aware of the way she dealt with Manhattanville and many of her classmates after graduation. Ethel is remembered to have attended only one reunion and given little if anything during college alumni fund drives.

"She just came flying into our first reunion wearing a fancy hat and outfit and looked around at everyone and said, 'So, isn't *this* terrific?' That was her big word for everything—*terrific*. She had a certain way of saying it. She knew how to make the entrance and wear the hat, the whole thing. Then she went off in a corner with one of her pals. That was the last time we heard from her, *ever, ever, ever!*" said a classmate involved in alumni activities. "Year in and year out nothing ever came in from her for the alumni's fund drive. Ethel was not one of those weeping the night that we sang serenades just before graduation. A number of girls who were close to Ethel felt they were forgotten by her after she left. She just flew off. Once she married Bobby Kennedy, Ethel never looked back."

PART VI

Bobby's Wife

35 * Engagement and Marriage

IN THE MONTHS immediately following graduation, Ethel did little except ponder her future with Bobby. She passed up a European summer holiday with friends and remained at home, spending her time riding, and helping her sister Pat prepare for her own wedding.

After Georgeann, Pat would be the second of the Skakel girls to marry. Her fiancé, Luan Peter Cuffe, was a bookish assistant architect from Ireland whose mother was a member of the radical Irish Republican Army. While he was getting his master's degree at Harvard's School of Design, Luan had been introduced to Pat by the mother of her Manhattanville roommate. The two had a whirlwind romance and, despite Pat's last-minute jitters, the Skakels announced her engagement on July 3, 1949, but with some reluctance. Big Ann had numerous misgivings, the main one being that, while Luan was well bred and highly educated, he didn't come from money, always a priority with her. Moreover, she was upset because Luan intended to take Pat back to Dublin to live. Pat, on the other hand, was ecstatic about her upcoming nuptials. She had made several visits to Ireland and had fallen in love with the country and its people, going so far as to speak with an Irish brogue. Moreover, Pat saw her marriage to Cuffe as a way to escape the dysfunctional Skakels and Greenwich. As Martin McKneally later observed, "Pat was more or less going into exile of her own choosing."

Despite Big Ann's disapproval, she gave Pat and Luan a spectacular wedding, with more than seven hundred attending the service and reception on October 8,

1949. There was a special papal blessing, and a close friend of the Kennedys, the Reverend Terrence L. Connolly, of Boston, officiated. The Mass was sung by Michael O'Higgins, a member of the Royal Irish Academy of Music, who was flown in from Dublin. Ethel, along with Georgeann and younger sister Ann, was one of the bridesmaids. After a honeymoon at the Cloisters in Georgia, the Cuffes sailed to Ireland aboard the *Mauretania,* soon taking up residence in a modest home in Carrig Gonn Killiney, County Dublin.

Back in Greenwich, Ethel, with no career in mind, had put her life on hold. With Bobby beginning his second year of law school, she was a bundle of pent-up energy. A number of her friends had already gotten jobs, many going to work for Father James Keller, the charismatic founder of the Christophers, a burgeoning anti-Communist Catholic religious movement. With the Cold War growing hotter, others were moving to Washington to work for the newly formed Central Intelligence Agency.

With nothing but time on her hands, Ethel began having second thoughts about marrying Bobby. She feared she couldn't live up to the Kennedy name. Would she be fully accepted by them? Would Joe and Rose treat her like a daughter or an interloper? Would the daffy Skakels embarrass the Kennedys? Did she have what it took to become a Kennedy?

It was during this period of indecision that Ethel actually thought about dropping Bobby altogether and becoming a nun. When word of her predicament reached Bobby's ears, he was concerned, asking his sister Jean on the beach at Hyannis Port one afternoon, "How can I fight God?"

"This was one of the few times in Ethel's entire life that she was truly introspective," said a close friend many years later. "This really was the biggest decision she ever made. Later in life she'd leave all decision-making up to Bobby and the Kennedy clan."

Ethel confided her concerns to several close friends. One, Maplehurst headmistress Mother Bourke, suggested that Ethel come to work at the school, which had now moved to Greenwich. Ethel gratefully accepted, and for the next few months she helped one of the younger nuns, Mother Marion Duffy, coach field hockey and assist with routine classroom chores. "Ethel told me she was in love with Bobby, but also made me very much aware that she was thinking about becoming a nun," Duffy clearly recalled. "She was very mixed up, so she went to her God to get an answer. She prayed in the chapel every day for an hour."

By Thanksgiving, Ethel's confidence had been sufficiently restored. She flew to Charlottesville and told Bobby she'd marry him and they immediately agreed on a June wedding. But when Bobby called his mother to tell her the good news, Rose Kennedy wasn't overjoyed. She wanted him to wait until after he had graduated from law school. "I had misgivings," she acknowledged later.

(Ethel later wrote off this important period of her life as uneventful. Once asked about the months leading up to her marriage, she replied, "I just sort of played around . . . . it's hardly worth mentioning.")

Ever the social climber, Big Ann was initially thrilled about her daughter's choice for a husband. Unlike Pat's marriage to Cuffe and Georgeann's to Dowdle, Ethel was entering the big time and through this, as a Kennedy in-law, Big Ann saw herself vaulting to the pinnacle of American Catholic society. George Skakel, on the other hand, wasn't as excited. He thought of his daughter's future father-in-law as "low-life, Irish trash." It would not be long before Big Ann herself would lose her wonderment and come to despise the Kennedys, too. But for now she was exultant.

She called "Smart Set" columnist Cholly Dearborn at the *Chicago Herald-American* and leaked news of the engagement, giving emphasis to the Skakels and their Chicago roots over the Kennedys. Under a headline that read, ETHEL SKAKEL'S ENGAGEMENT TO ROBERT KENNEDY STIRS SOCIETY, Dearborn noted that "the betrothal is of the greatest interest here because Ethel is a Chicagoan by birth. Ethel and young Kennedy have been keeping company for some time, therefore the betrothal was not unexpected. . . . You can be sure the wedding in June will be on an impressive scale. The Skakels are famous for their large, lavish parties. . . ."

Meanwhile, the formal engagement notice that appeared in newspapers across the country was a concoction of fiction and overstatement, showing the fine hand of Joe Kennedy, a master manipulator of the press, a born publicist. It said that Ethel "is now completing post graduate work at Columbia University" and that Bobby "served with the Navy for three years during the war . . . he traveled extensively as a writer of newspaper articles." In reality, Bobby's military experience was minimal; his journalism merely a perk arranged by Joe himself. And as far as anyone can remember, Ethel never did advanced work at Columbia. "She might have taken a few courses," said Courtney Murphy Benoist.

To celebrate the forthcoming nuptials, the Skakels threw a lavish engagement party in early January 1950 at Lake Avenue, inviting some two hundred friends and relatives. The meal was elegant, but most of the guests never got a chance at the enormous bowl of Beluga caviar that Big Ann had set out on a card table. Her sons and their pals had swooped down and taken the delicacy out to the garden, devouring it in minutes.

Meanwhile, Ethel went from guest to guest showing off an elegant jeweled compact. "Look what Mrs. Kennedy gave me," she trilled.

But the real centerpiece was the engagement ring, a tremendous marquise diamond. Unlike most young couples of the era, Ethel and Bobby did not window-shop together in the traditional romantic search for the perfect ring. One day, shortly before the engagement party, a gentleman from Cartier arrived at the Skakel home.

"He delivered a *huge* tray of rings," recalled Courtney Murphy Benoist, who saw the selection. "Ethel chose an exquisite diamond. It wasn't the biggest and it certainly wasn't the smallest, but it was beautiful. It was all done very privately, very low-key. None of it was pretentious. But you don't see very many trays of rings from Cartier's. The Skakels thought it was very generous of Bobby since the Kennedys were notoriously tight." Bobby, who wasn't present when Ethel made her choice, put the ring on her finger a few days later. Still, Ethel felt like a member of royalty. "I'm like a princess in a fairy tale," she squealed. Ethel and her old chums Pixie and Pan were all getting married within weeks of one another, and Ethel couldn't wait to show off her ring to them. One day they got together to compare stones. "Pixie and I were looking at our little rings and Ethel arrived with this huge diamond that you could land a plane on," recalled Pan. "She said, 'Oh, kids, I just had to have this one because my hands are so big,' which, of course, they weren't."

Shortly after the engagement party, Ethel and Bobby went on a weeklong ski trip to Sun Valley, Idaho.

It was an exciting time for the Skakels. In April, Georgeann had her first child following five years of trying to conceive. The Dowdles named her Georgeann and called her Little Georgeann.

By early May, complex plans for Ethel's wedding were in place. Big Ann had organized the massive affair, including a huge party at her home, with military precision. A small army of servants and cooks had been hired. Twelve hundred invitations had been sent out, placing a burden on the tiny Greenwich post office. An enormous tent of circus-like proportions would be erected on the grounds to handle the wedding feast. Entertainers were booked. One of the favorites was Joe Kennedy's close friend, Morton Downey, the Irish-American tenor, whose son, Morton Downey, Jr., would one day become a controversial television and radio talk-show host.

On the surface, relations between the Skakels and the Kennedys appeared amicable in those hectic and anxious weeks before the wedding. But tensions were already growing between the matriarchs of the two families. One issue in dispute was over where the Kennedys would stay. Big Ann had invited a number of old friends and relatives to lodge at Lake Avenue, but not the Kennedys. Her thinking was: they have houses and apartments everywhere, let them find their own place.

Betty Skakel Medaille recalled the controversy clearly years later. "The Kennedy clan decided that it would be *convenient* to stay at Lake Avenue, but Aunt Ann decided it *wasn't convenient*—not for her, not for the other Skakels, not for their friends. No one pushed Aunt Ann around, not even Rose Kennedy. Aunt Ann liked to have the privilege of inviting, and not have it wished upon her. The Kennedys didn't like it at all." Except for Jean, who would be a special houseguest of Ethel's, the Kennedys were forced to make other arrangements.

The week leading up to the wedding was filled with excitement. Rose threw a weekend house party at Hyannis Port for the bride and groom, the ushers, the bridesmaids, and other friends, most of whom stayed at a nearby inn. The young people sailed during the day and danced in the evening. Bobby and Ethel escaped from the throng for one night to dine alone at the Stork Club. The next morning their picture appeared in the *New York Mirror* with gossip columnist Barclay Beekman's explanation that they were making last-minute plans for the wedding.

Back in Greenwich, Big Ann made final preparations for the spectacular reception as the house filled with relatives from Chicago and friends from all over. Bobby arrived one evening with his rowdy Harvard football pals. "Just look at them," marveled Ethel's father to one of the guests. "This is the Harvard team and they're playing musical chairs." He couldn't believe how innocent it all seemed. Musical chairs was a far cry from the free-for-all bachelor party that was thrown for Bobby at the Harvard Club in New York.

The wedding festivities began on a typically wild and wet note—not due to the weather—a few hours before Ethel left for the church.

Long ago, Big Ann had determined that with her and the girls throwing so many parties it would be convenient and cost effective to have one room in the house equipped like a beauty salon. Using one of her many bogus business letterheads, Big Ann was able to purchase shampoo and cosmetics at wholesale prices, along with hair dryers and other tools of the trade. On the morning of the wedding all of the bridesmaids had their hair done at Lake Avenue by beauticians brought in from town. Afterward, they dashed outside to mix with the Skakel and Kennedy boys and as usual things got out of hand. "A lot of the bridesmaids got thrown in the pool," recalled a guest. "Needless to say, their hair was a wreck."

Rose Kennedy spent the night before the wedding at her home in Hyannis Port, arriving in Greenwich early in the morning. Joe Kennedy, who had spent the night with a female friend, arrived later in the day from New York. The Skakels' spread—the food, the decorations—was so elaborate and grandiose that Hearst society columnist Igor Cassini, alias Cholly Knickerbocker, rushed over to greet Joe, telling him, "I know why that son of yours is marrying that girl—*for her money!*"

Meanwhile, a special train from Boston had carried Bobby and some of his guests to Greenwich for the big day.

It was truly a wedding of royal proportions. Close to two thousand guests—socialites, diplomats, leaders of industry, politicians, entertainers, blue-collar friends from the old days, mostly Irish, mostly Catholic—were present, hundreds more than had been invited. Outside, a throng of the curious from town had gathered in hopes of seeing the famous faces.

The perfume of white peonies and lilies filled the air at St. Mary's Roman Catholic Church that Saturday, June 17, 1950, the day Ethel Skakel, twenty-two, was formally inducted into the Kennedy family with the blessing of the Pope.

George Skakel escorted his daughter to the altar around noon. A virgin, Ethel wore white, and so did all of the bridesmaids, which is unusual. Looking like a princess, Ethel walked down the aisle wearing a satin gown made with a fitted bodice finished with an off-the-shoulder neckline and a bertha of pointe de Venise lace embroidered with pearls. Her tulle veil was fastened to a headdress of matching lace trimmed with orange blossoms. She carried a bouquet of lilies, stephanotis, and lilies of the valley.

Pat Skakel Cuffe, who had flown in from Ireland, served as Ethel's matron of honor, and Little Ann was maid of honor. Both wore white lace over taffeta, their wide hats of white organza trimmed with pink gardenias and baby's breath. Ethel's six bridesmaids, similarly dressed, included Georgeann; her sister-in-law, Pat Corroon Skakel, drunk by the time the ceremony started; her cousin, Celeste Solari; Jean Kennedy, feeling victorious for having been the matchmaker; a somewhat dejected Eunice, who'd just been robbed of her jewels at the Ambassador Hotel in Chicago; and Pat Kennedy, whose romance with Jim Skakel was on the wane. Massachusetts Congressman Jack Kennedy served as his brother's best man.

The ushers included Ethel's three brothers, Bobby's younger brother, Ted, George Terrien, and Bobby's football pals, a motley pack of bruisers, wide-shouldered and beefy. "Where did Bobby get these characters?" Big Ann wondered aloud.

The Reverend Terence L. Connolly performed the ceremony and was the celebrant of the nuptial mass. Even he had to chuckle when he saw the George Skakel, Jr.–Lem Billings incident that could have touched off an old-fashioned donnybrook. Sitting behind Billings, whom he didn't know, the already inebriated Skakel tossed a few coins in the aisle. He leaned over and quietly asked the effete Billings if he wouldn't mind picking them up. When he leaned over, George kicked him in the behind, sending Billings sprawling as the wedding procession was starting. As Jim Skakel said later, "George would do anything to get the action going."

With her marriage to twenty-four-year-old Bobby, Ethel Skakel became the first woman to snag a Kennedy man since Rose was betrothed to Joe.

The *Boston Globe* called the wedding "the prettiest" of the year and noted that the marriage "unites two large fortunes." Friends of both the Kennedys and the Skakels, in fact, had debated which family was worth more. There was substantial belief that the Skakels had a larger net worth than the Kennedys.

When the ceremony was over, everyone rushed back to Lake Avenue for the party, where the guests ate off of gold plates. Food was heaped high and liquor and champagne flowed. At one point, Big Ann pulled Ethel aside. Knowing well the Skakels' proclivities for drinking, she warned her daughter, "You can't drink and take care of your husband, too." It was one of the few pieces of advice from her mother that Ethel took to heart.

In a big room on the second floor the wedding presents were carefully displayed for the guests to admire. Ethel was meticulous about knowing who gave each gift. She made a list. Later, a social secretary—a pal of Ethel's from college—addressed and sent thank-you notes.

Meantime, John Dowdle had been assigned to help Bobby and Ethel plan their honeymoon itinerary, a project he undertook with mischievous glee. On a number of occasions Bobby had stiffed Dowdle for ten dollars here, twenty dollars there. Rubbing his hands together devilishly, Dowdle viewed the planning of Ethel's honeymoon—for which Bobby Kennedy would foot the bill—as payback time. Everyone in the family, except possibly Ethel, knew what he was up to and approved wholeheartedly.

Ethel and Bobby had decided they wanted to spend their honeymoon in Hawaii, after which they'd leisurely drive back across the country. They would be gone for three months. Dowdle proceeded to book them into the most expensive suites in the plushest hotels: the magnificent Royal Hawaiian on Waikiki Beach and the Hanamaui, a swank resort hotel, on Maui. Dowdle made certain every conceivable costly extra was put on Bobby's tab, such as the daily supply of fresh orchids that filled the bridal suite.

After the honeymooners left for Hawaii, Georgeann had boasted to friends, "We took a great deal of pleasure in arranging the most expensive honeymoon because we knew it would annoy the hell out of Bobby."

If the hotel bills bothered Bobby, Ethel never made mention of it. Her letters from Hawaii to friends at home told of the wonderful time they were having, how happy they were. The honeymooners stayed in Hawaii about a month. Back in Los Angeles, they picked up Pat Kennedy's convertible for a leisurely drive East. Most honeymooners want to be alone, but when Ethel and Bobby reached Salt Lake City they got together with Courtney Murphy Benoist, who was now living with her family there. The threesome toured the state for a few days, visiting Great Salt Lake and other sites. They made plans to get together the following summer.

Ethel and Bobby's destination was Charlottesville, Virginia, where Bobby would finish his final year of law school, and where Ethel would begin to establish herself as a loyal wife, a terrible cook and housekeeper, a gracious hostess, and a fertile baby-making machine. In Charlottesville, her final conversion to Kennedyism would be completed. The road ahead appeared smooth and paved with gold.

36 * Charlottesville

BY THE TIME the newlyweds arrived in Charlottesville, the Korean War had started, and Ethel and Bobby were fearful that he might be called to arms. Bobby felt his brief stint in the Navy had been enough; he had no interest in wearing a uniform again. His goals now were to finish law school, start a family, and begin a career.

But the Korean "police action," as the politicians were calling the conflict, was having a shattering effect on the early months of Ethel and Bobby's first year together. At home, his father was railing about America's involvement in the war and, at Bobby's invitation, would make his views public in a speech at UVA, condemning President Truman's doctrines.

Every morning Bobby and Ethel walked hand-in-hand to early Mass at Holy Comforter, the small, neo-classical Roman Catholic church near the university, to pray for a quick end to the war. They'd then spend a few minutes in contemplation, admiring the huge oil painting of Christ with his arms extended. Their prayers were answered. Bobby was never called to serve.

The Kennedys had set up housekeeping in a small, one-and-a-half-story, whitewashed brick Colonial-style home surrounded by shrubs and trees on Cameron Lane in a fashionable section of town near the law school. "Can you believe this?" Ethel asked visitors. "This place could fit in the living room of one of our guest houses; it'll have to do until Bobby graduates." To some of Bobby's less fortunate law-school friends, already raising children and living in cramped off-campus apartments, the Kennedys' modest home seemed like a palace.

One of their first acquisitions was an ugly, untrained English bulldog whom they named Toby Belch. Within days of the dog's arrival, the rugs were soiled and the house reeked of urine and feces. What's more, the feisty dog started attacking the antiques and reproductions that the owner, a Bostonian named Ed O'Donnell, had left behind. Recalled Ann Marie O'Hagan Murphy: "I told Ethel, 'For God's sake, get rid of that dog because he's chewing on absolutely everything,' and she said, 'Oh, he's just going to be fun.' I was a friend of Ed's and I told Ethel, 'He's wrecking Ed's furniture,' and he *did* wreck it. Ethel's philosophy was 'I'm not going to worry about it.' Then, of course, when they moved out, there was a big to-do about the damage. There was talk about a lawsuit, but I think they settled." In many ways Cameron Lane was a mini–Lake Avenue.

The Kennedys' irresponsibility came as no surprise to their friends. Ethel's rooms at home and at school were always a mess and so were Bobby's. His last Charlottesville landlord, Shatze Sommers, was overjoyed when he married Ethel and vacated the five-room second-floor apartment that he shared with George Terrien. Bobby had ruined the wooden floors with athletic cleats and left cigarette burns on the mantel, among other damage.

Others had the same take on Bobby in those days. "From the start I didn't like him very much because he didn't respect people's property," said law-school classmate Gerry Tremblay, who became a lifelong friend of the Kennedys. "I was a poor kid. I didn't have any money. My wife and I were just married and we had a nice coffee table that someone had given us. Bobby would come to visit and he'd put his big, old, dirty boots on it. I didn't like that and neither did my wife. Although our apartment was rather austere, we didn't like to abuse any of the furnishings in it. I thought, 'What the hell is it with this guy?' Bobby had a lot of money and should have acted differently because of his upbringing. He had a beat-up Chrysler convertible that had belonged to his father. The top wouldn't go up and the interior of the car was a mess. Bobby's dogs had ripped up the upholstery and there was dog hair all over everything, but he didn't care. When we went to the movies he'd say, 'Hey, Gerry, you got a couple of bucks?' I'd never get paid back. That was the way all of those Kennedys were, they never traveled with money."

His personal appearance also meant little to him.

"Bobby was really sloppy," recalled Ann Marie O'Hagan Murphy. "Not long after they were married, Bobby and Ethel came out to my family's farm. Bobby was wearing an old pair of gray slacks with the edges fraying where he had cut them off to make them into shorts. The pants had big holes in them and he wasn't wearing underwear. My father said, 'You better go home and change your clothes.' He actually kicked him out. At the least Bobby could have worn a jockstrap, but he didn't give a damn about clothes or anything. Ethel thought he was cute no matter what."

After a few months of matrimony, though, Ethel saw to it that Bobby bought a wardrobe befitting his station in life, and when he balked about wearing his new clothes, she'd buy him more.

"Ethel definitely had an influence over the way he looked and dressed," said Gerry Tremblay.

Even Bobby's own mother noticed the changes Ethel had wrought. One of the reasons for her "admiration" of Ethel, Rose Kennedy noted years later, was because she had "managed to get [Bobby] to pay attention to clothes, even to the extent that eventually [he] became known as being quite well dressed. I have always felt that appropriate dress and grooming are part of good manners and that good manners are important."

Friends observed that Ethel was Bobby's opposite: extremely confident, outgoing, active, energetic, a stylish dresser, a party giver, and social butterfly, but not very sophisticated. In many ways, she was her mother's daughter.

Like Big Ann with George, Ethel was also intensely serious about her relationship with Bobby. "She was desperately, desperately in love with him," said Charlottesville friend Sue Drake.

37 ✳ *Settling In*

CHARLOTTESVILLE WAS A quiet, segregated Southern city. In the fall of 1951, it had a population of about twenty-five thousand, about 20 percent poor blacks who lived in shacks near the railroad tracks. Ethel's only contact was hiring them as domestics.

"Ethel didn't care a whit about civil rights in those days," said George Terrien. "I don't think it bothered her one way or the other about having colored girls as servants. It never did."

Besides, Ethel needed as much household help as she could muster since she had neither the inclination, nor the need, to cook, clean, shop, or do other chores despite having lots of free time during the day while Bobby was in class. The only dish she could put together and get out of the oven without burning was an appetizer called Cheese Dreams, which tasted like glue and raw dough. Finally, Bobby had had it with Ethel's efforts in the kitchen and persuaded his bride to give up cooking altogether after she prepared a meal that consisted of four vegetables but no meat. Ethel's concept of housecleaning was to, as Terrien put it, "haul a bunch of people in, have them take everything out, have it all cleaned, and then have them bring it all back."

"She was one of those women who could not cope with the kitchen," said Sue Drake, whose husband, Phil Drake, was a classmate of Bobby's. The Drakes had gotten married a year before the Kennedys, and Sue was working part time to help make ends meet. Like the Tremblays, they were a bit envious of Bobby and Ethel's immense financial resources. "Ethel entertained constantly, but she wasn't very good at it because she was still trying to figure out how to cook," Sue Drake recalled. Ethel depended on friends like Sue to keep the fledgling Kennedy household functioning smoothly. Having a circle of handmaidens and acolytes to serve her would continue through Ethel's life.

• • •

Having fun was always a prerequisite for Ethel. As soon as she arrived in Charlottesville, she set out to find an appropriate place to ride and play tennis. As Ellie Tremblay recalled, "Ethel had a lot of time on her hands to fill."

Ethel decided that she and Bobby should join Charlottesville's exclusive Farmington Country Club, whose main building, erected in 1803, was designed by Thomas Jefferson. Farmington's golf course was considered one of the best in the region, the tennis courts were superb, and the view of the rolling Virginia countryside was spectacular. Negro waiters in starched uniforms served mint juleps to gracious women in straw hats and bourbon to gentlemen in blue blazers. Blacks and Jews were not permitted to join the club or be invited as guests. The Skakels had belonged to restricted clubs for years, and so had the Kennedys. Joe Kennedy's anti-Semitism was well known—he'd often refer to Jews as "sheenies"—and Bobby emulated his father's stance on such issues in those days. Through the university, Ethel arranged for a student membership that gave her and Bobby all of Farmington's benefits at a reduced rate. Both would remain active, happy members of the club until they left Charlottesville.

Knowing Ethel loved to ride, Ann Marie O'Hagan Murphy introduced her to Elliewood Keith, who had a big horse farm outside Charlottesville. The two got along famously, and Ethel was given access to the stables and the horse of her choice. Murphy's father also introduced Ethel and Bobby to Charlottesville's hunt-club set.

Many of Ethel's college friends, following the Sacred Heart tradition, continued their Catholic Action activities now that they were out of school and beginning families or careers. Ann Marie, for one, had taken a first-aid course and was volunteering her time by driving poor pregnant women from rural areas to Charlottesville for prenatal care. She also was performing postnatal care and donating her time at the local hospital. "This was just a natural follow-up to the Catholic Action I had done at school," said Murphy. "But in Charlottesville Ethel never did anything like that. She'd say to me, 'Let's go play tennis,' and I'd tell her, 'I can't.' She'd say, 'Oh, do it later because I want to play now.' I'd tell her that these women had appointments, that they didn't have phones, that I had to get out there and get them into the doctor and then take them back home. And Ethel would say, 'Oh, forget it, come on, let's play tennis!' "

Most weekends, Ethel and Bobby used one of the Great Lakes Carbon planes to fly north to either Greenwich or Hyannis Port, or south to the Kennedy's Palm

Beach digs. If they stayed in town, Ethel threw small dinner parties, usually inviting the Drakes and Tremblays, Ann Marie, and George Terrien. "Everybody liked her, but Ethel never had very many intimates in Charlottesville," said Sue Drake. "She was devoting all of her time to Bobby. He was the most important person in her life."

It was during those get-togethers that Ethel, while playing parlor games, displayed the scrappy and pugnacious side of her personality that often galled her Charlottesville pals. The games—Charades, Twenty Questions, Sardines, Indirect Questions, Ambassadors—were a Kennedy tradition that Ethel had quickly adopted. In order to keep up with Bobby, she had begun reading almanacs, encyclopedias, newspapers, and general-interest magazines. "She took it quite seriously. She told me she was 'reading and trying to learn more.' I remember her saying, 'I just gotta keep up with them [the Kennedys]. I have to be on top of *everything!*' " recalled Ann Marie O'Hagan Murphy. And Ethel's studying paid off because she usually won. If she didn't, she'd force her opponents to continue playing long into the night until she did win.

Ethel and Rose, equally competitive and assertive women, once got into a debate over whether Paul Revere's midnight ride was on April 19 or April 18, which Ethel claimed it was. "Ethel dear," Rose responded, "one of my brothers was born on the nineteenth of April and it's been a big celebration half my life, so you're wrong." Ethel wasn't about to concede, even to the woman whom she revered. "Do you mind if I get the book?" she asked as she barreled her way to a shelf. Ethel, it turned out, had the correct answer. Revere's ride began on the evening of the eighteenth.

Friends felt that Ethel and Bobby made a perfect couple because they were equally competitive. Gerry Tremblay got a taste during a visit to Hyannis Port. Near the Kennedy house was a deep gravel pit. "I'll bet I can jump further down than you can," Bobby boasted. "I said, 'No you can't.' So I ran like hell and jumped over the precipice and landed at the bottom. Then Bobby jumped and missed the bottom by three or four feet. He didn't land quite as far as I did, so he said, 'Okay, let's do it again.' I said, 'Hey, Bob, I only have to beat you *once!*' But he wouldn't give up. 'Let's do it again. Let's do it again.' He was like a child. Suddenly he'd changed the rules and it was two out of three."

Ethel was ruthless on the tennis courts at Farmington, where the Kennedys played doubles—usually with the Drakes.

"She wanted to win—*demanded* to win. It was a lot easier to *let* her win than to try to beat her, which we could have done. So we purposefully lost," acknowledged Sue Drake. "Ethel had a lot of self-confidence. I never saw her as a naturally fine athlete, but she was determined to excel, and she did."

One afternoon Ethel's brother George, who wasn't very good at tennis and had a bum leg to boot, was playing doubles with Bobby and Ethel. The only thing George Skakel had going for him on the court that day was his beautiful Scandinavian female partner—one of his many mistresses—who moved like a gazelle. She'd lure Bobby to the net, and Ethel in from the back court, while Skakel lobbed ball after ball over Ethel's head, scoring point after point. The Kennedys were angry, especially when they spotted George and his girlfriend laughing at them. Bobby flung his racket on the court, picked up his balls, and stormed off, with a seething Ethel in tow. "It's *our* court, so you better watch your manners!" Skakel yelled mockingly. "Yeah, well they're *my* tennis balls and *we're* leaving!" Bobby screamed back petulantly.

In recounting the episode to a friend, George Skakel doubled over with laughter. "Bobby's such a chicken-shit little bastard. He thinks he's such a tough guy. I can't figure out what Ethel sees in that little prick." As George Terrien noted, "None of the Skakel brothers liked Bobby. But I don't think it bothered Ethel one bit."

Years later, in the early 1990s, long after Ethel had established herself as a Washington monument, she still had the same ferocious desire to win on the courts. Visitors to her private tennis court at Hickory Hill received prematch briefings from an employee. The bottom line was: lose to Mrs. Kennedy, or risk getting disinvited.

"Ethel always had that arrogant side to her personality, bordering on being outright nasty," observed a lifelong friend. "From her Charlottesville days onward it became more intense because she was always trying to prove that she could be a Kennedy—could be competitive like a Kennedy, combative like a Kennedy, cold and calculating like a Kennedy. She felt she had to prove that to Bobby, prove it to her in-laws, Joe and Rose, and to herself, on a daily basis, *all* of her life. She succeeded."

38 * Perfect Partner

ETHEL WORKED HARD to become the Perle Mesta of UVA, throwing parties related to Bobby's involvement with the Student Legal Forum.

The purpose of the forum, which had been languishing for several years, was to bring interesting speakers to the university. Bobby, who saw the SLF as an opportunity to get some attention, used the power and prestige of his name to get elected president. His father's prominence and connections all but guaranteed a headline-making list of speakers. That year they included Sen. Joseph McCarthy, Ralph Bunche, Supreme Court Justice William O. Douglas, even Joe Kennedy himself.

Ethel decided that before each appearance, a select group of students and faculty would be invited to the house to meet the guest speaker over drinks, followed by dinner. Ethel wanted those gatherings to be memorable. Ann Marie O'Hagan Murphy's mother suggested an Austrian cook who had recently moved to Charlottesville and was earning a reputation for her exquisite European dishes. The woman agreed to cater the first party, which was a huge success.

But several months later she telephoned Mrs. O'Hagan. "She said, 'I'm terribly embarrassed to tell you this but my bill to that young Kennedy girl has never been paid.' Mother, who was very proper, was horrified," Ann Marie recalled. "So she came to me and told me to call Ethel, which I did. Ethel told me, 'Oh, of course it's been paid. That's ridiculous.' I said, 'Well, Ethel, you check and make sure.' A couple of months later this woman called my mother again. She still had not been paid." Whether Ethel paid the chef or not, in later years she would get a reputation for being difficult with help and stiffing vendors.

One of Bobby's early speakers was Congressman Jack Kennedy, about to embark on his first Senatorial campaign. Ethel had overseen preparation of an elaborate dinner for Jack that was scheduled for sevenish. By seven forty-five Jack still hadn't arrived and a frantic Ethel and a furious Bobby decided to go ahead and serve dinner.

As the others ate, Bobby and Ethel huddled in the kitchen. "How could that son of a bitch do this to me?" Bobby yelled, pounding the table. "I can't believe this," hissed Ethel in agreement. "I'll kill Jack! I swear it." Bobby feared that he'd be left in the lurch at the last minute without a speaker.

As everyone was nervously finishing dinner, the front door opened and the handsome Congressman strode in, acting as if nothing was amiss.

Ethel and Bobby turned from Jack, their faces frozen in disbelief, to his companion, a heavily made-up beauty with wild hair who was dressed in a short, tight black skirt, tight purple sweater, and platform high heels.

"She was," recalled Ann Marie O'Hagan Murphy, "a bimbo like you have never seen. She was French and pretended she couldn't speak English, but she obviously understood everything that was going on. Ethel and Bobby were furious."

"Where the hell have you been?" Ethel sputtered.

"Well, we had to stop at the motel and check in," Jack explained, growing more sheepish as his sister-in-law's wrath intensified.

"You know I told you I was fixing up the guest room for you. I had flowers in the room and everything!" Ethel said.

"Well," said Jack with finality, bringing an end to Ethel's scolding, "I'm staying at the motel."

Recalled Murphy: "Ethel had worked very hard because usually they didn't have houseguests. She'd fixed up one room and she had no idea that he was coming down with anybody. She'd tried hard to make things nice for him. After all the commotion, Jack went and gave a wonderful talk. But it was quite a scene at the house."

Another guest of Bobby's who sparked controversy was Joe McCarthy, then at the peak of his power.

McCarthy had become a close friend of Joe Kennedy's—and therefore his aims and goals were supported by Bobby, Jack, and the rest of the clan. Jack had met McCarthy in the South Pacific during the war. Later, McCarthy and the Kennedys had started socializing, and Joe even had a couple of dates with Jean and Pat. McCarthy once laughingly boasted that if things got really bad for him he always could marry a Kennedy girl. Later, McCarthy and Jack served together in Congress; they both used their wartime experiences—Jack's PT 109 story and Joe's tailgunner tale—to enhance their images and aid their elections. After McCarthy made his historic speech charging that Communists had infiltrated the State Department, Joe Kennedy decided that Joe McCarthy was definitely his kind of politician: a conservative Irish Catholic, an isolationist, a rabid anti-Communist.

Following his father's lead, Bobby, who would eventually work for McCarthy, had become an ardent supporter of the senator and McCarthyism. Ethel felt the same way. "She was strongly Catholic and she felt that Communist teachings were against the Catholic religion," Gerry Tremblay observed. Ethel's mother had contributed heavily to the anti-Communist Christophers, headed by Father Keller, a one-time candymaker and

Maryknoll missionary. For a time, Keller, a close friend of McCarthy's, had rent-free offices in Great Lakes Carbon's Midtown Manhattan headquarters.

Prior to getting married, Ethel's sister Pat had become one of Keller's top speakers, lecturing to young people that "Christians should work as hard for Christianity as Communists were working for communism." At Keller's direction, Pat Skakel had also infiltrated Manhattan's Jefferson School of Social Science, described in feverishly patriotic prose in *Look* magazine as a place where "young Commies are trained." As part of her spy network, Pat had enlisted the help of her gun-toting brother George, and Martin McKneally. "The people at the school thought Pat and the rest of us were Communist sympathizers," recalled Alice ("Appy") Whitney Lorillard, a socialite friend of the Skakel and Kennedy girls. Appy, who had converted to Catholicism through the good graces of Pat Skakel and Sargent Shriver, recalled that Pat's group not only developed intelligence about Jefferson School students but waged a dirty-tricks campaign. "The school sent out petitions for various Communist causes," she said. "At the end of classes each night, we'd collect all of the school's literature and pamphlets and throw them away. We thought it was loads of fun. Father Keller was happy as a clam."

Jack Macrae, a Greenwich boy who dated Ann Skakel when she was in high school and he was at Harvard, remembered discussions at Lake Avenue that "Joe McCarthy was, in the Skakels' eyes, a great person. It was that horrendous time when the Rosenbergs were executed and I remember that that didn't seem to bother Ethel or Ann a whit," he said.

When Bobby mentioned to Ethel that he thought he could get McCarthy to speak at the university, she was thrilled; such a visit would be a major coup for Bobby. McCarthy accepted and Ethel immediately dove into planning her most lavish party to date.

At the Kennedy house that evening, McCarthy was in an exuberant and playful mood. Ethel and Bobby weren't big drinkers, but Ethel kept refilling McCarthy's glass. "I found him rather terrifying, a terrible fanatic," said Sue Drake, who was helping Ethel with the party.

As McCarthy got progressively inebriated, he asked everyone to gather around the sofa. "Let me show you what I have here," he said, slurring his words, as he opened his briefcase with shaky hands and retrieved a dark metal object.

"It was a loaded gun," recalled Sue Drake, still shaken by the memory years later. "It was shocking. He showed it to us and we stood around gaping—and Ethel just laughed. The gun didn't phase her a bit. She *liked* McCarthy. I could tell Bobby was intrigued with what power had done for McCarthy."

Next to Joe McCarthy, Dr. Ralph Bunche was Bobby's most controversial guest. Bobby had extended the invitation with the full knowledge that the visit by the black Nobel Prize winner and director of the United Nations' Department of Trusteeship would cause trouble on the all-white campus. Bunche's agreement to come to Charlottesville, announced in a banner headline in the March 9, 1951, issue of UVA's *Cavalier Daily,* caused a firestorm of protest by segregationists, who had the backing of a state law that banned blacks from white meeting halls. But Bobby stood firm. He and another member of the Student Legal Forum fought for, and eventually received, the support of the university. In late March, Bunche spoke before an integrated audience—about a third black.

It had become traditional for Bobby, Ethel, and their friends to take the guest speaker to Farmington Country Club for drinks or a late supper. "But the manager of the club told Bobby he couldn't have a black guy," recalled Gerry Tremblay. "That was a blow to Bobby." But Bobby and Ethel maintained their membership.

Looking back over that year, Sue Drake observed that Ethel never offered an opinion about the people Bobby invited to speak. "She just entertained them. My analysis is simply that Ethel worshiped Bobby and she would do anything for him and she wasn't about to criticize his opinions or anything else about him. She was totally under his spell."

39 * First Stork

IN JUNE 1951, 124 young men graduated from the law school at the University of Virginia. Bobby Kennedy ranked fifty-sixth in that group, with a mediocre grade-point average of 2.54. Bobby didn't wait around to get his diploma. A month before graduation, he and Ethel quietly vacated the house on Cameron Lane and flew north to the Skakel estate in Greenwich, where they moved into one of the two guest houses to await the birth of their first baby.

When Ethel had joyously revealed her pregnancy to Bobby the previous winter, around the time of his twenty-fifth birthday, he had been elated. Not only was he the first Kennedy male of his generation to get married, but now he would be the first to father a member of the next generation. He would finally gain his father's attention and respect by making him a proud grandfather.

Ethel, too, was proud. She had quietly pledged when she married Bobby to have more babies than his mother because she knew such a feat would impress the matriarch, prove to Rose that she had the Kennedy grit. Now she was about to start fulfilling that promise. Ethel and Bobby's timing couldn't have been better. As Rose later noted, "Joe and I began to wonder when we were going to have grandchildren. Bobby blazed the trail."

Beginning in the late 1950s, when Bobby first started making his mark in Washington, an avalanche of glowing newspaper and magazine articles were written about Ethel, the sprightly young Kennedy wife who seemed to live in cute maternity outfits. The stories, written mainly by Catholic women reporters who idolized the Kennedys, helped establish Ethel's all-American image.

The fact is that Ethel never looked forward to her early pregnancies. She actually abhorred any form of physical discomfort, and had an extremely low threshold for even the most minor ache or pain.

"Ethel was sick and quite miserable through that first pregnancy," said Sue Drake. "She was basically terrified by the whole thing. She wanted to do what was right, but she was scared."

As Drake and other friends recalled, Ethel stopped virtually all forms of physical activity, acting more like a patient preparing for major surgery than a joyful mother-to-be—the picture that has been part of the Ethel Kennedy myth for so long.

Now, on the verge of giving birth at Lake Avenue, she was anxious and blue, according to friends who saw her.

Ethel was almost two weeks overdue when she finally went into labor. "The whole family was in the sitting room watching television," recalled a relative, "and Ethel just started screaming bloody murder. Bobby was there and helped her get in the car and they rushed her to Greenwich Hospital."

On July 4, 1951, three months after her twenty-third birthday, in a very painful and physically debilitating delivery that would leave her in pain for days, Ethel gave birth to a healthy daughter whom she and Bobby named Kathleen, after his late sister.

But Ethel came out of the delivery room still anxious. Bobby, who had never seen her that way, felt helpless and telephoned his mother in Hyannis Port. On her advice, he called the other important woman from his childhood, Luella Hennessey, who had been the Kennedy family nurse since the late 1930s, "an integral part of our family . . . the person we looked to first when any one of us needed skilled and loving nursing care," as Rose Kennedy put it. Over the years the nurse would attend the births of twenty-six of the Kennedy grandchildren, including all of Ethel's. Of all the Kennedy women, Ethel was her favorite.

"A day or two after the baby was born, Bobby called

me and said, 'Would you come down right away and take care of Ethel? She really needs you,' " the nurse recalled years later.

What Hennessey encountered in Ethel's sunlit, flower-filled private room at Greenwich Hospital was a depressed young woman upset about the recent past, gloomy about the future. "Ethel had a lot of problems," the nurse said. "I wouldn't call it a nervous breakdown. I would say it was exaggerated anxiety. It was a very difficult, quite hard delivery for Ethel and she was suffering when I got there." According to Hennessey, Ethel's perineum had been torn during the delivery and she also had suffered "an uncommon, unexpected internal injury because the baby was big and Ethel wasn't. It caused lots of pain and discomfort and it worried Ethel quite a bit because it could have been permanent. Ethel's quite a private person and I don't think she ever told anyone about it, not even Bobby."

After a few days, Ethel's pain subsided, and the injury healed, but her anxiety lingered. Adding to her troubled mood was the fact that she couldn't nurse Kathleen, who had to be fed by bottle, according to Hennessey.

Always private, rarely communicative about her inner feelings—typical Skakel and Kennedy traits—Ethel suddenly opened up to the nurse.

"She told me Bobby was studying all the time and they just had that little house in Charlottesville. She had friends down there, but nothing like her friends from Manhattanville. With her old friends she could discuss intimate things. In Charlottesville, Ethel didn't have that luxury. She didn't have her mother or father or an aunt or an old friend to help her. She felt she had been thrown into pregnancy far away from home. Nothing in her life was settled and that bothered her. She was concerned that she didn't have her own home with Bobby to go back to. She didn't feel it was natural going back to her parents' house."

After hearing her story, Hennessey came away with a different view of Ethel than most of her friends had.

She saw her as emotionally immature and isolated, unhappy with certain aspects of her marriage. "Ethel always put on such a good front for everybody, no matter how she really felt," said the nurse. "But she was really blue."

Two weeks after giving birth, Ethel took Kathleen home to Lake Avenue. While Ethel waited in a wheelchair, her father went to the hospital office to deal with her discharge. "Every time I've taken my children down here to Greenwich Hospital," he told Hennessey, "I've always had to pay the bill. But today it goes to Robert Kennedy." On the big day, though, Bobby was out of town on Kennedy family matters and didn't turn up until later, after George Skakel had picked up the hospital tab. When she got home, the first thing Ethel did was order a dozen red roses for Rose Kennedy, a tradition that she'd follow after each of her eleven births.

For Ethel and baby Kathleen, the reception at Lake Avenue was subdued. "Mrs. Skakel didn't seem worried about Ethel's physical and emotional state, whatsoever," recalled Hennessey, surprised by the family's reaction. "There just wasn't a lot of warmth."

The nurse was billeted in one of the guest houses with the baby, while Ethel and Bobby stayed in the main house. Each morning Kathleen was delivered to Ethel, and each afternoon and evening she was taken back to the cottage for her naps and sleep. Bobby seemed delighted, happy that his first child was a daughter. Hennessey recalled him remarking, "You can cuddle and pick up a little girl. Little boys are different. You can love a little girl." Bobby thought long and hard on whom to name as his firstborn's godfather, finally choosing Joe McCarthy.

After several weeks, Luella Hennessey was relieved of her duties. She returned home, and the Kennedys and their new baby moved into one of the guest houses, next to the Dowdles. "They lived there while Bobby studied for the New York Bar," said Sue Drake. The Drakes had moved north to nearby New Rochelle and Bobby and Phil Drake cracked the law books together. "That's what that summer was devoted to, a whole group of them studying for the bar."

At summer's end, Bobby and Ethel decided they needed a break; it had been such a difficult and stressful year. Leaving the baby in the care of a nurse and the Skakel family, they headed west to visit Ethel's Manhattanville pal Courtney Murphy Benoist in Salt Lake City. There, they also met up with Bobby's college chum Dean Markham, who worked as a salesman in his in-laws' fabrics business. The foursome drove to Moab, where Ethel made her first visit to the Skakel Ranch, and the friends drove into the Mojave Desert, quenching their thirst with canteloupes grown at the ranch.

After two weeks, Bobby and Ethel, relaxed for the first time in months, returned East—he to begin his career, she to start the full-time job of being a Kennedy wife and mother.

40 ✻ *Alexandra and Joe*

IN GREENWICH, ON a beautiful Indian summer day in October 1951, in the first weeks of her second pregnancy, Ethel's sister Georgeann went sailing on their mother's boat, the *Ann,* with her husband, Johnny, and her brother George. As the day progressed, Georgeann became increasingly ill. At first she thought she was seasick, or that she was getting the flu. She was nauseous, had a terrible headache, a painful sore throat. Concerned about his wife, Johnny Dowdle instructed George to head for home. By the time they reached Lake Avenue, Georgeann had a raging fever and a rash.

Frantic with worry, Dowdle telephoned the family doctor, who rushed to the house. His examination showed that Georgeann had rubella—German measles—which could cause damage to the baby. His diagnosis floored the Skakels and devastated Georgeann. While the doctor tried to reassure Georgeann, she fell into a dark depression.

Next to Georgeann and her husband, the hardest hit by the horrendous news was Ethel, who was still recuperating from her own difficult pregnancy and delivery three months earlier. Ethel had hoped to get pregnant immediately. Now, having had contact with Georgeann, she faced the possibility of contracting the same dreaded disease. As always in the face of adversity, Ethel went to church and prayed.

Ethel's fears about the future were well founded. Just two months after Georgeann's diagnosis, Ethel learned that she was pregnant, too. Not only did Ethel now fear for the health of the baby she was carrying, but other factors in her life were causing enormous stress for her.

Despite all of the people around her, Ethel felt isolated, mainly because she seemed to have little or no time with the most important person in her life. Virtually from the moment Kathleen was born five months earlier, Bobby had been traveling. First, there was a trip to San Francisco arranged by his father to report on an international peace treaty involving Japan. Bobby was home only a short time before he left Ethel again, this time to accompany Jack, who was prepping himself for a planned Senatorial race, on an extended fact-finding trip through the Middle and Far East. Ethel had essentially been left to fend for herself, shuttling gypsy-like between the Skakels' house on Lake Avenue and the Kennedys' place in Hyannis Port because Bobby still hadn't settled on what he wanted to do and where he wanted to live. When he returned home from the trip with Jack, his father arranged through the good graces of Joe McCarthy to get Bobby a $4,200-a-year-job in the Justice Department's Internal Security Division. For a brief time, Ethel was joyous, thinking that her young family would finally have some permanency. But Bobby stayed in the job only three months, quitting to become Jack's Massachusetts Senatorial campaign manager. As Rose Kennedy herself noted later, Ethel and Bobby had "barely settled" into their lives when the campaign started.

Pregnant and anxious, Ethel was now expected to join the other Kennedy women on the stump. This would be her political coming-out for the Kennedys; she'd have to prove what she was made of.

"Ethel was scared," recalled Martin McKneally. "But Bobby put intense pressure on her to get involved in the campaign. To Bobby, Ethel's problems were secondary to Jack's political career. Bobby knew Jack's win or loss wouldn't hinge on whether Ethel was involved or not. It just boosted his ego to have her fat and pregnant and on the stump. He could point to her and say, 'Look at the one I got.' Like a faithful dog is what she became. It was as if Ethel had taken a blood oath."

In the months since she had been taken ill, Georgeann had tried to take her mind off of the worst-case scenario. She had even made plans—once the baby came—to attend the Republican National Convention, scheduled to open in Chicago on July 7, 1952. Georgeann and the rest of the Skakels—except for Ethel, who was now an ordained Democrat—were hoping to finally see an end to the twenty-year Democratic reign that began in 1933 with FDR's election. The Skakels had their money on Eisenhower and Nixon.

But on June 21, 1952, Georgeann's—and Ethel's—worst nightmare came true. After being rushed to Greenwich Hospital, Georgeann gave birth to a daughter who was severely handicapped—the child, who was named Alexandra, was born blind, deaf, stunted, and retarded.

When Ethel heard the news, a friend said, "she made her hand into the shape of a gun and put it to her head. Then she cried."

But for the Skakels, with their strong Catholicism, pulling the plug was never a consideration.

"The doctors were instructed by Georgeann to allow the baby to live no matter how defective it was," said Martin McKneally. "Georgeann—all of them—had an absolute conviction that they had no right to interfere with her life."

The christening, which under better circumstances would have been at St. Mary's, the Skakels' church in Greenwich where Ethel was married, was held for reasons of privacy at the Dowdles' new home, a beautiful, elegantly furnished, antique-filled, Billy Baldwin–decorated English Cotswold manor house with stables, guest house, swimming pool, and tennis court. It had been a recent gift to Georgeann from her parents. She'd named the place Sursum Corda, a Latin phrase meaning "lift up our hearts."

"We went out there for the christening and it was horrible," recalled Mary Begley. "You could hear this poor little thing breathing all over the room because she probably should have been in an oxygen tent. She had terrible problems. We all saw her in Georgeann's bedroom and it was horrifying. All of the Skakels were there, Ethel and Bobby, all of them. They were all stiff-upper-lip and let's-make-the-best-of-it."

Ethel, then six months pregnant, was visibly upset.

"Her hands were trembling and her lips were quivering and I thought she'd fall apart but she held herself together. Ethel, like all the Skakels, had the ability to hide her emotions," recalled a relative who was present. "Ethel was a wreck. She looked at Alexandra and I could tell she was thinking about the baby she was carrying. She looked at Georgeann and was thinking, 'That could be me.' I remember Bobby whispering, 'Let's get out of here.' "

For Bobby, Alexandra's birth reawakened horrible memories of his own retarded sister, Rosemary, whom his father had quietly ordered lobotomized and institutionalized. Bobby distanced himself from the Skakels' problem with Alexandra and as usual, Ethel obediently followed suit.

As Martin McKneally later observed, "The Skakels now had their own Rosemary, but only the inner circle knew about it."

After the christening, Ethel never again saw her retarded niece. Georgeann sought the help of medical experts, but nothing could be done for Alexandra. Georgeann also sought her family's counsel, including

Ethel's. But a family insider said, "Ethel just didn't want to get involved; didn't want to give her approval or disapproval. Bobby had told her it wasn't any of her business and she did what he told her to do."

In late 1952, after much soul-searching, Georgeann had her retarded baby placed in Uville, a Catholic hospital for the terminally ill, near Boston. Georgeann, who would eventually have six children in nine years, made a few visits but became so emotional each time that she had to stop going. But a photograph of Alexandra was always on display in the library at Sursum Corda.

Tragic births would continue to plague the Skakel family. Pat Skakel Cuffe's eighth and last child, Sarah, was born retarded, attributable to a lack of oxygen flow to the brain at birth. She, too, was eventually institutionalized. One of Pat's sons was born with a club foot like his mother, and one of Georgeann's sons was born with a similar deformity.

"Privately, Ethel always feared she'd have a retarded or handicapped child," said a longtime friend.

(In September 1991, Alexandra died at age thirty-nine of natural causes in a Lowell, Massachusetts, nursing home. Over the years, her institutionalization had cost the Skakel family $3 million. At the request of Alexandra's sister, Little Georgeann, Ethel helped with the funeral arrangements, even forcing a Greenwich florist to open his shop at two A.M. so the flowers could be selected. The next day Ethel stood with her head bowed, silently praying, as Alexandra was laid to rest in the Skakel family plot at St. Mary's Cemetery. "Aunt Ethel told me after the service that Alexandra had weighed heavily on her through the years," Little Georgeann said. "Aunt Ethel said, 'I don't think God will ever forgive me.' ")

In spite of the tragic birth of Alexandra—or perhaps because of it—a pregnant, heartbroken Ethel immersed herself wholeheartedly in Jack Kennedy's Senatorial campaign. Through the summer of 1952, in the last months of her pregnancy, she campaigned vigorously in Massachusetts, helping Rose, Jean, Pat, and Eunice organize tea parties for potential voters and contributors.

At just one event, the women purportedly served up more than eight thousand cups.

Bobby, Ethel, and some of the other Kennedys and staffers had moved into a rooming house on Boston's Marble Street. Every night Bobby and longtime Kennedy operative Kenneth O'Donnell went out and made speeches while Ethel worked late at campaign headquarters, putting in ten- to fifteen-hour days.

Ethel had just finished giving her first campaign spiel for Jack in the town of Fall River when she started to go into labor and was rushed to the Boston hospital where Kennedy family nurse Luella Hennessey worked.

"Ethel didn't say much about Alexandra, but I know it was causing her a lot of distress," recalled Hennessey, who met Ethel at the hospital and stayed with her through the delivery.

On September 24, 1952, Ethel gave birth to her second child, a healthy boy.

"All of her prayers had worked," stated Donovan. "As soon as she was told the baby was fine, she visibly relaxed. Bobby was the one who wanted to name him after Joe, his brother who was killed in the war. Everyone was just so happy."

Two months later, there was reason for more joy among the Kennedys. In November 1952, by a slim margin of only 70,737 votes, Jack defeated three-term Massachusetts Senator Henry Cabot Lodge, Jr. Nationally, the Skakels' Presidential candidate, Dwight Eisenhower, won the White House. Lodge placed part of the blame for his loss on "those damned tea parties" that Ethel had been so active in organizing. As a note of thanks, Jack declared that Ethel helped "drown Senator Lodge in seven hundred gallons of tea." Rose Kennedy said that the thirty-three teas the Kennedy girls gave were attended by some seventy thousand guests. "The close matching of the figures is, I daresay, coincidence, but I also think that the tea parties helped," said Rose.

Ethel had soundly proven herself a political asset to Bobby and the Kennedy clan.

41 ✻ Family Feud

WHILE ENDEARING HERSELF to the Kennedys, Ethel had all but alienated her own flesh and blood.

"The whole family's view was that Ethel had now become a Kennedy, period, and they were sad about that," said Mary Begley. "They would have liked her to have been a little more loyal. As a result, the Skakel's were very cavalier about the Kennedys."

Ethel's sister-in-law, Virginia, who had married Jim Skakel about a month before Georgeann gave birth to Alexandra, expressed the view years later that the Kennedys, Bobby in particular, acted superior to the Skakels, and often showed outright contempt for them:

"In all those years, Bobby probably said only three words to me. I only saw Rose Kennedy at the Skakel house once in the two years I lived there, and that was a brief visit. So the Skakels didn't give a damn whether Jack won or lost the Massachusetts Senatorial race, and they didn't care about Ethel's involvement in the campaign. The only talk about the Kennedys was the jokes the Skakels made about them. There was no closeness between the two families at all."

At one point, the Kennedys threw a big costume party at the Plaza Hotel in New York to raise money for their favorite charity, retarded children. Some of the Skakels went for kicks. "It was the first time Joe and Rose appeared at the same party in years, and we were all in a state of shock," one of them recalled. "Teddy was there making a complete horse's ass out of himself. They had Nat King Cole entertain and Teddy, wearing a cowboy hat, stepped up to the mike and started singing.

He looked like a complete idiot. We thought the Kennedys were a bunch of dolts."

Ethel's brother George once participated in a regatta with Jack Kennedy off Martha's Vineyard. Jack was at the helm of the boat, shouting orders to George on how to adjust the sails. Ethel's brother believed that if he followed Kennedy's commands, they'd lose rather than win the race. In his tough-guy manner, Skakel turned to Kennedy and said, "Look, Jack, are you going to keep screaming at me how to trim this sail, when I know damned well better than you how it ought to be trimmed?" Jack Kennedy glared at Skakel. "Shut the hell up and do as you're told!" the former PT 109 skipper barked. With that, George Skakel, Jr., gave Jack Kennedy the finger and jumped overboard, swimming two miles to shore, leaving Kennedy furious and without a crew.

To tick off Ethel, meanwhile, the Skakels took great pleasure in making fun of Bobby in front of her.

"They called Bobby 'Boobie,' " chuckled Mary Begley years later. "And they used to call Joe Kennedy 'Old Monkey Glands.' "

Big Ann harbored the most disdain for the Kennedys, and as a result her relationship with Ethel deteriorated steadily in the early 1950s. She found Joe Kennedy's private life—mainly his womanizing and his marital arrangement with Rose—morally repugnant. As a staunch Catholic, Big Ann saw him as a venal, licentious reprobate who would never repent for his sins. He was, in her mind, a religious hypocrite, a rogue Catholic who was an insult to her staunch religious beliefs. She'd also lost any respect she might have had for Rose. "Big Ann had little or no regard for Rose because Joe was out and around town, messing around all the time, and was very flagrant," said John McCooey, who would marry Ethel's sister Ann. "Big Ann couldn't stand the fact that Rose was a tool of Joe's. Big Ann was never a tool of George's."

Big Ann's worst fear was that Bobby had inherited his father's genes. It made her both sad for and angry at Ethel. "Why did I ever let her marry into that family?" was her constant refrain.

Another trait of the Kennedys that grated on the Skakels was their notorious cheapness. It wasn't long after they were married that Bobby began nagging Ethel about money. Her extravagance would be a source of irritation and conflict throughout their marriage. When Ethel's bills began flowing in from stores in Palm Beach, New York, and Boston, Rose Kennedy ordered Bobby to get his bride in line. Bobby's warnings, however, were met with blank stares from Ethel, who had no conception whatsoever about budgeting money. When one of the Kennedys called to tell her that her checking account was overdrawn, Ethel was shocked. "It can't be," she responded with all innocence. "I still have some checks left."

One evening at the dinner table at Hyannis Port, Joe Kennedy angrily brought up the subject of frivolous spending. Glaring, he turned to Ethel and declared her the worst of the lot, a wild spender with no regard for the value of a dollar. Knowing that Joe's angry criticism would devastate Ethel—she'd been working so hard to earn his respect—Bobby told his father that his point had been well taken. But Ethel jumped up from the table and ran from the room, tears brimming in her eyes, her face crimson with embarrassment.

Despite her conflict with her daughter, Big Ann was livid when she learned how Ethel was being treated. On one occasion, she angrily telephoned Rose and warned, "If Bobby can't treat Ethel in the manner to which she's accustomed, we'll just take her back."

Every so often Big Ann gave a luncheon for some of the other mothers-in-law, gatherings that Rose rarely attended. But one afternoon the Kennedy matriarch arrived at Lake Avenue for a showdown. "Mrs. Kennedy came specifically to try to curb Ethel's spending, and Big Ann wanted no part of the curbing," recalled John McCooey, whose mother, along with a half dozen other women, was present for the show. "Rose told Big Ann that Ethel was spending too much and that she'd have to cut it out immediately. Big Ann said, 'I thought you Kennedys had nothing but money. If Ethel wants to spend, and Bobby's supposed to be so rich, then let Ethel spend.' Rose said, 'But Bobby doesn't have any money.' Rose was angry and nervous. She kept getting up and she'd walk around complaining about Ethel's spending and then she'd sit down again and continue her harangue. When Rose left, Big Ann and the others sat around the table for another hour, laughing their heads off. We later found out that Rose was there at Joe's urging. But Big Ann won because Ethel kept on spending."

Jim and Virginia Skakel experienced the Kennedys' frugalness as they were checking into a bungalow at the Beverly Hills Hotel. When Virginia Skakel gave the bell captain a ten-dollar tip, he looked shocked. "Aren't you Mrs. Skakel? The Skakels who are related to the Kennedys?" When she said she was, he confided, "Not one of us will pick up one of the Kennedys' bags. They don't give us more than a fifty-cent tip. The last time I told one of them, 'Keep it! You need it more than I do!' Why are they the way they are with all the money they have?" Giggling, Virginia responded, "Sometimes I think that's why they have so much money and I don't."

Rose constantly rode Ethel about her financial irresponsibility, sending her notes detailing where to get the best bargains, along with coupons that she'd clipped. Once, Rose noticed an expensive Jaeger Le-Coultre clock on a night table in a maid's room at Ethel's house. Furious, she took Ethel aside. "You can get a good electric clock for four ninety-five."

Big Ann felt that the Kennedys had undermined her mother-daughter bond. "I barely know Ethel anymore since she got in with that crowd," she confided to Martin McKneally. "She's becoming a stranger to me."

But neither Ethel nor her mother confronted the problem. When Ethel did make one of her infrequent visits home, Big Ann often berated her in front of family and guests, yelling at Ethel to clean up her room or make her bed, treating her like a naughty child rather than a young mother married to a scion of one of America's most powerful families. "I couldn't believe it," Virginia Skakel said. "It was definitely weird."

While Rose bristled over Ethel's spending habits, she

also found her daughter-in-law charming, vivacious, completely loyal, competitive, tough, and as devout a Catholic as herself. Rose accepted Ethel as one of her own.

Ethel's relationship with her father was paramount. "She respected and loved him tremendously," Virginia Skakel observed later. "They went on long walks together in the woods. I remember seeing Ethel when she was very pregnant walking with her dad hand-in-hand. There was a great attachment with her father, while her mother screamed at Ethel all the time."

Years later Ethel recalled her father as "reflective and extremely kind, probably the greatest Christian soul I ever knew, an extraordinary human being." She also recalled their walks, which she found somewhat tedious. "He'd stop and you'd have to admire a tree until it drove you *bonkers*."

In the end, though, Ethel would live her life more like her mother.

Ethel's decision in the early 1950s to drastically cut her family ties had much to do with Bobby's feelings about the Skakels.

"Bobby had reached a point where he couldn't stand being in the presence of any of them," recalled a longtime Kennedy confidant. "I remember him once telling Dean Markham, 'If I wasn't married to Ethel, I wouldn't give those micks the time of day.' "

Bobby knew he'd never be fully accepted by the insular Skakels. But, according to Martin McKneally, "Bobby didn't care. His whole attitude was, 'I have brothers, I have sisters, I have parents, I have money, I have power, I have prestige—I don't need you people.' He was an arrogant son of a bitch. But Ethel was madly in love with him. His family made him even more attractive to her. She wanted to please him in every way."

In Bobby's estimation, the Skakels were loose cannons with a potential for scandal that could impact the Kennedys adversely. Ethel knew her family's potential for mischief better than anyone. The Kennedys' apprehension would prove to be well-founded.

42 * Lake Avenue and the Fifties

JIM SKAKEL WAS twenty-nine when he started dating beautiful nineteen-year-old Virginia Weiman, a Methodist from Cartersville, Georgia. Virginia's aunt, Francis Luro, and her husband, Horatio Luro, a well-known horse trainer, had met Jim at Hialeah Race Track, where he was a regular, and were impressed with the tall, handsome young man. They told Virginia, "He's got a great family. They're a bunch of fun. They're off the wall. You're going to love them." A blind date was arranged and soon the two were going together. But whenever Virginia asked Jim about his family, he remained mum. "I'd say to Jim, 'What are they like?' He'd say, 'I don't want to talk about them.' I'd say, 'Well, if we ever have children, what are they going to look like, monkeys?' And Jim would say, 'Maybe so.' He never once discussed his parents, Great Lakes Carbon, the mansion in Greenwich, or the fact that he had a sister named Ethel who was married to a Kennedy. It was all very odd."

After months of subtle pressure from Virginia, Jim finally invited her for a weekend at Lake Avenue to meet his family. They were greeted at the front door by Big Ann, who said hello and thrust a gift-wrapped book into the young woman's hands. It was a copy of Dr. Norman Vincent Peale's *How to Improve Your Personality*.

Virginia saw the writing on the wall and cut short her visit to Greenwich.

"They were loud and boisterous and they all just ignored me," she recalled of the visit. "Ethel and Bobby were at the first dinner and didn't say one word to me. I knew I could not break the wall they built around themselves. It took ten to fifteen years alone just to get to know them. They were so private. So secretive."

Despite being a problem child, Jim had always remained Big Ann's favorite son, and over the years she had done everything in her power to keep him out of the clutches of the many women who had pursued him.

When young women came to the house, Big Ann would instruct them to freshen up in one of the bathrooms. When they'd come out, she'd make up a story that Jim had to leave. She'd tell Jim the same thing about the girls. Many of Jim's blossoming romances were aborted by Big Ann in that fashion. "He was her heart. She didn't ever want to lose him," Virginia said years later.

One evening during dinner at the Huntington Hotel, in Pasadena, California, "Jimmy showed up a half hour late with his suit and tie messed up and dirty, and drunker than a hoot owl," recalled Great Lakes Carbon executive Jay Mayhew. "Mrs. Skakel was putting her arms around Jimmy, and kissing him, and making excuses for him, and saying, 'Oh, Jimmy darling, what have you been doing?' I looked at George and I could tell he was disgusted as hell with Jim, but he just shook his head. Jim was Mrs. Skakel's favorite. I never saw any of that type affection from her toward any of the other children."

Despite Jim's behavior, George Skakel felt he was the brightest of his three sons and hoped that one day he would take over the company. On one occasion, in the early 1950s, the senior Skakel summoned Great Lakes Carbon attorney Tom Hayes into his office, confided that "my own son won't talk to me," and instructed the lawyer to "get Jim back." Hayes gathered that Jim was angry at his father for devoting all of his time to building Great Lakes Carbon and not enough to him when he was growing up. Hayes met with Jim several times at one of Jim's hangouts, the Ritz Bar, in Manhattan. "There was some softening and they eventually talked together," Hayes said later. But Jim would never have much to do with Great Lakes Carbon—at least while his father was alive.

Not only had Jim now decided to get married, but he'd chosen a girl who wasn't a Catholic, which drove Big Ann up the wall. "In the Skakel family," Virginia observed, "there were two things that were important—Jesus Christ and Great Lakes Carbon."

Jim and Virginia were married at her grandmother's house in Miami on May 24, 1952. "Big Ann and all of the Skakels never got off their knees the whole time during the ceremony," recalled Virginia Skakel, laughing about the "grotesque" affair years later. "Mr. Skakel and I were the only non-Catholics there." Except for Pat, who remained in Ireland, and Georgeann, who was expecting (Alexandra) at any minute, all of the Skakels attended. Ethel, pregnant, was there without Bobby.

At the reception, Big Ann got into an argument with Virginia's aunt. Knowing that the woman had been married three times, Big Ann declared, "I will *never* ask you to my house. I don't condone divorce." Mrs. Luro, shocked by Big Ann's outburst, looked her up and down and said, "I doubt if I would come anyway." Remembering that scene years later, Virginia said, "My aunt could not believe those people. When the party was over my grandmother said to me, 'Jesus! We'll probably see you in a month. You'll be back soon.' There were bets on how long Jim and I would last."

After their European honeymoon, Jim and Virginia moved into his boyhood room on the third floor of the Lake Avenue house. A few days later Big Ann, on her daily inspection of the house, marched into Jim and Virginia's assigned bathroom and stopped dead in her tracks. "Virginia Skakel! We have got to talk! Now!" When Big Ann found her cowering daughter-in-law, she thundered, "This is *not* allowed in my house! I want it *out* of here."

The item in question was a douche bag.

The rigid Catholic environment at Lake Avenue persisted in the early 1950s. Big Ann continued to maintain strict rules governing anything of a sexual nature. None of the Skakel girls, or any female guests, were permitted to wear slacks in the house. Only dresses were sanctioned. Shorts were allowed for athletic activity. Tight bathing suits were banned. At breakfast the women had to be in dress clothes; no pajamas, robes, or nightgowns were permitted.

The word *sex* was never used. "The Skakels never spoke of it," Virginia said later. "It's like sex never existed. It was taboo."

Big Ann also demanded that Virginia convert to Catholicism and enrolled her in classes at Ethel's alma mater, Manhattanville. Eventually, Jim and Virginia separated and subsequently divorced. The two would remarry and have a family, but only after Big Ann had joined her Maker.

• • •

Big Ann read hundreds of books on fine antiques, and hired renowned interior decorators like Elsie de Wolfe and Billy Baldwin to educate her. She also attended lectures at the Metropolitan Museum in New York.

"Big Ann's taste was perfect," observed Mary Begley, "but all very guided."

At Lake Avenue, Big Ann had her Venetian Room, with Venetian furnishings and paintings, and her Orange Room, decorated with French Provincial pieces. "It was absolutely unreal," said a family friend. "Beautiful. In perfect taste. But it wasn't like a museum in spite of it all. She did a remarkable job. In the 1950s, she paid fifty thousand dollars for *one* antique music stand, so she had better have known what she was doing." Big Ann was also infatuated with decoupage and retained a noted artist of the medium, Maybelle Manning, to decorate the grand piano, the dining room table, and Ethel's room, which was maintained intact even though she was long gone.

Big Ann was thrilled when, through her shrewd bargaining, or expert knowledge, she was able to buy a fine antique at a flea market price.

Once, on an antiquing expedition through New England, she came upon a shop in Boston whose entire contents she wanted. After dickering over price with the owner for hours, she finally wore him down. He agreed to ship it all the following week, cash on delivery.

George Skakel, Sr., was all too aware of his wife's obsession with antiques, but for the most part he looked the other way, as he did with her intense Catholicism, viewing both interests as innocent, if somewhat annoying. Every so often he'd take devilish pleasure in playing a practical joke. Big Ann happened to be out the day the antique-laden truck from Boston pulled up at Lake Avenue. "Hey, Mack," asked the driver, "where should I unload this stuff?" Skakel, who was working in the garden in his old clothes, ambled over to the truck. "You been paid yet?" he asked the driver, making himself sound like one of the hired help. When the driver responded that he was supposed to pick up a check, George Skakel cackled. "Well, I'll tell you," he said, wiping his brow, "I've worked for these here Skakels for twenty years and I still ain't seen a dime yet." With that, the driver got back in the truck and drove off with Big Ann's beloved bargain antiques, leaving George laughing hysterically. Big Ann was furious.

When she wasn't redecorating, Big Ann kept up with her neighbors by subscribing to every house tour in the area. "She got a kick out of seeing how other people did their places," said Mary Begley. Big Ann's favorite was the Rusk Rehabilitation Garden Tour, sponsored by the Gimbel family, who always got the owners of the most spectacular houses in Greenwich to open their doors. Lunch was held in a tent on the grounds of Chieftains, the Gimbels' magnificent Greenwich estate.

Big Ann, who tried to keep the grounds of Lake Avenue pristine, had a group of men working for her whom she called "the road gang"—local laborers whom she'd periodically check on throughout the day to ensure that they were earning their keep, making the rounds of her estate in a surplus Army Jeep. Big and beefy, she resembled a prison matron overseeing a work detail. The road gang tended the grounds and Big Ann's full-sized, commercial nursery, located not far from the main house. Mrs. Skakel had business stationery made up for the nursery to enable her to purchase all of the plants, shrubs, flowers, and related supplies at wholesale prices.

"She used to buy out whole stores," said a Skakel family member. "She'd find a business that was in trouble—a dry-goods store, a baby clothing store, a jewelry store—and she'd buy all of the stock. I don't know what the hell she did with all that stuff. It was *weird* now that I think back about it, but we were all amused. It was just one of Big Ann's pastimes; instead of playing golf or tennis she was out buying the contents of stores. What a *strange* life."

One Christmas Big Ann went to a toy shop on Manhattan's Upper East Side to shop for presents for her growing contingent of grandchildren and the offspring of friends and relatives. As the store manager listened solemnly, Big Ann brazenly described in detail her orphanage for poor Catholic children that she ran, emphasizing the fact that the kids would have to go without toys that holiday season unless someone opened his heart. "I'll buy most of everything in here," she said meekly, "if you'll only give me a price break." She put on such an act that the shopkeeper's eyes clouded up. "I started to crack up," recalled Virginia Skakel, who had accompanied her. "She whispered to me not to laugh, not to open my mouth. But she got away with it. *She was incredible!*"

43 ✻ *Washington Bound*

NOW THAT JACK had a job as a U.S. Senator for the next six years, Bobby needed one, too, so he once again turned to his father for help. About a month after the election, in December 1952, Joe Kennedy telephoned Joe McCarthy, who'd just won reelection.

It was only natural that the senior Kennedy would go to his demagogue friend for help. During the recent campaign, the two men had had some mutually beneficial dealings. As a longtime supporter of McCarthy's tactics and philosophies, Kennedy had discreetly offered the Senator strategy and advice, and quietly contributed a substantial sum to McCarthy's coffers.

McCarthy returned the favor by selling his own Republican Party in Massachusetts down the Charles River at Kennedy's behest. Kennedy was well aware that Henry Cabot Lodge, Jr., would get an enormous boost from having the immensely popular Irish-Catholic McCarthy visit Boston and environs and give Lodge his endorsement. To avoid that, Kennedy offered McCarthy a handsome contribution in exchange for staying out of Beantown. It worked.

Now that the Republicans had won the White House and captured the Senate, McCarthy was made chairman of the powerful Permanent Subcommittee on Investigations of the Senate Government Operations Committee, dubbed the McCarthy Committee.

Who better to put on the committee's payroll than Bobby, an ambitious young man with a law degree and the influential family name? Also Bobby and Ethel were fervent supporters of McCarthyism, Joe Kennedy pointed out.

Soon, the committee would stage Capitol Hill's most disturbing and dramatic spectaculars ever: the Army-McCarthy hearings. If he got the job, Bobby would have instant fame, be on the front pages every day.

At twenty-seven, Bobby desperately wanted the post. He also appeared to have a real feel for the sort of thing McCarthy was doing. During the Kennedy-Lodge race, for instance, Bobby had ordered the publication of a study purporting that Lodge was, as young Kennedy put it, "soft on communism." Bobby also fervently maintained that hunting down suspected Reds was "an important domestic issue." He was McCarthy's kind of man.

But as it turned out, Joe Kennedy had put in Bobby's bid for the job a bit too late. McCarthy had privately decided to hire another young lawyer who'd recently made quite a reputation for himself for having a brilliant legal mind and a taste for blood. Roy Marcus Cohn, twenty-five, had made his mark as a savvy, hard-nosed prosecutor by helping to send convicted spies Julius and Ethel Rosenberg to the electric chair. Now working for the Attorney General in Washington, Cohn, a closeted homosexual and a Jew with anti-Semitic leanings, was McCarthy's first choice.

The day Joe Kennedy telephoned McCarthy, Roy Cohn happened to be in the Senator's office. As Kennedy implored the Senator to give Bobby the job, McCarthy handed a note to Cohn. "Remind me to check the size of his campaign contribution. I'm not sure it's worth it."

Had McCarthy not already made up his mind about Cohn, it might have been a toss-up between the two young knights. Both the boyish Kennedy and the darkly sinister Cohn were equally arrogant and ruthless. They also shared the same Democratic Party affiliation, which didn't seem to bother the Republican McCarthy one bit, as long as they played his game.

Beyond his fondness for Cohn, McCarthy felt that Bobby lacked experience for the job. At the same time, the Senator, coming under intense scrutiny from the media, moderates, and the left, feared that such a Kennedy appointment would look like a political payoff.

McCarthy offered an alternative plan. He'd hire Bobby as an assistant to committee general counsel Francis D. Flanagan, a former FBI agent. Later, Bobby could move up as he gained experience. The arrangement also allowed Bobby to report directly to McCarthy and not Cohn, whom Bobby already despised.

Joe Kennedy telephoned his son and advised him to take the Senator's offer. Bobby reluctantly agreed. Luckily Bobby and Ethel didn't have to live off his starting salary, $95.24 a week.

44 * First Home

IN JANUARY 1953, Ethel, Bobby, and their babies, Kathleen and Joe, moved to Washington. Ethel was delighted. For the first time in their two and a half years of marriage, they'd finally have a permanent home and a life somewhat removed from the influences of Lake Avenue and Hyannis Port.

Bobby was pleased, too, excited about the prospects of independence, making a name for himself, and of forging a close political alliance with his brother, whom he would now see on a daily basis.

But, in typical Kennedy fashion, he was adamant to Ethel that the rent on their new home be reasonable and that the house be in Georgetown, where Jack lived. Bobby gave Ethel a rent budget of five hundred dollars a month, a respectable sum to most people in the early fifties, but peanuts to someone with Ethel's extravagant habits.

Ethel still had a difficult time understanding the Kennedys' penny-pinching mentality. Still, she knew she'd have to be more prudent if she wanted to keep Rose and Bobby off her back. One of her cutbacks that year was not giving her mother a Christmas present. "Mrs. Skakel was in high dudgeon because Ethel had had the gall to tell her she couldn't afford a present," recalled Mary Begley. "Big Ann went into a complete rage. I remember her saying, 'Ethel damned well better give me something.' She felt her daughter was getting more like the Kennedys every minute."

At first Bobby, Ethel, and the kids moved into a residential hotel, while Ethel house-hunted. She finally found one of the few detached houses in Georgetown, a charming, furnished four-bedroom on S Street, footsteps from the entrance to the majestic grounds of Dumbarton Oaks. She charmed the owner into dropping his rent, which brought the monthly payment in line with Bobby's budget. Ethel was ecstatic; she finally had her own home.

But there were times during that period when she was filled with self-doubt. Was she bright and savvy enough to handle the Kennedy political life? At one point, she sought her brother Jim's counsel. He was not one to mince words. "You're married to a Democrat, so behave like a Democrat," he told her. "Whatever your husband says—that's it. You're not there to think." Jim Skakel felt that by marrying Bobby, "Ethel had taken the Kennedy loyalty oath and that was it."

The normally gregarious Ethel was cautious when it came to making new friends. Said one close friend who eventually fell out of favor after devoting years to Ethel, "She wanted a return for her investment of time in a person. And she wouldn't welcome you officially until Bobby gave her the okay. She demanded style. Loyalty. She only admitted people who were amusing, funny, bright. She always had semi-glamour girls as her friends—blonde and blue-eyed, cute and perky, all-American good looks. She liked that type and she had them around because Bobby wanted them there, too."

One of her first buddies in Washington was Sarah Davis, cute, kicky, and creative, who had dropped out of Bennington College in her freshman year to marry a handsome Princeton graduate, Spencer Davis, a former Naval officer who had started to make his way as an investment broker. On the recommendation of a mutual friend, Sarah threw a small dinner party for Ethel and Bobby, and the two women hit it off instantly. But their relationship wasn't firmly bonded until the following weekend when Sarah, at Ethel's invitation, joined the gang to play touch football in Georgetown.

Sarah amazed Ethel and Bobby with her prowess on the field. Unlike Jackie, who once asked Kennedy friend Ted Sorensen, "When I get the ball, which way do I run?" Sarah could throw and catch, and didn't mind roughing it up with the guys. Ethel and Sarah's friendship was finally cemented when Sarah got a charley horse in one of her legs, but continued to play, showing the kind of spunk that Bobby and his family appreciated and expected.

The two young women became virtually inseparable, lunching and shopping together and talking on the phone for hours. Because of Sarah's flair for fashion and design, she became a valuable asset to Ethel, who constantly consulted her. "They were like ham and eggs," said a mutual friend. But by the early 1970s, Ethel and Sarah's relationship came to an end. Later, Davis told a confidante, "My friendship with Ethel was a painful part of my life and I don't even want to think about it."

More than a few of Ethel's friends would fall by the wayside as Ethel's power grew and her tastes changed. The path to Ethel's door would eventually be littered with the victims of her quirky and erratic personality and Bobby's controlling influence.

• • •

During those early days in Washington, Ethel's ebullience and euphoria manifested themselves in a determination to live as grandly as she could within the financial constraints that Bobby and Rose were forever mandating.

Inevitably, Ethel violated the limits almost as soon as they were imposed. She immediately hired a staff of servants who wore a different color uniform each day of the week. Ethel also became a familiar face at the many antique shops in Georgetown, and the antique shows, such as the one at the Shoreham Hotel, where dealers remembered her spending freely. Like her mother, Ethel had developed a passion for antiques and became expert at bargaining.

"Ethel had what I'd call WASP good taste," said a friend. "She never really cared about antiques, she wasn't *that* intellectual. But she had this incredible ability to pick up just a smattering of knowledge here and there and then make you *think* she was an expert."

Ethel was always alert for an interesting find. While

getting her hair done at Elizabeth Arden's, she fell in love with a French antique bench with pink brocade that was part of the furnishings and decided she had to have it. Ethel befriended the decorator, Catherine ("Boots") Treat, emphasized that she was a Kennedy, and got the bench. As time passed, Ethel would often use the Kennedy name with merchants and vendors to get things at wholesale, at cost, or even for free.

In New York, she'd make the rounds of her favorite antique and interior decorating shops: Garrick Stephenson's, on East Fifty-fifth Street, which specialized in Louis XVI furniture; the Upper East Side location of Jansen, owned by director-producer Leland Hayward's wife, Pamela—later Pamela Harriman.

The bills would come in and Bobby would be livid. At Jansen, for example, Ethel was late in paying for thousands of dollars of merchandise.

Among Sarah Davis's talents was painting, and Ethel had commandeered one or two of her friend's canvases to hang on her walls. After a couple of years, Sarah, who was not in the Kennedys' financial league, sent a modest bill to Ethel for her works. But when Bobby came across the invoice he hit the ceiling. "What do we owe Sarah Davis two hundred and fifty dollars for?" he demanded. When Ethel quietly explained that it was for the wonderful picture he'd always admired that hung in the dining room, Bobby smirked. "Sarah never got paid," said a mutual pal. "Ethel never fought Bobby over such matters, even if it meant hurting a friend."

A friend of Ethel's was a real-estate agent and had heard of a property that she thought Ethel and Bobby might be interested in buying. The friend mentioned the house to Ethel, but instead of going through Ethel's chum, Bobby called the sellers on his own in hopes of avoiding paying the agent's commission. When the friend complained to Ethel, Bobby got on the phone. "He really let her have it," recalled a principal. Bobby yelled, "This whole time you've only been after us for our money!" The friend was so upset that when Bobby hung up she ran to her room in tears.

Ethel loved simple, elegant, expensive sportswear that showed off her slim, athletic figure. When she couldn't find what she wanted in Washington—in those days there were only a few interesting specialty shops—she'd zip up to New York with one of her pals.

"At Bergdorf's, Ethel hit the shoe department like the Marines at Guadalcanal, buying expensive Delman shoes in every color," recalled one of her shopping companions. "She'd buy five of everything. Ten of everything. Ethel was very acquisitive. And she'd get hell from Bobby for it. He couldn't understand why she had to have six of everything." Bobby began asking Ethel's friends, "Do you spend like she does? How do you manage?" Finally, frustrated, he ordered Ethel to have all the bills sent directly to the Park Agency, the Kennedy family business office, at 230 Park Avenue.

While Rose was critical of Ethel's spending habits generally, she thoroughly supported her daughter-in-law's desire to look attractive. In fact, it was Rose herself who told Ethel that Joe always liked women in good-looking clothes, and that he'd compliment her when she wore a particularly stunning dress. She advised Ethel to do the same, leaving it understood that all of the Kennedy men were notorious womanizers like their father and that the Kennedy women should do everything in their power to make themselves alluring to their husbands.

45 ✻ *Ethel and Jackie*

NOT LONG AFTER settling into her new home, Ethel began throwing dinner parties, attempting to establish a reputation as a popular hostess. Ethel's first Washington soirée, taking place not long after she and Bobby moved to Georgetown, was in honor of St. Patrick, except that Ethel's curious telephoned invitation instructed the female guests to wear black, not green.

Jack had asked Ethel to invite the new woman in his life, Jacqueline Bouvier, whom the junior Senator from Massachusetts had recently taken to Ike's inaugural ball. Ethel's party was the first occasion for the future sisters-in-law to meet, and it would turn out to be a far from auspicious introduction.

It was a cold March evening, with ice and snow still on the ground from a recent late winter storm. Jack, whose chronic back condition was acting up, was in a great deal of pain that night. He had arrived early, alone, and was limping around on crutches, wearing old bedroom slippers, drinking with the other guests: Kennedy hanger-on Lem Billings; Bobby's boarding-school chum Dave Hackett; Jim Buckley, a future U.S. Senator from New York, who would eventually marry Ann Cooley, who had gone to Manhattanville with Ethel, and Ann Marie O'Hagan Murphy, among others. Jackie was one of the last to arrive, pulling up dramatically in a chauffered Rolls. As was her style, she made a stunning entrance. Like all of the other women at the party, she had obediently followed Ethel's directive to dress in black.

There was only one exception to Ethel's mandate: Ethel herself. She swooped into the party, a mischievous smile on her face, wearing, as Ann Marie O'Hagan Murphy recalled, "the most gorgeous, diaphanous chiffon dress—layer, upon layer, upon layer—of all shades of *green*. Now, that was typical of Ethel. No one was allowed to wear green, we were told. But there she was, glimmering like an emerald." In coming years, Ethel would use such gimmicks to earn a reputation as an offbeat hostess; invitations to her parties were in demand because guests never knew what to expect.

At Ethel's party that St. Patrick's Day, Jackie seemed to go out of her way to ignore her hostess. While the gregarious Ethel entertained, the aloof Jackie spent most of the cocktail hour alone, warming herself in front of the blazing living room fireplace; the house was always cold in winter because Bobby wanted to save on heating bills. "Jackie wasn't *just* being aloof," recalled one of the guests. "She was taking all of the heat to warm herself. And by standing in front of the fireplace, she became the center of attention, which was very typical of Jackie."

A few of the guests also noted that Jack was hardly paying attention to Jackie, and vice versa, which seemed odd at a time when the two were believed to be seriously in love and talking marriage.

When the butler came into the living room and announced that dinner was being served, there was a sudden commotion in a corner of the room. Suddenly Bobby retrieved Jackie's fur from a closet and put it over her shoulders. Moments later Ethel and Bobby saw Jackie to the door and she abruptly left.

"Ethel came back into the house and she was livid," recalled Ann Marie O'Hagan Murphy. "Jackie had accepted her invitation to come for drinks and dinner and then suddenly said that something came up and she'd have to leave. Ethel was furious because a beautiful dinner had been prepared and the table had been set for the right number of people, and now one of them was missing. Ethel felt that the whole dinner party was ruined by Jackie. Davey Hackett and Lem Billings were trying hard to lift her spirits, but everyone was stunned by Jackie's performance."

Ethel's St. Patrick's Day party set the tone for the chilly relationship that she and Jackie would have over the years. It was readily apparent to everyone present that the two had little affinity—let alone affection—for each other; the gulf between them would widen even more after Jackie married into the Kennedy family that fall. Jack and Jackie had met while she was working as the inquiring photographer at the Washington *Times-Herald,* on the rebound from a broken engagement. By the time of Ethel's party, Jackie had decided that she wanted to marry Jack, despite warnings about his womanizing from Lem Billings and others. But Jackie didn't care. "She wasn't sexually attracted to men unless they were dangerous like her father," a Kennedy family friend observed. "It was one of those terrible Freudian situations."

In the weeks and months that followed Ethel's party, the Kennedy gang got together on Saturday afternoons to play touch football at the Georgetown Recreation Center, a few blocks from Ethel and Bobby's place. Jack brought Jackie, who played halfheartedly. For the most part, she sat glumly on the sidelines and watched while Ethel roughed it up with the men. Jackie eventually put her foot down, refusing to play after breaking an ankle.

"Ethel made jokes that Jackie wouldn't play because she was afraid to smear her makeup," one of the female players recalled. "I remember Ethel, who rarely wore lipstick, shaking her head in wonderment, saying, 'Jackie thinks she's a queen. I can't figure out what Jack sees in her.' "

When Jackie made her first visit to Hyannis Port that summer, Ethel, who was also there, used the occasion to make fun of her blatantly, referring to Jackie as "the Debutante." Ethel mocked Jackie's trademark breathy voice and drew guffaws from her Kennedy sisters-in-law by noting that Jackie pronounced her name as *Jacqueleen*, which, Ethel howled, rhymed with *Queen*. The girls were in stitches when, during a conversation about their goals in life, Jackie mentioned that she'd once dreamed of being a ballet dancer. Staring wide-eyed at Jackie's slender size-eleven feet, Ethel muttered, "With those clodhoppers of yours? You'd be better off going in for soccer." On another occasion, Ethel commented to Jean about Jackie, "I don't think she has blood in her veins."

For her part, Jackie considered Jack's sisters and Ethel to be crude and boorish. "I'm not going to be what *they* want me to be," she later told a friend. "I won't cut my hair. I won't have twenty-five kids." She would later refer to Ethel as a "baby-making machine—wind her up and she becomes pregnant." Jackie later confided her dislike of Ethel to her friend Truman Capote, who wasn't fond of her himself. "Ethel Kennedy has the mind-set of a vulture," Capote once declared. "She's the most highly competitive and insanely jealous human being I have ever met. Jackie would give a party . . . and a week later Ethel felt obligated to throw a shindig . . . she was obsessed by Jackie. Anything Jackie did, she could do better."

To Ethel, Jackie was an alien from another planet. But in many ways the two young women were very much alike: rich, spoiled, and, as time would prove, ill-starred.

Jackie was born on July 28, 1929—fifteen months after Ethel—in Southampton, a wealthy resort town, a zigzag across Long Island Sound from Greenwich. Her mother, vivacious, social-climbing Janet Lee Bouvier, was the daughter of another self-made millionaire in the mold of George Skakel and Joe Kennedy. Jackie's stockbroker father, John Vernou ("Black Jack") Bouvier, was a handsome rogue of thirty-eight, sixteen years his wife's senior, when he married her. Unlike the sexually naive and religiously repressed Ethel, the precocious Jackie enjoyed shocking her friends with stories about her father's sexual exploits. Unlike Ethel, Jackie was a child of divorce; her mother had left Bouvier to marry the wealthy Hugh Auchincloss. To Ethel divorce was anathema. And while Ethel, the virgin, was still being properly courted by Bobby, Jackie had already spent a year alone in Paris, had been dubbed "Queen Deb of the Year" by New York columnist Cholly Knickerbocker, and had won *Vogue*'s sought-after Prix de Paris.

"Ethel and Jackie could never be friends," one family member observed. *"Never."*

About a month after her St. Patrick's Day party, Ethel became pregnant for the third time. The following month, Jack asked for Jackie's hand in marriage, but the details were tabled until the *Saturday Evening Post* published a story about "The Senate's Gay Young Bachelor." Once the magazine hit the stands, the wedding plans became public.

In the weeks preceding the biggest wedding of the year, there were a number of parties, including one given at the Hyannis Port home of the Harringtons, friends of the Kennedys. Ethel was there and was a major player in what Rose Kennedy later described as a "notorious" scavenger hunt. The rules called, in part, for the players to hunt for the "longest object" they could find. Pat Kennedy, who was then dating the actor Peter Lawford, accompanied by the very pregnant Ethel, snatched a driverless bus at the terminal in Hyannis. "She drove it right to the Harringtons' and parked it in the driveway," said Ethel, who also recalled how one of the Kennedys stole a policeman's hat. "By the time they got home there were three squad cars of policemen talking to Grandpa."

The wedding, with some eight hundred guests present in the church and twelve hundred at the reception, was held on September 12, 1953, with Bobby as best man and Ethel as one of the bridesmaids. The ceremony was presided over by then Archbishop Cushing, who read a special blessing from the Pope. That night Jack and Jackie went into New York, spending their wedding night in the Waldorf-Astoria's honeymoon suite before flying off for an Acapulco honeymoon.

On their return, they rented a two-bedroom house in Georgetown, within walking distance of Ethel and Bobby's; Jack's choice of location, not Jackie's. To keep peace, though, Jackie accepted a loan of drapes and slipcovers from Ethel, even though the two women had completely different tastes. "Jackie," said a relative, "felt Ethel had no class, no finishing." Jackie thought of Ethel as "the type who would put a slipcover on a Louis Quinze sofa and then spell it 'Louie Cans.' "

By the time Jack and Jackie had bought their first home near Thirty-third and N streets, about a block from Bobby and Ethel's recent O Street rental, Ethel had come to admire Jackie's skills as the first lady of her household, describing her sister-in-law's place as "heaven and so supremely well organized. I always get depressed getting back to my madhouse."

Ethel wasn't exaggerating. As Skakel family friend Mary Begley observed, "If you walked into one Skakel house, you walked into all of them: servants running around, no meals on the table, crazy, undisciplined.

Ethel's house may have been a little grander, a few more servants, but it was about the same."

Jackie devilishly documented on canvas what she saw as her sister-in-law's disorganization. Her painting showed children running wild, servants coming and going, and the house in a general state of disarray. Like a badge of honor, Ethel proudly hung the painting in a prominent spot in her very disorganized home.

46 * Marrying Them Off

BETWEEN 1954 AND 1958, the rest of the Kennedy and Skakel children would get married.

In June 1954, Pat Kennedy, the most attractive of the Kennedy girls—tall, auburn-haired, violet-eyed—married Peter Lawford. Pat had been starstruck since childhood, when her father was in the movie business, and she had met a number of Hollywood celebrities. Rose Kennedy was violently opposed to Lawford because he wasn't a Catholic, and Joe disliked him because he was an Englishman; the patriarch was still smarting from the negative treatment the British accorded him when he was ambassador. Pat and Peter settled into a Hollywood lifestyle on the beach in Malibu. They had four children between 1955 and 1961. But the union was troubled due to Lawford's obsessive womanizing and bizarre sexual proclivities. The Kennedys made every effort to avoid a scandal, sending both Bobby and Ethel in as peacemakers, but in 1966 the Lawfords, after a long separation, were divorced. It was later revealed that Lawford had helped procure women for Jack Kennedy.

A couple of months after the Kennedy-Lawford merger, Big Ann and George Skakel reluctantly announced the engagement of their youngest, Ann—the prettiest of the Skakel girls—to John Henry McCooey, a good-looking, brash Irishman of twenty-five, a Georgetown University graduate who was the namesake and grandson of the late Democratic party boss of Brooklyn.

McCooey was not greeted with open arms by the fiercely Republican Skakels, although eventually he would turn out to be as much of a Kennedy detractor as the Skakels.

Party affiliation, however, had less to do with Big Ann and George Sr.'s dismay about McCooey than their daughter's decision to quit Manhattanville, where she was a junior, to marry him. A week after the engagement announcement, Big Ann and George took Ann off to Europe in an unsuccessful effort to change her mind.

On October 2, 1954, Ann Skakel stood on the altar with John McCooey in St. Mary's Roman Catholic Church, where Ethel, Georgeann, and Pat had their weddings. The Reverend John J. Cavanaugh, the former president of the University of Notre Dame, officiated; Ethel, to whom Ann would always be devoted, was matron of honor; the bridesmaids included Georgeann; Ann's sister-in-law, Pat Corroon Skakel; and Ann Reynolds, who was engaged to Rushton Skakel. The Skakel boys—Jimmy, George, and Rushton—were among the ushers.

It was another spectacular Skakel wedding, but nowhere near as extravagant and elaborate, or as publicized, as Ethel's, who had become an instant celebrity by marrying a Kennedy. The Skakels' wedding gift to Ann, however, was certainly extraordinary: a solid gold, seven-piece service—appraised at thirty thousand dollars at the time—that had once been a gift to the Queen of England. In time, the McCooeys' marriage would also fall apart.

The only member of the Skakel family still to get married was Rushton, who would tie the knot in 1955 with Ann Reynolds, another Manhattanville graduate. The closest Kennedy woman to Ethel, Jean, would marry Steve Smith in 1956. And in 1958, the youngest Kennedy boy, Ted, would walk down the aisle with Joan Bennett.

47 * Kennedy vs. Cohn

WHILE JOE MCCARTHY and Roy Cohn were conducting their highly publicized witch-hunts at the Voice of America, State Department, and other government agencies, Bobby was involved in more mundane matters. He'd hoped to participate in McCarthy's major investigations, but as it turned out Bobby was assigned to assist committee investigator La Vern Duffy find ways to shut off the shipment by America's allies of strategic materials to Soviet countries.

Bobby was quoted several times in the press, particularly in the *Boston Post,* which favored the Kennedy family. As a sop to Old Joe, McCarthy invited Bobby to be at his side when the senator announced that a large group of Greek shipping magnates had agreed to stop carrying goods to Communist China; an agreement reached, in part, because of young Kennedy's research. Even Roy Cohn, who couldn't stomach Bobby, described him as "a vigorous prosecutor" during that period. In recognition for the "excellent" work he'd been doing, Bobby received a $7.35-a-week raise, bringing his annual salary to $5,334.57. Not long after, he was given another raise of $2,000.

Ethel couldn't have been prouder, periodically showing up at the committee offices with girlfriends in tow to catch a glimpse of Bobby, in shirtsleeves, at work. Breathlessly, she'd introduce her pals to Joe McCarthy and Roy Cohn, and ask them to sign autographs.

It was during those visits to Bobby's office that Ethel, who'd been working hard on improving her husband's public image by upgrading his wardrobe, noticed that while he now wore suits, white shirts, and ties to the office—articles she'd personally selected—he still chose to wear white sweat socks, giving him the look of a bumpkin as he walked determinedly down the halls of the Senate office building. Thereafter, before he left for Capitol Hill each morning, she'd personally inspect him from head to toe to make certain he was color coordinated. Ethel's visits to Bobby's office in those days set the pattern for his entire career. She'd usually be seated in the first row at his hearings—nervously at first, more confidently later, eventually abrasively and arrogantly—cheering him, offering moral support. For now, though, Bobby's profile was low and his public appearances scant.

While Ethel was exuberant about Bobby's close association with McCarthy, her father was not, and this caused more family friction. While strongly opposed to communism, George Skakel despised McCarthy and his tactics, referring to the Senator as "a worthless rattle brain." Skakel had been mortified when Ethel had told him that Bobby had gone to work for the Senator.

George Skakel rarely entertained confrontation, but he clearly made his displeasure known to Ethel, whom he loved dearly. During the time Bobby was affiliated with McCarthy, George Skakel, Sr., and Big Ann never once visited their daughter and her family in Washington.

Despite the high esteem in which he held McCarthy, Bobby suddenly quit the subcommittee after only seven months. Most knowledgeable sources agree that he resigned in a snit because Roy Cohn wielded the power that Bobby coveted. Bobby turned in his resignation on July 29, 1953, using the excuse that he intended to enter private law practice. Years later, in his book, *The Enemy Within,* he blamed Cohn for his decision to quit, though even then he equivocated. Rather than admitting that a power struggle and feud existed, he asserted that he left because most of the subcommittee's investigations were based on "some preconceived notion" of Cohn's. By blaming Cohn for the subcommittee's problems, he gave "McCarthyism" and the Senator a clean bill of health, blaming McCarthy only for "allowing the committee to function in such a fashion."

Bobby was unemployed for only a few weeks when his father came to his rescue once again by hiring him as his assistant on the Commission on Reorganization of the Executive Branch—the so-called Hoover Commission, headed by eighty-year-old former President Herbert Hoover. Bobby quickly grew bored in the musty atmosphere of the commission. Anxious for more action, he also became irritable and temperamental.

One night Bobby showed up at Jack's house with his face bruised and bloodied. Ethel was horrified and rushed to his side, thinking he had been mugged in the street. Actually, he'd been playing touch football with Teddy and some friends and had gotten into a fistfight with a few Georgetown University students who had ignored Bobby's request to stop hitting baseballs into the midst of their game. Bobby, in one of his dark moods, threw the first punch. "That must have been a rough game of touch," Ethel said quietly over dinner, but Bobby pretended not to hear her and never gave her an explanation for what really had happened.

• • •

Bobby's angst ended with the start of the new year, 1954. He had a new job, and a namesake. On January 17, after an easy pregnancy, Ethel delivered her third child, their second son, Robert F. Kennedy, Jr. As usual, Luella Hennessey was there to hold Ethel's hand and to comfort her.

Preparing to return home after a week's stay at Georgetown University Hospital, Ethel grew concerned about how Kathleen and Joe would react to the new baby. She finally came up with a plan, and used it for every subsequent birth. "When she'd get home all the children would be waiting as she carried the baby up the walk," Hennessey said. "They'd just go mad about it and want to hold it and talk to it. And Ethel would say, 'Look at what the new baby brought home to you.' They'd each get a basket with a gift and then they'd each kiss the baby and say thank you. It was quite a good idea."

Hennessey remained with Ethel and the baby for several more days. In eighteen months, she'd return, when Ethel would give birth on June 15, 1955, to number four, the third son, David Anthony Kennedy.

• • •

Within a couple of weeks of leaving the Hoover Commission, Bobby received a job offer he couldn't refuse. The three-member Democratic minority of the McCarthy subcommittee had gotten authorization to hire their own counsel. When Bobby heard about the position, he immediately called his father, who made a few discreet inquiries and virtually overnight secured the job for his son. Bobby now returned to the subcommittee with a bit more power, and just in time for its biggest show ever.

On April 22, 1954, the Army-McCarthy hearings began, mesmerizing the nation for thirty-six days, attracting as many as 20 million viewers to the televised proceedings. The hearings, which were the beginning of the end for McCarthy, focused on his allegations that Communists had influenced the Army. Denying the charges, the Army counterattacked, accusing McCarthy and Cohn of using their influence to get better military treatment for Cohn's pal, G. David Schine, who'd worked as a committee investigator before he was drafted.

As minority counsel, Bobby had little to do but sit behind the three Democratic Senators, acting as a glorified gofer, spending most of his time coming up with questions for them to ask.

Each day Ethel would leave the children with their nurse and drive to Capitol Hill, where, for the first time, she was noticed by the press, the beaming, pert wife of the young Kennedy boy. Like the rest of the country, Ethel sat transfixed. But all of her attention was riveted on Bobby.

It wasn't until a week before the hearings concluded that Ethel's hero emerged from virtual anonymity.

On Friday June 11, Bobby and his nemesis, Roy

Cohn, almost got into a fistfight outside the hearing room. That day Senator Henry M. Jackson, using questions supplied by Bobby, heatedly went after Schine and a curious fifteen-point plan he'd conceived for promoting democracy in places that appeared likely to fall to communism. Cohn was furious at what he later called a "burlesque" by Bobby. He noted that every time Bobby handed Jackson a question, the Senator "would go into fits of laughter." When the session finally ended, a fuming Cohn confronted Bobby. As their shouting match grew louder, a crowd, including a number of reporters, gathered. "There's only one way to settle this," Cohn said, and he started to throw a punch at Bobby. Two spectators grabbed Cohn, Bobby ducked, and the blow missed. Cohn later stated that since touch football wasn't one of his "long suits, I probably was the gainer in the stopping of the fight." The next day the front-page headline in the *New York Daily News* read: COHN, KENNEDY NEAR BLOWS IN "HATE" CLASH.

La Verne Duffy, who eyewitnessed the showdown, recalled later, "Ethel just loved it. I looked down and I saw her fists clenched. I was worried she was going to jump into the middle of the brawl and kick Cohn in the balls. She was Bobby's staunchest defender."

48 ✳ A Last Good-bye

FOR MONTHS DURING 1954 and 1955, George and Big Ann shuttled in one of Great Lakes Carbon's converted World War II B-26 attack bombers between Connecticut and California, where George was putting the finishing touches on his latest venture, the private and commercial development of thousands of acres of the verdant Palos Verdes peninsula, just south of Los Angeles.

George Skakel's leap from coke and coal into the more glamorous world of Southern California real estate had come about unexpectedly during the company's search in the early fifties for diatomaceous earth, a type of dirt used as a filtering agent in the manufacture of some of Great Lakes' products. While core-drilling in the Palos Verdes hills, Jay Mayhew struck a large deposit of diatomite on land that Great Lakes Carbon had leased from the estate of the late economist Frank Arthur Vanderlip. When George Skakel learned that the Vanderlips would rather sell than lease, an extremely favorable price was negotiated and Skakel picked up thousands of acres, including two miles of highly desirable land fronting on the Pacific Ocean for a thousand dollars an acre, a cool $9 million, which he paid in cash. Skakel quickly sold just one acre to Shell Oil for a hundred times what he had paid for it.

As it turned out, the moisture content of the diatomaceous earth was too high, so Skakel shut down the mining operation and set up a real-estate development division. Hiring the best architects and engineers, he envisioned beautiful homes, golf courses, tennis courts, swimming pools, and upscale shopping centers, all sitting high above the Pacific, and within easy commuting distance of Los Angeles.

By the time the land purchase was consummated, Skakel had already turned over much of the day-to-day operations of Great Lakes Carbon to George Jr., who succeeded his father as president in April 1953, with George Sr. now serving as chairman.

"My father needed a new challenge," said Rushton Skakel. "The Palos Verdes project became his baby."

Once Skakel decided to develop the property, which eventually would earn tens of millions of dollars for the company, he and Big Ann became regular transcontinental commuters. Skakel even installed a custom lift in the belly of one of his planes to make it easier for his wife to get on and off.

George Skakel loved to fly, and he was one of the first businessmen to make regular use of airplanes for business travel. As early as 1920, when he was just starting out, he'd wangle his way aboard the biplanes that crisscrossed the country carrying mail and were later bought by barnstormers and charter pilots, many of whom received handsome fares from George Skakel to ensure that he got to a meeting in a distant city on time.

As the years passed, Skakel decided it was more convenient to have his own planes, so he began buying surplus military aircraft from the government for a song and had them converted to civilian use. When the planes weren't being used for business, they became an integral part of the company perks the Skakels enjoyed. They'd fly anywhere on a lark, particularly the brothers who worked for the company. George Jr., now president of Great Lakes Carbon, was constantly taking off with his chums for weekend hunting, fishing, and skiing jaunts. A practical joker, George would sometimes have his friends arrive at the airport dressed for skiing and hours later they'd find themselves disembarking at a sun-baked airstrip in Cuba.

The Skakel planes also were a source of constant family friction, particularly among the Skakel girls—Ethel, Pat, and Ann—whose husbands didn't work for Great Lakes Carbon and who therefore were ineligible for company benefits. Ethel's lack of access to the planes rankled Bobby.

"The Kennedys didn't have a plane before Jack became President because they were too cheap to buy one," said George Terrien. "So they were always trying to get freebie rides on the Skakel planes." Remembering Christmas 1954, Mary Begley said, "Bobby had deigned to accompany Ethel to Greenwich, but then he wanted to get the hell back. I remember Bobby saying, 'We've got to get back to Washington. We'll take the plane.' He didn't even ask Mr. and Mrs. Skakel for their permission. Ethel's brothers, all of them, abhorred Bobby's pushiness when it came to the planes. They also were furious that Ethel never once spoke up in defense of her family's feelings, which she was well aware of."

Instead of being a source of luxurious pleasure for the family, the planes, as it turned out, sparked enmity and greed. And in the end, they also would become the cause of crushing tragedy.

• • •

On the evening of Sunday, October 2, 1955, George and Ann Skakel threw a first wedding anniversary party at Lake Avenue for Little Ann and her husband, John McCooey. With another trip to California set for the next morning, the senior Skakels left the festivities early. They had a full schedule ahead of them. This time out George had meetings scheduled with Marcel Breuer, the noted Bauhaus-trained architect and designer, who'd been retained to work on the Palos Verdes project. George also planned to make a stop in Salt Lake City to meet with Jay Mayhew, and Big Ann was looking forward to a layover in Chicago to visit Florence Kumpfer.

Monday, October 3, 1955, dawned fair and warm. Little Ann decided to see off her parents at Bridgeport Airport, the starting point of their flight to Los Angeles. The plane was already on the tarmac waiting for the Skakels' arrival. Following custom, the old man chatted with Joe Whitney, the pilot, and Johnny McBride, the co-pilot, both veterans of the Skakel fleet. Whitney reported that the weather looked good, that the intense safety check, which had been designed by son-in-law Johnny Dowdle, had been made, and that the ship was fueled and ready for takeoff. Little Ann hugged her mother—"Say hello to Aunt Florence for me"—and kissed her father on the cheek. Then she walked to the passenger area to watch the plane take off.

George Skakel was quite fond of the old bomber, but others found the plane uncomfortable. Passengers were forced to sit in the bomb-bay section and had to crawl on their bellies to get from one end of the ship to the other. And a few had recently questioned its safety. About six months before the Skakels took off that October day, Great Lakes attorney Tom Hayes and another company executive, Danny Crimmins, had taken a flight aboard the plane that had left them feeling intensely uneasy. "We smelled gas, fuel fumes," said Hayes years later. "I told one of the pilots and he said 'Ah, Nah. I don't think so.' But I became afraid to fly in it."

George and Ann Skakel buckled their seat belts. Joe Whitney switched on the engines and throttled the big plane onto the end of the runway, awaiting clearance to begin his takeoff, as Johnny McBride made a last-minute instrument check. He held up his thumb to indicate that everything was okay. A few minutes later the control tower radioed permission for them to depart. From behind the fence, Ann McCooey watched as the old plane lumbered down the runway and lifted off. Its first stop would be Tulsa, for refueling. She gave one last wave, went to the car, and was driven back to Lake Avenue by one of the Skakel chauffeurs.

49 * End of an Era

A MAID ANSWERED the telephone at Sursum Corda early on the morning of Tuesday, October 4, 1955. Big Ann's social secretary was on the phone asking to speak to Georgeann. "She's still asleep," the servant responded. "Please wake her. It's important." Georgeann picked up the phone in her bedroom. "I'm terribly sorry to bother you so early," the secretary said, "but what's all this nonsense I hear about your parents being dead?"

Georgeann froze, then immediately jumped to the conclusion that it was someone's idea of a sick practical joke. "That's absurd," she said, annoyed, and hung up the phone. But a few minutes later, when the maid brought her the morning paper, the eldest of the Skakel children learned the horrible truth from the *Greenwich Time*. The front-page banner headline blared, MR., MRS. SKAKEL, 2 PILOTS DIE IN PLANE CRASH . . . EXPLODED IN MID AIR OVER OKLAHOMA; WERE FLYING TO COAST ON BUSINESS TRIP.

The story went on to say that George and Big Ann, both sixty-three years old, had been killed instantly. The crash had occurred at about eleven-fifteen P.M., Eastern Daylight Time, not long after the plane had taken off from its refueling stop in Tulsa during a torrential rainstorm. Joe Whitney had radioed to Oklahoma City airport that he was having some sort of trouble and needed to land immediately, but he was advised that the weather made an instrument approach hazardous. That was the last contact with the plane. Moments later farmers in the rural area three miles north of Union City heard an explosion and an eerie, screaming whine. Thinking it was a meteor, or even a flying saucer—the UFO-sighting hysteria was at its peak in that part of the country—they called the police. The first to reach the wreckage, scattered over a wide area of a muddy field, were Oklahoma state highway patrolmen.

Somehow, among the molten and smoldering pieces of twisted metal, they found what was left of the bodies. Had one of the rescue workers not stumbled across a Diners Club credit card with George Skakel's name on it, and Joe Whitney's wallet, it might have taken hours more for authorities to make an identification.

As she read the story, Georgeann began trembling so hard that her husband thought she was having a convulsion. He ordered her to take a stiff drink and lie down, but she knew she had to get the family together as quickly as possible. She picked up the phone and started dialing.

Her brother Rushton was already at his desk at the Great Lakes Carbon facility in St. Louis, unaware, like the others, of his parents' death. When Georgeann told him what had happened he felt ill, paralyzed, his eyes filled with tears. "Oh, wow, it was such a shock. I couldn't believe it," he said later, recalling the moment.

Rushton got on a plane and headed north to Lake Avenue, where the Skakel family and close friends had begun to gather. The lights burned bright late into the night at the mansion, where George Jr. had taken charge of overseeing the return of his parents' remains and the arrangements for the funeral. Outside, police and private guards were posted to protect the Skakels' privacy.

Meanwhile, the inner circle had started gathering in Big Ann's sacred library: George Jr. and his wife, Pat, who was drinking heavily; a red-eyed Rushton and his wife, Ann, who'd just arrived from St. Louis; a shocked Little Ann, the last of the children to see her parents alive, and her husband; and Jim Skakel, now separated from his wife, Virginia, who'd been located in Atlanta and was on her way to Greenwich. Also en route were Pat and Luan Cuffe, who were trying desperately to get a flight from Dublin. Martin McKneally had arrived and so had George Terrien, who'd flown down from the company's offices in Canada. There were priests to give solace, and friends and business associates to offer whatever assistance they could.

Only one family member was conspicuously absent—Ethel. Mary Begley, who was at the house that horrible night, recalled the scene years later:

"George had called Ethel in Washington, but Bobby got on the phone and said, 'No! Ethel's *not* coming to Greenwich. She will come *after* you make the funeral arrangements. She will come *only* for the funeral. But she's *not* coming up now!' Bobby didn't give a reason. Maybe he was being protective of her, no one knew. The Kennedys didn't give reasons for what they did. George and Rushton and Georgeann—all of them—were furious with Bobby. They were all saying, 'Ethel should be here. . . . Why does she put up with him? . . . Why doesn't she just come up here on her own? My God, Mother and Father are dead!' I do remember them saying of Bobby, 'It's so typical of that little Napoleon to not let her come.' But Ethel always deferred to Bobby, a vindictive little soul."

Begley herself had been tracked down by Georgeann

at Yankee Stadium, where she and her husband had been watching the final game of the World Series between the Yankees and the Dodgers. During her frantic drive back to Greenwich, Begley had remembered a recent, curious conversation she'd had with Big Ann who, surveying all of the antiques, books, artifacts, and *objets* she'd accumulated over the years, said suddenly, "Dear God! You spend the first half of your life collecting and the second half of your life getting rid of it all." Looking back now, it seemed to her as if Mrs. Skakel, not an introspective woman, had some premonition of what was to come.

While flying north to be with Jim and the others, Virginia Skakel had dozed fitfully, remembering a recent surprise visit she had had from her father-in-law. George had taken it upon himself to fly down to Miami on the B-26 to talk to Virginia in hopes of bringing about a reconciliation with his son. Over cocktails at the Old Forge on Forty-first Street, he told Virginia, "The whole family wants you to stay. Jimmy's a wonderful person. Why don't you give it another chance?" Although she was touched, Virginia's answer was no. "Mr. Skakel," she said, "I don't think it's going to work. I just think it's best we part when we're young." A crestfallen George Skakel flew back home that night. It was the last time Virginia Skakel saw him alive.

She arrived at Lake Avenue just as four mortuary employees were carrying the two caskets bearing the remains of George and Ann Skakel into the house.

"A dynasty was gone," she thought. "The mother and father had run everything."

When the caskets were brought in, the Skakel brothers and sisters knelt down and said the rosary. "But they showed no emotions," recalled Virginia Skakel. "They were absolute basket cases, but you'd never know it."

At Georgeann's direction, the caskets were moved into the library and placed in the same spot where, displayed every Christmas, was an extraordinary nativity scene designed by artists from the Metropolitan Museum of Art featuring priceless Neapolitan religious figures that Big Ann had collected over the years.

• • •

Since George Skakel wasn't a Catholic, how could he be buried in a Catholic cemetery, next to his wife? Word began emanating from Lake Avenue, to the disbelief of many, that just prior to taking the ill-fated flight George had promised Big Ann that he would convert; the story even had it that he had a rosary in his hand when he was found. If anyone questioned how the beads could have survived the explosion, fire, and impact, no one raised their voices.

"There were three witnesses—a Trappist monk, a local pastor, and another priest—who heard my father say he would convert," Jim Skakel maintained years later. "My father said, 'When I come back from California, I'm going to be baptized.' "

Discussing his father's purported decision later, Rushton Skakel, curiously chuckling, said, "It was a miracle."

Bob Skakel, George's nephew, scoffed at the reports. "I think it's something his children wanted to believe," he said. John McCooey said he'd never heard a word from George Skakel regarding his conversion plans. "But it doesn't really matter if they made it up. It was just nice that he could be buried next to her. I know my wife Ann was very pleased that he was allowed to be buried as a Catholic."

In the end, though, the question was irrelevant. According to Martin McKneally, the Church decided to waive all the rules because of Big Ann's longtime friendship and affiliation with Catholic leaders. "It was all myth," McKneally said. "But the family started believing it themselves."

The funeral service was held on Friday, October 7, with hundreds of friends and business associates present for the solemn requiem High Mass at St. Mary's Roman Catholic Church. Some twenty-five priests were on the altar, and the Manhattanville choir sang. The immediate family sat in the front row. Ethel had finally arrived with

Bobby the night before. "I hugged her, but she didn't say a word," recalled Virginia Skakel. "There were no tears from her, or from any of them. Instead of crying, they laughed. It was their way of coping. It was the only way they could cope."

When everyone had left the cemetery, an enormous purple wreath was placed at the grave. It had been sent by the man who for years had operated a service station in town and had profited handsomely from repairing the many wrecked and dented Skakel cars.

Back at Lake Avenue, where every room was filled with flowers, the Skakels threw an old-fashioned Irish wake. "The house was crammed with so many people it was like the black hole of Calcutta with a cocktail-party atmosphere," recalled Ethel's cousin Betty Medaille. "Ethel and Bobby didn't want to mingle with the herd. Ethel had the look of someone who wished she wasn't there, which I could understand."

Being around the Skakels had always made Bobby uncomfortable and moody, but the funeral was more than he could bear. Ethel had hoped to stay a few days with her brothers and sisters, but Bobby was adamant about leaving. As usual she gave in, and the two of them departed for New York City. That evening, Ethel accompanied Bobby—at his urging—to dinner at his father's favorite restaurant, Le Pavillion, at Fifty-seventh and Park, both acting as if nothing had happened. Family members were incensed.

After dinner Bobby telephoned Ethel's pal Sarah Davis in Washington. Davis expected to hear sadness in his voice, but instead he sounded normal, and he had a request. When they arrived in Washington, would Sarah please meet Ethel at the airport and take her for a round of golf at Bethesda Country Club? Bobby told Sarah he thought such an outing would take Ethel's mind off the tragedy, so the next day Ethel and Davis played eighteen holes. Not once did Ethel discuss her parents or what had happened to them. "She knew they were in heaven, so she knew they were just fine," said Davis later.

• • •

Back in Greenwich, Connecticut, Georgeann had taken on the responsibility of closing down the Lake Avenue house. Her first act was to give the staff a month to get things in order, along with their salaries in advance. Later she'd deal with the task of distributing and selling off the furnishings and putting the place on the market. She also decided to stay away from her parents' house, now so devoid of life. A month passed. One morning, as she was opening the mail, Georgeann was surprised to find a bill requesting payment for several servants who, it appeared, were still working at the house. Thinking there was a mistake—after all, she'd personally given them notice—Georgeann dashed over to Lake Avenue to find out just what was going on.

When she arrived, she was dumbfounded to find life going on more or less as usual. Locating the majordomo, Georgeann demanded an explanation. She was informed that because a guest had remained in the house after the funeral, a guest who required constant attention—meals, cleaning, the full range of services—the staff had just assumed that the Skakel family wanted them to remain on duty.

Just who *was* this guest? Georgeann demanded, her voice and blood pressure rising. At that moment, she turned to see the mystery tenant bounding down the staircase, offering her a big smile and a hearty hello.

"What the hell are *you* doing here?" sputtered Georgeann.

"I came to the funeral and I decided to stay because it was more convenient than a hotel," was the response of her sister Ethel's brother-in-law Ted Kennedy.

Georgeann raced home and told Johnny Dowdle what had just happened. "That cheap son of a bitch!" he shouted. Ted moved out.

Dissension also developed between Georgeann and Ethel over the division of the priceless furnishings, antiques, first editions, and art that their mother had collected.

Ethel and Bobby were still living with their four children in a rented townhouse in Georgetown, but were making plans to buy a larger house, and Ethel wanted some of her mother's better pieces to furnish the new place when the time came. But Georgeann felt she had precedence: she had acted as surrogate mother for Ethel and the others when they were growing up, and she had taken on the responsibility of dealing with various aspects of her parents' estate after their deaths. Georgeann stood firm, and Ethel got only a few pieces.

"Against everybody's wishes," Little Georgeann acknowledged later, "my mother got a lot if it—the furniture, paintings, mirrors, books. The sisters and brothers were a little pissed off because the things weren't equally distributed."

Surprisingly, none of the children wanted the remarkable and magical house where they had grown up. "It would have been like living in a hotel," said Jim Skakel. An anachronism by the mid-fifties, the Lake Avenue estate remained vacant for some five years, until it was finally sold for a mere $350,000. By the nineties, the asking price was $25 million.

Meanwhile, because the Skakels were killed together, the estate tax bill was enormous. The family, feeling they were being treated unfairly by the Internal Revenue Service, which pushed hard for payment, now had to come up with millions of dollars in cash or face legal action and huge penalties. "They were in a cash bind because they spent everything they made," said Tom Hayes later. In order to pay the IRS, the family had to dissolve Great Lakes' Canadian operation, headed by George Terrien. Georgeann also came through with an infusion of cash by using money from her trust fund to buy a hefty chunk of her deceased parents' Great Lakes Carbon stock. As a result, she became the company's single largest stockholder, which would cause untold problems and great conflict within the family that would reverberate into the next generation.

Since Ethel hid nothing from Bobby, the Kennedys were well aware of the Skakels' money bind, and Bobby saw an opportunity to pick up some bargains. The Kennedys were specifically interested in the Palos Verdes property, the promised land to which George and Big Ann were bound when their plane went down. Assigned to make the deal was Jean Kennedy's husband, Steve Smith, the tough and shrewd grandson of an Irish immigrant.

"Bobby made an effort through Steve Smith to buy the whole real-estate division for the Kennedy family," John McCooey said. "Steve could smell an opportunity and thought he had a chance to do some cherry picking. But it didn't come to pass because the Skakels saw that if something was worth a dollar, the Kennedys wanted to pay a dime."

PART VII

Chief Counsel's Wife

50 ✻ Hickory Hill

NEAR THE END of the Eisenhower era and the beginning of Camelot, Bobby reigned as the nation's ace rackets-buster. Ethel had three more babies in three years, and the Kennedys finally got a home of their own. For Ethel, it was the happiest of times.

Since being named to the high-profile post of chief counsel of the Senate Permanent Subcommittee on Investigations, popularly known as the Senate Rackets Committee, Bobby, now in his early thirties, had quickly gained national prominence. His boyish face was featured regularly on the nation's front pages and on the evening newscasts. The runt of the Kennedy litter finally had his own spotlight, squaring off in the hearing rooms of the U.S. Capitol with thugs, mobsters, and corrupt union bosses.

Ethel too was beginning to garner media attention, a reflection of Bobby's growing fame. While he appeared on page one, she was starting to show up regularly on the society and women's pages. Reporters could hardly miss her: the bouncy little brunette rushing into the Senate hearing room each morning with a cute friend or an attractive Kennedy in-law.

"I like to see Bobby in action," Ethel told a reporter. "I wouldn't think of missing a session."

Later, when her brother-in-law had become President, Jack heaped praise on Ethel for appearing at those hearings regularly and showing her loyalty. "Every day for nearly two years Ethel sat watching Bobby," Kennedy declared. "She even looked at me once in a while. [Jack had been one of the twenty-six Senators on the committee.] With that loyalty, I decided she was my kind of sister-in-law." Ethel had already started proving herself, as one Skakel put it, "more Kennedy than thou."

Dulled by years of Mamie Eisenhower, the press corps found in Ethel a whole new kind of Washington wife: cute, trendy, full of pep. With a house full of kids and pets, and married to one of those handsome, rich Kennedy boys, Ethel possessed all of the ingredients necessary to make for rattling good newspaper and magazine copy. Many of the women reporters covering the Washington scene found Ethel more natural than her haughty sister-in-law Jackie, and they gave her more upbeat, less critical coverage.

The image the press presented was that of the wholesome, fifties, TV-sitcom housewife and mother: Donna Reed Goes to Washington.

"I just can't understand why anybody would want to write about me," Ethel said.

But privately she savored every moment of the limelight. "She told me she was tired of being overshadowed by Jackie all the time," noted one of her pals. "Ethel clipped every story ever written about her. The woman had an ego."

While she feared speaking publicly, worried she'd make a gaffe that would anger Bobby, Ethel would sometimes throw a bone to the newshounds. After Bobby's chief adversary Jimmy Hoffa was arrested, a pinch Bobby had orchestrated, Ethel told reporters it was one of the most thrilling moments of her life. "I'd never been to an arraignment," she gushed. "It was very exciting!" But her appearance had infuriated Hoffa's attorney, Edward Bennett Williams, who, upon seeing Ethel at the courthouse, brushed passed her, mumbling, "Why aren't you home with the kids?" (For years, Ethel would have it in for Williams, going so far as to try to have him fired as Georgetown University's counsel before they eventually made peace.)

Unbeknownst to most of the other spectators and press, Ethel spent much of her time at Bobby's hearings trying to overhear what others were saying about him. She'd then give him a summary of the critiques.

During the committee's two-hour lunches, Ethel usually went home and oversaw lunch with the children—a cook made it, a maid served it, and afterward two nursemaids put the little ones down for their naps. With everything under control at home, Ethel drove back to the Hill for the remainder of the day's hearing.

At night Ethel had the help prepare two dinners, one that she would have with the children and the second for her and Bobby, who rarely got home before ten. After they had a drink or two, the cook prepared Bobby's favorite meal, a medium steak, and chocolate ice cream with chocolate sauce for dessert, which they'd eat in the dining room under the big chandelier. Before going to sleep, Ethel and Bobby watched clips of the day's hearings on the eleven o'clock news and joked about the high pitch of his voice. Lights out was at midnight. Then they were up again before six for an early horseback ride before Ethel drove Bobby back to the Hill for another day of hearings.

By the time Bobby was pursuing Hoffa, the Kennedys had moved across the Potomac from their rented house in Georgetown to Hickory Hill, a small (by Lake Avenue standards) Civil War–era estate hidden from the road by huge trees and carefully trimmed ancient boxwoods in McLean, Virginia, a conservative Republican enclave much like Greenwich.

The most recent occupants of Hickory Hill had been Jack and Jackie, who'd gotten the place as a gift from Joe Kennedy. Jackie had adored Hickory Hill, which was only three miles from Merrywood, her girlhood home. But after she lost a daughter during an emergency cesarean in the late summer of 1956, she couldn't bear to live there anymore. Once she recovered from the trauma, she and Jack, who'd recently lost his bid for the Vice Presidential nomination in the 1956 race, moved back to Georgetown, where Caroline and John Jr. would be born.

After Jack and Jackie vacated Hickory Hill, Joe Kennedy gave the estate to Bobby and Ethel, who needed the space for their mushrooming family. The two-and-a-half-story, white brick Georgian house and the six acres of gently rolling countryside it sat on were perfect for them. There was plenty of room for the kids and pets to romp, and for Ethel to throw boisterous parties—shades of Lake Avenue.

Around the same time Ethel and Bobby took over Hickory Hill, a house came up for sale next to Joe Kennedy's place in Hyannis Port. The old man bought it and gave it as a gift to Bobby and Ethel. They were first of the new generation of Kennedys to have their own home there, marking the start of what came to be known as the "Kennedy Compound." Ethel was overjoyed to have a home right next door to her in-laws, whom she worshiped. "It makes me feel like a real daughter now," she told a friend.

Meanwhile, her own family continued to grow. Ethel had her fifth child, Mary Courtney, on September 9, named after Ethel's college chum Courtney Murphy Benoist. Conducting hearings on the West Coast, Bobby came home for the birth but quickly departed. Ethel, at twenty-eight, was now the mother of three boys and two girls, the oldest going on six. Over the next three years, she'd have two more children, Michael LeMoyne, in 1958, and Mary Kerry, in 1959, seven in her first nine years of marriage.

Besides the children, the menagerie at Hickory Hill, which would multiply and grow more exotic over the years, initially included: a two-hundred-pound Saint Bernard named Meegan, an "all-American poodle" of mixed breed named Ruffie, and two horses for Ethel, Shillelagh and Magic Pulse. Ethel's stable also included a pony named Toby, who would pull the children in an old wooden-wheeled cart, and two boxers, Angus and Shell, and their six puppies, who belonged to the Kennedys' horse groom. Soon there'd be a two-year-old sea lion named Sandy who ate ten pounds of fish a day, lived in the swimming pool, and escaped one day just before Christmas. "It's like the National Zoo around here sometimes," said Dee Dunworth, Ethel's secretary at the time.

Over the next decade, Hickory Hill, with Bobby and Ethel in residence, would become the most famous Washington address next to the White House. Hickory Hill would be to the nation's capital what Lake Avenue was to Greenwich, a place of high jinks and a source of gossip. The similarity between the two households was uncanny, if not surprising.

Despite all of the hired help, Hickory Hill was usually a mess, and would get progressively worse over the years. Ethel thought one of the funniest moments at the Senate hearings was when a tough Portland nightclub owner swore to Bobby that his joint was "as clean as your home." Ethel, who took the word *clean* literally, remarked guilelessly, "If he could have seen what the kids had done to the house that morning, he wouldn't have thought the comparison was so good."

Insiders who knew Ethel intimately choked back laughter when the Home Fashion League of Washington, a group interested in promoting good taste and design, chose her as its Outstanding Homemaker of the Year for 1958. Ethel, who got a silver bowl, was praised at a luncheon by the league's president for her ability to maintain a "functional, smooth-operating home." At the time, Ethel didn't even know where the butter was kept in the kitchen. But in her best self-effacing manner, she graciously accepted the honor:

"It's the first time I ever received an award. I'm so excited," she told the gathering. "When my husband left me this morning he said, 'They haven't seen the house yet so you'd better get that award before they do!' He told me to hustle over before you changed your minds."

Typical of the ambience at Hickory Hill was the zaniness that occurred late one spring afternoon in 1957 when Ethel played hostess to three hundred guests from the Tenth District Women's Democratic Club of Virginia. Just before the women arrived, water began seeping from a third-floor bathroom to the second floor. Ethel rushed upstairs and found that one of the children had turned on all of the taps. Ethel returned downstairs just in time to find four-year-old Joe pouring a soda on the white damask sofa in the drawing room. During the party one of the Kennedys' big Saint Bernards roamed—and urinated—freely among the guests. At eight, when everyone was leaving, five-year-old Kathleen decided to troop off the grounds and down Chain Bridge Road with her little brothers, Bobby and Joe, behind her. One of the departing guests spotted the little band and ushered them home.

As George Terrien noted, "Three weeks after Ethel moved in, Hickory Hill was like Lake Avenue all over again, out of control, and it would stay that way. In every way imaginable, Ethel would run her place just the way Big Ann did. No discipline, no controls. It was another Skakel household all over again."

51 ✻ *An Embarrassment for Bobby*

AS POINT MAN for the Rackets Committee, one of Bobby's prime targets was the International Brotherhood of Teamsters. Bobby had been told by a friend, Clark Mollenhoff, Washington editor of the *Des Moines Register,* that his own investigations had suggested a potpourri of illegal activities: embezzlement, intimidation, and mob infiltration within the union. On Mollenhoff's advice, in part, Bobby began a systematic probe of the union's leadership: Jimmy Hoffa and Dave Beck, the international's arrogant, melodramatic president.

A month after the televised hearings—during which Beck and his son, Dave Beck, Jr., repeatedly invoked the Fifth Amendment under a barrage of tough questions from Bobby—a bizarre event took place in Greenwich. Bobby had always thought of his in-laws as a potential source of embarrassment. But this particular incident also raised serious questions among the Kennedys about Ethel's prudence and common sense. It seemed that every time she felt she'd proven herself to the Kennedys something would happen, usually having to do with her own flesh and blood, that would place her back at square one.

The incident in question occurred during one of the many wild parties thrown at the sprawling Greenwich estate of Ethel's brother George and his beautiful, alcoholic wife, Pat, described as "the golden couple, fun-loving, wild, anything for a laugh." On one occasion, a guest crippled from the waist down by polio and confined to a wheelchair was pushed into the Skakels' pool. Another time, at a party for an important Great Lakes client, a soused Pat Skakel tore an emerald and diamond necklace worth thousands of dollars from around her neck and threw it in the pool, where it disappeared.

Knowing Bobby's feelings, Ethel had distanced herself from the family's shenanigans. But on a Saturday evening in mid-August 1957 she threw caution to the wind and became an active participant in one of George and Pat's nutty party stunts. Wary, Bobby had shrewdly stayed away that night, claiming business appointments in Washington.

It began when Clara Gildemeister, the society editor of the *Stamford* (Connecticut) *Advocate*, telephoned the Skakel house to check reports that a big soirée was scheduled. Pat Skakel confirmed some of the details: the party was being given in honor of Ethel, who was three months pregnant, and that Bobby would be there, too.

Then she added the kicker: "Dave Beck is coming."

What a great story, thought Gildemeister. The good guy and the bad guy at the same party. Excited by the scoop, Gildemeister arranged to have a freelance photographer attend. That evening, he took pictures of the guests. But when he asked to photograph Dave Beck, he was told that the Teamster honcho was not feeling well and had left early. However, he was invited to take a picture of Dave Beck, Jr., and his wife. Also in the photo were George and Pat Skakel, their little girl, Kick—and Ethel.

Back at the paper someone checked and learned that the younger Beck wasn't married. Something was fishy. The picture was held, but the story ran on Monday morning and was picked up by the Associated Press, which reported, "Dave Beck, Sr., and Dave Beck, Jr., labor leaders under fire of the Senate labor rackets committee, were present at a party which also was attended by Robert F. Kennedy, chief counsel for the rackets committee, it was confirmed here today." The story also quoted Dave Beck, Jr., as saying of Bobby, "Although our policies differ, socially we get along famously."

When other reporters began making inquiries, Pat Skakel fessed up. "It was all a gag," she reluctantly admitted. "All I can do is apologize. It was a prank—just a prank. All of my two hundred guests were in on it and went along with it. Everyone at the party knew it was a gag, except apparently the photographer. I'm sorry for any inconvenience the gag caused." She disclosed that the couple in the picture were actually Skakel friends Paddy and Peggy Loughran, daughter of the legendary New Jersey Democratic boss and one-time Jersey City Mayor, Frank Hague. Mary Begley, who was at the party, acknowledged years later that the Skakels pulled the stunt specifically to embarrass Bobby. "Until that party I had never thought that Ethel was that goofy to go along with something like that," Begley added. "Ethel, George, and Pat thought it was amusing, but Bobby was incensed." So was the *Stamford Advocate*. Embarrassed and furious, the paper's managing editor, E. R. McCullough, ran a page one apology to the Becks.

Ethel had gone along merrily with the prank. "It was crazy," she said in dismissing the incident.

"Ethel was acting under Bobby's instructions when she told the reporter that the stunt was a dumb thing to do," said George Terrien years later. "But privately Ethel thought it was great fun. Bobby was furious and told Ethel, 'If those bums you call your family ever do anything again like this to embarrass me or my family you're going to be in real deep shit. You're in deep shit anyway.' "

In the end, though, it would be the Kennedys—not the Skakels—who would do themselves in with their own highly publicized scandals.

52 ✻ *A Tangled Web*

ETHEL AND GEORGEANN were both pregnant in 1957, Ethel with her sixth and Georgeann with her fifth. Georgeann's husband used to quip that Ethel would grab the brass ring in the baby race between the two sisters because Bobby "wants to show his family he has the biggest balls."

By the fall of 1957, Georgeann was the mother of three daughters: Little Georgeann; the institutionalized Alexandra; Ann; and a son, John, who was born with the foot deformity.

Georgeann, who'd gotten pregnant three months ahead of Ethel, thankfully had a smooth time and an easy delivery. On Friday, November 8, she gave birth at Greenwich Hospital to a healthy boy, whom she and her husband named Jimmy after her brother.

Elated about having another son, Johnny Dowdle, a vice president at Great Lakes Carbon and a special assistant to George Skakel, Jr., went on a nonstop, three-day bender, accompanied by his brother-in-law, Rushton Skakel. "John [Dowdle] was an alcoholic, but he hadn't had a drink in a long time," Rushton Skakel said later. "I went to wild parties with him Friday, Saturday, and Sunday. In my mind, it didn't translate into a problem."

That Sunday night, Dowdle, who was wan and had always seemed somewhat sickly, returned exhausted to

Sursum Corda. He spent some time with seven-year-old Little Georgeann and then father and daughter napped together. When they awoke, the child sensed that her father wasn't feeling well. He told her he had a slight pain in his chest. He asked her to go to her room so he could rest.

After a fitful sleep, the child awakened before dawn, padded down the hall to the bathroom, opened the door, and found her father lying on the floor in his underwear.

"I thought that Daddy was playing a game," she said years later. "But in fact he wasn't breathing."

At thirty-nine, John Dowdle had died of what the family said was a massive heart attack.

The house was soon filled with shocked Skakel friends and relatives. Little Georgeann, not told what had happened to her father, was sent off to spend a week with close family friends, while Rushton Skakel was given the unenviable task of telling Georgeann that her husband and the father of her newborn was dead.

On the day of the pontifical Mass and funeral, all of the family was there, including Ethel and Bobby. Jim Skakel and Pat Skakel Cuffe, who'd flown in from Ireland, brought Little Georgeann home, telling her, as she recalled years later, " 'Your daddy's in heaven.' And that was that."

Dowdle's sudden death floored the Skakels. But the widow's impetuous decision a few months later to marry Bobby's chum George Terrien, whom most of them had come to abhor, left the family shocked and fragmented. As an outsider, Terrien was viewed by the suspicious Skakels, especially Ethel, as an opportunist who had insinuated himself into the family's inner circle, securing a cushy job for himself with Great Lakes Carbon.

"That bastard is out to marry a rich girl, it doesn't matter who," Ethel told Martin McKneally. "He'll take advantage of Georgeann. It's pathetic." Ethel also feared that Georgeann, who'd essentially been on the wagon since she had her first child seven years earlier, would start drinking again if she married Terrien, a heavy drinker himself.

Despite his growing dislike for Terrien, Bobby ordered Ethel to stay out of it. She was now a Kennedy, not a Skakel.

If Ethel and her siblings could have had a say as to whom Georgeann married, they would have chosen Martin McKneally. Despite his true sexual preference, McKneally had quietly worshiped Georgeann for years.

"Despite what they have said over the years, I think the Skakel boys knew all along that Martin was gay and accepted it," said Mary Begley. "But they were very fond of him and certainly preferred him to Terrien as a husband for their sister." McKneally acknowledged years later that had he been given half a chance he would have married Georgeann. "But Terrien stepped in there and took her away before any of us could say boo. He wanted her *money*. Had George Skakel, the father, been around, things might have been different."

The only member of the family who didn't seem to mind was Rushton. Just three months after John Dowdle's death, Georgeann confided to Rushton that she and Terrien were in love. "I said, 'Boom! Don't wait a year. Marry him now,' " Rushton remembers.

Despite the family's hostility, Terrien moved into Sursum Corda a day after Dowdle's death. Ethel, her siblings, and their friends were appalled.

"I was kicked out of my bedroom and George took over my bedroom and I was moved into the nursery," Little Georgeann recalled. She firmly believed that her mother had decided to marry Terrien as a form of escape. "Mother was a forty-one-year-old alcoholic with five kids who was scared to death and George was a known quantity," she said later. "But I don't think she was ever really in love with him. There were only two men she ever really loved—her father and my father."

In the period just before the wedding, the George Skakel, Jrs., the Begleys, and Claire and Tom O'Neal, who headed RKO General, flew to New Hampshire on a Great Lakes Carbon plane and held a summit meeting to discuss possible ways of stopping the wedding. But

Georgeann found out and flew into a rage, and at that point there was nothing anyone could do.

On October 4, 1958, a very disgruntled Skakel family and their friends gathered at St. Paul's Church in Glenville to witness Georgeann Skakel Dowdle become Mrs. George Terrien. "I certainly was well aware that Ethel and the rest of them didn't want me to marry Georgeann," said Terrien later, "but I told all of them to fuck off."

Terrien's brother served as best man and Little Georgeann and her sister Ann were their mother's attendants. But none of the other Skakels participated. Ethel and Bobby, along with the others, just sat in the church fuming. "Ethel was quite bitter," recalled her brother Jim. "She said, 'This is just revolting. How can this go on?' Ethel finally told Georgeann what she thought. I felt, 'Who the hell is Ethel to comment on why two people should get married?' My answer to Ethel was, 'It's none of your business.' " Privately, Jim believed the marriage was one of convenience, that Terrien wanted to marry a rich woman and Georgeann got to keep the Great Lakes perks by marrying Terrien, a company vice president and director. "All of that was important to her," he said.

After the ceremony, performed by Big Ann's close friend, Rev. James Fox, abbott of Our Lady of Gethsemane Abbey, the Trappist monastery in Kentucky, everyone returned to Sursum Corda for a small reception. "My God, George and Big Ann's wake three years earlier was a happier affair," said Fox.

While the gloomy party was underway downstairs, the newlyweds were upstairs in their bedroom arranging the pièce de résistance of their questionable union. At that moment no one in the family was aware that Terrien had insisted, and Georgeann had agreed, to have reciprocal wills drawn up. Terrien had asked Dick McAvoy, Great Lakes Carbon's corporate counsel, to prepare the papers quietly and bring them to Sursum Corda for signing immediately after they said their vows. The candles on the wedding cake were still warm as McAvoy witnessed the new Mrs. Terrien putting her signature on the paper authorizing that all of her fortune go to her husband, and only her husband, upon her death. Terrien signed a similar will, though he had virtually nothing to his name.

In years to come, Georgeann Skakel Dowdle Terrien's will would cause enormous dissension and would even lead to violence within the family.

The day after the wedding the Terriens left for a honeymoon in Spain. When they returned, said Little Georgeann, "Mother suddenly looked around and said, 'What the hell did I do?' And she dove into the bottle."

Ten months later Terrien formally adopted Little Georgeann and her brothers and sisters. On August 22, 1959, Georgeann gave birth to her sixth and last child, a daughter, who was named after Terrien's mother, Des Neiges.

A few weeks later, on September 8, Ethel had her seventh child, a daughter, whom the Kennedys named Kerry.

At Sursum Corda, George and Georgeann Terrien drank constantly. In her sober moments, Georgeann often warned her children never to get in a car with a Skakel—or their adoptive father—at the wheel for fear that someone would get killed because of their drinking. Her fear nearly became a reality shortly after Des Neiges was born. The mishap occurred in Vermont in a snowstorm with George Skakel, Jr., at the wheel. Because of her stepfather's irresponsibility, Little Georgeann was riding in the backseat. Terrien was seated between George and Pat Skakel in the front seat. All of them had been drinking when they slammed head-on into another car.

"We always had 'walkers' with us—a drink that you walk out of the house with," said Little Georgeann. "Everybody always had a drink in their hand and it was always in a glass and it was always in a car."

Little Georgeann remembered seeing the approaching headlights and hearing the crash. She came to in a lot of pain. She crawled out of the car and found her stepfather, her uncle, and her aunt bleeding profusely. "There wasn't much left of the face of the driver of the other car, but he was still alive," she said. "The ambulance came and they had all the plugs in George [Terrien] and I was very sure he was going to die and this wasn't very long after I found Daddy dead on the floor." Terrien spent almost two months recovering in a hospital; George and Pat each suffered broken noses.

When Bobby heard about the accident, he turned to Ethel and said, "Watch, they'll all kill themselves and then we won't have to worry about any of them anymore." Ethel remained silent.

53 * A Murder in the Bronx

ALTHOUGH THE NEAR fatal accident in Vermont did not become public, Ethel continued to fear that a scandal involving the Skakels would jeopardize her still-tenuous position in the Kennedy clan and cause irreparable damage to her marriage.

Avoiding such a situation became a priority by 1958 when Jack Kennedy, having won a resounding reelection to the Senate, quietly began planning for a 1960 Presidential run. Bobby, still chief counsel for the rackets committee, would be actively involved in Jack's campaign.

It was during this time that Ethel received horrific news from Rushton and Georgeann about the teenage son of their first cousin Betty Skakel Medaille, a poor relative whom Ethel had ignored over the years.

Unlike Ethel, Betty had faced incredible hardship. By the time she was eighteen, she had married "a good for nothing" named Alvin Zar and had had a baby. The Zars were subsequently divorced. At the start of World

War II, Betty met and married another man of little means, George Medaille. In search of work, they migrated to New York City, moving into a five-floor tenement on West 102nd Street. George Medaille was often unemployed, and Betty was constantly pregnant—she would have nine children in all.

During those difficult years, she often found herself skimming the society pages and the gossip columns for items about her millionaire relatives living a short train ride and a world away in Greenwich. Virtually destitute, she eventually contacted her uncle George, Ethel's father, who generously offered her financial help, sending his niece a monthly check for $125. When George Skakel died, her cousins Rushton and Georgeann made certain the checks continued to be sent. Only Ethel remained aloof.

"She had nothing in common with me," said Medaille years later. "I was a poor relation—dirt poor—and poor relations can be embarrassing."

On February 11, 1958, Betty Skakel Medaille went to her seventy-five-dollar-a-week job as a charge-plate puncher in a downtown credit agency. Her husband, George, was working the four-to-midnight shift as a desk clerk at the Manger-Vanderbilt Hotel at Thirty-fourth and Park, where his take-home pay was sixty-eight dollars a week. Eight of their nine children, ranging in age from two to eighteen, were at home: an eighty-dollar-a-month, six-room, first-floor flat in the bleak Highbridge Housing Project in the Bronx.

While Betty Medaille was at her dreary job dutifully cranking out charge plates for less than two dollars an hour, Ethel was at Hickory Hill in the ninth month of her sixth pregnancy. A staff of servants and a coterie of friends were catering to her every need as she waited to go to Georgetown University Hospital, where a private suite and private nurses were ready for her arrival. The only similarity in the otherwise disparate lives of first cousins Betty Skakel Medaille and Ethel Skakel Kennedy was the fact that both were perpetually pregnant.

Before she left for work that February afternoon,

Medaille did some chores around the apartment with the help of her son, a stocky, bespectacled, moon-faced fifteen-year-old, Francis Michael Medaille. A month earlier the teenager had been expelled from Cardinal Hayes High School in Manhattan for causing trouble and failing three classes. Twice prior to being expelled, he had run away from home. Despite his poor behavior and grades, young Medaille was known as "the Professor" among friends and acquaintances. He was highly intelligent, articulate, and an avid reader—among the meager possessions in his family's apartment was a bookcase filled with Shakespeare, Homer, and Dickens. But a sudden change had come over the boy in the past year or so, evidenced by his running away, his failing grades, and his destructive acts at school. Once his mother came home from work, opened the refrigerator door, and found a dead shark on the shelf.

Thin, fragile, and worn, Betty Skakel Medaille went to work that February day anxious about her son and worried about leaving him alone. But the family couldn't make ends meet without her small weekly paycheck.

After his mother left the apartment, Mike Medaille wandered outside, where he encountered strawberry-blonde seven-year-old Kathleen Hegmann, a playmate of one of his sisters. She and her family, nine children in all, lived two floors above the Medailles.

Mike told Kathleen that there was a box on the roof of their building that he had to get and he offered her a lollipop and ten cents if she'd help him carry it down. They rode up together on the elevator to the fourteenth-floor roof, the last time Kathleen, a student at Sacred Heart Parochial School, was seen alive.

Late that afternoon, Kathleen Hegmann's twelve-year-old sister ran into the family's apartment. "Mother," she cried, "there's a little girl on the ledge and I think it's Kathy."

Mrs. Hegmann ran to the living room window and her husband went to the one in the kitchen. "My husband screamed, 'My God, it is Kathy!' We both ran downstairs but it was too late." Their little girl's broken body lay on a stone canopy a few feet from the kitchen window and just above the building's entrance.

As the hysterical Hegmanns and their shocked neighbors gathered outside, Mike Medaille walked up to Det. John Murphy at a nearby precinct house and coolly told him, "I just pushed a girl off the roof."

In a signed confession, the boy said, "I grabbed her by the throat and I choked her. I choked her and I knocked her down—choked her again and picked her up. I carried her to the edge and pushed her off."

Not long after, Deputy Inspector John Halk ordered the teenager to reconstruct the crime for detectives. "He didn't even flinch when we walked up to where the corpse was still lying. I've never seen anything like it before."

The Medailles, notified of what had happened, arrived home in time to see their son being taken away in handcuffs.

Betty Medaille didn't know where to turn. But as soon as the story appeared in the papers the next day, she got a telephone call from Rushton Skakel. "He asked me how he could help. He asked me what he could do. He said he was there for me. After that Rushton went out of his way to be helpful and kind."

Rushton Skakel recalled later, "My heart went out to Betty and so did Georgeann's."

Cynical New Yorkers were shocked by the cold brutality of the murder, which played on the front pages for days. Headlines screamed: MOTHER'S AGONY: "WHAT SHOULD I HAVE DONE?"; ON THE ROOF: A BOY OF WILD COMPULSION; PSYCHIATRIST LOOKS AT SCHOOL TERROR; SHE WAS JUST TOO YOUNG TO KNOW OF EVIL.

Overnight the ghastly crime became a national story, appearing in the weekly newsmagazines and in papers around the country. "This case got an appalling amount of publicity," said Betty Medaille years later. "I was literally shocked into stillness. I couldn't breathe. I couldn't hear. I couldn't see. It was just dreadful. *Dreadful.*" But none of the papers ever connected Medaille to the Kennedys or the Skakels.

Georgeann Dowdle, at Sursum Corda planning for

her marriage to George Terrien, read the terrible news and offered comfort and aid to her cousin. "Georgeann said, 'Why don't you come and spend some time with me,' and I did. This was an extraordinarily kind invitation because our contact up until that point had been casual. Not everyone would stick their neck out at a time like that," Betty said.

Georgeann and Rushton alerted other members of the Skakel family to their cousin's plight, and they responded by expressing concern and willingness to help her in any way possible. "They all asked what they could do," said Betty Medaille. All of them wanted to help. Except for Ethel.

"I was present when Georgeann called Ethel to tell her what Betty's son had done," said George Terrien. "Georgeann thought that Ethel, through the Kennedys, might be able to get some expert help for the kid, a psychiatrist, a lawyer, whatever. But Ethel was beside herself. The first thing she said was, 'I have to let Bobby know. We have to keep this quiet. My God, Jack'll have a fit!' "

Meanwhile, Mike Medaille was committed to Bellevue Hospital for a psychiatric evaluation. "If it is determined that the boy had capacity and knew the nature of the crime," declared Magistrate J. Randall Creel, "he will burn in the electric chair."

Ironically, the same day that follow-up stories about Medaille's indictment on first-degree murder charges were running in the papers, a wire service photo also was published of a jubilantly smiling Ethel lying in a hospital bed holding her newborn son, eight-pound Michael LeMoyne Kennedy, in her right arm as a proud Bobby patted the baby on his tummy. The caption under the picture read: HERE'S ANOTHER KENNEDY.

The baby's baptism, conducted by Archbishop Amleto Cicognani, was held in the chapel of the apostolic delegation in Washington. Georgeann, in one of her few visits to Hickory Hill, attended as the baby's godmother, with Ted Kennedy as the acting godfather. Ethel and Bobby invited *Life* magazine to photograph the event for an article called "A Debut into a Burgeoning Family: The Clan Takes in Bob Kennedy's Son." Jack, whose daughter Caroline was four months old, was quoted as saying, "Mother and Father seemed to get so much happiness out of us that all of us want a big family, too. Bob and Ethel will get there first, but all of us will be close behind."

The upbeat piece showed the Bob Kennedys seated on a couch at Hickory Hill, a glowing Ethel holding Michael in a blanket on her lap, Bobby gazing adoringly at her, surrounded by their other five children and the Saint Bernard named Meegan. The layout appeared in *Life*'s April 24 issue, which appeared on newsstands a week after the court-appointed psychiatrists determined that Mike Medaille was insane when he killed Kathleen Hegmann. He was committed to the Matteawan State Hospital in Beacon, New York.

After her son was incarcerated, Betty Skakel Medaille learned from Georgeann that Ethel wanted the scandal kept under wraps.

Said Medaille: "Ethel was aware of Michael's situation and she was worried it might affect Bobby and Jack politically. Her attitude was that Bobby didn't need any of this poor white trash scandal attached to his family, that it would cause political problems.

"But Georgeann felt that Ethel was out of line. Georgeann thought that was the most ridiculous thing she ever heard, the idea that the son of an Irish bootlegger could be sullied by anything like an insane murder."

When Betty Medaille visited her son at Matteawan, she'd often stop in Greenwich to see Georgeann, Rushton, and Ethel's sister Ann, with whom she also became friendly. But Ethel never once spoke to Medaille.

A year after Mike's incarceration, the Medailles moved to Garden Grove, California, where their lives stabilized. There, she helped care for George Skakel's aging, spinster sister Margaret—Ethel's and Betty's aunt.

At twenty-one, Mike Medaille was released from Matteawan. "He became a child of the sixties and seventies," said his mother later. "He demonstrated and burned draft cards." She saw him for a brief time after he was released and once again in the early 1980s. In 1993, she did not know whether her son, going on fifty, was alive or dead.

As Ethel had hoped, the press never connected the Medaille case to either the Skakels or the Kennedys. Her efforts to keep everyone quiet had been successful.

Years later, another murder, involving another young female victim, this time in Greenwich, would envelop the Skakel family once again. This time the finger of suspicion would point at one of Rushton's sons, and Ethel would again fear scandal.

54 * *Winning the Big One*

FROM DECEMBER OF 1958 through the early spring of 1959, Ethel, pregnant with number seven, lived in fear that her children might become targets of revenge from the men Bobby was vigorously pursuing. At one point, he had received threats that acid would be thrown in his children's eyes if he didn't lay off. The FBI was notified and security tightened around Hickory Hill.

Despite the threat, feisty Ethel and her little band sneered at the bad guys. Sometimes, with the kids in the car, she'd lead a cheer against Bobby's enemies.

At a stoplight near Jimmy Hoffa's Washington headquarters, Ethel would ask, "What's up there?" and four pint-size Kennedys would respond, "The Teamsters' Union."

"And what do they do there?" Ethel would chant.

"Work overtime to keep Jimmy Hoffa out of jail," the kids replied.

"And?" prodded Ethel.

"Which is where he belongs!" they all squealed.

Like her father, who sometimes used the Skakel children in business as a public relations gimmick, Ethel was now making her kids part of their father's act.

On Friday, September 11, 1959, three days after Ethel gave birth to Kerry, Bobby resigned as chief counsel of the Senate Rackets Committee, a day after the panel concluded its three-year inquiry. The committee's purpose, he asserted, "has been fruitfully realized" with the passage of a labor reform bill and exposure of union corruption and racketeering. Bobby, whose two years of work on the committee had propelled him into the public consciousness, was immediately offered a hefty advance from Harper and Brothers to write a book about his work. Lost in the hoopla surrounding the publication of *The Enemy Within* the following year, though, was a $150,000 lawsuit filed by a Catholic missionary alleging that Bobby had stolen the title from a book the Reverend Raymond de Jaeeger had written eight years earlier about the rise of communism in China.

On his own, Bobby could now focus his aggressiveness, energy, and drive on his brother's bid for the Presidency.

On January 2, 1960, Senator Jack Kennedy, forty-two, formally threw his hat into the Presidential ring in front of several hundred cheering supporters in the Senate Caucus Room. He was one of the youngest and best-looking Presidential hopefuls in the country's history, and one of the few Catholics ever to seek the job.

As in past races, the Kennedy women worked long and hard. Ethel, still trying to prove herself, was at the front of the pack. She had become a first-rate campaigner, making appearances and giving pep talks for Jack wherever Bobby asked her to go. In Texas, campaigning with Eunice and Lady Bird Johnson, Ethel made appearances in thirteen hot and dusty towns—from Amarillo to Waco, and Lady Bird was duly impressed. The only friction between the two women occurred when Ethel stubbornly refused to wear a ten-gallon hat because she felt it made her look silly. For now Ethel and Lady Bird were a mutual admiration society.

"Before the bunting comes down and 'The Yellow Rose of Texas' fades away, I want to tell you how delightful it was to share the Texas campaign trail with you," Lady Bird wrote to Ethel. "Your sense of humor made it all the more pleasant. Tell 'Bobby who sent me' that you left Texas full of admirers and anytime he wants to do something about Mr. Hoffa, you are entitled to make the announcement."

Ethel responded enthusiastically, noting that she had been treated like royalty in Texas; she joked that it was difficult returning to the compound. Whatever would happen in November, she felt the Texas campaign had been unforgettable and that she would miss Ladybird's insight and knowledge of politics.

Because of Ethel's enthusiasm, spunk, and high spirits, she became the darling of the press corps, with news photographers dubbing her "Miss Perpetual Animation."

Jack cited Ethel's hard work with a gift—a map of the United States dotted in red to show the many places she made stops for him.

Back at Hickory Hill, Ethel's staff—a governess, a secretary, a housekeeper, a gardener, and several maids—cared for the household and the children while the mistress of the house was stumping for her brother-in-law.

While Ethel crisscrossed the country beating the drums for Jack, the Skakels as usual threw their support behind the Republican candidate, Richard Nixon. During Jack's earlier Congressional campaigns, he did receive some financial support from Ethel's father, but that was only after Joe Kennedy himself was forced to come to George Skakel hat in hand. To the Skakels, that alone made the contribution worthwhile.

Ethel took her family's decision to remain staunchly Republican in 1960 as a personal slap in the face and a vote of no confidence for her husband and the father of her children. The Skakels' refusal to cross party lines for Jack was a slight that she would never forget.

Years later, Jim Skakel summed up the family's views on the political differences between the two families:

"Bobby was brought up in one party and we were brought up in another. Our values were different," he explained. "We felt the tradition of the Democratic Party was to soak the rich and that the rich were the cause of all the problems." Jim said his sister never tried to coerce the family. "If she had called me up and said, 'Jim, vote for Jack,' I would have told her she had the wrong number. She knew her conversation wouldn't carry any weight with us."

On election day 1960, Jack Kennedy, who cast his ballot in Boston, went to sleep at four A.M. An hour and a half later, with Bobby monitoring the returns, Jack took Michigan, which put him over the top. The next morning President Eisenhower sent President-elect John Fitzgerald Kennedy a congratulatory telegram and a sullen Richard Nixon conceded defeat.

Immediately after the election, Jack offered Bobby the Cabinet post of Attorney General of the United States. If it hadn't been for Bobby's hard work, Jack felt, he never would have won. He felt his brother deserved a payback. But Bobby, still strategizing, feared that accepting the job would be publicly viewed as blatant nepotism, causing a scandal before Jack even had a chance to move into the Oval Office. "If you announce me as Attorney General, they'll kick our balls off," Bobby told Jack, who replied, "You hold on to your balls and I'll make the announcement." Deep down, Bobby disliked the idea of being in his brother's shadow again, rather than on his own. During one family discussion, Eunice, knowing her brother's feelings, jokingly brought up Jack's offer, saying that Bobby "can throw all the people Dad doesn't like into jail. They'll have to build more jails."

It wasn't until the morning of December 14, when Jack told Bobby he needed him "completely and totally and absolutely,'' that Bobby relented. ''Let's grab our balls and go,'' Jack said, and the nomination of Bobby was announced moments later to reporters outside Jack's Georgetown house. Later, Bobby said the appointment showed that Jack had ''the guts of a burglar'' for giving a family member a Cabinet post.

On the same day that Bobby was named Attorney General, the nation's highest law enforcement officer, Ethel was being fined forty dollars in absentia by an Arlington County, Virginia, court judge for going seventy in a forty-mile-an-hour stretch of the dangerous George Washington Memorial Parkway. Ethel also was charged with not having a Virginia permit. It was typical Skakel behavior. Ethel's lawyer appeared in court and paid the fine because his client was already basking in the sun at the Kennedys' Palm Beach home, still celebrating Jack's victory and nurturing the tan she kept year-round. ''I am just delighted,'' she said of Bobby's appointment.

PART VIII

Attorney General's Wife

55 ✱ *A Sexy Inauguration*

ON JANUARY 13, 1961, with Ethel and Jean Kennedy Smith watching attentively, Bobby appeared before the Senate Judiciary Committee. It was expected that the Republicans on the panel would give the Attorney General–designate a tough time over the nepotism issue. But the only criticism came from Everett Dirksen, the floor leader, and Nebraska's Roman Hruska, both of whom questioned Bobby's relatively brief legal experience. Hruska wanted Bobby to explain how effective he thought he could be since he had never tried a suit, chosen a jury, written a trial brief, or negotiated a settlement.

"I can't make up for the fact that I have only had ten years out from school," Bobby stated. "But I think that what I have done or what experience I have had in those ten years will be of tremendous help and make a tremendous difference in this new position."

Questions also were raised about Bobby's finances and whether any of his holdings would conflict with his job. He disclosed that he had sold his stock to conform with the conflict-of-interest laws. Now, he said, he owned only government and municipal bonds and cash. He also acknowledged receiving about a hundred thousand dollars annually after taxes as a beneficiary of two major irrevocable trusts set up in 1926 and 1936 for him and each of his brothers and sisters by Joe and Rose Kennedy.

Bobby's answers seemed to satisfy everyone. After just two hours of gentle probing and lots of praise of his character and ability, all fourteen committee members voted to approve the nomination.

At thirty-five, Bobby became the third youngest Attorney General in history and the only one whose brother was also President.

A week later at a luncheon Jack Kennedy said jokingly, "I don't see anything wrong with getting Bobby a little legal experience as Attorney General before he goes out to practice law."

After the confirmation hearing, Ethel went in search of a "historic old desk" for her husband's new office. She eventually found a six-foot-square mahogany desk used by Amos T. Ackerman, the first Attorney General to head the Justice Department when it was created in 1870.

Inauguration Day, January 20, 1961, was bitterly cold in the nation's capital. More than six inches of snow had blanketed the city the night before, delaying by two hours the star-studded Democratic fund-raising party arranged by Frank Sinatra and Peter Lawford. Because of the storm, Ethel had stayed with Kennedy family members in Georgetown to avoid being snowed in at Hickory Hill. Ethel was almost as anxious as Jack that morning; her inaugural dress and beaded gowns for the five inaugural balls were in the trunk of her dressmaker's car, which was buried under a mound of snow. Luckily no water had seeped in and the wardrobe was delivered in pristine condition.

Despite the fact that the Skakels were dyed-in-the-wool Republicans, none of them was able to resist a good party, even if it was a Democratic bash. Since Jack's inauguration promised to be a humdinger, Ethel's siblings put aside their political differences and across-the-board animus toward the Kennedys and blithely accepted invitations to attend all of the inaugural events. One gossip columnist reported that "the pretty wife of Robert Kennedy . . . wangled the invitations. But she issued a warning. None of the gals must wear Nixon earrings." Georgeann, making one of her rare ventures out of Sursum Corda, came to Washington by train, fearful of flying. Also down for the week were Ann and John McCooey; George Jr. and Pat Skakel showed up, as well as Ethel's brothers Jim and Rushton, with their wives.

But Bobby, who despised them all, wouldn't allow the Skakels to stay at Hickory Hill, so Ethel had to make other arrangements.

The George Skakel, Jrs., whom Bobby resented the most—he had never forgotten the Dave Beck party incident in Greenwich—stayed with Sarah and Spencer Davis in the tony Spring Valley section of Washington. "Ethel adored George, but it was hard for her because he wasn't Bobby's cup of tea," Davis said later. "They didn't get along at all, so they stayed with me. Whenever George came to town Ethel would see him, but on her own, without Bobby."

At the last minute George decided to skip the inauguration swearing-in ceremony altogether.

"He told me afterward that he gave his ticket to some black man who he ran into on the street," said Bettan Olwaeus, a Swedish beauty, one of Skakel's girlfriends during his marriage.

While George passed up the official inauguration, he wouldn't have missed the parties, which were right up his alley: lots of women and lots of booze. During the festivities, Bobby spotted George pawing one of the Hollywood guests, sexy Kim Novak. Furious, he ordered Ethel to put a leash on her lecherous brother. Jim Skakel, who was watching the scene, gleefully recalled, "George was giving Kim Novak a kiss and Ethel stormed over and said, 'None of that here! Find someplace else!' Ethel broke it up. I said to myself, 'Holy, man! You don't want to bring a good-looking girl to a party around my sister.' " But on their way into town for the parties, Ethel had told Jack's boyhood friend Paul "Red" Fay, just appointed Under Secretary of the Navy, that she had a surprise for him. Fay's wife, Anita, a close friend of Ethel's, could not be with him that night. "I hope you are going to constantly be thinking of things you can do for old Eth because I have really got a prize for you when we get to the gala," Ethel whispered mysteriously to

Fay. When they arrived at the party, Ethel pulled him aside. "Before we go up to the box, I got something down here that I want to give to Red." Ethel led him to a tall, shapely blonde draped in fur. "If she'll have you," said Ethel, pointing to Angie Dickinson, "here is your date for the evening." Ethel then sat back to enjoy the show with Bobby, Jean and Steve Smith, and Angie and Red Fay (who later would often entertain the Kennedys with his rendition of "Hooray for Hollywood").

In the next box sat the jubilant new President and his glowing First Lady. Later that night, according to Peter Lawford, Jack Kennedy had a "ménage à trois" with two of six Hollywood starlets whom Lawford had arranged for Jack to meet at a party at the home of columnist Joseph Alsop. In the realm of philandering, George Skakel, Jr., and Jack Kennedy were like blood brothers: their womanizing was already well known to insiders, including Ethel. As Bill Whiteford, a longtime playboy pal of George Skakel's, noted years later, "Sometimes it seemed that George and the Kennedy brothers were having a contest to see who could screw the most women."

For Ethel, Jack's inauguration was another triumph. Even right-leaning *New York Journal American* TV columnist Jack O'Brian observed, "Ethel (Mrs. Bobby) Kennedy is the owner of the most sincerely happy personality this side of Dinah Shore."

56 ❋ Glamour Girl

OVER THE NEXT eight years Ethel would become one of the most flamboyant hostesses Washington had ever seen, supplanting such warhorses as Perle Mesta and

Gwen Cafritz, who had ruled during the Truman and Eisenhower eras.

While Jackie tended to draw back from the limelight, Ethel jumped in with both feet, even supplanting Lady Bird Johnson, who, while popular, was not a big draw among Washington's New Frontier movers and shakers.

Barbara Gamarekian, who had worked in the Kennedy White House Press Office before becoming a Washington correspondent for *The New York Times*, said Ethel was a frequent stand-in for Jackie, who sometimes feigned illness to avoid appearances. "In one instance, we had a photo shoot set up with a little girl who had some disease. I had to call Ethel at the last moment because Jackie wanted to play tennis. Then I had to take the photographers on an around-about route to the girl so they wouldn't see Jackie on the court. Ethel was a great stand-in and she loved it."

Ordinarily the Attorney General's wife was considered just another VIP spouse in a city full of them. But Ethel broke all the rules. "Simply by being the sister-in-law of the President, and carrying the name of Kennedy, Ethel bears a certain ready-made glamour," noted Hearst White House correspondent Marianne Means. "She attends every event that she can possibly squeeze in."

In the first year of her reign, Ethel threw a constant round of parties at Hickory Hill. "It would be easy to make Washington social life a full-time job," she allowed. "I like people and parties." She also was involved in dozens of official functions and trips: she was honored by nuns and missionaries for her "Christian excellence," she christened the nuclear submarine *Polaris*, and she traveled with Bobby to the Ivory Coast republic, where her "charm," *Life* magazine noted, "turned out to be a secret weapon of major dimensions." When Ethel heard that the wife of the subprefect in one village had ten children, she quipped, "I'm jealous." In her rare free time, she swam and sailed at Hyannis Port, skied near Aspen, and celebrated her eleventh wedding anniversary with an outdoor party for two hundred where she received a toast from Vice President Johnson. Along with

Bobby, Judy Garland, and Kay Thompson, Ethel sang an impromptu rendition of "The Trolley Song."

Ethel also rode in a show ring for the first time in a dozen years, as a surprise entrant at the Washington International Horse Show. She jumped over ten fences, toppling a brush and rail obstacle, and losing her black bowler hat before an audience of twenty-five hundred. Still, Bobby yelled praise to her, "Ethel, you did fine." She then changed from her riding attire—canary yellow breeches, black boots, and yellow-collared black coat—to a long, black velvet sheath topped by a black beaded jacket with a diamond four-leaf clover in her hair, and diamond three-leaf clover on her lapel. In that outfit, she presented the first Joseph P. Kennedy Memorial Trophy to the show's winner.

Ethel seemed constantly in movement. "I don't know whether energy is a state of mind or whether one is just born with it. I think I was born with it," she explained.

57 ✻ The Other Mrs. Kennedy

WHEN SWISS-BORN MRS. Norman Paul moved to Washington in the mid-1950s with her physician husband she quickly noted how unfashionably the city's political wives and socialites were dressed. There was, she saw, a wardrobe crisis in the nation's capital. Mrs. Paul was fifty-one and had studied art but never clothing design. In 1959, she rented a little shop at 1661 Wisconsin Avenue, named her place Saint-Aubin de Paris, renamed herself Madame Paul, had little gold cards printed up, hired an assistant from the Dominican Republic who spoke little English, and opened for business.

Not long after, Jackie Kennedy, window-shopping a few blocks from her home on N Street, strolled in. The de Gaulles were visiting Washington and Jackie needed a hat for the occasion. She spoke to Madame Paul about her needs and left explicit instructions written in pencil on pink paper, requesting that she make a copy of a certain hat using the same material as the original.

Madame Paul, who specialized only in dresses, had her seamstress whip up a hat that pleased Jackie. "Maybe you can do something with Ethel," she told the dressmaker.

Ethel, who had been buying off the rack at Saks and Bonwit's, was soon making regular weekly stops at Madame Paul's, usually accompanied by Sarah Davis. "Sarah was a very good influence on Ethel," observed Madame Paul. "She had very good taste." Ethel became such a regular at the shop that she showed up one day with her own personal coffeepot.

Ethel brought other Kennedy women to Madame Paul—Joan, Eunice, Jean, even Rose—and many friends, including journalist Anne Chamberlin, a Time-Life reporter, who soon wrote a glowing profile of the designer in *Ladies Home Journal* headlined, SHE DRESSES THE LADY PIONEERS OF THE NEW FRONTIER, which made Madame Paul famous overnight.

Soon items about Ethel and her dressmaker began appearing in leading fashion journals. Referring to a three-week South American trip Ethel had planned with Bobby, *Women's Wear Daily* noted, "Mrs. Kennedy has packed lots of dresses, suits and coats from Mme. Paul." Above the item was a sketch of Ethel, looking like a Barbie doll cutout, labeled ETHEL IN THE PINK. The sketch had Ethel wearing one of Madame Paul's designs—a side-buttoned and -stitched, low-belted pink sharkskin coatdress. WATCH ETHEL EMERGE AS AMERICA'S GOOD WILL AMBASSADRESS, the paper predicted cutely.

Another time *WWD* called Ethel "the All-American girl," noting that in her closet were items from Oscar de la Renta, Dior, and Mollie Parnis. "She buys good

American clothes and wears them well with innate breeding and good taste," the trade paper gushed.

But to Ethel's chagrin it was always Jackie who made the best-dressed lists, who was elected First Lady of Fashion, who was never photographed wearing the same outfit twice, and who was now spending over forty thousand dollars a year on clothing.

Unlike some of the other women who had descended on Saint-Aubin de Paris, Madame Paul personally liked Ethel because she didn't act snobby and was willing to take fashion advice.

"People said Ethel didn't have the best taste in terms of fashion," Madame Paul said years later. "Ethel liked green because she loved trees, but that color didn't look good on her and I turned her toward pinks and reds, which were becoming."

Madame Paul found Ethel the perfect customer because she had simple tastes and a good figure to fit. "She had a very strong little body, with little breasts, an athletic body like a young boy's. She was not frilly. 'Don't put any ruffles on it,' she always told me. She liked classic clothes like those from Chanel.

"Many times Ethel saw a dress in a shop or a magazine that she liked but she didn't want to pay extraordinary prices for it so she'd tell me, 'Madame Paul, why don't you make a copy for me.' I didn't do exactly the same, but something similar."

Every year Madame Paul flew to Europe, for the Paris and Italian shows. Before one of her trips Ethel sent her flowers from the Park Avenue florist Irene Hayes, Wadley & Smythe. Attached was a short note asking her to make copies of the latest from top designers such as Dior and Givenchy. She also requested, tongue in cheek, that she bring back a Frenchman for her.

Women's-page reporters, keeping an eagle eye on Ethel, soon caught on to her game. A sharp reporter noted that Ethel had arrived at a function in what looked at first glance to be a Chanel suit, piped in gold braid with gold buttons. "But no one else in the world has one just like it. She doesn't have to worry about Seventh

Avenue in New York copying it, or someone else copying the copy, or copying the copy of the copy. Her own Mme. Paul did it locally."

Ethel drooled over Madame Paul's well-made, inexpensive, and authentic-looking knockoffs. But she also bought originals at wholesale whenever she could. Ethel's modus operandi was simple. "She'd go into a store like Saks and try on an expensive designer dress that she liked," a friend said. "If it looked good on her, she'd give the salesperson an excuse for not buying it. But she'd get the style number off the ticket. She'd then call a broker in New York, who'd get it for her at cost plus ten percent. She felt you were a fool if you bought clothing at retail." In some cases Ethel got dresses directly from designers. She became a good friend of Oleg Cassini—Jackie's official designer as First Lady—and other couturiers who would work with her, pricewise.

When Ethel's schedule became impossibly full, Madame Paul often made special trips to *"Ickoree Eel"* to discuss designs and fabrics and do fittings. Often, a Hickory Hill secretary telephoned Ethel's itinerary to Madame Paul, who'd recommend what she should wear and then make it: a yellow shantung suit for a breakfast with the First Lady at the Sheraton Park Hotel; a raspberry silk suit for a White House diplomatic reception; a hot-pink-and-white-print afternoon dress for a benefit at Hickory Hill.

Ethel's closets quickly filled with Madame Paul's designs. Finally, she devoted one large closet exclusively to her favorite dressmaker and even put a sign on the door with Madame Paul's name on it. In just a few years, Ethel had bought more than a hundred outfits from her. Unlike her sister-in-law Jackie, who would sell her used clothes on consignment at a chic thrift shop in New York, Ethel held on to her things. Said Madame Paul: "When I visited Ethel I'd say many times, 'Ooohhh, you still have this dress and that dress,' and she'd say, 'Yes, I still wear that.' Some she wore many, many times. She kept her clothes a long time. I never asked her, but I don't think she ever donated any of her clothes to charity."

Ethel, known to be tough on people who worked for her, treated Madame Paul with kid gloves even though one member of the circle said she "made that little woman sew her fingers to the bone and then tried to get it for free."

With Bobby running the Justice Department, Ethel had no qualms about using Jack's position as President to help her pals. Once, when Madame Paul complained of a backache, Ethel telephoned the White House and got Jackie on the phone. "Madame Paul is in terrible pain," Ethel exclaimed. "I wonder if Dr. [Janet] Travell [Jack's personal physician who treated his back problems] is around." "Ethel," Madame Paul recalled, "immediately took me to the White House. Dr. Travell did a very good job because in the next few days I was already on my feet. I think she gave me a shot in the spine."

Ethel regularly sent Madame Paul invitations to official Kennedy functions that others would die to attend. Madame Paul also was on Ethel's VIP Christmas card list, and the recipient of cute thank-you notes. In one, Ethel said that a new white fur ski hat she'd purchased conveniently hid her hair and made people look at her head instead of her feet, which were always in motion.

When Ethel traveled with Bobby to Greece in 1962 as part of a world tour, she sent back a black-and-white picture postcard showing a peasant woman riding on a donkey with all of her worldly possessions aboard. Ethel warned that this is what happened to Greek couturiers who sold a design to one special customer and then knocked off copies for her friends.

58 ✻ Handmaidens

ETHEL HAD BECOME a fashion trendsetter with her tanned legs, chic little dresses, simple gold jewelry, and short white cotton gloves that she donned even if it was ninety-five degrees.

Washington insider and journalist Barbara Howar, a friend of Ethel's during the Kennedy and Johnson years, observed, "It was fun merely to watch everyone dashing about frenetically . . . ordering from Ethel's seamstress those sleeveless little gabardine dresses in the right shade of pink at just the right height above the knees; placing multijeweled pins at the exact same spot on the chest . . . the women of Washington, myself included, trying to garb themselves exactly in what eventually became a national craze for women to have the 'Kennedy look.' "

Women also started redecorating their homes in "breezy" Ethel Kennedy fabrics. " 'PYG' is what I called them—pink, yellow, and green people," said Howar.

Some Washington women even had babies at the same time she did, using the same obstetrician and hospital, "something that required true planning even though [Ethel] gave everyone ample opportunity to follow her example," Howar noted.

There was a small group of women around Ethel who were dubbed the "S.S. girls" because their first or last names began with the letter *S* and because they protected and defended their territory—namely Ethel—as fiercely as the elite German S.S. troops of the Third Reich had guarded their Führer. Besides Sarah Davis, there was Sue Markham, wife of Bobby's pal Dean Markham, who worked at the White House (and later for

Great Lakes Carbon); Sue Wilson, wife of Donald Wilson, appointed by Jack to be deputy director of the U.S. Information Agency; and Liz Stevens, wife of television producer George Stevens, among others.

"Like Ethel, they were all bright-eyed, perky, and so energetic it seemed as if each of them took an equal dose of speed in the morning," said one observer. They rode shotgun around Ethel, jealously guarding their territory. They were Ethel's groupies, her handmaidens, the palace guard wearing the same Madame Paul dresses, Roger Vivier shoes with gold buckle, and bouffant flip.

Each had different responsibilities. Astronaut Scott Carpenter's wife, Rene, doubled as a traveling companion and hairdresser for Ethel. Liz Stevens was in charge of the children and functioned as "a loving aunt." Kay Evans, the wife of columnist Rowland Evans, oversaw the smooth operation of Hickory Hill when Ethel traveled. Those women became celebrities of sorts themselves, getting their names and pictures in the paper when they appeared at an event with their leader. Sarah Davis, for example, got a mention in the *Washington Post* when at a social event she had to scurry around to find an appropriate pair of shoes for Ethel, who had left hers at home.

Later, looking back on that period, Sarah Davis observed that "it was a very exciting atmosphere—beautiful lunches, interesting guests, and Ethel was always very funny."

"It was bizarre but it worked for those women because that's what they wanted—to be part of the inner circle," said Barbara Howar. "It was all part of the Kennedy mystique."

"There were people in Washington who would fall on swords for her," said Howar. "The real truth is that Ethel was a user—a big user. She knew what she wanted from you, and she would give something back and that would be an invitation to Hickory Hill."

To Ethel, Hickory Hill was her fiefdom, she was the queen, and many of those around her were jesters in her court. One of them was Dean Markham.

During a trip to Europe, Ethel had met one of the famous matadors, Manuel Benitez, known as *El Cordobes*. He was the idol of the jet set, and when he told her he was planning a visit to the United States, she promptly invited him to come see her and Bobby at Hickory Hill. Ethel planned a big dinner party in his honor but it snowed and he canceled. Ethel was miffed. Dean Markham, seeing her agitation, went out and returned a short time later dressed in a matador's outfit that he'd rented. "Dean was a wonderful, adorable person, who loved Ethel and Bobby," said an insider. "But he felt pressured to do things like that quite often, things that he probably would have just as soon not have done because they made him look foolish."

One of those who desperately wanted to get into the circle was the wife of the head of one of the regulatory agencies in the Kennedy administration who was always asking Ethel's pals, "What can I do? What do you need?" When she finally got her chance—one of the handmaidens asked her to pick up a dozen pair of black stockings for Ethel—the anxious woman made the fatal mistake of putting a signed note in the box to get Ethel's attention, which meant that Ethel would have to take the time to send a thank-you note. "Ethel didn't have time to deal with that sort of thing," said a member of the old inner circle years later. "The girls all went crazy and closed that woman out after that."

Once, at the annual pet show that Ethel threw for charity at Hickory Hill, Barbara Howar received a nasty kick from a pony and had to be rushed to a hospital in an ambulance. A few days later a dozen China roses arrived at Howar's with a note from Ethel saying how sorry she was about what had happened.

"What was interesting was that at the bottom of the note Ethel wrote, *Don't respond to this*. What she was saying was, 'We're not going to be chummy over this. Here are the flowers. Click.' Of all of the Kennedy women, Ethel had the most arrogance and considered herself the truest Kennedy."

59 * Bay of Pigs

THE KENNEDY BROTHERS landed on their feet running.

At Justice, Bobby pledged to continue his war on labor corruption and organized crime. He'd even put together a hit list of Mafioso targeted for prosecution.

At the White House, Jack increased the U.S. presence in Southeast Asia by sending "advisers" to help train the Laotian Army. He also promised to play catch-up after the Soviet Union took the lead in the space race by sending Maj. Yuri Gagarin into orbit in a Sputnik named *Vostok.*

All of that was public. But behind closed doors, from his first day in office, Jack had been involved in a top-secret plan to overthrow Cuba's Communist leader, Fidel Castro.

The operation involved an invasion of Cuba by anti-Castro exiles at the Bay of Pigs. A few weeks before the April 1961 assault, Jack brought Bobby in on the plans. He had delayed notifying him because information about the operation was on a need-to-know basis, and Jack knew Bobby was busy putting together his team at Justice, so he'd kept him out of the loop until the last minute, a decision Jack would come to regret when the invasion failed; Bobby, Jack came to believe, could have offered valuable advice and counsel.

Even Jack's trusted appointee at Navy, Red Fay, hadn't been told. The night before the Cuban patriots were scheduled to land, Red and his wife, Anita, were eating hamburgers and hotdogs at Hickory Hill when

Bobby revealed the invasion plan. Fay was humiliated, and angry at Jack for not having briefed him.

Intensely anti-Communist, Ethel was particularly scornful of Castro. For years, the Skakel family had had a long and happy history in Cuba under the Batista dictatorship. Great Lakes Carbon had maintained an office in Havana—the company sold filters used in Cuba's sugar industry—and the Skakels had close friends there. Ethel was concerned for their safety. She prayed that Castro's regime would be overturned at whatever cost.

After George Skakel, Sr.'s, death, some of his children continued visiting the island despite the political dangers. George Skakel, Jr., for one, often went there to hunt for quail on a preserve situated on a penal colony off the mainland, or to go after wild boar in the Cuban bush. His frequent companion on those trips was Louis Werner II, the Midwestern bureau chief for the Central Intelligence Agency, who used a position in the post office as a cover for his clandestine activities.

Because of the sensitive business and social contacts the Skakels had maintained in Cuba, George was often able to supply the CIA through Werner with valuable intelligence information about Castro's activities, the country's sugar production, and other such data, some of which was used plotting the ill-fated Bay of Pigs invasion. Jim Skakel later confirmed that Great Lakes Carbon, which had offices worldwide, routinely supplied intelligence information to the CIA and other U.S. government intelligence agencies.

The day Castro took over, George Skakel, Jr., was vacationing in Cuba with Werner, another friend, Don Tase, and their wives when they were confronted by a band of armed soldiers who demanded their customized forty-two-foot Chris-Craft, the *Virginia,* owned by Jim Skakel, and named after his wife. The revolutionaries had seen the high-speed boat in action and wanted it then and there. "They were pointing tommy guns at us and I must say I was a little nervous," recalled Tase later. "But George told them, 'Go to hell. We're goin' fishin',' and that's exactly what we did. They looked dumbfounded."

Shortly afterward, Jim Skakel, who also was in Cuba at the time, got a call from the other side—a CIA agent who wanted to borrow the boat for clandestine operations. Jim agreed, and the craft subsequently was used to take 157 people safely off the island. Back in Florida, the CIA held on to the craft, arming it with machine-gun mounts and new engines. After making numerous calls to get his boat back, Jim gave up and never saw the *Virginia* again. "I figured they were in enough trouble without me going after the damned boat," he said later.

After the Bay of Pigs fiasco, Jack assigned Bobby, CIA director Allen Dulles, and others to investigate why U.S. intelligence experts had underestimated Cuba's power to crush the invasion.

Bobby found some comfort in the fact that at least one of the Skakels had suffered. "When Bobby heard what had happened to Jim's boat he gloated," recalled George Terrien. "Bobby told Georgeann, 'The Bay of Pigs was all worth it just to nail one of your brothers.' "

Meanwhile, Ethel played her own role in the Cold War when, in the winter of 1962, she was quietly recruited as figurehead for a program to compete with the Soviets for the hearts and minds of some five thousand foreigners in Washington who formed part of the international Diplomatic Corps. The idea was to wine and dine and entertain them like the Russians had been doing. Pedro Sanjuan, deputy to the chief of protocol at the State Department, recommended Ethel as the front for the operation. "Very few people are the embodiment of the optimism and the contagious enthusiasm of the 'New Frontier' that Mrs. Robert F. Kennedy is," he wrote in a memo. "Therefore we would like to ask her to be our Honorary Sponsor. This will not take any of her time unless she desires to take part in these arrangements." Ethel was thrilled.

60 * Hickory Hill Comes to Justice

WHILE BOBBY HAD surrounded himself with many highly competent associates from his Rackets Committee days and from Jack's campaign team, he was still a hands-on Attorney General. He had started putting in twelve-hour days and six-day weeks, going home to Hickory Hill for dinner and then returning to the Justice Department until close to midnight.

As a result, Ethel and Bobby were spending less time together. Since July 1951, when her first child was born, Ethel had been pregnant an average of once every fifteen months. She had had babies in 1951, 1952, 1954, 1955, 1956, 1958, and 1959. But in the period between the beginning and end of Camelot, a span of about twenty-eight months, Ethel would have only one baby.

Because work was occupying so much of his time, Bobby and Ethel began bringing some of Hickory Hill to the Justice Department.

For a time, Bobby was chauffeured to work each day with his favorite pet, a fourteen-month-old, sad-eyed, black Newfoundland named Brumus who was constantly at the Attorney General's side, even during the filming by the U.S. Information Agency of a visit to the Attorney General's office by a group of Brazilian students. As the cameras whirled, Bobby solemnly poured the dog a drink of water from a silver pitcher into an ashtray, to the delight of his guests. But FBI Director J. Edgar Hoover began raising questions about the propriety of a pooch in the hallowed halls of Justice. An obsessive bureaucrat did some quick research and discovered that there was a law banning all but Seeing-Eye dogs from public buildings. Now facing a maximum fine of thirty days in jail and fifty dollars, the Attorney General of the United States decided to leave Brumus at home.

Bobby also caused consternation when he started tossing the pigskin around his office with his deputy, former All-American football star Byron ("Whizzer") White. "One of these days," grumbled an aide, "it's going to go out the window." When White had to drop out of the sessions, Ethel drove three of the children in to play with their father, once in front of a startled visitor from Great Britain.

On one occasion, Ethel convinced Bobby to have a midwinter "cookout" in the Attorney General's office, using the fireplace to grill hamburgers and hot dogs. When Bill Geoghegan, an assistant Attorney General, questioned the decorum and suggested that precooked chicken might be more appropriate, Bobby wrote him a memo: *You're getting old and crotchety. We will not get to the Moon first with this attitude.*

Late one afternoon Bobby was changing clothes in his office to attend a formal dinner when Ethel appeared with all seven children. Out of control, they started pushing intercom buttons, going through files, and galloping up and down the halls, yelling and listening for their echoes. FBI agents swarmed in when they pushed a button under Hoover's desk. The tumult finally ended when Ethel and a nursemaid rounded up the herd and carted them back to Hickory Hill.

Like her mother and father, Ethel had a laissez-faire attitude with her own children. "I just don't believe a child's world should be entirely full of 'don'ts.' We think it's possible to have discipline and still give the children independence without spoiling them," she said.

61 ⁕ Everybody into the Pool

SOCIAL LIFE AT Hickory Hill became more like Lake Avenue. But now, instead of cars being driven into the water by spoiled children, the best and the brightest of Camelot were being tossed into the drink fully clothed.

Ethel's people-dunking parties became infamous overnight, like the goldfish-swallowing and telephone booth–stuffing stunts of college sophomores. While Ethel thought it was hilarious to see serious types such as presidential adviser Arthur Schlesinger, Jr., soaked to the skin, others viewed the activity as boorish, foolhardy, and an embarrassment to the Administration.

One who held that view was Schlesinger's then-wife, Marion Schlesinger, a writer who observed years later that "Ethel was childish and self-indulgent. She created a certain atmosphere of fun and games as it were, and everything was done on a lavish scale. It was like a great big party all the time, extravagant and excessive, too much of everything. Everyone was attracted to Ethel, but that was because of Bob's p-o-w-e-r."

Arthur Schlesinger, on the other hand, viewed Ethel as "the best thing" that had ever happened to Bobby. "Her jokes diverted him. Her social gifts offset his abiding shyness. Her inextinguishable gaiety lightened his times of moodiness and pessimism. Her passion moved him . . . when he married Ethel he blossomed."

Either way, the swimming pool high jinks made Ethel the best-known party giver in America, which to her was quite a distinction.

To the men around Ethel—Bobby's aides and advisers—the ritualistic dunkings became a mark of initiation into a very exclusive club, branding them as genuine Kennedy insiders. Those who didn't get tossed into the water felt left out and, like Sen. Kenneth Keating of New York, expressed disappointment.

In a tongue-in-cheek "Dear Ethel" letter, the distinguished Senator wrote:

> I was delighted to read in the *Herald Tribune* that your party went off so swimmingly—which compounds my woe at not having been able to be on hand in my Hickory Hill formal attire (black tie and bikini)!
>
> I hope the mad rumor isn't true—that you're changing the name of Hickory Hill to Drip-Dry Manor!
>
> Best wishes to you and the General and *please* don't leave me out of your next party!

Even that era's stolid, gray *New York Times* seriously reported Arthur Schlesinger's first dunking, which occurred during a garden party and dinner dance for some three hundred guests that Ethel and Bobby had given for the Peter Lawfords.

"A source close to the family said Mrs. Kennedy, in evening attire, plunged into the water after a leg of a chair slipped off a plank placed across the pool's edges. The same thing happened to Mr. Schlesinger and Mrs. [Sarah] Davis. All three changed clothes and returned to the party. But another guest, Lt. Col. John H. Glenn, Jr., kept his chair upright, although its legs were but three inches from the edge of the plank," said the United Press International dispatch that the *Times* ran.

U.S. News & World Report devoted a whole page to "Fun on the 'New Frontier': Who Fell, Who Was Pushed." The story even included an aerial photo of the Kennedys' pool.

Washington Evening Star society reporter Betty Beale, who broke the pool-dunking story, concluded that "John Glenn bears a charmed life . . . Ethel Kennedy likes to live dangerously . . . and poolsmanship is an integral part of Hickory Hill."

After the party, Ethel, with a wink, suggested that it was she who shoved Schlesinger.

Later, Lee Udall, wife of Interior Secretary Stuart Udall, claimed responsibility. "All these years Ethel has been taking the rap for me," she said. "I was dancing by, and he was standing there holding forth and being so Arthurish, and something came over me. I just stuck out my arm and pushed him and danced away. He never knew."

Gerald Tremblay, Bobby's pal from law school, who was a frequent houseguest at Hickory Hill during those days and was present when the first dunking happened, noted that while Ethel enjoyed the stunt, Bobby didn't. "They were kind of acting wild and Sarah [Davis], who was a good-looking gal, got thrown in the pool wearing a dress," Tremblay recalled. "She came out of the water and thought it would be kind of wild to jump into Bobby's arms all wet and she did and he really got ticked off." Davis later denied that the incident with Bobby ever took place.

While men like Schlesinger were avid fans of Ethel and her style, some of their wives, like Marion Schlesinger, were less than enamored. In that category was Violet Marshall, wife of Burke Marshall, one of Bobby's most trusted and respected aides at Justice.

"She was not the sort of person I could discuss gardening with, or what I had just read, unless it was some really sensationalistic book," Violet Marshall said years later. "Ethel also comes at you in kind of a gushy way. I suppose it's insincerity because how can anybody know and like that many people? It's a social mannerism that she has. It's an act. She'd point to someone who was in the gathering and tell you what that person had just done, what he was known for, what he just said, and wasn't that a clever thing to say. That sort of thing. Gossip. And I was supposed to feel flattered by that."

With the passage of time Violet Marshall also came

to the realization that Ethel could, at times, be mean-spirited and rude.

She felt the sting of Ethel's wrath one summer's day at Hyannis Port. As soon as the Marshalls had arrived, Ethel jumped on Violet to join in a mixed doubles match. Violet, who had agreed to the visit "under duress from my husband, who was Bobby's closest confidant" had not come prepared for tennis; she was wearing colorful shorts rather than tennis whites and didn't have her racket.

Before Violet could raise a winning argument, she was out on the court teamed with Edwin Guthman, Bobby's press secretary at Justice. The two-set match didn't turn out the way Ethel had hoped.

"Though Ethel is a better tennis player than I, and she *thought* she was, and in fact she *knew* she was, somehow we managed to win," Violet Marshall said.

After the match the players shook hands, but Ethel didn't seem very happy. As she once said, "I like competition but I like to win better." Everyone returned to the house to prepare for dinner, which was equally as unpleasant and embarrassing because Joan Kennedy, who was intoxicated, used the occasion to tell Violet Marshall and anyone else in earshot that her marriage to Ted, who also was at the table, was in trouble.

With everyone seated at the table and "with all kinds of currents and crosscurrents going on," Ethel suddenly glared at Violet Marshall and in a fury bellowed, "Never, never, ever wear yellow shorts on my tennis court!"

"I was completely crushed. To say I lost my appetite is putting it mildly," she recalled. "I was so hurt because it was all so unexpected. I'd seen Ethel hurt other people in the past with little barbs here and there. But I never expected *that*. It was mean-spirited. My partner in tennis said, 'Talk about sore losers!' "

On the way home Burke Marshall attempted to pacify his shaken wife. "Well," he said, "that's Ethel."

After the incident at the Cape, Violet Marshall made a pledge to herself: "I'll never in my life play tennis again with Ethel Kennedy."

62 ✳ A Question of Arson and Adultery

BY JANUARY 1962, Bobby was ranked as the second most powerful man in the Kennedy Administration and Ethel was considered the most popular and visible woman next to Jackie.

Unlike previous Attorney Generals, Bobby had become involved in affairs of state far beyond his bailiwick. He had a say in almost every level of decision-making, from foreign policy, to intelligence, to the farm program. Jack trusted Bobby implicitly, and credited him, more than anyone else, for helping win the White House. The President actually believed that the only people he could confide in, could seek advice from—could fully trust—were members of his own family. Bobby topped the list.

It was no surprise then that Jack gave Bobby and Ethel a plum assignment in early 1962, an unprecedented fourteen-nation, twenty-eight-day goodwill trip, a journey of Presidential proportions. While the trip was billed as an informal tour with the emphasis on meeting young people, the host countries viewed Bobby and Ethel as they were meant to—as stand-ins for the President and First Lady, and they would be welcomed as such. Like Big Ann, Ethel was willing to leave her children behind for extended periods so she could be with her husband.

It was a hectic time for Ethel. With the trip looming, she had to pull together a new wardrobe and had assigned Madame Paul to come up with the designs. She also bought a brown wig at Elizabeth Arden's knowing she'd have difficulty fitting in sessions with a hairdresser or finding Western hairstylists in Asia. From her circle of S.S. girls, she chose Susie Wilson—whom Bobby thought was cute—as her traveling companion. "I was there to give Ethel a hand," said Wilson later. "She always had to be dressed wonderfully and I was there to say, 'What do you want to wear today?' or, 'Let's close up these suitcases.' " At the same time, Ethel was busy planning an important Kennedy family charity fund-raiser at the Washington premier of Irving Berlin's new musical, *Mr. President*. In Palm Beach, her father-in-law, recovering from a serious stroke, expected her to fly down and pay homage to him. Moreover, Ted was being primed to run for the U.S. Senate seat for Massachusetts once held by Jack. Ethel thrived on the action, the excitement, the pressure.

In the midst of all this frenzied activity, Ethel took a call on the morning of January 9 from Georgeann that left her completely undone.

With increasing dread Ethel listened silently as her sister recounted how the night before their brother George had been discovered with another woman in the guest house on their Greenwich estate by his wife Pat. There was nothing surprising about that. Ethel knew that Pat Corroon Skakel had confronted her husband's philandering before. Once, on the sidelines of the polo field in Greenwich where George played on a team that he named "The Patricians" after his wife, Pat Skakel caused a nasty scene by screaming "Whore!" at one of his girlfriends in front of a shocked crowd of onlookers, then raced off in a car that contained the woman's change of clothes. Georgeann herself had recently banned George from Sursum Corda after she returned home from Sunday Mass to find him and one of his girlfriends skinny-dipping in the pool. Until now, though, the Skakels' marital difficulties—her drinking and his philandering—had never gone beyond screaming matches and accusations. But the ante had just gone up. Georgeann now told Ethel that the beautiful guest house where George had had his most recent frolic had been reduced to a charred shell, and all available evidence pointed to his enraged wife as the cause of the fire. Georgeann thought Ethel should know the story right away.

Pale and shaken, Ethel hung up the phone. Again, a

scandal within the Skakel family threatened embarrassment for the Kennedys.

Ethel had no choice but to tell Bobby what had happened. She knew he'd want the matter kept under wraps at all costs. She went to church that day and prayed that everything would turn out okay.

Earlier that morning, in an effort to contain the situation, George Skakel himself had taken matters into his own hands. He placed two telephone calls. The first was to Mary Begley's husband, John, a trusted friend who had once worked for Great Lakes Carbon.

"We were in our pajamas and getting into bed when the phone rang," Mary Begley remembered. "All of a sudden John was getting dressed and I said, 'Where the hell are you going?' Smiling, he said, 'There's a problem with George and I gotta help him out.' When John got home he told me that George had a gal in the guest house and John had to help get the dame out because Pat was roaming around. John drove in through the Skakels' back driveway, picked her up, and took her home. He never would tell me who she was. This all happened before the fire started."

The second call Skakel made, around two A.M., was to his brother-in-law George Terrien, a drinking buddy of Pat Skakel's. George Skakel was contemptuous of Terrien and often used him for dirty jobs.

"George told me Pat had discovered him with some broad in the guest house and Pat had burned down the place," Terrien said. "He said, 'Get your ass over here and take care of things. You know what to do.' He wanted me to mollify the police and the firemen. He wanted me to perform miracles. He wanted the whole thing covered up. He told me. 'I don't need Ethel and Bobby crawling up my ass over this.' "

By the time Terrien reached Vineyard Lane, more than three dozen firemen were fighting the blaze in subfreezing temperatures.

The fire was calamitous. It destroyed thousands of feet of rare home movies of the Skakels dating back to their days in Chicago. Also burned was footage of Jack

Kennedy's visit to Indochina when he was a Congressman. The flames melted numerous equestrian and sports trophies won by Ethel, obliterated priceless pieces of art that had been lovingly collected by Big Ann. The house, reduced to a shell, had been a showplace with two immense bedrooms, a sauna, two baths, and a huge two-story living room with a stone fireplace. Equipped with a pair of professional thirty-five-millimeter film projectors and a large screen that came down from the ceiling, the Skakels often viewed first-run features loaned to them by their close friends, the Skourases, who were in the movie business. Everything was lost.

While the fire burned out of control, George Terrien wandered around the periphery listening for talk about arson, looking for any incriminating evidence.

"In the bushes I found a couple of pieces of women's clothing that the babe must have ditched when she left the place. I gave the stuff to George the next day," he said. "I had to do whatever I could to keep the whole thing quiet."

By the time the blaze was brought under control shortly before daybreak, four firemen had suffered minor injuries and all that was left standing of the house were portions of the four walls, a loss of more than a hundred thousand dollars.

The rubble was still smoldering when Pat Skakel told the Terriens over drinks that she was responsible for the fire.

"Ethel must have called Georgeann and myself a dozen times that day to find out what was going on," said Terrien. "She kept asking, 'Do the police know what happened yet? Do the police know who did it?' She was damned worried. She told me, 'George, do whatever you have to do.'

"Ethel also telephoned Pat and screamed and hollered at her. I went over to Pat's and she was crying and drinking and calling Ethel a 'bitch' for worrying more about how all of this would look for herself and Bobby rather than giving a damn about how badly her own brother was mistreating his wife by fooling around with other women."

Mary Begley, who saw Pat Skakel immediately after the fire, said, "She was very willful, drinking heavily and acting very cavalier, giggling a little bit about it. She'd get a little smirk on her face and say, 'Now, wasn't that too bad about the fire.' "

Jim Skakel arrived from his home in Bel Air to survey the scene. "It looked like Germany after the war," he said later.

While Greenwich police and fire officials heard "skuttlebutt and rumors" of arson, no formal investigation was ever conducted. The nasty affair was completely put to rest when George Skakel decided not to file a claim with his insurance company.

"He didn't want any investigators nosing around because he knew Pat had started the goddamned fire and it would be highly embarrassing if she got arrested," said George Terrien. "So George decided to cover the loss out of pocket. He told me, 'I don't need to add insurance fraud to arson and adultery.' Afterward Ethel called Georgeann and expressed relief that George had decided to drop the matter. During the entire episode, Ethel was worried that the whole thing would get into the headlines."

Luckily for Ethel, the national press once again ignored a scandalous episode involving the Skakels. In early February she and Bobby took off on their successful world tour.

63 ⁕ Seducing the Press

ETHEL'S FEARS THAT her family's wrangles would become public and cause embarrassment for the Kennedys were, for the most part, unwarranted. Many of Washington's most influential columnists, commentators, editors, and reporters had a gentlemen's agreement with Jack and Bobby not to report awkward or prejudicial stories of a personal nature.

Ben Bradlee, then chief of the Washington bureau of *Newsweek* and later executive editor of the *Washington Post*, was a close friend of Jack's and had direct knowledge of the President's womanizing. In the same month that Pat Skakel had purportedly burned down the guest house because of her husband's adultery, Jack Kennedy had begun an affair in Washington with Bradlee's sister-in-law, Mary Pinchot Meyer, a romance that blossomed in the Bradlees' carriage house, and continued in the White House when Jackie was traveling. Yet Bradlee, lauded years later for overseeing the *Washington Post*'s Watergate exposé, agreed never to report anything he knew about Jack from their social connections.

Ethel, meanwhile, was successful in controlling just about everything that was written about her and Hickory Hill.

"She was very careful. Anybody who talked was dead," declared Barbara Howar. "If Ethel wanted a story to get out, she put it out herself. You did not go out there and then talk about what you heard or saw—or you did not get invited back. Everything that went on at Hickory Hill was sacrosanct. She liked to have publicity when she was doing something with all the kids, and the animals and her women friends. It was all a colorful smoke screen that kept Ethel herself from being scrutinized."

In exchange for their discretion and loyalty, certain prominent journalists were given direct access to Bobby and Jack, and were on Ethel's exclusive party guest list.

As Washington correspondent Douglas Kiker, who had worked for the *New York Herald Tribune* and NBC, noted later, "If a bomb had ever gone off at Hickory Hill on a summer weekend, three-fourths of the most powerful print and broadcast journalists in America would have had to be replaced. It's never been a secret that relationships between reporters and their sources often become incestuous, but the situation at Hickory Hill between Ethel, Bobby, and the press was extreme. As a result many of those people in their reporting wound up promoting the Kennedys and building false images and myths about them that became part of Kennedy history and legend."

For journalists, Hickory Hill was a seductive environment, a place where they rubbed shoulders with the best and the brightest: Hollywood celebrities, cabinet members, Supreme Court justices, sports stars. Journalists sat by the pool and chatted with Bobby, played doubles with Ethel, tossed a football with Jack, drank the Kennedys' liquor, and ate the Kennedys' food.

"Hickory Hill was the place where you really wanted to be," said Barbara Gamarekian, who, after leaving her press job at the Kennedy White House, covered events at Hickory Hill for *The New York Times*. "Hickory Hill rivaled any White House party. It was seductive to everyone, especially journalists, and Ethel always had the latest gossip."

To stay on Ethel's good side, to continue being invited to the dinner parties, the barbecues, the intimate gatherings, all a reporter had to do was wave the Kennedy banner, be obeisant and completely loyal. "A lot of big-time journalists played by Ethel's rules and compromised themselves to be part of that circle," Douglas Kiker asserted.

Writer Sophie Burnham, one of the few magazine journalists to secure a lengthy interview with Ethel over the years, recalled sitting with her by the pool at Hickory Hill one pleasant spring afternoon, participating in the same media "adulation" that "inside made me sick to my stomach." The Kennedys, she noted, "knew perfectly how to charm the press. There they were—Ben Bradlee, all those guys—being charmed by John Kennedy and Bobby. The adulation was shameful." Burnham, on the other hand, had come away from her chat with Ethel feeling "horrified and speechless" at some of the extreme views Ethel held on issues ranging from sports to sex. But the article generated more mail than *Family Circle* had ever received about one story. "Fifty percent thought Ethel was absolutely wonderful," Burnham noted, "and fifty percent said she was the most shallow, stupid person they had ever read about."

The list of media biggies who were frequent guests at Hickory Hill—and personal friends of Bobby and Ethel—included NBC's David Brinkley, CBS's Roger Mudd, NBC's Sander Vanocur, *Look* magazine's Warren Rogers, *Life* magazine's Anne Chamberlin, *The New York Times*'s Anthony Lewis, influential columnists Rowland Evans, Joseph and Stewart Alsop, Joseph Kraft, Mary McGrory, the *Washington Post*'s Richard Harwood, writer William Styron, humorist Art Buchwald, to name a few. The power, glitz, and glamour of the Kennedys were aphrodisiacs that few could resist.

"There were a lot of journalists who probably crossed the line with Bobby and Ethel in terms of friendship and socialization," said Vanocur later. "The whole idea of journalists being close to politicians in Washington is nothing new. The funny thing about it all was that the people we worked for wanted us to have these connections. Nobody ever said stop."

"Ethel was a super-good politician and public relations person," observed Richard Starnes, the Scripps-Howard Washington correspondent assigned to cover the Kennedy Administration's enforcement of desegregation at the University of Mississippi. For months Starnes had tried unsuccessfully to do a profile on Bobby but couldn't get past his press person, Ed Guthman. It wasn't until after Starnes wrote an especially positive story about how federal marshals under Bobby's direction handled the rioting on the Ole Miss campus that he received a personal invitation from Bobby to come to Hickory Hill to do an interview.

"Although Ethel met me only briefly the first time I was out there, the next time I went—months and months later—she remembered me immediately. I had my then-wife with me and Ethel turned to her and said, 'Dick wrote such a wonderful piece about Bobby.' Ethel got my name right. That impressed me. She knew what was important. She came on as being very gracious and warmhearted."

Ethel's parties were amusing diversions filled with surprises, much like the ones her mother threw at Lake Avenue. Often, she'd slip into the dining room just before dinner was served and rearrange the placecards, causing chaos by putting the wrong sets of people together. Guests were always expected to perform and participate—tell a story, sing a song, debate a subject. One couldn't slip in and out of Hickory Hill quietly. One of Ethel's curious dinner-party games was dubbed "I'll tell you one, if you tell me one." The rules were simple. Ethel would compliment a guest for something he or she had recently done—written an interesting column, hosted a fascinating TV program—and then she'd expect a compliment about herself in return. Guests frequently were left feeling ill-at-ease because they couldn't think of anything Ethel had done to warrant a kudo. "I was always embarrassed because she would say something nice about me, that one of her sisters-in-law had seen a show I did that they liked, and I could never come up with anything for her," recalled Roger Mudd. "I always felt like a total dummy."

The Hickory Hill journalists were encouraged to bring their wives or girlfriends. Everyone's secret was kept. But quite often the men were invited on their own by Ethel to play tennis with her, which caused some dissension and jealousy. While some of the women became chummy with Ethel, others found her shallow and vacuous.

One, Polly Kraft, an artist who was married to political columnist Joseph Kraft, saw Hickory Hill as "a terribly glamorous, exciting, irreverent, cheerful place, full of hope. Ethel, however, was the absolute antithesis of what I am. She was either amazingly innocent, or naive, or maybe even square. Intellectually, she had no depth."

On the other hand, Susie Wilson, wife of journalist Donald Wilson, bonded instantly with Ethel. The two had met by accident one afternoon in a parking lot in downtown Washington in the late fifties as Ethel was rushing her daughter Kathleen, who'd fallen off a horse, to the doctor. "Would you help me carry her?" Ethel asked Wilson. While they waited around for the results of the X rays, the two women chatted and Ethel's eyes lit up when she learned that Susie's husband was *Life*'s Washington bureau chief. "The next day Ethel called and invited my husband and me to Hickory Hill for the afternoon to thank me for helping carry Kathleen up the stairs. If somebody had asked me why she *actually* called, I would have thought she was far more interested in Don and his position than in me."

Following the lunch at Hickory Hill, the Wilsons and the Kennedys became new best friends, a relationship that was beneficial to both sides. Don Wilson got access to the Kennedys and *Life* was able to do a number of exclusive and very positive features on Ethel, Bobby, and the children, puff pieces such as "Ethel Kennedy and Her Children: Full Life of a Famous Wife" and "*Life* Goes to the Christening of Bobby Kennedy's Son: 'Good Baby,' Says Uncle Jack," among others.

When Jack was elected President, Don Wilson was named deputy director of the United States Information Agency, and Sue Wilson accompanied Ethel and Bobby on a couple of major trips, including the Kennedys' triumphant round-the-world journey in early 1962.

"I felt I got so much from knowing Ethel," Wilson

said years later. "She taught me a lot about love, a lot about faith, a lot about relationships. She was a very loving human being and very uncritical of people except for those who held different political views than the Kennedys did. Ethel wasn't Jackie in any way. Jackie was much more of the intellectual and the cultural maven. There wasn't much introspection with Ethel. She never looked back."

David Brinkley's wife, Ann, a writer, also forged close ties with Ethel and became part of her circle. But unlike Susie Wilson, who remained friends with Ethel for years, Ann Brinkley's friendship was ended by Ethel when the Brinkleys' marriage of more than twenty years fell apart.

Overnight, Ethel began inviting Brinkley's new girlfriend to Hickory Hill instead. Ann Brinkley was hurt and angered when she learned that one Mother's Day Ethel, David, and his girlfriend had a picnic at Hickory Hill using Ann Brinkley's picnic basket for their food.

"Ethel had decided that since I was no longer married to David, I was not worthy of her friendship. At first I was deeply hurt and puzzled—later, I was amused. Though I had been a devoted friend and helped on many Kennedy projects, Ethel cut me cold," she said.

64 ✻ *Ethel's Enemy List*

WHEN IT CAME to dealing with the news media, Ethel's intense loyalty to Bobby manifested itself over and over in different ways.

According to Gerald Tremblay, Ethel once took a poke at editorial cartoonist Herblock, who had been critical of Bobby's authorization of wiretapping. Years later, Herblock denied the incident ever happened. According to Tremblay, Ethel was at a party when the cartoonist approached her, unaware of her anger. As he graciously extended his hand to her in friendship, Ethel planted her fist into his midsection.

"When Ethel hits you, she *hits* you," said Gerald Tremblay, Ethel's escort at the party, who wasn't particularly shocked by her behavior. "No one could openly criticize Bob without Ethel getting mad," he said. "Bobby probably wouldn't have been as furious about that cartoon, but Ethel had a mind of her own. If somebody crossed Bob, she put the black dot on your hand; she gave you the kiss of death."

Ethel was equally defensive of herself and other members of the Kennedy family. Once, a few days after a reporter wrote that she was "not noticeably adept at the Georgetown style-and-art small talk," Bobby slipped him a note warning him to stay out of her way.

When Susan Sheehan of *The New Yorker* wrote a particularly hard-edged profile of Ethel for *The New York Times Magazine,* Ethel sent her an "unusual" eleven-page, handwritten letter on delicate pink stationery. Rather than responding to Sheehan's description of her as extravagant, competitive, and "an intellectual lightweight," among other things, Ethel chose to defend the Kennedy sisters—Jean, Pat, and Eunice—whom Sheehan described as "too aggressive and masculine."

Ethel's extreme loyalty did not escape the more perceptive journalists covering Washington. UPI's venerable Helen Thomas noted that Ethel's "impulses are all positive and partisan. In her view, people are either for or against you. . . . When it comes to the Kennedy family, she is a 'team' player as contrasted to her sister-in-law, Jacqueline, who prefers solo flights. She is much more help 'politically' than Jacqueline, and carries her load willingly for the party."

Over the years, Ethel would repeatedly show herself ready to sever instantly long and close friendships with journalists if they wrote or reported something she perceived to be negative about Bobby or the other Kennedys. Among those blacklisted by Ethel from Hickory Hill were Joseph Kraft and Roger Mudd.

A product of Columbia and the Institute for Advanced Studies at Princeton, Kraft was fascinated by Bobby's take on issues, and savored his wit. A year younger than Kraft, Bobby marveled at his political commentary and analysis, was delighted by his *New Yorker* pieces, and impressed by his clout as a nationally syndicated columnist.

While Hickory Hill's main attraction for Kraft was Bobby, he also got a kick out of Ethel's irreverence and her uninhibited behavior. Though he didn't feel completely comfortable around her—he had problems relating to anyone who didn't know what lox and bagels were—he'd accepted her as a friend. The Krafts became frequent dinner guests at Hickory Hill, and over the years, Kraft supported Bobby when he ran for Senator and later for President. When Bobby was killed, Kraft was devastated. He rode the funeral train from New York to Washington with Ethel and served as one of the pallbearers.

On June 7, 1973, a few days after the fifth anniversary of Bobby's death, Ethel turned to the op-ed page of the *Washington Post* and saw a column by Kraft headlined RECOLLECTIONS OF ROBERT KENNEDY. Written at a time when the Nixon administration and the nation were paralyzed by Watergate, Kraft's piece was a poignant reminder of how much the country had lost with Bobby Kennedy's death.

In an attempt at fairness, Kraft also mentioned some of Bobby's weaknesses as well. On Vietnam, the columnist said Bobby "had been a piano-wire hawk. . . ." During his war on organized crime, he had "promoted wiretapping and other invasions of privacy. . . ." And few of Bobby's supporters "would now defend the Southern judges he appointed as Attorney General on the theory that Senator James Eastland could be bought off." But the overall thrust of the column was positive and compassionate.

"His inclination was to tell the truth to others and

himself," Kraft concluded. "Stiff self-isolation was not in his being. So when he was wrong, he could adjust his position without making it seem, as more recent leaders have made it seem, that it would be the end of the world."

Fiercely protective of Bobby's memory, blinded by her loyalty, Ethel saw none of the positive. Instead she locked on to the few criticisms like a heat-seeking missile and slammed the door forever on her friendship with Kraft.

She never called him to complain; he would not become aware of her fury until later. Instead, she raised the issue with her personal adviser—and Joe Kraft's longtime friend—Burke Marshall, who was now at Yale. The first volley in Ethel's campaign to blackball Kraft came two weeks later.

On June 22, 1973, the *Washington Post* printed a lengthy letter from Marshall denouncing Kraft's column, headlined: RFK DEFENDED ON WIRE-TAPPING AND APPOINTMENT OF JUDGES IN THE SOUTH. Marshall wrote:

"I know it is now fashionable in writing about Robert Kennedy to stress wire-tapping and bad judicial appointments in the South, and not his public accomplishments. But this is inaccurate in the particular, and grossly unfair in the balance. Mr. Kraft especially should know better." Marshall then went on to shoot down each of Kraft's criticisms.

"Obviously, Burke wrote the letter at the instigation of Ethel," said Kraft's widow later. "Joe was extremely hurt and bewildered. Joe felt his friendship with Burke predated any relationship he had with Ethel. Joe wrote Burke and said, 'How could you have done this to me?' Joe's relationship with Burke was never repaired after that."

At the same time, Ethel closed off all communication with the Krafts and forced their mutual friends to take sides.

"There was a very quiet closing of the ranks around Ethel—the ranks being Art and Ann Buchwald, Liz and George Stevens, and my cousin Kay [Mrs. Rowland Evans]," Polly Kraft said sadly. "Nobody would ever,

ever talk about it. When they entertained and when Ethel came they never invited us. We were absolutely blacklisted. I never had been aware that Ethel could be so vindictive. We didn't know that side of her."

Ethel was on the warpath. On one occasion, she walked into a party at the Robert McNamaras', spotted the Krafts, and stormed out.

By this time, Ben Bradlee had become executive editor of the *Washington Post*. With his pal Jack Kennedy long dead, Bradlee felt no strong allegiance to Ethel. In fact, according to Bradlee watchers at the *Post*, he didn't particularly like Ethel and savored printing juicy gossip about her and the doings at Hickory Hill. "You didn't invite Ben, Sally [Quinn, Bradlee's wife], and Ethel to the same small dinner party," said a writer and observer of the Washington scene. "In fact, Ben always kidded George Stevens about having 'his head halfway up Ethel's ass.' I said, 'Ben, that's the most horrible expression I ever heard,' but he laughed and said, 'Well, it's true.' " When someone leaked the McNamara party incident to the *Post* it became the lead gossip item under the headline NOT FORGOTTEN—NOR FORGIVEN. The *Boston Globe* and other papers picked it up, further enraging Ethel.

Not long after, Ethel walked out of another party, this time after checking the placecards and seeing the names Polly and Joe. It wasn't until later that she learned they weren't the Krafts.

Her next act was a clumsy attempt to bar Kraft from the prestigious RFK Journalism Awards luncheon that year. The awards were the brainchild of some of the reporters who covered Bobby's ill-fated presidential campaign, and the presentation of the prizes had become a prestigious affair with hundreds of submissions from reporters, and a big do at Hickory Hill—an opportunity, as the event brochure stated, "to help forward the causes that Robert Kennedy believed in, worked for, and articulated so well."

"Mrs. Kennedy told the journalists to remove Kraft's name," revealed Ruth Darmstadter, who was executive director of the awards program at the time.

"They said if you touch him we're all walking out. They couldn't tolerate that she would take that kind of stand."

Roger Mudd, an active member of the awards committee, said, "We responded to her as a board that if she intended to exercise veto power over who we invited we would resign. Ethel eventually backed off."

A compromise was ultimately reached between Ethel and the journalists that allowed her to invite her own guests but forbade her from vetoing Kraft or anyone else invited by the committee.

Hurt and baffled by Ethel's actions, Joe Kraft opted to stay away from the luncheon. Ethel felt victorious.

The first person who dared have the Krafts and Ethel together at the same dinner party was Valerie Cook, wife of a *Newsweek* reporter, who invited them on behalf of her guest of honor, former Nixon Administration honcho Donald Rumsfeld. After the Krafts accepted, Cook telephoned Ethel, who agreed to come. "Just don't put us in the same room," she barked.

Afterward, Kraft unexpectedly ran into Ethel at the Kennedy Library in Boston. "Oh, hi kid," she said, caught by surprise. Kraft looked at her pleadingly, hoping to end their feud. "Come on, Ethel," he said, giving her a kiss on both cheeks. But she pulled away and rushed off. It was the last contact they had.

Later, Polly Kraft took a hard look at what had happened. "All Joe and I could say was that Ethel, in a sense, had done us a favor. It seemed ridiculous, but we seriously began to wonder whether those people who sided with her were actually afraid of her. Were they so insecure that they cared that much? It taught us that we could exist quite well without them. You go on, and it really matters almost not at all, except it hurts in the beginning because people won't talk.

"The other thing that hurt Joe was that he believed if Bob had been alive none of this would have ever happened. He wouldn't have minded what Joe had written. He considered it a column about a man who was human. That's why he was so saddened by Ethel's reaction."

Roger Mudd had gotten to know Ethel while covering the Rackets Committee hearings as a young reporter for the CBS affiliate in Washington, WTOP-TV. After he joined CBS in 1961, as the network's Capitol Hill Congressional correspondent, he and his wife got the first of many invitations to Hickory Hill.

When the Mudds arrived at the front door excited and nervous that first night, they were greeted by Ethel and one of her little boys. "*This* is Roger Maris?" the disappointed youngster asked his mother, obviously expecting the Yankee slugger. Ethel shooed him away and introduced the Mudds to the other guests.

Before long the Mudds were among the regulars, and Roger became one of Ethel's Saturday morning tennis partners.

"I don't know of any other couple, or any other circle in Washington since, that was comparable to that salon," he said later. "It was an eclectic mix and the atmosphere was all so happy and jovial and a little scatterbrained. There was always so much going on—kids and dogs running in and out."

Because of his friendship with Ethel, Mudd easily got Bobby's cooperation for a special hour-long report on his Presidential aspirations. "It was a very difficult interview to do because Bobby was not very communicative," Mudd said. "None of the Kennedys were. They just didn't verbalize and did not like to talk about themselves because they thought it was Jewish psychiatry."

Despite Mudd's close relationship with Ethel, it took intense negotiations and lots of pleading before she agreed to sit for the camera, and in the end she said little.

After the Kennedys got a special viewing of the show at the CBS Washington Bureau, Bobby told Mudd he was pleased with the report. But Ethel wasn't; she was annoyed that Mudd had discussed the Kennedy family's enormous financial resources, even though he emphasized that Bobby and Ethel did not appear conscious of their money.

Ethel's criticism of the program didn't change her friendship with Mudd. When Bobby was shot in 1968, it would be Mudd who pulled Ethel through the shrieking mob so she could be at the side of her fallen husband. When one of Mudd's children was involved in a near-fatal accident in 1978, it would be Ethel who did everything she could to help the family. When Mudd needed a personal favor—a summer job for his son—it would be Ethel who arranged for the young man to work at Ted Kennedy's Senate office.

That changed, though, in 1979, after CBS did an hour news special, this time on Ted Kennedy's Presidential aspirations. Prior to agreeing to do the report, Mudd did a lot of soul-searching. "I had begun to see myself referred to in print as 'a friend of the family,' which was never true. I was more of a friend of Ethel's than of the Senator's. But I worried that if I did the report, critics would say, 'He doesn't come in with clean hands,' because of that friendship. I thought through it for a couple of days and then I said, 'You bet I can do it. Who knew as much about them as I did?' I found I was personally strong enough to do what I was paid to do, which was to ask the right questions. I thought, 'Jesus, if I'm not, I better resign.' "

Kennedy's people, who considered Mudd a friend, viewed his request as an opportunity to generate precampaign publicity for the Senator. They'd recently turned down a request from Barbara Walters for an interview, even though she came to the table with the backing of his sister Eunice Kennedy Shriver, who promised, "It would be a good piece. We can check out the questions in advance."

Mudd's program, "CBS Reports: Teddy," included a lengthy filmed interview with Kennedy at Squaw Island, with tough questions about his role in the death of Mary Jo Kopechne at Chappaquiddick a decade earlier. As part of the story, CBS lashed a camera to the front fender of a car and dramatically drove the same route Kennedy had taken that night. Kennedy had claimed at the time that he hadn't realized he'd gone off the macadam surface and on to a dirt road that led to the water. But CBS's re-creation contradicted him; the camera showed graphically how the car began bouncing when it hit the rougher surface.

After watching the program, Kennedy felt he'd been had. "That son of a bitch ambushed me," he said. But Kennedy remained friendly and cordial with Mudd.

Ethel, on the other hand, was beside herself.

"She never told me she was pissed off, but I never got invited back to Hickory Hill again," said Mudd, laughing about the incident years later. By then, Roger Mudd was philosophical:

"I didn't realize in the beginning that the reason I was welcomed at Hickory Hill was not because I was scintillating, or the best-looking guy, but because I was a prominent television journalist and was supportive of the Kennedy family. I now regard Ethel as very single-minded, loyal to the point of almost frenzy. The minute I gave signs of *not* being on the team—I was *off* the team.

"I came to realize that it was a professional mistake to have gotten close to Ethel."

Mudd subsequently ran into Polly Kraft at a party. "Well, *now* I know how you feel," he said.

65 ✻ *We Love Ethel*

AT THE END of February 1962, Ethel and Bobby returned to Hickory Hill elated and victorious from their world tour. They had been a hit. From Tokyo to Berlin, Hong Kong to Italy, the handsome young goodwill ambassador and his ebullient wife had been greeted like royalty by adoring throngs.

For Ethel, who was born to shop, a good part of her activity on the trip was spent buying things—silk and brocade yard goods in the Far East, a joke gift of sexy apparel from the House of Dior in Paris for Jack and Jackie to wear—"It's so silly I just can't stand it." She also brought home gifts bestowed upon her by foreign dignitaries for her children; Ethel's favorite was an Indonesian stuffed tiger "almost as big as a sofa and so fierce and spooky looking it's just unbelievable." Hearing that Bobby Jr. liked animals, the Indonesians also presented Ethel with a three-foot-long stuffed lizard. There also were Berlin bears for the boys, and dolls for the girls from Germany.

The trip, which cost the taxpayers a modest fifteen thousand dollars, had been a mixture of pure statesmanship on Bobby's part and vintage "I Love Lucy" on Ethel's.

In Rome, where she and Bobby had a private audience with Pope John XXIII, Ethel was involved in a zany traffic accident. She'd been window-shopping, followed by a coterie of reporters, when she fell in love with a bright green Vespa motor scooter in a showroom. Not long after, while having a bite in the Tuscan restaurant on the Piazza Fontanella Borghese, Ethel was surprised when the press corps showed up with the scooter as a gift because she had been such a "swell sport" throughout the trip. Ethel, who'd never driven a scooter, started the motor in the restaurant, which caused an Englishwoman sitting nearby to suggest, "What a charming idea, really, but wouldn't it be easier to ride outside?" Ethel then hopped on the Vespa, maneuvered out the door, and zipped into Rome's insane traffic to the cheers of Italian bystanders. Moments later she promptly crashed into a Fiat. Knocked to the ground, Ethel scrambled to her feet, smiling despite a bruised leg. "I just couldn't find the brakes," she apologized. A policeman who witnessed the fender bender said, "Mrs. Kennedy failed to slow down." But the matter was quickly settled and no charges were pressed because one of Ethel's escorts pulled out a wad of lire and paid off the other driver for whatever minor damage and inconvenience he had suffered.

A few days later reporters on the tour presented her

with an orange crash helmet emblazoned with the words CRASH KENNEDY.

In Honolulu, Ethel got dunked in the harbor a hundred yards offshore when the Navy boat that she, Bobby, and Susie Wilson had borrowed for a quick sail suddenly capsized in high wind and choppy waters. "Ethel wanted to swim back and I said, 'Are you nuts! I'm staying right here with the boat. I learned Lifesaving 101.' But she was ready to make a swim for it," said Wilson later. Luckily, two Navy pilots, waterskiing nearby, spotted their bobbing heads, directed their motorboat to the scene, and asked if they could use a lift. "We sure could," Ethel said.

In Berlin, at the German-American community school, Ethel urged a group of third-graders not to be discouraged if they did not always do well at their lessons. "After all, Bobby had to repeat third grade," she said brightly, a fact that had never appeared in any of the history books. Ethel's revelation embarrassed and annoyed the Attorney General.

In Tokyo, during a visit to the University of the Sacred Heart, whose superior had been a teacher at Manhattanville, Ethel delivered a speech that veered toward the "Twilight Zone." "I always thought that the United States was more liberal than this country, but it's not true. At Manhattanville, in my day, we were very virtuous. I understand now that you are allowed to get married." The reporter for the *Journal-American* wrote that her "train of thought was a bit hard to follow."

At the Zen Buddhist Temple of the Green Pines, where a Japanese politician had arranged for a three-hour, thirteen-course lunch, Ethel began to weary of the traditional kneeling position. She turned to a Japanese woman at the luncheon. "Are your legs getting tired?" When the woman responded politely, "No, are yours?" Ethel said firmly, "I can do it as long as you can!"

The rest of the time she spent shopping at Mitsukoshi department store, where she stocked up like a typical American tourist on battery-powered toy animals, a toy train that whistled, blew smoke, and "made lots of noise," kimono-clad dolls, wooden clogs, bamboo baskets, chopsticks, and a chinaware sake set for Bobby. Then she rode the subway back to the U.S. embassy.

Later, she was the special guest on a popular Japanese TV show, "What's My Secret?"

"Ethel's ego was bursting out of control when she got home," recalled a friend. "She began believing her own reviews. After that trip, she really did think she had more going for herself than Jackie. She was saying, 'Can you believe this, little me from Manhattanville, little Ethel Skakel, who would have ever thought . . .' She said, 'My God, they treated me like a queen . . . my God, the world loves Bobby! We should be in the White House. We *will* be in the White House.' "

66 ✻ The Monroe Affair

"I WANT TO be played by Marilyn Monroe," Ethel said with a mischievous grin. "She'd do me perfectly." Ethel's fantasy game involved the casting of the film version of Bobby's best-seller, *The Enemy Within*. Bobby had dedicated the book to Ethel, "whose love through this long struggle made the difficult easy, the impossible possible." Ethel's tongue-in-cheek choice of Marilyn would prove to be both curious and ironic.

Twentieth Century–Fox had secured the film rights following publication in 1960. A number of writers had been mentioned to do the screenplay, but Bobby favored Budd Schulberg, who'd scripted *On the Waterfront*.

By the fall of 1961, Schulberg had a draft script in hand. Producer Jerry Wald had "planted stories" in *The New York Times* and elsewhere disclosing that Paul Newman had been signed to play the role of Bobby. Wald also let it be known that he wanted Robert Mitchum as a corrupt labor leader and Spencer Tracy to play a management character. The story line was centered on Bobby's conflicts with Jimmy Hoffa and Dave Beck.

With shooting tentatively scheduled to begin in the winter of 1961 in Washington and New York, Schulberg began holding meetings with Bobby and Ethel at Hickory Hill to get their input for the final draft of the script.

"Ethel was very supportive of the project," Schulberg remembered. "She'd read my script and had suggestions about the treatment of her and Bobby and their roles in some of the scenes. Ethel gently protested that the dialogue I'd written for them wasn't exactly the way they actually talked to each other. After a point, I had Ethel practically writing her own lines. She'd say to me, 'It should be more offhand. I wouldn't say it this way.' And she'd write it her way. I didn't think of Ethel as a great intellectual, but I did find her to be a very quick study and she had a very good memory."

Even if it was a joke, Ethel's talk about wanting Monroe to play her on film had gone beyond the private meetings with Schulberg at Hickory Hill. Bobby's assistant at Justice, Bill Geoghegan, began hearing talk about it around the Attorney General's office.

In the period between 1961 and 1962 when Schulberg was having his meetings with Bobby and Ethel, the screenwriter and others in the Kennedy circle had started hearing "gossip and innuendos" in Hollywood that both Jack and Bobby had become involved romantically with Monroe. "I thought it was quite ironic that the actress being talked about as an intimate of Bobby was the same woman Ethel was casting to play her in the film," Schulberg said later. "It was eerie."

In the end, Ethel never got an opportunity to see herself portrayed on screen by Marilyn Monroe, or anyone else, for that matter. Newman, for one, turned down the role because Hoffa had disappeared, and the actor felt the story was unresolved. While Bobby understood Newman's reason for dropping out of the project, the two got into a heated argument when Newman told Bobby that he planned to narrate a critical documentary of Kennedy's pal Joe McCarthy. Then, in the summer of 1962, Jerry Wald died, and the entire project was put on hold. Later, Schulberg said, Hollywood dropped the idea completely after veiled threats were made concerning labor problems at the studios if the picture was made.

Meanwhile, the rumors about a relationship between Marilyn and Bobby had begun reaching Ethel's ears. While the movie deal fell through, the actress Ethel hoped would play her would in effect come to haunt her.

Jack had been introduced to Marilyn in the late 1950s by his brother-in-law Peter Lawford. A heavy drinker and drug user, Lawford had kinky tastes and had cheated constantly during his marriage to Pat Kennedy, acting out his proclivities with prostitutes and mistresses. "Her Catholic upbringing, her nightly prayers, and her other acts of devotion were unnerving for him," Patricia Seaton Lawford stated.

The President, like many men, had long had his eye on Marilyn, America's premier sex symbol. Hospitalized for a back problem when he was a Senator, Jack had kept a pinup of her on the wall near his bed. The photo was of Marilyn in tight shorts standing with her legs spread, but Jack had hung it upside down so Marilyn's legs were in the air.

Ethel had been aware of Jack's cheating. When the subject was brought up in her presence during the 1960 campaign, she was quick to react. Ethel and a friend were being driven to the airport in New York by a young woman who, assuming Jack's philandering was an open secret, began jabbering about it. "Ethel was so furious, so upset," recalled the pal. "Because we were in a moving car Ethel couldn't get away. She finally told the girl, 'We're not talking about any such thing, don't be an idiot,' or something along those lines. She didn't like what was going on. But, boy, once Jack became President, he could have brought Hitler in there and she wouldn't have said anything. She turned the other cheek after that."

Ethel had met Marilyn for the first time on February

1, 1962, at a going-away party that the Lawfords threw for the Kennedys on the eve of their world tour.

While Ethel felt sisterly toward Pat Lawford, she despised Peter, and the feeling was mutual. "Peter hated Ethel," Patricia Seaton Lawford said. "He felt she was self-righteous and he called her 'Miss Skakel.' He said Ethel was always wagging her index finger at him in her mind." But Ethel and Lawford kept their feelings to themselves and tried to act civil in each other's presence.

A number of Hollywood's biggest names had been invited to the Lawfords' twenty-seven-room mansion on the Pacific Ocean for Ethel and Bobby's party. The brightest star among them was Marilyn, who, as usual, arrived late, driving up among the Rolls-Royces and Bentleys in a lowly VW. Stepping out of the little car wearing a clinging black dress, a mink over her shoulders, and bathed in Chanel No. 5, she was besieged by a horde of photographers who wanted to know who her escort was. "Oh, just a sailor I've been dating," she said, winking. Actually, he was makeup artist Whitey Snyder, who'd given her a lift.

Pat Kennedy Lawford, typically effusive, ushered Marilyn into the living room.

"I wasn't sure you would come, with this huge, huge crowd."

"Are you kidding?" Marilyn responded. "I'm dying to meet Bobby."

Pat told Marilyn that Bobby would be seated between her and Kim Novak at dinner. "Is that close enough?" Pat asked. Marilyn giggled. "Thanks a lot for Kim," she said sarcastically.

Besides Novak, the other glamorous guests at the party included Natalie Wood and Janet Leigh, but Bobby only had eyes for Marilyn.

Friends of Marilyn stated later that they had seen her with Bobby long before the Lawford party. To avoid any questioning looks from Ethel, Bobby feigned boyish bashfulness and had to be coaxed by his sister to talk to Marilyn.

Ethel watched from across the room as her husband

and the sex goddess sat intimately together on the floor. "What does an Attorney General do?" Marilyn wrote in lipstick on a cocktail napkin that she passed to Bobby. Later, Ethel watched, a smile frozen on her face, as Marilyn taught Bobby how to Twist.

By the end of the night, Marilyn had consumed much champagne and needed a lift home. Anyone could have taken her, but she left with Bobby and Ed Guthman, his press aide. "Bob asked me to come along, too," Guthman said later. "He didn't say why, but his reason was pretty obvious. He didn't want to be seen going off alone in a car at night with Marilyn Monroe."

With Bobby driving, Marilyn beside him, and Guthman in the backseat, the three went directly to her Brentwood home and dropped her in the care of the housekeeper.

The next day Bobby and Ethel flew to Honolulu, the first leg of their trip.

• • •

While Bobby had lost much of his taste for George Terrien after his questionable marriage to Ethel's sister Georgeann, he still talked to him; after all, the two went back a long way. Sometime in mid-1962, as Terrien later remembered, he and Bobby were reminiscing on the telephone about the old days, when the Attorney General made a startling confession.

Said Terrien: "Bobby was sounding very macho and full of himself. Out of the blue he said, 'George [Skakel, Ethel's womanizing brother] would keel over if he knew who *I* was screwing.' First of all, I was flabbergasted that Bobby used that word because he rarely used that kind of language. Secondly, I thought he was joking because as far as I was concerned, and everyone in the family was concerned, Bobby and Ethel had a good marriage. She idolized him. We all knew Jack was fucking around, but I couldn't conceive of Bobby having a thing with anyone but Ethie. So I said, 'You are the biggest bullshitter in the world. You wouldn't have the balls to play around.' And he said, 'Just tell George I've had Marilyn's pussy.' I said, 'What the hell are you talking about?

Marilyn who?' And Bobby said, and he was laughing, 'You know, the woman Jack used to jack off over. Marilyn Monroe. After he finished with her, she fell for me. I think she's in love with me.' I told Bobby, 'You're full of shit,' and he laughed and that was the end of the conversation. I thought he was full of shit then, and I think he's full of shit now. I can't imagine Marilyn Monroe getting into bed with that little jerk."

But Terrien immediately telephoned George Skakel to pass on Bobby's boast. "George fell over laughing," Terrien recalled. He couldn't stand Bobby and the idea that Bobby would be having a thing with Marilyn Monroe was too much for him. 'She wouldn't fuck him even with my dick,' George said, dismissing what Bobby had to say as 'pure bullshit. Show me the pictures and just maybe, *maybe* then I'll believe it.'

"I also told Georgeann about it and she laughed. She said, 'They [the Kennedy men] are a bunch of sophomoric brats. Don't believe it. I don't. Ethel would giggle if she heard that one.' As far as I was concerned, none of the Skakels ever put any credence in the story. Whether Ethel did, I don't know. Never in a million years would I have brought it up to her and neither would her brothers or sisters."

After the Lawford party, Ethel didn't see Bobby together with Marilyn for another two and a half months. That occasion was also the first and last time the principal players in the drama—Ethel, Bobby, Marilyn, Jack, and Peter Lawford—were ever seen together in public. The date was May 19, 1962. The location was Madison Square Garden. The event was the star-studded celebration of Jack's forty-fifth birthday before an audience of some twenty thousand loyal Democrats. At Lawford's behest, Marilyn had agreed to sing "Happy Birthday" to the President. For insiders, the event seemed like a sick practical joke being perpetrated on the American electorate, who were unaware of the behind-the-scenes shenanigans.

As usual, Marilyn was late and Lawford, the emcee, joked about her tardiness. Jack, Ethel, and Bobby laughed when Lawford announced, "Mr. President, on this occasion of your birthday, this lovely lady is not only pulchritudinous but punctual. Mr. President—Marilyn Monroe!" All eyes turned but she did not appear. Other entertainers performed in the meantime. Then Lawford was at the microphone again. "A woman of whom it may truly be said—she needs no introduction," he teased, but Marilyn was nowhere to be seen. Finally, after a few more acts appeared, Lawford announced, "Mr. President, because, in the history of show business, perhaps there has been no one female who has meant so much, who has done more . . . Mr. President . . . the *late* Marilyn Monroe!"

Marilyn finally appeared from the wings in what later would become known as the "Kennedy dress": a twelve-thousand-dollar shimmering, beaded Jean Louis original that appeared to be painted on her body. In fact, Marilyn had to be stitched into the dress, which was made with special panels to cover her breasts and genitalia because she refused to wear panties or bra. A small slit at the bottom of the dress allowed her the freedom to take small, mincing steps.

Watching her walk onstage, Jack commented to another guest, "What an ass. . . . *What* an ass."

With Ethel seated beside him, Bobby said nothing.

In a whisper-soft, little girl voice, Marilyn looked at Jack and sang "Happy Birthday" as no one ever had sung that song before.

After the applause died, she sang another song especially written for the occasion by Richard Adler to the tune of the Bob Hope theme "Thanks for the Memory." Marilyn then led the audience in another rendition of "Happy Birthday."

Afterward, the President came to the stage. "Thank you," he said. "I can now retire from politics after having 'Happy Birthday' sung to me in such a sweet, wholesome way."

Jackie, aware of her husband's affair, was noticeably absent; she'd spent the day horseback riding in Virginia.

Backstage, Marilyn needed to recover from the performance. She had to be literally cut out of her dress and bathed with cold towels to lower her body temperature.

She then left for a party where Jack and Bobby were waiting at the penthouse apartment of United Artists executive Arthur Krim.

There, with Ethel looking on, Bobby danced with Marilyn at least five times, a fact that did not go unnoticed by Dorothy Kilgallen, who gleefully noted the fact in her gossip column the next morning. Bobby cockily walked around arm-in-arm with Marilyn, a scene witnessed by other party goers, including important journalists. At one point late in the evening, a candid photo was taken of Marilyn huddled with Jack and Bobby, the only published shot of her with both brothers. In her skintight gown, her right breast was pointed at Bobby and her left at Jack. One of the reporters at the party, UPI White House correspondent Merriman Smith, approached Bobby and Marilyn and the Attorney General was forced to introduce them. Later, he grew concerned when he caught sight of Smith talking to Marilyn and taking notes. He also was anxious about the photo that had been taken.

The distinguished Adlai Stevenson, like all of the men that night, was overwhelmed by Marilyn. He later wrote to a friend, Mary Lasker, telling her that he finally got to talk to Marilyn "after breaking through the strong defenses established by Robert Kennedy, who was dodging around her like a moth around the flame."

Also present was Arthur M. Schlesinger, Jr., who noted later in his biography of Bobby that he himself "had never seen anyone so beautiful" as Marilyn. "Bobby and I engaged in mock competition for her; she was most agreeable to him and pleasant to me—but then she receded into her own glittering mist."

In fact, Marilyn did more than "recede," as Schlesinger put it so poetically. Sometime after one A.M. she and the President actually disappeared from the party, followed by Secret Service agents. The two went to Kennedy's private suite at the Carlyle Hotel, supposedly for their last rendezvous. Marilyn did not return to her own Manhattan apartment until several hours later.

It had been quite an evening.

The next morning Ethel and Bobby returned to Hickory Hill.

Ethel was irate at Bobby's behavior with Marilyn, but did not make an issue of it at the time. A few days later, though, she telephoned her sister.

"Ethie told Georgeann she was furious with Bobby and 'would have liked to scratch that tramp's eyes out,' " George Terrien recalled. But Ethel was a good Kennedy wife. She kept her mouth shut and looked the other way, like they all did."

Ethel turned to affairs of state to keep herself from dwelling on the suspected affairs of her husband. Her first priority was to write a speech that she had to deliver on May 27, 1962, to the graduates of St. Bernard College, operated by the Catholic Benedictine order, in Cullman, Alabama. It was Ethel's first commencement address; she also received an honorary degree of doctor of humanities.

Through the summer of 1962 Bobby's relationship with Marilyn continued, while Marilyn's emotional and physical condition deteriorated. Her career had gone down the tubes; she was depressed over her relationships with Jack and Bobby, and she was drinking heavily.

During that period—beginning in June and into late July—Marilyn made numerous telephone calls to Bobby at the Justice Department, and she received calls from him. An unpublished photograph taken at the Lawford home during this time reportedly showed Peter standing with Bobby and Marilyn, who was wearing a skimpy robe and holding a bottle of champagne. The snapshot suggested that Bobby had been making trips to California on the sly without Ethel's knowledge. A friend and neighbor of Marilyn's asserted that she'd seen Bobby and Marilyn hug, kiss, and drink wine together. Meanwhile, Marilyn was affirming to friends the rumors they were hearing—that she'd been passed from Jack to Bobby.

Bill Geoghegan said he once heard from powerful Washington attorney Edward Bennett Williams that Peter Lawford had urged Monroe "to fall all over Bobby at a party." Williams, according to his biographer, Evan Thomas, was intrigued with the lives of the Kennedys, and had learned that Bobby and Jack had become involved with Monroe. On one occasion, Williams had a meeting with an investigator who needed advice because he'd been hired by Joe Kennedy to spy on Monroe and didn't know what to do. Williams never revealed how he advised the man, according to Thomas.

One of the more interesting pieces of the Marilyn-Bobby puzzle was the mysterious undated handwritten note purportedly signed by Jean Kennedy Smith that was found among Marilyn's papers.

Of the Kennedy sisters, Ethel had always been closest to Jean, her roommate at Manhattanville, and the one who prodded the relationship along between her and Bobby. Yet the note, if genuine, bore the address of the Kennedys' Palm Beach home and suggested strong approval of a relationship between Bobby and Marilyn. The writer stated to Marilyn that "you and Bobby are the new item" and invited her to join Bobby for a Kennedy family visit.

No one had ever been able to give a credible explanation for the note, and Jean Kennedy Smith said she had no recollection of ever having written it. But all that changed when the note came up for auction years later in May 1994, sparking a flurry of gossip items in newspapers. Jean, then serving as U.S. Ambassador to Ireland, sent a fax to the *Washington Post* claiming that the note's language had been misinterpreted. "The suggestion that the letter verifies an affair is utter nonsense . . ." she wrote. "I am shocked anyone would believe such innuendo about a letter obviously written in jest." Jean's response, however, confirmed for the first time that she had in fact written the mysterious missive, prank or no prank.

As Marilyn's emotional state worsened, she began making odd and contradictory statements. She told some friends that Bobby might divorce Ethel and marry her, still others that Bobby had cut off their relationship and that she was thinking about exposing the Kennedys. In early August, several days before the end, Marilyn asked Mickey Song, a Los Angeles hairstylist for the Kennedys, to come to her house. He thought she needed her hair done, but instead Marilyn began probing him about the Kennedy marriages. "What about Bobby and Ethel? I can't believe that's a happy marriage. What does he see in her?" Later, Song said he felt Marilyn was seeking information to use against the Kennedys.

On August 3, Dorothy Kilgallen ran a blind item about Bobby and Marilyn's relationship. It said, "Marilyn Monroe is cooking in the sex appeal department. She has appeared vastly alluring to a handsome gentleman. A handsome gentleman with a bigger name than Joe DiMaggio in his heyday—so don't write her off."

That same day Marilyn learned from the Hyannis Port compound that Bobby, Ethel, and several of the children had flown to San Francisco, where the Attorney General was scheduled to address the American Bar Association. Marilyn made several calls to the St. Francis, where they were staying, leaving messages for Bobby. Agitated, she took sleeping pills that night but was awakened constantly by an anonymous female caller who said, "Leave Bobby alone, you tramp. Leave Bobby alone."

The next morning, August 4, Marilyn, looking sick, described the telephone calls to her friend Jeanne Carmen. "Marilyn said she couldn't tell who it was. She didn't think it was Ethel," Carmen said.

Sometime on August 4, at Lawford's request, Bobby quietly slipped into Los Angeles and met for the last time with the distraught Marilyn.

Late that night, at age thirty-six, a depressed Marilyn Monroe died after taking too many sleeping pills.

One of the conclusions of British writer Anthony Summers, who did one of the most extensive investigations of Marilyn's relationship with the Kennedy brothers for his biography *Goddess: The Secret Lives of Marilyn Monroe,* was that "for many months she engaged in intermittent sexual encounters with both the President and Robert Kennedy. . . . The Attorney General, never the womanizer his brother was, may have begun his relationship with Marilyn as a rescue mission, an attempt to steer her into emotional calm. Soon, though, perhaps initially tempted to follow his brother merely in grasping the sexual prize, Robert then fell for the flickering light of Marilyn's fragile spirit. Their affair lasted for months. Then, alarmed by the flood of reports that criminals were hoping to take advantage of the Kennedy follies, the Attorney General tried to sever the connection. It was not easily done."

Despite numerous unofficial scenarios by credible writers like Summers, and by various researchers and private investigators who have alleged everything from a murder conspiracy involving Bobby and Peter Lawford to a Kennedy-instigated massive cover-up, no formal conclusion has ever been reached about the circumstances surrounding Marilyn's untimely death, and it remains as much a mystery today as it was on that August night in 1962.

The question of a Kennedy cover-up of the Monroe affair—this one with Ethel as a possible prime player—arose again in 1985, when "ABC News" chief Roone Arledge suddenly and inexplicably killed a "20/20" investigative segment on the relationship between the Kennedy brothers and Marilyn, much of it based on Summers's reportage. Arledge claimed that he axed the segment because it "set out to be a piece which would demonstrate that because of alleged relations between Bobby Kennedy and Marilyn Monroe, the Presidency was compromised because organized crime was involved . . . [but the piece did not] live up to its billing." He labeled the story "gossip-column stuff."

Arledge's ruling infuriated ABC producers and reporters involved in the piece. Correspondents Sylvia Chase and Geraldo Rivera left the show in protest, as did segment producer Lowell Bergman. Mild-mannered Hugh Downs, "20/20" co-anchor, angry over the decision, stated bluntly that the segment was "more thoroughly documented than network coverage of Watergate as its height."

Others connected with the project have long suggested that Ethel's close friendship with Arledge and her other important connections at the network were the real reasons for the story being dropped.

A dozen years before the "20/20" piece, Ethel had been seen on Arledge's arm in Washington and New York. *Parade* magazine, with a weekly circulation of millions, had even mentioned that the two were dating.

Ethel had additional tentacles within the network. Her son-in-law Jeff Ruhe, then married to Courtney Kennedy, was Arledge's assistant. Moreover, David Burke, one of the top vice-presidents of the news division, had been Ted Kennedy's chief aide.

"There's no doubt in my mind," speculated a "20/20" staffer involved in the project, "that Ethel learned what was in the piece during the reporting and editing stages. After all, her son-in-law was working next to Roone, for God's sake. Then Courtney talked to her mother and to Jeff, and Ted said something to David [Burke], and Ethel got on the horn to Roone. Whichever way it happened, the Kennedys did a quick bit of lobbying and the piece was killed."

• • •

While Bobby's brief affair with Marilyn has become part of legend, it wasn't his first, nor would it be his last, fling with another woman, despite his choir-boy reputation. During his eighteen years of marriage to Ethel, Bobby had occasionally bedded others, and carried on numerous flirtations. Some of his paramours were even reported to have been members of Ethel and Bobby's social circle.

Said a former Hickory Hill insider, a high-profile Washington woman, a chum of Ethel's who claimed knowledge of Bobby's indiscretions:

"Just like Jack, Bobby thought nothing of doing the wives of friends. He felt honor-bound to have a sample of them, and never gave it a second thought.

"These women were like a great silver tray of little canapés and when Bobby felt like popping one in his mouth he did. Bobby was never in *love* with any of them, and Hickory Hill was never threatened.

"One of the tacit understandings in that circle was that you protected Ethel from anything that might hurt her. There was lots of whispering about Bobby playing around, but Ethel heard what she chose to hear. She knew what was going on, but she didn't bring it to the surface. Ethel threw her formidable energy behind Bobby, and he never would have left her.

"For a woman, it was a red badge of courage to get fumbled up by Bobby, and it was understood that if you went off with Bobby, you covered for him."

The women who were named as having had flings with Bobby offered vehement denials. After making their denials, each would then point the finger at another woman, claiming that *that* woman had been involved with Bobby. One added, "In his own subtle way, Bobby was as bad as Jack, but his sexual appetite wasn't as voracious."

As for Ethel, sex had never been of great importance, one of her close friends observed. "She got pregnant eleven times, but you don't have to be bothered with sex while you're pregnant—and I believe that was her feeling. Bobby just came home and did his little husbandly thing and she tolerated her little wifely thing and always it resulted in a pregnancy because both of them wanted to have lots of children."

Bobby had developed quite a reputation as a "grabber," according to Dean Martin's ex-wife, Jeanne, who had been at parties at Peter Lawford's house with the Kennedys. She recalled that Bobby had no qualms about flirting with a woman in one room while Ethel was in the next. "I have a friend who was in the library with him," Martin claimed, "and before she knew it the door was locked and he threw her on the couch. It was so blatant."

Ross Traphagen was part of the group of young men that included Bill Geoghegan at Harvard, whom Ethel and Jean Kennedy sometimes dated when they were at Manhattanville. Years later, when Traphagen had become a prominent attorney, he was at a party in Washington with his wife when they encountered the Attorney General on the prowl. Traphagen's wife was initially glad to see Bobby because she had been a friend of his sister Jean's and knew some of the other Kennedys and Skakels from her days as a student at Noroton, the Sacred Heart school in Connecticut.

"It was a private dance and Bobby Kennedy showed up in a limousine without Ethel, who was away," Traphagen recounted. "Bobby stood in the corner of the room acting like Napoleon—a little man, eyeing the various women in the place. He finally cut in on my wife and within five minutes said, 'Why don't you come home with me? I have my car outside. Ethel's away.' It was terribly brazen, but typical of what I'd heard about the Kennedys. My wife was obviously upset. I didn't want to make a scene, so I didn't confront Bobby with it. I thought what he did was typical Kennedy. Typical Bobby."

Many attending a Hawaiian theme party given by Madelin Gilpatric and her husband, Roswell, deputy secretary of defense, were shocked by Bobby's blatant attentions to another woman in Ethel's presence. *Washington Star* society reporter Betty Beale said that while French ambassador Herve Alphand did a hula dance with Bob McNamara's wife, "Bobby [Kennedy] was sitting on the floor next to one of the Hawaiian dancers, putting his hand up her skirt. That was the only example of tastelessness at that fun party."

Meanwhile, Ethel once telephoned journalist Nancy Dickerson to tell her that Joe Kennedy was offering a thousand-dollar prize to the sister-in-law "who gave the most scintillating dinner for ten and provided him with the best dinner partner. I was [Ethel's] candidate and she wanted to book me 'before Eunice gets you.' "

During a cookout at Hickory Hill—while Ethel was vacationing in Hyannis Port—Bobby, then a U.S. Senator, went for a motorcycle ride with Polly Bussell, a beautiful blonde Radcliffe graduate in her early twenties who worked on scheduling in Bobby's Senate office. Journalist Douglas Kiker, who had occasionally dated Polly and was present at the party, said that Bobby and

Polly, both in bathing suits, had driven to a nearby wooded area when a McLean police car pulled in.

"When Bobby saw the cops, he took off into the underbrush, leaving this tall blonde in a bikini standing there," Kiker said later. "So here was Polly all alone on her motorcycle. The cops escorted her back into Hickory Hill. After they left, Bobby reappeared out of the bush. It was the Chappaquiddick syndrome long before Chappaquiddick. The way Polly told it to me, it was just a flat-out innocent ride on a motorcycle, but that's how Bobby handled it."

Bussell, who had been personally hired by Bobby after he met her in July 1966 at the Martha's Vineyard home of writer William Styron, confirmed later that she had taken Bobby "for a couple of motorcycle rides," but said her memory wasn't clear about the incident at Hickory Hill.

Bussell had received a number of invitations from both Bobby and Ethel to parties at Hickory Hill. "I spent much more time with Robert Kennedy than with Ethel," she said. "I felt I was definitely a friend, but not necessarily with her." Ethel had given Polly special instructions not to tell any of the other office staffers about the invitations so they wouldn't be jealous. A Hickory Hill insider noted that Bobby often told Ethel which women to invite to parties. "They were the cute blondes, the ones Bobby liked to have around him, and Ethel never seemed to object. She always went along with whatever he wanted."

But Bobby had a double standard, whether it involved Ethel or other men who cheated on their wives.

Once, at a party in Greenwich, Bobby became outraged when he saw Ethel dancing with Ray O'Connell, a New York businessman. Helen Downey, a friend of the Skakels, remembered being shocked by Bobby's performance. "Ray tapped Ethel to dance and sort of gave her a little pat on the behind because they'd known each other for years," Downey said. "Bobby came over and grabbed Ethel and said, 'Listen, why are you acting like a whore? I don't want to be married to a whore. Get out of here. You're not dancing with anybody.' I was just so surprised at the way he behaved. It was shocking. Ethel looked dumbfounded."

Another time, during a South African fact-finding trip, Bobby discovered that a friend, a Washington journalist, had been cheating on his wife. When Bobby returned home, he told Gerald Tremblay, who also knew the writer, that he had been repulsed and wanted nothing more to do with the man. "When this thing about Marilyn Monroe came up, I was astounded because if that was true, it would have made Bobby a hypocritical guy and I had never thought of him that way," Tremblay said.

In the future, Ethel would be faced with more rumors about Bobby's womanizing—with another actress and with one of their friends.

In October 1962, two months after Marilyn Monroe's death, Ethel became pregnant for the first time in three years, the longest she'd gone during her years of marriage to Bobby.

67 * Ethel, The Omnipotent

BY 1963, THE Kennedys seemed invincible. Following in the footsteps of his brother Jack, thirty-year-old Ted had been elected to the U.S. Senate from Massachusetts, swept into office easily in November 1962 on a tide of pure golden Kennedy élan. Entering his second full year in office, Jack was enjoying his highest popularity ratings ever. And political pundits were already forecasting something far greater for Bobby after the '64 Presidential race, which many felt Jack already had in the bag. From the Kennedy camp came predictions that Bobby would snap up the governorship of Massachusetts, then the Presidency—no later than 1972.

Camelot, it appeared, was here for a long, long time.

As for Ethel, she had risen to the occasion as the New Frontier's most favored lady. The very name Ethel had become as synonymous with the Kennedy mystique as Jackie's. It was as if there were two First Ladies in town.

Newsweek. McCall's. Life. Sunday magazine supplements. Nationally syndicated columns. From Bangor to Bellevue, Portland to Pocatello, housewives—voters—were being given weekly, if not daily, doses of Ethel: her activities, her views, even her favorite recipes. Because the Kennedy Administration had been promoting physical fitness, journalists began pointing to "petite and peppy" Ethel as the Kennedy woman more in tune with health than any of the others. Hearst's *Journal-American* in New York advised readers to "Stay in Trim with the New Frontier Diet," which stressed that Ethel "never counts calories . . . she claims that lots of exercise and a simple, nutritious diet with lots of fruits and gallons of milk" keep her "healthy and trim." Marguerite Higgins noted that one clue to Ethel's health and exuberance was the lazy Susan in the middle of the dining-room table at Hickory Hill that held bottles of vitamins for each of the Kennedys.

Despite her claims of a healthy diet, Ethel admitted to Agnes Murphy, who wrote the "At Home With . . ." column for the Sunday *New York Post Magazine*, that she had a sweet tooth. "I simply love desserts! My favorite? Chocolate roll, filled with chocolate and vanilla ice cream. With whip cream on the outside, and yes—also with chocolate sauce."

The Sunday supplement *This Week* ran a feature under Ethel's byline about fitness and motherhood. Boasting that all of her children were able to swim by the age of three, she said, "I turned them over on their tummies in the bathtub and told them to kick their feet." Noting that she and Bobby played games such as Kick the Can and Chase One, Chase All with the children, Ethel declared, "There is too much at stake in the world for us to deteriorate into weaklings, which will, in turn, affect our mental and moral strength."

Ethel's exuberance had also manifested itself in the occasional use of government perks that sparked Bobby's enmity. Nothing seemed to irk Bobby more than to see official cars being used for personal errands. It was, he felt, bad public relations. He didn't want the voters to get the impression that the Kennedys were living high off the hog. Ignoring Bobby's feelings, Ethel continued to ride around town on the taxpayers' tab, but made it a point to do it behind her husband's back.

Every winter when it snowed in Washington, Ethel telephoned the Justice Department's motor pool demanding that a car and driver be delivered to Hickory Hill posthaste. She'd pile a couple of the children in the backseat with her, throw a sled or two in the trunk, and order the chauffeur to proceed to hilly Battery-Kimball Park in Washington, where she'd rendezvous with her pals and their children.

"Ethel would have the driver sit in the car at the base of the hill and she and I and the children would have a grand time sledding down," one friend recalled. "Then we'd get into the warm car with the kids and the sleds and Ethel would have the driver take us back to the top. He'd then drive down to the bottom and wait for us. We did it over and over again through the afternoon. It was a riot. But then Ethel got hell for it from Bobby and Jack."

It was during those informal get-togethers with her girlfriends—outings with the children, shopping excursions—that Ethel showed herself to be as much of a Catholic crusader as her mother had been. When she saw a potential target for conversion, she zeroed in with missionary zeal. Susie Wilson, born a Jew and raised an Episcopalian, recalled Ethel espousing her belief that "People who lived according to Ethel's faith would find a reward in heaven." Following several trips abroad together, Ethel remarked to Wilson, "Susie, you're the only person who has met two Popes and hasn't converted yet."

Sarah Davis also was exposed to Ethel's proselytizing, even to the point of being offered incentives if she agreed to convert, a method that Big Ann had used in her heyday.

"Ethel did her best to make me turn Catholic," Davis said years later. "Ethel believed that if she got me to join the Catholic Church she'd be assured a place in heaven. That's why she really wanted me to do it. At one point she gave me *Imitation of Christ* and Thomas Merton's *Seven Storey Mountain* to read. But the major incentive was that if I agreed to convert she'd pay for my kids to go to private school. At the time, we didn't have the money for private schools. But my husband then started to make money and the kids, who started in public schools, all went to private school anyway. Ethel gave it a shot when the kids were really young but never brought it up later."

Ethel was more successful with Paul and Gertrude Corbin. A close and valuable political operative of Bobby's, Paul Corbin was at one point accused of being both a member of the American Communist Party and a rabid supporter of Joe McCarthy's. He was disliked by others in the Kennedy camp for his arrogance. Arthur Schlesinger, Jr., for one, called Corbin a "natural-born con man." Gertrude Corbin, though much older, had become close to Ethel, volunteering her time at Hickory Hill for whatever Ethel needed done: opening correspondence, working on charity functions. The Corbins idolized the Kennedys. Their Virginia home was a shrine to Ethel and Bobby, the walls covered with photos and other Kennedy memorabilia. When Ethel began proselytizing, the Corbins listened attentively.

"Ethel was responsible for us converting and becoming Catholics," acknowledged former Presbyterian Gertrude Corbin years later. "Ethel and Bobby were there at the conversion. Ethel felt very proud. Ethel became my [Catholic] godmother. If I wanted, I could go to her with personal problems. I always felt that Ethel would have made a great nun."

Religion aside, Ethel was still the capital's best-known party giver and funster. But her bashes had become a bit more subdued. The pool dunkings had ended, mainly because the publicity had infuriated the President. Later, Ethel admitted that the pool shenanigans were "awfully unfortunate. I don't like that subject at all. They probably hurt Bobby." But the parties at Hickory Hill continued on a weekly basis.

In early 1963, Ethel threw one for Gen. Maxwell Taylor, chairman of the Joint Chiefs of Staff, that had all of the capital buzzing. Arriving guests were greeted by a dummy dressed in a U.S. Army general's uniform hanging from a tree by a parachute harness; Taylor's place at the table was marked by the traditional champagne-filled large bowl used by a paratrooper to celebrate his first jump. Joan Kennedy, who'd recently been quoted by a national magazine as saying that Jackie owned three wigs—wigs were fairly new as fashion accessories in those days—sat down to find her place marked by three miniature hairpieces. And CIA chief John McCone found a black box at his dinner place that suddenly exploded open, revealing a green hand that reached out and closed the lid.

At another party, they made Vice President Johnson, whom the Kennedys barely tolerated, red with anger and embarrassment.

"After the party got rolling pretty good," recalled Jim Skakel, "Ethel got up on a chair and she was feeling pretty good and she said, 'I'm giving a toast to the second most important man in the Western world.' " Rushton Skakel, who also was at the party, said that before Lyndon Johnson could move toward the microphone, "Bobby rushed up to claim the number-two spot. LBJ was so shocked he couldn't believe it. His temperature either went up or down."

While Johnson may have taken a dim view of Ethel's sense of humor, most everyone, it seemed, fell for her high jinks, even intellectuals like Rose Styron, a poet and the wife of writer William Styron. Ethel and Rose, the mother of four, had first met at the birth of Camelot, and usually saw one another during the summers when the

Styrons held forth at Martha's Vineyard and the Kennedys vacationed across the water at Hyannis Port.

"Ethel was someone who was always game to have a good time," Rose Styron said later. "We would go to the beach and everybody would sleep on our lawn and there were a lot of high jinks and a lot of fun that Ethel was always a part of. My view of her was so two-dimensional—so much as a sport and an athlete."

One summer day the Kennedys, the Styrons, and other friends decided to go to a private beach on the other side of the island. Knowing it was a long, rocky road down to the sand, Ethel commandeered a van from one of the Styrons' neighbors, loaded it with kids, food, and beach gear, and, followed by Teddy, Eunice, and others in a car, headed out for the day. The first mishap occurred upon arrival, when Ethel raced onto the beach. The van got stuck in the sand and had to be dug out. After that, everything went swimmingly, with lots of fun and games for the kids and the adults. At the end of the day, with plans for everyone to have dinner back at the Styrons', Teddy took it upon himself to round up the crew. "We better get back," he yelled, "and get dinner started."

Ethel said, "I'm coming too. I'll get everything."

Recalled Styron: "Ethel really was the great organizer of all this and she collected everybody. We all got back to the house and put dinner on but suddenly we noticed that someone was missing. 'Well, where's Eunice?' Teddy asked. And nobody could find Eunice. About an hour later, after it had gotten dark, Teddy came out to me in the kitchen and said, 'Rose, you won't believe what's on the front porch.' There was poor Eunice, drenched because it had started to rain, wrapped in a tiny little towel, and nothing more, looking so distressed no one could believe it.

"Eunice had been behind a dune sunbathing in the nude and Ethel had picked up everything on the beach, including Eunice's bathing suit and shoes, and thrown them in the van with everyone else's stuff. Eunice had to walk barefoot back up this rocky path and all the way out to the main road; she had to hitchhike twice. She got one ride after another until she got home.

"The Kennedys all thought it was the funniest thing that ever happened. Poor Eunice was torn between weeping and fury."

Out riding one afternoon in 1963 near Hickory Hill with a couple of her children, Ethel came upon an upsetting sight—an emaciated horse locked and tied in a chicken coop. Horrified, she galloped home at once and ordered her groom, Richard Mayberry, to bring the animal back to Hickory Hill so it could be cared for.

The horse's owner, Nicholas Zemo, a trainer with a record of animal cruelty charges, was furious when he learned of her mission. He demanded that the animal be returned instantly. Ethel refused, reporting Zemo to the county animal welfare league instead.

When the horse died of malnutrition and a severe anemic condition a week later at Hickory Hill, the league brought another cruelty complaint against Zemo.

Thus began a bizarre, often comical legal battle between Ethel and Zemo that would involve two trials and stretch over almost four years. Zemo was handed a suspended $250 fine and a six-month suspended jail term. He then sued Ethel for $30,000—the cost of the horse. Overnight, Ethel, who was eventually exonerated, became the unofficial patron saint of the nation's nags.

Behind the scenes, though, Ethel found the whole scenario a big hoot, according to her chum Sue Markham. "We knew this was going to get Ethel into trouble, but somehow we couldn't stop laughing to keep from crying," Sue said later. "Here was this horse, looking like a bag of bones in a comic strip, standing there, or trying to, with all the fat, sleek Kennedy horses with their initialed blankets on them, and Ethel had stolen it and, well . . . it was just so funny that there was no way we could stop laughing even when we were being serious, like Charlie Chaplin movies where you laugh while somebody falls off the Empire State Building."

At one point, during the height of the publicity surrounding the case, Ted Kennedy was introduced at a

National Press Club luncheon not as the Senator from Massachusetts, but rather "as the brother-in-law of an admitted horse thief." Quick on the uptake, Kennedy said, "It must be hereditary—I understand Ethel's grandfather really was a horse thief."

While Ethel and Ted found the case a big joke, Jack was livid. Columnist Joseph Alsop's wife, Susan Mary Alsop, recalled being seated next to the President at a White House dinner when the subject of Ethel and the horse came up.

"I had a little too much to drink because you always do at the White House, you're so nervous and you gulp down everything that's passed to you," she said. "I told the President this story about his sister-in-law and instead of laughing, he was furious. I told him he was being stuffy. Imagine, saying such a thing to the President of the United States. He talked to the person on his other side for a while, and then a little later, he turned back to me.

" 'You know why we disagree,' he said, 'about whether this story is funny or not? It's because you like Ethel as a friend, and of course you want to protect her, but you're not responsible for what happens. I happen to love her, and also to be responsible because I'm the President and she's my sister-in-law.'

"I felt so badly afterward because of course I'd thought he was worried about the publicity. Not at all. He was worried about Ethel. He knew she had a propensity to do things impulsively."

When the horse-rustling case was finally concluded, Ethel quipped, "I don't think Bobby's going to let me off the property again without my keeper."

And that was certainly the wish of some of Ethel's neighbors in McLean who were furious about her habit of riding roughshod over their property, much like she had done as a girl in Greenwich.

One neighbor, Hope Johnston, who had grown up in Greenwich and knew the Skakels well, lived midway between Hickory Hill and the home of Ethel and Bobby's good friends Red and Anita Fay.

"To get to the Fays' place, Ethel would just ride right through my lawn and leave big hoofprints behind," Hope Johnston said later. "She'd do it periodically with whole troops of kids on horses. You could hear them coming—clop, clop, clop—and then they'd cut across the lawn. Of course, the horses left their stuff all over the place, too. She just didn't give a damn. One neighbor used to go after her with a broom. What she did was typical Skakel, typical Kennedy. She had no respect and it would make my husband hit the ceiling."

But Hope dared not complain to either Ethel or Red Fay. Hope's husband was then a Navy captain at the Pentagon and Fay was an undersecretary of the Navy. Fay had once boasted to Johnston that he "was the only person in the Defense Department who [Secretary of Defense Robert] McNamara couldn't fire because he was such an old friend of Jack's." There was no way Johnston, who later became an admiral, was going to go up against that kind of clout.

One night the Johnstons were having dinner when they heard the screams of fire engines racing up the street and stopping at the Hickory Hill stables. Thinking the place was ablaze, they ran outside and found the firemen laughing hysterically.

"It was the first frost of the season," recalled Hope Johnston, still chuckling years later. "The horse manure had been piled up outside. The manure is hot, and when you put it in the cold air, it smokes. One of Ethel's maids saw all that steam coming out of the horse manure and thought the stable was on fire so she called the firemen. What a crazy place that Hickory Hill was."

68 ⁕ Family Affair

ETHEL'S EUPHORIA OVER the boundless political successes of the Kennedys was once again threatened by her own family's peccadillos and the threat their exposure posed to her in-laws.

The latest bit of unhappy news that Ethel received from Greenwich was the breakup after almost ten years of her sister Ann's marriage to John McCooey. To Ethel, divorce was sinful and utterly scandalous. Moreover, she knew it would infuriate her mother-in-law, the devout Rose Kennedy.

The McCooeys' union had been rocky from the start. Immediately after their marriage, they had moved into one of the guest houses at Lake Avenue, living under Big Ann's controlling thumb. Her parents' death a year after the marriage left Ann traumatized. In 1958, after trying unsuccessfully for several years to conceive, she finally gave birth to a son, John Jr.

But by 1960 her marriage was about to veer off track. That spring, at a dinner party held at the Greenwich home of friends, Ann met William M. Fine, a charismatic New York businessman whose high-profile jobs had included being publisher of *Harper's Bazaar*. Like Ann, Fine was married. He and his attractive wife, Patricia, and three sons lived in Darien, an affluent community much like Greenwich. Like the McCooeys', the Fines' marriage was on the rocks.

"Bill and Ann were drawn magnetically to each other that night," recalled Bev Keith, a close friend of both couples. "I remember being very surprised because

Ann really wasn't Bill's type. He liked more glamorous women."

But Bev Keith wasn't entirely shocked. "In those days, we called Greenwich 'Grimwich' because the people there didn't seem to have a handle on real life," she observed. "There were lots of parties, drinking, and fooling around. It was a very hypocritical place. Once, our friend Bob Mathias, the Olympic star, a big, good-looking guy, came to visit and the women went bonkers over him, practically handing him their panties."

While friends of Ann's weren't shocked by her affair, they were surprised at how open it was. "It was almost as if Ann didn't care who knew," a pal recalled later. "She told me about the beautiful letters Bill wrote to her and the attention he was giving her."

And then Ann got pregnant. She was in Florida with a friend from Greenwich, Sally O'Brien, when she got the news. Sally's husband, Royall O'Brien, the baby's godfather, said it was well known that the baby was Fine's. "Ann acknowledged it from the beginning," he said.

John McCooey was stunned.

"I knew the baby wasn't mine," he said later. "I knew the affair was going on. One day before the birth of the child, Ann came to me and said, 'I want a divorce' in favor of Bill Fine. I said, 'Does Bill Fine know?' and she said, 'Of course he does.' I had somebody call Fine to check to see if he knew that Ann intended to marry him. Fine then called up Ann, got her on the phone for an hour, and just slaughtered her. He told her, 'Are you crazy? I have no intention of marrying you.' "

Ann had the baby, a girl whom she named after herself and her mother, at Doctors Hospital in Manhattan. She then returned to the McCooeys' home on Winding Lane in Greenwich, where she lived for six months before permanently separating from her husband and renting a townhouse on Manhattan's Upper East Side.

The Skakels were aghast. Ethel, for one, stopped talking to her sister for more than a year. Worried that Ann's problems might become public—a Hearst gossip columnist had the story and was threatening to print it—Ethel asked Bobby to meet with John McCooey to work out a quiet divorce settlement.

A meeting eventually took place in Kennedy's suite at the Carlyle Hotel. "Bobby was changing to go out and he was in and out of the bathroom taking his bath," recalled McCooey. "He definitely could have lived without that meeting. He was Attorney General and he had plenty on his plate without me. But he had promised Ethel he'd talk to me; he was interjecting himself for Ethel's sake. In his own inimitable way he tried to persuade me to give Ann a divorce. 'Let's have no mess here,' he told me. He wanted to have it peaceful. I said, 'There is no mess, there will be no mess.' I told him Ann could have a divorce anytime she wanted. 'All she has to do is give me custody of our son.' Bobby asked me to think about what he had said, to give it some serious thought. We couldn't reach a conclusion and I left after about an hour."

Ann had made a number of financial demands on McCooey, which she eventually dropped. When McCooey saw that it would be all but impossible for him to get custody of his son, he dropped that demand. Several years after their separation, Ann went to Mexico and got a divorce on the grounds of incompatibility. Later, the McCooeys' marriage was formally annulled by the Catholic Church.

Ann subsequently married her divorce lawyer, Peter Ryan, but that marriage also ended in divorce after almost a decade. After his second wife died, John McCooey married Helen Downey, a New York real estate woman, one-time actress, and longtime friend of the Skakel family.

• • •

At the same time that Ann's marriage was disintegrating, Ethel learned that her brother George had left his wife, Pat, and was having an affair with Bettan Olwaeus, a beautiful Swedish stockbroker with the investment firm of Bear, Stearns in New York.

While Ethel loved George, she had come to realize that he was a loose cannon who couldn't be trusted, especially with the family business, which he was running when he wasn't playing. Luckily, he had competent executives who steered him away from questionable deals, such as one to develop a chain of resorts catering to sixties swingers, a far cry from his father's lucrative love affair with coal dust.

Bettan was a guest at one of those legendary wild parties thrown by George and Pat Skakel when he met her. "He was concentrating on Swedes in those days," recalled Bill Whiteford, a longtime friend.

George's relationship with Bettan was unusual in that she was single. Most of his affairs had been with the wives of his wealthy friends. "George was totally amoral," said Whiteford years later. "I never could figure out how all those guys handled it. There were a lot of husbands who were afraid to come out and say anything against George because he could be very intimidating. But some of them were good sports about it."

One husband even allowed George to sleep with his beautiful wife on the deck of a yacht while the husband slept alone in the master cabin.

George didn't make his move on Bettan until long after the party in Greenwich, when Whiteford, Bettan, George, and his girlfriend of the moment spent a wild weekend together in the backseat of a taxi in Bermuda because all the hotels were full, it being Rugby Week.

Back in New York, George began dating Bettan, who quickly fell head over heels for him.

"George was charming, sweet, spontaneous," she recalled fondly. "But he drove me through heaven and hell the whole time we were together."

Over the next two years, with George dangling the promise of marriage, Bettan enthusiastically participated in George's bacchanalia.

George lived and played on a grand scale, thanks to the fortune his father had amassed. With the business in good hands, he'd take his friends on trips to far-flung spots on a moment's notice aboard the Great Lakes Carbon planes. For one weekend of fun, they'd fly off to Hong Kong. Several times he flew a crowd to Belgium just for Thursday-night parties. George's gang went hunting for wild horses in Utah, trapped wildcats in Colorado, and participated in orgies of eating and drinking. On a good day, George consumed as much as two bottles of vodka, though he never seemed drunk and was not considered an alcoholic in a family of them. And, of course, there was plenty of sex.

Yet George, indoctrinated well by Big Ann, was still a fervent Catholic who interrupted his revelry to go to Communion, Confession, and Mass. "I would go with him rather reluctantly," said Bettan later. "It was so hypocritical."

His religious beliefs notwithstanding, George's wildness was nonstop. At the Hotel Plaza Athenee in Paris, where friends maintained a sumptuous apartment, George drove through the lobby and up the grand stairway on a motorscooter wearing only his underwear. As a result of that evening's excesses, the friends were evicted after fifteen years in residence.

Friends and family members saw George as crazy and self-destructive, a man who got perverse pleasure out of putting himself into dangerous situations, risking death, and sustaining serious injuries.

In a Paris restaurant, he slipped and fell from a tower of chairs and tables he had built to demonstrate what it was like climbing aboard an elephant. He broke his leg and suffered a limp for the rest of his life.

In Utah, George had gotten permission to hunt for wild horses on the Ute Indian reservation. The hunts were another excuse for George and his pals to go wild. All of his girlfriends would show up and George would jump from tent to tent where the women slept. During one of the post-hunt dinners, George and a three-hundred-pound Ute named Boone began tossing a knife back and forth between them. George added to the danger by being the first to put a flip on the knife, which Boone managed to catch by the handle. He then flipped it back at George, who feared that the blade would wind up in his hand if he caught it, so he let it go. "That knife sliced into the calf of George's leg like a knife into butter," recalled Bill Whiteford. "It cut right to the bone, a big piece of meat just hanging there."

Mal Stevens, a former football coach at New York University and a prominent Park Avenue physician who was a guest on the hunt, said, "All right, George, let's go into my tent and get you sewed up." According to friends, Stevens had gone on a number of George's trips and had sewn up lots of casualties.

One afternoon in Aspen, George and his gang piled into and on top of his car and recklessly drove along the sidewalk to the Top of the Horn Restaurant for lunch. Just as George was preparing to order, a young policeman, who had witnessed George's driving and was livid, stormed over to the table.

"You know, pal," the officer said, "what you did is unconscionable. You could have killed someone. I'm taking you in."

"Well, I'm not going," George said firmly, looking back at the menu. "And don't go for your gun either because I'll put it down your throat. Somebody better be ready to die, because I'm taking you with me."

Bill Whiteford, who was present, said, "I was sure George had had it. But by God, the cops actually left. George turned back to the rest of us at the table and burst into his maniacal laugh. He loved it. He just loved it."

But Bettan saw a softer, more sensitive side to George Skakel, Jr., whom she felt was a "very unhappy and lonely man." After seeing *Days of Wine and Roses*, the Jack Lemmon–Lee Remick exploration of alcoholism, Bettan said, "George just absolutely hated it. He felt the story was too close to home and he wasn't only referring to the situation with his wife, Pat. I'd never seen him look so sad."

Of his six siblings, Jim was George's favorite, Bettan said, "but he loved Ethel a lot. They didn't see each other much and he rarely talked about her. He certainly avoided going to Washington because he didn't like Bobby and he often wondered how in the world Ethel could have married him."

During the two years of their affair, George kept

showing Bettan divorce papers that he said he intended to file. Then, he promised, they'd be married and move into a beautiful new home in Palos Verdes. But George was lying through his teeth. He had revealed to Bill Whiteford, quite gleefully, that the divorce papers he was waving in front of Bettan's eyes were bogus. "You know, Willie," he confided to his chum, "you got to do these things sometimes. I don't mean to marry every girl I go to bed with."

Finally Bettan had had it with George's empty promises. She gave up her job, her friends, her apartment—she and George had never moved in together because he actually felt it was immoral to live with a woman out of wedlock—to return to Europe for a year to visit her family, to ski, and hopefully to forget about him.

"I had two incredible years with him," she said years later. "It was hard to live under those circumstances because he was not really free to get married, but I don't regret any of it."

• • •

Meanwhile, Ethel and her brother Jim had completely stopped speaking. Jim's wife, Virginia, said that brother and sister "had grown apart after Ethel got so politically opinionated" following her marriage into the Kennedy family.

When he wasn't off on some wild exploit such as harpooning whales in the Azores, Jim worked on and off for Great Lakes Carbon, collecting a sizable paycheck and other perks. At Virginia's urging, however, he agreed to move to California, in part so they could distance themselves from the rest of the Skakels. Jim had been drinking heavily and his health was poor; Virginia felt they could find a better quality of life on the other side of the country, far from Greenwich and Washington. They moved into a pretty home near the exclusive Bel Air Country Club, where Jim spent his days on the links and his nights at the bar. At home, Virginia had become a virtual recluse, spending most of her days in a bathrobe with all of the shades down.

In the quarter century that the Skakels lived in Bel Air, Ethel visited her brother and sister-in-law no more than three times, and she always arrived unannounced on their doorstep acting gruff and tactless.

Virginia Skakel recalled one such horrible visit: "I was in my nightgown, my hair was in rollers, I had grease all over my face and my kids were hanging on me like some poor white trash. I didn't dress every day. I just didn't want to go out. My hair was a mess. I was a chain-smoker and I had cartons of cigarettes lying around. The house was filled with cigarette smoke because the windows weren't open. I actually lived in the den of the house and that was the only room I could invite her into.

"So I finally opened the door and Ethel says sarcastically, 'Gee, kid, you look just like Lana Turner,' which did not turn me on. I was terribly annoyed. 'Where's the coffee, Virginia?' Ethel said. 'Why are you in this dark den? Don't you want some air? You can't breathe in here! *Where's the coffee?*' She was so pushy and aggressive. I was so mad I was literally shaking.

"She just stared at me and said, 'I just wanted to see you and Jimmy. Well, gee, kid, tell me what you and Jimmy have been doing?' I told her everything was fine and she said, 'Well, Virginia, bring the children in here so I can see them.' So these five snotty children wander into the room and I said to one of the boys, 'Earl, this is your godmother.'

"Ethel kept asking about Jimmy and where he was. I didn't tell her that when she knocked at the front door and he saw it was her, he ducked out the back door. He just couldn't deal with her."

One evening Ethel bumped into Jim and Virginia at the bar at the Bel Air Hotel. Ethel was seated with some friends at a table and Jim was in his usual spot, at the corner of the bar, drinking alone while Virginia sat with some friends. Ethel asked Virginia to tell Jim that she was there, that she'd like to see him. "I went over to Jim," Virginia Skakel recalled, "and said, 'There's Ethel, aren't you going to say hello?' and he said no. And that was it."

Over the ensuing years the relationship between Ethel and her brothers and sisters was to deteriorate even further.

69 ✻ Life and Death

IN THE MIDST of all of the Skakel family turmoil, Ethel had become pregnant with her eighth child, one more than Big Ann, one less than Rose.

She wasn't the only Kennedy wife carrying a child in 1963. Jackie and Joan were each due to have their third. "We're all simply delighted to be pregnant again," enthused Ethel that spring. "I think Eunice and Jean are rather worried about having three high-strung sisters-in-law on their hands."

But Joan would suffer a miscarriage in mid-May. And, in August, Jackie would face the tragedy of losing her second and last son, Patrick Bouvier Kennedy, who died less than two days after his premature, cesarean birth.

After the depression and difficult delivery she had experienced with her first, Ethel had undergone five relatively easy pregnancies and normal deliveries, although the last one, Kerry, had been delivered by cesarean section because of numerous complications. Now, this latest pregnancy was beginning to look difficult, too. Bobby, grown accustomed to a wife who ran strong virtually up to the moment of delivery, was concerned that she wasn't her usual buoyant self, especially when she started bailing out of routine family activities.

She suddenly began to avoid the traditional weekend touch football games at Hickory Hill that were played between teams captained by Bobby and Ted. She stopped playing tennis with Bobby, whom she usually beat. Through most of Bobby Jr.'s ninth birthday party Ethel was in bed, coming downstairs only to watch him blow out the candles. On the night of the Democratic National

Committee's Second Anniversary Inaugural Salute to Jack, she left early, complaining that she wasn't feeling well.

"Ethel was under a lot of stress and anxiety during that pregnancy," recalled George Terrien. "She was still dealing with her anger and suspicions about Bobby and Marilyn, and she was furious over what was happening with her sister Ann and her brother George. She had become very testy, very nervous. It was not a good time for Ethel to be carrying a baby."

Terrien's observation was supported by Greenwich friends of Ethel's who saw her for the first time in years during this period and were shocked at how tense she appeared.

"She was under incredible pressure just being the Attorney General's wife and having to live in the spotlight like she did," believed Pixie Meek's brother, Sam, who ran into Ethel a few times in Greenwich. "And she was always concerned about what the Skakels would do because the Kennedys didn't want any kind of unsuitable behavior. In general, she was starting to show the strain of the marriage. You could read it on her face."

Pressure or not, Ethel was determined to beat Rose's childbearing record. She had told friends that while she didn't really care whether number eight was a boy or a girl, she was really dreaming of having twins. Having a multiple birth would, of course, place her neck-and-neck with her mother-in-law in the baby-making sweepstakes. Then she'd have a few more to solidify the number-one spot.

But besides breaking Rose's record, Ethel simply enjoyed having babies. "She was always joyous when she learned she was pregnant," said Sarah Davis, who saw Ethel through her first nine. "There was a little spell there where she went about two years without being pregnant and she was telling me how worried she was. She wanted to make sure she kept having children. She had a compulsion to have many, something I could never understand."

The press continued to portray Ethel as a doting,

devoted mother. Just a few months before Ethel was scheduled to deliver, Hearst's Ruth Montgomery received an invitation to Hickory Hill. "Life with Bobby and Ethel Kennedy is a perennial day camp," she wrote. While Bobby went horseback riding every morning with six of the children, Montgomery noted, one of the youngest ones was always left behind with Ethel. "He loves his mommy," Ethel gushed. "He actually has me all to himself for an hour."

An hour, if he was lucky. Ethel's calendar was normally so full that her current brood often saw her only at breakfast—lots of greasy bacon, eggs cooked in lard, glazed doughnuts, and ice-cold milk popped in the freezer for fifteen minutes before being served.

Or, the little Kennedys saw their mother if she was carpooling that day, or at bedtime, but only if she and Bobby didn't have an evening social obligation, which was rare. Like both of their parents, the young Kennedys of Hickory Hill spent most of their childhood being cared for by hired help.

Sarah Davis saw it somewhat differently. "Ethel did everything for them. The children had lunch with us every single day, like it or not. She adored playing with her kids." Still, Davis also knew that "Ethel worshiped Bobby above all humans on earth," her children included.

Gerald Tremblay, a frequent guest at Hickory Hill, said he never got the feeling that Ethel was a bad mother. But he saw that "her personal involvement was minimal. She always had lots of help to do it. I was there a number of times when Bobby came home from a trip and I can remember the children running to him with their complaints about what went on when he was away. Bobby was the disciplinarian, and he was a good disciplinarian, not one who shouted at the children. Bobby talked to them rather softly but made them mind. Ethel wasn't like that. Ethel couldn't get into the disciplinary act. She didn't know how to cope with all the complexities of raising all those children. So she'd have someone take care of them while she played tennis. I think the children suffered somewhat."

Still, Ethel had handsome children and she fawned over them like any adoring mother would. She had portraits painted of them that hung throughout the house. She also had canvases of generic children on the walls, painted by French-born New York artist Maura Chabor, whom Ethel had begun to promote. At one point, Ethel telephoned Sarah Davis with another idea to memorialize her offspring. "Kid, would you get heads for the kids if you were me?" Davis thought Ethel was referring to a particular brand of skis. "She actually was talking about having sculptures made—you know, busts."

Three traits that Ethel endeavored to instill firmly in her children were competitiveness, superiority, and religiousness—just as Big Ann and Rose had done with their large broods.

Ethel's pugnacious style of letting her children know that they were special was often accomplished at the expense of other youngsters. "Ethel was always very much like that," said a friend years later. "If you'd go skiing with them, Ethel's kids always got the first choice of rooms and I'd get the last." More telling was Ethel's occasional abusive treatment in deference to her own children. In one instance, Ethel actually slapped the daughter of a pal, even though it was her own children who were acting rowdy. "I was seated right behind Ethel, who turned around as fast as she could and just sort of slugged me across the face and told me to shut up," the girl said years later. "I was petrified and scared. I don't remember if I cried, but it was a shock."

Another time, on a charter flight to Aspen that had gone off-course, "Ethel lost her cookies completely and started screaming at me to take care of the young kids," a friend of the Kennedy children said. "She yelled that the reason we couldn't find Aspen was all my fault, and really threatened me. When we had to land somewhere else, she said I was going to be stuck in that place and I'd never get to Aspen. She was just very mean; she was always very scary as far as being a mother, especially when it wasn't one of her kids. She had so many kids. She was out of control, and the kids were out of control."

From the day they were baptized, Ethel raised her children to be staunch Catholics. She took them to Mass regularly and made certain they received all of the required training and guidance. "Ethel's kids said their prayers before breakfast and before lunch and before naptime and before dinner," said Sarah Davis. "Ethel gave them a very good Catholic upbringing."

Following Skakel and Kennedy tradition, Ethel in 1963 sent her daughters, Kathleen and Mary Courtney, to a Sacred Heart school, fashionable Stone Ridge, in Bethesda, Maryland. The other school-aged Kennedys—Joe, Bobby Jr., and David—went to Our Lady of Victory, in Georgetown.

With the Kennedy Administration battling segregation in the South, Bobby was shocked to learn that Our Lady of Victory had only white students, sparking accusations by Southern congressmen that he was sending his children to a segregated school while advocating integration for others. Though billed as integrated, the mother superior of Our Lady of Victory admitted, "We have no Negroes here. If any Negroes applied who were members of our parish, we would accept them. . . . Apparently there are no Negroes in our parish, since none have applied."

For a time in the spring of 1963, Bobby seriously considered taking the boys out of the Catholic school for political reasons—against Ethel's wishes—and enrolling them at the non-Catholic Landon School, an expensive private academy in Bethesda that billed itself as having a policy of never denying admission to boys for reasons of race or religion. After the contemplated transfer was disclosed, the school was deluged with calls from black parents inquiring about enrolling their children. It was then revealed that Landon, like Our Lady of Victory, had no black students. Two days later, the Justice Department announced that the Kennedy boys would remain at Our Lady of Victory. But after several months the Kennedys quietly enrolled Joe, a sixth-grader, and little

Bobby, a fifth-grader, at the integrated Quaker's Sidwell Friends School in Georgetown.

After the transfer came to light, the principal of Our Lady of Victory said the Kennedys had decided on Sidwell not because of racism but because the classes were less crowded there, and the school had a more active athletic program. She also noted that the Kennedy children missed school frequently because of colds, and Sidwell had a tutoring system for students who fell behind in their work. Meanwhile, David remained at the Catholic school, and Ethel, in defiance of her detractors, registered Michael in first grade there.

Although Michael and Kerry, the youngest of her brood, could have gone to the elite White House nursery school with their cousin Caroline, Ethel chose to keep them at home. "They can learn more there," she said.

Meanwhile, home had become quite crowded. With the new baby imminent, space in the house was at an even greater premium. The children were now forced to share bedrooms, doubling and sometimes tripling up. "There's long and loud discussions nightly over who sleeps with whom," Ethel said. As a result, she decided to go ahead with a major expansion of the historic house, which would include the addition of four more bedrooms.

Ethel was at the Kennedy compound on July 4 watching Bobby play with a few of the other children when she went into labor. Getting the kind of VIP treatment usually accorded a First Lady, Ethel was transported by Air Force helicopter to St. Elizabeth's Hospital in Boston's Brighton section, where Dr. Roy Heffernan, the gynecologist who had helped deliver four of her children, was waiting. He'd raced to the hospital behind a police escort when he got word that Ethel's time had come a week early. After examining her, he quickly concluded another cesarean was warranted; he feared the likelihood of a breech birth, among other possible complications.

While Bobby paced nervously, Ethel was wheeled into an operating room and administered a spinal. At her side was the reassuring Luella Hennessey. Three other doctors and two nurses, all Irish, were there to assist Heffernan. Ethel remained conscious during the forty-two-minute operation, which culminated at 6:48 P.M. with the birth of a healthy six-pound, fourteen-ounce boy, her fifth male child, who cried lustily. He was the second to be born on the Fourth of July.

Red-eyed and weary, Bobby got a quick peek at his new son and then telephoned his bedridden father at the compound to give him the good news.

"They tell me he was the best-looking child ever born at St. Elizabeth's," Bobby boasted to reporters. "He's got a strong face just like his grandfather. He's got a lot of character. He's a very good-looking baby. And, oh, he's got black hair."

Ethel took nine days to recover, sleeping as much as possible, understandably, perhaps. After all, practically the only time she wasn't on the run was when she was in the hospital recovering from a delivery. During her hospital stay, Ethel and Bobby batted around a long list of names for the newborn, finally agreeing over the phone on Christopher George.

A week later a crowd of two hundred cheered Ethel and little Christopher's arrival at St. Francis Xavier Roman Catholic Church, in Hyannis Port, for the baby's baptism, officiated by Richard Cardinal Cushing of Boston.

"Holy mackerel, Ethel, you've done it again!" Bobby declared wryly.

As Jack left the church following the ceremony on his way to Hyannis Port Country Club for a round of golf, he took note of his latest nephew. "He looks like a pretty good baby, but of course we'll know later."

Christopher George Kennedy would be the only one of Ethel's children born during Jack's tragically aborted White House years.

70 ✻ *Dallas*

ON FRIDAY MORNING, November 22, 1963, Bobby telephoned Ethel and told her he planned to have lunch at home with two associates, Robert Morgenthau, the U.S. Attorney in New York, and Silvio Mollo, the chief of the criminal division in the Manhattan office, who had been participating with Bobby in two days of intensive sessions about organized crime.

It would be a nice break for his colleagues, Bobby thought, to get away from the office and relax by the pool with Ethel before the afternoon conference resumed back at Justice. Although Thanksgiving was just a week away, it was sunny, with temperatures in the balmy sixties.

Ethel was delighted by Bobby's request; she could show off her new baby to the visitors. She told the cook to prepare lunch for four, then played a quick game of tennis with a friend.

About the same time Bobby and his colleagues were getting out of his government car in the driveway at Hickory Hill, Jack and Jackie were stepping into an open Lincoln Continental limousine for a ten-mile motorcade through downtown Dallas, a route lined with thousands of mostly smiling, cheering, flag-waving Americans thrilled to see their President.

Jack's two-day appearance in Texas was a mission of mercy, both for himself and for the state's badly divided Democratic organization. The Democratic Governor, John Connally, and the Democratic U.S. Senator, Ralph Yarborough, were at each other's throats, and unless there was a truce, Kennedy faced the certain loss of Texas in the Presidential election, just a year away.

Jack was well aware of the fierce anti-Kennedy sentiment in the Lone Star State, which he had won in 1960 by the slimmest of margins, a mere 46,233 votes. Since then, his support in the conservative state had worsened. The Bay of Pigs fiasco, the Administration's liberal stance on civil rights and social welfare, all contributed to his problems. Despite the thousands on hand to welcome him, Dallas was a city seething with extremist groups and disgruntled loners, many with a grudge against the President. His visit had even been preceded by the circulation of a wanted poster with his picture on it. Texas friends had thought the trip ill-advised, and some of Jack's aides agreed. But the President wasn't overly concerned about his safety. In fact, he had always felt Bobby was more vulnerable because of his ongoing war with organized crime and labor racketeers. The President had decided to give Texas his best shot, his eye already on the main prize—the state's twenty-five electoral votes, which he hoped to win in November 1964.

But fate interceded. President Kennedy's life ended—and history was changed forever—at one-thirty P.M., in front of a downtown Dallas office building known as the Texas School Book Depository. There, a twenty-four-year-old ex-Marine, one-time Soviet defector, and Fair Play for Cuba activist named Lee Harvey Oswald had fired a cheap mail-order rifle out of a sixth-floor window, leaving a massive, gaping, and fatal wound in the head of the forty-six-year-old President.

Four minutes later, as the car carrying the President, the wounded Governor Connally, and a blood-spattered, panic-stricken First Lady raced toward Parkland Hospital, United Press International moved a rare flash on the newswire saying that the President had been shot.

One of the first people at Justice to get the news—from a UPI machine in his office—was FBI Director J. Edgar Hoover, who despised the Kennedys as much as they hated him. Hoover immediately telephoned the Attorney General's office and got Angie Novello, Bobby's secretary, who confirmed that she'd heard what had happened but didn't have it in her to call her boss.

"The President has been shot," Hoover said matter-of-factly. "I'll call him."

A White House operator patched Hoover through to extension 163, a white telephone in a wooden box at the shallow end of the swimming pool at Hickory Hill. It was one of two outdoor phones (the other was near the tennis court) that had been installed by the Army Signal Corps in 1961 so Jack and Bobby could have instant access to one another, a Kennedy hotline of sorts.

Bobby had just taken a swim, changed into shorts, and was having chowder and tuna sandwiches with Ethel, Morgenthau, and Mollo at a table near the pool when the phone rang.

" A maid, or perhaps a houseman, came over and said, 'Mr. Hoover's on the White House phone,' " Morgenthau recalled.

Not wanting to interrupt the men's conversation, Ethel got up to answer it herself.

As she walked to the phone, Bobby looked at his watch, decided they'd been away from the office long enough, finished his sandwich, and got ready to head back to the house to change before returning downtown.

The White House operator said, "The director is calling." Ethel said, "The Attorney General is at lunch."

From everything she'd heard about Hoover from Bobby, Jack, and the others, Ethel had grown to resent the director, too. Once, at a party, she had teased Hoover about Los Angeles Police Chief William Parker, who often was critical of the bureau. "Don't you think Chief Parker is a wonderful man? Don't you think that if you ever retired, he'd be the man to replace you?" Hoover had turned red with fury.

Even though Hoover was waiting impatiently on the line, Ethel wasn't about to disturb Bobby's lunch. But the operator told her it was urgent.

Holding out the phone, Ethel said, "It's J. Edgar Hoover." Because it was the first time the director had ever called the Attorney General at home, Bobby grabbed the phone. At that moment, Morgenthau saw one of the men who was painting the new addition at Hickory Hill running toward them with a portable radio in hand.

"I have news for you," Hoover said, emotionless.

"What?" asked Bobby.

"The President has been shot."

Bobby froze. "What? Oh. I—Is it serious? I—"

"I think it's serious," the director responded. "I'm endeavoring to get details. I'll call you back when I find out more." Later, Bobby recalled that conversation vividly. He said Hoover was "not quite as excited as if he was reporting the fact that he'd found a Communist on the faculty of [Washington's predominantly black] Howard University."

At that same moment, Morgenthau suddenly realized what the housepainter had said: " 'They say the President is shot.' It didn't sink in."

Bobby started walking toward Ethel and his guests. "He clapped his hand to his mouth," Morgenthau recalled. "Ethel realized what had happened . . . or at least had an idea . . . and she ran over to him." Bobby stopped suddenly and screamed, "Jack's been shot! It may be fatal."

Morgenthau and his aide went inside the house, leaving Ethel and Bobby alone, holding one another.

Just three days earlier, the grounds of Hickory Hill had been filled with joy as Ethel and dozens of friends helped Bobby celebrate his thirty-eighth birthday into the wee hours. In a prescient moment, Ethel had suddenly looked around her, taking in the joyous scene, and said offhandedly, "It's all going too perfectly."

Bobby tried not to fall apart. There was too much to do.

He wanted to be at his brother's side as soon as possible, so one of his first acts was to call Bob McNamara and ask the Defense Secretary to get a plane ready. His next move was to find out all he could about Jack's condition, Jackie's state of mind, the capabilities of the doctors at Parkland, the availability of a priest, and how the other family members were holding up.

Instead of panicking, Bobby had taken over the

family reins. Meanwhile, Ethel stood by, frozen, wringing her hands.

Bobby was in the midst of dressing for the flight to Dallas when the White House extension in the bedroom rang. The caller was Capt. Tasewell ("Taz") Shepard, the President's Naval aide at the White House. Bobby listened tensely. "Oh, he's dead!" Bobby exclaimed. Ethel burst into tears. "Those poor children," she sobbed, thinking of six-year-old Caroline and three-year-old John-John.

Ethel would never forget Bobby's next words. His brother, he said, "had the most wonderful life."

Bobby wandered through the house in a state of shock. Friends began arriving and television sets were turned on to the horror in Dallas. Bobby had returned to the pool area when the White House extension rang suddenly. It was Hoover again, with old news that Jack's wounds were critical. "You may be interested to know," Bobby responded icily, "that my brother is dead!" He slammed down the phone.

Of all days, November 22 was Ethel's turn to drive the afternoon car pool. Devastated by the events of the last hour, she felt she couldn't face the task of dealing with the children and thought it would be better if friends picked them up. But Bobby insisted she go so the children could hear from their mother, not from strangers, what had happened to their uncle in Dallas. It was decided that Dean Markham, one of the first to arrive at the house, would pick up the boys, and Ethel the girls.

Pulling herself together as best as she could, Ethel telephoned Mother Mouton, the headmistress at Stone Ridge, and told her that she would soon be there for Kathleen and Courtney, along with their cousin Maria Shriver, thus saving the grieving Eunice from the burden. Ethel also called the White House and offered to take Caroline and John, but Maude Shaw, the children's nurse, refused to let them go without Jackie's permission.

Meanwhile, the Sacred Heart nuns, having heard only reports that the President had been shot but not killed, had already taken many of the Stone Ridge students into the chapel to pray for his recovery. When Ethel arrived at the school, she announced herself to Mother Mouton and then disappeared into the chapel herself, kneeling and praying until the children arrived. Outside, as they were walking to the car, Ethel stopped, put her arms around them, and told them what had happened.

As Ethel was driving home, Lyndon Baines Johnson was being sworn in as the grieving nation's thirty-sixth President in a brief and hurried ceremony aboard *Air Force One*. Moments later it was announced that Lee Harvey Oswald had been arrested.

By the time Ethel got home with the children, Hickory Hill had become a virtual armed camp, secured by Fairfax County, Virginia, police who had taken up posts around the estate. Until Jack's assassination, and despite the many enemies Bobby and the Kennedys had made, there had never been regular security at Hickory Hill. Security was something the Kennedys didn't believe in. "Ethel and Bobby were never afraid," observed a friend later. "Anybody could have walked in that door. Nobody thought about it."

Shortly after six P.M., *Air Force One* landed at Andrews Air Force Base in Maryland, and a half hour later the ambulance bearing the President's body, his widow, Bobby, and close associates arrived at Bethesda Naval Hospital, where an autopsy would be performed. By early evening Ethel and other members of the Kennedy family had set up shop in the hospital's seventeenth-floor VIP suite.

There, Ethel saw Jackie for the first time since the gunfire. "Oh, Jackie!" she cried, embracing her sister-in-law. Ethel told Jackie she was confident Jack was in heaven. "He is just showering graces down on us," she declared.

"Oh, Ethel," Jackie said, "I wish I could believe the way you do." Then Jackie, still wearing the suit with Jack's blood on it, told Ethel how "wonderful" Bobby had been to her. "He'll always help you," Ethel responded.

Meanwhile, as the President lay in state only hours after his death, the Kennedys and close friends gathered for dinner in the White House family dining room. Some suggested that Bobby get away for a while. His sister Jean, for one, was fearful that Bobby would get into a fight with Lyndon Johnson, who would be moving into the White House at any moment. By this point in time everyone had decided to refrain from talking about the events in Dallas. Ethel was even able to bring some semblance of merriment to the grim scene. The wig she was wearing was snatched off her head and passed from head to head, eventually finding a home on Robert McNamara's pate.

Later, after midnight, Bobby accompanied Jackie to the East Room, where the casket had been placed. Jackie had a number of personal items that she wanted to put in the open coffin—three letters, a pair of Jack's cuff links, a piece of scrimshaw. As they knelt, Bobby took off his PT 109 tie pin and put it into the box along with an engraved silver rosary that had been a wedding gift from Ethel. Then they left, Jackie carrying a lock of her husband's hair.

Two days after the assassination, on Sunday, November 24, more horror erupted in Dallas. As millions watched on television, Lee Harvey Oswald was shot to death as he was being escorted by Dallas police to another jail. His killer was a Kennedy admirer, Jack Ruby, a Dallas nightclub owner who would become a player in the various assassination conspiracy theories.

The latest violence left Ethel distraught and uncomprehending. She pulled Arthur Schlesinger aside outside the White House Treaty Room, where she had been watching a rerun of the Oswald shooting, and asked him for answers, but he had none to give her.

As Jackie worked on producing the state funeral, she and Ethel got into a debate of sorts over the design and language of the Mass card. Three prayers had been presented to her, including one that had been used on the card at Ethel's parents' funeral eight years earlier. Jackie rejected them all, saying she had no intention of pleading with God to allow Jack into heaven. But Ethel protested. Surely there *had* to be a mention of God. Jackie eventually gave in. Then there was a dispute over the design of the card. Jackie wanted a black border; Ethel was opposed. The card, she felt, should not look sad—"not reminding you of death." Jackie disagreed, but it was too late for the printer to include a border. Later, Ethel, along with Bobby, decided that Communion should be offered, but Cardinal Cushing and Washington Archbishop Patrick O'Boyle disagreed; it might take too long if a large number of people decided to take it and they'd never get out of the church. It was finally decided that only the family would take Communion.

Jack Kennedy was buried on Monday, November 25, 1963. The Skakels put aside their enmity and were in attendance.

"He's in heaven looking down on us," Ethel told her sister Georgeann after the funeral. "Bobby and I will be with him one day ourselves. We will all be together."

But on earth, the lights of Camelot had gone out forever.

71 ❋ *After Jack*

"KENNEDYS DON'T CRY," Bobby taught his children, and he tried to live by those words in the weeks and months following his brother's death. But it wasn't easy. Friends described him as "shattered," "wounded," "in pain."

A journalist friend who visited Bobby at Justice a few weeks after the assassination was shocked at how he looked: "Desolate, bleak, a vacuum . . . crushed beyond hope, mentally, spiritually, and physically."

Unlike her husband, who was far less simplistic in his faith, Ethel truly believed that Jack was now happily ensconced in heaven. Often she would say that he was now looking down at them, causing Bobby to roll his eyes. "*That's* the wife of the Attorney General speaking," he'd mutter.

But precisely because of her piety, her strong beliefs, and her devotion to her husband, Ethel, more than anyone, would help bring Bobby through the torturous aftermath of Dallas.

"The Skakels are pretty emotionless people and they all were brought up by Big Ann to believe that the soul lives on after death so Ethel felt no real lingering upset after Jack was killed," recalled George Terrien. "Bobby, though, was depressed, darkly so, for the first time in their marriage. Getting Bobby back on track was the biggest challenge Ethel ever had to face at that point in her life. She came through swimmingly."

The Thursday after Jack's funeral was Thanksgiving, and the Kennedys had decided to carry on with life, to have an old-fashioned turkey feast at Hyannis Port.

"It was well understood," Rose noted later, "that we would go ahead with Thanksgiving as usual . . . with every one of us hiding the grief that gnawed on us." The Shrivers, the Lawfords, Ted and his family, along with the widow Jackie and her children, John-John and Caroline, came for dinner. But Bobby had chosen to stay away, spending the holiday at Hickory Hill with Ethel and the children.

At one point during the long weekend, Ethel quietly stole away and drove to Arlington Cemetery, where she briefly visited Jack's grave, standing well back from the picket fence that surrounded it so she wouldn't draw attention. Dressed in black, wearing a lace mantilla on her head, she prayed for several minutes, a rosary in her hand.

Among the hundreds of mourners who were at the cemetery, several women spotted Ethel and approached her. She quietly thanked them for showing their respect and asked that they pray for Jack's soul.

Over the next weeks, Bobby struggled with his grief, but Ethel continued to prod him back toward the world. For example, she cajoled him to go to New York to represent the family at the ceremony to change the name of New York International Airport to John F. Kennedy International Airport. And at the Justice Department, a Christmas party had been planned long before the assassination for some seven hundred underprivileged children. Ethel persuaded Bobby to attend. With Ethel by his side, he put on as cheerful a face as he could muster, talking to the children, tousling their hair. At one point, as someone in a tiger suit handed out toys to the children, Ethel brought over four-year-old Kerry, who caused her father to guffaw when she said, "You're not a tiger—you're a man. Tigers don't go like that."

A friend of the family, watching the scene, noted later, "Without Ethel, Bobby might have gone off the deep end."

Ethel also convinced Bobby to appear at a Washington orphanage Christmas party. As he stood facing the group, a little boy broke through the ranks and ran up to him, teasing, "Your brother died! Your brother died." Everyone in the gathering froze. But Bobby lifted the youngster and held him closely and said softly, "I have another."

Bobby tried as best as he could to keep in touch with the daily business at Justice and the transition of his brother's administration, but it was clear he had removed himself because of his suffering, leaving the department in the hands of Deputy Attorney General Nicholas Katzenbach. One continuing concern, though, was J. Edgar Hoover, a longtime friend of Lyndon Johnson's. Bobby was still angered over the brusque manner in which Hoover had communicated the news from Dallas. Moreover, he felt that the bureau was again running without oversight now that Jack was gone. Rumors of all kinds were flying about the escalating feud between Hoover and Bobby. One even had Ethel claiming that Hoover had bugged Hickory Hill so the new President could listen in on Bobby's most intimate conversations.

In late December, Bobby and Ethel left Washington for Palm Beach, where most of the clan had gathered. Ethel even managed to convince the grieving Jackie, who had come down with her children, to go shopping with her on Worth Avenue. But when a crowd gathered, they ducked into a car and returned to the Kennedy home.

By the start of the new year Bobby had begun to emerge from the darkness that had engulfed him. But the changes in him were noticeable: gray now showed in his thick, light brown hair; he'd lost a considerable amount of weight; he appeared more reflective, less aggressive.

In January, accompanied by Ethel, Bobby surprised friends, family, and colleagues by agreeing to undertake a diplomatic mission to Asia, where he spoke to large groups of students in Japan and Manila—a trip that Jack had planned to make. After his talk in Manila, Bobby was mobbed by cheering students. "It really wasn't for me," he said of his reception, his eyes welling with tears. "It was for *him*."

For Ethel, the trip seemed no different than their world tour in those heady days shortly after the inauguration two years earlier. She was inexhaustible, jubilant. In Kuala Lumpur, she visited an orphanage and gave out candy; she spent time with hospitalized aborigines; at the Mandarin Palace restaurant, she sailed through a nine-course luncheon with diplomatic wives and female civic leaders; she swam with Bobby at the Selangor Country Club.

Prior to leaving, Ethel had read about the existence of Indonesia's rare and exotic Komodo dragons, actually ten-foot-long, carnivorous lizards that weighed as much as three hundred pounds. She had mentioned to her brood, half kidding, that a dragon would be fun to have as a pool companion, and they had clapped their hands in agreement. By the time Ethel and Bobby arrived in Malaysia, Prime Minister Rahman, the Tunku of Malaysia, had learned of her interest and offered her a smaller, less fierce Malaysian lizard—with the stipulation that the dragon fly back with the Kennedys on the same plane. Since they had to make several other stops, Ethel, who wasn't up to dragon-sitting, diplomatically declined the offer.

By the time she had returned home, word of her refusal had reached the ears of officials at the Washington Zoo, who were in despair. Ethel's aborted dragon adoption soon involved assorted State and Justice Department diplomatic officials, and various and sundry foreign emissaries. Not to be outdone, President Sukarno of Indonesia, who was Rahman's arch enemy, had now offered up two of the Komodos. Zoo officials then agreed to trade four white whistling swans and one Malaysian duck for the dragons if the diplomats could pull off the transfer.

When the dragon deal had finally been consummated, Ethel, who had started it all, had one request: "Could I have them out at the house for a few days for the children to see?"

By late winter Bobby was clearly on the mend emotionally, and political pundits had begun speculating on his future. Nineteen sixty-four was a Presidential election year, and polls already were proclaiming him the favorite choice for Vice President, but he felt that was Lyndon Johnson's decision to make. Or at least that's what he said for public consumption. In truth, Bobby had no desire to be Johnson's running mate. For the first time in his life, he had decided to go it alone, to seek his first elective office. He no longer wanted—or needed—to be the "second most powerful," as he had been when he was in his brother's shadow. He was biding his time. When rumors began circulating in February that he planned to run for office in New York—probably for the U.S. Senate seat—he denied them outright, saying his only alternatives were the governorship of Massachusetts, travel, or teaching.

Meanwhile, Bobby returned to Justice and took back the reins from Nick Katzenbach. The word went out that he was in control when, on the second night after his return, he put in a late-night telephone call to a colleague demanding to know how one of his pet organized crime probes was going. The last outward vestige of his mourning was a black tie adorned with a PT-boat clip.

Ethel was relieved to see Bobby finally emerge from his cave. "I think it's been really rough, really the roughest of all, a terribly hard experience for Bob—but very good for him too," she said. "His whole life was wrapped up in the President . . . he was just another part of his brother—sort of an added arm. Bobby never thought about himself—or his own life. So when the President died—well, it was like part of Bobby died, too."

Just before the first anniversary of Jack's death, Bobby and Ethel received an invitation from Lady Bird Johnson to visit her and the President at the White House. But Ethel passed the word through Bob McNamara's wife that "they still can't quite emotionally bring themselves to accept," according to the First Lady's social secretary, Bess Abell.

In fact, Bobby's emotional wounds from Dallas would never completely heal.

• • •

Along with his gloom, Bobby felt a strong sense of responsibility for Jackie and her two young children. He was determined, despite the dark cloud that hung over him, to help get the widow through their mutual nightmare.

In order to accomplish this, Bobby began spending an extraordinary amount of time with Jackie—which did not go unnoticed by Kennedy family members, friends, and observers.

Rose, for one, was well aware of Bobby's attentiveness. Later, she would describe him as Jackie's "main pillar of strength . . . adviser, protector, confidant. . . . She had no really close male kin . . . so it was natural and fitting that she should turn to Bobby in this time of sorrow and reconstruction in her life."

Jackie would later say of Bobby: "I think he is the most compassionate person I know."

The press, keeping a close eye on the former First Lady's movements, noted that just four months after the assassination, Bobby had accompanied Jackie from a ski vacation in Stowe, Vermont, to Antigua. Ethel, who had been scheduled to go with them to the Caribbean, canceled her reservation at the last minute and returned to Hickory Hill.

Meanwhile, in Washington, Bobby had begun sending Ethel home from evening social engagements so he could escort Jackie back to her place.

It was apparent to many that Ethel, always extremely possessive of Bobby, had become unhappy with the situation.

"He's spending an awful lot of time with the widder," Eunice said to Ethel one afternoon while getting their hair done at Elizabeth Arden in Washington. As one friend put it years later, "I know Ethel was very pissed about all the attention Bobby was giving Jackie, but she was a good sport about it."

Mary De Grace, who worked for Ethel in Hyannis Port, said that during this time there was visible tension between the two women. One evening, Ethel briskly left the dinner table when Jackie entered the room.

In the summer of 1964, Jackie moved from Averell Harriman's Georgetown home that she had been occupying since the assassination to an apartment at the Carlyle Hotel in New York where the Kennedys had maintained a residence for years. A Washington writer who would work in Bobby's Senate campaign recalled seeing Jackie and Bobby together in a banquette in the hotel's piano lounge.

Stanley Tretick, who had photographed the Kennedys for *Look* over the years and had become a friend of both Bobby's and Jackie's, observed later: "Bobby was getting a lot of criticism for spending so much time with Jackie. Once, he looked at me and said, 'She's lonely.' "

In the end, Bobby and Jackie pulled themselves out of the malaise they shared. Once that happened, life for Ethel returned to a semblance of normality.

72 ✻ To the Senate

IN MARCH, ETHEL received the first good news in months. In the midst of all the tumult, she had become pregnant with number nine—the magic number. Early the following year, if all went well, she would finally tie her mother-in-law's childbearing record.

But more sorrow was in store. In May, Joan had another miscarriage. The following month, while she was awaiting Ted's arrival at a Massachusetts political convention where he was being renominated for a full Senatorial term, the private plane in which he was flying crashed. Ted's aide and the pilot were killed. Near death himself, Ted was rushed to the hospital, his back and ribs broken, a lung punctured. Bobby raced to be at his brother's side. Later that night he told a friend, "Somebody up there doesn't like me."

At this point, the Kennedys and the world began to wonder, "Is this family jinxed?"

But by late summer, following trips with Ethel to Warsaw, where she danced merrily at a Polish wedding, to West Berlin, to Greece, and to Rome, where Pope Paul presented her with a silver plaque engraved with biblical scenes, Bobby had decided to make his big political move.

After rejecting any future role in the Johnson Administration—actually LBJ didn't want him as anything more than campaign manager—Bobby resigned as Attorney General.

On August 25, at the age of thirty-eight, he announced his candidacy for the U.S. Senate seat from New York then held by sixty-four-year-old Republican

Kenneth B. Keating, a one-time conservative who had recently gained a more liberal image because he refused to back the GOP's ultraconservative Barry Goldwater against Lyndon Johnson. A week later, Bobby received his party's formal nomination at the State Democratic Convention and Ethel, who had curiously registered as an Independent, was ecstatic.

For the first time in their fourteen years of marriage, Ethel would be on the road campaigning for her husband, not another Kennedy. And, as in some past Kennedy campaigns, she'd hit the trail well into another pregnancy. But her current brood, as she noted to a reporter, were "not too enthusiastic about all this. You know, children don't like change."

The day Bobby announced his candidacy under a broiling sun on the lawn at Gracie Mansion, Ethel spent a half hour posing for photographers and never had a hair out of place. She said she found being a political wife "very mixed up and crazy but very enjoyable."

Bobby immediately hit the campaign trail. Ethel wouldn't see him for another two weeks when she was shocked to see the toll the campaign had already taken. He'd shaken so many hands that his own right hand had become swollen and tender.

Bobby's advisers felt that Jackie would make a wonderful asset to his campaign, but he had rejected every idea, ranging from the former First Lady's appearance in TV campaign spots to being at his side when he went to church. Ethel noted that while other members of the Kennedy family would campaign for Bobby, Jackie would not because she was still in mourning. Jackie, however, did offer advice to Bobby, such as how to smile his way through a long day of campaigning. "You could turn on a very low-level smile," she said. "It's the really broad smiles that tire you out. A gentle little smile would wear better." Jackie had wanted to attend some of Bobby's rallies surreptitiously, and had even discussed with him the possibility of wearing a wig or a turban, but that was ruled out. At one point, however, she did show up at Bobby's campaign headquarters and was almost knocked to the ground by a surging crowd of several hundred admirers and dozens of photographers. Despite her offer of support, Jackie had had it with Kennedy political circuses. She wanted to spend time deciding on her own future. Privately, Ethel was furious with her. Later, Ethel would only say, "Jackie could have helped Bob get a lot of votes. Everyone knew that, and Jackie would do anything for Bob and offered to do anything that would help. But we couldn't ask her or let her go through that. It would have been too cruel—it would have brought back too many memories. Jacqueline has suffered too much already."

As soon as the campaign got underway, Bobby was immediately branded a carpetbagger by elements of the press and his political rivals—with good reason. His only claim to residence in New York at the time of his announcement was the Kennedys' elegant three-bedroom suite 11E at the Carlyle. At campaign stops, he faced hecklers carrying signs that read: GET A ROAD MAP AND GO HOME, CARRY ME BACK TO OLD VIRGINNY, and TAKE YOUR CARPET AND BAG IT. Unflinchingly he declared, "I shall devote all my efforts and whatever talents I possess to the state of New York."

Ethel branded the charge "a false issue. Bobby spent more of his life here than anywhere else," she claimed. "He is no Johnny-come-lately to the state of New York. He has spent twenty of his first twenty-eight years in New York. He went to school in Riverdale and Bronxville." She also pointed out that she considered herself a New Yorker by adoption because she had once lived in Larchmont and Rye. Ethel pledged that if Bobby was elected, her ninth would be born in a New York hospital; if Bobby lost, she'd give birth in Washington.

In order to give the public and the voters the perception that they were actually becoming citizens of New York—and to establish the required formal residency for candidacy—Ethel and Bobby signed a two-year lease on a 130-year-old, white frame, twenty-five-room, French Provincial and Chippendale-furnished estate called Marymeade, in Glen Cove, Long Island.

The Kennedys' New York manor sat on five acres with an eighty-by-forty-foot swimming pool, a two-story playroom wing (complete with a kitchen and spiral staircase leading to the children's bedrooms), and a separate playhouse. But Ethel had already enrolled the children in classes in the Hickory Hill environs. In actuality, the Kennedys spent little time at the Glen Cove estate. Except for campaign and media events, they were mostly at the Carlyle or in Virginia.

While Ethel claimed that she disliked speaking publicly, she always came alive and turned in stellar performances. Ethel also thrived on the recognition factor of being a Kennedy in the national spotlight. "She sure did enjoy her power," said a pal. "She liked the idea of people turning around and pointing and saying, 'That's Ethel Kennedy.' She ate it up."

A reporter who had followed Ethel on the campaign trail in New York also noted her self-assurance: "She talks about the things she knows best—children and families—and when she refers to her husband, it is unaffectedly 'Bobby,' not 'Mr. Kennedy' or 'the next Senator of this great state.' On the campaign trail she is very much in charge." Ethel generally got along well with the press. The only thing that seemed to aggravate her was when reporters used the word *condition* to refer to her pregnancy. "Why is it that the English language is so poor we have no graceful way of saying someone is expecting a child?" she demanded of one journalist.

Ethel was in her second trimester when she hit the bricks for Bobby, showing up at rallies in chic but simple maternity dresses, a wonderful campaign tactic.

She claimed she wrote her own speeches, submitting them for approval to Steve Smith, Bobby's campaign manager. "I deliver the speech by phone to him, and he criticizes my diction as well as the content."

On a street in Brooklyn, she mounted a sound truck and told a crowd of more than four thousand, "You'll help him and he'll help you later." At the Seventh Annual Steuben Day Parade on Fifth Avenue, Ethel candidly confronted Bobby's adversary. "Shame on you for calling my husband bad names," she told Keating, rubbing one index finger with the other as a child would. At another stop, the very pregnant Ethel said the only time Bobby was stumped by a question was when a Columbia University student asked, "What do you intend to do about the population explosion?" She said Bobby looked at her and was at a loss for a reply. At the Rockville Centre Diocese, a thousand waving, autograph-seeking nuns turned out to hear Bobby speak and to see Ethel. When Bobby was about to leave, he saw Ethel surrounded by a mob of nuns. He watched for a moment while Ethel continued to sign her autograph. Finally, he had had it. "Ethel, let's go. *I'm* the candidate!"

When she wasn't stumping for Bobby on the streets of New York, she was holding massive campaign teas and coffee klatches at the house in Glen Cove to stimulate Democratic women's interest in Bobby's candidacy. The spacious rooms of the rented house were now filled with Kennedy family pictures, which visitors viewed as if they were touring a gallery or a museum. On display on the living-room wall, for example, was a photograph of little David at the White House that bore the inscription, *A future President inspects his property,* signed by Jack. When guests arrived, Ethel talked—from prepared text—about a spirit that Jack had instilled in the country, "a spirit we can all be proud of . . . of an individual forgetting about himself, to reach out and help those less well off. . . . It touched the lives of everyone in every walk of life. All I ask is that you try to keep that spirit going."

During one such gathering, in her eighth month of pregnancy, Ethel shook the hands of eight hundred female members of the Yorkville Neighborhood Club who filed past her on a long reception line in the dining room where seventeen servants were on hand to help the ladies with cakes, cookies, and coffee. Another time, Ethel, along with her sister Ann McCooey, the only Skakel who ever turned out for a Kennedy campaign, calmly greeted eight chartered buses carrying hundreds of wives of congressmen, assemblymen, senators, judges, and dis-

After fleeing the ravages of the Civil War in Mississippi, Grace Mary Jordan, daughter of a wealthy plantation owner, migrated to Chicago, where, on November 18, 1873, she married James Curtis Skakel, an abusive alcoholic. George, the second of Curt and Gracie's four children, became Ethel's father.
(COURTESY OF ROBERT SKAKEL)

Right: Ethel's mother, Ann Brannack Skakel, right, as a child. Her sister, left, was Ethel's namesake. The family lived in the Irish Catholic ghetto of Chicago's South Side. Their father, Joe Brannack, was an alcoholic who worked at menial jobs. His wife, Margaret Hughes Brannack, eventually separated from him and lived the rest of her life with Ethel's parents.
(COURTESY OF GEORGEANN DOWDLE)

Looking regal, Ethel's mother, Ann Brannack, around the time she met her future husband, George Skakel, just before the outbreak of World War I. Tall and slender at the time, she gained as much as fifty pounds with the birth of each of her seven children, eventually becoming known as "Big Ann" to friends and family.
(COURTESY OF GEORGEANN DOWDLE)

The palatial home on Lake Avenue in Greenwich, Connecticut, where Ethel spent her childhood. Her father bought the mansion for a song at the height of the Depression from the widow of the founder of the Simmons Mattress fortune. The estate was the setting of wild parties, and Jim and George Skakel, Jr., terrorized the community with blazing guns and fast cars. (MICHAEL FORESTER)

In many ways life at Hickory Hill, the McLean, Virginia, estate where Bobby and Ethel lived and raised their enormous family, was much like Ethel's childhood world at Lake Avenue: lots of kids, pets, and parties. (AP/WIDE WORLD)

Left: Master of his destiny: George Skakel, Sr., Ethel's father, strikes an appropriate pose. As a young man he helped found Great Lakes Carbon Corporation, initially a three-man coal brokerage, which grew to become one of the largest privately held companies in the U.S. (GOLD & STETTNER)

Right: "Big Ann" Skakel, Ethel's mother, sitting in her enormous library filled with religious books, many of them first editions and authors' manuscripts. A staunch Catholic who constantly proselytized, she instilled a religious fervor in Ethel. Many say it has been Ethel's strong religious beliefs that have carried her through so many tragedies. (GOLD & STETTNER)

The Skakel girls at home in Greenwich, circa 1950: vivacious and wild Ethel; troubled and alcoholic Georgeann; serious, academic Pat, born with a club foot, and "Little Ann," the baby of the brood, considered the prettiest with her golden hair and blue eyes. (GOLD & STETTNER)

Ethel in her high school graduation picture, spring 1945. She drove the nuns and her schoolmates up the wall with her antics at Maplehurst, a Catholic girls' school.

A top-ranked equestrian, Ethel began riding as a youngster. Horses were her life until she met Bobby Kennedy. (COURTESY OF GEORGEANN DOWDLE)

A joyous Ethel and Bobby visiting the Skakels in Greenwich shortly before their wedding. Soon the Skakels would come to loathe Bobby and the Kennedys. Ever loyal to Bobby and the clan, Ethel would begin to sever ties with her own flesh and blood. (GOLD & STETTNER)

Ethel gazes with awe and respect into the eyes of her future father-in-law, Joseph P. Kennedy, who made a rare appearance at the Skakels' house to attend the christening of Ethel's sister Georgeann's first baby, Little Georgeann Dowdle. (GOLD & STETTNER)

Ethel with sisters Ann, left, and Georgeann, right. Far right is George Terrien, Bobby's University of Virginia law school roommate, who eventually married Georgeann and became a featured player in the Skakel family drama. (GOLD & STETTNER)

Skakel family and friends about to embark aboard another pleasure flight on one of the Great Lakes Carbon planes. Air tragedies eventually claimed the lives of Ethel's parents in 1955 and her brother George Skakel, Jr., in 1966. Pictured here from left: Ethel's father; John and Georgeann Dowdle; Ethel; Pat's husband, Luan Cuffe, an Irish architect; Big Ann; a family friend; Pat Skakel Cuffe, Rushton, and Jimmy. (GOLD & STETTNER)

Bobby and the Skakels celebrate Christmas 1950 in front of the big tree in the library at Lake Avenue. Bobby next to Jimmy; Pat Corroon Skakel, wife of George Skakel, Jr., holding their firstborn, Kick; the Skakel patriarch next to Ethel; Ann, Rushton, George Jr., Georgeann and John Dowdle, and Big Ann holding Little Georgeann. (GOLD & STETTNER)

Wedding day, June 17, 1950. Ethel and Bobby emerging from St. Mary's Roman Catholic Church in Greenwich. Ethel's dream to snag a Kennedy had finally come true.
(UPI/BETTMANN)

It was 1960. Jack Kennedy was the Democratic Presidential candidate and Bobby had just been named Father of the Year by the National Father's Day Committee. Ethel and Bobby dine on the terrace at Hickory Hill with their seven children.
(AP/WIDE WORLD)

Standing next to Jack, Ethel joins the Kennedy clan and friends for one of their many get-togethers. Photo was taken soon after patriarch Joe Kennedy suffered a stroke. (COURTESY OF THE JOHN F. KENNEDY LIBRARY)

Ethel, center, mourns at Jack Kennedy's funeral. Bobby would fall into a deep depression but with Ethel's help and faith would emerge and run for the Senate. (COURTESY OF THE JOHN F. KENNEDY LIBRARY)

Despite the dark cloud of Jack's assassination that hung over Bobby, he felt obligated to help Jackie through their mutual nightmare. The two, seen here leaving her Georgetown home, often spent long hours together. (AP/WIDE WORLD)

"Now, on to Chicago!" Bobby Kennedy declares after winning the California Presidential primary. Moments later, on June 5, 1968, he would be shot by twenty-four-year-old Jordanian Sirhan Sirhan, and Ethel's life would become a living nightmare. (UPI/BETTMANN)

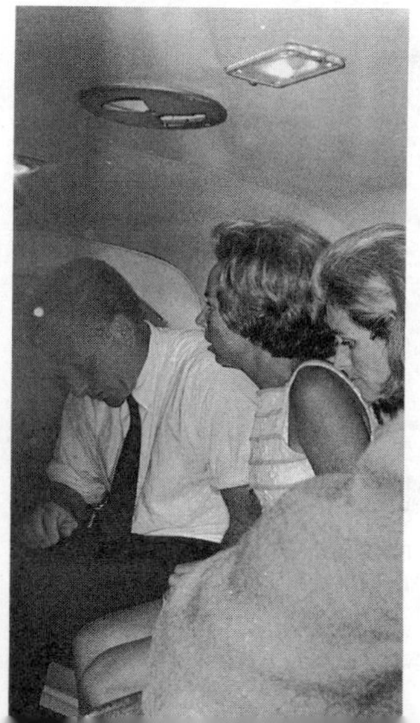

Ethel, in a state of shock, rides in the ambulance with mortally wounded Bobby. All efforts to save his life, though, fail and he is pronounced dead on June 6, 1968. (UPI/BETTMANN)

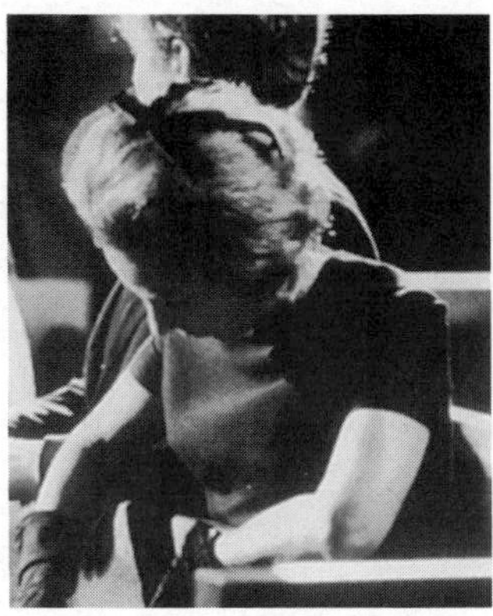

Above right: At St. Patrick's Cathedral, Ethel prays. A staunch Catholic, she will always believe that Bobby is in heaven. (ARCHIVE PHOTOS) *Above left:* Memories of 1963: Jackie, Caroline, and John-John bid a sad farewell to Bobby. Not long after Bobby's death, Jackie married wealthy Greek Aristotle Onassis. (ARCHIVE PHOTOS)

Ethel, the veiled widow, carrying her eleventh child, a heartrending image the world will never forget. (ARCHIVE PHOTOS/ARCHIVE FRANCE)

Above left: Ethel and Bobby Jr. arrive at Barnstable, Massachusetts, court in August 1970 for his hearing on a marijuana possession charge. The judge eventually dropped the charge. (AP/Wide World) *Right:* At Bobby's gravesite for the sixth anniversary of his assassination, widow Ethel and troubled son David smile for photographers, but privately their relationship was stormy. (UPI/Bettmann)

After he died of a drug overdose in Palm Beach, David Kennedy's body is borne by family members and friends for a private Mass at Hickory Hill. Ethel, whose relationship with David became intolerable after Bobby's assassination, is visible third from left walking next to Eunice. (AP/Wide World)

Top left: ABC News chief Roone Arledge was linked romantically with Ethel by the media, but he was actually just another one of her many escorts. A controversy was sparked when he killed a "20/20" investigative segment about Marilyn Monroe, Jack, and Bobby. (AP/Wide World) *Top right:* John Glenn, a former astronaut and later U.S. Senator, was one of Ethel's close friends and helpmates during the troubled period after Bobby's death. (UPI/Bettmann) *Above left:* Ethel's close relationship with singer Andy Williams prompted much media speculation of a marriage, but Ethel would never give up the Kennedy name to remarry. (Archive Photos) *Above right:* Frank Gifford, another man in Ethel's life, was actually just a close friend. His daughter eventually married one of Ethel's sons. (AP/Wide World)

Ethel was presenting awards at a Special Olympics event in Connecticut the day the Chappaquiddick incident became public. Here, the car carrying the body of Mary Jo Kopechne is pulled out of the water. (UPI/BETTMANN)

Ethel, center of every Kennedy triumph and tragedy, accompanies Ted and Joan into church for the funeral of Mary Jo Kopechne. (UPI/BETTMANN)

An ever-loyal Kennedy, Ethel makes a very public appearance in Palm Beach to show her support for nephew Willie Smith, charged with rape and later acquitted. At left is Willie's mother, Jean Kennedy Smith, who introduced Ethel to Bobby in the mid-1940s. (AP/WIDE WORLD)

Above left: Martha Moxley, the Greenwich, Connecticut, teenager whose murder still remains unsolved. (Courtesy of Dorothy Moxley) *Above right:* Ethel's nephew Tommy Skakel, one of two suspects in the Martha Moxley murder. He has professed his innocence and has never been charged. (The National Enquirer)

A policeman stands guard over the scene where Martha Moxley's battered body was found. Police theorized that the murder weapon was a golf club belonging to the family of Ethel's brother Rushton, who lived nearby. (The National Enquirer)

As a college girl, Ethel once marked her own route across Central Park in a car to get to a horse show at Madison Square Garden on time. Here, she carefully backs up a new convertible not far from the Kennedy compound.

Ethel and the woman she most revered, matriarch Rose Kennedy. When Ethel married Bobby, she pledged to have more babies than her mother-in-law, and she did—eleven in all. (AP/Wide World)

Above left: Ethel with her son Representative Joe Kennedy at Hyannis Port, 1993. (Rex/USA) *Above right:* Ethel and Ted were on hand for the first preview of the play *Private Lives* in New York. (David McGough/DMI)

Ethel shares a moment with President Bill Clinton after he paid tribute to Bobby during a memorial Mass at Arlington National Cemetery. (AP/Wide World)

trict leaders from all of the boroughs. "In this case," Ethel quipped, "I believe in busing."

Ethel and Bobby took great advantage of their brood during the campaign. One day the whole family gathered in the game room to be filmed for a campaign commercial directed by Leland Hayward. "Well, here we are," said Ethel, "just an average American family."

During one tea at the house, Ethel shifted the center of attention from herself to the back lawn, where four-year-old Kerry, wearing black trousers and a scary Halloween mask, was playing with fifteen-month-old Christopher as the guests oohed and aahed.

By now, Bobby was aware of the political asset he had in Ethel. Between the beginning and end of his short campaign, Ethel appeared with him at more than a dozen rallies and she hosted nine "at-homes," a grinding schedule for anyone, much less a pregnant woman.

Besides Ethel, he also got an enormous amount of help from his mother, now seventy-three, and his sisters, who got involved in everything from the at-home teas to street-corner rallies.

Everything didn't always go according to plan. At one reception, the rooms were well stocked with food and drink, the bartenders were in their uniforms, and the cute campaign girls were in their electric-blue dresses. The candidate was there and so was his wife. Suddenly, Ethel wondered aloud where the guests were. That's when someone realized that the invitations hadn't been sent. As Ethel grinned devilishly, Bobby gritted his teeth.

Ethel hustled friends with Hollywood connections to get celebrities involved in the campaign. When Gerald Gardner, who was writing a book about the campaign, said he might be able to get Robert Morse, Ethel was thrilled. "I *love* that boy," she exclaimed. "Bobby and I went backstage after *How to Succeed* and met him."

During the entire campaign Bobby canceled only one appearance—a rally in Union Square in New York on September 28, the day the Warren Commission released its report on Jack's assassination. The memories were too disturbing for Bobby to appear publicly. Both Bobby and Ethel had declined to read the report, though Bobby had been briefed on it and said he was "completely satisfied" with its findings. He was firmly convinced that Oswald was the lone assassin.

On November 3, 1964, Election Day, Bobby's nine-week campaign was over. Unlike most candidates, he was unable to be photographed casting a vote for himself when the polls opened. Nor was Ethel. The husband-and-wife team, who had fought the carpetbagger charge throughout the campaign, were not registered to vote in New York, but rather in the Kennedys' real home state, Massachusetts.

Bobby had breakfast with a group of supporters, thanked his staff, and then went to the Bronx Zoo with Ethel and the children. "Please do not feed the candidate," Ethel joked to her gang, who held bags of peanuts. That night she and Bobby dined on beef Stroganoff. Afterward, Bobby went off to visit Jackie in her Fifth Avenue apartment. Later in the evening, he paid a brief visit to his stroke-paralyzed father, who had been brought down from Massachusetts for the election results. Two weeks earlier Joe Kennedy had taken a turn for the worse, but he still wanted to be close to Bobby, his eldest surviving son, the new family head, whose chances for victory weren't considered as good as Ted's were in Massachusetts, where he remained hospitalized.

Bobby had no reason to worry. With the Kennedy name, sympathy for Jack, and riding on the coattails of President Johnson—who was celebrating one of the greatest Presidential landslide victories in American history—Bobby overwhelmed Keating, garnering 719,693 votes. He'd won his first elective office, and his last.

There was jubilation in the seventh-floor Kennedy suite at the Statler-Hilton, which was packed with celebrities.

"We made it!" Marlene Dietrich exulted, as a delighted Shelley Winters allowed a friendly gentleman to inscribe the name of longtime Kennedy aide Pierre Salinger on her bosom with a ballpoint pen.

When the votes that put Bobby over the top came

in, Ethel was in another room with the children, the girls in pink coats with pink velvet collars, the boys in semi-Beatle haircuts. Ethel herself had on a shocking pink sheath, looking as one observer noted, not much older than a teenager.

While Ethel glowed that night, the reality was that it had been an exhausting two months for her. But she spoke only of how rough it had been for Bobby. "It was such a hard campaign for him, I think, because while he would do anything when he was doing it for his brothers—Jack or Teddy—it was different for himself," she said. "I think the only thing that carried him through was his belief that he has to carry on his brother's ideas and work."

With Ethel at his side, Bobby, still wearing his black mourning tie, went down to the grand ballroom to speak to several hundred cheering campaign workers. After he spoke, the crowd called for Ethel. "Thank you," she said, "for making this such a happy night. We will try in the next six years to make it happy for all of us."

When a reporter asked her whether she saw the Presidency in Bobby's future, Ethel laughed ingenuously. "My goodness," she said, "we never think about such things. We live one day at a time."

• • •

Early in the evening of January 10, 1965, six days after Bobby was sworn in as the junior Senator from New York, and in the midst of the heaviest snowfall of the winter, Ethel entered Roosevelt Hospital in Manhattan. News photographers had been alerted and were awaiting her arrival. Ethel posed, smiled, and then was taken to a private room in the obstetrics section of the hospital, accompanied by Luella Hennessey.

Eight hours later she gave birth to an eight-pound boy, her sixth son and ninth child, by cesarean delivery, her third in a row. Bobby was not at the hospital when the baby was born, but arrived about the time she was leaving the recovery room, and spent an hour with her.

After fourteen and a half years of marriage, Ethel

had finally succeeded in meeting one of her primary goals, producing as many children as Rose.

The *Daily News* noted in its headline that the new baby "Gives Ethel and Bobby a Baseball Team." By the time she was through having children, Ethel would have enough to make up a football squad.

On January 17, with Ethel still recuperating in the hospital, the baby was baptized at St. Patrick's Cathedral. The sacrament was administered by the Skakel brothers' old pal, the Very Reverend Msgr. William J. "Billy" McCormack. The baby's godparents were his sister Kathleen and brother Joe.

Ethel and Bobby had decided to name him Matthew Maxwell Taylor Kennedy, after their close friend, the U.S. Ambassador to South Vietnam.

Bobby saw the historical and political significance in the birth of Max, as the boy would be called. "Teddy was the ninth child in our family and he became a United States Senator. It would be nice if the baby decided to be a Senator, too."

Two days after the christening, Ethel left the hospital, promising to be back very soon.

"Children," she said, "are cheaper by the dozen."

PART IX

Senator's Wife

73 ✻ *Camelot vs. The Great Society*

ONLY HOURS AFTER Bobby was sworn in as the junior Senator from New York on the evening of January 4, 1965, he and Ethel attended the Women's National Press Club's annual party for new lawmakers of the Eighty-ninth Congress. Bobby brought the house down when he spoke about his political future. "I have absolutely no Presidential ambitions," he declared, an impish smile spreading across his face, "and neither does my wife—*Ethel Bird*."

Wisecrack or not, Bobby's comment underscored two truths that Washington insiders had become well aware of over the past year: Ethel's undeniable popularity and power, and the rancor that existed between Bobby and Lyndon, and therefore between Ethel and Lady Bird. After Jack's death, the surface friendliness between the two women had all but vanished.

Over the next few years of the Johnson Administration, a catty rivalry would exist between the two camps, the one at 1600 Pennsylvania Avenue, and the other at 1147 Chain Bridge Road, in McLean.

For her part, Lady Bird Johnson loved Texas and would have preferred going back to the Lone Star State. Ethel, on the other hand, savored Washington life and thrived on the power, the competitiveness, the intrigues. But each woman was fiercely loyal to her husband, and they became immersed in a game of one-upmanship—a low-key feud that provided fodder for Washington's gossip machine, though it never became public.

"It was *war*—the Great Society versus Camelot," an astute Washington observer declared later.

As Barbara Howar, the self-described aribiter of Texas and Washington taste, noted, "Loyalty to both [the Johnsons and the Kennedys] was impossible. To give Lyndon his due by day and mingle socially in the Kennedy world at night required Olympian stamina."

Howar was one of the few who was able to swing both ways without suffering too badly, at least for a time. As a popular party giver, she brought Johnson and Kennedy people together under the same roof, and she was the *only* LBJ insider to be invited to an anniversary party thrown for Bobby and Ethel by Ted and Joan.

Once, at a bash at the French embassy, Howar was on her hands and knees helping Lynda Bird Johnson look for a lost contact lens when the President's daughter let the First Family's true feelings be known. "Don't get your dress dirty," she said snidely. "Your Kennedy friends won't dance with you."

Meanwhile, Ethel consistently invited the young, sexy, and energetic Howar to Hickory Hill parties, always making certain the papers played her up, which infuriated Lyndon.

When Howar eventually ran afoul of the Johnsons, Ethel was ebullient. "She was even nicer to me after that," Howar said.

The pettiness of both the Johnsons and the Kennedys was underscored by LaDonna Harris, who at the time was married to another freshman Senator, Fred R. Harris of Oklahoma. When Bobby entered the Senate, LaDonna Harris became one of Ethel's new best friends. As a result, the Harrises were frequently invited to Hickory Hill and Hyannis, aggravating the President and his wife no end. Ethel was quite aware that the Harrises were close to the Johnsons and the Humphreys.

"Lyndon and Lady Bird didn't like our relationship with Ethel and Bobby," LaDonna noted years later. "When we'd visit them at Hyannis, Lyndon would actually *call us* there just to let us know that he knew we were with the Kennedys. Sometimes we felt as if we were in the middle of a snowball fight."

Because of her intense competitiveness and feverish

defensiveness, Ethel seemed always to be involved in one feud or another. As one member of her circle at the time said, "Underneath that cheerful exterior, there was real anger. It was always there ready to surface like an armed submarine."

One of her rows involved the Kennedys' old pal Red Fay, who had stepped down as Navy Undersecretary after Jack's death. In Ethel's view, Fay had violated two key commandments of being a member of the Kennedys' inner circle: discretion and secrecy. Three years after the assassination, Harper & Row published *The Pleasure of His Company,* Fay's memoirs about his friendship with the Kennedys. In the preface, he described the book as "the journal of a friendship." But Ethel saw it as a stab in the back because Fay had written about private conversations and embarrassing incidents.

Ethel was particularly incensed by Fay's description of a Kennedy dinner at which the patriarch criticized the young people for their extravagance.

Bobby had gotten a look at the manuscript before publication, according to Arthur Schlesinger, and "landed on [Fay] as if it were the only book through which posterity would ever know his brother." Bobby demanded that Fay cut nearly 40 percent of the book, which Fay refused to do, making just a few excisions.

After the book was published, a friend of Ethel's revealed years later, "The Fays were off Ethel's list." (When Bobby was assassinated in 1968, Fay came to the funeral and eventually his friendship with Ethel resumed. But by that time, the Fays had returned to California and they rarely had occasion to see Ethel.)

Paul Newman also became a target of Ethel's wrath. Several years back he had incensed her by pulling out of the planned *The Enemy Within* film project. More recently, Newman had infuriated her once again by enthusiastically joining a group of intellectual and celebrity liberals—Gore Vidal, James Baldwin, Joseph Mankiewicz, and Nat Hentoff—in a Democrats for Keating Committee.

Now Ethel had it in for Newman. She released her

dark rage one sunny afternoon under the guise of a friendly game of tennis.

"From the moment they got on the court, Ethel wouldn't let up on Paul," recalled LaDonna Harris, who witnessed the match. "Ethel has an unhealthy kind of competitiveness, a masculine kind of meanness, real tough-guy stuff. I was shocked at her treatment of Paul. She told him he was a lousy player. She teased him nonstop—hard teasing, real mean teasing, hard-hitting. He just didn't know how to deal with it. He finally walked off the court. He had tears in his eyes."

Another target was the gentlest and most fragile of the Kennedy women, Joan, Ethel's jilted and alcoholic sister-in-law. Joan was constantly comparing herself to the other Kennedy women and finding fault with herself. She viewed Rose as a saint, Jackie as the consummate sophisticate, and Ethel as the epitome of motherhood. "I just couldn't keep up . . . the Kennedys are so good at everything and I'm a flop," she once said. After she had two consecutive miscarriages, Joan told a friend, "I always admired Ethel and wanted to have as many children as she had."

Joan had good reason to feel intimidated by Ethel, as evidenced by an incident at a dinner party at Joan and Ted's house. Besides Ethel and Bobby, the other guests included Senator Birch Bayh; Eunice and Sargent Shriver; the Harrises, and a couple of Harvard psychiatrists who had been invited by Eunice.

"Out of the blue Ethel started criticizing Joan on the way she had set the table, the salt serving she'd used, just about everything," recalled LaDonna Harris. "It was totally uncalled for, totally unnecessary, and it made everyone feel self-conscious and uncomfortable. Joan tried to ignore it, but it made her feel terrible. She was near tears. I always felt sorry for Joan because Ethel was always too mean to her."

On another occasion Ethel attacked the way Joan had dressed for an afternoon of boating. "Joan showed up wearing a beautiful leopard print bathing suit with a hat and matching scarf looking like she just stepped out of *Vogue,*" said LaDonna Harris, who once again was present. "As soon as Ethel saw her, she went after her with a vengeance. 'Why did you dress up? . . . Did you think someone was going to be taking pictures? . . . Maybe I should dress up like a model too. . . .' She was just so mean for no reason, taking these backhand slaps at Joan just because she looked so glamorous."

Friends believed that Ethel targeted Joan because she wasn't strong like the other Kennedy women. "Ethel despised weakness of any kind," George Terrien observed. "It was just so un-Kennedy in her mind. So she took it out on Joan whenever she could. That was the same attitude she had with her own sister Georgeann, who was an even bigger boozer than Joan."

Richard Burke, who served as a senatorial aide to Ted and had close ties to the family before he suffered a nervous breakdown, remembered that Ethel "had a very condescending attitude toward Joan because Joan was really sick. Ethel didn't deal very well with anybody's illness. It was like Ethel had two personalities. She could show compassion and be very attentive to people who were ill, but if they were people who were close to her, or people she relied on, she took that as weakness and acted resentful toward them. That's the way she treated Joan, in a condescending manner, like a little girl."

Ethel's anger toward Joan also stemmed from jealousy. "There was no question," said a member of Ethel's circle, "that Ethel wasn't crazy about her friends becoming too friendly with Joan and her pals. At parties, Ethel always kept tabs on who was there for her and Bobby, and who was there for Joan and Ted."

Whenever Rose Kennedy had a special guest at Hyannis, she'd usually invite Ethel *and* Joan. To Ethel's dismay, Rose was quite fond of Ted's wife. In Joan, Rose saw a dignity that she felt Ethel didn't possess. Rose once described Joan as "strikingly beautiful," a woman who "caused heads to turn wherever she went," a view she would never hold of Ethel.

But because of how intimidated and nervous she felt in the presence of the Kennedy women, Joan, who was drinking heavily, usually begged off. Ethel was usually put in the position of having to cover for Joan, which she was loath to do because it involved lying to Rose, the woman she most admired and most feared.

"Ethel would come into my office and say, 'Did you tell the guests that Joan isn't coming?' She'd put it off on me to make some excuse for her," recalled Barbara Gibson, one of Rose Kennedy's secretaries. "Ethel treated Joan like a sick child; they all did. Ethel and the others tried to hide Joan's drinking problem from Rose as a means of protecting Rose, not for Joan's sake."

When Ted Kennedy considered making a run for the Presidency, members of the family met with the doctors who were treating Joan for her alcoholism. The reason for the secret summit, held in a private suite near National Airport, was to determine whether Joan could hold up through the demands and rigors of a Presidential campaign.

Eunice immediately rallied to Joan's side. Jean, who had introduced Ted to Joan, said that she'd help Joan as much as she could. Ethel's feelings were clear, too. While she conceded to help, she had extremely negative views about alcoholism, having come from a family of heavy drinkers. She strongly believed that Joan's problem would be a major deficit for Ted, and she expressed her misgivings in front of Joan. "It could be dangerous," she said to those in attendance.

To be a woman in the Kennedy family was a tough chore, noted Ethel and Bobby's pal Gerald Tremblay. "Joan couldn't stand it, she couldn't weather the storm. Ethel, on the other hand, was a master at being a Kennedy. Both Jackie and Joan retreated, but Ethel didn't retreat."

74 ✻ A Premonition

FOR ETHEL THE summer of 1965 began with a premonition.

One night, when Bobby was away on Senatorial business, she shot up from a deep sleep. She had dreamed, or thought she had, that something terrible was about to happen. She got out of bed, checked on the children, then returned to her room, but had difficulty getting back to sleep. The dream had left her with a sense of foreboding. Still thinking about it the next day, she telephoned her sister. "I remember Georgeann telling me that Ethel was quite frightened," recalled George Terrien. "She said that the dream had involved injury or death to someone close to her. Georgeann had told her not to worry, that it probably had to do with all the stuff she was still feeling about Dallas and Ted's plane crash. But Ethel was unnerved, certain it was a premonition of some sort."

At the end of June Ethel and Bobby, seven of their nine children, and a few close friends, flew West for a weeklong adventure that would include riding the rapids on Idaho's treacherous Salmon River, ominously known as "The River of No Return."

The trip—they'd made a similar one the year before—had all been Bobby's idea; Ethel had initially balked. Why did they have to go to some godforsaken place in the middle of nowhere? Even though she'd flown all over the world with Bobby, Ethel had an intense fear of flying that had started with the death of her parents a decade earlier. Now, in order to fly, she required a drink or two and sat clutching her rosary with white knuckles until the plane landed safely. After Ted's recent air tragedy, her dread had only worsened.

Before leaving for Idaho, Ethel telephoned her sister again. "I still can't shake that feeling," she said. "I hope we make it. If not, I'll see you in heaven."

On July 1, a dozen Kennedys and their friends—former astronaut John Glenn, Jr., singer Andy Williams, mountain climber James Whittaker, and Lem Billings—were ferried safely from Sun Valley eighty miles northwest to a place called Jackass Flats. The flight had been a tricky one. The route called for the small planes to fly into a canyon, tilt ninety degrees for hairpin turns, and then come down over a rise before landing. Ethel, who wanted to get it over with, was the first one in, arriving ashen-faced; Bobby came in on the second flight. Grinning broadly, aware of her fear, he teased her: "How was that?" Ethel was still shaking. "Never again!" She shuddered. "Never again!"

Despite her anxiety, the trip went off without a hitch. Over the next week, the Kennedys and their chums battled the rapids in inflatable yellow boats without incident. Afterward, the Kennedys left Idaho for western Canada, where Ethel and Bobby received a tumultuous welcome from some four hundred thousand spectators on hand for the Calgary Stampede.

By the time Ethel got home, her sense of foreboding had evaporated. "That dream I told you about," she said to a friend, "it's all forgotten."

But a month later, when three of her children were injured within days of one another, Ethel's uneasiness returned. "I knew there was something to it," she told Georgeann. "That dream, it's with me all the time now."

The first injury involved eleven-year-old Bobby Jr., who required a hundred stitches for severe leg lacerations and a severed tendon suffered when he crashed through a window after jumping off a garage roof in the Kennedy compound.

The more serious injury, one reminiscent of Ethel's childhood, was suffered by fourteen-year-old Kathleen who, like her mother, had become an accomplished equestrienne. During the past summer, Kathleen had won four blue ribbons for excellence in horsemanship, but her riding days were almost ended on August 29.

While competing at Sea Flash Farms in West Barnstable, Kathleen's mount, Attorney General, failed to clear a hurdle, tripped over the barrier, and somersaulted over the girl, leaving her unconscious and bleeding internally. An ambulance rushed her to Cape Cod Hospital, which was fifteen miles away. Meanwhile, authorities tried to find her parents. At that moment, the Kennedys and six of Kathleen's brothers and sisters were en route to Hyannis Port from Sag Harbor in rough seas and strong winds aboard the seventy-foot yawl, the *Neris*. An appeal went out to Coast Guard patrol vessels to try to intercept the Kennedys' boat and notify the family of the accident.

After a three-hour search the boat was located near Buzzards Bay Light. A coxswain aboard a Coast Guard cutter yelled through a bullhorn that Kathleen had been hurt, the extent of her injuries not yet known. Bobby felt he should be at her side, but the eight-to-fifteen-foot waves and thirty-knot winds made it difficult for him to transfer safely from the schooner to the cutter. Rather than wait, he decided to swim to the boat. In a near-panic over Kathleen's accident, Ethel tried to restrain him, demanding that he at least wear a life jacket. Bobby protested that it would interfere with his swimming, but relented when Ethel threatened to go with him. Placing a small orange floater around his neck, he dove into the rough water. Waves washed him fifty yards through a boiling sea toward the cutter, and within minutes he was safely aboard.

Shortly after the cutter left for Woods Hole, the winds picked up and a gust sent a boom slamming painfully into twelve-year-old Joe Kennedy's chest, stunning and knocking the boy flat on the deck. Ethel administered first aid, but luckily he was not seriously injured.

"It was that dream," Ethel told her sister later. "I could feel it."

The cutter carrying Bobby reached Woods Hole

four hours after Kathleen's accident. State police rushed Bobby, still in sailing garb and bare feet, to the hospital where Kathleen had now regained consciousness and was being treated for a mild concussion, a contusion of the bladder, and internal bleeding. In a nearby room, Bobby Jr. was still recuperating from his badly cut leg. Several hours later the *Neris*, under Coast Guard escort, limped into a protective cove near Woods Hole, her sails torn. Frantic with worry, Ethel was taken by police escort to the hospital. By the time she got there, Ted Kennedy had had two Boston doctors flown to Cape Cod to examine Kathleen. Surgery wasn't necessary, and Kathleen made a quick recovery.

In Washington, President Johnson had heard about the Kennedy mishaps and, despite the animosity that existed between the two sides, dashed off an encouraging note to Ethel and Bobby: "Take heart. Children do grow up despite roof tops, horses and boats. My devotion to the children and my sympathy to you both since I know no remedy for the grey hair these incidents promote."

To Kathleen, he had sent a bowl of yellow Texas roses in the shape of a horse, along with some words of guidance: "It's no fun to part company with a horse, especially in mid-air, and I speak from experience. But the best thing to do is pick yourself up, brush yourself off, and start all over again. And I know you are the girl with the spirit to do it."

The President had also sent notes and flowers to Bobby Jr. and Joe, both of whom responded that they were making quick recoveries.

When Kathleen was finally declared out of danger, Bobby went off to a clambake for friends and former campaign supporters. Ethel relaxed by playing golf, but her dream of a few months back was uppermost in her mind. She was clearly worried.

"I believe it was a warning," she told Georgeann. "What next?"

75 ❋ Knacky Baby

BOBBY'S CAREER AS the U.S. Senator from New York had little if any impact on life at Hickory Hill. Though he and Ethel had bought a five-room apartment in the fashionable United Nations Towers, they spent little time there. The apartment was far too small for the family, and was used strictly as a way to stave off critics who were keeping the carpetbagger issue alive. The Kennedys had shopped for quite a while before settling on the $68,000 co-op: three bedrooms, a kitchen with a combination bar and pantry, and a living room, two walls of which were a continuous stretch of floor-to-ceiling windows running almost fifty feet across.

While Ethel stayed at Hickory Hill, Bobby usually commuted to New York several times a week to work out of his office on East Forty-fifth Street, using the apartment as a pied-à-terre. By spring 1967, Bobby had become the largest Senate employer: his staff now numbered sixty-three members, fifteen more than New York's senior Senator, Jacob Javits.

In Washington, Ethel showed a distinct lack of interest in activities for Senate wives. She was usually missing from the weekly Red Cross meetings, where the wives wore seersucker dresses and made bandages. At Senate receptions, Ethel could never remember the names of the Cabinet members' wives and was constantly giggling and asking LaDonna Harris for help.

Meanwhile, Ethel continued to throw huge parties for friends, and galas for charities, at Hickory Hill. In the spring of 1966 alone, she had picnics and cookouts for hundreds of children—all the while trying to oversee her own uncontrolled brood. At one event, Ethel had to rush out in the yard when someone told her that ten-year-old David was risking a broken neck by jumping higher and higher on a trampoline while overhead a small car supported by ropes carried young guests back and forth across the lawn. She chaired benefits for the Stone Ridge School and rubbed some liberal guests the wrong way by having black maids with little doilies on their heads serve coffee in the dining room. Her big party of the year, a virtual reunion of the old JFK crowd, was the seventy-fifth birthday for Ambassador-at-Large Averell Harriman, with music supplied by a combo from Peter Duchin's orchestra.

Ethel's social life had become so full and she was at the hairdresser so often that she finally had Evelyn, co-owner of Christy's Hairstylists in McLean, install a special telephone for her use only.

Ethel had come to be known as a "knacky baby," a description coined by members of Washington's swinging sixties set. While Bobby was making headlines with his increasingly negative views about the Vietnam War, Ethel was making news of her own by occasionally wearing "way-out," skimpy dresses. She showed up at an elegant farewell dance for McGeorge Bundy with Bobby and a suitcase. While Bobby mingled with the guests, she ran upstairs and changed. When she came back down she started a near fashion riot, shocking the more conservative women of LBJ's crowd with a futuristic outfit that could only be described as Flash Gordon flapper. While other women wore floor-length chiffons, Ethel had chosen Courrèges boots and a straight shift of black and white blocks on vinyl with spaghetti-thin shoulder straps studded with rhinestones. "Is it linoleum?" one guest asked. Ethel told friends she'd bought the dress at a hip new store in New York called Paraphernalia, "where everything is so way out it's in—I decided to wear it because everybody was talking about Vietnam. I thought we all needed a change of pace, so I put on my new dress." One Congressman's wife, looking askance at Ethel, said, "If I wore those short-short skirts, my husband would lock me up."

While the press and outsiders only saw Ethel's wacky and wild side, a few of her closest friends perceived something different. They had started to interpret her growing flamboyance as a shield for what they saw as insecurity and resentment—insecurity about her abilities, resentment at the limitation of her role as a Kennedy wife. As a woman of the clan she was restricted from having a career of her own, or from even expressing herself in ways more serious than party giving and outrageous dressing.

"Poor Ethel had to wear vinyl dresses and toss people into swimming pools to call attention to herself. All the Kennedy wives were squelched," said a member of Ethel's inner circle.

LaDonna Harris had a similar view. "Women's lib was making itself known. All of us were beginning to blossom out, to become full participants in what was happening, to grow. But Ethel seemed to be afraid. Her life revolved around being very supportive of Bobby, a role she was very schooled in."

Only on rare occasions did Ethel make her feelings known on political or social issues. After having read a *New York Times* story about a family-planning program run by the Peace Corps in Bombay, Ethel hit the ceiling. Vehemently opposed as a Catholic to any form of birth control, she wrote an irate letter to U.S. Peace Corps Director Jack Vaughn complaining about fifty-two U.S. volunteers assisting in vasectomy operations. But Ethel never made Bobby aware of her correspondence with Vaughn, which would have been viewed harshly by him as a violation of the code of silence imposed on Kennedy wives.

For the most part, though, Ethel obeyed the unwritten family rules. LaDonna Harris recalled an incident that she felt underscored the restrictions imposed upon Ethel. At a small dinner party at Rose's house, the conversation turned to Bud Wilkinson, the University of Oklahoma's star head football coach, who had been a consultant to President Kennedy's physical fitness program. All of the women agreed that, while Wilkinson was a superb athlete and leader, he was too much of a conservative, too right-wing in his views. Jackie then admitted that she and Ethel had expressed their feelings about Wilkinson's politics in the form of "unsigned poison pen letters to the President." Harris said she was dumbfounded when she heard the story. "I felt it was really sad that Ethel had to put her thoughts in writing in little secret notes, that she felt she didn't have the right to be *openly* critical and express her views. It was kind of pathetic."

76 * Death Wish

IN JULY 1966, Ethel received good news from her doctor. She was pregnant with number ten. If all went well, she'd finally surpass Rose's record by one sometime the following spring.

Ethel's joy, though, would last less than two months when a succession of tragedies would strike the Skakel and Kennedy families, a sequence of deaths and injuries that would continue virtually unabated for a period of twenty months, culminating with fatal gunfire in Los Angeles.

Ethel's dream, she later would tell confidantes, had turned into a living nightmare.

Ethel's brother George, now forty-four, had been the president of Great Lakes Carbon for more than a decade, and despite his imprudence and indiscretions, the company had fared well. Recently, George had authorized the $20 million purchase of the 4,600-acre Camarillo Ranch about thirty miles from Los Angeles for the development of expensive tract homes.

But playing hard was still his first priority. The latest adventure on his itinerary, scheduled for September

1966, was a ten-day elk hunting trip on a ranch he was thinking of buying in Idaho, not far from where Ethel and Bobby had run the Salmon River rapids a year earlier.

But George was having trouble rounding up his usual gang of merrymakers. More and more of his friends had come to realize that being in George Skakel, Jr.'s, company could be a life-and-death proposition.

In June 1966, his pal Bill Whiteford had married Bettan Olwaeus, George's former girlfriend, and they were now living in Colorado. George called and asked them to come to Idaho with him. The old gang, including some of the other Swedish girls, would be there; he promised lots of fun and games.

"My dad, who found George despicable," said Whiteford, "called me up and said, 'If you go on that trip you're a lot dumber than I ever dreamed you were because that son of a bitch is up to no good. Don't go! If you do, you deserve what you get, and that's gonna be a set of horns.' " As a result of Bill's conversation with his father, chairman of Gulf Oil, Bill and Bettan gave George their apologies.

While the Whitefords and even Jim Skakel had bowed out, George was able to pull together a gregarious crew of about twenty friends. Most of them had flown out of Westchester Airport with Skakel aboard one of the Great Lakes Carbon planes, a Convair 300. The plane took them first to St. Louis to pick up some more pals and then flew on to Boise, where the crowd boarded three small planes chartered from the Johnson Flying Service and one owned by Skakel. By the time they got to tiny McCall, Idaho, in the late afternoon, George was suffering from a terrible toothache, which he had treated by a local dentist. He instructed all of the others, except for three, to complete the final leg of the trip, a thirty-minute flight from McCall to the Shepp Ranch in a primitive area about thirty miles east of the town of Riggins. They left around six P.M.

Less than an hour later, a single-engine Cessna 185 took off carrying George, his tooth fixed, and three companions: Dean Markham, forty-two, a father of five, who now ran Great Lakes Carbon's Washington, D.C., lobbying office; Lew Werner, also forty-two, George's CIA pal from St. Louis; and Earl Ranft, at sixty-four the oldest of the group, a veteran sportsman who had been a close friend of George Skakel, Sr.

It was going on eight when off-duty Air Force Master Sergeant Donald Adams attempted to land the plane in a tight canyon.

On the ground, a crowd that included George's thirteen-year-old son, Mark, Lew Werner's wife, and several of George's Swedish ex-girlfriends watched in horror as the plane, loaded with guns and liquor, came in too high and overshot the short runway. Attempting to abort the landing, the pilot tried to pull up and make a last-minute turn, but the small craft was trapped by the nearly vertical walls of Crooked Creek Canyon.

As the plane made its final pass before crashing, those on the ground could see George Skakel, Jr., looking out of the window, wearing "that terrible grin he'd get on his face when he was looking down the muzzle of a police revolver," one of them recalled.

That night a search party of George's pals went into the canyon and found the bodies and what was left of the plane, which had hit trees and slammed into the bank of Crooked Creek.

"It did more than telescope," said a member of the party, New York businessman Tom Wyman, who was a State Department official during Jack Kennedy's administration. "The plane disintegrated." The next day a helicopter was sent into the desolate area to pick up the bodies.

Ethel was at Hickory Hill when the call came informing her of the crash. She was devastated. While she knew what a liability George could be to the Kennedys, she loved her brother intensely. After pulling herself together, she made two calls, one to try to reach Bobby, who was en route to Manchester, New Hampshire, to deliver the keynote address at the New Hampshire state Democratic Convention; the other to her sister Georgeann.

After talking to Ethel, Bobby canceled his speech and flew to Massachusetts to pick up two of the Markham children and bring them back to Washington. His deep sorrow, he later told friends, was for Dean and his family, not for his brother-in-law.

"That lunatic always had a death wish," Bobby told a colleague later, unforgivingly. "He took my best friend with him."

At Hickory Hill, a note arrived from the White House:

"Lady Bird and I just heard the news of the loss of your brother. Our hearts are with you, and we pray to God and ask him to sustain your faith and your courage at this lonely time," the President wrote.

In Colorado, Ted Kennedy was on a four-day Western campaign trip when his office reached him and he grabbed the first commercial flight back to the capital. He was still suffering pain from the broken back he had suffered in his plane crash less than two years earlier. Air crashes had now claimed the lives of three Skakels and two Kennedys—beginning with Joe Kennedy, Jr., in 1944.

Ethel, Bobby, and dozens of family friends attended services for Dean Markham in McLean. The mourners then boarded a Great Lakes Carbon plane that took them to Watch Hill, Rhode Island, where Markham was buried. Then the mourners flew on to Greenwich, where, on September 28, 1966, more than two hundred gathered at St. Mary's Roman Catholic Church in Greenwich to say a final good-bye to George Skakel.

"It was," said a Skakel family friend, "quite a bizarre affair. Father Bill—Billy McCormack—who used to hang out with the Skakel boys in the old days, led the Requiem Mass. But there in the church the only thing that was on everyone's mind was that George Skakel was the world's biggest sinner and was probably burning in hell at that very moment. The service was made even more strange by the bevy of George's blonde, blue-eyed babes sitting in the pews crying their eyes out—the Swedish Mafia, as we called them.

"After the service, I was standing with Ethel and even she was amused by the fact that there was this klatch of beautiful blondes who had been her brother's girlfriends. Despite what Bobby felt about George, Ethel adored her brother, and deep down she thought he could do no wrong. The sad part was that George took good friends like Dean Markham with him when he went."

Sarah Davis, who also attended the funeral, said that Ethel handled her brother's death as she had her parents': "With incredible grace and incredible bravery. She never got maudlin or dramatic. She never shed tears that anyone saw. She dealt with it by ignoring it. She tried to find something else that was fun to talk about or do. That's the way she was about death. I envied her strong religious beliefs because I thought it's what got her through all the bad things in her life."

At Rushton Skakel's house in Greenwich, the future of Great Lakes Carbon was being hammered out "while my brother George's body was still warm," said Jim Skakel, still angry years later. Now, with George dead, another faction of the family, the Solaris, which Big Ann's sister Ethel had married into, was making a move to take over after years of feuding with some of the Skakels. But not Rushton Skakel. Now in a controlling position, he appointed his cousin Joe Solari, Jr., whom he affectionately referred to as "a skinny Guinea flop wop" to be the new president of Great Lakes Carbon. Ethel and the others were furious.

Several months after George's funeral, his wife, Pat, who had eighteen volatile and rocky years of marriage, made a surprise appearance at the restaurant-casino that Bill and Bettan Olwaeus Whiteford owned in Vail. "I was apprehensive when I saw her come in," Bettan said later, "but we sat at the bar and talked for a long time and she admitted that she knew George had loved me. We talked about her kids and what had happened. It was all very civilized. I think she was trying to resolve in her own mind the kind of life George had."

Eighteen months after the crash, Lew Werner's widow filed a $1,375,000 negligence suit in U.S. District

Court in Boise, Idaho, against Great Lakes Carbon and two subsidiaries, Rancho Palos Verdes Corp., which owned the plane, and Rancho Idaho, Inc., which had leased it on the day of the crash. In December 1970, after a costly and nasty legal battle between old friends, Great Lakes Carbon finally agreed to pay Anne Werner and her children the sum of $90,000.

Others, like Susie Markham, remained quiet and embittered. "Down in the depths of her heart she was very, very upset that George had taken Dean with him," said a friend of the Markhams. "George was a wild man."

Despite his craziness, George Skakel, Jr., was remembered fondly, not so much by his widow or friends or for that matter even some family members, but by some of the biggest names in journalism who had palled around with him from time to time.

Sportswriter Red Smith wrote: "Big George was all man, all sportsman, all battle and we could not afford to lose him."

William Buckley wrote in his nationally syndicated newspaper column that had George not been related to Ethel and Bobby, his death would not have been noted on page one of the nation's newspapers. But on his own, Buckley wrote, George Skakel had "an energy to his life which, in this jaded age of a general fatigue and instant ennui, of philosophical weltschmerz and forty-hour weeks and unconditional surrender to television sets and the passive life, made him seem almost the eccentric, out of harmony with the rhythm of a senescent world, made him, too, impulsive, in mischievous and irresistible ways."

77 ✻ *Thanksgiving Ride*

ETHEL WAS STILL in mourning when more tragedy struck the Skakels on Thanksgiving 1966, a sunny, unseasonably warm day in Greenwich. It had been two months since George's death, and his widow and four children had been trying to bring some semblance of normalcy back into their tumultuous lives. Pat Skakel had planned a big Thanksgiving feast later in the day at her Vineyard Lane estate, with the children, other family members, and friends. Ethel, as usual, was spending the holidays with the Kennedys.

At noon, the sun warm and bright, Pat Skakel's eldest daughter, Kick, home from Catholic boarding school, decided to put down the top on the new Mustang convertible that her father had given to her as a "sweet sixteen" birthday present. Kick had asked her cousin, Little Georgeann, to go cruising with her, but she had declined. "To be around Kick was like being around Uncle George," Little Georgeann noted later. "She was always living dangerously. Mother made it perfectly clear—Kick's a bad influence."

At about one o'clock that afternoon Kick and her mother jumped into the new car to visit old family friends, Royall and Sally O'Brien, who lived nearby on Pecksland Road. Sally had been a year behind Ethel at Manhattanville, where she had often played tennis with her; Royall had been a Georgetown University pal of Rushton's and years later, when Ann McCooey's daughter was born, the O'Briens were named her godparents. The O'Briens also were active in the Whitby School, the first full-time Montessori program in the United States, which Georgeann had helped establish years earlier in converted stables at Sursum Corda.

The O'Briens were outside enjoying the holiday weather and tending their garden when Kick Skakel and her mother drove up. The couple had gone to George Skakel's funeral and felt enormous sympathy and compassion for the family over their loss. On the grass nearby, Sally O'Brien's mother was playing with her three granddaughters, Hope—called "Hopey"—who was six, Sarah, who would celebrate her eighth birthday in a few days, and nine-year-old Morgan.

Everyone chatted about the weather and after a few minutes it was decided that Pat Skakel would join Sally and her mother for a walk around the neighborhood. Kick asked if she could take the three O'Brien sisters and their two playmates, the Martin girls who lived across the street, just down Pecksland Road in the car to pick up her sister Susan Skakel, who was visiting a friend. Sally O'Brien consented. Everyone left, and Royall O'Brien returned to puttering in the garden.

An hour and a half later, he was still working in the front yard when Kick Skakel pulled up in front of the house, long after she had promised to return. He immediately noticed that his daughters weren't with her. With growing concern Royall O'Brien watched as the teenager got out of the car, walked up the path to the front door, and knocked. The women were still on their walk, so no one answered. Wondering where his brood was, he yelled to Kick, who apparently hadn't noticed him, "Hi, I'm over here. Where's everyone?"

At that point, growing more apprehensive, O'Brien had wandered over to the convertible and looked inside, where he was shocked to see Susan Skakel slumped in the front seat holding Hopey in her lap.

His daughter's eyes were closed.

"What *happened?*" he asked anxiously. Kick, who appeared calm at that moment, said simply that the child had fallen out of the car.

"Hopey was out, but she wasn't bleeding. I didn't ask too many questions," said O'Brien years later. "I jumped right in the car and drove down to Greenwich Hospital."

A half hour later his wife and Pat Skakel arrived at the emergency room and joined O'Brien and Kick, who by now was agitated and upset.

"It was horrible. We were frantic," O'Brien said.

The doctors had tried unsuccessfully to revive the little girl, who was in a deep coma.

O'Brien remained by his daughter's side constantly. "Hopey's hand held my finger," he recalled. "She gripped me very tightly. But a few days later, her grip had loosened. She died on the seventh day."

Throughout the horrific ordeal the O'Briens had not paid much attention to anything but their daughter's plight. They had not questioned their other daughters about what had happened; they had not read the newspapers, nor were friends and family telling them about any reports or rumors they were hearing about the cause of the accident. The family, everyone felt, had enough heartache and grief to contend with.

The day after the accident, on Friday, November 25, the *Greenwich Time* led a roundup of Thanksgiving Day accident stories with the O'Brien case.

The story quoted Greenwich police as saying that Hope O'Brien "was thrown out of a car . . . when the car passed over a man-made bump in the road. . . . Miss Skakel told police her car was traveling at between 15 and 20 miles an hour when it went over the bump, which is designed to slow traffic."

While Kick Skakel had given her story, there was nothing attributed to the O'Briens. For some reason, neither the police nor the press had bothered to contact them. Also curious was the lack of biographical detail about the Skakel girl. There was no mention of the fact that she was a member of Greenwich's legendary Skakel family, or that her aunt was the nationally prominent Ethel Kennedy, wife of the world famous U.S. Senator from New York. Two months earlier, such facts had been well placed in the stories about Kick's father's death.

A month after Hope O'Brien died, an investigator

for the Skakels' auto insurance company telephoned Royall O'Brien to get details about the accident in preparation for a financial settlement. It would be the first time that O'Brien would question his daughters—who had been eyewitnesses—about what had occurred that afternoon in Kick Skakel's car. "It was just something I had never thought about doing before," he explained years later. "When Hopey was in the hospital, we were there most of the time and in and out of the house a great deal. There wasn't a lot of discussion at that point concerning the actual accident and how it happened. I also felt it was a sensitive subject to bring up with the girls."

The story the O'Brien children finally told their father and the insurance investigator, a scenario O'Brien said was supported by the Martin girls, turned out to be different from the account that Kick Skakel had given to the police, at least the one that was quoted in the *Greenwich Time*.

With the O'Brien and Martin youngsters as passengers, according to Royall O'Brien, Kick Skakel picked up her sister Susan as she had promised. But instead of returning immediately to the O'Brien house, as she also had promised, she drove around the neighborhood, finally stopping on Fox Run Lane near her own home. By that time most of the little ones had squeezed onto the trunk of the car with their legs dangling in the backseat.

With the kids piled on the trunk, with the car in drive, Kick began to alternate quickly between stepping on the gas pedal and hitting the brake, causing the car to jolt and the children to rock back and forth. The Martin children and the two eldest O'Briens, fearing they'd fall off the car, plopped down into the rear seat. But little Hopey, giggling with delight, stayed where she was, pretending she was on an amusement park ride. Then, at fifteen to twenty miles an hour, Kick hit the speed bump and Hopey was thrown off the car—not out, as the newspaper had reported—and hit her head on the street.

"That's the *real* way it happened," said O'Brien with finality. "I have never had a reason to question my daughters' account. They were eight and nine years old at the time. They gave me the innocent truth. They would have had no reason to lie. They couldn't have made up a story like the one they told me."

There were other shockers for O'Brien in the wake of the accident. Just twenty-four hours after Hope O'Brien was critically injured, the Greenwich police returned Kick Skakel's recently issued driver's license to her.

On December 1, the day the child died, Greenwich Police Chief Stephen M. Baran, Jr., whose department had never once questioned the victim's family, denounced speed bumps as road hazards. The front-page headline in the *Greenwich Time* read: BARAN DEPLORES ROAD BUMPS AS GIRL SUCCUMBS.

The story reiterated Kick Skakel's account that the O'Brien girl had "bounced out of the car . . . was thrown out of the car"—not off of it—and there was no mention made of the stop-and-go game described by the O'Brien sisters. Also still missing was any biographical information about the Skakel family.

Asked whether any charges would be brought against the Skakel girl, Baran said he doubted whether any negligence was involved, but that a coroner's inquest would be held in a few days.

Kick was cleared of any blame.

"We were never invited to be present," O'Brien said later. "We were never in any kind of court over this case." By 1993, the Greenwich Police Department had disposed of all records of the case. Retired Chief Baran had died in February 1992. And copies of the *Greenwich Time* for the period when the inquest was held were missing from the files of the Greenwich Library.

Kick Skakel was devastated by the accident. Little Georgeann recalled getting a tearful telephone call from her in early December 1966. "She called me at the pay phone at school during study period and told me that Hopey had died. Kick was crying. She's paid hell for it every day of her life. It was horrible for everyone involved."

In the wake of Hopey's death, O'Brien emphasized,

the Skakel family offered an enormous amount of sympathy. But the O'Briens were naturally angry.

"Pat Skakel tried to be very solicitous," said O'Brien years later. "I only saw her once after the accident and that was when I went over to tell her not to call our house anymore. She was calling constantly and it was upsetting Sally. I was contacted by all of the Skakels and they were very solicitous, too. The only one who didn't call was Ethel. She's a very unemotional type, a *frightening* personality."

In the end, the Skakels' insurance company settled the case with the O'Briens for twenty-five thousand dollars.

Every Thanksgiving since his daughter's death, Royall O'Brien checks the weather. He's found it ironic that there's not been a Thanksgiving since that ill-fated one in 1966 that has been nice enough to drive around with a convertible top down. "I've become *very* conscious of that fact," he said.

A decade later another girl would die in Greenwich, a death also allegedly linked to one of the Skakels—a nephew of Ethel's. Once again charges of a cover-up, of power and influence, would be heard.

78 ✻ Record Breaker

ON THURSDAY MARCH 23, 1967, Bobby left Washington with six of his children, on Easter break from school, and his brother Ted, for a long weekend of skiing in New Hampshire. Ethel, very pregnant, but not due until early May, had decided to pass on the trip. She felt she needed some time alone, some rest.

But several hours after Bobby and the gang departed, Ethel began to feel the first pangs of labor. Believing she must be mistaken, she telephoned her obstetrician, Dr. John Walsh, who had also brought Jackie's two children into the world, and asked with a giggle whether it was possible. He wasted no time getting to Hickory Hill. Yes, he told her, she was in labor—six weeks early. Ethel was taken to Georgetown University Hospital where, at 3:37 A.M., on March 24, she broke Rose Kennedy's record by giving birth by cesarean section to her tenth, a five-pound, four-ounce boy.

Several hours later Ethel realized that she'd left home so quickly she didn't even have a change of clothes with her. She telephoned Hickory Hill and ordered what she needed. Young Joe, now fifteen, jumped into the Kennedys' chauffeured car and delivered a fat suitcase to his mother; he was the first of his siblings to see the latest addition.

Meanwhile, Bobby, having gotten word, got out of bed and began the long trek home by car, private plane, and a commercial flight, making it to the hospital by three-thirty the next afternoon. After an hour's visit with Ethel, he told reporters, "My mother said if she had known it was going to be a race, she wouldn't have stopped at nine."

What Bobby didn't tell the press—nor would Ethel—was that the baby's life was in jeopardy during its first few hours of life. He had been born with congested lungs, the same problem that had claimed the life of Jack's infant son, Patrick. It had been touch and go as the life of Ethel's newborn hung by a thread. Luckily, she had not gone to New Hampshire with Bobby or the baby probably would have died, not able to get the kind of expert medical help offered at Georgetown, where highly skilled doctors and nurses pulled the baby through. "I'd just as soon not go through that again," Ethel would tell a friend later.

A week later, with the infant's health improving, Ethel went home without the baby with instructions to stay in bed. Lonely because Bobby had gone out of town, she telephoned Fred Harris, complaining that she needed some companionship. "I'd just like you to stay around and carry me up and down the stairs when I feel like seeing some different scenery," she said. Harris, the gallant Senator from Oklahoma, agreed. The joke around town for the next several weeks was that, "Fred Harris carried a lot of weight with Ethel."

On April 13, Ethel and Bobby arrived at Georgetown Hospital in cream and blue chauffeur-driven convertibles to pick up tiny Douglas Harriman Kennedy, named after former Treasury Secretary Douglas Dillon and roving Ambassador Averell Harriman, the infant's honorary godfathers. After twenty days in the hospital he'd gained seven and a half ounces. Ethel proudly paraded her latest in front of two dozen photographers. When Ethel was asked what she'd learned about children from her first to her tenth, she declared, "Just keep each one happy."

By this point in time, Ethel's determination to produce even more children was viewed by friends and relatives as bizarre. Marion Schlesinger, for one, interpreted it later as "a form of exhibitionism." Privately, others made fun of Ethel, calling her "a cow," "a peasant," and worse. Some even analyzed her drive to become pregnant as a convoluted way of *avoiding* sex. "Sex was never important to her, but having babies *was*, for some bizarre reason," offered a member of her circle years later. "Bobby and Ethel were in love, but it wasn't what today they'd call a 'hot' relationship. The baby thing gave Ethel some sort of identity. In Bobby's case, I think Ethel's baby-making made him look and feel more macho and virile."

Ethel's chum LaDonna Harris agreed. "There was a lot of affectionate teasing and patter between Ethel and Bobby, but no warmth, no hugging, no kissing," she said. "I never saw anything intimate or sexual. They were more like brother and sister."

• • •

Less than two months after giving birth, Ethel was back in action, accompanying Bobby on yet another physically demanding vacation, this one involving running the rough water on the upper reaches of the Hudson River.

Waving aside the warnings of local residents that shooting the rapids was madness, Bobby and Ethel proceeded with their adventure. It almost turned out to be their last.

On May 6, in forty-degree water on a cold and cloudy day, Bobby lost control of his kayak, was thrown headfirst into the water, and swept for a half-mile past partly submerged boulders. Onshore, Ethel watched in horror as Bobby hurled by, only his head, shoulders, and the top of his life jacket visible in the white foam. An unsuccessful attempt was made to throw him a line as he was borne along helplessly by the rapids, almost slamming into several boulders before finally reaching calmer waters, where he was able to swim to shore. He'd been in the water for only several minutes but an hour later, as he drank a cup of hot chocolate, he was still shivering.

The next day, not to be outdone by her husband, Ethel decided to take to the water herself as Bobby and some of their children watched from shore.

Against the advice of several boating experts, Ethel had persuaded Jim Whittaker and University of Denver ski coach Willie Scheffler to take her down the seven-and-a-half-mile course in a canoe.

Not long after Ethel got in the tiny boat, a thousand people waiting at the finishing line at the tenth annual White Water Derby near Riparius, New York, heard an ominous announcement on the address system: "A rescue party's been sent up the river to get Mrs. Kennedy, who is on a rock—she's having a bad day."

Bobby paced nervously, now sipping from a can of beer, waiting for Ethel to appear. Seven of the Kennedy children who had also made uneventful trips down the rapids, as had Ethel's nieces, including Caroline Kennedy, and two nephews, Stephen Smith, Jr., and Chris Lawford, also waited tensely. There had been so many accidents in recent months that they all expected the worst.

Ethel's canoe had overturned in the freezing water three times. The last incident had left her and Jim Whittaker stranded on a boulder and clinging to the boat about a mile from the end of the course. They were more lucky than Scheffler, who had swum through the rapids, striking his head on a rock, but he was not badly injured.

Ten minutes later the rescue party reached Ethel. Precariously she was taken aboard another canoe and brought downstream to calmer water.

With typical Kennedy bravado, expressing none of the fear she felt, she joked about the near-tragedy: "My advice is, don't ever go on the river with a mountain guide and a ski expert," she said through chattering teeth.

The adventures Ethel had shared with Bobby could be viewed as an outgrowth of her childhood love of daredevil stunts. But many of the challenges she now met were for Bobby, to prove to him her more-Kennedy-than-Kennedy spirit—from having all those babies to risking her life in the air, on land, and on sea.

"She was absolutely, completely, totally, and utterly loyal to him," said Gerald Tremblay. "She gave him her undying support and love."

That fact was underscored to Tremblay one afternoon at Hyannis Port. "We were out on a little sailboat," he said. "Suddenly, we came about and the thing tipped over. Ethel had been wearing Bobby's sunglasses, and they fell off and into the water. She yelled, 'Oh, my God!' I thought, 'Jesus, there's no way she's going to get those back.' But she dived in and went under and was gone for over a minute. I was waiting and waiting for her to surface, and suddenly I thought, 'My God, she's drowned. She's been underwater too long. For what? A pair of sunglasses?' I dove under and looked for her and I couldn't see anything. And then she suddenly popped up—with the sunglasses in her hand! She was excited that she had found them. All I could say was 'Wow!'

"What went through my mind when she dove in for those glasses was that she was going to catch hell from Bobby if she had lost them, and knowing him he *would* have given her hell. She had independence, but in that relationship she was the submissive one."

79 * Final Meal

THE TRAGEDIES THAT haunted the Skakel family in 1966 continued unabated into 1967. Friends began to wonder aloud, "What's going on here? Are they cursed?" The Skakels were now thought of as star-crossed characters in an F. Scott Fitzgerald novel, leaving a trail of disaster behind. And the worst for Ethel was yet to come.

Not long after the Kick Skakel accident, her brother Mark was nearly killed. He and a friend, Dion Lowery, went to a wooded area in Greenwich, pried open some shotgun shells with a penknife, laid down a trail of gunpowder leading to a saltshaker, and then Mark struck a match. The ensuing explosion had sent glass shards into Mark's face and body. His injuries required intensive hospital care.

By May 19, 1967, he was well enough to return home and his widowed mother, Pat, still recuperating from her husband's death and the O'Brien girl tragedy, decided to throw a little party for her son. She invited two close friends for dinner, Hilbert Heberling, a captain on the Greenwich police force, and Heberling's wife, Anne, a nurse who worked part-time for one of Pat Skakel's doctors.

Heberling, who had a policeman's Irish brogue right out of Central Casting, had known the Skakel family for years. The Heberlings got to the Skakel house at about five-thirty, and were soon joined by George Terrien.

"I had a few drinks. My wife had a few drinks. George Terrien had a few drinks," recalled Heberling, who was off duty that night. "That family and Pat had a history of drinking, but she had nothing to drink that night except soda of some sort. She was not under the influence. She was happy that her family was home and they were all together."

Kick Skakel had made shish kebab. Early in the meal, Pat suddenly got up and excused herself from the table.

"After about ten minutes I said, 'Where's Pat?' and my wife told me she had to go to the ladies' room," recalled Heberling. "I said, 'Gee, she's been gone an awful long time.' It was just instinct to go after her."

He found Pat sprawled on the hallway floor, just outside the bathroom door. From the way she looked, he knew she was dead.

"I put one and one together and figured she might have choked on a piece of meat. I put my hand down her throat and got it out—a cube of meat from the shish kebab. I yelled to my wife to call the police and to call the Terrien family, since George had just been there. The kids came running in and they were crying, hysterical. George Terrien called the Skakel family physician, who arrived to console the family about the time the ambulance did. When the police arrived I told the captain, 'She's gone.' "

Almost nine months to the day that George was killed, his widow had died at age thirty-nine of asphyxiation caused by a piece of meat lodging in her larynx.

Georgeann Terrien telephoned Ethel at Hickory Hill to deliver the bad news. Ethel got on the first flight to Greenwich. But Mary Begley, looking back over that terrible period of time beginning with Ethel's brother's death and ending with her sister-in-law's, felt Ethel had "distanced herself as much as she could from the family, gracefully."

For the Skakels, the Kennedys, and the Corroons, Pat's funeral service—a Requiem Mass at St. Mary's Roman Catholic Church—was a bizarre reunion of friends and family.

The four Skakel children—Kick, seventeen; George III, sixteen; Mark, thirteen; and Susan, eleven—were suddenly orphans. The Skakel and Corroon families had to make some quick decisions about the children, not an easy task. Some of the Corroons, multimillionaires in the insurance business, were embittered. Over the almost two decades of Pat's marriage to George, Pat's five brothers and two sisters had observed quietly as their sister was battered emotionally by George's womanizing and wildness. Some family members felt that George's excesses were the reason for Pat's alcoholism. "My sister," said Lawrence Corroon years later, "was a wonderful woman."

After Pat's sudden death, the Corroons did not want the Skakels to have any role whatsoever in raising Pat's children, who had been out of control for some time.

No one even thought of suggesting that Ethel take the children. As one of Ethel's close friends at the time said later, "Ethel would *never* have taken Pat's kids, and it would have been miserable for the Skakel kids to have lived at Hickory Hill. Actually, Ethel never liked anybody else's children but her own. She never really wanted to have anybody else's around, unless it was the Kennedy cousins, of course. There wasn't anything she wouldn't do for them."

Although Rushton Skakel expressed interest in adopting his brother's orphaned children, it was quickly decided that they would live with Pat's brother, Richard Corroon, and his wife, Nancy, who had recently lost two of their four daughters in accidents.

• • •

Just a month after Pat Skakel was buried, with the family still in a state of utter shock, Ethel and Bobby celebrated their seventeenth wedding anniversary at Hickory Hill, one of the biggest parties Washington had seen in years.

Ethel's timing, Skakel family members and close friends felt, was in poor taste. "But Ethel had this eerie ability to bury bad news," said George Terrien. "She'd stick her head in the sand. It was amazing. The crowd in Greenwich were shell-shocked that she'd be partying a month after Pat died. Georgeann was furious. I remember she said, 'She's not one of us, that's for sure. She's one of those goddamned Kennedys.' "

The anniversary party started with little soirées all over town, the most posh thrown by Alice Roosevelt Longworth, at her Embassy Row home.

"Ethel Kennedy disappeared at least three times during the evening to change her dress," reported *Washington Evening Star* society columnist Ymelda Dixon. "The first dress, a short beaded one, seemed too heavy, the next, short and blue, was too something, and the third one, also short and blue, she made do with."

Dixon noted that while Ted was in Massachusetts awaiting the birth of a new baby, the rest of the Kennedys were out in force—from family matriarch Rose to her daughter Pat—"looking sensational in a short, pink tunic, with beaded bloomers."

Meanwhile, back at Hickory Hill, Ethel had outdone herself. The infamous Kennedy swimming pool had been cordoned off and large movie screens were placed in each corner as projectors whirred simultaneously. The three hundred guests, including such Ethel "sparklies" as Andy Williams, Carol Channing, Jack Paar, George Plimpton, Buddy Hackett, Kirk Douglas, Walter Cronkite, and David Brinkley, were delighted watching specially edited newsreel footage of Adolf Hitler having a temper tantrum to the dance music; a home movie film of Ethel and Bobby doing the hula; Civil War scenes running in reverse; and rare family footage—Kennedys clowning, nearly drowning each other in swimming pools, marrying, climbing mountains, and shooting rapids. In the background Peter Duchin's orchestra played until three A.M., when a jukebox took over.

At sunrise, Father's Day, Ethel oversaw the serving of scrambled eggs and bacon. At noon, bleary-eyed, she and Bobby, their children, and close friends drove to nearby St. Luke's Catholic Church for Douglas Harriman Kennedy's christening.

Afterward, over champagne and black caviar on toast rounds, Ethel opened a pile of christening gifts and proudly displayed the anniversary present she'd given

Bobby: a beautiful piece of polished Steuben glass in the shape of a rock, from which emerged a letter opener–sized silver sword.

"Isn't it lovely?" Ethel asked, and everyone nodded.

It was the last wedding anniversary she and Bobby would celebrate.

PART X

Presidential Candidate's Wife

80 ✻ Hat in the Ring

DURING THE LATE winter of 1967 and the early spring of 1968, Bobby debated whether to follow in the footsteps of his dead brother and run for the Presidency.

He had listened to much advice, pro and con, from his brain trust. For many of his advisers, the memories of Dallas, little more than four years earlier, were still too vivid, and they counseled him not to run. Leading that faction was his brother Ted, who was convinced the family was cursed.

But Ethel, along with the Kennedy sisters and their mother, eagerly pushed Bobby in the other direction. "He has lots of ideas, he's had them right along," Rose Kennedy said. "He is young and has great hopes for the Democratic Party."

Still, Bobby was torn. And time was running out. The campaign had already started.

Bobby feared that his late entry would cause turmoil, split the party, strengthen Republican support; he again feared being called "ruthless" and opportunistic, of jumping in only because of a vendetta against Lyndon Johnson, the still undeclared candidate for renomination. By this point, Johnson's popularity had dropped to virtually zero in a country torn apart by the war in Vietnam, racism, and violence in the streets. In secret, the beleaguered Texan had all but decided not to run. Bobby also questioned the ethics of breaking the solemn promise he'd made the previous November to anti-war candidate Eugene McCarthy. The soft-spoken, low-key Minnesota Senator—who'd recently made a strong showing against LBJ in the New Hampshire primary, garnering 40 percent of the vote—had come to the Kennedy camp offering to stay out of the race if Bobby decided to enter. Bobby had given him the green light.

Ethel was furious at those who now were advising Bobby against running, lashing out at Kennedy advisers such as Ted Sorensen.

It was Ethel, in fact, who first gave out hints that Bobby was thinking about taking the Presidential plunge. Sailing off Hyannis one afternoon with Fred and LaDonna Harris, Ethel suddenly turned to Bobby and said, "Explain to them how it's so unusual for a person to run against an incumbent President of his own party."

In the end, it was Johnson's war policy, McCarthy's remarkable showing, and Ethel's intense lobbying that finally convinced Bobby to throw his hat into the ring. "Without any question, Ethel was a major factor," said Fred Dutton, one of Bobby's top political advisers.

Bobby scheduled his historic announcement for the morning of Saturday, March 16, 1968. The day before, a very reluctant Ted had been dispatched to Minnesota to give Gene McCarthy the bad news. Before leaving Hickory Hill for the U.S. Capitol, Bobby was so nervous and tense that he needed Ethel to help him get dressed.

It wasn't until they were all in the car heading for the Capitol that Ethel was certain her agonizing was over. "That shows you how great Bobby is," she said later. "He heard out all the arguments, then he made up his mind, and did what he thought was right." In turn, Bobby said of his wife, "She's a great supporter for a husband. She always thinks I'm right and they're wrong."

Standing at the same podium where Jack had announced his Presidential run little more than eight years before, Bobby told a national television audience:

"I do not run for the Presidency merely to oppose any man but to propose new policies. I run because I am convinced that this country is on a perilous course and because I have such strong feelings about what must be done . . . to end the bloodshed in Vietnam and in our cities . . . to close the gaps between black and white, rich and poor, young and old, in this country and around the world. . . . I run for the Presidency because I want the Democratic Party and the United States of America to stand for hope instead of despair, for the reconciliation of men instead of the growing risk of world war."

Dispensing with what political correspondent David Broder of the *Washington Post* termed "the nostalgic rhetoric of the earlier Kennedy era," Bobby shrugged off any support for the President or McCarthy by proclaiming, "I am in it to win."

Just as he had predicted, Bobby's decision immediately plunged the Democratic Party into its most bitter internal battle in a generation. But his announcement came as no surprise to the American electorate. In the wake of Camelot, most people accepted as a given that Bobby Kennedy, inheritor of his brother's torch, would sooner or later make his charge on the White House.

If he won in November, Bobby would be the youngest man ever to be elected President, a hundred and seventy-five days younger than Jack was when he was sworn in.

Bobby's campaign would last just eighty-five days.

The candidate's greatest cheerleader sat in the front row with her head held high, beaming. As usual Ethel was tanned, coiffed, and chicly dressed, surrounded by nine of the ten little Kennedys; Douglas Dillon was at home in his crib. At the moment Bobby was announcing his candidacy, the world was unaware that Ethel had just learned she was pregnant with number eleven. Her pregnancy, though, would be kept secret for now.

While Bobby grappled with reporters' questions about political opportunism, eight-year-old Kerry raced around the Senate chamber, and five-year-old Christopher stood up on his chair and stuck out his tongue at his father. "Chris," said Ethel, pulling him down, "this is your *last* appearance." While she was trying to quiet him, four-year-old Matthew Maxwell lunged at his brother, got him in a hammerlock, and had to be disengaged. Moments later Christopher, back in action again, kicked a woman reporter in the shin. "Listen to your daddy," Ethel pleaded frantically.

Once again Ethel, who had visions of moving into the White House the following January, was the only member of the Skakel family supporting a Kennedy candidacy, although her sister Ann would attend a few campaign functions.

As her brother Jim Skakel observed later, "The crowds, the press, the hyper state. It was as bad as cocaine. Ethel liked the fast lane. They [Ethel and Bobby] started believing those things about themselves, and she became that, she lived that mentality. You could not debate with her. There was no two-way street."

81 ✳ Save the White House

MEMBERS OF ETHEL'S inner circle became hysterical when they contemplated the strong possibility that their madcap buddy, with the enormous, undisciplined brood, had a good shot at taking up residence in the White House in the very near future.

"Ethel thought she was going to be the First Lady, no doubt about it," said one of her ladies-in-waiting years later. "She desperately wanted it. She was already talking to us about living in the White House, and that was even before Bobby hit the campaign trail. I remember her saying, 'We Kennedys *always* get what we want.' Power, power. She was a power-mad woman. Power and money were what was important to her."

With the press, though, Ethel spoke modestly, insisting that she'd "not even thought" about being the First Lady. "I just think about getting through Indiana first," she said, referring to Bobby's first primary test.

"We all loved her and wanted Bobby to win," added Ethel's friend "but we couldn't help from laughing when we thought about her and that family occupying the White House. After a small birthday party at Hickory Hill she needed a cleaning service to come in. We figured, 'If Bobby wins, the White House will be destroyed.' "

Journalists were also mindful of the consequences. Paul Healy of the *New York Daily News* wrote early in the campaign, "If Ethel Kennedy becomes First Lady, the White House will have the swingingest First Family since Teddy Roosevelt's day."

While Ethel was dreaming about moving into the residence at 1600 Pennsylvania Avenue, ten-year-old Michael Kennedy had given an "exclusive" interview to a half-dozen women reporters who had visited Hickory Hill. One of them, veteran Washington reporter Sarah McClendon, recalled the boy saying, "My father will be in the White House but we won't have to move out of this house—this is what I have heard."

When Ethel hit the campaign trail, she surrounded herself with her handmaidens. For wardrobe, she had Sarah Davis and Madame Paul, who was ordered to lower all of Ethel's hemlines an inch or two because her miniskirts rode too high when she sat on speaker's platforms, a lesson Ethel learned during Bobby's Senatorial campaign. In addition to Madame Paul's creations, Ethel also wore designer dresses she'd picked off the rack at shops like Bonwit Teller's in New York. Ethel carried so much clothing with her that fellow travelers on the campaign couldn't recall her wearing the same outfit more than once in a three-week period.

Rene Carpenter, astronaut Scott Carpenter's wife, helped with Ethel's hair on the road.

What Ethel really needed, though, was a full-time luggage attendant. After a night at the Kansas Governor's mansion in Topeka, Ethel and Bobby left behind his shirts and socks, and her cosmetics, bathrobe, and a pair of diamond and ruby bracelets.

Pierre Salinger's wife, Nicole, assisted in organizing things at Hickory Hill, while her husband, who had been White House press secretary for Jack, was now helping to manage Bobby's campaign. Liz Stevens was in charge of the children. As journalist Judith Martin, who later became known as Miss Manners, noted the day after Bobby threw his hat into the ring, "There are always plenty of Washington women for whom no task is too menial and no work day too long when it's for Ethel Kennedy."

Shortly after Bobby announced, one of Ethel's most trusted secretaries, and a governess, had decided to leave, not a surprise in a household with a revolving door for the help. It had become so bad that a joke circulated among Ethel's pals that every Spanish couple in the world had worked for her except for Juan Carlos and his wife, Sophia.

To replace the most recent defectors, Ethel hired sight-unseen a good-looking twenty-one-year-old college dropout, former Boy Scout, and devout Catholic named Bob Galland to look after some of the boys and teach them camping and sailing for the duration of the campaign. But Galland quickly learned that he essentially had been employed as a baby-sitter. Ethel was desperate for someone to watch over the young ones while she was traveling with Bobby. "You will get the kids up and you will put them to bed," Ethel instructed Galland. "You will eat three meals a day. You will sit at the table." Before he could say "RFK," Galland was installed at Hickory Hill, sleeping in a bedroom one room away from Ethel and Bobby's.

In return, Galland received $67.50 a week after taxes plus room and board "for twenty-four hours a day, seven days a week, of service. It was ridiculously low and I didn't always get paid on time," he said later.

"She had school people, yard people, tennis people, garden people, horse people, people to feed animals, drivers, kitchen help, butlers, two secretaries, three maids. The amount of food and wine and whiskey that went through that house was astronomical and no one was responsible. There was a lot of money being spent and Ethel wanted to know why. She'd say, 'I know there's a problem here. Let's see if we can get it straightened out.' Then the word would come down from her to turn lights off. It was gag on gnats and swallow elephants.

"She wasn't the easiest person to work for. As an employee of hers you quickly learned what Ethel liked and didn't like. If she didn't like something as mundane as your tie she told you so and you took it off, simple as that. If you were supposed to be somewhere at eight, it didn't mean eight-fifteen. She was very strict, very strong-willed. If you did not perform like you were supposed to, you knew it quickly."

Galland soon realized that there was little, if anything, he could teach the Kennedy kids, whom he found undisciplined, spoiled, and arrogant, for the most part. "You're talking to young Bobby and he's just gotten back from Africa with Lem Billings after a three-month tour the year before and I'm going, 'Jesus Christ, what am I going to teach this kid about? Raccoons?' None of my experience made any impression at all on them. They'd already done it—camping, sailing, kayaking, mountain climbing."

82 ✻ More Bombshells

FOURTEEN DAYS AFTER Bobby announced his decision to run, Lyndon Johnson went on television and stunned the nation. "I shall not seek and I will not accept the nomination of my party as your President." Earlier that day, March 31, Johnson had seen a Gallup poll showing that only 26 percent of those questioned favored his handling of the Vietnam War. Acknowledging that there was "division in the American house," the President said he was withdrawing in the name of national unity. The Democratic race would now come down to Kennedy, McCarthy, and Vice President Humphrey.

Moments after Johnson's speech concluded, Bobby

landed at JFK International on a flight from Phoenix. "The President withdrew," campaign aides told him. "You're kidding," Bobby mumbled, wondering what the impact would be. By the time he arrived at his apartment in the UN Plaza, a celebration was under way, presided over by Ethel. One of the campaign workers, Bert Drucker, happened to walk into the kitchen with Ethel at one point. "Are you going to be my bartender?" she asked. Drucker said he'd be happy to. "Let's open some champagne," she urged. At that moment Fred Dutton walked in. "Oh, Ethel," he said with concern, "the Senator doesn't really think it's a night for celebrating—*not champagne.*" Ethel turned to Drucker without missing a beat. "Scotch?" She then went to the liquor cabinet and brought out a good bottle. "Well," she said after glasses were filled, "he never deserved to be President anyway."

Bobby asked for a meeting with Johnson to find out how active he would be in the campaign now that he no longer was a contender. "I won't bother answering that grandstanding little runt," growled the President. But the two did meet a few days later. Johnson said he intended to stay out of the fray.

"At first glance," contended Jack Newfield in *Robert Kennedy: A Memoir,* "Johnson's withdrawal appeared to benefit Kennedy. But in the long run it did not. The speech deprived Kennedy of two great issues—the war and Johnson's record. . . . And, in a mysterious way, it made Robert Kennedy the magnet for much of the free-floating venom in the country that had previously been directed at the President."

Four days after Johnson's speech, on the evening of April 4, Bobby was en route to Indianapolis from Terre Haute, when he got a call on the plane from Pierre Salinger. The Reverend Dr. Martin Luther King, Jr., had been shot to death as he leaned over the second-floor railing outside his room at the Lorraine Motel in Memphis. On the ground in Indianapolis, Ethel had gotten word of the King murder and was frightened that she and Bobby might become the target of angry blacks. She suggested that everyone go back to the hotel, where they would be safe. But Bobby, never known for cowardice, was scheduled to speak at a street rally in a black neighborhood, and had every intention of doing so. He sent Ethel back to the hotel and carried on with his plans. When he told the gathering about the shooting, a gasp surged through the crowd and there were a few shouts of "Black power!" But there was no violence.

Kennedy's speech, for the most part extemporaneous, lasted about eight minutes and came from the heart:

"For those of you who are black and are tempted to be filled with hatred and distrust at the injustice of such an act, against all white people, I can only say that I feel in my own heart the same kind of feeling. I had a member of my family killed, but he was killed by a white man. But we have to make an effort in the United States, we have to make an effort to understand, to go beyond these rather difficult times. . . .

"What we need in the United States is not division; what we need in the United States is not hatred; what we need in the United States is not violence or lawlessness, but love and wisdom, and compassion toward one another, and a feeling of justice toward those who still suffer within our country, whether they be white or they be black."

The murder of King by James Earl Ray touched off rioting in cities across the country that night, including the nation's capital, but there were no problems in Indianapolis. Bobby had spoken, the crowd had heard and believed him. It was one of his finest moments.

At two A.M., from his hotel room, Bobby had a telephone conversation with Coretta Scott King, offering her whatever help and assistance she required. She told him she needed extra phones to handle the volume of calls. She was shocked when, an hour later, the installer arrived at her house. Several days later Bobby and Ethel went to King's funeral. "We embraced each other," Mrs. King said of Ethel. "It was a natural reaction from her to me, and I had that kind of warm feeling about her as a woman who reached out to me."

• • •

After the King incident, the campaign resumed. Bobby's first primary—the first big test at the polls since he had announced his candidacy—was back in Indiana, where the voters would cast their ballots on May 7.

In Indianapolis, Ethel made a series of shotgun appearances. At most of the stops, she seemed nervous and signed autographs with a shaky hand. At the Eli Lilly Pharmaceutical plant, the staunch Catholic backed away from a picture with workers making birth-control pills. Despite her glee over Bobby's candidacy, Ethel clearly was not happy. She complained that the Indiana papers were "so awful I can't think of a bad enough word to describe them." Every day there was a negative editorial and nasty cartoon. Ethel asserted that the people of Indiana didn't "appreciate Bobby for what he is. . . . It's so hard to get across what he stands for."

Ethel had good reason to be angry. Indiana was not Kennedy country. Richard Nixon had beaten Jack there in 1960 by a quarter-million-vote margin. Despite Ethel's feelings about the Hoosiers, she went over well with the dowdy Indiana ladies who, surprisingly, liked her short skirts. "Isn't she cute," they oohed and aahed. "Did you see her pretty dress?" But one newspaper columnist noted that Ethel was wearing a huge seven-carat diamond ring, which infuriated her, because it emphasized the Kennedys' wealth.

The press contingent following Ethel saw her as tense and cranky. Normally outgoing, she was reluctant to talk about anything substantive.

"She is terrified . . . that she might hurt Bobby," wrote *Women's Wear Daily*.

Ethel's fear went back to 1966, when Bobby had thrown his support behind a man named Ben Silverman, who was seeking an important judgeship. Being interviewed at the time about her coming week's activities, Ethel had said, ". . . and after that we'll go campaign for Ben Silverman, whoever he is." Bobby and Silverman were furious.

In Indianapolis, Ethel almost got into a fight with a

local TV reporter. She visibly paled when the newsman said that many of Bobby's fellow Senators considered him "worthless." What he meant to say was "ruthless." Losing her composure, Ethel's eyes became icy and her hands trembled. Her voice tight, she declared, "I would use 'brilliant' to describe him myself because that's what he is." She moved away quickly.

Throughout the campaign, Ethel gave the press a hard time for writing negatively about Bobby. On one campaign flight she marched down the aisle and threw a crumpled copy of a story she didn't like in the face of the *Washington Post*'s Richard Harwood.

Meanwhile, reporters were constantly trying to analyze her. Clare Crawford of the *Washington Daily News,* for one, wrote, "It's not accurate to say Ethel has an inferiority complex. But for one of the most famous women in the country, the mother of ten healthy children, a well-dressed and good-looking woman, an acknowledged gracious and entertaining hostess, she seems afraid of being found in some way wanting."

The campaign was only a month old, but Ethel was concerned about the physical and emotional toll it was taking on Bobby. "Seeing the strain it puts on him is the worst thing about the campaign trail," she said. "But the pleasure is seeing him and watching the crowds react to him."

Even though she was carrying a baby, Ethel didn't seem to worry about the rigors of the campaign on herself. When she wasn't pumping potential voters' hands—she lost dozens of pairs of gloves to souvenir hunters during the campaign—she burned her enormous energy in other ways. During one three-hour layover in the town of Snowball, New Mexico, she executed six tough ski runs instead of resting, and during a seventy-five-minute layover in Kansas City, Missouri, she spent her idle time walking briskly around the immense airport parking lot. Bobby was exhausted at the end of each campaign day, but Ethel never stopped for a moment.

83 ✻ "Old Moms"

BEFORE JOINING THE campaign, Ethel had given explicit instructions to her staff at Hickory Hill to make certain the older children diligently followed their father's activities in the newspapers and on television. "One of her rules was, 'You will watch the six-o'clock news every night because your father might be on,' " said Bob Galland. "We did that religiously. They'd get real excited to see their parents. There was a lot of elation—'Yea, there's Dad! This is great!' "

On several occasions the children went on the road with their parents, and it was because of their presence that many women voters identified with Ethel, despite her $750 Courrèges outfits and her Elizabeth Arden wigs. "She sure don't look like she's had no ten children," one woman said admiringly.

One photo from the campaign showed little Chris, Max, and Michael on Ethel's lap in a convertible surrounded by hundreds of citizens trying to grab the candidate's hand. The children appeared disoriented. Another was of David stumping from the back of a train, looking embarrassed and uncomfortable. The only time during the Indiana campaign that Ethel felt truly awed was when she encountered a woman in a receiving line who had far surpassed her own childbearing record. Turning to her handmaiden of the day, Sue Markham, Ethel whispered in wide-eyed admiration, "She's had eighteen children. *Imagine*."

Through the campaign Ethel was rarely home, despite her proclaimed yearning to be with her kids. "There were times when she would arrive at Hickory Hill in the middle of the night, sleep in late, stay for a day or so, and you wouldn't see her. Then she'd be gone," recalled Bob Galland. As a result there were some problems.

The oldest and youngest of Ethel's brood were fine. Kathleen, almost seventeen, was finishing her last year at Putney, a fashionable, progressive school in Vermont. Joe, going on sixteen, also was away at boarding school, his father's alma mater, Milton Academy. The youngest children, year-old Douglas; three-year-old Matthew Maxwell; Chris, nearly five; Kerry, eight; and ten-year-old Michael, were in the care of two nurses as well as a young woman secretary. After only a short time on the job, however, she announced her intention of leaving once the campaign ended.

But the middle children—Courtney, going on twelve; David, almost thirteen; and Bobby Jr., fifteen—were virtually left to fend for themselves, with little or no supervision, parental or otherwise.

"It was incredible," said Galland. "There wasn't anybody to say, 'Don't do that.' The secretary who was leaving was younger than me and I was only twenty-one, so it was hard to control them."

It was clear that the children missed their mother and father, and the middle boys began acting out their anger and frustration.

On the road, however, Ethel played up her role as the doting mother. At one stop she said, "I plan to remain active in my husband's campaign [but] I want to spend at least three or four days a week at home with my children." During a stop in Davenport, Iowa, she said she felt she could best help Bobby by keeping the home fires burning brightly.

"I try to keep our family life happy and easygoing so he doesn't have to worry," Ethel proclaimed. "It's important for him to know the children are well. He worries so much if he isn't sure things are just right at home. Of course, we do have quite a bunch to keep track of. It's a difficult thing for us going at such a rapid pace, but that isn't the worst part of it. We miss our children when we're away from home. Of course, I miss Robert when I'm home and not with him. It seems I'm caught in the middle."

Back at Hickory Hill, things had gotten out of control. One of the Kennedys' neighbors, seventy-one-year-old Jack Kopson, a construction superintendent, claimed he was being harassed by neighborhood youngsters poking at his doors and windows between midnight and four A.M. He also charged that his one-story brick house, which sat on three acres and backed on Hickory Hill, had been vandalized night after night for weeks. Cherry bombs had been placed in his mailbox, and a firecracker was taped to his living room window. When it exploded his whole house shook, he said. Moreover, debris had been thrown on the front steps, lime on the neatly manicured lawn, and an expensive signpost had been knocked down.

Kopson was sure that David Kennedy was involved, and believed his older brothers were as well, although Joe and Bobby were often away at boarding school.

The incidents, reminiscent of the kind of mischief carried out by Ethel's brothers years earlier in Greenwich, almost resulted in tragedy. On the night of April 12, Kopson became so angry that he fired shotgun blasts into the ground, just two feet from young David Kennedy.

"I didn't want to hurt him, only to scare him and his two older brothers [Bobby Jr. and Joe] from coming around my place," said Kopson, who had been a neighbor of the Kennedys for a dozen years. He was also a longtime Democrat and political supporter of Jack's and Bobby's.

One night, Kopson arranged for his son-in-law, Robert Meyers, to hide in a truck across the street from his house and watch for the vandals. The youngsters were nabbed and hauled into the house.

"David Kennedy was the spokesman for the group," Kopson said. "He denied everything. He's a slick one. He said they had been hearing about mailboxes being ruined."

Kopson said he had attempted to talk to Ethel about the problems, but every time he telephoned the Kennedys' private number, he had to go through a battery of operators and finally was referred to a downtown Washington, D.C., office, where a secretary listened to his complaints but did nothing.

"Mrs. Kennedy ought to come on home and watch her children instead of traipsing all over Indiana," Kopson declared at the time. "There is no upbringing over there. No one is controlling those kids."

Around the time of the Kopson incidents, just a few days before the voters in Indiana went to the polls, David and a classmate were picked up by Fairfax County, Virginia, police after throwing a rock through the windshield of a passing car near Hickory Hill.

The driver, Leoneo L. Correa, a McLean builder, jumped out and chased the boys, catching David's friend. A short time later David himself was nabbed by the police as he sat in a field near Hickory Hill. The boys admitted throwing the stones but did not know which one had actually hit the car. Several days after the incident, Correa dropped his complaint on the condition that the Kennedys and the parents of the other boy pay for the damage and confer with police on their sons' behavior.

In Indianapolis, Bobby said that David felt "very badly about what he has done and has apologized to all concerned and I want to add that he is a good boy and has always been a source of great joy and pride to all our family and has never been involved in any trouble whatsoever prior to this incident." He added that he and Ethel and their son would "appear at the appropriate time and place to meet the requirements of the law."

On their return to Hickory Hill, Bobby and Ethel showed little concern about David's behavior, however. "David was chided and ridiculed by the Senator and Mrs. Kennedy, but not for what he did," Bob Galland said later. "The Senator and Mrs. Kennedy felt Dave was stupid to get caught. I think the Senator took Dave aside and they had a chat while the Senator was putting on a suit getting ready to go somewhere, but that was it."

Remembering those days twenty-five years later, Galland said, "David was the one always getting into trouble, whether it was of his own doing, or he got blamed by the other kids." But Galland felt all of the Kennedy youngsters were problems. "Their philosophy was, 'Let's see what we can get away with.' "

As for Ethel, Galland viewed her during his six months of employment—admittedly one of the most turbulent periods in Ethel's life—as a distant, detached, and standoffish mother. "It may have been the only way she could deal with so many kids. She'd fool with the babies. I don't mean take care of the babies. I mean visit with them. She didn't get them up and get them dressed. She was not like my mother and probably not like most mothers."

But on the campaign trail, Ethel—who often referred to herself as "Old Moms"—boasted about her role as a mother and claimed that her children "were not hard to handle. They're all so busy with their own interests. Little Bobby loves animals; Joe goes sailing." She said the most important quality to develop in children was "responsibility."

"Sometimes it backfires," she added. "We sent the top four out to California on their own to go skiing. They were supposed to call the minute they landed at the San Francisco airport. That should have been at eleven. By twelve, I was pacing; by one, everybody was going mad. At two the phone rang. It was Kathleen, who said, 'It's okay. You can stop worrying about David.' I yelled, 'David!' And then Kathleen explained calmly that they'd left him at the airport. He was fine—he just sat right there waiting for them to remember him."

84 * The Jackie Problem

ETHEL SEEMED TO show little concern about her children's behavior, writing it off as youthful Kennedy exuberance. She was more bothered about Jackie's behavior, and the impact it would have on Bobby's campaign.

At the time Bobby announced his candidacy, Jackie, widowed for less than five years, had started seeing Aristotle Onassis, one of the world's wealthiest men. While Onassis was usually discreet, he had gossiped about Jackie at a cocktail party in Paris a few days after Bobby hit the campaign trail, and the conversation had reached Bobby's ears. Onassis had expressed the view that Jackie "is a totally misunderstood woman . . . she needs a small scandal to bring her alive, a peccadillo, an indiscretion. . . ."

When Bobby heard the comment he was furious. Jackie was a Kennedy; there would be no scandal, he declared. Moreover, Bobby felt personally wounded by Jackie's relationship with a man he found despicable.

When Bobby announced his run, Jackie was in Mexico and released a statement saying, "I will always be with him with all my heart, I shall always back him." While Jackie was conscious of, and sensitive to, Bobby's concerns about Onassis, she was also determined to live her own life and not be dominated by the Kennedys.

Disapproving of her new relationship, Ethel and Bobby had sarcastically started calling Onassis "that Greek." They watched with concern, along with other members of the clan, as Jackie visited Onassis's secluded island of Skorpiós, his apartment on the Avenue Foch in

Paris, and went nightclub-hopping with him in New York, where he spent time at her duplex on Fifth Avenue.

At one point, Ethel paid a visit to Jackie and pleaded with her not to marry Onassis, saying that it would hurt Bobby's campaign and injure the family name. But Ethel, who never felt any real connection to Jackie, and the feeling was mutual, left without any concessions.

Next, Bobby met with Jackie. When she told him that marriage to Onassis was a strong possibility, he was outraged. Afraid to alienate her, Bobby controlled his anger. Jackie's allegiance was too important to him and his career, so he jokingly said that such a union "could cost me five states." Sympathetic to his situation, Jackie agreed to put off making any announcements until after the November election. She told Onassis of her conversation, but he was dubious about the arrangement. Bobby, he said, is "making it too fucking easy. He just sees me as the rich prick moving in on his brother's widow woman. Sooner or later it will come to a test of wills."

In the end, none of the Kennedys could stop Jackie. On October 20, 1968, on Skorpiós, thirty-four days before the fifth anniversary of Jack's death, the thirty-nine-year-old widow married the sixty-two-year-old billionaire. Ethel would always remain bitter about Jackie's decision.

Some years later, when Ethel heard that Onassis had died, she told a servant, "Maybe I can get out of the funeral. I'll call Ted and see if I can get him to represent the Kennedys."

• • •

In the weeks before Dallas, *Look* magazine had been working on a feature about Jack and John-John, a cover story entitled "The President and His Son." When Jack was killed, the issue had already gone to press, and couldn't be stopped. The upbeat piece, with a picture of the little boy in shorts smiling at his proudly beaming Presidential dad, took up the whole cover, appearing on newsstands a few days after the assassination. It caused a lot of talk and embarrassed *Look*.

Now, almost five years later, *Look* had another cover

piece in the works, this one on Ethel, whom editors at the magazine now viewed as the next First Lady of the land. When Bobby decided to run in mid-March, *Look* editors had quickly assigned the story—to be headlined "Ethel's Kennedys: How She Manages Them"—to its crack pictorial-reportage team of Laura Bergquist and Stanley Tretick. They scheduled the Ethel cover for the June 25, 1968, issue, which would hit the stands a week after the June primary in California.

Later, the ironic timing of those two covers would become eerily apparent.

Tretick had started photographing Bobby for United Press International as early as his Senate Rackets Committee days, and more recently had shot Bobby's Senate campaign, and the two had become good friends. Along the way, Tretick and Bergquist had been invited to Kennedy functions and dinners, becoming a part of the elite circle of journalists at Hickory Hill. By the time the *Look* editors came up with the idea for the cover on Ethel, Tretick and Bergquist had what everyone in the news business could only dream of—complete access to the Kennedys. If Bobby was elected President, he had promised Tretick the job of official White House photographer.

For the *Look* story, Ethel had decided it would be easier if Stan and Laura spent time at Hickory Hill and watched the family in action. Bergquist could freely take notes and Tretick could shoot candid pictures. Kennedy insiders already were touting the article as "the best thing ever done on Ethel," who *Look* said "remains probably the least known Kennedy."

When the story appeared a week after Bobby's death, Ethel was portrayed as a happy, busy, concerned mother—bathing and feeding her children and asking questions about their schoolwork. No mention was made of the problems she was having with the adolescents. Those stories wouldn't become public for years, when the young Kennedys began to speak out candidly. All in all, the *Look* story read as though it had been blue-penciled by Ethel herself, perpetuating all the old images and myths. Bergquist painted Ethel as "ebullient, gregarious, terribly friendly . . . vulnerable . . . a funny combination of very mod and old fashioned . . . shrewd and naive . . . puritanical and open-minded . . . ferociously candid. . . . Above all she shies from self-revelation which perhaps accounts for the astounding Ethel-gap in the Kennedy literature."

Years later, Tretick talked about the Ethel cover-story assignment, and the view he and Bergquist had of her at the time.

"I never bought that she was a great mother. The operation at Hickory Hill was too loose. The kids all went their separate ways. It was like bedlam, everyone running around crazy. When Bobby was around, the kids were much calmer. I don't think he would take any shit from them. He was like a father and mother, good with the kids, very loving with them, and when he said do something, they did it.

"One night about ten o'clock Ethel was going to fix food for us, but she said I don't know how to fix shit. She couldn't handle anything in the kitchen. Pots and pans were all over the place. Bobby looked at her and said, 'Mother of the year.'

"I was never around when Laura interviewed Ethel, but I was there shooting sometimes when Laura was watching the kids. Insane's the word for it. Laura's comment was, 'Jesus, why am I subjected to this.' I remember that our view of Ethel was, 'God, it's going to be bedlam, just nuts, if she goes to the White House because that place will become a real zoo. Crazy. Nuts.'

"Ethel as First Lady would have been pretty high-handed, too. She was a very demanding woman—'I'm the queen.' My general feeling was that Laura had found Ethel difficult. I don't think she was very fond of her. We *all* knew Ethel was difficult. *Any* story you ever did on the Kennedys with Ethel involved was pandemonium. It's unbelievable what you'd have to go through."

Like so many others, Tretick was eventually dropped from Ethel's A-list. In his case, she had hated a photo he'd taken of Bobby on the broad shoulders of his pal Rosey Grier, wearing Grier's thick glasses. According to Tretick, Ethel had Frank Mankiewicz "disinvite" him from a special memorial service for her husband. "I said to myself, 'Well, that's Ethel. She's displeased with something, so she made her feelings known.' I had heard that she could be vindictive. It was very hurtful to me. It was never the same for me after that. I'd see her from time to time and she'd say hello and smile—but that was it."

85 * *Winning and Losing*

THE INDIANA CAMPAIGN had been difficult, but in the end Bobby had blitzed the Hoosier State and won the primary with 42 percent of the vote, despite Ethel's earlier concern. That same day Bobby also won the District of Columbia, beating Hubert Humphrey 62.5 percent to 37.5 percent.

Ethel was thrilled that the blacks and the white blue-collar workers had come out for Bobby. "Don't you just wish that *everyone* was black," she crowed.

Later, during a party at Hickory Hill for more than five hundred wives of newspaper editors, Ethel approached Flaxie Pinkett, a black real-estate woman and D.C. civic leader, who was supporting Bobby's campaign, and asked her to recite the pro-Kennedy speech she had been giving. Ethel liked Flaxie's words so much that she used similar material in her own speeches. "Ethel," said a friend who witnessed the scene, "seemed to suddenly be discovering the Negro."

On her return from Indiana, word had finally leaked out that Ethel was pregnant with number eleven. Maxine Cheshire reported on May 9 that "close friends . . . are saying [she] is expecting 'sometime near the date of the inauguration' "—as if it were a given that Bobby would be the one sworn in. Ethel refused to confirm or deny the pregnancy story. "I never answer that question and I'm not going to answer it now," she firmly told a reporter. But Bobby, in Hyannis for a quick visit with his father at the Kennedy compound, confirmed but declined to elaborate. "Further information will have to come from Mrs. Kennedy," he said. Kennedy's office in New York later disclosed that the baby was due in January.

During the campaign, Bobby had tickled the crowds and caused Ethel to beam when he engaged in a mock exchange with what he termed "all you Planned Parenthood people back there in the back row with your placards."

His comments were aimed at William Vogt, a former director of the Planned Parenthood Federation, who proclaimed that a man with ten children had the wrong image to be President. He charged that the election of Kennedy "would set back for years the attempts to achieve a rational population policy."

Planned Parenthood revolted Ethel as much as abortion did. And she found Vogt's disapproval just plain silly. "I wish their parents had limited their children," she spat back.

Later, when Ethel was asked by a reporter if she thought big families were truly advisable on the overpopulated planet, she said, "But what would we do without Teddy?" He would never have been born, she pointed out, if Rose had stopped at eight.

• • •

After Indiana, Bobby took his campaign by car and train through rural Nebraska, which he won on May 14, with 51.5 percent of the vote. McCarthy had surprisingly given up on the state altogether and moved on to Oregon and California.

In Colorado, Ethel pulled off one of her elaborate pranks, arranging for a mock political rally—complete with signs, cheers, and music—for Fred Dutton. When the six-car campaign train arrived in Dutton's birthplace of Julesburg, Ethel and some of the girls on the press staff had made up the signs and "Dutton buttons" and painted poster slogans on shopping bags. BEAUTIFY AMERICA, GET A HAIRCUT, FRED, read one sign. FRED DUTTON'S BROTHER FOR ATTORNEY GENERAL, read another. MAKE FRED, NOT WAR, proclaimed a third. Bobby got on the rear platform of the train, grabbed a placard that read, SOCK IT TO 'EM, FREDDY, and led a chant, "We want Fred!" Ethel insisted that Dutton give a speech using many of Bobby's phrases, his accent, and mannerisms. She still wouldn't let him go. "Hey, how about George Bernard Shaw?" she shouted. Dutton was forced to give the quotation from the Irish writer that was the signal in Bobby's standard speech for reporters to scramble back on the train.

Ethel went home for a few days, then flew to Portland with Gerald Tremblay, who was helping Bobby in the Oregon primary. "We took off from National Airport and she squeezed my hand the whole way. I thought her fingernails were going to go through my skin," he recalled. "She had her prayer beads and she was saying the rosary. She had a lot of fear going out there."

In Oregon, the Kennedy juggernaut met with disaster. Oregonians weren't Bobby's constituency; the state had few blacks, Catholics, or poor people. But there were lots of hunters who were against gun control, something Bobby felt strongly about since Dallas. McCarthy wanted a television debate and Bobby refused, which didn't help the Kennedy cause, either. On May 28, when the ballots had been counted, Bobby became the first Kennedy ever to lose an election. McCarthy had won, 44.7 percent to Bobby's 38.8 percent.

Ethel couldn't understand the defeat. "Such a small state," she said several times. "Do you really think it will make that much difference, if we win in California? That's the important state, more like the rest of the country."

86 ✻ California Sunshine

ON WEDNESDAY, MAY 29, the morning after losing the Oregon primary, Bobby Kennedy landed in Los Angeles to begin the grueling week of campaigning that would lead up to the Tuesday, June 4, California primary, his most important yet.

Bobby saw the loss in Oregon as a setback, but the multitude of Californians who would turn out for his speeches and motorcades restored his confidence. It was in Los Angeles that he got his biggest welcome as thousands of blacks, Latinos, and Oriental Americans lined the streets, a ton of confetti swirling around them. "Piss on Oregon!" some shouted as a smiling Bobby passed.

At Hickory Hill, meanwhile, Bob Galland received his latest marching orders from Ethel via Pierre Salinger's wife, Nicole. "Ethel wants six of the kids to campaign. Get yourself a new suit, pick up traveler's checks, and show up in Los Angeles," he was told. His charges included David, Michael, Kerry, Courtney, Christopher, and Max. The next day they flew out on American Airlines from Dulles and were met by Ethel at LAX, taken to the Beverly Hills Hotel, and installed in a three-bedroom bungalow. "They were excited to see their parents," Galland recalled. "Excited to be campaigning."

On Saturday, June 1, Bobby and Gene McCarthy, who had been slightly behind in the polls but gaining fast, finally had a much-heralded debate in San Francisco. Bobby had agreed to the nationally televised face-off, charging that the Minnesotan's "great crusade that began for the future of the United States is now involved in a campaign to distort and stop me.'' His statement was in response to a full-page anti-Kennedy advertisement that McCarthy had placed in the *Los Angeles Times* on May 30. While the press had hyped the debate to a point where some viewers expected fisticuffs, it was, in the end, bland and unenlightening. At the conclusion, each candidate was asked to state his qualifications. Bobby's response seemed unfocused. Asked why later, he said, ''You won't believe it, but I was daydreaming. I thought the program was over, and I was trying to decide in my mind where to take Ethel for dinner. . . .''

On the flight back to Los Angeles, journalist Jack Newfield stopped to talk to Bobby. For the first time he saw what the last few weeks had done to him. ''His face looked like an old man's; there were lines I had never noticed before. The eyes were puffy and red and pushed back into their sockets. His hands shook, as they often did when he was speaking in public. He was so tired. . . .''

The next day, Sunday, June 2, Bobby combined campaigning with some amusement.

''We had a motorcade in Orange County; all fun and games, and then we wound up at Disneyland, where we got a VIP tour for half a day,'' recalled Bob Galland. ''The kids were constantly badgered by the press. Cameras in their faces, microphones in their faces. The photographers would be walking backward taking pictures and the kids would run ahead and get down on hands and knees so a guy walking backward would stumble and fall over them. Ethel got a kick out of it.''

On the eve of the primary, Monday, June 3, an exhausted Bobby and Ethel traveled more than a thousand miles—from Los Angeles to San Francisco—then back south to Long Beach and San Diego.

During a rally in San Francisco's Chinatown, a cherry bomb exploded close to Bobby and Ethel's convertible. Then a string of firecrackers went off. Visions of Dallas. Ethel ducked, terrified, trembling, and pale. The press corps tensed, wondering whether bullets had been fired. But Bobby remained standing, motioning to a friend to hold Ethel's hand and help calm her.

By the time they reached Long Beach, Bobby was physically depleted. Like a hypoglycemic, he slurred his words, felt shaky. "I don't feel so good," he admitted to Fred Dutton. As the motorcade went through Venice, Bobby complained of an upset stomach and asked for ginger ale. In San Diego, he had to be helped to a dressing room at the El Cortez Hotel after getting dizzy and nauseous. Rosey Grier and Rafer Johnson waited while he vomited. A few minutes later he returned to finish his speech, looking sickly.

Bobby's previous campaign trips normally ended lightheartedly. Not this one. The subdued group boarded a plane for Los Angeles, Bobby sitting alone looking ill with Ethel. He finally asked the singer Rosemary Clooney to join them.

That night, the candidate, his wife, and the six children moved into director John Frankenheimer's Malibu beach house to relax, the first time most of the family had been together in weeks.

Primary Day, Tuesday, June 4, was smoggy and overcast, typical for Los Angeles.

At the Frankenheimers', the Kennedys slept late, while the kids romped on the beach. After brunch, Bobby walked down to the water with the writer Theodore White to gaze at the big white-capped waves. Spotting Bob Galland watching the children, he said, "Why don't you take the day off? Don't worry about the kids today."

Galland wandered back toward the house.

From the window, he could see Bobby and David talking together, then wade into the pounding surf.

"The water was freezing and it was rough and the wind was blowing and it was overcast," Galland recalled. "It was not a day for swimming."

Suddenly, tensing, Galland saw a big wave crash, sucking both David and Bobby under. "I could see them getting rolled around. Then I saw Bobby come up holding David."

Everybody ran down to the water's edge. Ethel touched the bruise—"a strawberry burn" was the way Galland described it later—that Bobby now had over his right eyebrow, caused by the rough sand when he went under.

"Everything's fine," Bobby said, calming the others, patting the stinging bruise. "The surf's just too rough."

They all walked back to the house to swim and lounge by the pool. Bobby tussled with the children. "Mummy's so tired that she's going to rest next week, and I'm going to take care of you myself. How do you like that?" They loved the idea, but they didn't believe him. Even they knew the campaign took priority.

Around three in the afternoon Ethel suggested to Galland that he take the children back to the hotel so they could rest. "She wanted the kids to come to the Ambassador Hotel that evening to partake in the election returns," he said.

By six-thirty, Bobby was dressed and ready to leave, but Ethel wasn't. It was decided that Bobby would drive into town with Frankenheimer and Dutton and that Ethel would follow. Thirty minutes later, with the polls closing in an hour, Bobby got off the elevator at the fifth floor and stepped into Room 516, the Royal Suite, already filling with family members—Teddy, Jean, and Pat; advisers Richard Goodwin and Ted Sorensen; and the inner circle of journalists—Jimmy Breslin, Stan Tretick, Pete Hamill, and others, all drinking and watching television.

Not long after he arrived Bobby learned he had won another primary that day, in South Dakota, with 50 percent of the vote. The Indians, he boasted, were behind him.

By the time the California polls closed at eight, the Embassy Ballroom downstairs was already jammed with supporters, campaign workers, and reporters. Upstairs, a party atmosphere reigned. At the Beverly Hills Hotel, Bob Galland noticed how tired the children were from their day at the beach. He telephoned Nicole Salinger and suggested that the two younger ones, Max and Christopher, remain at the bungalow under the care of an assistant, Diane Broughton, and he'd bring Kerry, Michael, Courtney, and David to campaign headquarters.

Salinger gave her approval, and Galland and the brood left by limousine, arriving at the Ambassador not long after Ethel.

Early projections by the networks showed Bobby winning California; he was in a jubilant mood. Still ahead, he knew, was the New York primary on June 18, then a ten-day trip to Europe, followed by a cross-country campaign in all the nonprimary states. But winning California was crucial. In the crowded suite, Bobby lit up a celebratory cigar and mixed with reporters, giving interviews to his network friends, including NBC's Sander Vanocur and CBS's Roger Mudd.

By ten-thirty, as Bobby talked to the press, Galland noticed that the children were exhausted. He suggested to Ethel that he take them back to the bungalow and that they watch the remainder of the festivities on television. She agreed, kissing each good-bye. Back at the hotel, they played with a little monkey that had been given to Kerry by someone earlier that day at the Frankenheimers'. Finally, Galland put Kerry, Michael, and Courtney to bed. The two younger ones, Max and Christopher, were already asleep as was Diane Broughton, in the other bungalow. Galland took off his suit and shoes and settled in front of the TV set. Across the room, David, playing with the monkey, casually watched the TV.

By eleven-thirty, Bobby knew he had won. He had a private meeting with an aide and then went into the bedroom to get Ethel, who was stretched out on the bed. "Are you ready?" he asked. She jumped to her feet, smoothed her orange and white minidress, and got into her heels. Her face was bright and alive. "Do you think we should take Freckles down?" Bobby asked her. Some weeks earlier McCarthy had said that Bobby would require a dog and an astronaut to win. Ethel laughed. Someone joked that the vote showed that not everybody disliked her husband. Ethel took a playful poke at the speaker.

The Kennedys left the suite.

87 * The Light Is Snuffed Out

ON HIS WAY down the hall, Bobby said that it had all been worth it. "I like politics," he said. "It's an honorable adventure."

They got on a service elevator and rode to the second floor with former FBI agent Bill Barry, Bobby's bodyguard, at their side. Only moments before, Barry had mentioned that he sometimes got mixed up in big crowds—". . . maybe I won't be able to react quickly enough . . ." he said. But Bobby had declined police protection and Barry had full responsibility for the candidate's safety. Rosey Grier and Rafer Johnson also helped with the crowds.

Bobby had ruled out any form of police security because he felt it placed a barrier between him and the public. "He was not going to be isolated, he was not going to be sealed off," Fred Dutton remarked later. A reporter who was covering the campaign, John Lindsay, felt that Barry had "an impossible duty" because "it was not possible to protect" Bobby from danger. Only two weeks earlier, Pierre Salinger had been warned by a friend that Bobby would be killed, and Salinger agreed that he knew Bobby was in danger, "but that it was impossible to run for President and not be surrounded by people all the time."

Since arriving in Los Angeles Bobby had made it clear that he didn't like having police around him, said former Los Angeles Police Sergeant Marion Hoover, who had initially been assigned to the candidate's detail. Hoover claimed that during one campaign stop Bobby had actually slapped the hand of an officer who had tried to assist him when he was engulfed by supporters and knocked to the ground. On another occasion, a pick-pocket grabbed Bobby's watch and tried to escape through the crowd. Hoover spotted the man and ordered him arrested. "With that, Kennedy blew up," Hoover recalled. "He came apart and began to scream at me, 'Get the hell away from me and stay away.' I remember thinking, 'I'm not taking this treatment from anybody.' I couldn't believe that a Presidential aspirant—especially a Kennedy—could make such a decision." Later, Los Angeles Police Chief Thomas Reddin declared that all efforts to protect Bobby had been flatly refused. "I got the impression that he wished to appear to be antipolice and antiestablishment, and not to need our help because politically it was the smart thing to do at the time."

The Embassy Ballroom was pandemonium when Bobby, flanked by Ethel and Steve Smith, stepped onto the small speaker's platform before a bouquet of microphones. Ethel waved to the crowd. Then Bobby spoke. He thanked everyone for the win, from César Chavez, who had helped bring out the Mexican-American vote, to the Dodgers' Don Drysdale, who had pitched his sixth straight shutout that night. "I hope that we have as much good fortune in our campaign," Bobby said to Ethel, whose "patience during this whole effort was fantastic . . . My thanks to all of you, and on to Chicago, and let's win there."

Flashing the V-for-victory sign, Bobby waded into the crowd on his way to give a press conference in a room on the other side of the hotel's kitchen. Bill Barry stopped for a moment to help Ethel down from the podium. In that split second, the candidate and his bodyguard, the candidate and his wife, were separated.

Back at the Beverly Hills Hotel, David Kennedy watched on TV as his father disappeared into the crowd.

"The speech was over and I got up and started switching the channels," said Bob Galland. "Then I saw that something had obviously happened."

As he stepped down off the podium, Karl Uecker, the assistant maître d' at the Ambassador, took Bobby's right hand and began leading him through a pantry area toward the Colonial Room, where the print media was waiting. On the way, Bobby turned to look for Ethel, and stopped to talk with the kitchen help, shaking hands with a seventeen-year-old busboy, Juan Romero.

Seconds later, a small, swarthy, twenty-four-year-old man named Sirhan Bishara Sirhan, dressed in blue and wearing a smile, stepped off a tray rack shouting, "Kennedy, you son of a bitch!" and shoved a .22-caliber Iver-Johnson Cadet revolver an inch from the Senator's ear and pulled the trigger, emptying the chamber of its eight bullets.

Bobby Kennedy threw his hands up toward his face, staggered back, and crumbled to the gray concrete floor, mortally wounded.

"Ethel was sort of with us because she knew us," recalled Roger Mudd later. "And we heard these shots. It was like Hades—this screaming that was going on. It was absolutely unworldly. It was just awful. You weren't prepared for it. The ring of people around Bobby's body got heavier and thicker and there was this screaming and guys just slamming at each other trying to wrestle Sirhan to the ground. Jim Wilson, one of the TV cameramen, was absolutely going out of his mind. He was so frustrated, so frozen.

"Ethel just grabbed on to my arm. She was just shaking and I sort of shouldered my way through, just sort of forcing, forcing, forcing and pulling her with me and yelling, 'Let Ethel through, let Mrs. Kennedy through!' and finally the crowd opened up enough for her to go through and she went through."

In the living room of the Kennedy children's bungalow, a horrified Bob Galland stayed frozen on the camera shot of Bobby on the ground in the eerie glow of a TV light for five or ten seconds too long, as twelve-year-old David, still dressed in his blue blazer and gray slacks and playing with the little monkey, watched.

"There was no doubt that the Senator had been shot. David saw it. There was definite shock there," recalled Galland. "I left the TV on five, seven, ten seconds too long. I'm standing there flipping around to catch other coverage and then just turned the damned thing off. I sat down with David and for a few awkward moments wondered what the hell I'm going to say to this kid now. . . . Jesus, I gotta do something. So I gave him a hug and said, 'David, let's just go for a walk for a while, wait and see what happens, other news reports'll come in.' He said something like, 'Oh, man, it's over . . . they got him, too.'

"He was not surprised his father was shot. I said to David, 'Let's get out of here.' I knocked on the door and woke up Diane [Broughton] and told her that the Senator had been shot. She fell apart, literally, wrapped up in a blanket, and started crying. I said, 'Knock it off. You got a job to do.' So she pulled herself together and walked me outside. I told her, 'Don't let anyone in the bungalow unless they're with me.' She said, 'Anyone?' My major concern, and it was definitely a concern, was I didn't want anyone coming in and waking up the kids, telling them their father's been shot. Then David and I went for a walk." (For years afterward, it was reported erroneously in many books and magazine articles that David had watched the assassination alone in a suite at the Ambassador Hotel. That story had originated from an article written by Dr. Gerald Caplan, a psychiatrist, in the September 1968 issue of *McCall's*. In the piece, headlined "Lessons in Bravery," which was picked up by the news media, the doctor attributed his information about David to campaign chronicler Theodore White. But White had made no mention of the incident in his book on the 1968 race. Galland said that White, who died in 1986, had looked in on David an hour or two *after* Galland had arranged for David to be put in another room at the Beverly Hills Hotel. "He probably found him there alone for a moment and the facts got mixed up about the time and location from that point on," Galland theorized.)

Back at the hotel, Juan Romero, the kitchen worker who had shaken hands with Bobby moments before the shooting, was now bending over the fallen candidate, putting a rosary in his hand. Bobby clutched the beads.

His lips moved, but nobody could hear what he was saying. Ethel, her eyes wild with fear, was kneeling in her husband's blood. "Get back, all of you," she screamed. "Get out! For God's sake, give him room to breathe." A cameraman yelled back, "This is history, lady." Bobby turned his head and seemed to recognize Ethel as she whispered to him, stroked him. His sister Jean, who first brought Ethel and Bobby together many years earlier, knelt beside her. Newsman Charles Quinn saw Ethel leaning over Bobby, whose shirt was open. Quinn noted that Bobby was still alive because he saw him fingering the rosary beads, which were lying across his belt. "Ethel looked up at me at one point and said, 'Oh, Chuck, please go away.' But I couldn't leave."

Several others had been shot along with Bobby. One, Ira Goldstein, a nineteen-year-old reporter for Continental News Service, had staggered to a chair, wounded in the left thigh, and asked, "How is Senator Kennedy? What happened to him?" Ethel, disoriented, in shock, heard him. "She said to me, 'How dare you talk about my husband that way,' and she slapped me across the face. And I said, 'I'm sorry, lady, but I was shot, too. I'd like to know how the Senator is.' And she said, 'Oh, I am sorry, honey,' and kissed me. At that time she was not in tears. She was a little hysterical, though, but she wasn't crying."

Less than a dozen feet away Bill Barry, Rosey Grier, and Rafer Johnson still struggled with Sirhan for the gun, pinning the tiny assassin on a steam table. There were shouts of "Kill him! . . . Get the gun, Rafer! . . . Get away from the barrel! . . . You monster! . . . You'll die for this! . . ."

A Christian Arab who had emigrated from Jerusalem in 1957 at age twelve, Sirhan apparently held Kennedy responsible for his people's problems. "I did it for my country," he screamed later on his way to jail.

In the ballroom, Steve Smith pleaded for a doctor over the public address system.

The word spread. "Bobby's been shot!"

"Kennedy Girls" in white blouses and navy blue skirts and straw skimmer hats burst into tears.

At 12:23 A.M., two ambulance attendants, Max Behrman and Robert Hulsman, arrived with a rolling stretcher. Bobby whispered, "Don't lift me, don't lift me," the only words Behrman recalled him saying. "Gently," Ethel implored, "gently," as they lifted Bobby on to the gurney and strapped him down. Before losing consciousness, Bobby, in terrible pain, said, "Oh, no, no . . . don't." They were the last words he would ever utter in public.

With Ethel, his sister Jean, Dutton, Barry, and a few others in close attendance, Bobby was wheeled to an elevator, where Behrman began to bark orders, infuriating Ethel, who shouted at him to be quiet. An argument ensued and one of the women in the entourage slapped the medic, who threatened to crush her head if she did that again. At one point, the men were moving the stretcher so fast it almost ran out of control. At the ambulance, Behrman declared that only Ethel could ride with Bobby. Ethel wanted Father James Mundell, a lay priest and friend of the Kennedys, to ride with her and Bobby, but he got lost in the crowd. Dutton pushed Behrman aside and squeezed in next to Ethel. Barry and *Look*'s Warren Rogers hopped into the front seat. The ambulance, lights and siren blazing, sped toward Central Receiving Hospital, a mile away. Seeing that Bobby was having trouble breathing, the medic tried to slap an oxygen mask on his face and head, where the bullet wound was. Ethel screamed at him and wouldn't let him touch Bobby. "I tried to check his wounds and she told me to keep my hands off," Behrman said. "I tried to put bandages on him but she wouldn't let me. She got so mad at me she threw my log book out the window." Suddenly Bobby's breathing turned heavy and Ethel let Behrman clap an oxygen mask over his nose and mouth. "Is he breathing?" Ethel cried. Behrman said he was.

The ambulance attendants wheeled the litter into Emergency Room No. 2 at Central Receiving, and lifted Bobby onto a padded aluminum table. As Ethel watched, nurses cut off his clothes to prepare him for a heart-lung resuscitator. His eyes were fixed and staring; he was nearly pulseless, his blood pressure close to zero. Dr. Vasilius Bazilauskas thought at first glance he was dead. "The bullet hit the switchboard," he said. He slapped Bobby several times on the face, saying, "Bob, Bob, Bob." The doctor then determined there was a heartbeat. He took the stethoscope and put it to Ethel's ear so she'd know he was still alive. "She listened, and like a mother hearing a first baby's heartbeat, she was overjoyed," he said later.

"Will he live?" she begged. The doctor told her that for now Bobby would be all right.

Outside the emergency room, meanwhile, Father Mundell was being blocked from entering by a policeman. Seeing them arguing, Ethel ran out and pushed the officer, yelling that she wanted the priest with her. The policeman shoved her in the chest. Dutton broke up the pushing match and the priest was allowed to enter the room, where he gave Bobby Absolution. At that moment another priest, Father Thomas Peacha, of nearby St. Basil's Parish, entered the room and performed the Last Rites of the Catholic Church.

Thirty minutes later it was decided to transfer Bobby several blocks away to Good Samaritan Hospital, where he would undergo surgery for removal of two bullets: one had entered the mastoid bone and lodged in the midline of the brain; another was lodged in the back of the neck; a third had grazed the forehead.

At one o'clock in the morning, Bobby was brought out on a stretcher with tubes running into his body and wearing an oxygen mask. Ethel walked next to him and rode in the ambulance with him. At Good Samaritan, he was rushed to ninth-floor surgery. Father Mundell had stayed with Ethel and now suggested that she lie down as other family members, Jean and Pat among them, joined her in the vigil.

Within minutes of Bobby's arrival at Good Samaritan, Ethel received a telegram from the President and Lady Bird: "We grieve and pray with you."

• • •

About that time, after having silently walked the quiet streets of Beverly Hills for more than an hour, Bob Galland and David Kennedy ended up behind the pool of the Beverly Hills Hotel, drinking Cokes.

"There were a couple of emotional minutes, there were tears; he brushed a half a dozen of them away and that was it. He was a Kennedy. He handled it like a big boy," recalled Galland. "I was surprised by his maturity, but he was evidently prepared in his own mind for the worst. I could tell it was definitely something he had wrestled with before. I wanted to know what had happened to the Senator but my responsibility was to David. At twenty-one, I was not prepared for this. David was obviously tired, so I left him sitting there and I went into the hotel lobby and told the guy I wanted a room closer to the front desk. I told him who I was and he gave me a key and I got David. He obviously wasn't going to go to sleep and I didn't want him waking the other kids. I stayed with him for a while, got him undressed, and put him to bed and told him if I heard any news I'd be back immediately."

Galland walked to the hotel restaurant, where he ran into John and Ann Glenn, who wanted to know how the children were. Glenn, remarkably calm, told Galland, "I just want to make sure I can reassure Ethel that the kids are fine." About that time, Galland recalled, Theodore White, who was working on his book *The Making of the President 1968,* also arrived at the hotel. The Glenns, White, and another couple tiptoed into David's room and sat in the dark as the boy slept. As Galland remembers it, "They were all hot to go wake up the other kids and I wouldn't let them do that."

At Hickory Hill, Bobby Kennedy, Jr., had watched most of the primary night on television, but had gone to bed after hearing that his father had won. He got up the next morning hoping to read about the victory in the paper but instead saw the headlines about the shooting. He lit a fire in the living room fireplace and fed the newspaper into the flames, page by page.

Like so many others on the East Coast, Ethel's pal Sarah Davis had gone to sleep happy with the knowledge that Bobby had won the primary, but unaware of the shooting. Sometime in the middle of the night the ringing of the telephone awakened her. It was Carmine Bellino, an investigator who had worked with Bobby on the Senate Rackets Committee. Bellino, brother-in-law of Bobby's secretary Angie Novello, told Davis what had happened. "Ethel," he said, "wanted you to know." He suggested that Davis get to Hickory Hill to help. Davis immediately turned on the TV and with her children, Jock and Tracy, watched a replay of the shooting. "We stayed up the rest of the night and cried," she said later. At Hickory Hill in the morning, she joined other members of the inner circle who were already planning for the inevitable.

Back in Los Angeles, Police Detective Sgt. Dan Stewart was ordered to get to Good Samaritan and help take charge of security. For the next twelve hours, he and his colleagues had problems with the Kennedys and their aides. "They didn't appreciate any of the police," he said. "They were pushy and at one point one of the cops knocked Jesse Unruh on his ass, just leveled him. They were trying to tell us how to run the show and we just said, 'We don't care what you guys did in Dallas, let's not have it here.' They finally eased up because they got a bar set up on a medical trolley in one of the waiting rooms and they started drinking. The booze was brought in through a back entrance by one of their people. They were abusive folks. Steve Smith, for one, was bad news. He said, 'I'm a lawyer, I'm this, I'm that.' I said, 'Just sit down there and have a drink.' The family wanted to run the show and tell us how to run our investigation."

At one point, Stewart was sitting next to one of the doctors handling Bobby's case. "I asked, 'How's he doing?' And the doctor looked at me and said, 'He's dead.' I said, *'Dead?'* Then he took me in the room and pointed to a screen beside the bed and said, 'Look at this. We've got a straight line.' He said, 'We're just pumping charges into the brain just to keep him going.' "

At 3:12 A.M., a team of six surgeons, brain and chest specialists, began a three-hour-and-forty-minute last-ditch effort to save Bobby's life in a ninth-floor operating suite as two grim-faced policemen stood guard outside with green surgical smocks over their uniforms.

A nurse tried to get Ethel to go back to the fifth floor during the operation. But she refused, sitting instead in a tiny room near Surgery, biting her lower lip until the double doors opened and Bobby was wheeled out. In the recovery room, she climbed onto a surgical table and lay there next to him.

At 7:20 A.M., Frank Mankiewicz, looking grim, told reporters that all but one fragment of the bullet had been removed from Bobby's brain. The good news was that Bobby was breathing on his own; the bad was that "there may have been impairment of the blood supply to the midbrain, which the doctors explained as governing certain of the vital signs—heart, eye track, level of consciousness—although not directly the thinking process."

At a command post established at a nurse's desk, an aide fielded phone calls for the Kennedys from well-meaning people with bizarre suggestions of how to save Bobby's life: magic words, herbs, onions and garlic, the position of people standing in his room.

That morning one of LBJ's aides visited the hospital. While he didn't see either Bobby or Ethel, he sent back word to the President that "things look quite gloomy . . . there is nothing anyone can do except pray . . . all of the Kennedy people are aware of the President's willingness to do whatever he can."

At the Beverly Hills Hotel, the Kennedy children were beginning to stir, and Bob Galland was a nervous wreck.

"Colonel Glenn had told me in the middle of the night that he would come by the bungalow in the morning and help me wake the kids and that he would tell them what had happened. He never did and I was really pissed.

"The kids came wandering in for cereal at different times. As gently as I could, I told them that after their dad's speech the night before somebody had shot him.

What could I say? I told them he was in the hospital, that their mother was with him. There was crying, but no screaming. Courtney or Kerry or Michael went in and told the little ones. It didn't matter to them; they didn't understand. But it mattered to Michael, to Kerry, and to Courtney—Courtney so much so that she was never close to me again for the rest of the time I worked for the Kennedys. She saw me as the one who gave her the bad news."

Finally, John Glenn arrived. He had been involved in making arrangements for an Air Force plane to take the young Kennedys back to Washington. Gathering the children around him, he said, "Everything's going to be all right. Mother's at the hospital. . . ."

Said Galland, "We got all of them dressed and we were gone before ten that morning. Colonel Glenn flew back with us. He would sit with the kids for a while. I would sit with them for a while. It was an in-flight refueling plane, not a passenger plane, so it was interesting for the children to wander around and explore it. There was no talk during the flight about their father."

At Good Samaritan, meanwhile, the clan was gathering to plan for the funeral that Ethel and the others now knew was inevitable. The doctors had told Ethel privately that there was little chance for Bobby to pull through. "I'll pray," she told them, her voice strong, her face tense.

Teddy, who had been Bobby's stand-in at the Kennedy campaign headquarters in San Francisco, became ashen and looked like he was going to faint when told of the shooting. "My God, how can this be happening," he groaned. Arrangements were made for an Air Force plane to fly him to Los Angeles so he could be at his brother's side.

Suddenly catapulted by tragedy to the role of acting patriarch, as Bobby had been when Jack was killed, Ted knew his first task was to call Hyannis Port to tell his paralyzed father and seventy-seven-year-old mother what had happened. But he decided to wait until morning, when more was known about his brother's condition.

Rose Kennedy had campaigned for Bobby in California, flying home to watch the primary on TV. Seeing that he was substantially ahead by eleven o'clock, she'd gone to sleep, fairly certain he'd won.

She'd gotten up at six to go to early Mass at St. Francis Xavier Roman Catholic Church and turned on the TV and heard the news. "My mind somehow would not allow me to think—that it could be anything really serious," she wrote later in her memoirs. "There had been an accident of some sort, perhaps during a victory celebration. I went on dressing, listening distractedly. . . ."

At that moment her niece Ann Gargan came in and told her that Bobby had been shot. By the time Teddy had called, his mother knew what had happened. Later, Joe, sitting helplessly in his wheelchair, wept after listening to Ted.

"It seemed impossible," Rose thought, "that the same kind of disaster could befall our family twice in five years. If I had read anything of the sort in fiction, I would have put it aside as incredible."

On the way to Mass she prayed, "Lord Have Mercy," and thought, *Oh, Bobby, Bobby, Bobby*. Later, she remembered keeping herself busy by sorting and rearranging things in her room. "I had to keep moving . . . I prayed . . . I still couldn't believe it, although I knew it was so."

She also thought of Ethel.

"Ethel was the most admirable of all. She and Bobby loved each other deeply—they loved being together, sharing everything; they had a perfect life. Much as I would grieve for Bobby and miss him, I knew she would miss him even more: not only for all they meant to each other but as the father of her ten children, with the eleventh to come posthumously. . . . I knew how difficult it was going to be to raise that big family without the guiding role and influence that Bobby would have provided. And, of course, she realized that too, fully and keenly. Yet she did not give way: She was calm and courageous, and I was very proud of her."

At daybreak after the shooting, the press descended on the compound and police sealed it off. But later in the morning newsmen witnessed a curious scene. The matriarch, wearing a long pink coat, white shoes, and sunglasses, was seen throwing a tennis ball against the wall of the house that Jack once lived in. She'd toss the ball and catch it, slowly, mechanically. When she realized she was being watched, she said, "Really, how can you be so unfair." No one answered.

Despite her recent dispute with Bobby over her relationship with Onassis, Jackie completely fell apart when she learned of the shooting. Ever since Jack's assassination five years earlier, she had lived in fear that the same fate would befall Bobby. Just two months earlier, a few weeks after Martin Luther King was gunned down, she had attended a dinner party in New York where she ran into Arthur Schlesinger and the talk turned to Bobby's campaign. "Do you know what I think will happen to Bobby?" Jackie whispered. "The same thing that happened to Jack. There is too much hatred in this country, and more people hate Bobby than hated Jack. I've told Bobby this, but he isn't fatalistic like me."

Jackie, in New York, had also watched the primary returns on TV and gone to bed before the shooting. She was awakened by a call from London. Prince Radziwill, husband of her sister Lee, had already heard the news across the ocean. He was horrified when he learned at that moment that he was the bearer of bad tidings. After hanging up, Radziwill grabbed the first flight to New York. Jackie pulled herself together and telephoned a close friend, Roswell Gilpatric, who had served in the Kennedy Administration as Undersecretary of the Air Force. He immediately made arrangements for Jackie to fly to Los Angeles aboard IBM president Thomas Watson's private leased jet. Jackie waited for Radziwill's arrival and they flew West together. On their arrival at LAX, they were met by Bobby's longtime friend Chuck Spalding. "What's the story?" Jackie asked frantically, wearing her trademark sunglasses to cover her eyes, red from crying. "I want it straight from the shoulder."

Spalding gave it her. "Jackie, he's dying," he said bluntly.

Despite their negative feelings about the Kennedys, and Bobby in particular, the Skakel family was horrified and heartbroken. Georgeann called Ethel in Los Angeles. Ann Skakel McCooey Ryan telephoned. Pat Cuffe made arrangements to fly in from Ireland. Rushton called. All of them offered her their prayers. But it was mostly the Kennedys and their friends who rallied around Ethel.

Even though Jim and Virginia Skakel were living in the Bel Air section of Los Angeles, they did not go to the victory night festivities at the Ambassador Hotel. Jim was in Portugal, but wouldn't have gone had he been home. And Virginia felt funny about showing up since she and Jim rarely talked to Ethel and were not supporters of Bobby's run for the presidency. But Virginia, despite some of her past run-ins with Ethel, was fond of her sister-in-law and thought of her as "charismatic, dynamic, a doer." On primary night, Kennedy family friend Ray O'Connell had called. "Ginny, come down to the Ambassador, Ethel wants you to be with us," he had said. Virginia told him that Jim was away and that she herself couldn't handle all the excitement because she was pregnant. "Well, so is Ethel," O'Connell responded jovially. But Virginia was adamant. The next morning, when she heard the horrible news, she rushed to Good Samaritan. "Jim had heard what happened to Bobby and was on his way back," said Virginia years later. "I sat at the hospital all day alone. All the Kennedy family were in Bobby's room with Ethel. They asked me if I wanted to go in and I said no."

Virginia, who had not known previously that Ethel was pregnant, realized the stress she was under and offered her the services of her own obstetrician, Dr. Blake Watson. The doctor, whose patients had included Pat Kennedy Lawford, had just delivered a baby at St. John's Hospital in Santa Monica when he got a call from Virginia at six A.M. "The police came and picked me up and took me to Good Samaritan and the family asked me if I would stay with Ethel. They wanted me to be around as a precaution. I went to see her and talk to her and she seemed, naturally, in shock."

Meanwhile, a tightly controlled Ethel, a ghostly-looking Ted, and the others discussed the funeral arrangements as Bobby clung to life in intensive care. Ethel, who had already come to grips with the worst, decided that the services would be held at St. Patrick's Cathedral, and the burial at Arlington National Cemetery, next to Jack. Because there were so many people who would have to travel between the two cities by plane, the idea came up of using a train to carry them all from New York to Washington. The high drama of a funeral train was not even considered, only the logistics of transporting the many friends and family members. The decision was quickly telephoned to Hickory Hill, where a scene of controlled chaos existed.

If all had gone according to plan, Bobby, Ethel, and the children would have been returning to Hickory Hill early on the evening of the fifth for a victory party. A crew of workmen had already spruced up the spacious lawns, cleaned the tennis courts, and decorated the swimming pool. Fresh slipcovers in spring patterns, flowers, cartons of food and liquor had been delivered in preparation for the welcome-home festivities. Now the house was surrounded by police and Secret Service men keeping back the press and hundreds of Washingtonians who had awakened to the horrible news and came to watch and to grieve.

All of Ethel's girlfriends—Sarah Davis, Sue Markham, Kay Evans, Ann Buchwald—had arrived early in the morning to help. One of the first to get there was Gertrude Corbin, whose husband, Paul Corbin, was an advance man for Bobby. At the time of the shooting, he was with Ted at campaign headquarters in San Francisco. "I was in bed watching TV. It was about one-thirty in the morning," Gertrude Corbin recalled. "I was shocked. I'd gone through it with Jack. I immediately called Lem Billings and told him what happened. I got dressed and rushed over to Hickory Hill about five A.M. Nobody was there except for the household help and a few others. It was very depressing for all of us." Nicky Arundel, a Kennedy friend who owned a radio station and was active in the campaign, said sadly, "We had plans to open our main headquarters in Richmond tomorrow."

The only children at home were Bobby Jr., who had decided not to go to Los Angeles, and the baby, Douglas, just fourteen months old. By midafternoon, the eldest of the children, Joe and Kathleen, arrived home from their boarding schools in New England. Despite the gloom that hung over the house, the Kennedy spirit seemed alive and well. At one point, the brothers Joe and Bobby Jr. played touch football. Kathleen went out with friends and returned with cartons of ice cream. Surly Brumus, appearing to miss his master, wandered forlornly, stopping to sniff an abandoned football. Staff members and neighbors supplied the police and federal agents with cold drinks and sandwiches, which they stashed for later in the Toonerville Trolley, a cart that in happier times the children used to ride around the grounds. Now law enforcement officers had wired it, equipped it with a sound speaker, and used it as part of a hastily rigged communications system.

Early in the evening, John Glenn, Bob Galland, and the six other Kennedy children landed at Dulles and were driven to the house.

On TV, Frank Mankiewicz was about to give the next-to-the-last update on their father's condition. At the time, none of the children at Hickory Hill, nor the reporters standing before Mankiewicz in Los Angeles, were aware that funeral arrangements were already in the works. But the close friends at the house in McLean knew. "Even though Bobby was still alive," Sarah Davis said later, "Bobby's funeral was basically being planned. We knew that he was going to die. All the grown-ups in the house knew, taking phone calls from Los Angeles, making phone calls to New York, getting St. Patrick's and the whole deal."

On television, Mankiewicz was saying, "The team of physicians attending Senator Robert Kennedy is concerned over his continuing failure to show improvement during the postoperative period. Senator Kennedy's condition is still described as extremely critical as to life. There will be no further regular bulletins until early tomorrow morning."

That night Bobby Jr., Joe, and Kathleen—accompanied by Lem Billings, Kay Evans, and a Secret Service agent—were flown to Los Angeles aboard the *Jet Star*, one of the planes in the presidential fleet. After refueling at Tinker Air Force Base in Oklahoma, it arrived in Los Angeles around eleven-thirty.

Sometime after midnight on June 6, the family and the doctors met to discuss Bobby's condition. In attendance besides Ethel were Jean, Pat, Jackie, and Ted. Also present was Dr. Blake Watson, the obstetrician who was keeping a careful watch over Ethel. "We were in intensive care while Bobby was on the table. Ethel was there beside him and I was behind her. The doctors were talking with the family about what to do, because all along there had never been any sign of brain waves. They all talked for a while and then all agreed to pull the plug.

"Ethel was very staunch and very self-controlled. She was very, very, very calm about the whole thing. It was only a few minutes after they took the apparatus off Bobby that he didn't breathe anymore."

Mankiewicz walked into the press room to announce that Bobby had died. He said the specific cause of death was "the gunfire attack . . . the bullet that went into the head near the right ear." No mention was ever made, or would it be, that the family had decided to speed his death.

Bobby's body was taken into the basement of the hospital for an autopsy. There, another angry confrontation would occur between a Kennedy aide and Detective Dan Stewart. "Myself and another detective [Bill Jordan] were the only two officers at the autopsy," Stewart said. "Suddenly this Kennedy aide walked in. I said, 'Who are you?' He said he had been asked to come down and watch over the autopsy for the family. Then he asked me who I was and when I told him he said, 'You can't be here. The family doesn't want you here looking at Bobby's nude body.' I said, 'Get the fuck out of here!' "

Officially at 1:44 A.M., on Thursday, June 6, 1968, Ethel Skakel Kennedy, pregnant with her eleventh child, became a widow. The one and only shining light in her life had been snuffed out.

PART XI

Widowhood

88 ❋ *Going Home*

FROM THE MOMENT Bobby was shot until he was buried, Ethel rarely left his side. In his death, as in his life, her sole wish was to be with him.

Around noon on June 6, Bobby's body was taken from the mortuary at Good Samaritan, where the six-hour autopsy had been performed, and placed in a blue-gray hearse for the ride to the airport. Outside the hospital a crowd of five thousand stood vigil, many weeping. Ethel got in the front seat with Ted for the thirty-minute ride to the airport, where thousands more waited in silence to say their last good-byes, some tossing flowers near the ramp leading to the plane. An airport lift truck raised the casket, draped with a purple cloth, to the front entrance of the jet. Ethel, Ted, and the widow's three eldest children rode to the doorway with the casket, while other members of the family, led by Jackie, entered through the plane's rear door.

Jackie had been apprehensive about boarding until she was assured that it was not the same plane that had borne Jack's body from Dallas. The plane carrying Bobby's body had actually been on its way to Japan with Kennedy's Cabinet and staff members when word was received that the President had been shot.

For part of the flight, Ethel lay against the coffin, at one point falling into a fitful sleep. Seeing her lying there, a passenger came forward and put a pillow beneath her head and rosary beads in her hand. Ethel awoke for a moment, looked at him, then fell back to sleep. Young Joe Kennedy stayed with his mother while she slept; it was he who had suggested the rosary beads.

His uncle Ted, the new family head, the sole surviving brother, also stayed next to the coffin for the entire flight. About an hour out of New York, Ted, too, fell asleep, snoring loudly. Others came forward and took turns lying next to the casket. Meanwhile, Pat, Jean, and Eunice sat with Kathleen, Joe, and Bobby Jr., behind the coffin.

For the first hour, two of the world's most famous widows, Jackie and Ethel, sat together talking quietly. Then the recently widowed Coretta King, who had flown to Los Angeles the previous evening, spent time with both Ethel and Jackie.

The flight, though, was not altogether solemn. "After we got ten or fifteen minutes up in the air," recalled George Plimpton, "the natural esprit of those people who surround Ethel and the Senator began to break out. People began to move up and down the aisle . . . when Ethel came through the plane . . . everyone saw that she was trying to put a face on all of this, and it gave them a release, I think, and they were able to start functioning."

At times, Ethel walked up and down the aisle asking friends where they were planning to stay in New York, and how they were holding up. She even managed to joke and banter a bit, discussing what she would wear to the funeral; personally she despised black, she said. Amazed at her apparent calm, many wondered how she could possibly act so normal, and worried what would happen in the future when the shock wore off. Some noted that it was the first time they had ever seen her appear so relaxed on a plane. "If Bobby had been alive on that flight," a friend who was aboard observed years later, "Ethel would have been strapped in, fingering her beads, a nervous wreck. During that flight there was a serenity about her I'd never seen before." It would not take a trained psychiatrist to figure out the reason—after all, the worst had already happened. What more was there for her to fear.

Dr. Blake Watson, who accompanied Ethel on the flight, said later it was virtually impossible to tell she had just undergone a trauma. "Physically she was fine, too, her blood pressure, everything. I was surprised. I admired her for being such a lady and holding up the way she did."

Sander Vanocur, one of the few journalists on the plane, remembered later, "Ethel tried to cheer up everyone. She tried to lift everyone's spirits in that moment of sadness and great grief for herself. People would come up to her and offer their condolences and she'd say, 'But are *you* all right?' She'd smile and they'd talk and she'd try to console *them*. It was a great act of dignity and courage on her part."

Part of the "NBC News" team handling around-the-clock coverage of the assassination, Vanocur went ahead and reported the emotional scenes he had witnessed aboard the plane. This infuriated Ethel, who prompted Mankiewicz to issue a statement: "Everyone who was on the plane was there on the basis of friendship," he said. "No one was there as a reporter. Everything was private, and that is how we intend to keep it."

Years later Vanocur, recalling the incident, said, "I'm sure I was told she was pissed. I called Steve Smith and said I was sorry if I had done anything that offended anyone. But I told him I thought the story should have gotten out. What was the sense of my going on the plane if I couldn't report it? No one ever said I couldn't. If it was appropriate or not to do, it never crossed my mind. I was a friend, but a reporter, too. This town was full of reporters who were [Kennedy] *friends*."

In the air, George Plimpton recalled, everyone felt insulated from the reality of what had happened and what was to come. But that began to collapse as soon as the plane began its descent into New York. "That was the end of conversation. It became so quiet you could hear the plane creak."

• • •

About a half-hour after Bobby passed away, Carmine Bellino had telephoned Sarah Davis, rousing her from a troubled sleep. He instructed her to go to Hickory Hill and put everything black that Ethel owned into a suitcase, take it to the Kennedys' apartment in New York, and wait for Ethel to arrive later that evening. Bellino also telephoned Ethel's friend New York socialite Natalie Cushing and told her to give Davis a hand.

As the Kennedy plane was leaving Los Angeles, Davis arrived at Hickory Hill. She was surprised to find so many new things in black. Then it struck her: Ethel had just been to Martin Luther King's funeral. It was all so sad and ironic, she thought. Madame Paul, meanwhile, had gone into action on her own. At dawn she had her seamstress working on a black dress for Ethel. "No one asked me, no one had to," she said later. "I always anticipated what Mrs. Kennedy would be needing and I made it up." Davis took the shuttle to New York, where Cushing had spent the morning shopping, sending over twenty more black dresses in big purple boxes from Bergdorf's for Davis's approval. Davis tried on all of them, chose the five she felt were best suited for Ethel, and had the others returned.

The next friend to arrive at the Kennedy apartment was John Glenn, who, before leaving Hickory Hill, had assigned Bob Galland to buy a new black suit for the funeral and escort some of the children to New York. Galland had been sitting with Glenn when the call had come announcing Bobby's death. The astronaut's calm response was, "It's over. End of that chapter. We'll move on from here." Galland, who would be one of the altar boys at the funeral, took the children to Pat Kennedy Lawford's Manhattan apartment.

In his zeal to make Ethel's imminent arrival go as smoothly as possible, Glenn made a preemptory decision: to remove certain reminders of Bobby from the apartment, specifically all of the Senator's clothing. Since the Kennedys had only three bedrooms, arrangements had been made to use other apartments in the building to house the many friends who were arriving from all over the world. One of those apartments belonged to Jackie's close friend Truman Capote, and that's where Glenn intended to leave Bobby's personal effects. Davis, who felt she knew Ethel as well as anyone, was appalled. Since marrying Bobby, Ethel had saved virtually everything from grocery store receipts to party swizzle sticks to a 1954 note from Saks Fifth Avenue demanding payment for a $47.15 unpaid bill. All of it she considered historic Kennedy memorabilia, not to be thrown away. The removal of Bobby's clothes at a time like this, Davis knew, would cause Ethel real anguish. She explained her view to Glenn and, after a few minutes, he agreed. They then proceeded to move everything back into Bobby's closets and drawers.

Glenn left to attend to other details, leaving Davis alone in the apartment to await the widow's return. Passing through the lobby, he noticed a vase of white peonies for Ethel. The Johnny Carsons, who also lived in the building, had arranged for them.

89 * Back in New York

IT WAS SHORTLY before nine, a steamy New York night, when the Kennedy plane touched down at La Guardia. More than a thousand Kennedy friends, politicians, and celebrities were waiting. A motorized lift moved to the front entrance of the plane, carrying Eunice Kennedy and her husband, Sargent Shirver, recently appointed as U.S. Ambassador to France, along with several of the Kennedy children and a Kennedy aide. From the plane, Bill Barry guided the casket onto the lift, with Ted's help. Ethel followed, along with Pat, Jean, Jackie, and the children. After the lift was lowered to the ground, Ethel leaned against the corrugated wall of the elevator for a few moments, staring down blankly at her feet, a dazed look on her face, her large black handbag dangling limply in her left hand. Seeing her state, Jackie moved quickly to her side, talking quietly, comfortingly. Moments later, the Archbishop of New York, Terence J. Cooke, sprinkled holy water on the casket, which was then placed inside the hearse for the ride to St. Patrick's Cathedral. Arrangements had been made from Los Angeles for Ethel to ride with the body. At first, John Rooney, the New York funeral director, balked. It was the only time in all of his years in the business that he had ever heard of such a thing. "Highly unusual," he called it. Ted slid into the hearse first, followed by Ethel. He put his right arm around her shoulder and held her. Her face was like granite.

Behind the hearse, mass confusion reigned. Many of the hired limousine drivers drove off with their vehicles empty, leaving famous friends and Kennedy relatives trying to hail rides. Sargent Shriver was forced to run alongside a crowded Cadillac, whose driver had opened its door for Eunice, but refused him. Jackie jumped out of a barely moving car when she spotted Robert McNamara. He darted between two cars to be at her side as she burst into tears and buried her head against his chest. Coretta King was forced to walk twenty cars to the rear with her party until she could find a vehicle. Andy Williams, who would be part of the service at St. Patrick's, and his wife, Claudine Longet, stood forlornly with their one canvas suitcase, waiting until a policeman could flag down an empty limo.

Finally, the motorcade of twenty-six cars, escorted by four motorcycle policemen and a police cruiser, began the drive to St. Patrick's, passing clusters of people waving silently. By the time they reached the cathedral at Fifth Avenue and East Fifty-first Street, a crowd of thousands was waiting.

Rose Kennedy, in black, had arrived ahead of the others and had already prayed. When she saw Ethel she put her arms around her and they talked quietly. As Ethel watched silently, the coffin was placed in the transept and Archbishop Cooke offered another prayer. While Ethel remained stiffly composed, Jackie wept as Rose comforted her. Then, a six-man honor guard was formed to maintain an all-night vigil, in relays of half-hour and quarter-hour watches. The members included McNamara, Ralph Abernathy, Walter Reuther, William Styron, Budd Schulberg, Arthur Goldberg, among others.

Ethel and the family then left the church. Only Ted remained behind until well after midnight—standing, pacing, praying.

• • •

Once Ethel left the cathedral, Secret Service agents kept in constant touch with the Kennedy apartment. Finally, they reported, "We're in the lobby." Fearing Ethel would be on the verge of collapse, an emotional wreck, Sarah Davis raced down the hall and stood before the elevator, prepared for the worst.

But when the door opened, Ethel was once again smiling and composed.

"She looked incredibly great. I couldn't believe it," Davis remembered.

Ethel gave her a big hug and squeezed her hand, comfortingly. Her first words were, "Hey, kid, have you got a beer in there?"

It could have been just another evening at the Kennedys', Davis thought, wiping away her own tears. "She was so steady, she was so very strong, she was obviously living on borrowed time," Davis said later. "Ethel wasn't shaky at all; she could get shaky very easily on a lot of different subjects, but she was not shaky then. It was almost like she didn't realize what had happened. That's the way it was for the whole time."

Ethel had arrived at the apartment with Rose and the Kennedy sisters. "They were acting the same as Ethel," said Davis. "It was like another big campaign thing. Everyone talked about everything but what had happened. I remember Rose Kennedy said to Ethel, 'I love that coffee table, where did you get it?' And Ethel said to me, 'God, kid, do you remember where we got it?' That was the atmosphere. That's the way they were. It almost made me turn Catholic because I thought, 'If you can take death that well, and be so sure that your beloved person is in heaven, well, that's the best thing I ever heard of.' "

Others began arriving at the apartment, including Dr. Blake Watson, who, like Davis, was astonished by the upbeat mood. "Sometimes you go into a situation like this and there is nothing but crying," he said. "But there was no emotion at all in that apartment. I talked to Rose Kennedy for quite a while and while she did say, 'What a tragedy it is,' she never once became emotional or shed a tear. Ethel was the same way. She sat around and greeted the different people as they came in, mostly different members of the family. I tried to get her to rest. Finally, at around midnight, I got her to go into the bedroom and go to bed."

Later, Rose looked around the room and said, "I'm so glad all you children are home again." One of the few guests who fell apart was Jackie, who was in a state of near collapse. She had to be taken home by Bob McNamara, who'd tried unsuccessfully throughout the evening to take her mind off of Bobby's death with forced patter.

While Ethel was sleeping, a touching letter had arrived from President Johnson and Lady Bird:

> Our hearts ache for you today. It is so painful to search for reason in what has happened and find none. We know what a blessing it must be to each of you to have each other.
>
> All of your children must find consolation in the knowledge that they were such a source of joy and pride to their father—and we know what strength they will give you, Ethel, in the agony of this hour.
>
> We look to faith and God to lighten our heavy hearts.

Moved by Johnson's words, Ethel sat down the next day and wrote a brief thank-you that she had hand-delivered to the White House. She expressed gratitude for the President's quick response in her darkest hour.

Meanwhile, members of the family had asked Dr. Blake Watson to stay and accompany Ethel on the funeral train, but he spoke to Ethel's regular doctor in Washington, and they agreed she could make the trip without him. The next day Watson flew back to Los Angeles, but he'd be left with a bad taste from his experience.

While he never billed the Kennedys for his time and services, he likewise never received a single offer of compensation, either. Although his return flight had been booked for him by the Kennedys, he paid for the ticket out of his own pocket and was never reimbursed. On his arrival in New York, the physician's luggage had gotten misplaced. His bag was found in the Kennedy apartment and returned two weeks later, his clothing crumpled in a ball. But he was hurt most by the fact that he never received a thank-you from Ethel. "I never had any letters from her afterward," he said with resignation years later. "I expected that maybe one of the Kennedys would send me a letter, or something, to thank me for taking my time off from my practice and going there and everything, but nothing was forthcoming. It was hurtful."

• • •

Ethel spent the early-morning hours with Sarah Davis, trying on dresses, discarding the ones she didn't find suitable. Adolfo arrived at the apartment to design a black pillbox hat and veil, which he promised he'd have ready before the next morning.

Then the hairdresser, Kevin, arrived to do Ethel's hair, and the hair of some of her friends.

"Ethel always wanted to look her best for Bobby," said Davis. "She did it for him."

Friends had begun streaming into the apartment, and Ethel greeted them with smiles and words of encouragement. "Don't cry now," she told one visitor, patting her shoulder. "We'll all have a good cry later."

"By afternoon that apartment was just a complete pushy madhouse; there were people all over the place," one guest remembered. "You know how Irish wakes are? It was sort of like that. Ethel was very strong, very pulled together. But I noticed that look she'd get in her face at Hickory Hill when she really wanted everyone to get the hell out and give her and Bobby some privacy."

When Teddy arrived, the two went into the bedroom. With Ethel lounging on the bed, Ted practiced reading the eulogy he planned to deliver at the funeral. "The bedroom in that apartment had become her sanctuary during those trying days," a friend said. "It was the only place she could get away from all the other people that were pushing around in the front of the apartment."

After listening to Ted, Ethel put on a black silk dress, black stockings, and a black ribbon in her hair. She left the apartment accompanied by some of the children, friends, and relatives to attend a private Low Requiem Mass at nearby Holy Family Church, where she and Bobby had met Pope Paul three years earlier.

Rather than drive, she decided to walk, a decision that was based in part on the public-relations value. "There always was a little drama in her and she knew all of the reporters and photographers were staking out the apartment, so she thought, 'Let's give 'em a real Kennedy show,' " a family insider said. Ethel walked at a brisk pace, her sons Joe and Bobby Jr. on either side, and Kathleen close by. Earlier, young Joe, for the first time in public, had given way to tears after serving on his father's honor guard at St. Patrick's. For a half-hour he had stood silently, moving his fingers over the coffin's mahogany surface. When he was relieved from duty, he went to the Communion rail with tear-filled eyes. In the ambulatory, he had put his hands over his face and wept. Bobby Jr. also stood in the honor guard and was later reduced to tears as he knelt to kiss the coffin. As Ethel's entourage neared Holy Family, an ugly scene was being played out by a Kennedy groupie, the recent wife of a close family friend. "She was just horrible," someone in the gathering recalled. "She kept pushing her way up so she could walk beside Ethel and get photographed. She just sort of took over and was ordering all the best friends around, and she was very much a newcomer on the scene. We were all nauseated by her and then finally someone told her to knock it off. Ethel tried to look calm but she was furious."

Meanwhile, four Army Green Beret sergeants approached Ethel and asked if they could join her. When one of them, Sgt. Maj. Francis Ruddy, explained that it was he who had placed the wreath on the grave at Jack's funeral, Ethel embraced him.

At the church, Msgr. Timothy J. Flynn asked Ethel who would act as altar boys. She pointed at Bobby Jr. and Joe.

After the service, Ethel and the children were driven to St. Patrick's, where they joined with thousands of mourners who had come to pay their final respects. Ethel led the children into pew seats beside the bier. Before sitting, she crossed herself and then sat, as if transfixed, staring at the closed coffin. For a few moments, she and the children bowed their heads, then stood beside the coffin. It was then that Courtney broke down and cried. In the process of comforting her, Ethel's strict composure and stoic dignity faltered and she wiped her own teary eyes, for the first time in public. Ethel touched the coffin gently, then with the index and middle fingers of her right hand, she blew a kiss to the casket and quietly left the church.

She went uptown to have lunch with the Douglas Dillons.

"The Dillons had caviar and champagne," recalled one of the other guests, "and Rafer Johnson was there and he had never tasted caviar before and wouldn't taste it even though Ethel tried to coax him and then started kidding him about it. It was all very weird because Ethel was acting so natural."

The Dillons' lunch was one of several upbeat events that Ethel attended in New York during those horrific few days. A friend remembered being with her when she was dressing to go to one of the parties. "She was trying to get dressed really quickly and was having trouble finding underwear and then she pulled out this gay flower-print bra and she put it on and I said, 'Ethel, are you wearing *that?*' And she whirled around and said, 'The merry widow. Bobby would *love* it.' "

During the funeral planning, Jackie had telephoned her friend Leonard Bernstein to get his help with the musical program. When Jack was slain, it had been Bernstein who was able to get the New York Philharmonic together with a chorus and soloist to perform Mahler's Second Symphony on CBS. Bernstein promised Jackie he'd do everything he could. But he immediately ran into a brick wall dealing with the leadership at St. Patrick's. In the midst of his discussions, he got a second call from Jackie. She told him that Ethel had certain wishes: that nuns from Manhattanville be permitted to sing things she had remembered from her youth, that Andy Williams be allowed to sing "Ave Maria," and that "The Navy Hymn" be sung. When Bernstein explained to Jackie that he was having enough problems with the monsignors—without the new requests—Jackie ordered brusquely, "You just insist. . . . You tell them that's Ethel's wish . . . it will make her feel so much better and bring her such comfort if she can have these things." Bernstein was most appalled about Andy Williams, who was not his idea of a serious performer. But he duly passed on Ethel's wish list. As he had expected, the church officials were horrified. "It's out of the question. We can't do it."

Friday night, Jackie went to meet with Archbishop Cooke to try to smooth out things, but he told her it was no longer necessary. Ethel had been there a half-hour earlier and had personally resolved the problem, using a bit of muscle. When Ethel brought up Andy Williams's name, the clergy around the table had adamantly refused. They couldn't permit him to participate because Williams was the son of a Protestant minister. They suggested a different soloist. Ethel, furious, banged her hand on the table and boomed, "Absolutely not! He's a close personal friend." A member of Bobby's staff said later that Ethel then threatened to "pull the funeral from St. Patrick's" if Williams wasn't allowed to sing. Ethel's hardball worked. The priests reluctantly consented to all of her demands. Ethel's only concession was that Williams could sing "Battle Hymn of the Republic" instead of "Ave Maria."

After the meeting she went into the cathedral and knelt

at the altar as Archbishop Cooke said a prayer. Leaving, she touched the flag covering the coffin, held the cloth in her fingers for a second, and left quietly.

Ethel then rushed uptown to a dinner and wake at Jean Kennedy Smith's house. One of the guests, Art Buchwald's wife, Ann, recalled Ethel bursting into the dining room shouting, "I won! I won!" as if she'd just come off the tennis courts at Hickory Hill. But Andy Williams, who also was at the party, had a problem. While he could sing "Ave Maria" blindfolded, the only lyrics he knew to "Battle Hymn of the Republic" were "Mine eyes have seen the glory." The Smiths didn't have a songbook with the lyrics, and it was too late to call a music store. Finally, John Glenn found the words in an encylopedia and dictated them to Williams, who jotted them down on a yellow legal pad. Because he didn't have a very good memory for new lyrics, he planned to write the words on cardboard shirt boards and use them as cue cards at the church.

Ethel's victory got the party rolling. The dinner, which had started glumly, was now lively, with people laughing and drinking. At one point, one of Jean's children, seven-year-old Willie Smith, who had two front teeth missing, came into the dining room to show his pet chameleon to the guests. He was still angry that it had only won second prize at the last Hickory Hill pet show. Art Buchwald, who had been one of the judges at the show, asked Willie if he could take a second look; maybe he had made a mistake. Willie put the lizard on the table as the women guests shrieked. "Oh, it *walks*," said Buchwald, acting startled. "I didn't know it *walked*." He told Willie it was definitely worth a blue ribbon, which he'd send him when he got home, and everyone clapped their hands.

Later that evening the gaiety evaporated when Ethel learned that the family of the man who killed Bobby had sent a telegram to her saying that they were praying for peace.

Ethel told a friend, "I never want to hear his name said to me again. Anyone who does is not a friend."

Then she went to sleep, prepared to bury Bobby.

90 ✻ The Funeral

MANY OF THE more than two thousand invited mourners, led by President and Lady Bird Johnson, began arriving as early as seven A.M. the next morning for the ten o'clock service at St. Patrick's. Outside, thousands had already begun lining Fifth Avenue to listen to the Mass over loudspeakers.

Back at her apartment, Ethel awoke refreshed from a solid sleep. It was, she would say later, a glorious day for a funeral. Sunny and bright, the skies blue, the clouds billowy white above the city. By the time she left the apartment, though, the heat had become oppressive. "Unreal," one of the mourners would complain.

Everyone had left the apartment to prepare for the funeral, leaving only Ethel, Sarah Davis, and a maid. Ethel seemed to dawdle, taking her time dressing. From all the choices she had, she'd finally selected the simplest black dress. Adolfo's hat, as promised, was in its box on the dresser.

At the breakfast table Ethel took her time as if she had the whole day to herself, leisurely eating her toast, sipping coffee, sprinkling salt and pepper on her eggs. Davis, getting nervous because of the time, suggested they hurry. Ethel smiled. "They're not going anywhere without me," she said with finality.

At that, Davis relaxed and the two women sat and chatted over coffee. The conversation was purposely casual, unimportant. "I took my cue from her," Davis said later. "I just kept on a very even keel."

• • •

At the cathedral, Ethel sat in the front row under hot television klieg lights. Next to her were some of the children—Joe, Kathleen, David, and Mary Courtney—along with Rose, Jackie, and her children. Later, friends said they were startled at how beautiful Ethel looked that day, despite the fact that she wore no jewelry or makeup. (She wouldn't wear makeup for at least a month after the funeral.) Few of her friends had ever seen her dressed in black. Yet, as Ann Buchwald noted, Ethel "looked just perfect."

There was a major difference between Jack's funeral Mass in Washington and the Mass for Bobby: Jack's was grim with references to the Day of Wrath, to retribution, and was said in Latin; Bobby's stressed a beginning of life and was in English. As Ethel told one of the priests before the service, "If there's one thing about our faith, it's our belief that this is the beginning of eternal life and not the end of life. I want this Mass to be as joyous as it possibly can be."

The most moving moment of the service was Ted's short eulogy, written by several of Bobby's top aides, Adam Walinsky, David Burke, and Milton Gwirtzman.

Standing tall and straight, obviously deeply shaken, only a few yards from his brother's flag-draped casket, Ted spoke eloquently:

"My brother need not be idealized, or enlarged in death beyond what he was in life, to be remembered simply as a good and decent man, who saw wrong and tried to right it, saw suffering and tried to heal it, saw war and tried to stop it."

As she listened, Ethel remained stoic. Nearby, Eugene McCarthy brushed tears from his eyes; Richard Nixon sat with his eyes closed, head bent; President Johnson sat grim-faced; Coretta King's eyes were hidden behind dark glasses. When Leonard Bernstein conducted a thirty-member segment of the Philharmonic in the mournful slow movement of Mahler's Fifth Symphony, Bernstein's body wrenched. Only Ethel remained resolute.

Archbishop Cooke, principal celebrant of the Mass,

issued a strong call in his eulogy for America to "find the courage to take up again the laborious work to which Senator Kennedy devoted all his energies. . . . We mourn Robert Kennedy and we know that America shall miss him. . . ."

Several of the Kennedy children then stepped to the altar with bread and wine for the Consecration. At the end of the service Cardinal Cushing spoke the Absolution, circling the coffin twice, anointing it with holy water, perfuming it with incense, intoning an ancient prayer: "May the angels take you into paradise; may the martyrs come to welcome you on your way, and lead you into the Holy City. . . ."

As Andy Williams, his shirt-board cue cards hidden from view, sang "Battle Hymn of the Republic," the pallbearers grasped the bottom of the coffin and the procession moved up the aisle led by Ted and Joe. Ethel, Bobby Jr., and the other children followed behind. Outside, the crowd watched silently as the procession emerged into the muggy air and the casket was placed in the hearse for the ride to Pennsylvania Station.

The twenty-one-car train pulled out shortly after one o'clock, a half-hour behind schedule, for the 226-mile journey to the nation's capital. A throwback to the trains that carried Lincoln, McKinley, and Roosevelt to their graves, the Kennedy train was scheduled to arrive at four-thirty, but more tragedy along the way would delay its arrival by five hours.

The casket was placed in an observation car with a rear platform bedecked with fresh green leaves. The last five cars were reserved for the clan, their special guests, and closest associates.

At the start of the trip, Ethel spent her time near the casket. But then she began to move through the cars, greeting everyone, thanking them for coming.

"Where are the advance men?" she asked, a reference to Bobby's last campaign. "Oh, I know, they're getting out the people." Rosey Grier acted as her escort. It was a difficult walk and even a professional athlete like Grier felt drained, having to stop for water on several occasions. "I felt so much for her," he said later. "I remember that anytime I would drift off into a really down feeling, she'd say, 'Now, Rosey, come on over here.' She'd keep pulling me back, you know. Pulling me back."

Awed passengers stumbled to their feet when they saw Ethel looming above them, her chiffon veil pushed away from her face. "Hello," she'd say, "nice to see you." When she entered the car where the four Army sergeants who had attended the service with her at Holy Family Church were seated, she declared, "There they are. You thought you could hide from me. Well, you can't." She kissed friends on the cheek, hugged others, patted backs. But the passengers couldn't help but notice that her hands trembled and that every so often her left arm shot out nervously, clutching at the suit jacket of Lem Billings, who had joined her.

Mrs. Martin Luther King, Jr., reacted with stunned silence when Ethel spotted her in a window seat and called, "There's our pal Coretta." When she ran into a physician friend, she quipped, "There's a doctor in every car, and every one of them has delivered one of my children." She was overjoyed to run into Mother Eleanor O'Byrne from Manhattanville, whom she introduced to Lem Billings. "She did me in at Manhattanville," Ethel said, laughing.

When Ethel got to Jose Torres, the boxer and writer who had stumped for Bobby and who had recently had surgery on his foot, she squealed, "Jose, where have you been? . . . Look at that, half a day campaigning for Bobby and look what happened, you have crutches." Then she pressed his strong hand in hers. After her long walk through the train—she'd spoken to nearly every one of the eleven hundred passengers—Ethel appeared exhausted and slightly disoriented. Suddenly, to no one in particular, she said, "Have you ever been to Disneyland? Disneyland is green and big and there's a mountain." Someone gave her a cup of soda. She pulled at the black stockings that had wriggled down around her ankles, and looked out the window, smiling and waving at the people lining the tracks, startled when she heard people calling her name. The train at times crawled and Ethel had become anxious. "If it keeps going like this," she said at one point, "we'll never get there. What about another train catching up with us?" She was reassured that the tracks in front and behind had been cleared.

After a ten-minute rest, she began the long walk back through the cars to the casket. In one particularly stuffy car jammed with people, she said, "You gotta be kidding. There are lots of other cooler cars, front and back. Why are you here?" No one answered. She turned to look at a heavily perspiring Frank Mankiewicz, who explained he was giving a press briefing.

When Ethel was stationed back with the casket, close friends and family members looked in on her every so often, or came to kneel by the casket themselves. One friend recalled Ethel sitting with one hand on the coffin with her eyes closed. As he watched he had the feeling she was drawing strength from Bobby in some deeply mystical way. Another friend saw most of the clan standing on the observation platform. Ethel was holding a rosary, resting her head against the casket, and crying quietly.

Outside, along the tracks, the throngs of mourners grew. Many people, ignoring police warnings, jumped onto the tracks to be closer to the Kennedy train as it passed. In Elizabeth, New Jersey, John Curia and Antoinette Severini, both fifty-six years old, were standing on the northbound tracks watching the Kennedy train and failed to hear the horn of the oncoming *Admiral*, a four-car express en route to New York from Chicago. The engineer hit the emergency brakes, but was unable to stop before striking the two, killing them instantly. Six others, including three-year-old Debra Ann Kwietek, a granddaughter of Mrs. Severini, were injured.

"It was a nightmare," said Bob Galland, who was looking out the window when the accident happened. "I was standing there with a couple of the kids. They saw the mangled bodies. I turned them away. I couldn't believe this was happening."

Young David, who had his head out the window,

witnessed the accident, appeared fascinated by the gruesomeness of it, and had to be pulled away and put in a seat by a Secret Service agent.

Ethel had her own air-conditioned compartment on the train but rarely spent time there. Next door was a similar roomette that was shared by Sarah Davis and Sue Markham. Ethel had made sure they got special attention, even though people like the Averell Harrimans, the Douglas Dillons, and the Robert McNamaras were sweltering in the coaches, the windows pushed up and the soot blowing in. Lauren Bacall, the actress, had just stopped in the Davis-Markham compartment to cool off and chew gum, when the accident happened. "I had never seen violent death before," said Davis, who was looking out of the window and saw the people on the tracks and the train approaching. "We were yelling, 'Go back! Go back!' We had this frantic look on our faces, and they were waving and waving and that train couldn't stop. George Kirkpatrick, who was in the compartment, pulled the shade down and wouldn't let us look one more second. It was the most horrible thing I'd ever seen."

In Trenton, there was another accident. A teenager, Joseph Fausti, was critically burned when he touched a high-voltage power line after he'd climbed atop a freight car to get a better view of the Kennedy train.

Both incidents were kept from Ethel until after the services in Washington. The next day she had one of her secretaries call Elizabeth General Hospital to authorize the purchase of a teddy bear for the little girl who had been injured.

In the last few hours of the ride, the mood on the train became more casual, with weary passengers demanding drinks and food in the club cars, even men and women flirting.

During the trip the train passed as many as two million people, prompting a French journalist onboard to begin his story with a line that Ethel would have loved. He wrote: "Robert Kennedy won the American election today."

• • •

A few minutes before nine-thirty the train finally pulled into Washington's Union Station.

An exhausted Ethel, accompanied by Joe, Bobby, Kerry, and Ted, walked through the station's red-carpeted concourse toward the hearse as the pallbearers bore the casket to the strains of the "U.S. Navy Hymn." Ethel had a few words with Vice President Humphrey; President Johnson, looking drawn and grave, nodded to her as hundreds of dignitaries watched.

Ethel got in the hearse for Bobby's final motorcade to Arlington National Cemetery. Tens of thousands lined the route to the Lincoln Memorial, where it stopped as another chorus sang "Battle Hymn of the Republic." Then the motorcade headed across the Potomac on the Memorial Bridge.

The hearse stopped about fifty yards from the Kennedy gravesite. Ethel, with Ted at her side, stood on the sloping hillside as the pallbearers moved the casket to the grave, feet from where Jack was buried, beneath an eternal flame. Washington's Patrick Cardinal O'Boyle said the final prayer, and the flag on the casket was folded into a triangle by the pallbearers. John Glenn handed it to Ted, who gave it to Ethel. Then she and Ted walked to the casket, knelt, and kissed it.

At 11:34 P.M. the coffin was lowered into the earth.

A half-hour later the widow returned home to Hickory Hill, her first time back in what seemed to her like an eternity. Accompanying her were several dozen friends, who stayed up until nearly four in the morning, eating and drinking and laughing.

Later that morning Ethel paid a visit to Bobby's grave. Then she returned home for a typical Sunday at Hickory Hill.

"I can see Ethel now," a friend said years later. "She had her hair in pigtails, little short pigtails, and she had on her bathing suit and she was getting sun. The whole gang was there, all the fancy people. Ethel had a big luncheon for them. Maybe Ethel cried her eyes out after we left. Maybe she broke down. I never saw it. It was bizarre. But that's the way she was about death."

91 ❋ Life Resumes

IN HER SECOND trimester of her eleventh pregnancy, Ethel needed as much rest as possible. The strain of the past few months had been incalculable, and friends and family feared for her emotional and physical well-being, concerned she'd fall apart déspite her outward calm. But Ethel held up remarkably well.

"She never collapsed because she believed with all her heart and soul that Bobby was in heaven and that she'd eventually be with him," George Terrien said later. "I talked to Ethie a week after the funeral and she sounded like a wife whose husband had taken a business trip and wasn't sure when he'd be back. There were never any histrionics, never any melodrama. She was cool and relaxed even though I heard an edge in her voice that wasn't there before. I asked her, 'Are you sure you're okay? Is there anything Georgeann and I can do?' She said, 'I know they're all up there in heaven together now—Mother and Father, and George and Jack, and now Bobby. Bobby's in good hands. I feel safe.' But we all still worried about her because her life revolved around him. We wondered how the hell she was ever going to carry on without him; how she would be able to handle all those damned kids; how the pregnancy would turn out; how she would make it through, heaven or no heaven."

Friends like Art Buchwald said at the time, "If she's downbeat, she never lets on."

Family members like Eunice feared Ethel would become an empty shell without Bobby in her life. "He was everything to her—the best sailor, the best skier. A hero who could easily climb Mount Everest if he wanted to . . . all the love and appreciation for which she seemed to have an infinite capacity came pouring down on him. . . ."

Friends, such as journalist Anne Chamberlin, also had difficulty conceiving of Ethel without Bobby.

"No one I know had ever beheld such a two-way case of total commitment," she observed. "They weren't the customary dutiful couple, marching in locked step, two-by-two, up the gangplank of the Ark, who daily stare out from the society pages of the Washington papers to reassure us that while all else crumbles, Marriage Survives in the Establishment. They actually *enjoyed* each other. Even if they dined at home alone, Ethel came downstairs dressed and perfumed as though it were their first date for the movies."

Others, like Burton Berinsky, who had worked for Bobby as a staff photographer when he ran for the Senate and traveled with him during the Presidential campaign, took a less romantic, somewhat embittered view. One of a number of Bobby's friends who adored him, but had little use for her, he said long after the assassination: "Ethel was nothing more than a satellite of Bobby, who was probably the most charismatic person I've ever met. Bobby had an aura about him, and Ethel was caught up in the aura. But by herself she was nothing; just this loudmouth, not very intelligent satellite. Everything she had came from Bobby."

In the days after the funeral, before she left for the Kennedy compound, Ethel was constantly surrounded by friends; none of them wanted to leave her alone for a moment, fearful she'd fall into a deep depression. A synthetically jolly atmosphere prevailed at Hickory Hill, which continued to serve as a country club for Kennedy friends. "It's a constant pilgrimage," said Kay Evans. "Ethel's friends flock to see her, not so much because it makes her feel better but because they feel better. They really want to touch base with her."

During those days, Ethel sunned by the pool, played tennis, lunched with pals, gossiped, cheered on the younger kids who swam and played touch football. She also caught up on pressing business. At her behest, Ted's aide David Burke called Joe Califano at the White House. Ethel had wanted to know from the President whether "there was any commendation for bravery that . . . could be appropriately awarded to Rafer Johnson, Roosevelt Grier, and Bill Barry" for their efforts in subduing Sirhan.

Ethel also wrote a heartfelt letter to the President, expressing thanks for his generosity. She was especially grateful for the use of Air Force One, and for LBJ's presence when the funeral train arrived in Washington so late.

That same day, after receiving her missive, the President wrote:

Dear Ethel,

I appreciate your letter more than I can say.

I am glad that you feel I was able to help when you needed it. Practical assistance of the kind I could give is necessary, but it is never enough to assuage the loss. Only time and faith can do that, and the support of people who love you.

Thank God you have so many who love you nearby, that you have been blessed with so many fine children, and with a strong affirmative spirit in yourself.

If there is ever anything I can do to help you or yours in the future, Ethel, I hope you will let me know. So long as I have the power to help, please know that I have the desire to do so.

In the deepest sympathy,
Sincerely,
LBJ

Ethel had decided it would be best for her three oldest to get away—and they had taken off for points across the globe. At the same time, she didn't want the responsibility of the children. Joe, who had made such an impressive showing during the funeral, went to Vermont for summer school, then on to Spain, to visit a bull ranch; Bobby Jr. flew off to East Africa for a month, visiting the Serengeti, Manyara, and Ngorongoro national parks; and Kathleen headed West, to teach at an Indian reservation, bent on starting at Radcliffe in the fall.

A contingent from the Secret Service remained at the house for a time. The younger children delighted in sneaking off the property to get ice cream without their assigned agent at their heels.

"It was a picnic atmosphere," recalled Bob Galland. "Eat what you want; do what you want; watch first-run movies down at the pool house. There were always a lot of people coming and going—movie star celebrities, political people—to give their condolences to Ethel; non-stop streams of people in and out of the house."

Because mail was pouring in from all over the world, as many as twenty-five thousand letters a day, staffers from Bobby's Senate office, campaign workers, and Ethel's ladies-in-waiting volunteered to open, file, and answer the cards and letters. Acting quickly, Congress passed a resolution granting Ethel free mailing privileges for six months. "It was very depressing for all of us, but Ethel seemed fine," recalled Gertrude Corbin, who spent several hours every day at Hickory Hill typing and answering phones side-by-side Liz Stevens, Kay Evans, Sue Markham, and others. "We used to have lunch together and Ethel would tell us about various things she wanted to do. She kept a stiff upper lip. There were so many friends around her to keep her from thinking."

Ethel wrote a number of thank-you notes herself, including one to New York Mets manager Gil Hodges, expressing gratitude for his canceling the game against the San Francisco Giants because of Bobby's funeral. She also was on hand for the sad closing of the Kennedy for President campaign headquarters in downtown Washington, shaking hands with each worker and thanking them for their loyalty. Meanwhile, Ted and Rose, in a videotaped message broadcast nationally, thanked the nation for its sympathy. "Ethel and the members of the family are doing well," Ted said. "We pray to God that the Lord will give them the health to carry on."

With Bobby's death, Ted became a virtual surrogate father for Ethel's brood. Other men in her sphere played a similar role: John Glenn; Dave Hackett, who played touch football with the children; Lem Billings, who took Bobby Jr. on a trip to Colombia; and Art Buchwald, who entertained the young ones with secret projects.

Ethel made a number of visits to the grave, and every morning went to Mass at nearby St. Luke's Catholic Church.

She had hoped to make a quick retreat to her house in the Kennedy compound at Hyannis Port after the funeral. But workmen, hired months earlier to make extensive renovations, were still busy, and the place was unlivable. If all had gone according to plan, the house would have become the Kennedys' weekend and summer White House. Ethel had contracted to have a huge dormer bedroom built over the garage for the boys, in space that had once served as a Secret Service security command post when Jack was alive. (Had Bobby lived and been successful in November, Secret Service agents likely would have taken it over again.) In addition, she had ordered new furniture, curtains, and upholstery, retaining Boots Treat, who had helped with the decorating at Hickory Hill and the New York apartment, to oversee the work. Ethel, then anticipating the happiest summer of her life, had wanted the house to be "bright, gay, and special," a haven for her and Bobby from the rigors of the campaign.

92 ✻ First Summer

FOR BOBBY'S CHILDREN, especially the teenage boys, the death of their beloved father had been devastating, a near mortal wound. Reeling from the blow, they began acting out their anger and frustration in a way that caused terrible dissension with their mother.

Ethel, too, had sustained unfathomable emotional wounds. As with the boys, her anger and frustration were also seeking release. In the immediate aftermath, she began taking out her rage on her sons, the most readily available targets. Once, when Joe hit little Kerry, Ethel forced him to walk up and down the stairs dozens of times. A week after the funeral, David celebrated his thirteenth birthday at a grim Hickory Hill party during which his brother Bobby spiked everyone's milk with a laxative. Bobby Jr. and David constantly got on their mother's nerves and she began ordering them out of the house. "Just leave home, get out of my life!" she would scream. On one occasion, when little Christopher fell at poolside and began to cry, Ethel's rage overflowed on him as well. "On your feet! You know how to behave. Now get out there and show some class!" she bellowed.

Friends of the Kennedy children who visited them said they were fearful of Ethel and tried to avoid her as much as possible.

Fractious, turbulent, unsettled, enraged by a private pain barely under control, Ethel and her brood arrived at the Cape to spend the summer sixteen days after Bobby was shot.

Accompanied by a Secret Service agent, Courtney and Kerry, and the dogs Brumus and Freckles, Ethel flew from Washington to Edgartown on Martha's Vineyard. With her small entourage, she passed anonymously through the airport, bustling at the moment with photographers and Hollywood and New York celebrities arriving in town for a wedding. At the Harbor View Hotel, she met up with a large contingent of the family—Joan, Jackie, Pat, and Jean, with all of their children. Ethel led the group to St. Elizabeth's Church, hoping to take Communion. But the curate, Father George Almeida, not expecting such a large crowd, ran out of consecrated bread and had to send to nearby Oak Bluffs for a new supply. To the priest's embarrassment, Ethel got tired of waiting and convinced the others to leave and receive Communion later. For weeks afterward, the priest—who had never met the Kennedys—feared that Ethel would complain and that he'd get a call from the Pope himself for allowing such a thing to happen with the world's most famous widow.

Back at the hotel, Ethel went to the front desk and requested a pink heating blanket. "We didn't have any," recalled Bill Thompson, a Maryland college student who was working at the hotel for the summer. "So we dashed somebody into town who ran around and finally found one heating blanket and brought it back. It was the wrong color and she was very upset."

The next morning, after attending Mass, Ethel returned to her room, where Thompson happened to be changing the bed linen. Years later, Thompson, who had become a reporter for the *Baltimore Evening Sun,* was still shocked by her curious behavior.

"She unlocked the door, walked in, looked at me but didn't say anything. She went over to her bed and proceeded to undress, down to her black underwear. I can't say I stood there and stared at her. I continued to do my work but we were in the same room and she was down to her bra and slip. It struck me as something somewhat memorable. I just figured that she had grown up having staff and that I was just another invisible person."

After leaving Ethel's room, Thompson was assigned

to clean Ted's, where he found the floor and tables littered "with lots of empty cocktail glasses. They must have had a party the night before." In one of the Kennedy bathrooms, he also found "an incredible mess. The tub was filled with long dog hairs where they had bathed Brumus."

As the Kennedys were walking to the dock to board the chartered sixty-foot yawl *Mira*, Ted realized he had forgotten a jacket with his eyeglasses. Thompson, who was helping them with their luggage, ran back to the hotel and found the jacket lying over a railing. "I ran down and handed it to him and he didn't even look at me or say thanks. The help was simply invisible to them. They left a ten- or fifteen-percent gratuity on top of their hotel bill."

With Ted at the helm, the *Mira* began the twenty-mile trip across Nantucket Sound to Hyannis Port. For most of the cruise, Ethel stayed on the stern, sunning herself in a white swimsuit.

At one point, Ethel became angry with Bobby and David and took action. Directing them below deck, she proceeded to beat them with a hairbrush, the first time they had ever been punished in such a way. When the boat docked, Ethel told them once again to leave home. This time they complied. Bobby Jr. spent most of the summer in Africa with Lem Billings, and David went to a tennis and ski camp in Austria with his cousin Chris Lawford. David later claimed he was seduced at the camp by a seventeen-year-old-girl who went after him after she found out he was a Kennedy.

Ethel's Hickory Hill staff had traveled north by car, bringing a ton of luggage, half a dozen horses and ponies, and many of the children's pets. Bob Galland, who had driven to the Cape in one of Ethel's cars, crammed with her things, hoped the summer would ease the pain he knew she was suffering. "She was haggard, tired, and ready for some calm," he recalled.

At Hyannis, the mood was tense, as Ethel issued multiple orders and directives, ranting if the staff didn't carry them out quickly. Shortly after arriving she fired her longtime horse groom on the grounds that he wasn't working hard enough. Fearing for their own jobs, the rest of the help kept a low profile.

Ethel's days and nights that first summer without Bobby rarely varied. She awakened early, went to Mass at St. Francis Xavier Church with some of the children, and was out in the yard by ten, phoning friends or writing letters. If a pen ran out of ink, she dispatched a member of the staff to go into town for half a dozen of her favorite twenty-five-dollar gold-plated Crosses. When her stationery supply became thin—black-bordered letter paper and brightly colored memo pads with *ethel* spelled out in bold lowercase letters—she'd have her secretary place a rush overnight order with an exclusive Madison Avenue stationer whose other clients ranged from Richard Nixon to playboy Porfirio Rubirosa. One of her notes, written during that period, received national attention when it was read by Coretta King to the thousands on hand for the Poor People's March in Washington.

She also had correspondence with the President.

"In the moments after your terrible loss," Johnson wrote, "world leaders sent many messages of condolence. It occurred to me that you and the children might like to have this volume which contains those expressions of loss and sympathy. All have been acknowledged."

Ethel responded with a note of thanks on her black-bordered stationery.

Most afternoons Ethel went sailing with children and friends, taking along an enormous basket of turkey, chicken, roast beef, milk, fruit, cookies, pie. What wasn't eaten was tossed away. She'd return home at sundown to bathe and dress for dinner. There were always guests because she refused to eat alone; she had even rented a small house outside of the compound for friends to use when they dropped by—and many came.

Priests and nuns were among the most frequent visitors, just as they had been at Lake Avenue in the old days. They came to offer comfort, and Ethel enjoyed their presence. Her brother Rushton also arrived, but he stayed on his boat, not in the compound. Ethel appreciated his interest but tended to avoid him. "There was a lot of drinking on Rush's boat," recalled one staffer. "Beer all afternoon and as soon as he tied up at the dock, whiskey. There was a lot of sitting around, and fooling around." The usual Hickory Hill crowd was ever-present—the Glenns, the Stevenses, the Evanses, the Buchwalds, and Andy Williams.

Ethel's moods swung drastically. One moment she'd appear to be blue, the next cheerful and ready for a party. On one occasion neighbors telephoned for the police because music was blaring from the compound. When officers arrived they found that Ethel herself was the culprit.

Despite being in the sixth month of pregnancy, Ethel was still eager to compete on the tennis courts. On one occasion, when she and Jim Whittaker were beaten by Buchwald and Williams, Ethel was livid, falling to the court and banging her head on the surface in frustration. She demanded a rematch, and the next morning smashed the ball into Buchwald's cheek before he had a chance to lift his racket; she and Whittaker took the set, 6–0.

Williams, whose seven-year marriage to Claudine Longet had begun to crumble, was a frequent guest at the compound that summer. Doing an engagement at a Boston summer theater, he was picked up by one of Ethel's drivers after each evening's show, brought back to the house, and returned to the theater the following afternoon. "Andy was there more than anybody else and he did stay in her house," Bob Galland said. The singer was not one of the more popular guests, at least in the eyes of the help. "He treated us with disdain," said Galland. "He would talk through you or around you, which didn't seem to bother Ethel, but made us feel badly. I know the kids didn't particularly like him, either. He didn't have anything he could share or do with them, and he didn't go out of his way to . . . he was just there to see Ethel."

Another frequent visitor was Robert Berks, the New York sculptor who had been commissioned to do a bronze bust of Bobby for display at the Justice Department and needed Ethel's approval of the proper likeness before he could cast it. Berks had previously created a famous bronze bust of Jack Kennedy. Ethel rejected one design after another, which Berks had based on hundreds of photographs that he'd bring with him to the house. The tension between the two was high. "Ethel didn't like the nose, or didn't like the hair. It became quite humorous after a while," revealed a friend. Ethel and Berks finally came to an agreement and the bust of Bobby was unveiled in January 1969.

At the end of the summer the older boys returned to the compound, their behavior not noticeably improved. One afternoon David and Bobby got together with some friends and the discussion, as it often did in those days, turned to drugs. Bobby, admitting that he'd given LSD to his parakeet, urged David to try mescaline. David was soon hallucinating, the drugs peeling away the thin veneer of control. "You're dying," he screamed at his brother hysterically, "just like Daddy."

Later, for the first time since Los Angeles, David made an awkward attempt to talk about his father's death with his mother. She refused to look at him. "It's not a subject I want to discuss," Ethel said firmly, pushing past him. He would not bring it up again.

93 ❋ *Money Matters*

WHILE ETHEL VACATIONED, there was growing speculation about her future; where she would live, and on how much.

The truth was that Bobby had not left her as wealthy as many thought. While his estate totaled $1,606,438, more than half that amount was already earmarked for debts and expenses. In the end, Ethel was left a relatively modest $358,842, with each of the children receiving $17,120. Not included in the gross estate was the Hyannis Port house, lot, and furnishings, valued at $111,500. Ethel and the children also shared in various trusts set up by Bobby and his parents, but those funds had been established to be doled out over time and were not easily accessible. After George Skakel, Sr., and Big Ann had died thirteen years earlier, Ethel's share of their estate remained tied up in stock and trusts, too. While she received regular dividends from her Great Lakes Carbon stock, the annual amounts were modest. Ethel needed to face the cold reality of cutting back on the extravagant lifestyle to which she had become so accustomed. Still, by most standards she was well off.

But on the advice of Steve Smith, who would keep close tabs on Ethel's financial situation—and would eventually come down hard on her—Ethel filed a petition in mid-August in Manhattan's Surrogate Court for permission to sell the New York apartment, which was in Bobby's name, and worth an estimated $150,000. Cited in the petition as the reason for seeking court approval of the sale was a "currently favorable" market for the apartment.

Rumors immediately flew that Ethel was planning to sell Hickory Hill, too. NBC reported that she had decided to leave McLean and return to Greenwich, where, the network said, she had bought a twenty-room, sixty-four-acre English Tudor estate with a guest cottage and stables for $1.5 million. The rumors had started in McLean when Ethel had the names "Hickory Hill" and "Kennedy" removed from the big white mailbox to protect her privacy. A similar rumor started in Greenwich, where the Skakels initially declined to deny that Ethel was the "mystery buyer" of the Tudor estate. *The New York Times* immediately jumped on the story with a lengthy feature on the beautiful homes of Greenwich and the "rationale" behind the report that Ethel had bought one.

But Hickory Hill had become as much a part of Ethel's identity and persona as the Kennedy name, both of which she had pledged she would never surrender, and her children felt the same way about the house.

Shortly after the funeral, they had held a family conference of their own at the dining room table and ruled out living in New York and Massachusetts. Not knowing their mother's plans, Kathleen and Joe decided to speak for their sisters and brothers and tell Ethel they wanted to remain at Hickory Hill. To their relief, there was no argument. "Hickory Hill will always be our home, especially with Uncle Ted living nearby. This is where we will stay," Ethel told them.

Ethel was angered by the erroneous news reports and instructed Ted's office to issue a public denial, saying that she "has not looked at any property, has not bought any, and will not buy any." Ethel's sister Ann said at the time, "Why should Ethel go back to Greenwich? It's like Thomas Wolfe says, you know!" Unlike the New York apartment, Hickory Hill had been deeded as a gift to Ethel in January 1965 by Joe and Rose; Ethel owned the place outright, her most valuable asset next to her chunk of Great Lakes Carbon stock.

While Hickory Hill would never go on the block, Ethel's financial advisers saw another way, in addition to the sale of the New York apartment, to generate money for her. They dusted off an unpublished magazine article written by Bobby a year earlier and shrewdly offered it for sale.

In April 1967, Bobby had been commissioned by *The New York Times Magazine* to write a several-thousand-word piece about the Cuban missile crisis, to be published in the issue of October 22, 1967, which marked the fifth anniversary of Jack's announcement that Soviet missile sites were being built in Cuba. In late August 1967, Bobby's office told the *Times* that he had already written about five thousand words and was only half finished. In October, after repeated inquiries about delivery of the piece, Frank Mankiewicz informed the *Times* that the Senator was reluctant to release the story, now twenty-five thousand words, because it might look like he was using inside information to advance himself for the 1968 Presidential nomination. The *Times* capitulated and the piece never ran.

After Bobby's death, Ethel found the unedited article, which had been forgotten, among his effects. About the same time, editors from *The New York Times Magazine* coincidentally approached Bobby's people once again to see if the story could finally be published. Seeing the renewed interest, the Kennedy money people put it on the block, touching off a strenuous bidding war that did not include the *Times* magazine.

The major selling point, of course, was Bobby's ultimate insider status; he'd kept detailed notes on the crisis and had put never-before-revealed material in the manuscript, including correspondence between Jack and Russian Premier Nikita Khrushchev. The key marketer of the piece for the Kennedy family was Ted Sorensen, who had served as a special assistant to Jack, and was currently both the attorney for Bobby's estate executors—Ethel, Ted, and Pat—and an editor at large of the *Saturday Review,* a magazine owned by the McCall Corporation. Within days *McCall's* topped all other bidders. The final selling price: a cool $1 million, the highest amount ever paid at the time for a manuscript of that length. The deal also gave the Kennedy estate approval of advertising copy, excerpts for serialization, and photographs. *McCall's* won all rights, including book publishing, serialization, films, and television. The article, with some editing by Sorensen, ran in the November 1968 issue of *McCall's*. After the book rights were sold, Ethel got actively involved in the production of *Thirteen Days*; she even chose the actual paper stock the publisher used and vetoed some of the advertising because it focused more on Bobby's role in the crisis than on Jack's.

Editors at the *Times* magazine were furious at the Kennedys' actions; after all, it had been the *Times*'s idea to have Bobby do the piece in the first place; the magazine had even supplied him with an outline. But, as one editor involved in the project noted years later, "This was no time for us to raise a ruckus; the *Times* didn't want to be accused of widow-bashing. But what the Kennedys did was, well, pretty sleazy." But Sorensen maintained after the sale that it was the duty of the executors "to maximize the estate, particularly when there are eleven minor children."

94 ✻ Number Eleven

ETHEL RETURNED TO Hickory Hill after Labor Day to await the birth of number eleven, "a Thanksgiving present," she enthused, noting that the child was due in late November. Meanwhile, most of the other children returned to school, leaving three at home during the day: three-year-old Max, five-year-old Chris, a half-day student at nearby Potomac School, and eighteen-month-old Douglas Harriman.

Ethel once again fell into her old routine: morning Mass at St. Luke's; afternoons with friends who couldn't help but notice that one of the pink walls of the pool house was now plastered with news photographs of Ethel and Bobby taken during the campaign.

Despite her doctor's warning to take it easy, she took an active interest in planning an interdenominational memorial chapel for Bobby in the White Mountains of New Hampshire, where they sometimes skied. She also kept close tabs on the effort to raise $3.5 million to pay off Bobby's campaign debt. And she was working closely with architect I. M. Pei on the design of a permanent marker for Bobby's grave. Her main focus, though, was on the establishment of the $10 million Robert F. Kennedy Memorial Foundation, a "living memorial" to Bobby that would be involved in journalistic and humanitarian endeavors.

As her due date grew closer Ethel became frightened. For the first time, she faced the reality of childbirth without Bobby. Moreover, she would never forget the problems surrounding the premature birth of her last baby, Douglas. And that birth had happened under the best of circumstances.

On the evening of Friday, October 11, still at least a month away from her due date, Ethel decided to kick up her heels a bit, accepting an invitation from Kay and Rowland Evans to attend a dinner party for twenty at their Georgetown house. She appeared relaxed and healthy and everyone was thrilled to see her back on the circuit. The next morning, though, Ethel awoke feeling odd. By noon she thought she'd felt the first mild tremors of labor, and immediately telephoned Ted and Dr. John Walsh. By six, she was in the labor room at Georgetown Medical Center. Ted had contacted Luella Hennessey at her suburban Boston home and arrangements were made for a police escort to take the Kennedy nurse to Logan International Airport for a flight to Washington. By the time Hennessey arrived, though, Ethel's false labor pains had subsided. Ethel was kept overnight for observation and released by eleven the following morning. Her doctors ordered her to remain in bed.

Hennessey was asked to stay on at Hickory Hill, which required her to take a three-month leave of absence from her hospital.

Hennessey recalled that Ethel was looking forward to the baby. "She had very strong faith and believed that if this is what the Lord had planned out for her, he would also provide for her. She was truly an optimist. Ethel talked as if Bobby was away. She never said, 'Oh, he's never going to come back, isn't it awful.' "

Each night one of the cooks would prepare a tray for a different one of the young children so they could have dinner with their mother in bed.

Said the nurse: "She would be so excited and joyful that whichever one it was was going to eat with her, and after the meal she would have a very private conversation with that child."

Every morning the nurse would have to insist that Ethel remain in bed and rest. "Ethel was a very active person and wanted to do this and that. We'd plan to have somebody over for lunch every day; she always had somebody with her—Elizabeth Stevens or Sarah Davis. One of them would come over every morning, go over the mail, see if she wanted to exchange anything at the store. They were very faithful friends. I'd make sure she'd have at least two hours of rest right after lunch. I'd draw the curtains, open the windows and have fresh air come in, and bundle her up as if it were evening, so she'd feel fine for the children when they came home from school.

"If it was a nice day she'd say, 'Bobby would be playing touch football with them today; the boys haven't played touch football all week, they haven't had any exercise, call Dave Hackett and see if he'll come over and play with them.'

"After school the children would have a brief visit with her. Ethel was such a strong personality that the children followed along with whatever she wanted. They never talked about what happened to their father. Bobby and Joe were at boarding school but came home for the weekends. I think Joe was affected the most; he seemed quieter than he used to, very sensitive, a lovely boy. David just tagged along, not quite up to it physically, it seemed. Ethel sought professional help for him.

"The whole family was afraid she'd go into premature labor. Senator Kennedy said to me, 'I don't know what will happen to Ethel if anything happens to this baby.' "

Ethel ventured out one evening a few days before Halloween. Wearing a pink gown, she attended a preview of the Lee Marvin and Jean Seberg musical *Paint Your Wagon* at the new Motion Picture Association building in downtown Washington. But she remained confined to bed the day Ted announced the formation of the RFK Memorial in a ceremony on the back lawn at Hickory Hill. November 20 was Bobby's forty-third birthday and from her bed Ethel helped plan a remembrance Mass that was held at St. Luke's. Afterward, a group of friends visited with Ethel, had a light breakfast, and Ethel received Communion. Jackie, who had married Onassis little more than a month earlier, sent a telegram but didn't attend.

Still confined to her bed on November 22, the fifth anniversary of Jack's death, Ethel missed the ceremonies at Arlington National Cemetery. Jackie also was absent, as were Pat and Jean. The three attended smaller memorial Masses in Manhattan. Ted prayed once at Jack's grave, once at Bobby's.

Thanksgiving came and went. Now Ethel and her doctors were hoping for a full-term birth, sometime in mid-December. The big news story at the time, besides her impending delivery, was the beginning of Sirhan Sirhan's trial in Los Angeles. But Ethel made a point of ignoring it. The world press, however, had begun speculating whether she would be called as a witness—she wasn't—and what impact the trial would have on her emotionally. The help in the house made certain she'd didn't see any of the stories in the papers or on TV.

Finally, early in the evening of December 11, eight days before the baby was expected, Dr. Walsh felt it was advisable to get her to the hospital and perform a cesarean the next morning. Accompanied by Luella Hennessey, Ted, Fred Dutton, and Rafer Johnson, she arrived at Georgetown Hospital in typical Ethel fashion, loaded down with five suitcases, one of them still carrying an identification tag from the Ambassador Hotel; her silk Porthault sheets and pillowcases, which she had laundered separately from other hospital linens, and a three-speed electric fan.

She had hoped to keep her arrival secret and was disappointed to find reporters waiting for her. She refused to acknowledge them and kept a stern look on her face.

Ethel was put in one of the maternity ward's exclusive sixty-dollar-a-day private rooms—the same one she occupied when she had her last child. It had recently been given a fresh coat of pink paint in readiness for her arrival. In the room was a bouquet of pink and blue flowers sent by Jackie. Hennessey was given a private room across the corridor.

"I said to her, 'I'll be right over there. If there's anything you're nervous about, just ask the nurse to awaken me and I'll come over.' " Besides Hennessey, there were special-duty nurses retained to attend Ethel around the clock.

She was wheeled into the delivery room shortly before eight in the morning, with Ted and Luella Hennessey on either side of the stretcher. Ted stayed in the operating room until Ethel got settled on the table and then he left. "She went through it like a soldier. She was happy that she had people with her whom she knew and trusted," Hennessey said.

Less than an hour later, Ethel gave birth to a healthy eight-pound, four-ounce girl, her fourth daughter. "I thought it would be very upsetting for Ethel when the baby was born because it would never see its father. It was kind of a traumatic few minutes, but then everything was fine," Hennessey said.

Waiting in Hennessey's room for word of the birth were Ted, Joan, and several of the children. "She looks just like Ethel and even has some hair," Hennessey reported to the family. Ted then went to the recovery room to stay with Ethel through the morning. "I now have sixteen children," he quipped, referring to his own three, Ethel's eleven, and Jack's two. As a precautionary measure, the baby was placed in an incubator to avoid the possible respiratory problems that cesarean infants sometimes develop. Ethel wouldn't get her first real glimpse of the infant until the next morning, when she held her and declared her "beautiful."

With Ted's help, Ethel named the baby Rory Elizabeth Katherine Kennedy; Rory, because it sounded close to Bobby (Ethel didn't like the name Roberta); Elizabeth for her friend Liz Stevens; and Katherine for her pal Kay Evans.

A week after she entered the hospital and six days before Christmas, Ethel took Rory home. On the way, she suddenly asked Ted, who was driving, to make a detour. Minutes later he drove through the gate of Arlington National Cemetery. Ethel walked to Bobby's grave, carrying the baby clad in a pink bonnet and frilly pink bunting. The widow and daughter stood quietly in the chill wind for a few moments, then she returned to Ted's station wagon and headed for Hickory Hill.

95 * Two Faces of Ethel

ETHEL'S PUBLIC PERFORMANCE in the wake of Bobby's death—that of the brave widow—had been convincing. Journalists filing year-after-the-assassination profiles of her, without exception, described the widow as the same old Ethel. All of them missed—or ignored—the fact that there was trouble behind the seemingly tranquil walls of Hickory Hill and Hyannis Port; that Ethel had become increasingly mercurial and temperamental; that her façade was beginning to crumble.

If any of those reporters were aware of the familial drama that was taking place at Hickory Hill and Hyannis Port—Ethel's extreme mood changes, her ongoing war with the older boys—none of them chose to let the public in on it. It was still a time when the Kennedys' privacy was respected by a mostly adulatory press.

As the torchbearer for Bobby, it was imperative for Ethel to keep up appearances.

"Ethel went from career wife to career widow overnight," George Terrien observed. "Now she could be more outspoken, more of an activist. That was a role she had long sublimated."

Members of Ethel's Mafia supported Terrien's assessment. They too saw a change in Ethel. "She became a little fiercer in speaking about things, especially things Bobby was interested in,'' said one pal.

The thousands of letters of condolences had changed: now she was in demand on the speakers' circuit; she was asked to lend her name to sundry charities. Some of those who demanded her presence were putting her in the same activist league as Mrs. Martin Luther King.

Ethel became active in Bobby's causes: the grape pickers' movement in California; the Bedford-Stuyvesant Restoration Corporation; John Glenn's first political campaign in Ohio, and John Lindsay's in New York.

With the conviction of Sirhan Sirhan, the demon of Los Angeles had been exorcised. Ethel had ignored the trial, but told confidantes that she had had disturbing and recurring dreams of personal retribution. ''I would like to see him burn in hell,'' she told her sister Georgeann after the trial. Initially sentenced to die, Sirhan would spend the rest of his life behind bars.

In February, Ethel was named by the Gallup poll, in a special survey, as the woman Americans admired most. She had even topped her mother-in-law; Rose had placed second.

Ethel found the honor rather amusing.

''I got it because of my cooking,'' she quipped cynically to friends. A couple of her boys toasted the event by getting stoned.

In April, Ethel received her second big accolade of the year: the cover of *Time* magazine, courtesy of Hays Gorey, a trusted journalist friend who had covered Bobby's campaign, had access to Hickory Hill, and therefore was able to get the widow's cooperation.

''What happens in the life of a Kennedy automatically becomes the object of universal fascination,'' Gorey wrote, noting correctly that ''the public does not know [Ethel] today. Perhaps it never did.'' He pointed out that Ethel's placement in the recent Gallup poll had been ''an assessment born of sympathy, not knowledge.''

Gorey had gotten an insider's look, at least as much as Ethel wanted him to have, of life at Hickory Hill without Bobby. This included Ethel playing the role of mother; Gorey was permitted to watch her bathe Rory. Although there were few revelations in the five-page story, Gorey was the first reporter to suggest that Ethel had been having problems with some of the children since Bobby's death. In describing Ethel and her brood, he wrote:

"She comforts, counsels and disciplines—quite strictly sometimes. 'Once in a while she gets sore as hell at them,' says a family intimate. 'Bobby never struck any of the kids. Ethel, I think, has.' "

In the piece, Ethel had recalled how much time Bobby had spent with his children. "If one of the boys was having trouble just catching a football," she said, "Bobby would go out and work with him on it, tell him what he was doing wrong and practice with him until he got it."

At Christmas, she said, the older boys had written papers about their father. The one *Time* chose to reprint was a heartbreaking piece, written by the troubled David. With the loss of his father, the boy wrote, there would be no more football, swimming, riding, or camping—the activities he and Bobby shared and loved. He was "the best father," David had concluded.

Ethel said she intended to bring up the children using the principles that Bobby believed in. "Sometimes a seed has to die before it takes," she said. "I will bring up the children the way he would have wanted. He has already established the pattern. They all understand that they have a special obligation. They've been given so much; they must try to give that again. . . ."

But Ethel's problems with the boys were continuing to escalate. Just a month before the *Time* cover story appeared, fifteen-year-old Bobby Jr. had been expelled from the Millbrook School, in New York, because of poor grades and behavior; Ethel had refused to come to his assistance, leaving it up to family loyalist Lem Billings to help him. Joe, the son Ethel most respected, had gotten terrible grades at his father's alma mater, Milton, where he had also become something of a pothead. In an effort to help salvage the boy, the school's headmaster, Tom Cleveland, asked him to move in with his family. They found Joe a somewhat eccentric houseguest: he feared silence and kept a radio constantly blaring; he kept a curious collection of old neckties; he had a hot temper; and he often veered between flaunting his family name and cursing it. Joe also showed signs of becoming a womanizer, boasting that he could get any girl he wanted. "Once a Kennedy, always a Kennedy," he declared.

Around this time a rumor began to spread that Ethel might become the next Kennedy to enter politics, challenging Virginia's powerful Republican Congressman Joe Broyhill. Ethel was touched but said she had no political ambitions, pointing to her small children. "You can see why right here." But the rumors and speculation continued to feed upon themselves, causing Ethel some embarrassment. She finally asked those involved to put an end to the gossip.

When the stories reached Rose Kennedy's ears, she made it abundantly clear to Ethel that her place was not in the political arena, but at home with her children. "Ethel has greater responsibility than almost any woman in the world—the moral education of eleven children," declared the matriarch, now seventy-seven. She said she was confident God was watching over Ethel's brood and "will endow them with a special sense of family responsibility and with an intense desire on the part of the older ones to be examples and guides to the younger ones." And she voiced unlimited confidence in Ethel. "She will never submit to despair or defeat but will always persevere in her faith, courage, and optimism."

For Ethel, the jock, the greatest honor of the year, aside from her mother-in-law's accolades, was the official renaming in June of D.C. Stadium, where her favorite team, the Washington Redskins, played, to RFK Memorial Stadium. The entire Kennedy clan, even a beaming Jackie, who despised football, was present for the ceremony. *Chicago Daily News* reporter Virginia Kay noted that "not all of Washington viewed the Kennedys with compassion or friendship." She reported that Liz Carpenter, Lady Bird Johnson's former press secretary, was at a party where the subject of the renamed stadium came up and had cracked, "What's left—the Potomac River?"

Standing next to Ethel at the stadium ceremony was thirteen-year-old David, wearing a cast on his right arm. He'd recently been injured when he collided with Redskin lineman Ray Schoenke during a touch football game at Hickory Hill. Ethel had taken to inviting the Redskins out to the house whenever they were available. "He pats the cast and tells all his friends, 'Ray Schoenke gave me that,' " Ethel boasted.

The memories of Los Angeles came swirling back when Ethel, along with a crowd of several thousand, gathered at Bobby's grave on the first anniversary of his death. Along with Ted, Ethel had planned the memorial Mass, which was held at twilight, with a choir singing folk songs. Ethel shed no tears. After the hour-long ceremony, she led some three hundred friends back to Hickory Hill for another wake. Every year thereafter there would be a memorial Mass and, as the years passed, they would become social rather than spiritual gatherings, an opportunity for the old New Frontier gang to eat, drink, and gossip.

Later in June—in what the media billed as her coming-out after a year of mourning—Ethel was the center of attention at a glitzy Southampton party to benefit the California grape pickers, one of Bobby's pet causes. Ethel arrived on the arm of the host, twenty-four-year-old Andrew Stein, New York's youngest assemblyman, whose oceanfront estate was the setting for the party. Rafer Johnson, now a Los Angeles newscaster, ran interference for Ethel as a horde of what were then dubbed the "Beautiful People," wearing designer dresses and DON'T BUY SCAB GRAPES buttons, descended on the famous widow. "Let's face it, there's a charity benefit every Saturday night in one of the Hamptons," remarked a guest, "but Ethel makes the difference." Ethel, who'd flown down from Hyannis Port, where she'd just begun her second summer vacation without Bobby, was her usual cheerful public self. She posed with Anne Ford Uzielli; she joked with old friends like Fred Harris, Judy Moyers, and a pal from Manhattanville who had picked her up at the airport. Despite Ethel's outward calm, though, she needed support. Pressing the hand of a close friend of Ted's, she whispered pleadingly, "Don't leave me." Listening attentively to a speech by a grape pickers' union official, Ethel let friends know that she planned a trip later in the year to visit grape boycott czar César Chavez, who had worked so hard to get the Chicano vote out for Bobby in California. Frank Mankiewicz, now working as a newspaper columnist, said, "I'm here asking for money for the grape pickers—at least twenty-five percent of what Pucci [the Italian designer of many of the dresses at the bash] got from this audience. We'd like to raise a hundred thousand dollars." But, despite the high rollers in attendance, all they got was sixteen thousand dollars. Ethel left early.

The next day's headlines read, ETHEL RETURNS TO SOCIAL LIFE, and conservative columnist William F. Buckley, Jr., who had once written endearingly about George Skakel, Jr., took his sister to task deftly for getting involved in the event. He warned, in an open letter to Ethel, that supporters of the ban-the-grapes movement were uninformed; that most of the pickers were not migrants.

Attempting to keep alive the annual tradition that Bobby had started, Ethel took the family on a July Fourth weekend rafting trip along the turbulent Green River in rugged eastern Utah. This was the first time the clan had gone on such an adventure with their uncle Ted as the leader, instead of Bobby, and the trip proved to be a disaster, at least in the eyes of the young Kennedys. Ethel's children and their cousins were still struggling to recover from the tragedy in Los Angeles. They had loved Bobby and looked up to him, but apart from Ted's own three children, the young Kennedys held a dim view of the new family patriarch.

"We all felt a lot of bitterness toward him," Christopher Lawford said later. "It was probably unfair. There was no real reason for it except that he couldn't fill Uncle Bobby's shoes and didn't try." Beside Ethel and Ted, the party included Joan Kennedy; thirteen Kennedy children and a dozen of their friends; two Congressmen and their families; and such old pals of Ethel's as Jim Whittaker and Lem Billings.

On past trips, Bobby had made certain that the young people mixed with their elders, but Ted made no such effort. Still struggling to cope with his own reactions to his brother's death, Ted lacked the strength to help the younger Kennedys with their wounds. Still angry years later, Chris Lawford charged that Ethel, Ted, and the other adults spent the four-day trip drinking, ignoring the young people. At one point, Bobby Jr. and David tried to draw their mother and the others into a water fight, the sort of thing that had been typical when Bobby was alive. But that was then. This time the adults were disinterested. When the boys continued to pester, the towering Whittaker threatened to throw Bobby and David forcefully into the churning water. After that the young people set up their own campsite. "We'd sit in the darkness," recalled Chris Lawford, "talking about what a drag the family was, what an incredible asshole Teddy was to let it happen, how it was never like this when Bobby was alive. . . ."

The trip had become controversial for another reason. A couple of months earlier, Ethel had been invited to the inauguration of Charles Evers as the first black mayor in Mississippi since the post–Civil War era. Having already scheduled the whitewater trip, Ethel asked Evers to change the date of his historic swearing-in to a more convenient time. When he refused, she sent her regrets. "We don't ask much of each other," Evers said, "but I know that Bobby would have come."

With all the dissension, Ethel returned to Hyannis Port from Idaho exhausted and wrought up; she hoped to relax by partying with her pals.

96 ✻ *Chappaquiddick Summer*

THE ONLY OFFICIAL event on Ethel's schedule in mid-July 1969 was an appearance at the opening of the first Connecticut Special Olympics for the Retarded, held on the grounds of the University of Connecticut, in Storrs. There to represent the Kennedy family's favorite charity and to present the young contestants with ribbons and certificates for their efforts, Ethel had gone to the games with Rafer Johnson and Boston Celtics star Don Nelson. She had tried to talk Ted into accompanying her, but the Senator had other plans for that weekend—a party in Edgartown, Martha's Vineyard, that was set to begin on the evening of Friday, July 18, and continue into the early-morning hours of Saturday, July 19. Those dates would later come to live in infamy for the Kennedy clan.

As Ethel was preparing to leave the compound for the games that drizzly Saturday morning, a chilling discovery was being made across the water, on Chappaquiddick Island.

Two teenage boys, walking across a narrow wooden bridge that spanned a tidal pool, spotted the outline of a submerged car. The boys alerted vacationers in a nearby house, who called the police. Minutes later, Dominic Arena, a former state trooper who'd been named police chief of Edgartown two years earlier, arrived at the scene. He jumped into the water to get a better look at the car, a 1967 black Oldsmobile, then radioed for a deputy and a diver from the fire department. As the diver went down, the chief asked his deputy to run a make on the car's Massachusetts plate, L78 207. Minutes later, the owner's name and address came back: Edward M.

Kennedy, Room 2400, JFK Building, Government Center, Boston, Massachusetts.

My God, thought Arena, another Kennedy tragedy. Meanwhile, the diver was making an even grimmer discovery. Inside the car was the body of a young woman, in rigor mortis; the position of her body clearly showed that she had made a desperate attempt to escape before the car had filled with water.

"Do you recognize her?" Arena asked when the diver surfaced with the body. "Is it one of the Kennedy clan?" Arena studied the face carefully, then breathed a sigh of relief. "Thank God," he said. "It isn't one of the clan."

Arena ordered his deputies to find Ted, while a tow truck—bearing the slogan YOU WRECK 'EM—WE FETCH 'EM—hauled the car out of the water.

Meanwhile, papers in the glove compartment led police to the victim's identity.

Her name was Mary Jo Kopechne, a petite, blue-eyed blonde who was a week away from celebrating her twenty-ninth birthday, but was still considered by friends to be somewhat unsophisticated, a quiet and serious only child. Her ties to the Kennedys went back five years to 1964, when she had been hired as a secretary in Bobby's Senatorial office. She fit the Kennedys' profile perfectly. Mary Jo was a Catholic, had attended parochial schools, and spent a year teaching at the Mission of St. Jude in Montgomery, Alabama. Moreover, she hero-worshiped the Kennedys, was a tireless worker and a dedicated loyalist; she stayed up one whole night at Hickory Hill typing Bobby's major anti–Vietnam War speech; she traveled for him, and he often consulted with her; Kopechne had not only typed Bobby's Presidential announcement but had helped in its phrasing. During the 1968 campaign, she was one of a handful of trusted staffers, known as the "Boiler Room Girls," who compiled data on how Democratic delegates intended to vote. When Bobby was killed, Kopechne had been devastated.

Police soon learned that the young woman had been in town at Ted's invitation to see the forty-sixth annual

Edgartown Yacht Club Regatta and to attend the party and cookout that had kept Ted from accompanying Ethel to the Special Olympics. Because of Ted's growing reputation as a womanizer, Kennedy aides moved quickly, albeit unsuccessfully, to quash growing suspicions about Ted and Kopechne's activities at the party, a reunion of sorts for the Boiler Room Girls and other Kennedy campaign workers. After some brainstorming, the Kennedy people decided that the most virtuous person they could compare Mary Jo to was the Senator's own sister-in-law. "She was like Ethel in that she would grimace if anyone said anything that was dirty or tasteless. You can spot people who are swingers and she was not one of them," asserted Wendell Pigman, a former boss of Mary Jo's when she worked for Bobby.

About the time Ethel was handing out awards to the disabled in Connecticut, Ted was walking into the police station in Edgartown to give a statement.

"I'm sorry about the accident," Arena told the Senator when he walked through the door of the police station.

"Yes, I know," Ted said. "I was the driver."

Arena didn't know whether he could take another shocker that morning.

He had never imagined that the Senator had actually been in the car. He had assumed that the girl had been driving alone.

Years later the chief recalled, "Nothing in my prior career as a police officer had prepared me for standing in a wet bathing suit and shaking hands with a United States Senator—and a Kennedy—who tells me he is the driver of a car from which I have just removed the body of a beautiful young girl. I was stunned." Looking at Ted, Arena noted that he didn't look like someone who'd just been in a fatal car-plunge accident.

From that point, events moved quickly. Word of the accident had leaked out and reporters began descending on the police station. The Kennedy family's top advisers, such as Burke Marshall, and Kennedy staffers, such as David Burke, had been activated, and were either en route to the compound or planning strategy in Washington on how to deal with the sudden crisis and the hungry media.

Meanwhile, Ted wrote a two-page statement about the accident with the help of attorney Paul Markham, the former U.S. Attorney for Massachusetts, who had been a guest at the ill-fated party. Ted's statement said that he was driving with Kopechne, "a former secretary of my brother," at around eleven-fifteen the previous night to take the ferry back to Edgartown when he made a wrong turn onto Dike Road, came to the bridge, and went over the side.

"The car turned over," he wrote, "and sank into the water and landed with the roof resting on the bottom."

The statement continued:

"I attempted to open the door and the window of the car but have no recollection of how I got out of the car. I came to the surface and then repeatedly dove down to the car in an attempt to see if the passenger was still in the car. I was unsuccessful in the attempt. I was exhausted and in a state of shock.

"I recall walking back to where my friends were eating. There was a car parked in front of the cottage and I climbed into the backseat. I then asked for someone to bring me back to Edgartown. I remember walking around for a period and then going back to my hotel room. When I fully realized what had happened this morning, I immediately contacted police."

To Arena and other investigators, the statement was a shocker because it showed that Ted had waited more than nine hours before reporting the accident. The Senator also never mentioned that there had been a party.

Ted told Arena he wanted Burke Marshall to read the statement first before it became an official part of the record, and he suggested that the chief return to Chappaquiddick to see that the car "got out and cleared okay." Ted also told the chief that he'd telephoned Mary Jo's parents. Kennedy refused to answer any further questions and, with Arena's help, was able to get a private pilot to fly him to Hyannis Port.

Before leaving the police station he telephoned his mother and told her about the accident. Rose immediately canceled plans to attend a bazaar at her church. She had known Mary Jo as "one of Bobby's most dedicated staff assistants" and remembered that "Ethel knew her well." The previous summer, after Bobby's death, Mary Jo had been a guest at Hyannis Port for a cookout and sailing. The matriarch, fearing that a major scandal was in store for Ted and the entire House of Kennedy, called her other surviving children—Eunice in Paris, Pat in California, and Jean in Spain—and asked them to come home. Jean's husband, Steve Smith, a smooth operator who handled the Kennedy family finances and other behind-the-scenes activities, would take charge of the crisis; he booked the first flight back. Rose was there to greet Ted when he arrived at the compound. "He was so unlike himself it was hard to believe he was my own son," she recalled later. ". . . He was disturbed, confused, and deeply distracted. . . . I was deeply distressed, especially in the wake of all the tragedies which preceded this one." Pat Lawford's son Chris recalled getting the news in Los Angeles: "Nobody said a word about what had happened. There were all these hushed phone conversations. And then my mother packed her bags and said she had to go to the Cape. That was the way we were always informed of crises—someone arriving in a hurry, or someone leaving in a hurry."

By the time Ethel returned from her duties at the Special Olympics and walked through the front door of her house in the compound, the story had already been broadcast on TV and radio, and had run with a headline of BULLETIN on the front page of the *Cape Cod-Standard Times*.

"At first she didn't know what to make of it; she didn't know what to believe; she couldn't process any of it," said a family insider years later. "Here was a woman who was still in a state of shock over the death of her husband; who had lost control of her children. And now the man who she was relying on to keep her on steady-ground—the only shoulder she had to lean on—seemed to be self-destructing before her eyes."

Ethel met with Ted and Burke Marshall. She knew not to ask questions. She was told to call highly placed friends in Washington who could offer advice and counsel. One of the first was Robert McNamara. "Come up here, Bob," she pleaded.

Before Ted went to the police station, David Burke had located Mary Jo Kopechne's parents, Joseph and Gwen Kopechne, in New Jersey, and the Senator had delivered the terrible news, leaving out one important fact: that he had been the driver. After hearing that Mary Jo was dead, Mrs. Kopechne fell into a state of shock. Marshaling his resources, Burke Marshall had gotten hold of another lawyer and trusted member of the circle, William vanden Heuvel, who had served with Bobby at Justice and was involved in his Presidential campaign. Marshall told him to get to the Kopechnes' home before the press did.

Meanwhile, Ethel had gotten additional marching orders. She was told to place another call to the Kopechnes. "She talked about faith, how it could help. She said, 'We will be at the funeral,' " Joseph Kopechne remembered.

Three days later, Ted, Ethel, and Joan flew from Hyannis Port to Wilkes-Barre, near the dreary mining town of Plymouth, in the mined-out anthracite hills of northern Pennsylvania, where Mary Jo had been born. The Senator, who had been in seclusion at the compound since giving his statement to police, was now wearing a neck brace as a result of the accident. It was a bizarre scene outside of St. Vincent's Church in Plymouth when the Kennedys pulled up.

"It was supposed to be a mournful occasion," wrote *Washington Post* reporter Richard Harwood. "But young people swarmed around his car, girls pinched one another, squealed and said, 'Isn't he beautiful? I saw him! I saw him!' It all caused people to remark that it was like a scene from an old campaign."

A woman even stood in the crowd holding a red,

white, and blue sign that read: KENNEDY FOR PRESIDENT, 1972.

Before the Mass, the Kennedy party and the Kopechnes met in the church rectory. Mary Jo's father remembered Ted as being "so emotional" he couldn't understand a word the Senator was saying.

Some seven hundred were in the church when Ted, Ethel, Joan, and Lem Billings took their seats in a pew near the front, across the aisle from the dead girl's parents. Mrs. Kopechne was near collapse; Ted looked straight ahead, grim-faced. Ethel too remained stoic. The previous day, she had infuriated reporters when she released a forty-word statement from the compound praising Mary Jo, never once mentioning the accident or her brother-in-law's involvement. "A typing exercise," said one angry journalist. "Mary Jo was a sweet, wonderful girl," Ethel had written. "She was just terrific."

A large number of Kennedy hands were on the scene in Plymouth, including men and women who had been at the party with Mary Jo, some now crying. Before the services they had viewed the body at the funeral home where Mary Jo lay in an open coffin, wearing a pale blue gown and clasping a crystal rosary. "This has been a year to learn a lot about Catholic funerals," said Adam Walinsky, who had been in the trenches with Mary Jo during Bobby's campaign. Two of the eight pallbearers were Kennedy aides—Mary Jo's boss, Dave Hackett, and K. Dunn Gifford, Ted's legislative assistant. While Kennedy aides told reporters that the clan had offered to pay for the costs of the funeral but had been turned down by the Kopechnes, they refused to discuss the nine-hour gap between the time of the accident and Ted's appearance at the police station.

After the burial, there was a buffet at which Mary Jo's father spoke with Ethel. "I thought I was talking to my sister," he said later. "That's the way she makes you feel. She's like that nice lady next door. She was interested in what was being done in the mines. She asked all about the area."

Three days after the funeral, Ted pleaded guilty to

leaving the scene of an accident and received a two-month suspended sentence and a year's probation; that night he appeared in a nationally televised speech, calling his conduct "indefensible" and asking the voters of Massachusetts to tell him whether he should resign from the Senate. A couple of weeks later the district attorney asked for an inquest, sparking Kennedy's side to seek a temporary injunction; the DA wanted to exhume Mary Jo's body for an autopsy and her parents filed a petition against it. The grim tale continued to unfold on and on through the summer and into the fall and winter.

It had become the biggest scandal the Kennedy clan had faced, but they weathered it, at least on the surface. Ted would be re-elected, with Ethel's help, to another Senate term in November 1970. But the echoes of Chappaquiddick would continue to resound down through the years and would eventually preclude Ted from ever becoming President.

Publicly, Ethel staunchly supported her brother-in-law through the bleak months of Chappaquiddick, defending him to friends, and foes, and later stumping for him on the campaign trail, always the consummate Kennedy loyalist. On the heels of the accident, when *Newsweek* ran a piece asserting that Ted's closest associates were concerned about "his indulgent drinking habits, his daredevil driving, and his ever-ready eye for a pretty face"—it could have been a description of George Skakel, Jr.—Ethel was the most outraged of all the Kennedys, angrily telling friends that Ted was being crucified.

"Ethel always had the philosophy that the Skakels and the Kennedys were above the law, that they were invincible. So that's the way she played Chappaquiddick," said one member of her circle later. "We're not talking about a rocket scientist here. We're talking about a nice Catholic girl who really believed that the Kennedys were everything that they set themselves up to be and that they were above any kind of law of any description."

Privately, though, Chappaquiddick had all but demolished Ethel.

It had been Ted who, after hearing that Bobby had

been shot, declared, "If I let go, Ethel will let go." She had believed him and relied on him to help her hold it all together. Now his pledge seemed empty.

"Ethel felt as if she had been abandoned by Ted," George Terrien said later. "She had a lot of anger—anger toward Ted, anger toward Bobby for dying, anger toward her sons."

Ethel told her sister Georgeann at the time, "First it was Father, then it was Jack, then it was George, then Bobby. Now Ted is being destroyed. I feel I've lost every man in my life who was ever important to me."

Ethel was also highly distressed over the question of Ted's morality, which had become the focal point of the whole Chappaquiddick affair. Had the Senator had an intimate relationship with Mary Jo Kopechne? That was the question on the minds of the investigators and the press at the time, and was still being asked by credible cover-up and conspiracy buffs long after the scandal had cooled. "Ted was supposed to be a role model for my boys," she told her sister. "Now look at him. He's a laughingstock. Why would they ever take him seriously? I'm at such loose ends."

Though she had always privately frowned upon Ted's womanizing and drinking, her strong religious beliefs carried her through and kept their relationship from falling apart. As one of her closest friends said years later, "Ethel took a very dim view of adultery and thought it a heinous, mortal sin. But at the same time she believed in reclamation of the sinner. Ted was her brother-in-law; he had been very attentive to the children; he did his best after Bobby died, the best he knew how to do. She forgave him the way she'd expect Jesus to forgive any erring human. She applied the parable of the stray lamb and became less critical of Ted because she saw him as an erring young fellow. And my God, with the Skakels, what the hell could Ted do that came close to what her brother George did? He was a fourteen-carat wild man. In the end, Ethel's attitude was that Ted would work it out in Purgatory."

• • •

For Ethel's sons, still reeling from the wounds caused by their father's death, the Chappaquiddick incident was the final straw. That summer, as their mother and the rest of the adults dealt with the clan's latest crisis, the boys, led by fifteen-year-old Bobby Jr., who had taken to dressing all in black, went wild in the streets of Hyannis Port. Their gang had been officially dubbed the Hyannis Port Terrors, the HPTs for short. Using one of their mother's expensive sheets with an RFK monogram, the boys painted *HPT Rules* on it and hung it from the steeple of a local Presbyterian church.

Along with pals, Bobby Jr. and David tossed firecrackers at passing cars, beached boats, firebombed the Hyannis breakwater, shot water balloons at police cars, had sex with local girls, and consumed a mammoth amount of marijuana, LSD, and amphetamines.

Later, they would pay the price. One of their buddies, a local cab driver who had allegedly paid Eunice's son Bobby Shriver ten dollars for a joint, turned out to be an undercover narcotics officer. Not long after the sale, as Ethel and her children were having dinner at the Shrivers' place in the compound, the police moved in and accused young Shriver and Bobby Jr. of possession of marijuana. Freaking out, Ethel chased her son through the house and slammed him into the bushes, screaming that he'd defamed the Kennedy name.

Publicly, Ethel issued a statement saying, "Naturally, I was distressed to learn last night that my son had been charged with possession of marijuana. . . . This is, of course, a matter for the authorities to decide. But Bobby is a fine boy, and we have always been proud of him. I will stand by him. . . ."

Ethel, Ted, and Sargent Shriver were present when the boys appeared at a private hearing in juvenile court in Hyannis Port, just one day before members of the Robert F. Kennedy Memorial Foundation were set to meet at a nearby hotel. As is routine in such cases, Judge Henry L. Murphy continued the case without finding. Both boys had denied the possession charge. The judge said that "unless they get into trouble again" they would not be subjected to further legal proceedings on the marijuana charge. At one point, Bobby Jr., wearing a cast on his right wrist to mend injuries suffered when he fell out of a tree a month earlier, spotted a chum in the crowd and flashed a grin.

After the court appearance, Ethel threatened to throw Bobby Jr. out of the family. She didn't have to. The sixteen-year-old took money from his own bank account, bought a used car, and drove to Los Angeles, the scene of his father's death.

Meanwhile, David and Chris Lawford hitchhiked to New York, panhandled for money, bought heroin in Central Park, and snorted it. They wound up at Pat Lawford's Fifth Avenue apartment, which was vacant; she had left for France saying she had to get away from the clan for a while. Her place quickly filled up with street people who had heard the boys were throwing a party. Neighbors complained, but the boys managed to get everyone to leave before the police were called. When David and Chris returned to the compound, Ethel acted as if she didn't know they'd been gone.

Other members of the clan, seeing the problems Ethel was having, began putting distance between their children and hers. Bobby Shriver said he'd gotten a sense that "the Bobby Kennedy family was dangerous."

• • •

Ethel was at Hickory Hill with a bad cold when she got word, on November 17, that Joseph Patrick Kennedy, eighty-one, had very little time left, and that the clan was gathering at the compound. Despite a high fever, she flew north to be with the family. By the time she arrived, the patriarch, an invalid since his first stroke in 1961, had already received the Last Rites. His condition, the family knew, had worsened during the Chappaquiddick affair. The entire family was there, each taking turns sitting at the bedside of the failing patriarch.

Shortly after eleven in the morning the following day, the grand architect of the Kennedy political dynasty died. Ethel was one of those in the room with him at the time. At his father's funeral, Ted, his voice breaking, read a tribute to the patriarch that Bobby had written. It had come from a collection of one hundred essays written about Joseph Kennedy by family and friends and privately printed in a book called *The Fruitful Bough*.

"I don't believe he is without faults," Ted read. "But when we were young, because of the strength of his character or the massiveness of his personality, they were unobserved or at least unimportant. When we grew a little older we realized he wasn't perfect; that he made mistakes, but by that time we realized everyone did. In many, many ways, to us he is something special."

97 * Letting Go

ETHEL'S BROTHER-IN-LAW Steve Smith, the clan's cold and calculating exchequer, had made the determination that Ethel was no longer a cost-effective line item on the Kennedy family budget.

When Bobby was alive, Ethel's spending, though carefully monitored and often criticized, had been justified for the most part. The big parties, expensive clothing, and trips were written off as publicity and promotion. After all, as the wife of the Attorney General, then Senator, and finally potential First Lady, Ethel had to uphold the Kennedys' royal image. Now, with her role virtually demolished, Ethel had become a financial liability to the family, whose coffers had been depleted by an estimated $8 million in the last two months of Bobby's campaign. Ethel's limited personal funds, too, had been somewhat diminished since she'd anted up a tidy sum of her Skakel money to help Bobby in his bid for the Presidency.

As one member of Ethel's circle put it, "All of her

life Ethel had been used to a high standard of living. Suddenly, before Bobby's body was even cold, the Kennedys began coming down hard on her to cut back. Here was a woman who had just lost the true love of her life, a woman whose children were freaking out. Now they were taking away from her one of the few things she had left and truly enjoyed—shopping and spending. I think it was the final straw."

Since Los Angeles, Steve Smith had given Ethel numerous warnings to downgrade her lifestyle, which now cost the Kennedy family about $650,000 a year. But Ethel was a typical Skakel—generous to a fault; a free spender. So she brazenly ignored Smith's pleadings, flaunting her conspicuous consumption: "I have twin butlers. When Steve sees them he thinks there's only one," she boasted to friends with a mischievous giggle.

Besides Smith, Rose Kennedy was constantly after Ethel about her spending. "She didn't approve of Ethel at all," said the matriarch's secretary, Barbara Gibson. "She thought that Ethel was too extravagant. When Ethel was staying at her house in the compound, she would invite Mrs. Kennedy to dinner and she'd send over the menu. There'd be dishes like lobster thermidor and beef Bourguignonne—three or four main courses—and Mrs. Kennedy would shake her head and say, 'Oh, my, aren't we rich.' Ethel also wore Liu, the same perfume as Mrs. Kennedy. But Mrs. Kennedy would get angry and say, 'She doesn't buy it by the ounce like me, she buys it by the quart!' "

"Mrs. Kennedy wasn't scrimping," recalled Noelle Fell, one of Ethel's secretaries in the seventies. "They'd come down to see her from New York, or sometimes they'd call, and really bitch at her because all of a sudden there was a ten-thousand-dollar food tab.

"She wasn't at all careful about her money, and the staff was free to run around with her credit card. There was a Giant gourmet supermarket in McLean, and I don't think there was anything that I couldn't buy there. She had unlimited credit and we'd pay with vouchers. At the end of the month the bill was sent to New York to be paid. Unlike other Kennedys, who were constantly freeloading at other people's dinners and parties, Ethel enjoyed entertaining at home, so she purchased immense amounts of food, wine, and liquor. She ordered cases of her favorite white wines, Pouilly-Fuissé and Casal. With friends constantly visiting, and with eleven children and a staff of ten to feed, the refrigerator door was always open.

"Food was always being wasted because at the last minute Ethel would decide to throw out the menu for the day. The chefs were ready to fix whatever, but she would get pissed with the menu for no rational reason and just tear it up and give them another menu. She was very demanding and went through a lot of chefs. It was unbelievable. And, of course, that made life hell for all of us.

"When we'd go to Hyannis Port, Ethel, of all the family, laid out a really good spread for everybody. She was never chintzy. Once a week, all of the families would get together for dinner at one of the houses in the compound. Ethel especially hated to eat at Jackie's and Eunice's because their meals didn't come near what Ethel served. When it came time for Jackie to host dinner, Ethel would say, 'Oh, God, I can't stand it there; I don't want to have a peanut butter and bacon sandwich.' "

Defying Smith, Ethel refused to cut back. On clothing alone, she was spending thousands, often doubling or tripling her costs because she was obsessed with having at least one backup for every favorite piece of clothing she owned, fearful that she'd either lose the original or leave it somewhere and not have a replacement.

"Oscar de la Renta was a favorite designer of Mrs. Kennedy," said Noelle Fell. "He had made her a skirt that she really liked, so she said, 'I have to call Oscar and have him make me another.' He came to the house and I remember him saying, 'My God, I can't get this material anymore.' Mrs. Kennedy begged him to try and he finally got it in France."

Ethel was buying the finest imported cosmetics. Her boudoir shelves were filled with bottles of Liu; she'd have Pierre Salinger buy ounces for her in quantity in

Paris. "She had oodles of bottles," recalled Noelle Fell. Ethel also used one of the most expensive bath oils, Floris Special #127, imported from England, which she bought once again in quantity from Dumbarton Pharmacy in Georgetown, the only shop in the capital that carried the floral fragrance. She spent thousands annually for the finest French linens from the firm of D. Porthault & Co. One set, with some custom work, had cost her almost five thousand dollars; Ethel had at least three dozen sets.

People from the Park Agency were calling Ethel two, sometimes three times a week, to question her spending, or were making personal visits to Hickory Hill to warn her that if she didn't get in line fiscally, there would be hell to pay. After each call, Ethel would hit the ceiling.

"It was violent," recalled Noelle Fell. "Whatever hell they gave her, she would take it out on the rest of us, as if none of it were her fault, as if it was all my fault, or the chef's fault, and of course it wasn't. She'd order a meeting of the staff and say, 'I've been told that our household expenses are way too high. Now what are we going to do about this?'

"She would go on a rampage and start pacing the whole house, screaming, 'Look at all this waste!' She'd rip open the refrigerator door and yell, 'Why do we need all this food?' She'd go down to the basement where her wine was stored and where there was a huge freezer, and she'd yell, 'Who are you dealing with? Why are my bills so high?' But that very night she would have caviar and lobster.

"She'd suddenly lay down new rules: the chef would not be permitted to buy the groceries anymore; a daily menu would have to be in her hands by ten each morning for her approval. Then she'd telephone New York and say, 'I've taken care of it.'

"Because she didn't know how to cut the budget, she'd turn off a lamp with a sixty-watt bulb in it. Meanwhile, the rest of the lights in the house were on and all the TVs were on. She'd take out her anger on the little children if they left a light on in their rooms. If she happened by, she'd shriek, 'Ah-ha!' when she caught them, and then she'd send someone down to the store to buy ten-dollar scented candles to use instead of sixty-watt bulbs. In the winter she'd have six heating pads in her bed but all the windows were open and the fireplaces were blazing. She had no clue as to what things costs and no clue on how to cut down on expenses."

Faced with her mounting bills, Steve Smith finally dropped the axe. Major cutbacks were put in place. Lem Billings, whom Ethel now relied on to help manage the older boys, acted as the family's hatchet man.

The press had been under the impression that Ethel had unlimited funds since she was both a Skakel and Kennedy heiress. Some expressed surprise when they suddenly spotted minute changes in her style of living.

"Ethel Kennedy with all her wealth is not met in New York by a limousine," society reporter Ymelda Dixon noted with surprise. "In fact, last week at La Guardia Airport, she was enterprising enough to grab the cab a D.C. news-hen had staked out."

The use of a cab versus a limo, though, was minor compared to other sacrifices Ethel was now being forced to make, including the unprecedented sale of fifteen paintings that had been hanging in the Kennedys' recently sold United Nations Plaza pied-à-terre.

She had quietly put the artwork, priced in the $1,000 to $10,000 per piece range, on the market through Jose Munoz, a friend and dealer in Georgetown who was given strict instructions at the time not to reveal the identity of the seller. The paintings included a Kennedyesque figure at the helm of a sailboat—Ethel had picked up the watercolor at a gallery in Cape Cod years earlier—and a large oil of a beach scene in the south of France that had hung over Ethel and Bobby's double bed. Another, which was originally to have been hung on the wall over a bureau in young Max and Chris's room at the Cape, depicted a racetrack scene with jockeys and their mounts in a paddock.

But the paintings she treasured most, and had been reluctant to sell, were done by Maura Chabor, a well-known painter of children (many resembling young Kennedys), whom Ethel had sponsored in the early 1960s in Washington after falling in love with her work at a Palm Beach gallery. Afterward, Ethel had bought a number of Chabor's works, chosen to match new decor at Hickory Hill.

As far as anyone knew, Ethel's forced art sale was the first time that Kennedy family personal possessions had been placed on the market.

Ethel also had to cut her staff by a third, getting rid of at least five people. But her most difficult divestiture was her beloved horses and the equestrian area at Hickory Hill. "The horses and the jumps and the fences were fairly expensive to maintain," said a member of Ethel's inner circle later. "The jumps and fences had to be painted; the grass had to be cut; the horses had to be fed and cared for. It was a big deal. Ethel was also involved in sponsoring some local horse shows and giving an annual Skakel Memorial Cup. To the Kennedys, it had all become too costly."

About six months after Bobby's assassination, Gerry Tremblay, in private law practice in Charlottesville, got a call from Lem Billings, whom he'd met at Hickory Hill.

"Lem told me they were cutting the expenses of the household and that Steve Smith had taken over the finances and there wasn't the dough there to handle a lot of the things that Ethel had been used to," Tremblay said. "Steve Smith had said to Ethel, 'Hey, you've got to cut back on this stuff.' He laid the law down. He was a pretty tough guy. Lem asked me if I knew anyone in this area, knowing that this was horse country, who might be willing to take the horses. He said they were willing to give them away in order to cut expenses; that Ethel just couldn't manage to continue to keep them.

"I was rather surprised that she wouldn't even be allowed to have the horses, and I recall that she was very distraught. I was saddened by the fact that, gosh, she was made to look almost like poor folks."

Tremblay mentioned to Billings that he had a friend, Mrs. Magruder ("Posey") Dent, a Charlottesville horsewoman who owned a farm. Dent had had a passing acquaintance with Bobby and Ted, and her in-laws had lived in Greenwich for years and knew the Skakel family.

Soon after, Dent got a call from Tremblay. "Gerry explained to me that the Kennedys had a legal theory conceived by the old man that was called 'the poor widow's theory.' What it meant was that the money was always left to the kids in trusts and it left the widow, especially if she was a wealthy woman in her own right, with nothing. It seemed so horrible, so nasty to me. Then Gerry told me that Ethel needed to get rid of the horses because she had been left virtually nothing."

Dent then spoke to Lem Billings. "I was so shook up by the whole thing," she said later. "I tried to be businesslike and Lem said, 'Of course you're going to charge us board for the horses until they're sold,' and I said yes, I'd charge some board and sell the horses as fast as I could. I was taking them on consignment."

Not long after speaking with Billings, Posey Dent and a friend, Phyllis Jones, took a horse trailer to Hickory Hill, to clean out Ethel's stable.

It was dreary and beginning to rain when they pulled off Chain Bridge Road and rattled down the driveway to the paddock and stables. Dent had hoped someone had telephoned ahead to tell Ethel she was coming; she feared that neighbors might think she was stealing the horses and call the police. As she got out of the cab of the truck, Dent felt a sense of desolation about the place, that all the joy that had resounded there through the years had vanished. There was an eerie, haunted quality that made her want to leave as soon as possible. No one seemed to be around, but as she walked to the stables she looked up at the house and saw Ethel peering out of one of the windows. The widow gave Dent a quick wave and then disappeared from view.

"It was a very sad moment, just awful," Dent recalled. "I didn't go in the house and she never came out. We never exchanged a word. I never ever heard from her before, during, or after."

After talking to Billings, Dent had expected to find

perfectly healthy horses ready for resale. But when she got to the stables she was horrified by what she encountered.

"Two of the Kennedy children's favorite ponies, Geronimo and Atlas, were in terrible physical condition. They hadn't been very well treated, they hadn't been taken care of. Either they were fed too much, or not exercised. Their feet were just abominably sore. They were really badly handicapped. They were both lame," Dent said. "The whole thing still makes tears stream down my face when I think about it. She wanted the kids to have horses and wanted them to grow up with horses like she did. But the horses weren't cared for and that property at Hickory Hill was *tiny* with this teeny backyard with all these horses stuffed in there." Another horse, a big gray mare that had belonged to Ethel's eldest, Kathleen, was in relatively good condition.

Nearby, neatly stacked for Dent, were a number of red tack trunks, with the initials RFK on them, ready to be hauled away, along with numerous pairs of children's and adults' riding boots, children's riding hats, and various and sundry equestrian gear—saddles, bridles, crops.

"I was instructed to take what's called 'everything,' " she said. Dent and her friend loaded the horses and gear into the van and returned home.

"There wasn't any point in charging them board for the ponies because they were in such bad shape as to make them unsalable," she said. "I turned them out on the green grass until their feet healed a little bit and then I gave them away to some little kids. My job, as Lem said, was just to get rid of the horses and the stuff so it wouldn't cost anybody anything. What they were eliminating was any more expense."

A few weeks later Dent received what she remembered as a "heart-wrenching" telephone call from Kathleen Kennedy. "Mrs. Dent, may I have my horse?" Kathleen pleaded. "My mother wouldn't tell me where it was."

Dent said she got the feeling that Kathleen had

suddenly learned that the horse had been given away behind her back.

Relieved that no one had bought the mare, Dent had the horse and tack shipped to Kathleen's school.

Some years later Dent ran into Bobby Jr., when he was in law school, and recounted the story to him. "He said, 'Oh, my God, Posey, one of those was my favorite pony.' He was so sad. It was awful," she remembered.

• • •

Because of the alcoholism Ethel had witnessed among some of her siblings, she had always kept herself distanced from drinking. While she wasn't a teetotaler, a drink or two was her maximum. As a political wife, social drinking was expected. But she never took it too far. As a close friend observed: "Ethel knew what drinking could do to you, so she was very wary of it."

Now Ethel increased her drinking. And, according to colleagues, she began taking sleeping pills to help ease her emotional pain.

One of Ethel's secretaries, according to Barbara Gibson, asserted that Ethel had begun using what Gibson described as a "potentially lethal combination" of a sleeping pill and wine before going to bed. Rose Kennedy's secretary asserted that Ethel "had to drug herself to sleep, though Ethel did it with what seemed to be an attempt at class and sophistication."

If Ethel's stock of wine became low, Gibson contended, "staff members, friends, and anyone else . . . had to scour liquor stores in an ever-widening area until her needs could be satisfied."

On one occasion, Ethel was at Logan Airport in Boston awaiting a flight when she made a hurried call to Ted's Boston office asking that someone meet her at the gate with a case of her favorite wine. When one of Ted's aides arrived at the airport, he learned that Ethel had assigned the task to two others as well. As Gibson put it: "She so feared being without her nightcap, she refused to trust the effort of just one person."

Because of how erratic Ethel could sometimes be, her employees gossiped about her in private. One trusted aide recalled to another how Ethel openly discussed her use of what were believed to be tranquilizers. "She'd say things [to the other employee] like, 'Oh, I had a little bluey this morning to get up, and I had to take a little pinky last night.' She described them as pinkies and blueys."

Despite the hell she went through in the wake of Bobby's assassination, though, Ethel never developed a serious drug or drinking problem.

98 ✻ Little Brown Bag

DESPITE ALL OF his efforts, Steve Smith ultimately waged a losing battle to impose fiscal restraint on Ethel, who had now devised a unique way to make it appear that she was cutting back. She just stopped sending a number of her bills to the Park Agency.

Ethel had started getting dunning letters from creditors for amounts as small as $11.45. That one was from President Nixon's New York business manager, Vincent S. Andrews, whose firm had arranged with a messenger service to pick up a movie in Manhattan for showing at a Hickory Hill party. Ethel had never paid the bill.

"Merchants began calling the Senate, that's how bad it got," chuckled Richard Burke, who had been an aide to Ted Kennedy. "Ethel was definitely unwilling to deal with any of her creditors. It got totally out of control. The house was in chaos and she was grabbing at anybody who could give her some administrative help. When the calls came in from the bill collectors, they came to my desk. I remember she owed one local grocer eleven hundred dollars and he was screaming on the phone for his money. I called the office in New York and asked why the bill hadn't been paid. Joe Hakim, an aggressive guy who was running the Park Agency office for Steve Smith, said, 'I'm looking at her account and we have no back bills. The problem is she doesn't send them to us.'

"Finally, I talked to the Senator and said, 'Hickory Hill is just a mess.' Steve flew down and talked to Ethel. She complained during the meeting that she didn't have enough to live on. She admitted that she'd let the bills pile up until it became a crisis, then they'd have to pay. She was acting like a little girl—'I have responsibilities. I need money for the children, for the house, for the servants.' Then Steve would point out all these excessive expenditures that she'd made, like flying everybody first-class to Aspen. And then when they got there, they had destroyed the place. The owner of one condo called me at the office and pleaded with me, 'You have to do something. Her kids threw a cherry bomb in the toilet and blew it apart. They just threw out the toilet.' We had to pay for it. I remember he sent us a bill for eight or ten thousand dollars. The Senator looked at me and laughed. He said, 'Talk to Steve in New York and let him deal with it.' Afterward the condo owner called and said, 'Never again, no more Kennedys, absolutely not.' "

At one point, Ethel wangled an invitation to borrow her pal Averell Harriman's Sun Valley ski cottage. The two had been friends for years. After Harriman's first wife, Marie, died in September 1970, he gave her wedding ring to Ethel because Marie and Ethel had been so close, and Ethel continued to wear the ring years later. She also had been one of the witnesses at Harriman's next marriage, to Pamela. But despite their close ties, Ethel and her crew all but gutted Harriman's Idaho getaway house, packing the tiny place with some thirty people, and abandoning it dirty, with cigarette burns in the rugs.

It got so bad that a number of real-estate agents were reluctant to rent to Ethel, who one year resorted to using the alias John Wilbur in order to get a place. The co-owner of the Aspen Club spa finally denied access to the Kennedys because, "The kids were utterly wild. If they ate a meal, half of it was ground into the carpet. They were like banshees."

Added Burke: "Ethel never really gave Steve an excuse for her spending. Steve finally said, 'She's not going to be controllable. She's just going to be like this. She can't be left to stay within a budget.' When the bills came, Ted often said, 'Why doesn't she use her own money? Skakel money.' Ted had a fondness for Ethel, but they weren't particularly close, as the public generally thought. He treated her almost like a sick sister, talked down to her. He couldn't call Ethel and discuss anything with her. It was always an afterthought to include her. Jean and Eunice were the important ones."

A number of small merchants in McLean were left holding the bag for months before they were paid. "For a while it seemed Ethel just paid her bills in January," recalled one McLean merchant, "which meant if you did something for her in February you'd wait a year to get paid." Don Burns, owner of Burns Brothers Cleaners, recalled that Ethel had been behind in her bill to him for as much as "several thousand dollars, that's not an exaggeration. We had a terrible time getting her to sit down and write the checks." He said he finally got the matter settled by demanding that her secretary be given the authority to write and sign checks for household account items. Besides the slow payments, Burns found Ethel extremely demanding. "One secretary would come in with a pile of clothing to be cleaned at three o'clock and another would come back for it a half hour later. There was no organization."

Among the many cars the Kennedys had at Hickory Hill, Bobby's favorite had been a 1966 white Ford convertible. After his death, the car developed mechanical problems and Ethel had one of her people call Bobby Jones at B & M Exxon, a couple of miles from Hickory Hill, to pick it up and check it out. The car, which still sported old New York plates from when Bobby was a Senator, was towed to the shop. "Nobody had put oil in it and they drove it and the engine blew," Jones recalled. He telephoned Hickory Hill and gave his diagnosis to a member of Ethel's staff, with a five-hundred-dollar repair estimate. "They were supposed to let me know what to do but they never did," Jones said. "The car sat on the lot for two years, abandoned. Finally, I called and said that if they weren't going to fix it I had to be paid for storage. Ethel signed over the title to me and I dropped a new engine in it and drove that car for four or five years before I sold it, which I wish I'd never done because those cars are classics today." Jones said he had done other auto work for Ethel. "It sometimes took two, three, six months to get paid."

Another McLean merchant who had sold Ethel half a dozen bathing suits was forced to wait six months for payment.

A local plumber said, "It got so I didn't want to go out there and do any work because it took so long to get paid. And the plumbing out at Hickory Hill was a mess."

A friend of Ethel's, unaware of her spending habits, happened to be in Best & Co. when one of Ethel's secretaries came in with a long list of items, which she told the saleswoman to put on Mrs. Kennedy's charge. After Ethel's assistant left, the saleswoman chuckled, saying, "I wonder when we'll get paid."

A prominent Georgetown antique dealer in the seventies, Peter Mack Brown, was paid late by Ethel for items she had purchased. On occasion, Ethel would also take pieces, such as an antique chair, "on approval, have a party, use it, and bring it back the next Monday," said Michael Lehman, a friend and longtime associate of Brown's. "Peter was very free about it. Customers would often take things out on approval. But I think it became kind of a habit with her; she was standing out, and because of her name she got away with it."

In trying to cut her expenses, Ethel had begun bargaining for better deals by invoking the Kennedy name and playing on people's sympathy about her widowhood. "Don't you realize who you're talking to?" she'd say to shopkeepers. "I'm Mrs. Robert F. Kennedy. Don't you know how much I buy from you? Can't I get a better price?" She felt victorious, said Noelle Fell, if she secured a 10 percent discount. Friends recalled that Ethel also attempted to trade on her name in order to secure goods, such as skis and tennis rackets, for free. "She believed that the name 'Ethel Kennedy' was a good endorsement for a product," a member of the circle recalled. "She was always trying to hustle that way."

Whenever there was a big event now at Hickory Hill, Ethel arranged through Ted's Senate office to get loaner cars from local dealerships to transport guests. "We'd go to a local Pontiac dealership and say, 'Listen, we'll thank you in the program if you give us ten cars,' " recalled Richard Burke. "Ethel used us [Kennedy's office] all the time. If there was an immigration problem with any of the people who worked for her, we were always involved with it. We were using Senate employees to do errands for her."

Mary DeGrace, who had worked as a laundress for Ethel at the compound for years, receiving only a minimum wage and only one gift, a picture of Bobby after his death, quit when Ethel accused her of conspiracy to rip her off. "She thought I was sending out too many things to be cleaned. Ethel came into the laundry room and told me, 'You must be in cahoots with the laundry man. My laundry bill so far this year comes to seven hundred dollars, and you're going to pay for it.' So I told her she could wish with one hand and shit in the other and see which one got filled up first. Then I threw down the iron and walked out the door."

Ethel's failure to cut her spending infuriated her mother-in-law. "The worst thing Ethel could do in Mrs. Kennedy's eyes was be extravagant," said Rose's secretary, Barbara Gibson. "That was a big thing with Mrs. Kennedy because she was really stingy. She hated giving things to people and she hated the idea of anyone taking from her."

Rose Kennedy was especially furious when she heard the stories about Ethel's shopping sprees. One, in particular, involved a fashion show in New York where Ethel bought a Mary McFadden dress in five different colors; and then, at Bergdorf's, snapped up a half-dozen of the same expensive belt in different hues.

In order to get Steve Smith and Rose off her back, Ethel devised another scheme, dubbed "shop-return," to give the Park Agency the illusion that she'd finally gotten into line fiscally. She began using her powerful and respected name—Mrs. Robert F. Kennedy—to buy, use, and return items with impunity. After a time, some merchants wanted to bar their doors when they saw her coming; others prayed she wouldn't return at all.

Ethel's first visit to Saks West-End, a tony designer boutique in Chevy Chase, Maryland, was a memorable experience, employees recalled.

After a bit of browsing, Ethel approached Jane Abraham, the assistant manager, telling her she needed a dress for an upcoming event. Ethel then proceeded to pick out four or five pieces, finally choosing a pretty $750 black organza with a white collar by Oleg Cassini. "She looked quite nice in it," Abraham recalled. Rather than paying cash or using a credit card, Ethel asked to open a house account, delighting the shop manager. Having a Kennedy woman as a customer, any savvy retailer knew, could only generate good publicity and more business, even though they could be difficult to deal with. The dress was wrapped and Ethel was ushered to her car with a profusion of "Thank you, Mrs. Kennedy, please come back again." After Ethel drove away, the shop's owners, Ernest and Henry Marx, were ecstatic. "Jane, you're wonderful," she quoted them as saying. "My God, you sold Ethel Kennedy a dress."

A week later, Jane Abraham was leafing through the newspapers and came across a picture of Ethel wearing the dress. Thinking it would be good publicity for the store, she clipped and filed the item. A few days later, one of Ethel's servants arrived at the shop with the dress. "The maid said that Mrs. Kennedy had not worn it and wanted to return it," Abraham said. "I thought to myself, 'What gall that woman has.' "

To make matters worse, Abraham said, "the dress looked like a limp rag, [it was] dirty and had food stains.

I said, 'Mrs. Kennedy was photographed wearing that dress. I have a picture of her wearing that dress. You better take it back.' " Abraham could tell that the servant was distraught knowing she'd have to return to Hickory Hill with the garment. "So I told her, 'Tell Mrs. Kennedy we're not in the used-clothing business. If there's a problem have her call me.' "

Abraham thought that would be the end of it, but was soon proven wrong. Another Kennedy housemaid arrived at the shop, this time with the dress on a hanger, in a plastic bag, sporting a little paper collar from a dry-cleaning establishment. "The dress was still a bit limp because the cleaner hadn't sized it, which would have restored some stiffness to the fabric," Abraham said. Once again, Abraham was forced to tell the Kennedy employee that the dress had been worn. "It's clean! It's clean!" she replied. "Wait here," Abraham told the maid. Furious, she marched over to her desk and picked up her pen.

"Dear Mrs. Kennedy," Abraham recalled writing. "I'm terribly sorry but the dress has been altered, the dress has been cleaned, and we are not a secondhand store. If you don't care for the dress after wearing it, why don't you try [selling it to] one of the secondhand stores. There's Encores, there's Think New, there's Next to New." To make her case as direct as possible, Abraham attached the clipping that showed Ethel wearing the dress. The saleswoman noted, "It happens to look wonderful on you and I'm sure that if you do wear it again you will get great pleasure from it. . . ."

When several months had passed and Ethel still hadn't paid her bill for the dress, Jane Abraham met with the Marx brothers. "I said, 'She didn't pay for the dress; who needs more aggravation from her.' They didn't know what to do because at that time the Kennedys were held in very high esteem in this town."

The owners were naturally disappointed that they'd lost such a well-known customer, but they decided not to press for the payment. No one in the shop expected to see Ethel again. But about a year later she marched in, eager to buy and charge more clothing. "We did not sell her another dress," Abraham recalled. "She left empty-handed." Abraham maintained that the management had decided not to allow her to shop or charge anything; she'd essentially been banned. "She was asked to take her business elsewhere. Ethel was not happy," Abraham remembered. "She raised her voice some; she got kind of sassy and snotty. But she didn't throw anything at me."

Ethel also shopped at the Chevy Chase, Maryland, Saks Fifth Avenue, where she had arranged to have selections of apparel delivered to Hickory Hill on approval.

"She always expected a great deal of attention, and that was kind of annoying," said a longtime Saks employee. "Her secretary often called and asked us to send out clothes to Hickory Hill on a consignment basis. Those orders were handled in a special book at the store. We would send out fifty things; one dress would be picked out and forty-nine would come back. In general, the [Robert] Kennedys' return rate was tremendous. It got to the point where, if a telephone call came in from Hickory Hill, the salespeople just weren't interested in encouraging her to take merchandise, or even telling her what they had in stock. The store suddenly felt the glory of the Kennedys was not the glory of Saks Fifth Avenue anymore, and was not cost effective.

"The major aggravation was that a lot of times the merchandise would come back damaged. Belts were missing or other things were missing from the dresses. Some of the dresses had been worn. The items weren't always returned in good condition. If it was an important dress, then it couldn't be easily replaced and that was the kind of thing that would happen. It was very annoying for the store and the salespeople because nobody makes money off of damaged merchandise. Saks would try to recover the belt. Someone would call Mrs. Kennedy and say the store had received the returned merchandise, but a belt seems to be missing from such and such a dress and the answer would be, 'We will look for it. If we find it, we'll send it back.' It never came back. If Ethel

Kennedy was running a ship, it wasn't very tight. Secondly, Ethel would keep the merchandise out of circulation for a lengthy period of time, and that doesn't help a [sales] department."

Other incidents involving Ethel's shopping behavior began to surface in the seventies. The talk emanated from merchants and salespeople who savored such gossip, especially about the rich and famous. Because of Ethel's prominence, the stories eventually came to the attention of gossip columnists, such as Diana McLellan, who wrote "The Ear" in the *Washington Star*.

Years later those stories couldn't be confirmed because the memories of the merchants and salespeople involved had become clouded, or because they didn't want to embarrass the woman whom they felt had suffered enough. As Alice Dineen, who had headed the Regency Room, the couture salon at the Chevy Chase Saks Fifth Avenue, and who had often served Ethel, put it, "She definitely had her foibles and eccentricities. In fact, she was unique. But she had terrible tragedies and I don't think she should be torn down. There isn't a woman customer alive that at one time or another doesn't give you a problem, especially people in prominent places like Ethel Kennedy."

When Bloomingdale's, the trendy New York department store, opened two stores in the affluent northern Virginia and Maryland suburbs of Washington, Ethel became a spirited customer. After a few experiences with her, though, the Bloomies people, like clerks at other stores, wanted to take cover when they saw her coming. One disturbing incident that made the rounds once again involved the return of merchandise. Not long after Ethel had purchased a comforter at the Tyson's Corner store, she returned it in soiled condition. She had it cleaned and then instructed one of her cooks to take it back and get the credit. The employee complained, but Ethel insisted, and with great embarrassment he followed her instructions. It wasn't until later, as Bloomingdale employees were putting the merchandise back in stock, that they noticed the stains. But store management refused to make a stink about it because of Ethel's prominence.

Around the same time, the *Washington Post*'s gossip column "VIP" reported that "when Bloomingdale's employees slip off to the Forty Carrots for a health-juice break these days they amuse each other with accounts of Ethel Kennedy's shopping problems in outfitting her younger sons. One source says that outfits purchased the day before the dedication of the JFK Library in Massachusetts . . . came back the day after. It was assumed they did not fit or weren't suitable."

On another occasion, Ethel arrived at the Bloomingdale's White Flint Mall store in Bethesda, Maryland, and, for some five hours, using the store's personal shopping office, At Your Service, bought several thousand dollars' worth of towels, glasses, sheets, men's shirts and sweaters, skirts, and women's sweaters, most of it on sale.

The saleswoman who accompanied Ethel recalled how difficult she was. "She would go into the fitting room and try things on and throw the garments she didn't like on the floor, and I had to come in and hang it all up. I mean she was a real slob."

A month after Ethel's shopping spree the saleswoman received a telephone call from the secretary of the store manager at the Tyson's Corner store in Virginia.

"She said, 'Did you sell all these things to Mrs. Kennedy? The chauffeur is here returning everything and half the things have no tickets on them, and half the things look worn, and half the things are disheveled, all balled up together. There's so much stuff here and he doesn't have a sales ticket,' " recalled the saleswoman. "Ethel had sent the whole shmeer back, every last piece, and wanted the credit. I said, 'Well, yes, she did come over here before Christmas and bought a whale of a lot of stuff.' She said, 'Well, it's all over here and I think the best thing to do is put it in a van and send it over there.' I don't think they wanted to take it back; they wanted to see what I had to say about the condition of the merchandise."

After talking to Tyson's, the saleswoman telephoned Hickory Hill and reached one of Ethel's secretaries, who explained that Mrs. Kennedy had changed her mind and decided she didn't need or want the merchandise. The saleswoman said it appeared that some of the clothing had been worn and, if that was the case, it would be sent back to Hickory Hill and that Bloomingdale's would expect payment.

"The secretary, who was very snotty, said, 'Oh, Mrs. Kennedy won't put up with that. She's not going to accept any of it back.' I said, 'Well, Mr. Bloomingdale and Mr. Traub won't put up with it, either.' "

About a week later, Ethel's purchases arrived at the White Flint store.

"It could have come from JCPenney's, for all I knew," recalled the saleswoman. "It was just a pile of clothing and household debris, including a toaster and some other stuff thrown in."

Most of the items, according to the saleswoman, were shipped back to Ethel. "Of course, she didn't pay her bill, and I heard New York closed her account," she said. "If there is an excessive amount of returns on an account, they close it."

Whenever she visited the Kennedys' Palm Beach mansion, Ethel's first order of business would be a trip to Worth Avenue.

"She'd go to the stores, Courrèges or one of those places, and buy sweaters, shorts, not dressy things, and she'd wear them during her visit and then when she left to fly home she'd leave them piled up in my office for me to return them," said Barbara Gibson. "When Mrs. [Rose] Kennedy found out, she told me to give the things to the chauffeur to return. The people in the stores were used to getting the stuff back. When they saw me or the chauffeur coming with the clothing, they'd laugh and say, 'Here she comes. Write Ethel a credit slip.' It really was a joke after a while. The store owners wrote it off as p.r. All those things that she went out and bought extravagantly, she would return. Ethel had gotten a reputation for not paying, for being very cheap."

By the end of the seventies, Ethel's arrogance toward merchants reached its zenith when she was sued by a small catering service for failure to pay a $535 bill for a rush Christmas dinner that she ordered while vacationing in Aspen with Ted and some of her children.

"Ethel had returned to the condo with some two dozen guests and had suddenly decided on a big Christmas dinner," said Noelle Fell. "She asked one of the maids, who was an excellent cook herself and could have prepared the meal, to get a caterer. Mrs. Kennedy was in a bad mood that day. David had been there and was causing a ruckus, so she was not very happy. The maid finally talked the caterer into preparing the dinner, but they told her that it would cost more because they had to pay their people overtime. The maid told Mrs. Kennedy and Mrs. Kennedy told her, 'It doesn't matter what it costs, just have it done.' "

But after Ethel and her guests ate the dinner, Ethel refused to pay the bill, claiming that Dean Small and Tom Gerlak, the owners, had overcharged her for the twelve-pound roast, green beans, a dip, chips, baked potatoes, French bread, and dessert—a huge walnut cookie cake with raspberry and pecan filling.

Small said he gave the bill to Ethel the day after Christmas. "She was really furious." He recalled her saying, "The whole meal's worth twenty-five dollars."

"Not only didn't she want to pay the bill," recalled Noelle Fell, "but she was pissed off at the maid because she had agreed to the price. Now that she had impressed her friends with the dinner, she didn't care what happened."

As the wheels of justice ground forward, Ethel tried to get out of appearing publicly in court, but the judge denied her motion to testify in depositions. Ethel gave the appearance that she was taking the matter lightly. Prior to the scheduled trial date, in an oblique reference to the case, she sent out valentines to friends showing her dressed in a maid's uniform, serving a turkey. The caption said she'd cater "even if you sue." A week before the trial Ethel reached an out-of-court settlement with the caterers "for a sum that was satisfactory to both parties," Small said at the time. "Le Cuisinier has no animosity toward Mrs. Kennedy. We feel we were just in what we did and what we charged. We'd serve her in the future—if the payment was made in advance."

99 * Ethel and Andy

WITH HER PERKS slashed dramatically and with the ongoing responsibility for eleven children, Ethel's future was looking less than bright. She needed a husband, members of her inner circle felt, and they had started suggesting she follow her sister-in-law Jackie's example and find a rich one.

"We hinted to her that she needed someone to make her life comfortable again," a pal said. "Ethel's response was, 'We'll see.' "

Early bets were being wagered on genial Andy Williams, whom Ethel had known since the mid-sixties when Bobby invited the singer and his pretty, Paris-born actress wife, Claudine Longet, into their group of celebrity pals.

Williams, who would become one of Ethel's favorites at Hickory Hill and Hyannis Port, had initially failed to see the value of befriending the Kennedys, according to his friend, TV producer Pierre Cossette.

"I was playing golf with Andy one day at the height of his television years," Cossette recalled, "and he says, 'God, I just got a call from Ethel and Bobby Kennedy and they want me to go down to Palm Springs. I have a lot of work to do and I don't want to go down there, and they keep calling.' "

For Cossette, the conversation was déjà vu. A few

years earlier his friend Peter Lawford had asked him for a favor: Could Cossette, then a talent manager, convince his client, popular singer Vic Damone, to fly up to Fresno and help campaign for Jack Kennedy? Damone's response was, "Jesus Christ, *Fresno?*"

This time around Cossette knew better. "You should pay attention to their call because that's how Bob Hope and Bing Crosby stayed stars for a hundred years," he advised the singer. "They developed all of those outside relationships that were not just show business. This is very, very key to your career and success. Bing has all kinds of friends in politics and so does Bob, and that just spreads out and boomerangs through all the media. So, Jesus, if Bobby and Ethel Kennedy are calling you, don't be a schmuck." Cossette continued, "Andy said, 'You really think so?' I said, 'I'm positive.' So he got in his golf cart and went down to the snack bar and called them. He came back and he said, 'Okay, we're gonna go.' When he came back from Palm Springs, he said, 'I love that Bobby and I love that Ethel. We spent four great days together.' So that was the beginning of the involvement."

The relationship between the Kennedys and the Williamses blossomed quickly. Andy and Claudine were usually at the top of the list for parties at Hickory Hill and weekends at Hyannis Port. The two handsome couples skied together at Sun Valley and Aspen, sailed off of Cape Cod, shot the rapids on the Colorado River, and cruised the Caribbean. Claudine and Andy even named the last of their three children after Bobby.

The couples had grown so close that some insiders began to suspect that a flirtation—possibly even more—had developed between Bobby and Claudine by the time Bobby had become a Senator.

Peter Lawford, the clan's sex guru, actually told confidants that Bobby had had a "brief, rather intense affair" with Claudine, who was fifteen years his junior, during that time. Lawford's last wife, Patricia Seaton Lawford, had heard about the affair from her husband. "Peter was definite that Bobby and Claudine had had an affair. Peter had probably heard it through some very reliable source who was present. I don't think Bobby would have picked up the phone and said, 'Hey, guess what, Peter, I slept with Claudine Longet last night.' Peter and Jack were more suited to each other. Peter's relationship with Bobby was more tense."

The closeness of the relationship between the two couples was indeed intense, underscored not only by their frequent visits and trips, but also by the enormous amount of Bobby and Ethel memorabilia that Andy and Claudine kept in their Beverly Hills mansion. Walls and tabletops were covered with silver-framed photos of the two couples together, or of Bobby and Ethel separately. Gold-tooled leather albums filled with snapshots of their shared trips and vacations were piled high on cocktail tables. When the Williamses separated after Bobby's death, Claudine left behind many photographs that had been signed by Ethel to Andy. The one picture Claudine took with her and treasured the most was of Bobby holding an umbrella in the rain. The inscription read, "If you ever need to share a raincoat . . ."

Andy had a special photograph, too. It was of Ethel, Bobby, and their children, and he kept it in his private office. "This is what you get, Andy, with Ethel," Bobby had written in one corner. In another part of the photo, Ethel had added her own comment; she'd drawn a heart pierced by Cupid's arrow, with the words "That's O.K., Andy. I think you'd make a great dad."

In 1971, when the Williamses were still only informally separated, Claudine explained away the intimate inscriptions by saying, "It's the sort of thing we were all always sending to each other. It was a game. An inside, hip sort of game."

But she did acknowledge that she had had a very special relationship with Bobby, one that didn't exist with Ethel.

"We could talk in the way a girl and a man can talk, the way women are almost never able to talk, the way I was never able to talk to Ethel . . . not chitchat," she said. "When Bobby died I lost interest in the Kennedys.

There was no one for me to talk to. I drifted away. There was just no one there."

Kennedy friends remembered that Bobby had been very attracted to Claudine, a pretty Parisian who was petite and wiry like Ethel and whose sharp, angular face had an almost Kennedy cast. An aspiring actress, Claudine had come to the United States after several theatrical appearances in Paris and Rome the same year that Jack had won the Presidency. In December 1961, Andy, then thirty-one, married Claudine, who was just nineteen. A huge success by that point, Andy was instrumental in helping his young bride's career get off the ground, playing sex-kitten roles on such TV programs as "Kraft Theater," "Dr. Kildare," "Combat," and "Rat Patrol." She also made a couple of films, most notably *The Party,* a zany beatnik farce with Peter Sellers. But none of her roles garnered much critical acclaim. It wasn't until 1977, two years after her divorce from Andy, that she received worldwide attention for a real-life melodrama: she was convicted of criminally negligent homicide in the shooting of her lover, Vladimir "Spider" Sabich, a professional ski racer, at his home near Aspen. Claudine testified that the gun had fired accidentally—a claim that was famously parodied in a "Saturday Night Live" skit. She eventually served thirty days in jail.

Friends recalled how Ethel had always grown dreamy-eyed whenever she heard Andy sing "Canadian Sunset," and "The Village of St. Bernadette," two of his big hits from the fifties.

"Andy offered the kind of clean-cut, all-American, low-brow entertainment Ethel savored," a mutual friend said later. "It was Ethel who had coerced Bobby into calling Andy in the first place and bringing him into their circle."

After they became close friends, Ethel often commented on how much Andy reminded her of Bobby; both were short, slight, and somewhat rugged-looking; both had toothy grins and dimples.

There were odd similarities in Ethel's and Andy's backgrounds, too, which they both felt connected them.

Like George Skakel, Sr., Jay Williams, Andy's father, had started out as a railroad man, a mail clerk, and like Ethel's father, he too had an entrepreneurial spirit. An amateur musician, he had trained his pretty daughter and four good-looking sons—Andy, born in 1930, was the youngest—to sing, hoping to get them into show business. He first booked them as a "family choir" into the Presbyterian church in their hometown of Wall Lake, Iowa. After that things moved quickly.

By the early fifties, while Ethel was learning to be a Kennedy wife, and Bobby was slogging through his law books, Andy, already known for his smooth delivery of love ballads and his relaxed and casual manner, had made his way to New York, where he scored a big recording contract, a regular spot on the "Steve Allen Show," and finally his own long-running, Emmy Award–winning variety show on NBC.

Over the years Andy had become a very wealthy man—at the height of his career he was the country's best-selling male vocalist—and had managed to amass an enormous art collection that included works by Frankenthaler, Diebenkorn, Oldenburg, Picasso, Pollock, and Klee. His art was one of the interests he shared with Ethel, along with tennis and dogs.

Rich, handsome, powerful, and as comfortable as an old shoe, Andy seemed a perfect marriage prospect for Ethel. Even his estranged wife Claudine agreed on that when Ethel and Andy were first linked romantically in the press in the early seventies. "If Ethel and Andy should get married, it would not make me unhappy," Claudine said. "It would be a great thing for America. I mean, having her marry such a wholesome boy-next-door type."

Not long after Bobby died, Ethel made Andy's rendition of "Battle Hymn of the Republic" the number-one song on her home jukebox and ordered a member of her house staff to buy up every Andy Williams record he could find on the Cape.

As early as the fall of 1970, Ethel's relationship with Andy showed signs of becoming seriously romantic.

When he hosted a Thanksgiving TV special at Washington's Ford's Theater, Ethel sat in the audience with her pal David Brinkley, her escort for the evening. But members of the audience noticed that Ethel only had eyes for Andy. When he sang the word *love,* observers agreed, he looked straight at Ethel with a meaningful smile.

A couple of months later, with Andy at her side, Ethel showed up in a sexy white hot-pants jumpsuit under a see-through skirt for a benefit at the new Kennedy Center in Washington. Photos taken of the two suggested nothing more than platonic friendship. But the *Washington Post*'s Maxine Cheshire, writing for the *Ladies' Home Journal,* reported, "Ethel and Andy held hands under the table and sipped champagne from a single shared glass." Later, Andy and Ethel were spotted being openly affectionate. When someone asked Andy whether he thought they'd get married, he said, "We just might. But first I'd have to work a few things out."

A deluge of items began appearing in gossip columns: Ethel spotted in the audience at a taping of Andy's show in Los Angeles; Ethel and Andy together at ringside for the Ali-Frazier fight at Madison Square Garden. In the summer of 1971 reports of an Ethel-Andy marriage began appearing. *The Lakes Region Trader,* a little paper in Laconia, New Hampshire, quoted reliable sources as saying that the two would tie the knot on a New Hampshire mountain over Labor Day and that a champagne party was being organized at the Waterville Valley Resort, owned by Kennedy-clan pal Tom Corcoran. A journalist trying to promote a Kennedy book was "telling pals that he believes Ethel and Andy will make an announcement any day." The pulp magazines also got into the act. The headline on the cover of the June 1971 issue of *Screenland* screamed: MARTHA MITCHELL TELLS US ETHEL KENNEDY AND ANDY WILLIAMS TO WED. (Martha Mitchell, wife of Richard Nixon's Attorney General, subsequently expressed shock that she'd been quoted by the magazine. "What in the name of God do I know about Ethel Kennedy?" she gasped when asked for comment. "I have never even heard this discussed and I have never met Andy Williams in my life.") Mrs. Mitchell also sent a note to Ethel explaining that she had never said anything of the kind. Ethel thanked Martha for replying to the story, and sent along another clip that declared: CARY GRANT LIFTS THE LID ON HIS ROMANCE WITH ETHEL KENNEDY.

Ethel's purported hunt for a potential husband had become a zany romp. The media was having a field day—and so was Ethel.

"She thought it was all a riot," recalled George Terrien. "She loved the attention she was getting; she loved the fact that she was suddenly considered a femme fatale."

Meanwhile, Andy played along, raving to his friends that Ethel was a great gal; so much fun, that they had so much in common, that she was a marvelous catch.

Claudine, though, didn't buy it. "Andy and I see so much of each other," she said at the time. "I kid him about what the fan magazines write. I say, 'I read that you are going to marry Ethel.' He says, 'Yeah, and you wouldn't believe the people who talk to me now who never talked to me before.' " Claudine felt Andy was "enjoying all the publicity and all those glamorous dinners." The bottom line was that she didn't see marriage in their future. "Not unless I have become insensitive to what my husband is thinking and feeling and I know I have not. . . ." Ethel and Andy, she believed, were not quite as well suited as many thought, either. "Ethel is so strong, so sportive," she said. "Andy has no taste for sports. He isn't coordinated. He is brilliant and creative, but not athletic. He is scared to death of water and he is no good at skiing."

Observed a friend of Andy's years later, "He was always quite an operator and Andy has always come first with Andy. The publicity value in whatever was going on between him and Ethel was enormous, great for the career."

Parade magazine touched on exactly that point in its

popular celebrity question-and-answer section on Sunday, August 29, 1971:

> . . . Mrs. Robert F. Kennedy has no press agent, nor does her involved, ebullient lifestyle need one. However, ever since the beginning of the singer's idolatrous friendship with the Kennedys, Andy's "relationship" with Robert and Ethel has always landed him in the news. . . . If Andy makes a "secret" visit to Hyannis Port, Mass., it suddenly turns out to be no secret. Ethel Kennedy is already heralded as a visitor to Andy's Las Vegas opening, though it hasn't happened yet. No one ever said that Williams isn't his own best press agent.

For months, Pierre Cossette had been reading the gossip items and hearing Andy's boasts about his relationship with Ethel. Having advised the singer more than a decade earlier to ingratiate himself with the Kennedys, Cossette was now finally about to meet the reputed woman of Andy's dreams.

"One day, in the midst of all that hullabaloo about the two of them, Andy says to me, 'Come on, I want you to come to Washington with me and meet her,' " Cossette recalled. "Andy said, 'Ethel's going to pick us up at the airport and we're going to stay at Hickory Hill, and we're going to play tennis and swim and eat.' I said, 'Okay.' At this point, I was kind of anxious to meet her. As a show-business guy, I knew all the show folks, but I didn't know very much about the political life. I had this image of the limousines and all that stature.

"So we get to the airport and I'm looking around and this old, beat-up station wagon with, God, a kid sticking out of it, and an old dog yappin', pulls up and I hear this voice, 'Andy! Andy!' And I say, 'Andy, who the fuck is that?' He said, 'That's Ethel.' I said, '*That's* Ethel Kennedy?' I couldn't believe it. I *could not* believe it. She looked like anything in the world other than Ethel Kennedy. I was absolutely stunned. Andy had been married to Claudine, a real beauty, and here's this chick who looked like Raggedy Ann. I was dumbfounded and Andy was laughing. He said, 'Well, that's Ethel.' And that remained Ethel for the twenty years I knew her."

Cossette, though, who would have some interesting adventures with Ethel through the years, did see almost instantly how she could be attractive to a man.

"She had enormous enthusiasm; the energy that came from her was huge. She was genuinely inquisitive but asked simple questions that were kind of unsophisticated for a woman of her stature. She had an absolutely, completely simplistic approach to everything. She'd look at you with those eyes and ask questions like a kid in seventh grade: 'Oh, gee, I didn't know that.' "

Once, when Cossette was visiting Ethel at Hyannis Port, he mentioned in passing that his friend, the singer John Raitt, Bonnie Raitt's father, was appearing at the local theater-in-the-round. Ethel was thrilled, bubbling over, jumping up and down, like a child. "Oh, John Raitt! I love John Raitt! You *know* John? We must go see John Raitt." That night, Ethel began coaxing Cossette to call Raitt for a get-together. "Let's take him out sailing on the *Resolute,*" she suggested. "I said, 'Jesus, Ethel, he's doing a show tonight.' And she said, 'Bring him out! Come on! Come on!' " That night, after the show, Cossette telephoned Raitt at his hotel and extended Ethel's invitation. "John, tomorrow we're going out with Ethel Kennedy. We're going to take a ride on her boat." Raitt was less then enthusiastic. He explained that he shouldn't be doing a lot of running around, that he needed to protect his voice for the show.

"We're talking *Ethel Kennedy,*" Cossette reiterated firmly. John Raitt relented.

"The next day John shows up and he's expecting this three-hundred-foot Kennedy-style yacht and she's got the *Resolute,* this little bullshit sixteen-foot boat that's got holes and fourteen kids in it," Cossette chuckled.

"So we get in this boat with the fourteen kids and the sixty-five sandwiches and the two dogs and it can barely keep afloat. I know John very well, and the one thing he does not like to do is perform without an orchestra, without lights, without a sound system. So Ethel says, 'Children, wait'll you hear this . . . wait'll you hear this, children. Mommy was there opening night at *Carousel* and John sang. . . . Do that one John, oh, you know, "My Boy Bill." Now John, how does that go? Oh, come on. Do it! Do it! Listen children, listen!' At this point John is absolutely staring knives at me. He couldn't believe what was happening. Ethel's saying, 'Now you must do this, you must do this for the children.' He's in this boat and he's now singing 'My Boy Bill' . . . When he's finished Ethel says, 'What's that thing you did from *Pajama Game?* Listen to this one, kids, you'll know this one,' and he's standing in this boat and she's now got him doing his entire repertoire, and, to my absolute amazement, John's getting into it. Ethel said, 'Isn't he wonderful, children?' And the kids couldn't have fucking cared less. They wanted to hear a little Simon and Garfunkel. When we got back to the house I said, 'Ethel, I have never in my experience seen anything like that. You'd make the greatest producer in the history of show business.'

"Ethel loved being around the show-business people. She was very entranced by their accomplishments. And they were drawn to her too because they knew they were greatly appreciated as artists.

"She had all the attributes of a celebrity and she was also just like the lady next door. She was either in a dirty old pair of Levi's with part of her ass showing, or she was in some kind of a gown that she put together in three seconds before she had to go on. She was a very unusual woman."

But she did not seem to be a woman in love, at least as far as Cossette could see. Cossette found no indication that the relationship between Ethel and Andy was anything other than platonic. "We used to hang out and we had a lot of fun and so on, but Andy never talked to me about a romance with Ethel Kennedy. I'd tease him about it—'Well, why won't you marry Ethel? You'd be king of Washington'—and he'd just laugh. Andy himself once said, 'It would take quite a man to marry Ethel.'

"They didn't have that kind of relationship," Cossette said. "It wasn't close. After Andy divorced Claudine, he had two great girls that he lived with for long periods of time. One was a therapist in a hospital and an interior decorator; the other one worked in Andy's company."

Through the years, Ethel and Andy remained close friends. At his fifty-third birthday party at Washington's Jockey Club, she affectionately pushed his face in the cake, which wasn't as bad as the time she poured red wine over his head at a party and stained a priceless Persian carpet.

Sixteen years after his divorce from Claudine, Williams, sixty, married a pretty Aspen hotel hostess who was twenty-five years his junior. Claudine had also remarried. After serving her jail term for shooting the skier, she tied the knot with her defense attorney.

100 ✻ *Dating Game*

THROUGH THE SEVENTIES and eighties a number of prominent men were linked to Ethel, such as *Look* magazine's Warren Rogers. Like Andy, he was an old friend of Ethel and Bobby's. According to members of Ethel's circle, Rogers had been dating Ann Brinkley, ex-wife of NBC's David Brinkley, until Ethel had "stolen" Rogers away from her.

One of those Ann Brinkley had confided in was Coates Redmon, who had handled organization and press for the Robert F. Kennedy Journalism Awards, and was constantly having nasty run-ins with Ethel. "I suppose the reason Ann talked to me about what happened with Warren was because I was having my own personal hard time with Ethel at the time. Ann had an antique store in Georgetown and I was in there one day and she told me totally gratuitously and in a rueful way that Ethel had stolen Warren. Ann considered Ethel an absolute rat."

Another friend said, "Warren was attractive. Ann thought she had a corner on him and Ethel threw herself at him."

Speculation about a romance between Ethel and Rogers began in the spring of 1970 when the two showed up together at the Shoreham Hotel's Blue Room to hear singer Jack Jones. "Weight-conscious women in the Blue Room enviously eyed Mrs. Kennedy, the mother of eleven children, as she danced cozily with Rogers," wrote *Washington Star* society reporter Gwen Dobson. "She wore a form-fitting pale pink dress. . . . Romantic speculation was rife among observers who know Rogers was widowed about a year ago."

Eighteen months later Ethel was photographed standing with Rogers, smiling proudly, at his inauguration as president of the National Press Club.

Rumors also flew that Ethel was romantically involved with New York attorney William vanden Heuvel, a longtime aide of Bobby's. At the time, vanden Heuvel, a Catholic, was separated from his wife. Friends of Ethel's tried to promote the "romance" with the press, telling the *Washington Post*'s Maxine Cheshire that vanden Heuvel "is being mentioned more and more frequently as a suitor with serious intentions about Ethel Kennedy." Cheshire quoted one intimate of Ethel's as saying, "He makes a wonderful substitute father for Ethel's children. He's in a position to devote himself to helping her bring them up the way she wants." Cheshire wrote that a friend of vanden Heuvel had telephoned him to ask about the rumors and he replied, "It would be the most wonderful thing in my life. Why don't you call and ask her? If she says yes, call me back." Everyone jumped on the story, even after vanden Heuvel denied the *Washington Post* account that he and Ethel actually were considering marriage. Once again *Screenland* was on the spot with "exclusive" photos the magazine claimed were of Ethel and vanden Heuvel attending a charity ball in New York. The man turned out to be Lem Billings.

Hollywood gossip columnist Dorothy Manners quoted a close friend of Ethel's as saying of the vanden Heuvel speculation, "Ethel is an old-fashioned Catholic. She has never gone along with the innovations within the church. . . . So, it would be a terrible wrench in her devout beliefs to marry a man whose wife is still living even though vanden Heuvel is himself a Catholic. I don't see a marriage there myself."

Names of other purported suitors—New York Governor Hugh Carey, Los Angeles businessman Don Klosterman, ABC news and sports executive Roone Arledge, Norton Simon president David Mahoney, sportscaster Frank Gifford—continued to surface, making Ethel seem like the world's most sought-after merry widow.

Like many of her other suitors, Gifford had been a friend of both Bobby and Ethel's, having gotten to know them when Bobby was Attorney General, even though Gifford had been an avid supporter of Richard Nixon in the 1960 campaign. One afternoon at Hyannis Port, sailing aboard the *Resolute* with Ethel at the helm, he saw how crazy she could be. Ethel and Eunice had begun playing a game of chicken in their respective boats, heading straight at one another. "I took only one look at the set of Ethel's jaw and thought, 'Oh, my God, she's not going to back off!' I know nothing about sailing, but something told me no rule of the sea would come into play here," Gifford recalled. "At the last minute, Eunice swerved. Ethel did not even blink. Had both of them been alone on those boats, I suspect that would have been the end of the boats." Not long after, Eunice got her revenge. Ethel, Gifford, and others were having cocktails when Eunice came through the French doors with a garden hose and soaked Ethel and everyone present. "No one [laughed] harder than a thoroughly drenched Ethel," said Gifford.

Gifford had become a frequent dinner guest at Hickory Hill in the mid- to late-seventies, and Ethel's pals were putting out the word. "If he wasn't married, she'd grab him in a minute." Gifford was in the process of getting a divorce from his wife, Maxine, who had multiple sclerosis. Like Ann Brinkley, she had once been close to Ethel, but that was before Frank and Maxine split.

"Mrs. Kennedy was crazy about Frank," recalled Noelle Fell. "Big-time, teenager crazy. When she knew he was coming for dinner, she'd giggle, she couldn't stand it. 'Oh, God,' she'd say—and go make herself up. All the members of the staff would say, 'Frank Gifford's coming; she'll be in a good mood now.' Mrs. Kennedy would look the best she could for him. In the years I worked for her I would have said he would be her pick, even though I believe it was all one-sided."

At a dinner party at Hickory Hill, recalled a friend from college, Ethel let everyone know how she felt about Gifford. "She set up a table for just the two of them. It was very private and she never gave it a thought how it would look to everyone else who was present." By the late seventies, Ethel and Frank began appearing together in public, dining and dancing at Georgetown bistros. While nothing ever came of Ethel's friendship with Gifford, her son Michael married Gifford's daughter Victoria in 1981. The two met in 1974 when Victoria worked as an intern in Ted Kennedy's office while staying at Hickory Hill.

For a time, there was talk that Ethel might become the First Lady of New York. Hugh Carey seemed to have dropped his longtime date, Anne Ford Uzielli, in favor of Ethel. She and Carey had started seeing a lot of each other and were, for a time, spending every weekend together. Friends were saying the Governor was soundly smitten. "Ethel is really incredible," Carey told a friend.

Ethel thrived on compliments from her male friends, and they were quick to oblige her. "She liked to hear how pretty she looked, what a good athlete she was," Fell said. "They knew that's what she expected. She just loved attention from the men."

On one occasion, Ethel arrived unexpectedly at the

Kennedys' oceanfront estate in Palm Beach with a man, infuriating Rose, who had been staying at the house at the time. "Mrs. Kennedy made her leave because she didn't like the idea of her having a boyfriend by the pool," recalled secretary Barbara Gibson. "Ethel and the man were openly showing affection and Mrs. Kennedy disapproved."

Another time, Ethel had mailed out Valentine's Day cards with a photo of her sitting on Rosey Grier's lap and the words "Won't you be my Valentine?" Somehow one of the cards got into the hands of Rose. "Mrs. Kennedy had a fit," said Barbara Gibson. "She wrote to Ethel saying, 'I don't think it's wise to spend the Kennedy money on things like this.' "

Ethel loved being around men. She had started playing doubles once a week at indoor courts in McLean, just her and three fellows. "Women's tennis bores the tears out of me," she said, although in the mid-seventies she had become an ardent fan of Martina Navratilova, whom she found "magnificent." Ethel was the only woman on the board of the RFK Foundation. She let it be known that she found most women uninteresting and unintelligent, and scoffed at the growing feminist movement. "I just think we've lost what should be the main emphasis on motherhood and being good wives. People seem almost ashamed of it," she said. It was clear, friends observed, that Ethel was in conflict about her own role as a woman. While highly competitive herself, she retained old-fashioned notions about relationships and the roles of women and men. Some felt that Ethel's toughness and competitiveness actually frightened potential suitors. *Washingtonian* magazine, in a humorous article on dominant women who scare men, listed Ethel among the "Scary Emeritus" alongside Nancy Reagan.

Ethel had begun to advertise openly that she was available, though most of her efforts seemed in jest. At one point she had started wearing a bunch of tiny gold keys on a slender gold necklace ring. When she was asked what the keys unlocked, she responded, "Love," but she didn't say whose. One year she had a giant poster designed that superimposed pictures of herself and all of her children against a Mother Goose drawing. She then sent it to interested men with the following poem:

> There Was An Old Lady Who Lived In A Shoe.
> She Had So Many Children She Didn't Know
> What To Do
> She'd Marry ANYBODY—Even You.

During the height of her frenzied dating period, Ethel devoted an inordinate amount of time preparing for the man's arrival, sometimes hours, according to Noelle Fell, who helped dress her. In an effort to make herself more appealing, Ethel would wear his favorite color. Under her slinky dresses she had started wearing either padded bras, which she bought a dozen at a time from Saks Fifth Avenue, or special push-up supports to make her small breasts appear larger. She had also begun waxing portions of her body to get rid of body hair. "Her arms and legs were real hairy, and she had facial hair," Fell said. "She'd go into her bathroom, lock the door, warm up the wax, and apply it. You could hear her in there yelling 'Ouch! Ouch!' as she stripped it off because it hurt like hell. She would do that when she was expecting a man she really wanted to impress, usually on a weekly basis."

In the end, despite all appearances to the contrary, Ethel never had any real intention of remarrying. She would always have one excuse or another for friends when a prospective candidate's name was brought up. "He's not Catholic," she'd groan. Or, "He's divorced, I can't marry him." She once joked to Frank Mankiewicz, "You know what'll happen. I just know it. In 1990, the Catholic Church will say that it's perfectly all right for a Catholic to marry a divorced person. And worse—they'll say it was all right all along! And there I'll be—too late!"

Mankiewicz said later, "Whenever I see someone linked with her, on the cover of one of those magazines they sell in grocery stores, I call her and kid her about it."

It had all been somewhat of a game. Ethel had

always known that she would dedicate her life to Bobby's memory. She talked to him constantly, and she had never removed her wedding rings. At a hockey match to benefit retarded children in Madison Square Garden in 1974, six years after Bobby's death, Ethel shook hands with a blind child. When he asked her whether she was Rose Kennedy, Ethel answered, "No, I'm Ethel, Bobby's wife."

"We'd be in a car looking for a parking spot," said a confidante, "and Ethel would say, 'Don't worry, Bobby will direct me to one.' She talked to him just as though he was right there. In a restaurant she'd say, 'Bobby, what should I order . . .' To the children she'd say, 'Your father won't like this, he'll be mad.' In discussions with friends, she'd say, 'The Senator would never agree with this.' It was eerie and it was quite sad." Ethel had become so obsessed with the correctness of a painting of Bobby that she went through two artists before she finally unveiled the final version at the Justice Department in March 1975. It was a boyish portrait of Bobby—hair windblown, hands stuffed in the pockets of rumpled khaki pants. It was a painting that she felt showed his "compassion, significance, and concern and really catches Bobby's spirit."

Friends said they would be shocked if Ethel ever had a physical relationship with a man after Bobby's death. Ethel's brother Jim Skakel said, "We nicknamed her 'The Virgin of McLean.' "

Ethel had turned both Hickory Hill and her home in the compound into shrines to Bobby. There wasn't a room in either house that didn't have photographs of Bobby plastering the walls or spilling over tabletops; there were literally hundreds of them. Inside her closets were life-size photos of Bobby that often frightened guests who happened to open one of them unawares. Attending a party at Hickory Hill, Barbara Howar had somehow wandered upstairs and into Ethel's dressing room and bathroom. "There were pictures of Bobby. She also had a tape that David Brinkley had put together for her of love songs from the fifties that she and Bobby must have liked. The label on the tape said, 'For Ethel to take a bath by from David Brinkley.' From her tub she could listen to music and see all of the photos. That bathroom was like a shrine. Ethel had become the keeper of the flame, to keep the legend intact—and the legend was falling apart. But she believed Bobby—and the Kennedys—were special and different, and she wanted to keep the lamp lit."

As one member of Ethel's circle said later, "The ghost of Bobby haunted Hickory Hill. How in the world any man ever thought they could win her and compete with Bobby Kennedy's spirit, I'll never know."

George Terrien agreed. "The whole Skakel family hoped she'd find someone and get married. But down deep we knew she never would. The Kennedy name meant too much to her. She sacrificed a lot in those years, but that's one thing she'd cling to until the day she died."

101 * *Anger and Fury*

RUTH DARMSTADTER, EXECUTIVE director of the Robert F. Kennedy Journalism Awards program, had for the most part successfully avoided contact with Ethel. A professional writer and researcher, Ruth had heard from colleagues how abrasive, sharp-tongued, and tyrannical Ethel could be, but had never had firsthand experience. Luckily, there had always been a buffer between her and the widow, most notably longtime family soldier Dave Hackett, executive director of the Robert F. Kennedy Memorial, the umbrella organization for the journalism awards and related programs. Hackett often boasted to his employees, "Don't worry, I can handle her."

But as time neared for the latest annual awards ceremony, Hackett developed serious stomach problems and had to be hospitalized. Others charged with keeping Ethel at bay managed to find their own excuses to distance themselves from her, leaving Ruth directly in the line of fire.

One late spring afternoon the telephone rang at the memorial's townhouse offices in Georgetown.

It was Ethel calling. Ruth, she said, needed to drop whatever she was doing and come help her at once. She had to make a quick decision on which tablecloth should be used at the forthcoming awards luncheon. She instructed the executive director to pick up a sample on hold at Lord & Taylor's in Chevy Chase and deliver it to Hickory Hill, forthwith.

"I've got another tablecloth here at the house," Ethel said. "I'm trying to compare the two to see which one is the best. I want you to help me choose."

Hearing Ethel's strident tone, Ruth Darmstadter's intuition told her that her days were numbered.

"We were on deadline. I was under pressure. But I didn't feel I could say no to her," she said later. "It was one of those 'Where does a two-thousand-pound elephant sit?' situations."

With trepidation, she picked up the tablecloth and drove out to Hickory Hill, her only visit there in the almost three years she'd worked for the program. She was greeted by a bubbly young secretary, Susie Wells, who worshiped Ethel and called her "Ma."

"Come on up," Wells said, pointing to the stairs. "Mrs. Kennedy's in her bedroom."

After a quick introduction, Ethel held up the two tablecloths.

"Well?" she asked impatiently, tapping her foot.

Darmstadter didn't know what to say as she looked from one to the other. The two tablecloths were exactly the same.

"Exactly," she emphasized, years later, *"absolutely*. No question about it."

Panic-stricken, she looked from one to the other,

and finally she turned to Susie Wells in mute appeal. After a long pause, Wells rescued her. "Well, Mrs. Kennedy, I sort of like the left one."

She nodded meaningfully at Ruth Darmstadter, who babbled her agreement. "Oh, yes, Mrs. Kennedy, definitely the tablecloth on the left."

Ethel, looking pleased, ushered the two women to her bedroom door. "Good," she said, "that was my choice too. Susie, have Lord & Taylor pick up the other tablecloth. Ruth, thank you for coming. Good-bye."

At the front door, Ruth Darmstadter looked at Susie Wells for explanation. The secretary merely shrugged.

Darmstadter was also asked but refused to pick up the liquor for the awards ceremony at a D.C. store, which would have meant breaking the law. Virginia state law prohibited transporting more than a gallon of alcohol from Washington to Virginia. The penalty was a maximum one-year jail sentence, a five-hundred-dollar fine, or confiscation of the car. "I could just see myself being stopped with liquor for two hundred people in my car going across Chain Bridge," said Darmstadter later. "I said, 'No, that was just out of the question.' When it came to breaking the law, I was not about to do it. I ended up buying it at a Virginia liquor store where there was no discount."

Darmstadter had made a wise decision. The Kennedy household had been under surveillance at the time by Virginia Liquor Board agents who had even staked out a liquor store in Georgetown hoping to catch a Kennedy employee making a purchase. "We've tried on several occasions to catch them, but unfortunately we've never had much luck," said Liquor Board enforcement agent Carl Hayden.

To Ruth Darmstadter and scores of others who had dealings with Bobby Kennedy's widow during the seventies and eighties—including some of her own children—Hickory Hill had, in many ways, become a disturbing and troublesome place because of Ethel's sometimes curious behavior and moods. Ethel had a deep reservoir of uncontrolled anger. Always annoyed, exasperated, and infuriated, she battered—emotionally and physically—those whom she had hired to help and serve her. Staff members and employees of the RFK Memorial and its subsidiaries, assaulted on a steady basis by Ethel's sudden onslaughts of denigrating comments and criticisms, were often reduced to tears; some were moved to consult doctors and psychiatrists with real and imagined stomach problems, and at least one required life-saving hospitalization.

Even apparently innocent activities could send Ethel into uncontrolled rages, especially if they had anything whatsoever to do with Bobby's memory or the Kennedy name.

Visiting Hickory Hill on a rare occasion, Peter Lawford was nursing a cup of coffee in the kitchen, idly watching a newly hired maid go about her job. The woman had picked up various scraps of paper, including notes written by Bobby years earlier that Ethel had never bothered to file. She was heading toward the trash can when Ethel, standing by the door watching, saw that she was about to toss the paper. As Lawford later recounted the incident: "Ethel screeched, 'What are you doing?' The maid said, 'I'm throwing this away, Mrs. Kennedy.' And Ethel said, 'You stupid nigger, don't you know what you're doing? You're destroying history. Get out of my sight. You're fired!' The woman fled in shock." On his return to California, Lawford, disgusted by what he had witnessed, mentioned the incident to his new wife, Patricia Seaton Lawford. "Peter was very upset," she recalled years later. "He had been very much into the civil rights movement and he hated what Ethel had said. He felt for the woman who was dismissed by Ethel that very day. Over the years he had seen a lot of self-righteous behavior in Ethel. He always called her 'Miss Skakel.' He had a real problem with Ethel and she barely tolerated him."

To others, it seemed incomprehensible that Ethel, who counted Coretta King, Rafer Johnson, and César Chavez among her friends, would shout a racial epithet, especially in light of Bobby's public stance and her devotion to his philosophies.

"I never heard her use *that* word," said Noelle Fell. "But she would say things like 'Those black people are stupid.' I really don't think she liked blacks or Hispanics. She couldn't stand it if they didn't speak English well or understand it. She would say something once and she didn't like to repeat herself."

Once, leaving to go on a trip, Ethel had asked one of the maids, who had difficulty with English, to bring her a jar of face cream. "When Mrs. Kennedy asked for something," said Noelle Fell, "it had to be right away. Mrs. Kennedy was in a hurry and when she was in a hurry everything flew." Moments later, misunderstanding Ethel's request, the woman returned with sanitary napkins. "That's not what I asked for!" screamed Ethel in a sudden fury. Shaken, the maid started to say she was sorry, but Ethel was already on her feet. "I'll show you 'sorry,' " Ethel said. Then, according to Fell, who was in the room with the two women, "Mrs. Kennedy hit her in the face, just slapped her." In shock, the maid ran out of Ethel's room, followed by Noelle Fell. "She was crying and she ran to the basement and said she was going to leave. I said, 'Mrs. Kennedy's not in a good mood today. I'm so sorry. She should never have slapped you. This is not called for. Let me talk to her.' She said, 'No, I'm never going to work here again. I don't want it. I don't need this. No one has ever slapped me.' "

As the maid stormed out of the house, the secretary raced upstairs to deal with Ethel. "She was still furious," Noelle said. "When she got in bad moods like that, she didn't just jump out of them." Knowing that that was not the right time to bring up the slapping incident, Noelle helped Ethel finish packing. Awhile later, with Ethel calmer, Fell said to her boss, "She's very upset that you slapped her. Do you think you want her to continue working here or do you really think she's that incompetent?" Ethel, now petulant, refused to answer. "She knew I had seen it and she knew she had lost her cool. I said, 'She's a very good worker; she's the only one who comes and goes at the time you want her; she's very valuable here. I don't feel like we can lose her.' " Finally, Ethel said, "I don't care what she does." To Noelle, that meant that Ethel wanted the maid to stay. "Otherwise she would have said, 'Fire her.' " The next day Noelle met with the woman and apologized for Ethel. "I didn't tell her that Mrs. Kennedy had said, 'I don't care.' I told her, 'She really wants you back.' "

Over the next week the maid stayed out of Ethel's way. A few weeks after the slapping incident, while Ethel was throwing a party, the maid suffered a minor injury and Ethel made a big todo over her in front of the other guests and announced that she personally would drive her to the emergency room at Fairfax Hospital. "Mrs. Kennedy was a great actress," said Noelle Fell. "She was trying to show her guests what a nice boss she was. I remember her saying—and I laughed to myself when I heard it—'I have really valuable people working for me. She's one of the best. I'm going to take her to the hospital myself.' But if she didn't have an audience—watch out!"

Besides her household help, many of whom feared and despised her, Ethel's tyrannical, mean-spirited manner also infuriated public servants such as cab drivers and policemen, sometimes getting her into trouble.

On her way to shop for gardening supplies in Barnstable, near Hyannis Port, one September afternoon, Ethel pulled her convertible into a No Parking space and Special Officer John Ebel, a young summer patrolman, ticketed her. Furious, she raced back to the car, grabbed the ticket, tore it methodically into dozens of pieces, and strode off. Shocked, Ebel reported what had happened to his superiors, who delivered a summons to Ethel at the compound, ordering her to appear in court on a charge of mutilating a parking ticket. "In nearly five years, this is the first complaint of a mutilated parking ticket I can recall ever seeing," said Omar Chartrand, clerk of the First District Court in Barnstable.

When she got home that day, Ethel was ranting and raving, recalled Noelle Fell. "She said she wasn't going to pay the ticket. She said she had just jumped out of the car for a minute and it wasn't right that she should be ticketed. She claimed they picked on her specifically. She was really ticked off."

Ethel, who had initially pleaded not guilty, didn't show up in court. But at the hearing, her Boston attorney admitted to sufficient facts of guilt. She was convicted and fined $31.25.

When Rose Kennedy heard about the incident she was beside herself, recalled Barbara Gibson. "It seemed to her that there was always some kind of problem with Ethel," she said. "Mrs. Kennedy had discussed with me writing a note to Ethel about the incident but then decided against it because she felt it would only upset her and not accomplish anything. Because Ethel had been left with all those children, Rose felt sorry for her. She would often preface anything about Ethel by saying, 'I don't know why Bobby had to go off and leave Ethel. It was so stupid.' It was like she was blaming him."

At Hickory Hill, Ethel routinely had members of the household staff telephone three or four different cab companies when only one taxi was required to pick up a guest; the first cab that arrived got the fare and the others were dismissed by the mistress of the house with an airy, "Well, you didn't come so we had to call another." On one occasion, she refused to pay the fare, claiming it was too high, leading to a violent physical confrontation.

Arriving at Hickory Hill from National Airport one evening, the cabbie pointed to the meter. "That'll be twelve dollars, Mrs. Kennedy." Looking in the rearview mirror, he saw fury stamped on her face. "Twelve dollars?" she shrieked. "I don't care what your meter says. *These things can be fixed!* You're taking advantage of me. All you cab drivers are the same. No matter if I can afford it. I don't like being ripped off." Noelle Fell, hearing the ruckus, ran outside. The driver, a Hispanic man who spoke only broken English, tried to explain, "I have to get paid, but you don't have to give me a tip. I just want what's on the meter." But Ethel, hysterical, was beyond reason. "No! No! No!" she screamed. "You ripped me off." With that said, she suddenly slapped him in the face, declared, "I'm not paying you," jumped out of the cab, slammed the door, and yelled to Noelle Fell, "Bring my luggage in this minute!"

"Mrs. Kennedy, who's got a pretty strong tennis swing, really hauled off and hit him with her open hand near his jaw," Fell said. "The poor man was flabbergasted. She hurt him. His face was red. His mouth was open. He said, 'I have to have the money.' I told him to wait a minute and I went into the house and I saw her and I could tell she was scared. I went to my purse and got the cash and paid him. When I came back in she asked me if I'd paid him and when I said I did she was furious, so pissed off that she looked like she wanted to kill me. 'How dare you pay him?' she asked. 'Well, it's not going to come out of my money.' She refused to reimburse me."

Fell said Ethel had frequent standoffs with other cabdrivers, but that she decided not to get involved in the future. "I figured she wouldn't show off so much if I stayed out of it, so I watched from the front door. She argued with them; said they were taking advantage of her; said she wasn't going to pay until they decided to charge her what she *really* owed, and then they could have their bosses bill her. It seemed to me she would always take on people who really couldn't afford to give her a break. She would fight with the people who were trying to make a modest living—the florist, the man who ran the wine and cheese shop, the cabbies."

• • •

The Sunday of the RFK Journalism Awards luncheon, Ruth Darmstadter drove out to Hickory Hill early to make sure everything was in order. As she calmly walked up to the house she thought, "Well, I survived. We're here. It'll go off." But her brief reverie was rudely interrupted by Ethel yelling at the top of her lungs from the tennis court, *"Rrrruuuutttthhhh! Where are all the chairs?"*

"What chairs?" a mystified Darmstadter asked. "The-chairs-for-the-people-who-are-coming-to-the-reception-so-they-can-sit," the exasperated Ethel explained slowly, as if talking to a child. Other than a few chairs set aside for elderly guests, Darmstadter told her, she had not been instructed to order extra chairs. Ethel muttered to herself and stormed off.

"Things still seemed to be going all right," Darmstadter recalled. But just as the party was about to begin the head bartender, looking alarmed, approached her. "There aren't any white-wine glasses," he said. Feeling her blood pressure soar, she told the bartender the glasses were on the list and the caterer was supposed to supply them. "There are," he intoned, "no white-wine glasses. Get them!" Like everyone else, the hired man knew of Ethel's temper and feared becoming a target, so he threw the responsibility onto Darmstadter.

Luckily, Darmstadter had asked her husband to accompany her to Hickory Hill that day to assist with any emergencies. In minutes, he was off in search of the glasses, but the only store he found open was a pharmacy that had a supply of tacky yellow plastic glasses with a little nineteen-cent price sticker attached. "Perfect," Ruth thought. "They'll go well with the deviled eggs and the peanut butter hors d'oeuvres on white bread with the crust removed." Darmstadter's husband was in the kitchen removing the price stickers from the glasses when one of Ethel's children marched by, looked at what he was doing, and warned gleefully, "Uh-oh. Mommy's not going to like those." Under his breath, Darmstadter mumbled, "Well, you know what Mommy can do with them."

The rest of the day was a blur for Ruth. "When the ceremony was over I just fled," she said later. "I got in the car and burst into tears and resolved to quit."

In the office the next day she announced her intention to Bunny Roncevic, office manager for the RFK Memorial, who gave her some advice. "Mrs. Kennedy has forgotten it already," Roncevic said. "It'll all blow over. Wait until Dave Hackett gets back and he'll handle it." Just then the telephone rang and it was an angry Ethel, demanding to know what she should do with all those horrible yellow wineglasses she had sitting around.

Two days later John Nolan, a Kennedy legal adviser, telephoned Darmstadter, saying he understood that things had not gone well and wouldn't Ruth like to talk about it. A day or so later Darmstadter met with Nolan and Hackett. "When I went in I had a job and when I came out I didn't," she chuckled years later. "They told me, 'We just think you're not very happy here.' I could see the handwriting on the wall. It was obvious I was being fired and it was obvious that Ethel had done it."

Darmstadter complained to the *New York Times*'s Jack Rosenthal, the incoming chairman of the journalist committee. "He said, 'Don't worry about it. Just leave it in our hands.' But when push comes to shove whose side are they going to take? The journalists wanted to be on the committee because it gave them access to the Kennedys in a way they could never have. I was certainly dispensable."

Darmstadter demanded and got a letter of recommendation from the committee signed by Paul Duke of PBS; Ed Guthman, Bobby's old press secretary at Justice, who was now at the *Philadelphia Inquirer*; Dorothy Gilliam of the *Washington Post*; Betty Cole Dukert of NBC, and Jack Rosenthal.

In the end, it was Ruth Darmstadter's choice of wineglasses that really rankled Ethel and did in Darmstadter.

102 ✻ Stomach Pains

MOST OF THE people who came to work for Ethel were initially charmed by her and mesmerized by the Kennedy mystique. Deep down, they hoped to move from being Kennedy employees to Kennedy friends, part of the clan's circle and legend. They certainly didn't come aboard because of the pay, benefits, or perks. The Kennedys were notoriously stingy with their help, and Ethel, always under the gun to cut back on her spending, was far from an exception. Once Ethel's employees realized what they had gotten themselves into, many were still willing to sacrifice their self-respect and their health just to have a little taste of what remained of Camelot.

When Ruth Darmstadter first heard that a job was open working for Ethel, she was thrilled, despite a warning from her predecessor, Margot Higdon, to "stay out of Ethel's way."

"The idea of working with the Kennedys was exciting; a true Washington glamour job," she felt.

Like Ruth, Noelle Fell had also jumped at the chance to work for Ethel, whom she initially thought of as "magnetic, strong, lovable, friendly, real, well-appointed. I was in awe of her." Fell said her optimism about working at Hickory Hill had not been clouded when she saw Ethel's treatment of Sandra Renzy, the woman Fell succeeded. "I saw Sandra in tears so many times," Fell said. "If Ethel was in a bad mood, no matter what Sandra did it wasn't good enough. If the wrong tea bag was put in Ethel's cup by the chef, it was Sandra's fault. Sandra would take the chef's recommendations of the day and bring it up to Mrs. Kennedy in the morning. If she was in a bad mood, she'd take the menu, cross things off, write things on it—get pissed off, get ticked off."

Coates Redmon, who was Ruth Darmstadter's successor as executive director of the Robert F. Kennedy Journalism Awards program, felt the same awe as the other women. But she too received a warning, this one from Bunny Roncevic: "When you go out to Hickory Hill, if you don't like her, and she doesn't like you, you're gonna know it. If that happens, for God's sake, do not take the job. Working for Ethel can be totally and utterly lethal. This is the way it is and we choose to work here."

But Coates, also a widow, considered Ethel "an

icon, and Hickory Hill a shrine." She came away truly impressed from her first meeting with the lady of the house.

"I had a tremendous amount of empathy for her," she said later. "She was just as advertised—peppy and cute and very friendly. I was thinking, 'Oh, I like this woman, and I can work with this woman, and I can see that she can be difficult because she's got a very high level of energy; she runs a big establishment; she's the nation's widow; she's famous and has famous friends.' I wanted to be her friend, to get along with her, and I was very predisposed to do so. I had a wonderful attitude about all the Kennedys. I saw them as attractive, smart, stylish."

At first, Coates thought it was "fun to be a part of the Kennedy satellite system . . . it was hypnotic." But before long she discovered that the only real pleasure to be found on the job was gallows humor. "We'd sit around describing ways to kill Ethel. We put together a joke list of tongue-in-cheek things to do to make Ethel love you, such as calling her husband Bobby instead of Senator Kennedy," she said.

Like Ruth Darmstadter, Coates Redmon's job entailed producing the annual awards ceremony, dubbed "Throw-up Day" by the anxiety-ridden staff.

During one of the event luncheons, Ethel was sipping the mussel soup when she noticed that John Seigenthaler, one of the guests at the head table, had suddenly vanished.

Seigenthaler, a former Justice Department aide to Bobby, had quietly left the table to go in search of Coates, whom he liked and expected would join him and Ethel for lunch. He was unaware that only moments earlier Ethel had told Coates that she wasn't welcome at the table, that her job was to organize, not socialize. Coates and her assistant, Caroline Bishop, had then retreated into the study, where Ethel's secretary of the moment—another beleaguered employee—was sitting at her desk. The three women were commiserating when Seigenthaler entered.

"What the hell are you doing in here?" he asked. "Why aren't you at the table?"

"Well, we've been disinvited," said Coates. "We're not allowed to sit down with you swells."

"Oh, you're kidding," exclaimed Seigenthaler.

"That's the way it is," said Bishop.

"Well, what do you expect?" said the secretary.

Redmon, Bishop, and Seigenthaler were now seated on the sofa, off to the side of the room, out of view of the entrance, when Ethel stormed in, leaned over the secretary's desk, grabbed her by the lapels of her blazer, lifted her out of her chair, and started shaking her violently, screaming, "Where's the food? Where's the food? The food isn't coming fast enough! Second course . . . Second course!"

Trembling, she whispered, "I don't know, Mrs. Kennedy. That's not my job."

"Well, find out! Find out! Go to the kitchen and find out!" Ethel screamed, continuing to shake her.

"Mrs. Kennedy, I'm not supposed to have anything to do with it," the secretary gulped.

"I'm telling you, go into the kitchen and find out this minute!"

Finally, Ethel released the secretary, who fell back into her chair, ashen-faced. As she turned to leave, Ethel came face-to-face with John Seigenthaler, who was all but speechless at the scene he had just witnessed. He had heard stories about Ethel's behavior in the past but had never put credence in them. Coates and her assistant, both of whom had been the brunt of such abuse in the past, sat quietly, watching the scene.

"Oh, oh, oh . . ." stuttered Ethel. "Oh, where were you, John?" Ethel asked, trying to appear composed. "Suddenly you were gone from the table."

"Well, I'm right here, Ethel," he responded calmly.

Unnerved, Ethel started to back up toward the doorway, telling Seigenthaler to "return to the dining room because the food's getting cold."

Then she suddenly turned and walked into a wall.

For everyone, the scene was highly embarrassing,

and Ethel, visibly shaken, left the room alone and red-faced.

"All right, now I see," said Seigenthaler somberly to the other women before making his way back to the dining room.

At another event, Ethel became enraged when she noticed that Caroline Bishop's adhesive name tag wasn't properly positioned on her body; Ethel wanted all name tags located directly over the collarbone. When she saw that Bishop's was an inch too low, she ripped it off her blouse and slammed it back in the proper place, using the full force of her palm. "It's supposed to be *there!*" she ordered as Bishop fell backward in pain. "*Don'tcha-know-how* you're supposed to wear it!" Ethel screeched before stomping off.

"She very nearly broke Caroline's collarbone," said Coates Redmon, who was present. "She can be violent."

One of the most embarrassing situations witnessed by staffers of the memorial involved Dave Hackett. Lore had it that Bobby and Hackett, who had met at Milton Academy, where they became the closest of friends, were the two boys portrayed in writer John Knowles's novel *A Separate Peace*. After Milton, Hackett had gone on to college in Canada with hopes of having a career of his own, but Bobby had convinced him to work for the Kennedy family in various political jobs. After Bobby's death, the family gave Hackett the job of running the RFK Memorial. But by the early eighties, insiders said, the Kennedys had decided to run the programs directly themselves and had no need for Hackett. There was anger on both sides, including a memorable screaming match in the street outside the memorial's offices between Hackett and a Kennedy family operative. On another occasion, the irate Hackett tossed all of the journalism awards program files into the trash. Coates Redmon, called from home by Bunny Roncevic, had to race into town and rescue the files before they were picked up by the trashman. Coates, who was working under Hackett at the time, said, "They just got rid of him. Dave never knew what hit him. It was sad."

Ethel's attitude, her constant mood changes, her sudden demands, all had a deleterious effect on the people who worked for her. Those on staff in McLean had begun calling the place "Hickory Hell." Those working for the RFK Memorial now referred to it as the "Hell Hole."

Noelle Fell, for one, suffered a sudden heart attack at age thirty-five. "We had just come back after a summer at Hyannis Port," she recalled. "I had been working very hard. It had been so hectic. The hours had become so unreasonable because there had been a lot of parties. I was there eighteen hours a day. There was never any relief.

"Suddenly I felt real bad and couldn't go to work. I called in and said I was sick and I didn't know what was wrong. I could hardly move. That night I had a heart attack and was rushed to Fairfax Hospital. Though I received a bouquet of flowers from Mrs. Kennedy, she never called me. When I got home she never contacted me. I had never worked for someone who was so noncaring. Mrs. Kennedy asked one of the maids to call me. When I told her to tell Mrs. Kennedy that I needed some weeks to recover, she was very upset and she said she would just replace me." Fell made a quick recovery, and Ethel took her back.

One of Ethel's favorite helpers was Susie Wells, who was hardworking, loyal, athletic, and cute. To show her appreciation, Ethel once gave Wells a puppy. She even made an appearance at her wedding. But even Wells, who had great affection for Ethel, suffered, according to other Kennedy employees. Coates Redmon said that Wells had experienced stomach problems from working on Ethel's annual fund-raising celebrity tennis tournament. Ethel sent her to her doctor.

Bunny Roncevic, described variously as a "Kennedy priestess" and a "Kennedy nun," also complained of stomach disorders that she suspected were related to her work, colleagues said.

Coates, too, began experiencing stomach problems that she attributed directly to Ethel's constant raving and criticisms. "I had almost five years of it and it had a profound effect on me," she said later.

Coates said she had become so anxious that "I made an appointment to see Dr. Evelyn Nef," a respected Georgetown psychiatrist. At their one and only session, Coates described her symptoms. "Dr. Nef asked me what kind of stress I had and I said 'high stress.' I told Dr. Nef I had these pains in my left side and I said I suspected that they were psychosomatic. I said I wanted to discuss it because I didn't know what to do about it. She asked me to tell her about my professional life and I said, 'Well, for three months of the year I have to deal in a very intense way with Ethel Kennedy.' Dr. Nef said, 'Say no more.' "

As a seasoned observer of life at Hickory Hill noted, "Ethel's life was wonderful on the ascendancy with Bobby, but before they ever reached the tippety top, it was finished, and she became very angry at that. She had wanted her life to stay the way it had always been. She felt like fate had been so good to her that she was entitled to have fate continue to be good to her and then fate turned on her. Ethel's anger, Ethel's rage, was enormous, *enormous*."

103 ✻ Horror Hill

ONE MEMBER OF the Hickory Hill staff who truly got under Ethel's skin after Bobby's death was Ena Bernard.

A black woman from Costa Rica, Ena was utterly devoted to Bobby, and he considered her "our treasure," often exclaiming, "If it wasn't for Ena, this place would fall apart."

Ena had begun working for the family in the early

fifties when Jack, at Bobby's behest, had used the influence of his Congressional office to secure a green card for her. Later, as a publicity gimmick, Bobby arranged for Ena to accompany President Kennedy on an Alliance for Progress trip to her homeland, where she was accorded a virtual hero's welcome. Later, Bobby brought Ena's daughter, Josefina, to the United States from the Bernards' hometown of Heredia.

Ena always had a bright, cheerful room on the third floor at Hickory Hill, and traveled with the Kennedys to the Cape and elsewhere. When Bobby died, Ena was heartbroken. At every memorial service, she was in attendance, usually standing with her arms around one or more of the children, tears in her eyes.

Ethel, though, had come to loathe the aging nanny and housekeeper.

She was actively thinking of sacking the woman, who was approaching seventy. Noelle Fell said that when she was hired, the outgoing Sandra Renzy had told her, "Make sure this doesn't get back to Ena, but Mrs. Kennedy wants to get rid of her so bad that you'll start taking over some of her duties. This will give Mrs. Kennedy a reason to let her go; she can tell her she wants her to retire."

The cold war between Ethel and Ena added to the high level of tension in the household. The friction also touched off frequent skirmishes between Ethel and the older children, especially Joe and Kathleen, who were adamant that Ena be retained. They loved and revered the heavyset woman who had watched over them from the time they were toddlers; she was a beloved presence in their lives, someone who had been always there to cuddle them when no one else was around. Later, as they became young adults, they often went to her for guidance and advice instead of to their mother. All of the Kennedy women would have given anything to have had Ena to take care of their own children when she was in her prime. As Pat Kennedy Lawford once said, "Everyone who wondered how Ethel could raise eleven children knew when they saw Ena in action."

When Bobby was alive, Ethel had smiled and tolerated Ena, knowing how fond he was of her. But in truth she had always felt jealous of her. It was typical of Ethel, always so possessive of Bobby, to harbor such feelings. She had felt the same way about Bobby's longtime secretary, Angie Novello, too. Since Bobby's death, Ena had become the self-styled majordomo of the household, which infuriated Ethel. When Ethel had one of her tantrums, or did something embarrassing, Ena gloated. Noelle Fell, who witnessed this ongoing battle between the two women, recalled Ena saying, "The thing I miss most about the Senator is that he used to put her in her place. This would never go on if the Senator was alive. He would take her by the shoulders, sit her down, and give her a talking to. He'd tell her what was expected and she'd do it."

It was clear to Noelle that Ena loved Bobby and hated Ethel "with a passion." Ena could be highly critical of Ethel. She said she thought Bobby had done too much for her, coddled her. On one occasion, Ena confided to Noelle, "You know the reason why Mrs. Kennedy had so many children? Because that was her way to make sure her marriage stayed together."

Noelle said, "Mrs. Kennedy would get ticked off at Ena and yell, 'Get out! I don't need you here.' Mrs. Kennedy felt Ena was a thorn in her side because Ena knew too much about the family, that she was a snoop who always had her ear to the door. I'd say to Ena, 'Why do you stay?' And she'd say, 'I stay because the children want me to stay.' She did treat the children very nicely. And she was bound and determined to stay until the day she died because Senator Kennedy had helped bring her into the country and she felt she owed him her life."

Richard Burke, Ted Kennedy's personal assistant in the mid-seventies, was also aware of the conflict. "Ena really called the shots," he said later. "She was the one everybody always went to; nobody went to Ethel. Ena was the person who was always there for the kids. I never saw the kids running up to their mother; they always went to Ena first. The older kids shied away from Ethel, avoiding her like the plague. So Ena was really the center for the children. She also knew everything that was going on in that house; she was aware of it all.''

Some members of the Hickory Hill staff felt Ena had become as autocratic and critical as the actual mistress of the house. Not long after Noelle Fell was hired, Ethel told her, ''It won't be long now before she's gone. I'm fed up with her.'' But Joe, in his midtwenties, interceded on Ena's behalf. On one occasion Noelle overheard an argument between mother and son. ''You can't get rid of her,'' Joe beseeched. ''We all love her.''

''This is my house and I'll do what I want!'' his mother screamed. But in fact she had conflicting feelings about Ena.

''Mrs. Kennedy would get upset with herself and say, 'I don't know why I just don't get rid of her, but the kids like her,' '' said Fell. ''She kind of took out the animosity she had toward Ena on others who worked at Hickory Hill. There was a tremendously talented laundress who also was a wonderful seamstress who would work down in the basement all day and come up only for lunch. All she did was wash, iron; wash, iron. But Mrs. Kennedy was always so offensive to the woman that it came to the point that the woman would ask me to bring the things upstairs because she refused to have an encounter with Mrs. Kennedy. It was people like her who took the brunt of Mrs. Kennedy's feelings toward Ena.''

Because of Ethel's behavior, morale at Hickory Hill in the seventies was at its lowest ebb. Ted Kennedy had asked Richard Burke to give Ethel as much help as he could with staffing and organization, but Burke soon threw up his hands in despair.

''There was a period of time when she was going through new people every week,'' Burke said. ''She was unable to deal with hiring people, and I was interviewing people for her. It got totally out of control. The house was in chaos. She was in chaos. Finally, I just said, 'I can't help you anymore.' ''

It had become difficult for Ethel to get help because

stories about the household's turmoil had become known.

A Chevy Chase employment-agency manager recalled one experience ruefully:

"I remember sending a cook to Ethel's house and I remember the woman coming into the office not long after, pulling her hair out and saying, 'I just can't go back there again. It's constant chaos. That woman, with all of her kids and all of her dogs, is absolutely insane. I just can't take it. I can't take it!' I really thought she was going to have a breakdown. The woman was a wonderful cook who couldn't believe it when Ethel demanded that a variety of inappropriate sauces be served with different dishes. I couldn't help but laugh. This woman was an artist in the kitchen and she couldn't believe how someone like Ethel could have such bad taste in food. After all that hell we were put through, Ethel never paid the agency its fee."

Things got so bad that Ethel was forced to resort to running blind advertisements in the employment section of the *Washington Post*. Paul Nass, a young chef, had the misfortune to answer one of those classifieds. He called and was invited to Hickory Hill, where one of Ethel's secretaries begged him to take the job, they were so desperate. The last cook had quit after only a month. Like so many others before him, Nass was excited by the prospect of working for Ethel Kennedy, despite warnings that it could be hell, that he'd be on call twenty-four hours a day. "A lot of people who go to work out there are just like me. They all hope they'll meet Ted Kennedy and he'll say, 'Hi, won't you come work in the White House?' "

Nass lasted exactly twelve hours—from seven-thirty in the morning until seven-thirty that night—when he threw off his apron and told one of Ethel's children, "Tell your mommy I said bye."

During the time he was there—the job paid $180 a week for six twelve-hour days—he had been forced to cook breakfast after breakfast for Ethel and each one of the six Kennedy children who were home that day. The only words he heard directly from Ethel were, "Hi," "Close the door," and "Who dared park in my spot?"

When the family wasn't around, staff members sat in a circle and bemoaned their fate. Between complaints they offered Nass tips: he should always have a good supply of cold Heineken beer at the ready for Ethel after she got off the tennis court; and while the children always got plastic utensils and paper plates, their mother required a pink linen napkin and place mat to match the dining room's draperies and paint.

By lunchtime, Nass was still serving breakfast. Looking ahead toward dinner, he noticed the only meat in the freezer was pork chops, that the cupboards contained little more than Duncan Hines cake mix. By late afternoon, Ethel had still not given him the dinner menu. She said she was having a network TV executive over and wanted a fancy roast or steak. While she pondered a menu, she suggested that Nass make her a bacon, lettuce, and tomato sandwich as a snack. Each of the children then demanded a BLT, too. "They should raise pigs out there," Nass said later. "They eat so many BLTs." Finally, Ethel set down her dinner instructions on a note card engraved with her name. She instructed the chef to serve up plates of caviar and, if there was none, to have "Governor," another servant, run out and buy some. After reading Ethel's note, Nass took his leave, thinking, "They ought to call that place Horror Hill, not Hickory Hill." He never returned. A few days later another blind ad for a cook appeared in the newspaper.

• • •

In the years after Bobby's death, the house he loved had become a smelly zoo. The dogs roamed freely indoors, urinating and defecating on the rugs and furniture with abandon. "There was even poop from the turtle Carruthers on the rugs," said a frequent visitor. Bobby Jr. had brought home the enormous turtle from Kenya in hopes of winning the biggest turtle prize at the annual pet show at Hickory Hill, which Ethel was still throwing as if nothing had changed. When Carruthers died, Bobby put him in cryonic suspension in the basement freezer. As a

Christmas gift one year, Lem Billings gave Ethel a baby pig, whom she named Billings, and whom she allowed to run loose in the house, making a mess and leaving a horrible smell. Ethel finally gave Ena the responsibility of making certain the little porker was fed and taken outside. "They tried to feed it on the patio and make it go to the bathroom outside," said Noelle Fell. "It was wintertime and about two weeks after Ethel got the pig, someone left it outside one night and forgot it and the next morning they found it frozen. I'm not sure whoever left the pig there didn't do it on purpose. Mrs. Kennedy should have given it away, but instead it died. Ethel was furious. She demanded to know who was responsible for leaving Billings outside, but nobody fessed up."

A beautiful oriental rug, a gift from the shah of Iran, was thrown into the basement, "stained with dog wee-wee," one of Ethel's friends recalled. Noelle Fell said the dogs also went under the table in the dining room during the now infrequent dinner parties Ethel threw. "They would go doo-doo. No one would dare say anything to Mrs. Kennedy, who would try to cover up the mess with her foot. But everyone could smell it. I'd think, 'Oh, my God.' "

In the kitchen, the appliances had become outdated and the tile floor was worn through to the wood underneath. The immense commercial stove and grill was old and dirty. The insides of the kitchen cabinets were filled with crumbs, grease, and grime. The two big refrigerators and an icemaker creaked and groaned.

One summer, Ethel invited her pal Liz Stevens to stay at Hickory Hill while she was at the Cape. Stevens, who lived in Georgetown, immediately accepted the gracious invitation, which would permit her and her children to swim in the Kennedy pool and play tennis on the Kennedy court.

"She brought all of her clothes and she brought all of her own beautiful pots and pans and a beautiful polished stainless-steel salmon poacher because she didn't want to use Ethel's kitchenware," said Noelle Fell. "She said, 'I refuse to use hers. This stuff is so dirty I can't stand it.

I don't know how Ethel can live here. If I was living here, my staff would have to clean this mess up. How come they don't do this?' I said, 'They're very busy, they're always busy, and Mrs. Kennedy has never said anything.' She said, 'I can't stand it. It's a wonder this place is not full of roaches.' Mrs. Stevens got very upset because the kitchen looked like it was in a poorly run restaurant. If it had been inspected it would have been condemned. Liz being Liz, she just said to her husband, 'I can't stand it. We're going to have to get a crew to come in here to clean. I'm not moving in here. Bring my clothes back home and I'll come back in a few days.'

"The Stevenses brought in a crew to clean up. They even put new paper in the cabinets and had everything that Liz didn't have any use for taken out and boxed. She did the same thing in Mrs. Kennedy's bedroom. Her bedroom wasn't dirty but it wasn't up to Liz's standards, either. About a week before Ethel got home, Liz had her staff put everything back the way it was and took her own things home. She would never have said anything to Ethel and she knew we wouldn't tell. Mrs. Kennedy never knew what happened."

Conditions in Ethel's house in the compound were not much different: the pets ran wild and made messes, the place needed major repairs.

"One of the men whom we used for handy work went over there and he could see the sky through the roof when he was in the attic," recalled Barbara Gibson. Because Ethel was short of funds, she couldn't afford to pay for the repairs, or didn't care to. Gibson mentioned the situation to Kennedy nephew Joe Gargan in hopes of getting financial help from the Park Agency. Gargan also sent an appeal to all of the family members. "It had words to the effect that here is the widow of Bobby Kennedy, the Senator from New York and Presidential candidate, who has holes in the roof of her house so that the rain comes through and you can see the sky," recalled Gibson. "The only one who called was Jackie and she told him, 'Joe, I will buy Ethel a new roof. This is ridiculous.' And she did. Ethel got a new roof courtesy of Jackie."

While Jackie felt compassion for Ethel, and was willing to come to her aid financially, she had decided to keep her distance socially. At one event at the Metropolitan Museum in New York honoring Bobby's Bedford-Stuyvesant project, reporters noted that Ethel and Jackie had arrived separately and never spoke to each other. When photographers pressed Ethel to pose for a picture with Jackie, she replied that she felt the crowds were too big and it would be impossible for them to get together. Jackie's whispered response was drowned out by the loud music. "The two women," wrote a *Washington Post* reporter, "never managed to exchange even a smile through the mobs." Several days later, though, the *Washington Post* ran a correction stating that the sisters-in-law "did meet and exchange greetings and kisses."

Jackie had made it a strict rule not to allow Caroline and John Jr. to fraternize with their Hickory Hill cousins. That became very clear when Ethel extended an invitation to her niece and nephew to come and stay for a couple of weeks. "Jackie said, 'No way,' " recalled Richard Burke. He said that Caroline had previously spent some time there "but with all that stuff going on out at Hickory Hill—especially with the problems the boys were having—Jackie just didn't want Caroline and John there."

Jackie wasn't the only member of the clan who was wary of the happenings at Hickory Hill. Ethel's sister-in-law Eunice also kept Ethel's children at arm's length. One afternoon, Burke said, he was driving Maria Shriver, Caroline Kennedy, and Sydney Lawford to the Shrivers' Maryland estate, Timberlawn, and the girls were talking about the family, specifically the Bobby Kennedy branch. "They were saying what a mess they all were and how their mothers wouldn't let them go near Hickory Hill. There was definitely a hands-off attitude on the part of those three mothers—Eunice, Jackie, and Pat."

104 ✻ *Bad Boys*

WITHOUT BOBBY AT the helm, Ethel's life had spun out of control. The ongoing mayhem at Hickory Hill was only one reflection of her inner chaos; another sign, far worse, was the way her relationship with her three older sons had deteriorated. If she wasn't having screaming matches with them, she was ordering them out of the house. All semblance of parental authority had vanished.

"Ethel had a knack for throwing the kids out," said Patricia Seaton Lawford. "Peter and I would be sitting at home in our bathrobes and the doorbell would ring and it would be Bobby."

Peter Lawford eagerly shared with Bobby his own favorite pastimes, getting stoned and hanging out at Hugh Hefner's place, surrounded by willing women.

Defiant and angry, struggling with intolerable loss, Bobby and David intensified their use of drugs. While Joe stayed with marijuana, Bobby and David had begun moving into the danger areas: popping pills, snorting cocaine, and shooting heroin.

Just two weeks after Bobby's year-long probation from his 1970 marijuana bust ended, he was arrested in Hyannis after a run-in with a policeman. Patrolman Frederick Ahern had asked the seventeen-year-old Kennedy to move along because his car was blocking traffic. Bobby, sitting with a girl, refused to budge. Noticing that the boy's eyes were bloodshot, the officer asked the long-haired, grubby-looking teenager whether he was drunk. According to Ahern, Bobby answered no and then spat at him. In court, he claimed the officer was lying, pleaded no contest to the charge of loitering, and paid a fifty-dollar fine.

Bobby and Joe also had a series of motor vehicle incidents. In the same month, Joe had an accident on the West Coast and his brother was cited for speeding on the East Coast.

Bobby had spent his senior year at the Palfrey School in Watertown, Massachusetts, and Lem Billings had made arrangements for him to live at the home of friends, the Brode family.

The woman of the house, Joey Brode, a school-teacher, said that during the entire year Bobby stayed with her family, Ethel had never once called to inquire about her son. "I never knew Ethel," she said later. "Bobby never talked about his mother. It's certainly true that they were alienated.

"I was like a parent to him. The one thing that I tried to do—and it seemed to be successful—was to feed him. I loved to cook and he loved to eat. One of the things that happened that year that really was quite wonderful was that he gradually became very much a part of our family. When he came to live with us he was the type who would grab food and run. Here he was able to relax and eat dinner with us and have conversations. It was a nice thing because there was a lot of tension in Bobby—caused by the death of his father, by the attentiveness of the press, and the difficulties of being young. He was finally able to relax with our family."

During the time Bobby lived with the Brodes, he had stopped using drugs and had not gotten into trouble. But once he returned to his mother's jurisdiction, the problems started all over again. That summer at Hickory Hill he and David grew a marijuana patch that was discovered by Richard Burke as he was helping to get the grounds ready for Ethel's annual pet show. Ethel's secretary, Caroline Croft, told Burke, "They grow it all the time. And smoke it." In the fall, as a freshman at Harvard, Bobby had been arrested for driving sixty-five miles an hour in a thirty-five-mile zone in Waterville, New Hampshire, where the Kennedys skied. He failed to show up in court, pleaded guilty, and paid a thirty-dollar fine.

His brother Joe, meanwhile, had collided with a car in a busy Berkeley, California, intersection, and then struck a second vehicle. Joe's head hit the windshield, causing minor chest, skull, and neck injuries.

Joe had just arrived in Berkeley after a couple of months at the Massachusetts Institute of Technology. After some psychiatric counseling he'd dropped out of MIT, feeling he needed to distance himself from the clan. Never a particularly good student, Joe had gone to Milton Academy, his father's alma mater, for a time, but was forced by poor grades to leave before graduation, eventually earning his high school diploma from the Manor Hall Tutoring School in Cambridge.

He had worked for a time in his uncle Ted's 1970 Senate reelection campaign, and for the RFK Memorial. In February 1972, Joe had accompanied his mother and uncle to Bangladesh, but refused to return home with them. Instead, he bought a motorcycle and rode through the central states of India. He was on a Lufthansa flight headed home when five Palestinian terrorists hijacked the plane, rigged the aircraft with explosives, and held Joe and other passengers hostage for eighteen hours. "It wasn't the worst moment of my life," he said at the time. He also stated, "I've been scared before, but it never lasted as long."

Arrangements were then made by Ethel and Ted to enroll the troubled and aimless young man at the University of California at Berkeley. He registered for only a few courses, but rarely attended classes. Joe spent most of his time watching TV in his room at the home of Diane Clemens, a Berkeley history professor, who found him erratic and obnoxious, often breaking house rules by smuggling in girls. More worrisome for Clemens was the time Joe threatened to kill her eleven-year-old daughter after the youngster had mischievously locked him in his room. The husky six-footer angrily smashed his way out and chased the child, threatening her. He later apologized profusely. On one occasion, he mysteriously disappeared for a couple of days. Clemens got word to the Kennedys, who instructed her to look for him but warned her not to call the police, fearful of the publicity. Joe never revealed where he had been.

When Ethel learned that Joe had dropped out of Berkeley altogether, she had Ted use his influence with San Francisco Mayor Joseph Alioto to give her son an $8,976-a-year job in a federally funded program to control TB and VD in black neighborhoods. The hiring sparked anger from at least one San Francisco supervisor, who questioned the twenty-year-old's qualifications for the job. But Alioto, a longtime Kennedy ally, said he stood firmly behind the hiring, saying he was "impressed" with Joe. Young Joe sounded like a veteran politician when a reporter asked him about his controversial job. "You realize the mistrust of higher officials and what government is doing among these people," he said. "They see countless programs being cut by the [Nixon] Administration and feel helpless."

Despite the smooth patter, Joe quickly lost interest in the job and quit. He'd been in Berkeley only a few short months when he told Diane Clemens he was returning to Boston. Clemens tried her best to get him to stay, concerned that he'd hurt himself or someone else if he didn't pull himself together.

Several months later, back East on Nantucket on a muggy August afternoon, her fears became reality.

A Jeep Joe was driving overturned, leaving eighteen-year-old Pam Kelley, a close pal of the Kennedy kids, paralyzed from the chest down.

Joe had been cutting through woods, spinning the Jeep in circles. "Everyone was acting crazy," Kelley recalled later. Joe swerved suddenly to avoid an oncoming car; the Jeep flipped, landing in a ditch and tossing all six occupants to the ground. Eighteen-year-old David, who worshiped his older brother, was also hurt. He suffered a fractured vertebra and had to be placed in traction. The doctors prescribed morphine to kill the pain, and David took as much as he could get. Three other friends, including Pam's sister, and another girl, the daughter of a *New York Times* reporter, suffered minor injuries. Pam, the most critically injured, would never walk again.

A week after the accident, twenty-one-year-old Joe Kennedy was found guilty of negligent driving, a misdemeanor carrying a maximum jail term of up to two years, a three-hundred-dollar fine, or both. Joe, who pleaded innocent and did not testify, was let off with a hundred-dollar fine and a brief scolding by a judge who had been a friend of his father's and had gone to college with his late uncle, Joe Kennedy, Jr. To many Kennedy-family critics, it was Chappaquiddick all over again.

"I would hope you would use your illustrious name as an example that could be an asset to the young people of your age instead of becoming involved in cases that bring you into court," said Nantucket Judge C. George Anastos. "I knew your father in Washington. We did not always agree on matters, but he was a fine man. You have a fine mother."

Ethel's eyes filled with tears when the judge, who had been an attorney for Joe McCarthy in the Army-McCarthy hearings, mentioned Bobby. Joe, whose relationship with his mother had never been worse, played the loving son for the reporters who packed the courtroom, leaning over and kissing her on the cheek after hearing the sentence. But throughout the three-hour trial, mother and son, Ted, and Steve Smith had sat emotionless as prosecution witnesses such as Sandra Peterson, a tour-bus driver, took the stand. She told the court she came upon the accident scene, saw "bodies lying all over" and spoke to Joe, who said, "It was all my fault."

Ethel never liked the now-paralyzed Pam Kelley, daughter of a bartender whose home was located near the Kennedy compound. Ethel had always suspected that Pam and her sister had tried to seduce her sons. But after the accident that garnered front-page headlines for weeks—and before the settlement—Ethel had suddenly begun showering attention on the Kelley girl. Ethel visited Pam every day at the hospital, once with Rose Kennedy at her side. Ethel brought Pam flowers, straightened her room, and every night had a first-run movie shown there. Knowing Ethel's past feelings, those around Pam questioned her sincerity. Pam later told writers Peter Collier and David Horowitz, "Everybody would gather there, even the nurses. While they were watching, I'd ease into the wheelchair I was trying to get used to and go out in the hall and smoke a cigarette while they watched the film. They never missed me."

Two years later, the Kennedys settled with the Kelley family for nearly $1 million.

"For Ethel it was all like a bad dream," recalled George Terrien of that period in the seventies. "Ethel refused to admit to herself that her sons were boozing and using drugs. She just felt they were bad boys who wouldn't listen to her; just like her brothers, who had disobeyed Big Ann. Kids were out of control all over the country, but Ethel had closed her eyes to all of it. It was easier for her to throw them out of the house, or turn them over to Teddy, or that Billings character. After Chappaquiddick, Teddy had enough problems keeping himself under control, and we all thought Billings was a deviate. Ethel washed her hands of those boys. But that was typical Skakel—ignore the two-thousand-pound elephant in your living room."

By the time David recovered from the injuries he had sustained in the Jeep accident and returned to boarding school, he considered himself a "chipper," street talk for a heroin user who believed he could take the drug or leave it. In actuality, he was hooked. A couple of months before graduation—as part of his senior project—Ethel and Ted arranged for David to take a part-time job in Nashville at the *Tennessean,* published by family friend John Seigenthaler. David showed up looking like a junkie. Another young man recovering from a drug problem, John Warnecke, whose father had designed Jack's grave at Arlington National Cemetery, was also in Nashville at Seigenthaler's invitation, and the two young men became friends. Warnecke's clearest recollection of David was how, when he took off his jacket, syringes and packets of white powder fell out of the pockets like loose change.

"We'd talk and he'd say how the family treated him so bad," Warnecke recalled. "He was the one taking the heat from Ethel. It became clear that he thought of himself and in fact was what they call in family therapy 'the designated sick one,' the one whose sickness allows everyone else to feel healthy by comparison."

The only real joy Ethel experienced during this period was the marriage of her firstborn, and even that happy occasion was marred. An hour before twenty-two-year-old Radcliffe senior Kathleen said her vows with twenty-five-year-old Harvard graduate student David Lee Townsend, at Holy Trinity Church on November 17, 1973, Ted's twelve-year-old son, Teddy Jr., was having his cancerous right leg amputated at nearby Georgetown University Hospital. Ethel knew the operation was scheduled but had refused to cancel the long-planned wedding. A grim-faced Ted, still desperately trying to play the role of surrogate father to Ethel's brood, bravely came to the church immediately after his son's surgery, leaving Joan at the boy's bedside.

105 * Zany Playgirl

ETHEL, APPROACHING FIFTY, continued to act in as capricious and kooky a manner as ever.

"My mother's not involved in anybody's life except her own," David told his friend Nancie Alexander, a born-again Christian and a hairdresser. "We have a whole slew of people raising us and she's not one of them. My mother loves to be busy. Just look at *People* magazine and you'll see her playing tennis and skiing. But she's not around for us."

On one of her frequent ski trips to Mount Tecumseh,

in New Hampshire, Ethel suffered a painful leg fracture. Two expert skiers who were behind her saw the middle-aged jock do a cartwheel and land on her back on the icy, steep slope. "Please help me, please help me. Oh, it hurts so much," she cried as they came to her rescue. For a couple of months, Ethel was in a cast, getting around merrily in a special wheelchair that was a gift from friends; it had been one of President Eisenhower's old golf carts, and it still had the general's five stars on the side.

When some old Greenwich friends read about the accident, they laughed. Years earlier, they remembered, Ethel had been skiing in Vermont, had fallen, and had screamed out in pain. When the ski patrol reached her, she told them she thought her leg was broken. Three rescuers strapped her into a toboggan and brought her gently down the precarious slope. It was only when they got her to the bottom that she stood up, smiled, and jauntily walked away, leaving them exhausted, dumbfounded, and angry. "Ethel faked the injury. She just wanted to know what it was like to come down on a toboggan," said a friend years later.

In terms of her driving record, Ethel appeared to be racking up as many motor vehicle violations as her sons. It was like the old days in Greenwich. On skiing vacation in Waterville, New Hampshire, a state trooper clocked her doing eighty-four in a fifty-five-mile-an-hour zone. Ethel pleaded guilty by mail and was fined thirty dollars. A local newspaper, obviously immune to the Kennedy mystique, asked, "Why was Ethel doing eighty-four? Some people spend all their lives under sixty m.p.h. Maybe she had to get the beer. Something like that, probably."

When she was nabbed on the speeding charge, a gossip column lumped her in with a couple of fading pop stars who had recently made the news wires for auto-related incidents. Four months later David once again was arrested, this time by Virginia state police, for doing ninety-two in a fifty-five-mile-per-hour zone in his year-old Toyota. He was held briefly in Shenandoah County jail, charged with reckless driving and failure to have a driver's license and registration in his possession. He pleaded guilty and was fined fifty dollars.

While novelist Pearl S. Buck of *The Good Earth* fame predicted in her curious 1970 book, *The Kennedy Women: A Personal Appraisal,* that Ethel had the "strength and dynamism" to become the symbolic leader of the Kennedy family, and the Gallup poll continued to put Ethel on its "Most Admired Women" list (though she had dropped to second-string status by 1974, behind the likes of child-star-turned-diplomat Shirley Temple Black and actress–stroke victim Patricia Neal), Ethel was acting more like a zany playgirl than a contender for the matriarch's throne. "Honestly, Ethel," declared the *Washington Star*'s gossip columnist Diana McLellan cattily, "you *can't* carry your drink outside. Not even if you're you. Not even in Georgetown. Not even from Clyde's [a popular bar]. There are these things called city ordinances, and, alas, they even apply to you."

Ethel's life now seemed to revolve around her annual Pro-Celebrity Tennis Tournament at Forest Hills, which she started in 1972 when the Kennedys suddenly realized they couldn't raise enough money privately to fund the RFK Memorial. From a distance, she also oversaw the memorial's annual journalism and book awards. But playing continued to occupy most of her time. On the tennis court, she once bounded through a tough match suffering from two bruised ribs she had gotten when Eunice jabbed her during a touch football game a few days earlier. In winter, she skied in chic Aspen with other "sparklies" and eventually bought a condo there after her family had "trashed" a couple of places, and realtors had adamantly refused to rent to her anymore. Spring and summer she sailed. Reporters from the supermarket tabloids descended on Hyannis one weekend when the *Resolute,* with Ethel at the helm, capsized and sank after she ran it aground, dumping the widow and her eleven guests into the water. The tabloid crowd had descended because one of those reportedly dunked was "Charlie's Angels" star

Farrah Fawcett-Majors, whom Ethel had befriended at a tennis tournament.

And every so often Ethel, who had become a darling of the paparazzi set, pulled off a banal stunt or practical joke that became the talk of the Kennedy cognoscenti.

One of her victims was singer Neil Diamond who, while singing his hit "Sweet Caroline" to some four thousand guests at a fund-raiser on the grounds of the Shrivers' estate in Maryland, was suddenly drenched in beer by Ethel because he hadn't sung her requested tune, "New York Boy."

After prominent Washington lawyer Edward Bennett Williams's home was hit by burglars, he received a mysterious telegram saying the loot wasn't as valuable as originally thought. Thinking the wire was from the thieves, Williams turned it over to police, who traced the telegram to Ethel. (She kept a stack of blank Western Union forms on her desk for just such occasions.)

George Plimpton, having had just undergone gall-bladder surgery at New York Hospital, was coming out of the anesthesia when his hospital room door suddenly burst open and a six-foot, helium-filled red balloon floated in, compliments of Ethel.

Luciano Klosterman, the young, beautiful wife of Los Angeles businessman Don Klosterman, an old friend of Ethel's, had been warned that in order to gain Ethel's respect and friendship she'd have to pass some sort of a test. Luciano hit the jackpot a few days after she arrived at the John Gardner Tennis Ranch in Carmel, where Ethel was vacationing. After a night out with Ethel and other chums, Luciano volunteered to drive Ethel back to her bungalow. She pulled her rental car to the curb, next to a wide patch of beautiful flowers that led to Ethel's place. "No, no, no—I don't want to get out here," Ethel scolded Luciano with a wink. Luciano got the idea, wheeled the car around, jumped the curb, plowed through the plantings, and delivered Ethel to her front door. "We ruined everything," Luciano chuckled later. "But I passed my test."

On another jaunt to the West Coast, Ethel had stayed

at the home of an old friend, Los Angeles Rams owner Carroll Rosenbloom. After an evening on the town with Pierre Cossette, she discovered that she had forgotten the keys to the Rosenblooms' house, and no one was home. Accompanied by Cossette, Ethel tiptoed around the sprawling Beverly Hills house in hopes of finding an unlocked window, every so often climbing onto Cossette's shoulders, trying unsuccessfully to force one. "This is absolute insanity," Cossette had warned her. "There's private security. The Beverly Hills cops. Probably dogs. We're going to get ourselves killed." When Ethel finally realized she couldn't break through a window, she decided to gain entrance by smashing her way through the door. To accomplish this, Cossette attached the steel cable from the winch on his brawny Chevy Blazer to the two huge handles on the Rosenblooms' double front doors. "Go ahead! Do it! Do it!" Ethel insisted. "Pull the damned door off the hinges."

"I was laughing—but she was really serious," said Cossette. "Later, she acted like one of her big disappointments in life was not pulling the doors off of Carroll Rosenbloom's house in the middle of the night."

106 ✻ Martha Moxley

HALLOWEEN HAD ALWAYS suited Ethel's prankster style. When Bobby was alive, and the children were small, Hickory Hill at Halloween was festooned with ghosts, goblins, and skeletons. Ethel invited her pals and their offspring to lively parties; the little ones passed spaghetti tendrils from hand to hand in the dark, screaming with fear and delight; there were best-costume contests, usually won by the Kennedy kids, and bobbing for apples. Overseeing it all was a wildly enthusiastic Ethel, dressed like a wicked witch, clapping her hands, egging everyone on.

Now, with only Rory, Douglas, and Max still at an age to enjoy the holiday, celebration rites had been severely curtailed. Ethel either sent the young ones to friends' homes after a small party at Hickory Hill or let them go trick-or-treating with a governess.

But Ethel herself still loved Halloween and every year she recruited a friend or two to celebrate with her, showing up in costume on the doorsteps of pals in Georgetown, or surprising neighbors in McLean.

Halloween night 1975, which fell on Friday, October 31, was no exception, despite the curious comings and goings at Hickory Hill earlier in the day.

"Something had happened and Mrs. Kennedy was very upset, very agitated," said Noelle Fell years later. "Senator Kennedy, looking very serious, had been at the house, meeting with her in private, and there were all these hush-hush telephone conversations.

"Late in the afternoon I happened to overhear her call a friend and say, 'I've got to get out of here. You've got to come trick-or-treating with me tonight, and I don't want to bring the kids. It's just going to be you and me.' I had gone home and gotten my daughter, Danielle, and a couple of her friends and brought them back to Hickory Hill so the kids could look at each other's costumes, and I took some pictures. Afterward they went trick-or-treating with the governess. Mrs. Kennedy, still very distressed, put on her witch mask, got dressed in black, grabbed a broom, and went out with her friend."

A terrifying event had occurred that day hundreds of miles away in Ethel's hometown of Greenwich.

Not far from Rushton Skakel's elegant home, in the exclusive enclave of Belle Haven, teenager Sheila McGuire had made a gruesome discovery. Shortly before one P.M., while walking through a cluster of evergreens, she stopped suddenly and clasped her hand to her mouth. On the ground, under a pine tree, was the body of a girl. She was lying on her stomach, her blonde hair matted with blood, her jeans pulled down to her knees. She was fifteen-year-old Martha Elizabeth Moxley, whose frantic mother, Dorthy Moxley, after searching through the night without success, had reported her daughter missing just before dawn. The McGuire girl, a friend of Martha's, had been participating in the search when she stumbled upon the body.

In Greenwich, the night before Halloween was known as "doorbell night," a time when the local kids played pranks on their neighbors. A pretty, popular sophomore at Greenwich High School, Martha had spent the evening with a group of neighborhood teens. Among them was Ethel's seventeen-year-old nephew, Tommy Skakel, Rushton's son.

When police searched the crime scene, which was on the edge of the Moxleys' property, diagonally in back of the Skakels' house, they found what they believed to be the murder weapon, a broken golf club.

The attack had been so vicious and brutal that the club had been shattered. Two pieces were found near Martha's body; the third was missing. Detectives quickly learned that Tommy Skakel had been the last person seen with Martha Moxley that night. A police search of the Skakel home turned up a set of golf clubs similar to the portion of the club found near Martha's body.

Tommy Skakel soon became one of two prime suspects in the girl's murder. He has consistently professed his innocence and has never been charged.

• • •

A year earlier, Martha's father, David Moxley, had been promoted to head the New York office of Touche Ross, one of the Big Eight accounting and management consulting firms, and had moved his family to Greenwich from Piedmont, California, a small, affluent community, south of Berkeley. The Moxleys had been attracted to Greenwich for the very same reasons George Skakel, Sr., and Big Ann had been years earlier: the town was close to Manhattan, and there was no state income tax in Connecticut. Like the Skakels, the Moxleys had gotten a good buy on their new place—a rambling three-story stucco Mediterranean with six bedrooms and twelve bathrooms, in need of work, on three overgrown acres.

Dorthy Moxley enrolled Martha and her older brother John in the Greenwich public schools, and then jumped into the job of renovating and redecorating her new house.

"We loved Greenwich from the moment we moved in," she said later. "We felt comfortable. The people were so kind. Martha loved her schools and her friends. It was a very positive atmosphere." Their community, Belle Haven, had its own private police force, and guard posts kept out interlopers. The neighborhood appeared crime-free.

After the Moxleys moved in, their neighbors Cissy Ix and her husband, Bob, president of Cadbury Schweppes U.S.A., threw a cocktail party. Among the guests was Rushton Skakel.

Like Ethel, Rushton had gone through hell in recent years. His wife, Ann Reynolds Skakel, had developed cancer around the time Jack Kennedy was assassinated. She suffered until her death at forty-one, in 1973, leaving him a widower with six sons and a daughter. Her illness and death left the children and their father, a recovering alcoholic, traumatized.

While Rushton's wife was in Greenwich Hospital dying, Rushton and Ethel's sister Georgeann Terrien was in an intensive-care room down the hall, having had a lung removed because of cancer. (Along with her heavy drinking, she was also a chain-smoker.)

Rushton Skakel took an instant liking to the Moxleys. He sponsored the family for membership in the fancy Belle Haven Club, and David Moxley for membership in New York's prestigious University Club.

"Rush was very, very good to us," Dorthy Moxley said. "In the beginning, he really was just so nice and kind."

But after their initial meetings, the Moxleys and the Skakels had very little social contact. Soon, Dorthy Moxley began hearing stories about the Skakel boys, particularly Tommy and his fifteen-year-old brother, Michael, who had a reputation in the community for their wildness, just as Ethel's brothers Jimmy and George had years before.

"They didn't seem to act like everybody else in that neighborhood," she reflected. "They just didn't do things like other people. Our kids got up in the morning and went to school and came home at night when they were supposed to and I was there. My husband went to work and came home at the end of the day. They had a housekeeper and no mother and Rush was always off somewhere. Every once in a while I'd see one of the children straggling home, but that was about it."

Rushton's house was typically Skakel; no one was in charge to establish discipline or controls for the children. It was much like the home Rushton himself had grown up in not far away on Lake Avenue.

Because of the problems, Rushton had been forced to hire housekeepers to help care for his large brood. And like Big Ann, who had retained Martin McKneally to serve as a tutor and companion for her sons, he had begun hiring teachers from a local private school for the same purpose. The latest was a Williams College graduate named Kenneth Littleton, age twenty-three, who taught science and coached baseball at the nearby Brunswick School, where Tommy was a tenth-grader. Rushton had offered the young man a hundred dollars a week and free room and board. Littleton had started working with the Skakel boys in early October, but it was only hours before Martha Moxley was murdered that he had actually taken up residence in the Skakel house on Otter Rock Road. Like Tommy Skakel, Littleton would become a prime suspect in the girl's death. Like Skakel, he has always professed his innocence and has never been charged.

Shortly after the Moxleys moved to Greenwich, Martha entered ninth grade at Western Junior High School, where she was thought of by teachers and friends as an intelligent, confident girl. Known as "Mox," she played the piano and took violin lessons. All of the boys found her attractive. She had long, blonde hair and blue eyes and stood five foot five. "Martha was very popular and very outgoing," recalled Joe Romanello, a close friend and classmate. "In the ninth-grade yearbook, she was just all over the place." At graduation, after having been at Western less than a year, Martha was voted the girl with the best personality.

Two months before the murder, Martha had started her sophomore year at Greenwich High School. She had also begun seeing a boy, Peter Zaluca. "She talked to him all the time on the telephone. They'd get together at school. He'd come to our house. She'd go to his. They'd see each other on weekends. It was a puppy love kind of thing," her mother recalled.

As far as Tommy Skakel was concerned, Dorthy Moxley believed that her daughter had had little or no contact with him until a week or two before she was found dead. Martha had gone to a party at the home of a neighborhood friend. "She had stayed out very, very late, and didn't get home until three o'clock in the morning," Dorthy Moxley said. "It was the first time she had ever done that." After her daughter's death, she found Martha's diary and felt a chill when she read one of her last entries, dated right after the party. "Martha mentioned that she thought 'Michael Skakel was okay,' but that she knew she 'had to be careful of Tommy.' "

• • •

Thursday, October 30, had begun routinely. Martha and her brother John had had breakfast with their mother; their father was in Atlanta on business, expected home the next day. Almost two years older than his sister, John Moxley was looking forward to varsity football practice in the afternoon; the next day, a public school holiday, a big game was scheduled at the Greenwich High School stadium. Martha, who hoped to be a cheerleader next season, told her mother she and her best friend, Helen Ix, were going "hacking" in the neighborhood that night; that meant spraying mailboxes with shaving cream, hanging toilet paper from trees, innocent mischief. Dorthy Moxley walked the children to the front door, and gave each a kiss good-bye. She spent the rest of the day puttering around the house and lunching in town with a friend.

Martha got home from school late in the afternoon. Shortly before seven, Helen Ix and Geoffrey Byrne arrived to pick her up. Dorthy Moxley, on the phone in the front hall, heard her daughter debating whether to wear her new shearling lamb jacket or her old down parka; she finally settled on the latter. Over her shoulder, Martha said she'd be home early, waved good-bye, and left. It was the last time Dorthy Moxley saw her daughter alive.

Outside—it was now around seven o'clock—Martha and her pals met up with a few more friends, including Jackie Wettenhall, a neighbor, whose father was president of the National Dairy Corporation. For about two hours, they wandered the winding, tree-lined streets of Belle Haven.

During that time, the Skakels were having dinner at the Belle Haven Club with their new helper, Ken Littleton; their father, Rushton, was away on a hunting trip. The group included Tommy and Michael Skakel; their sister, eighteen-year-old Julie; her friend, Andrea Shakespeare, sixteen; and a Skakel cousin, fifteen-year-old Jimmy Terrien, one of George and Georgeann's sons. When they got back to the house around nine o'clock, Littleton went upstairs to Rushton Skakel's room, where he planned to sleep until his employer returned home. Minutes later Martha and her friends arrived at the Skakel house and were invited in. After a short time the crowd moved outside and got in a van belonging to the Skakel family. Martha sat in the front seat, between Tommy and Michael, listening to music.

It was close to nine-thirty when Jackie Wettenhall announced she had to go home. About the same time Julie Skakel drove her friend Andrea to her house. Minutes later Rushton's two oldest boys, Rushton Jr. and John, sauntered over to the van to get their cousin Jimmy so they could drive him back to Sursum Corda. Michael joined them, leaving behind Tommy, Martha, Helen Ix, and the Byrne boy.

Around nine-thirty, Helen Ix and Geoff Byrne left

for home, too. Only Tommy and Martha remained, police later ascertained.

It would have taken Martha less than five minutes to walk from the Skakel house to her front door.

Dorthy Moxley was painting in her bedroom about ten o'clock when she was suddenly startled by a commotion in the yard. "I think that's when Martha was being killed," she said later. "I heard all this noise. I didn't hear Martha screaming. I heard voices, and I heard the neighborhood dogs barking. If that's when Martha was being killed, it may have been more than one person involved. I went downstairs and I turned on the outside light and I looked out the window."

But she didn't see anything out of the ordinary. Switching off the light, she decided to call it a night. She took a shower, got into her pajamas and robe, and went downstairs to watch television. Around ten-thirty, her son John arrived home. "You know, it's funny, but Martha's not home yet," his mother remarked. "But I wasn't really concerned," she explained later, "because, aside from the party a week earlier, Martha had never been a problem about getting home at a reasonable hour. Besides, she was off from school the next day." John, however, said he'd go out and look for her. A half-hour later, he returned, said he couldn't find Martha, and went upstairs to bed. His mother returned to the TV, watched the eleven-o'clock news, and then fell asleep with the set on. Around two A.M., she awoke with a start, the TV screen filled with static and noise. Groggy, she went upstairs, expecting to find Martha asleep, but her bed was empty.

Growing concerned, Dorthy Moxley went back downstairs and began telephoning the homes of her daughter's friends: the Ixes, the Wettenhalls, the Zalucas. When she learned from Helen Ix that Martha was last seen with Tommy at about nine-thirty, she immediately dialed the Skakel house, rousing Tommy's sister, Julie. It was the first of several telephone conversations she had with her between two and three o'clock in the morning. Each time, Julie said that Martha wasn't there.

During one call, the worried mother asked the teenager if she would look in the van in the driveway to see if her daughter might be there. "I knew Martha was getting to like beer and I thought maybe she had a couple of beers and passed out." Julie checked the van and reported it was empty. Calling back again, Mrs. Moxley asked to talk to Tommy, who came to the phone and said he had no idea where Martha was. The last time she called the Skakel house, Julie suggested that Mrs. Moxley telephone her aunt Georgeann Terrien.

"I had never met the woman; I knew nothing about the Terriens. She was a little groggy because I had awakened her," recalled Dorthy Moxley. "I told her who I was and apologized for calling at that hour and I told her I was looking for my daughter and that she was last seen with Tommy Skakel. She said, 'Oh, that darned kid, he's always doing something; he's always into mischief.' She asked me to wait a minute and came back and said, 'No, nobody's here.' I don't know what time this was but Jim Terrien wasn't home when I called. She asked for my number and told me she'd call back. She said she was going to go down to the guest house because she said sometimes the kids went there. A few minutes later she called back and said no, she was sorry, but no one was there, either. She seemed irritated at the fact that I might think that Martha was there, but she wasn't mad at me. I think she was mad at the kids."

Shortly before four o'clock, now frantic with worry, Dorthy Moxley called the police and reported her daughter missing. Minutes later an officer arrived, asked her some questions, looked through the house and in the yard. "He gave me the feeling that he thought she was just at a friend's house, that she just hadn't bothered to call home," she recalled. "I told him it really wasn't like her and that I had called all of her friends."

After the officer left, Dorthy Moxley tried to pull herself together. She thought, "Kids today are drinking beer. Kids are into drugs. Martha could have tried something." She went into the library and lay down on the window seat, eventually falling into a fitful sleep.

At daybreak she awoke and saw that Martha had still not returned. She quickly got dressed and walked over to Rushton Skakel's house, where she was greeted in the driveway by their large, snarling mutt, whom she had to keep at bay. "I was scared to death of that darned dog, but I thought, 'I have got to get past him and get in that house because that's the last place Martha was.' I finally knocked on the door and talked to Michael Skakel. He said Martha wasn't there. Then their gardener looked in the van. She wasn't there, either."

By the time she got back home, friends were calling to see if Martha had arrived safely, shocked when Dorthy Moxley told them she hadn't. Meanwhile, John Moxley had gotten up. While nervous about his sister's whereabouts, he had to get to school for his team's pregame warmup, and left the house. By that point, Dorthy Moxley's friends, knowing how upset she was, began arriving: Jean Walker, Marilyn Robertson, Jane Wohl. They sat, drank coffee, and tried to reassure Dorthy that Martha was safe.

At twelve-fifty in the afternoon, the doorbell rang. Jean Walker, wife of "Beetle Bailey" creator Mort Walker, accompanied Dorthy to the door.

Sheila McGuire was standing there crying.

"I found Martha," she said.

"Where?" Mrs. Moxley asked.

"Out under the tree," the teenager said.

"Well, is she okay?" Dorthy Moxley asked.

"No," Sheila sobbed.

As Dorthy Moxley started to go out, Jean Walker grabbed her hand. "Why don't I go and look," she said.

While she waited in the hall with her friends, Jean Walker followed Sheila McGuire onto the Moxley grounds.

A few minutes later Mrs. Walker returned to the house.

"It's Martha," she said quietly. "She's dead."

As Jean Walker went to phone the police, Dorthy Moxley found a chair in the living room, where she sat frozen throughout the day, even as her house filled with policemen, neighbors, and friends.

Shortly after Martha's body was discovered, David Moxley called home from a phone booth at the Atlanta airport to let his wife know he was about to board a flight for New York. Marilyn Robertson, who had answered the call, hesitated and then told him that his daughter was dead.

Even in her paralyzed state, Dorthy Moxley thought, "My God, why did you have to tell him?"

Moments later, John Moxley came into the house, crying, "My sister . . . my sister . . ."

After hearing the horrifying news that Martha Moxley had been found murdered, Georgeann telephoned Ethel at Hickory Hill. "My wife told Ethie that the Moxley girl had been hanging out with Tommy the night of the murder," George Terrien said. "Ethel was a nervous wreck. Georgeann told me later that Ethel said she was going to call Ted right away. She also called her other advisers. She said, 'We can't let this touch the Kennedys.' "

• • •

During the course of the investigation, and later, critics asserted that police didn't do all they could to solve the case. At the same time, some investigators felt intimidated by the Skakels' power.

The autopsy, conducted by Dr. Elliot Gross, Connecticut chief medical examiner, showed that Martha had died as a result of a fractured skull and brain injuries. The killer or killers, in a frenzy, had battered Martha's head with a Number 6 Tony Penna model golf club; she had been hit at least a dozen times, and stabbed through the neck with the shaft of the club. But there was no evidence of a sexual assault.

There had been two assaults on Martha, investigators theorized. The first occurred in the driveway of the Moxleys' home, about a dozen yards from Walsh Lane, or inside the Moxleys' circular driveway. The more violent of the two attacks was believed to have happened some feet away, under a weeping willow tree. The killer or killers then dragged Martha by her hair through weeds, grass, and brush to the spot where she was found. Near the body, police recovered an eleven-inch section of the golf-club shaft. Some distance from the Moxley driveway a smaller piece of the club's shaft was found, along with the club's head. The club's handle was never found. The time frame of the murder, as theorized by investigators, coincided with the noise and barking dogs Dorthy Moxley had heard that night.

Combing the neighborhood, conducting interviews, police quickly learned that Martha had last been seen with Tommy Skakel.

Detectives Jim Lunney and Ted Brosko went to the Skakel house to ask questions and look around, but had no reason to get a search warrant. When the officers arrived, the Skakel children invited them in; their father, still away on his hunting trip, would not return until November 2.

Tommy told the police that he had left Martha at nine-thirty on the lawn of his house and returned to his home to write a report about Abraham Lincoln for school. Police later checked with the school; Tommy had never been given such an assignment. His tutor-companion, Ken Littleton, said he had checked Tommy's room about the time Tommy claimed he was there; Littleton said he was missing. He claimed he didn't see Tommy until ten-thirty that night, when Tommy came into the den where Littleton said he was watching *The French Connection* on television. Littleton said the two had a normal conversation during the commercial. Reviewing that night, Detective Carroll thought the questioning of Tommy and Ken Littleton hadn't been thorough enough. The police also never determined what clothing Tommy had been wearing the night of the murder.

In a storage bin in the house, officers Lunney and Brosko discovered part of a set of Tony Penna golf clubs, similar to the broken golf club—the murder weapon—that was found near Martha's body. The clubs had belonged to Rushton's late wife, Ann, and carried a tag with her name.

In a later report, Detroit Homicide chief Gerald Hale, who had been brought in as a consultant, stated that Martha had been killed with the six-iron belonging to that set. The part of the murder weapon that was missing, Hale asserted, was the piece that would have had Mrs. Skakel's nameplate on it. He also noted, based on "an extensive survey," that there were "no other Tonny Penna golf clubs" in the entire Belle Haven area.

"There was never any question that a Skakel club was the murder weapon," said Donald Browne, the local prosecutor.

Despite finding the golf clubs in the Skakel house, neither Lunney, Brosko, nor any other Greenwich officer had immediately searched for other evidence, such as the missing piece of the murder weapon.

The reason for this failure was simple: initially the Greenwich police could not bring themselves to believe that the murder could have been committed by a local resident. Greenwich, and Belle Haven in particular, was populated by wealthy, powerful professionals, not the sort of people who commit such violent crimes. And that naive assessment applied to the entire Skakel clan, despite the fact that their long history of eccentric, occasionally violent behavior was well known to the local police and longtime residents of the community.

In the first twenty-four hours of the investigation, the police were, as Detective Steve Carroll said later, "very disorganized." Instead of focusing on suspects, teams of detectives, each looking to make the big collar, eliminated them. One theory was that an outsider, possibly a hitchhiker, had come in to the community under the cover of darkness, avoided detection from the private security force, killed Martha, and fled. Several suspects were cleared through lie-detector tests, or alibis.

With outsiders ruled out, the police finally began to focus on locals; one, another neighbor of the Moxleys, was a single twenty-seven-year-old Columbia University graduate student, who was subsequently cleared.

When Rushton returned from his hunting trip that Sunday, the police were there to greet him. "Since the golf club which was still at the Skakel home was similar to the one that caused the death of Martha Moxley, investigators proceeded to the Skakel home in an attempt to obtain the golf club," Detectives Lunney and Brosko wrote in their report.

Since they didn't have a search warrant, Rushton signed a consent form giving the detectives permission to search the house. But the police never made a formal search, according to Tom Keegan, who was the chief of detectives at the time. The reason, Keegan said, was because "Rushton Skakel was totally cooperative at the beginning and gave us carte blanche inside the house." Detective Lunney, who participated in the search, gave a different reason: "We were afraid if we asked him . . . . he might have said, 'Get out,' and we'd lose what access we had." According to Hale, "When it came to the Skakels, the Greenwich police were treading lightly." As Det. Steve Carroll observed later, "Maybe it was the Skakel money. Maybe it was their position. But I believe I was subconsciously intimidated by them." Police left the Skakel house that Sunday with a No. 5 Tony Penna iron that had Rushton's dead wife's name on it. When, six months after the murder, a search warrant was finally sought by Greenwich police, the state's attorney's office rejected the application. The reason? Too much time had elapsed.

Two days after Rushton returned home he took Tommy to Connecticut state police headquarters, where a lie-detector test was administered; the results were inconclusive because, it was said, he had not been sleeping well and was too tired to answer the questions properly. Five days later he was retested and passed, according to Keegan.

• • •

Fear, shock, anger, and one rumor after another rippled through Greenwich in the days and weeks following the murder.

Even Rushton's brother Jim Skakel had heard enough conflicting stories to stay out of the matter. Initially, he had contacted a friend who was head of investigations at Pinkerton, filled him in on the situation involving his nephew and the victim, and asked him to take a quick look and report back. "Just don't get my name mixed up in it," he instructed. "He got hold of me a couple of days later and said, 'It's a complete mess; there are all kinds of wackos involved, all kinds of stories flying around, and that Greenwich police force is screwed up. Don't go near any of it.' So I just forgot about it. I just hoped things would come out okay for my nephew."

Martha's high school friends had heard all sorts of wild stories about Tommy. The rumors were untrue, but inevitable in such a controversial case.

Martha's friend, Joe Romanello, said: "In 1975 we were a bunch of teenagers who didn't remember Chappaquiddick. The stuff hadn't come out about Jack or Bobby, so we weren't biased at all. But at the same time we said, 'There's a lot of money here. This is Ethel Skakel Kennedy's family. This is the Kennedys.'

"There hadn't been a murder in Greenwich in years. It shocked the conscience of the town. I can remember going to the football game that next day and they had a moment of silence, and everyone was a mess. The adults were worrying about their children and the effect a murder was going to have on us and trying to cope with something most people who lived in that kind of environment never had to deal with. Having grown up in Greenwich, it's a very insulated, antiseptic town, real New Englandy, very wealthy, very staid, a town that doesn't like to air out its laundry."

Not long after the murder, having heard all of the rumors, Romanello, who later became a criminal attorney in the Greenwich area, went to Greenwich Police Headquarters with four or five friends of Martha's from school.

"We were just very confused, very upset with the whole situation, and nothing seemed to be getting done," Romanello said later. "We had heard a lot of rumors about the Skakels . . . so we went marching into the police department and we demanded to see the head of the detective division, Tom Keegan. We told him all the things that we had heard and he became very upset. I remember thinking, 'We must be right because why would he get so angry at something like that.' Maybe that was a wrong conclusion and now, years later, I'm an attorney and I wouldn't draw that conclusion. We also hit him with the fact that this kid had left the country. He said, 'Do you know what Tommy Skakel looks like? Did you ever meet him? Do you know who he is?' He was just very upset; that how could these kids get this information; how the hell did they draw the conclusions they were drawing, and also, my God, if they know, everyone else is going to know. The man seemed obsessed with trying to find this girl's murderer and he seemed frustrated at his inability to do so."

Two months after the murder, Greenwich Police Chief Stephen Baran publicly blamed the rumors on "the shock that results from a crime of this nature." He said Martha's murder didn't happen "because of the kind of town we have. . . . This kind of crime happens because there are people, people with serious problems. Everything that can be humanly done is being done. I still have confidence that the case will be solved."

• • •

In the immediate aftermath of the murder, before police began taking a cold, hard look at Tommy Skakel as a prime suspect, members of the Skakel family were extremely cooperative with authorities, and were passionately sympathetic to the Moxleys' plight. David and Dorthy Moxley received messages of compassion from virtually everyone in the family, with the notable exception of Ethel, who had decided as a Kennedy to keep her distance; the danger of the case blowing up in the Skakel family's face—and tarnishing the Kennedy name—was much too great.

"We never heard from Ethel Kennedy; she never called; there was never a note," Dorthy Moxley said later. "But Rush and the others were wonderful in the beginning. I remember seeing Tommy at Martha's funeral and I went over to him and gave him a hug. I didn't know Tommy, but I felt since he was the last one to see her it must have been hard on him to know that she'd been killed; I did not even remember thinking that he was the one who—maybe—had killed her. I remember Rush used to come over and visit and tells us how sorry he was; he came over one night and said he'd just been to an A.A. meeting and he came in drinking a big glass of bourbon. He said, 'This is really terrible what happened to Martha. I wish it could be solved. I hope you don't think it was Tommy.' "

On one occasion, not long after the murder and before Tommy became a suspect, Rushton Skakel extended an invitation to the Moxleys to spend a weekend with his family at their country home in Windom, New York, which the Moxleys accepted. Another time, knowing John Moxley was seeking a job for the summer, there was promising talk from Tommy Skakel that his family might be able to get him one as a batboy with the Boston Red Sox. "John was excited," Mrs. Moxley recalled, "but then Tommy came to the door one day and said they couldn't get it for him. Later, when I thought about it, I felt we were being placated by them."

The Skakels' cooperation with authorities started coming to a close at the beginning of the new year. In mid-January of 1976, two and a half months after Martha's murder, the investigators, with little evidence to go on concerning Tommy or anyone else, decided to take a close look at the Skakel boy's past. They wanted to see his medical records, his school records, any psychological records. Initially, Rushton Skakel agreed to the request; he gave permission to the various schools Tommy had attended to turn over their files. All of them cooperated except for the Whitby School, the little Montessori school that had been founded almost twenty years earlier by Georgeann Terrien. It was the school where Tommy had spent most of his years; the school he attended after his mother became ill and the family began to disintegrate emotionally. Shortly after asking for the files, the police received a call from attorney Christopher Roosevelt, a member of the Whitby board. A former Justice Department attorney, Roosevelt rejected the request for the records and advised Rushton, who also served on the board of the school, to get a good lawyer to look after his son's interests.

On the afternoon of January 21, Rushton Skakel personally delivered a letter to the police chief rescinding his authorization for Tommy's records. He also let it be known that he had hired a criminal attorney, Emanuel Margolis, of Stamford, Connecticut. Rushton dropped off the letter at the police department's complaint desk and then went home. An hour later, Dorthy Moxley was sitting in her home when an ambulance screeched to a halt in front of the Ix house across the street; moments later the attendants carried out Rushton on a stretcher and took him to Greenwich Hospital. He had suffered chest pains while visiting the Ixes and required sedation.

Ten days later, Margolis rejected police requests to administer sodium pentothal, the so-called truth serum, to Tommy. The lawyer said he had made the decision after consulting a psychiatrist. He also refused to allow detectives to conduct another interview with Tommy. To Margolis, the discovery of the golf clubs at the Skakel home—which police saw as important—proved nothing. "Golf clubs were left all over the property all the time," he said. "Anyone could have picked one up from the grounds."

A couple of days later Rushton appeared at the Moxleys' house to, as he put it, "set the family's mind at ease." He told David and Dorthy Moxley that his son had undergone an unspecified examination and that the results were negative. But Skakel said the results hadn't been turned over to the police because his attorney had advised against it.

To the Moxleys, Rushton's decision to stop cooperating with the authorities strongly suggested that the finger of guilt was pointing at Tommy.

"It got so I couldn't even talk to the man," Dorthy Moxley said later. "I couldn't be in the same room with him. How could I be in the same room with a man who I thought was covering up for someone in his house? I remember one time my husband and I were playing tennis and Rushton was on the next court and I thought, 'I just can't play. I just cannot be anywhere around that man.' "

With the investigation turning up little or no new leads, Greenwich police welcomed the arrival of Gerald Hale from Detroit. Police from Nassau County, New York, also were consulted. Meanwhile, the Moxleys, desperate for a solution, had turned to psychics. "My sister and brother-in-law got in touch with some of the best—if there is such a thing as some of the best—psychics and I know that a couple of times the psychics asked about a bloody sweater," said Buck Jolgren. "The psychics told them they should look in certain places. They also pointed the finger. That was pretty wild and way out, but the stuff was being fed to the police department."

Five months after Martha's murder, there appeared to be a major break in the case. Helen Ix and Geoffrey Byrne, who had been with Martha the night of the murder, told Hale that they had witnessed a shoving match between Tommy and Martha outside the Skakel house.

"This, after careful questioning consisted of Martha pushing Thomas and Thomas pushing Martha," Hale wrote in his report. "At one point, Thomas pushed Martha down and either fell or got down on her. This point is not clear as it happened partly out of view of Helen and [Geoff] behind a brick wall." Tommy later told the *Greenwich Time*, "I don't remember anything like that."

By the spring of 1976, Tommy Skakel felt he was being harassed by the police and had decided to leave the Brunswick School. He tried to enroll in a private school in New York but parents who had heard about the Moxley case threatened to withdraw their children if he was admitted. Instead, he enrolled at Vershire Academy in Vermont.

Around that time he also took a trip out of the country, to visit his aunt Pat Skakel Cuffe in Ireland. Rumor had it that he had fled the country, but a Skakel relative maintained years later that the trip had been planned long before the murder.

Meanwhile, Tommy's tutor-companion, Ken Littleton, had lost his job at the Skakels' following a falling-out with Rushton, who subsequently refused to pay Littleton's last month's salary. The headmaster at Brunswick interceded on Littleton's behalf, and Skakel finally paid him. "I never understood why he turned against me," Littleton said later. "I think he wanted to separate himself and his family from me when the police began pressuring me." For months, police had tried unsuccessfully to coax Littleton into giving them a formal written statement. He told detectives he would not supply "circumstantial evidence" against Tommy because he said he believed Tommy was innocent. "I just didn't think Tommy could have done it," Littleton said.

Police thought they saw a break in the case that Bicentennial summer of 1976, one that might have cleared the cloud that had been hanging over Tommy Skakel.

The Moxley task force received a report that Littleton had been arrested and charged with grand larceny. He had been accused of stealing four thousand dollars worth of items from stores and a boat while working on Nantucket. He had buried at least one of the items. Littleton had told Massachusetts authorities that he was drunk at the time of the break-ins. He pleaded guilty to the larceny charges and received a suspended sentence of seven to ten years in prison and five years of probation.

For the first time, police began taking a hard look at Littleton; like Tommy Skakel, he now had become a prime suspect in the case.

That October, Littleton agreed to take a polygraph test. He was given the test three times, the report stated, "and it was the opinion of the examiners that Kenneth Littleton was not truthful in answering key questions." Littleton, though, scoffed at the results, claiming that the interpretation of his answers was affected by his recent legal problems in Massachusetts. The state police report of the polygraph tests said that Littleton had continued to deny any "involvement or knowledge" regarding the murder. Littleton's attorney, John Meerbergen, who at the time described the case as "too hot and heavy," advised his client not to submit to a sodium pentothal test, which Greenwich police had requested. Police hoped the test would bring out something in Littleton's subconscious about the night of the murder. The lawyer said his client had "no need to prove his innocence."

Because of his arrest on Nantucket, he lost his job at Brunswick. He was next hired at the private St. Luke's School, in New Canaan, Connecticut, but was dismissed after Greenwich police paid a visit to the school. "It just didn't seem like a good situation for us," said a school official. "I told Ken that once he cleared up this Nantucket business, he could re-apply. He's an extremely competent science teacher who had a great relationship with the kids. And he was well thought of by other teachers."

Months passed. Now unable to get a teaching job, Littleton became a salesman.

Tommy Skakel continued his studies and graduated from Vershire Academy.

There were no new leads. The police were stymied.

Eighteen months after the murder, *The New York Times* did an update: WHO KILLED MARTHA MOXLEY? A TOWN WONDERS. Around that time, recalled Ted Kennedy's aide Richard Burke, Rushton Skakel had been invited by Ethel to an event at which the Senator was scheduled to be present. "Ted knew about her brother's trouble. He said to me, 'Just make sure that guy [Rushton] doesn't get near me.' Ted didn't want him near him because the press was there and he didn't want to wind up in a photograph with the father of a suspected murderer."

• • •

For years the Martha Moxley case remained open but dormant.

Tom Keegan, who rose to police chief, retired from the force, moved to South Carolina, and was elected to the State House of Representatives. Lunney, Carroll, and the other detectives on the case also retired. Along with the police, the two young men who had been the primary suspects tried as best they could to get on with their lives.

After attending Ithaca College, Tommy Skakel traveled extensively; he went through Europe and Africa. In Mexico he contracted malaria and would suffer from raging fevers. In May 1989, he married Anne Maitland Gillman of Boxford, Massachusetts. The two had met in New York, where she was working for a clothing firm, Banana Republic Design. They had a big wedding in Greenwich that was attended by many of Tommy's Kennedy cousins and his Aunt Ethel. Tommy also became a father. By the late 1980s and early 1990s, he had become involved in commercial real-estate brokering, and in the venture capital business. One of his associations was with a group of New York entrepreneurs doing business in the Soviet Union. "Tommy introduced us to a lot of very important people that included his cousin Bobby Kennedy, Jr., who was in environmental law, and Bobby's brother Michael Kennedy, who was in the petroleum business," said one of his colleagues, Harvey Hamment. "My wife and I had even gotten an invitation to have dinner with Tommy's aunt Ethel Kennedy, in Virginia, but I couldn't go because I had an appointment in Moscow. Tommy was a pleasure, a real gentleman. I never knew he had been connected to a murder case until I read about the case later."

Kenneth Littleton, meanwhile, reportedly developed a drinking problem.

Feeling that the investigation had destroyed his life, Littleton temporarily left the country for Australia.

Two years after their daughter was killed, the Moxleys moved from their house on Walsh Lane in Greenwich to the Upper East Side of Manhattan. Losing himself in his work, David Moxley rose quickly through the ranks, serving as managing partner of Touche Ross USA and managing director of Touche Ross International. Later, he became senior adviser to Kansas Senator Robert Dole in his aborted 1988 Republican presidential bid. In November of that year, at age fifty-seven, Moxley died suddenly of a massive heart attack, just a month after being named managing director of the prestigious New York law firm of Lord Day & Lord, Barrett Smith. He was buried next to his daughter at Putnam Hills Cemetery in Greenwich.

While the case had long faded from the police blotter in Greenwich, there wasn't a day when Dorthy Moxley didn't think about Martha, but she had given up all hope that her daughter's killer would ever be found.

As far as she was concerned, the file had been closed.

• • •

Another criminal case, in the spring of 1991, this one involving another nephew of Ethel's, William Kennedy Smith, had the instant effect of sweeping cobwebs from the Martha Moxley murder-case file.

Thirty-year-old Willie Smith, son of Jean and Steve Smith, was a fourth-year medical student at Georgetown University. He had been accused of rape at the Kennedys' Palm Beach estate during Easter. His accuser was thirty-year-old Patricia Bowman, an attractive single mother whom he had met at a club called Au Bar during a night out with his uncle Ted. For the Kennedys, the Willie Smith case was Chappaquiddick all over again. The international press descended on the rich Florida resort. Charges flew of a Kennedy cover-up involving Ted, other family members, and hangers-on. Headlines in publications ranging from *The New York Times* to *The National Enquirer* screamed: TEDDY'S SEXY ROMP; KENNEDY RAPE SCANDAL; KEY DETAILS OF WEEKEND AT KENNEDY ESTATE REMAIN MYSTERIOUS; FOR KENNEDY, NO ESCAPING A DARK CLOUD. There was a titillating, bitterly fought trial, televised nationally, at which Willie was eventually acquitted. Throughout the proceeding, Kennedy women sat in the courtroom en masse to show their support for Willie. "Ethel and Eunice are frequently in attendance at the trial, although they seem to absent themselves if there's a good chance that they might have to hear testimony about whether their nephew can get hard or not," noted one journalist. "If you're in the press row you sit right behind them and look at their hair. They could both use a good hot-oil conditioner."

In Greenwich, news of the William Kennedy Smith rape charge and acquittal reawakened memories of the Martha Moxley case. As Buck Jolgren pointed out, "We had friends calling us from all over the country after this thing involving the Kennedys in Palm Beach, saying, 'God, here we go again.' " Similar comments echoed throughout Greenwich among people familiar with the Moxley case; friends and neighbors of the Skakels and the Moxleys; retired cops; attorneys and prosecutors. One, Royall O'Brien, whose little girl Hope had died in the Skakel speed-bump accident nine years before the Moxley murder, says he thought, "Here's another one."

There also was a resurgence of bizarre rumors: that Rushton Skakel had been using a golf club as a walking stick; that Tommy Skakel was thinking of taking a job with a company that manufactured golf clubs.

Following a tip about the long unsolved case, *The National Enquirer* dispatched a team of reporters to Greenwich. Tying the Moxley murder in with the publication's ongoing coverage of the Willie Smith scandal, the *Enquirer* wrote in its issue of May 7, 1991: "In a case that chillingly echoes the reported rape at the Kennedy mansion . . . a Kennedy cousin is a prime suspect in the savage murder of a teenage girl . . . Thomas Skakel . . . quickly became the 'No. 1 suspect'—and he remains a top suspect today, said Jim Lunney, a police detective who worked on the investigation." An *Enquirer* reporter reached Tommy Skakel, who said, "I didn't kill Martha Moxley. I don't know who did it."

After the story ran, Greenwich police began getting calls from people who had new leads. State's Attorney Donald Browne said he believed the tips, which he didn't view as significant, had been prompted by the fierce interest in the Palm Beach rape case.

For a number of years, Leonard Levitt, an investigative reporter, had been probing the Moxley case for the *Greenwich Time*. He'd interviewed virtually everyone involved—detectives, family members, suspects. As far back as 1982, the newspaper had requested that the police department make public its files on the case under Connecticut's Freedom of Information laws, and subsequently some four hundred pages of documents were turned over. The police were permitted to withhold any documents and portions of documents they believed could jeopardize an eventual prosecution. Keegan, then chief of police, refused to release more than four dozen documents, including witness statements. Many of the documents that were made public had large portions blacked out. The paper also got Hale's confidential summary of the case.

But nothing had appeared in print.

On April 18, 1991, Dorthy Moxley told the author of this book, the only journalist outside of Levitt to call her in years, "The Greenwich paper won't do the story. That's what Levitt says. Every time he writes something they give it to their lawyers. Then it gets right down to the wire and nothing happens."

Apparently spurred by the *Enquirer* story and subsequent newspaper accounts—the *New York Post*, for one, ran a story on May 1, 1991, with a headline that read, FLA. CASE REVIVES PROBE OF KENNEDY KIN IN '75 SEX SLAY—the *Greenwich Time* finally ran a massive, detailed story about the police investigation.

The headline on the June 2, 1991, story, written by Levitt and *Greenwich Time* reporter Kevin Donovan, said, MOXLEY MURDER CASE STILL HAUNTS GREENWICH. The story maintained that there "appears to have been no coverup by the Greenwich police." But it acknowledged that after the discovery of the golf club at the Skakel house, the police did not immediately conduct a formal search. "Doing so," the paper concluded, "could have produced evidence related to the murder or helped clear one or both of the two chief suspects." The paper also said that contrary to rumors that the Skakel family hampered the investigation, they cooperated with authorities for the first few months.

After the *Greenwich Time* story ran, more new leads were telephoned to police headquarters, and a police hotline was opened. Two detectives were reassigned full time to the case. Dorthy Moxley increased to fifty thousand dollars the twenty-thousand-dollar reward that had been offered by the state since 1978 for information leading to the arrest or conviction of the murderer. In a letter to the *Greenwich Time*, she wrote, "I want to know why Martha deserved to die. What did she do? If she hadn't done it would she be alive today? Would the killer do it again if he had the chance? Are you sure he wouldn't do it again?"

In mid-1991, Dorthy Moxley received a letter from novelist Dominick Dunne, himself a parent of a daughter who had been murdered. Dunne met briefly with Mrs. Moxley at an airport restaurant, had her describe for him the events surrounding the death of Martha, and then went home and wrote a best-selling novel, *A Season in Purgatory*, about a murder, a cover-up, and a powerful Irish Catholic family. Mrs. Moxley found little in the book that resembled the real story of her daughter's death, but she was grateful for the publicity the book sparked about the unsolved murder. "People talk to Dominick all the time," she said. "Some things the police were very interested in."

In April 1993, Dorthy Moxley was chatting with her old friend Cissy Ix, who was still a neighbor of Rushton Skakel's. In 1983, ten years after his wife's death, Skakel had remarried. Now, suffering from prostate cancer, he had put his Greenwich home on the market for $5 million and planned to move permanently to Florida, where he owned a condominium. Mrs. Ix told Dorthy Moxley that, in the wake of the renewed publicity about the murder, Rushton had hired a private investigator, Jim Murphy. "You should really talk to him," Cissy Ix urged. But when Dorthy Moxley called Jacob Zeldes, the lawyer her husband had retained years earlier, he advised her not to talk to Murphy. "You can't," he said. "They're not cooperating with us. We just can't cooperate with them." Frustrated, Mrs. Moxley decided to call Murphy anyway, thinking, "Someone has to start cooperating around here." She had one telephone call with Murphy's associate, who she said told her, "We can definitely prove that not one person in the Skakel family had done anything to hurt Martha."

"I told him, 'If you can do that, then go to the police.' He said they couldn't because the Skakels' attorney, Manny Margolis, didn't think that was the thing for them to do. By the time I got off the phone, I was in tears."

At the suggestion of the police, Dorthy Moxley sent a registered letter to Rushton Skakel in April 1993. "I said to him that I was confident that he was convinced no one in his family had anything to do with Martha's death, and wouldn't he please permit the boys—Tommy, Michael, Jimmy Terrien—to be interviewed by the police; that the police said their lawyers could be present and could stop the questioning at any time; let's do this so we can all get on with our lives. Rush never acknowledged my letter. If the Skakels had nothing to do with Martha's death, why aren't they going to the police, why aren't they proving it and getting this monkey off their backs?"

At the time of the Willie Smith case, Jim Murphy said, there were so many rumors starting up again about the Skakels' alleged involvement in the Moxley case that "it was creating a great deal of tension within the family. They were asking, 'What do we do? How do we defend ourselves?' So our mandate was to flush out the truth and, if that truth should have been that one of the Skakel children was involved, then so be it; then let's identify that and let's put together a credible defense, if there is one. If that is not the case, then let's do as thorough and accurate and objective an investigation as we possibly can and come up with as much factual information as we can to stop the rumors. That mandate, though, has got to be balanced with the reality that Mr. Skakel never believed that any of his children had anything to do with Martha Moxley's murder."

As of Halloween 1993, the eighteenth anniversary of Martha Moxley's murder, the case remained unsolved.

107 * More Scandal

IN 1977, AS the Skakels dealt with the fallout from the Moxley case, the Kennedys were rocked by more scandal—the publication of Judith Campbell Exner's tell-all book about her secret love affair with Jack.

Two years earlier, the Senate's Church Committee investigation had smeared the story of the affair across the nation's front pages. Exner's name had not been revealed by the committee, but was quickly leaked by Republican sources fearing a whitewash. Exner, who was attacked by the press and the Kennedys as a "Mob moll," "tramp," and "party girl," now decided to break her long silence.

The result was *Judith Exner: My Story,* which became an instant best-seller for publisher Grove Press.

"I knew them when the dream of Camelot was real—Jack Kennedy, Frank Sinatra, Sam Giancana, and John Roselli," Exner wrote of her relationships with the President, the "chairman of the board," who introduced Exner to Jack in Las Vegas in 1960, and the two Mafia chieftains.

The vast majority of the Washington press corps had known about Jack's affairs for years, but had protected him. But for the first time, because of Exner, the American public was now getting a keyhole view of Jack's extramarital sex life. Exner's tale was only the beginning—soon Jack was being linked in the media to other beauties—Angie Dickinson was one; Marilyn was yet to come. The press was riding high in the post-Watergate era; no person or institution was sacred, not even the martyred President.

The Kennedys were aghast—the foundation, the

very cornerstone of their structure, was crumbling around them. In the face of the scandal, they circled the wagons. One Kennedy loyalist, denying any knowledge of the affair, said the only Campbell he was aware of was the soup.

As usual, though, the biggest defender of the faith was Ethel. In private, to her journalist friends, she angrily denounced Judith Exner's story as a sordid lie. Moreover, she threatened to sever Kennedy family ties with any journalist who joined the media mob that was now exposing Jack's bedroom romps.

When Exner's book was published, Ethel's friend Barbara Howar was working for a CBS-TV newsmagazine called "Who's Who," which also starred Dan Rather and Charles Kuralt. Unlike the investigative "60 Minutes," "Who's Who" did *People* magazine–style profiles on celebrities. Since both shows utilized the same facilities, Howar had become friendly with the "60 Minutes" crew. She recalled that when the Exner story broke, veteran "60 Minutes" correspondent Mike Wallace had decided to pass.

"Mike wouldn't do Exner and I remember he said to me, 'I'm gonna do you a favor, kid; I'm gonna let *you* do Judith Exner,' " Howar said later. "Well, the word came back that Ethel was leading the campaign and that your children would never play with another human again if you did the story. I was so frozen and it got so bad that finally Walter Cronkite said to me, 'If you don't want to do Judith Exner, I can understand that.' Walter bailed me out and he did it.

"Now I look back and I wish to fuck I'd done Judith Exner. But we still thought the Kennedys sacred people; the whole world did. We didn't know. We suspected but we didn't know. All the way down the line that was poor editorial judgment."

Another journalist who felt Ethel's bite during the Exner controversy was Larry Stern, an editor at the *Washington Post*. One of his colleagues, Bob Woodward, had heard about Exner's forthcoming book and was interested in doing the story. Stern got a copy of the proposal but mischievously chose an awkward moment to hand it over to Woodward—a party where Woodward was chatting up Ethel.

"When she saw it," Stern said, "she began shouting and screaming. Then she grabbed her jock-of-the-week escort and left."

A few years later, Ethel was once again on the warpath, battling the producers of a TV miniseries called "Blood Feud," which dealt with the struggles between Bobby and Jimmy Hoffa. In a tough letter to Al Masini, the executive producer, Ethel charged that the four-hour program distorted history, and lacked integrity. She wondered what had happened to responsible journalism.

If the media's way of handling the Exner book and the Hoffa film were infuriating to her, it was a good thing Ethel couldn't see ahead to the early nineties, when fictional and speculative accounts of the Kennedys' lives exploded on the scene, ranging from Oliver Stone's *JFK* to the USA Network's *Marilyn & Bobby: Her Final Affair,* to Joe McGinniss's *The Last Brother*. Still carrying the banner, according to insiders, it was Ethel who had convinced Ted not to cooperate with McGinniss, and it was Ethel who ordered others not to talk to him. As one intimate of Ethel's put it, "She was in there tooth and nail shutting down the avenues. She had gone crazy over the prospect of Joe's book. Ethel was the one in the family who was smart enough, cunning enough, to know that you don't let Joe McGinniss in with Teddy, as flawed as he is. When the bad reviews of Joe's book started pouring in, Ethel was jubilant."

108 ✻ David's Drugs

DEFENDING THE KENNEDYS' honor against the likes of Judith Exner and others should have been the least of Ethel's concerns in the late seventies, a time when Bobby Jr. and David, now in their early twenties, were moving deeper into the nightmare world of hard drugs.

To outsiders who read the warning TRESPASSERS WILL BE EATEN, Hickory Hill still appeared to be the same warm, hospitable place it had always been: the young ones, Rory, Doug, and Max, still romped on the grounds. Friends of Ethel's, a much smaller group now, played tennis, swam, and dined with her. Ethel threw fund-raisers for political cronies. Each year the best and the brightest turned out for the annual RFK journalism and book awards, and Ethel's pet show, which made headlines in 1978 when a runaway elephant almost flattened the First Family's daughter.

Ethel's relationship with Jimmy and Rosalynn Carter, the first Democrats to inhabit the White House since the Kennedys and Johnsons, had been less than amicable from the start. Ever since the 1976 Democratic Convention, Ethel had quietly seethed, believing that the former Georgia Governor had snubbed the Kennedys by not giving Ted a role and by giving family members lousy seats. Rumors had circulated that, for the first time, Ethel had voted Republican.

Now, with Jimmy Carter in the White House, Ethel was getting the cold shoulder. She had sent the one-time peanut farmer a syrupy "Dear Mr. President" letter inviting him to participate in the seventh annual Robert

F. Kennedy Tennis Tournament and a "gala dinner dance" at the Rainbow Room in New York. She complimented him on his tennis game and his dancing ability and promised that if he accepted, he'd have his choice of dancing with Dolly Parton, "Cheryl Tiggs"(sic), and even little, old Ethel.

Two weeks later, Carter wrote back, saying, "It is too early to make a definite commitment. . . . However, Rosalynn and I have both noted the days . . . on our calendar . . . and plan to get back in touch with you. . . ." In a postscript, Carter added, "Your remarks about the reputation of my tennis game and dancing ability are flattering. I must say that my dancing partner is superb! (An unbiased observation, naturally!)" Not long after, Carter sent Ethel what appeared to be a form letter with her name typed at the top and his hand-stamped signature at the bottom. Carter said the two-day tournament happened to "fall in the brief period of time that we can plan to be away on vacation. I know you will understand how important we feel it is to set aside some time for our family. . . . Perhaps we can join you next year!"

Friends said Ethel was raging after she read the letter. "That cracker has not a whit of class," she told a pal.

But Ethel, keeping up an appearance of cordiality, did extend an invitation to the President's ten-year-old daughter, Amy, to attend the pet show at Hickory Hill. A background memo on the event was prepared for Rosalynn Carter by a White House assistant who wrote, "It's like a big outdoor fair . . . the Washington Redskins, Mr. Rogers, 'Annie' and her dog, Art Buchwald, and others will be there . . . there will be games and pony rides."

Ethel had made no mention of a three-ton Indian elephant named Suzie that she had borrowed from the Ringling Brothers and Barnum & Bailey Circus.

Irritated by one of the Kennedys' barking dogs, Suzie got away from her handlers as she was being loaded into a van and barreled headlong into the midst of the festivities and the celebrants—Amy, among them. A

Secret Service agent responsible for the presidential daughter's life broke a finger and wrenched an ankle when he grabbed Amy and lifted her over a fence as the pachyderm, "moving fairly rapidly," came "relatively close" to her. A Secret Service official said the situation "called for some pretty quick action, and the agents responded." Before Suzie was stopped, she had crashed though a fence on to the property of one of Ethel's neighbors. "I understand our neighbor came out of his house, just stood there for a moment, shook his head, and went back inside," Ethel told a reporter. When Amy got home she told her parents what happened. "It was pretty scary," she said.

A few days later, Ethel wrote a mea culpa to the First Lady, calling Amy a great sport, plucky, self-possessed, and courageous in the face of Suzie's stampede. She also complimented Mrs. Carter for her abilities as a mother.

Everything appeared as usual at Hickory Hill. But in truth, life inside the big house had become a bleak affair because of David's and Bobby's drug problems. The one sunny spot came in November 1977, when Ethel became a grandmother for the first time. Kathleen's baby girl, Meaghan Ann Kennedy Townsend, was the first of a new generation of Kennedys.

Having dropped out of Harvard, David was spending his time living between Hickory Hill and New York where, stoned most of the time, he crashed with friends and family members. While still in Cambridge, his psychiatrist had given him prescriptions for Percodan. In March 1976, strung out and debilitated, he developed pneumonia and had to be admitted to Massachusetts General Hospital. A month into his hospitalization, doctors discovered that he had suffered inflammation of the lymph glands as a result of the antibiotics. A few days later, Ethel celebrated her forty-eighth birthday at a lively party at Hickory Hill.

"David was Mrs. Kennedy's least favorite," recalled Noelle Fell. "He was an embarrassment to her. He kept his room in the house, but she couldn't have cared less whether she talked to him or not, whether he ate dinner with her or not. At dinnertime, she'd say to the children, 'Okay, it's ready,' and she'd make certain everyone was at the table with her. But she didn't do that with David. If there was any company, she'd tell David to go upstairs, like a child."

Because Ethel refused to allow David to use any of the family cars, or to give him pocket money, he'd beg the help for both, then drive across the Potomac in a borrowed car to score heroin with borrowed money. Other times he'd leave for a day or two to buy drugs in New York. Most, if not all, of the staff at Hickory Hill, having had no experience with drug addiction, thought that David was an alcoholic.

Then, early one morning in the summer of 1978, the truth hit home.

The day staff arrived at Hickory Hill to find two important, longtime Kennedy family friends pacing nervously in the first-floor TV room. One was the imposing Supreme Court Justice William O. Douglas, and the other was Gertrude Ball, who handled business for the Park Agency and the Kennedy Library. Both had rushed to the house after getting word of a break-in while Ethel was at the compound.

"Oh, my God, something terrible has happened," Ball told the staff. "We have got to call the police."

David claimed he had surprised a burglar who had smashed his way in through a third-floor window and that the two had had a bloody fight before the intruder fled. The story sounded plausible. It wasn't the first time Ethel's house had been invaded by the kind of psychotics who harass famous people. A year or so earlier, a man had climbed a fire escape, gotten into nine-year-old Rory's room, awakened her, asked directions to her mother's room, and then walked in on Ethel, who had just gone to bed after a party. More recently, a strange woman had gained entrance to Ethel's house in the compound, made a series of telephone calls to New York, and then tried to walk off with Noelle Fell's little girl, who looked like Rory and was the same age. Police nabbed the woman, but no charges were filed in either case because Ethel didn't want the publicity.

Therefore, when David reported his encounter with the intruder, no one had any reason to doubt his veracity. They all knew that, for some unknown reason, despite all of the past incidents—not to mention the assassinations and a frightening 1974 kidnap threat against all the Kennedy children—Ethel had refused to install even the most basic form of security system in her homes.

While demanding that the police be summoned, neither Gertrude Ball nor Justice Douglas had bothered to go up to the third floor to check David's story. Knowing it was all but impossible for anyone to gain entrance there, Noelle Fell told the two to hold off sounding the alarm, and raced upstairs to see for herself what had happened.

"The window was broken, the room had been turned upside down, and there was blood on the floor," she said later. "There also were needles and vials on the floor. It was now ten o'clock in the morning and David was in his bed sleeping with a girl and I couldn't wake up either one of them. I went downstairs and I said to Gertrude Ball and Justice Douglas, 'Please don't call the police. This was not the work of a burglar. This was David's doing. This was drugs.' "

Justice Douglas stood there, seemingly uncomprehending. Shocked, Gertrude Ball asked Noelle what she should do. "I think you should call Mrs. Kennedy," the secretary suggested. "No, *you* do it," Ball responded, wanting to avoid an embarrassing confrontation.

Noelle reached Ethel at Hyannis, where David had now been banned by his mother because of his behavior.

"I told her what had happened. I told her that it was really David, not a burglar; that David must have been looking for drugs or shooting drugs and that he had probably freaked out. She didn't say a word. Then I asked her what she wanted us to do. She said, 'Go tell David to clean the room.' I said, 'I beg your pardon?' I told her that David was asleep with a girl next to him. She said, 'Well you go tell David to clean his room.' I thought to myself, 'What the hell good is that going to do? This poor kid is sick.' So I told her it might be better for me to have David call her after he got up, but that I wasn't about to tell him to clean the room like he was a five-year-old. Besides, if I tried he'd probably punch me in the face. I told her Gertrude Ball and Justice Douglas were there and wanted to call the police. That really upset her. She said, 'No, no, no, no, no. Don't call the police whatever you do! I just want to make sure David goes and cleans up his own mess.' Mrs. Kennedy then asked to talk to Gertrude Ball and told her the same thing—have David clean the room, don't call the police."

As Noelle Fell recalled, Justice Douglas, who had been listening, still seemed unable to understand what was going on. "Are you sure we shouldn't call the police?" he asked once more. Noelle Fell said, "What for? It wasn't a burglar." Gertrude Ball grabbed her purse, steered the perplexed Supreme Court justice to the door, and left.

Moments later Noelle Fell placed a call to Ted's house, a few miles away, to tell him what had happened.

"There's nothing I can do," he said with finality. Fell had telephoned the Senator because he had taken on the responsibility, at Ethel's request, to keep a watch on David that summer. Initially, David had been ordered to stay at his uncle's house in McLean, not at Hickory Hill. Ted had even assigned George Dalton, an old drinking buddy of Jack's, and now Ted's majordomo, to baby-sit David. The idea was that Dalton, a tough, retired military man, would guard David around-the-clock, not let him out of his sight, and thereby force him to kick his drug habit. The day before the plan was scheduled to go into effect, David pleaded with his uncle to allow him to stay at Hickory Hill, at least for a few more days. "I promise to be a good boy," he told his uncle. "I promise I won't get into any trouble."

David spent just two days at Ted's house before returning to Hickory Hill. He spent a day there under the watchful eyes of Noelle Fell, then took one of his mother's credit cards and left for New York.

His parting words were, "My uncle's as bad as I am; he can't do anything for me." Ted's efforts to help David came at a time when the Senator himself had begun experimenting with cocaine, according to Richard Burke.

Still at the Cape, Ethel was livid when she learned that David had left Ted's house.

"Mrs. Kennedy called me at Hickory Hill and demanded to know where David was," Noelle Fell recalled. "She said, 'I told you to watch him.' I told Mrs. Kennedy that there was only so much I could do. I told her quite bluntly that if she couldn't control her son, how was I supposed to do it? She said, 'How could you let him use my credit card? Where did he get the money to go to New York? Did you loan him money?' She was so pissed off at me that she wanted to come home and blow my brains out."

Minutes later Ted and George Dalton, both visibly agitated, showed up at the house. "If and when you hear from David," Ted told Noelle, "make sure he calls us."

Three days later David returned to Hickory Hill, but refused to go back to Ted's house.

In Noelle's presence, the Senator telephoned Ethel at the compound. "There's nothing I can do," he said. "You'll have to put him in a hospital."

But for the moment, no one did anything, and David continued his drug feeding-frenzy.

In early 1979, David abandoned Hickory Hill completely. Using money from his trust fund, he moved to New York, rented a penthouse apartment on East Seventy-second Street, partied nightly at discos, and for a time took up with pretty twenty-one-year-old model-actress Rachel Ward. That May, Ethel was furious and embarrassed when she saw tabloid photos of her fourth-born—long-haired, skinny, disheveled, about to turn twenty-four—slumped in a banquette at Xenon behind a drink- and cigarette-cluttered table with his arms around Rachel and another beauty. On one occasion at Xenon, David had flown into a jealous rage when he spotted French playboy Phillippe Junot, new husband of Princess Caroline of Monaco, paying too much attention to Rachel. Their fight over Rachel was duly reported in the tabloids and in *People* magazine. David's tempestuous relationship with Rachel lasted only five months. He said afterward, "Rachel wanted to get an apartment with me and settle down. But I knew I was too fucked up. I was back on smack. She had no idea what I was up to." Rachel said later, "We smoked joints now and then, but there was no suggestion of heroin. He ate like a pig and didn't take very good care of himself, but he was crazy, with a wonderful sense of humor, and he was always very merry."

On a warm evening in early September 1979, David, needing a fix, got behind the wheel of his sixteen-thousand-dollar green BMW sport coupe with expired Virginia tags and a pile of unpaid parking tickets in the glove box and journeyed from the safety of the Upper East Side into the crime-riddled streets of Harlem, where his father and mother had once campaigned for the poor black vote. Near the corner of Eighth Avenue and 116th Street, in a seedy shooting gallery known as the Shelton Plaza Hotel, David tried to make a buy. But something went horribly wrong. The first police on the scene found David in the lobby, bruised and dazed. As he told it, he had been driving near the hotel, was waved down by two pedestrians, forced into the hotel's lobby, robbed at knifepoint of thirty dollars, and beaten. But narcotics detectives, suspicious of why a rich white boy would be anywhere near the well-known drug spot, made a quick search and found twenty-five abandoned glassine envelopes of heroin on a third-floor landing. At first police sources said that David had been trying to buy cocaine, but quickly it was revealed that he was after heroin. "I'm a stoned-out junkie," he confessed.

The Kennedys were livid over the press leaks and soon police stopped talking. As one official said, "Police here know you don't mess around with the Kennedys."

David was never arrested and remained listed as a victim. "Our office issued a quick statement blandly explaining that David was on a leave of absence from Harvard and was simply in New York to visit friends," said Richard Burke. Burke was assigned by Ted—who two days after the Harlem incident got the green light from the clan to make a run for the presidency—to help set up a treatment program for David. David soon entered a drug rehabilitation program at McLean Hospital, near Boston. He was then moved to Massachusetts General, in very serious condition for treatment of an infection known as bacterial endocarditis, usually contracted through the use of contaminated hypodermic needles.

While David was hospitalized, Ethel, who had turned fifty, became a grandmother for the second time. Kathleen, having graduated from the University of New Mexico law school, gave birth to a second daughter, named Maeve Fahey Kennedy Townsend.

109 * Bobby's Drugs

AFTER DAVID'S RELEASE from the hospital, Ted assigned Lem Billings to be his guardian.

It was an unfortunate choice. Billings, whom the family had appointed surrogate father to Bobby after Los Angeles, had, in the boys' company, become a heavy drug user himself, and Bobby was in almost as bad shape as David.

Once fastidious, dressing in tweeds, Lem Billings had changed almost overnight. His hair was long, he wore beat-up clothes, and he talked the jargon of the street. At Bobby's urging, Billings—almost four decades older than his charge—tried everything from smoking marijuana and snorting cocaine to shooting speed and heroin. Friends felt that Billings had become as obsessed with Bobby as he had once been with Jack Kennedy. Billings also was an active promoter of Bobby's sexual escapades. He allowed Bobby to bring women back to the East Eighty-eighth Street duplex that they often shared, and he boasted that the boy was even more virile than Jack had been in his youth. While many believed Billings was asexual, there were others who maintained he was a homosexual. George Terrien, who knew Billings well, said, "Everyone knew Lem was queer—the Kennedys, the Skakels, everyone. I never could figure out why Ethel would let Lem have such an intimate relationship with the boys. She always remained blind to what he really was."

Somehow, through it all, though, Bobby continued in his studies—with much prodding and help from Billings—and graduated from Harvard. But afterward he made little headway: while his senior thesis, a biography of Federal Judge Frank M. Johnston, Jr., had been published as a book, it received negative reviews (Jack Kennedy's thesis had been promoted into a best-seller by his father and had Bobby been alive that might have happened again); his hopes for a Rhodes scholarship had been dashed when his application was flatly rejected by the committee; he spent several weeks at the London School of Economics, but dropped out (as Jack had done on the eve of World War II).

By the time David was being hospitalized after the Harlem incident, Bobby was enrolled in law school at his father's alma mater, the University of Virginia. But, despite denials to himself and others, he was still caught up in drugs.

Summers and holidays Bobby often stayed at Hickory Hill, mainly to spend time with his younger siblings, Rory, Dougie, and Max. His relationship with his mother was strained, though certainly better than the one she had with David. During those visits, Bobby was usually accompanied by Billings. The odd duo sat around either stoned or drunk. Ethel didn't say anything. To Ethel, Bobby was the namesake, the standard-bearer who could do no wrong, unlike his brother David. She held Billings in the same high esteem because of his long history with

Jack and the family. Others, though, now thought of Lem as crude, rude, an embarrassment.

One morning Billings, in a terry-cloth robe and towel, and Bobby, in a matching robe, sat at the breakfast table openly drinking straight shots of whiskey while Ethel and the younger children ate their bacon, eggs, and doughnuts. Billings had called for a cab to take him and Bobby to the airport, but they'd both gotten so soused by eight-thirty that they hadn't bothered to get dressed. When the taxi arrived, Billings lectured the driver for arriving too early, and then got into an argument with him over the fare. "That fucking son of a bitch," he bellowed when he returned to the table, "he wants to get paid for just fucking coming." Bobby and Billings started laughing again, joined now by Ethel.

Suddenly, Billings jumped up from his chair. "Ethel, why is this house so fucking hot?" With that, he took off his robe and let his towel drop.

One of the cooks, who had started to walk into the room with a pot of coffee, stopped in her tracks and let out a scream. Billings was standing stark naked in front of the family. Instead of taking offense, Ethel started laughing so loud and so hard she almost choked.

"Mrs. Kennedy wouldn't have taken that sort of thing from anyone, but she made every exception for Lem Billings," said Noelle Fell, who had witnessed the incident.

When Bobby entered law school, he had started dating a fellow student, Emily Black, a pretty, petite Protestant from an average Indiana family. At Bobby's urging, Emily had decided to convert to Catholicism. "My mother tells me that means I'll go to heaven," Bobby said wryly. Bobby and Emily tied the knot in April 1982. His plan at the time was to go to work for his father's old Justice Department colleague, Manhattan District Attorney Robert Morgenthau, as a twenty-thousand-dollar-a-year assistant DA, a prosecutor like his father. "If you want to compete with the best people," said Bobby, exuding confidence, "you go to New York. You can't bring out the best in yourself unless you do that." The couple planned to move into an East Side home and were already thinking of having five children. Emily planned to be a public defender. "She's interested in keeping people out of jail," Bobby said, "and I'm interested in putting them in." From all outward appearances, Bobby seemed to have pulled his life together.

But things didn't go quite as well as he had planned. While he got his law degree in 1982, he failed the New York bar exam. Because of his sporadic use of drugs, he was forced to take a couple of leaves of absence from his job in Morgenthau's office. He also lost his first trial as a prosecutor when a jury returned a not-guilty verdict in the case of a man charged with beating a co-worker in a Garment District fight. Having failed to pass the bar exam, he eventually was forced to resign.

The press wrote about Bobby's failures and Emily's successes as a legal-aid lawyer, which hurt Bobby's pride. The sudden death of his longtime mentor, Lem Billings, of a heart attack at sixty-five, hit Bobby like a ton of bricks. "I won't get over Lem's death any more than I will my father's," he said.

Friends noted that he had become despondent and was using drugs more frequently, venturing into Harlem like his brother to score. Emily, an innocent already lost in the powerful, moneyed world of the Kennedys, had no idea how to help him.

In May 1983, Bobby got a major shock when two pals were arrested on drug charges.

Fearing that his name would come up, Bobby pledged to kick his habit. But his attempts failed, and his behavior became more and more bizarre.

One afternoon in early August 1983, the Coast Guard found him aboard a small boat that had been adrift for some twenty hours about a mile off the coast of Hyannis. He was cited for operating the sixteen-foot Boston Whaler without registration, life jackets, and distress signals. The Coast Guard called Ethel, who confirmed buying the boat a year earlier for fifteen-year-old Doug. She said she had neglected to have it registered.

A month later, Bobby was arrested for heroin possession.

He had spent the nights of September 9 and 10 partying in New York, celebrating the twenty-third birthday of his cousin Willie Smith, and the forthcoming marriage of another cousin, Sydney Lawford.

On the evening of Sunday, September 11, 1983, Bobby was aboard Republic Airlines flight 967, making the hop between Watertown and Rapid City, South Dakota. He was en route to the Deadwood, South Dakota, home of a friend, Bill Walsh, a former Catholic priest, who was helping him kick his drug habit. Suddenly passengers heard a commotion in the rear of the plane. One of them walked to the restroom and found Bobby, now twenty-nine, sitting on the toilet, incoherent, cold, and clammy.

It took five minutes for two passengers and the stewardess to coax him out of the restroom and get him to lie down in a pair of vacant seats. They covered him with a blanket and administered oxygen; Bobby had lost muscle control, his eyes were dilated, his pulse weak.

When they asked him for his name, he said it was Bobby Francis.

An ambulance and police cars were on the tarmac when the plane landed. By that time, Bobby was in control enough to stand on his own two feet. Two policemen escorted him to a conference room, where he admitted his identity.

By the next morning, the Kennedy's well-oiled crisis-management team was in full gear. Bobby was flown East to New York, then driven to Fair Oaks Hospital, in Summit, New Jersey, a drug treatment center, whose patients had included rock star John Phillips and his daughter, Mackenzie.

Ted's office quickly issued a statement in Bobby's name: "I have admitted myself to the hospital for the treatment of a drug problem. With the best medical help I can find I am determined to beat this problem. I deeply regret the pain which this situation will bring to my family and to so many Americans who admire my parents and the Kennedy family. I am grateful for the support of my wife, Emily, the other members of my family, and my friends during this very difficult time."

Meanwhile, in the presence of a judge, Bobby's bag was searched. Slightly under a gram of heroin was found, a felony punishable by up to two years in jail and a two-thousand-dollar fine.

In February 1984, a month after his thirtieth birthday, Bobby pleaded guilty. His lawyer told the court that he was coming to South Dakota "for treatment, realizing he had a problem" with drugs. Bobby, who was sentenced to two years' probation and community service, had already started work as a volunteer for a legal fund devoted to environmental concerns. In June 1985, he was finally admitted to the New York State bar, and not long afterward, Emily gave birth to their first child, Robert Francis III. By then, Bobby, thirty-one, was a project director with the Natural Resources Defense Council. Once again, it looked as if Bobby had pulled his life together.

But not so, his brother David.

110 ✻ David Redux

AFTER THE HARLEM hotel incident and hospitalization, David went into a yearlong drug rehabilitation program in Sacramento, California. Aquarian Effort, as it was called, was run by a forty-one-year-old therapist named Don Juhl, who had treated celebrities such as Beach Boy Dennis Wilson (who eventually died of a drug overdose) and actor Jan-Michael Vincent.

The $100,000 fee that Juhl received for his services was not paid for by Ethel or any other member of the

Kennedy family; it came out of David's own trust fund. That was his Uncle Ted's idea; it was part of the clan's tough-love philosophy, and it made David furious because he felt the treatment was overrated as well as overpriced.

"I agreed to take it because my Uncle Ted told me to get my act together or I'd wind up in an institution for the rest of my life like his sister Rosemary," David told his best pal in Sacramento, Nancie Alexander.

"I tried to minister to him. I tried to care for him. All he wanted was his family's love and he couldn't get it," Nancie said later.

The object of much of David's anger and wrath was his mother. Often, he'd angrily denounced Ethel with a litany of complaints:

"She's oblivious to my problems," he told Nancie. "She doesn't love me. She never wanted eleven children. It was my father who wanted all those kids. It was part of his Kennedy dynasty concept. My father felt Uncle Ted and John didn't do their part, so my father made up for it. Those stories about what a big, happy family we had at Hickory Hill were all bullshit. Life at home was mayhem, a mess. My mother was always having screaming rages. The house looked like a shit-hole. She didn't know how to deal with so many kids. She didn't have the skills to raise eleven children. She didn't have the skills to run a house. If my father was alive, he'd never have sent me here."

Every published account of David's addiction implied he was driven to drugs because of the trauma of witnessing his father's death on television. David himself, however, scoffed at the armchair analysis.

"I am what I am because I come from a whole line of alcoholics," he said. "Just look at how many of us are fucked up. My brother Bobby's a junkie, but I take all the blame."

At one point, David even talked about attending a parole hearing for Sirhan Sirhan, for whom he showed no anger. "I'm out here. I'm a Kennedy. It would be interesting to go," he told Nancie Alexander.

During David's year in exile, Ethel had made several quick trips to see him. "She's just doing her motherly thing," he'd say. Her visits were always secret and tied to social calls on friends in San Francisco and in the town of Davis. "David desperately wanted his mother to be involved in his life," Nancie Alexander believed. "But it was clear to him that she was not going to be." After each mother-son get-together, David returned to Sacramento in a depressed state.

For a time in Sacramento, David worked on a construction job, then boasted about the prospect of becoming a millionaire as a distributor of Amway products. At the same time, he wrote a five-hundred-dollar rubber check for an overhaul on his BMW, even though he was living on two thousand dollars a month from his trust fund. For several months, he dated Nancy Narleski, a local girl, whom the Kennedys disliked; then began seeing Paula Sculley, a fashion photographer he had met in Aspen, whom the Kennedys did like. The two moved in together, and members of the clan, seeing how good marriage had been for Bobby, lobbied for David to do the same.

Off heroin, David drank and got high by purposefully putting himself into hypoglycemiclike states. He'd stop eating, become shaky, clammy, turn pale, and hallucinate.

"Because he couldn't get any drugs into his system, he allowed this to happen," Alexander said. "It altered his state of consciousness—and that was David's goal. I found out about his hypoglycemic game one day when I went over to his apartment. Paula, who was very, very good to David and took care of him, was really angry and she was saying, 'You do this on purpose. This is stupid. It's dangerous.' He laughed and said, 'I'm not diabetic, I'm only hypoglycemic.' Paula was furious and told him, 'It's still a deadly game.' "

Right after his $100,000 treatment ended, David was arrested for drunk driving, pleaded guilty, and paid a $380 fine. Don Juhl said, "As far as the problems of the past go, they're all over. He is in no kind of trouble."

In the fall of 1982, David left Sacramento with sketchy plans to return to Harvard and become a lawyer or a journalist.

"I went to cut David's hair the night before he left and to say good-bye to him," Nancie Alexander recalled. "I told him I'd take them to the airport. I borrowed my girlfriend's beat-up Volkswagen van, but when I got to David's place, I had to wake them up. When we finally got to the airport, I saw something strange happen. Here's David running to the ticket counter with his beautiful black leather jacket on, and his shirttails flying, and his hair all messed up, and the ticket agents are being very rude to him. You could see them thinking, 'Look at this punk kid.' All of a sudden he gave his name and it came up on the computer screen. *Kennedy, David.* And they suddenly realized who they were dealing with. I was standing right next to David and I saw this look come across his face. It was a look of disappointment. All of a sudden they realized he was a Kennedy and they were very nice and very polite and falling all over themselves to help him with his luggage. And that upset him because David thought he was nothing, that he didn't deserve any fanfare. He hated being sick, and believed that he wasn't good enough to be a Kennedy. I kissed him good-bye and then I watched him board the plane, and then I cried."

Nancie Alexander never heard from David again. That poignant moment at the airport was the last time she saw him alive.

In Boston, David got an apartment on Beacon Hill with Paula Sculley and worked as a clerk-intern at the *Atlantic Monthly*. With a year to go toward his undergraduate degree, he re-enrolled at Harvard, but dropped out after a semester.

Since 1980, Peter Collier, a contributing editor at *California* magazine, and David Horowitz, a *Rolling Stone* writer, had been working on a landmark book, *The Kennedys: An American Drama*. David, along with other members of his generation, had talked openly to the authors. When *Playboy* ran an excerpt from the book in May 1984, "David was bitterly criticized for breaching the family faith," the authors wrote in a note to their book. "The word used in condemning him was *treason.*"

The Kennedy family called the piece "absolutely inaccurate, the lowest form of journalism, except to call it journalism dignifies it."

Paula Sculley said that Collier and Horowitz had called David continually before he finally relented and allowed them to interview him.

Said Sculley: "I met Horowitz the same day David met him and we gave him dinner at David's apartment in Boston. I left as soon as I saw his tape recorder. I didn't even want a cough of mine on the tape. When David read the article in *Playboy,* it devastated him beyond belief. David made a mistake by talking. Everyone makes mistakes, but David didn't realize until too late how big of a mistake he had made."

Back on drugs, David sought help once again, this time spending a month at St. Mary's Rehabilitation Center in Minneapolis, where he checked in under the name David Kilroy.

On April 19, 1984, he was released. The next day he flew to Palm Beach to spend Easter with his family.

"I saw him when he left and he was in very good spirits," said Paula Sculley. "The treatment had done him a lot of good. It had been the best place in the world for David. He was completely clean of drugs when he went to Florida. He had plans for his life. He was going to write John Seigenthaler to see if he could spend the summer working at the Nashville *Tennessean,* and he was thinking about going to Boston University to study journalism, which was something that really interested him. But the article in *Playboy* was the down point in his life. It was like taking ten steps back."

In Palm Beach, David checked into a $292-a-night two-room suite at the Brazilian Court Hotel because he was told there was no room for him at the Kennedys' North Ocean Boulevard estate. For a time his favorite younger brother, Doug, now a seventeen-year-old senior at Georgetown Prep, stayed in a room across the hall from him.

For the next five days David drank and used drugs heavily, hotel employees said later. David, they said, was at the hotel bar by eight A.M. drinking double vodkas and grapefruit juice and by nine A.M. looked "like a transient on the street." He was still going strong by midnight.

From his brothers and sisters who had visited him at the hotel, Ethel learned that David was on a marathon bender.

On Tuesday, April 24, she telephoned a Palm Beach attorney and family friend, Howell ("Mickey") VanGerbig, frantically asking whether there was anything she could do to help her son. She said David was in "bad shape," that he had been "very abusive" to members of the family, and "was upsetting them." VanGerbig said Ethel was "very, very confused" during the several conversations they had that day. He asked her if she knew of any drugs David might be using and she told him he was taking Mellaril, a tranquilizer. Ethel said she had talked to David about VanGerbig and told him that he would be "a good person to help," that she had "begged" her son to get in touch with the lawyer and that David had promised he would call and arrange to have dinner with him that night. He never did. "I called her back that evening and said that what I'd try to do is have breakfast with him in the morning, and go over and get him and see what the situation was. . . . " VanGerbig also advised Ethel to contact Dr. Sheldon Koningsburg of New York, who was "very savvy on drugs." He also told her something she already knew: "Avoid publicity."

That night David talked to a drug counselor and admitted he'd had nine or ten drinks and a lot of cocaine.

At nine A.M. on Wednesday, April 24, Paula Sculley was running out of the door of the apartment she shared with David in Boston when the telephone rang. It was David calling to tell her that he planned to fly home that day with his cousin Sydney Lawford. They talked for a few minutes about a vacation in the Bahamas scheduled to start in early May, and David said when he got back home he planned to go to his A.A. meeting.

"He sounded perfectly happy, normal, sober," Sculley claimed.

Just before eleven-thirty, the hotel manager's secretary, Josephine Dampier, got a call from Ethel, who wanted to make sure David made his flight back to Boston.

"Mrs. Kennedy said no one from the family had seen him since the day before, and when she called his room, no one answered. She asked us to check on him," Dampier said later.

While Ethel stayed on the line, the secretary dispatched another employee, desk clerk Elizabeth Barnett, to go to Room 107 and check on David. Barnett, accompanied by a porter, stood outside ready to knock.

"I had an ominous feeling," she said. "Call it a mother's gut instinct or whatever, but I knew what we would find. We knocked, but there was no answer. I opened the door a little and peeked in, but I didn't see him. The beds were made up, and a green duffle bag was on one and a dollar bill on the other."

She stepped into the room. The shades were drawn. Clothes were scattered around. Then she saw David. He was sprawled on his back, fully dressed, lying on the floor between the two beds. She bent down and felt David's neck for a pulse. There was none.

Barnett ran back to the front desk and reported to Josephine Dampier what she had found.

"I told Mrs. Kennedy we'd call her right back because we had to get the paramedics," Dampier said.

Ten minutes later hotel executive Gerald Beebe called the Kennedy estate.

"We have found your son and the paramedics have arrived," he told her.

"He's dead, isn't he?" Ethel said.

"I'm sorry, yes," Beebe responded.

"She made a mother's sound, a strange sound, like a gasp, and hung up the phone."

Caroline Kennedy and Sydney Lawford, still in their bathing suits, arrived at the hotel and identified the body. They were followed shortly by Jean Kennedy Smith. A priest, Father Dan O'Brien, from St. Edward's Catholic Church, where the clan worshiped when in town, anointed the body before it was removed.

Afterward, Paula Sculley said of her last conversation with David, "I didn't know he was going to die or otherwise I would have talked to him forever."

David's body was taken to the Palm Beach County Medical Examiner's Office. There, Joe Kennedy, now thirty-one, married, a father, and head of a public-interest company to help the poor obtain fuel to heat their homes, paced back and forth while the autopsy was conducted.

Cause of death was an overdose of cocaine, the powerful painkiller Demerol, and the tranquilizer Mellaril, the coroner said. In David's room, police found 1.3 grams of high-grade cocaine. Investigators would once again probe the possibilities of a cover-up: had someone flushed drugs down the toilet before the police arrived? Had a syringe and other evidence been removed from the room?

After the autopsy, David's body was placed in a black station wagon and driven to a West Palm Beach funeral home.

In three weeks he would have turned twenty-nine.

"It is a very difficult time for all the members of our family, including David's mother and his brothers and sisters, who tried so hard to help him in recent years," Ted said in a statement released by his Washington office. "All of us loved him very much. We trust in God, we all pray that David has finally found a peace that he did not have in life."

Within hours of David's death, Ethel talked with Rev. Gerald Creedon, who had been affiliated with St. Luke's in McLean. "She showed remarkable inner strength and confidence," he said. "She seemed more concerned with other members of the family and how they were taking the loss. She is supportive of them. Ethel's faith is remarkable and very real, not a cold faith." He added, " 'Why me' has never been in Ethel's vocabulary."

On the drive to Hickory Hill for a private funeral service, Ethel asked that the clan stop at Arlington National Cemetery so she could pray at the graves of David's father and uncle. At the house, Ethel spent time alone in a room with her son's coffin. That night there was yet another wake: ham, turkey, macaroni casserole, tomato aspic and lasagna were heaped on buffet tables. Composed, stoic, Ethel told a friend that she believed David had joined his father in heaven. On April 27, 1984, David was buried alongside his grandfather, family patriarch Joseph P. Kennedy, in the family plot at Holyhood Cemetery, in Brookline, Massachusetts. A Mass card, pale blue in color, carried a passage from John Donne's Holy Sonnet X: "Death be not proud." David had written it out himself in a childish hand and drew a swirling, decorative border. He had given it to his mother sixteen years earlier when his father was killed.

Ethel's brother Jim and his wife, Virginia, were still living in California when they heard the news. Virginia called Hickory Hill.

"Ethel, I just wanted you to know that we are thinking about you, and you are in our prayers," she said. "Gee, kid, thanks so much," Ethel responded. "Thank Jimmy for thinking of me, too. It's great to hear from you. Sorry you couldn't make the funeral, but I'll call you when I'm on the West Coast."

Virginia felt like crying, but she remembered clearly that "Ethel was strong as a horse."

"I said, 'You know, Ethel, Jim said a very interesting thing. He said that maybe David's death will cause the other children in the family to wake up if they have a problem; ours in the Skakel family and the rest of yours.' She said, *'I beg your pardon. Just what does Jimmy mean by that!'* I said, 'Well, think about it. There are a lot of kids in this family, and who knows how they're going to turn out.' But Ethel was angry and that was the end of the call."

III ✻ *End of a Dynasty*

WHEN DAVID WAS born in June 1955—the Kennedys' fifth-wedding-anniversary present—Ethel had a large pool of relatives and friends from which to pick a godmother: her three sisters-in-law—Jean, Pat, and Eunice; her own three sisters—Georgeann, Pat, and Ann; plus an endless list of friends. In the end, though, she selected her oldest sibling, Georgeann, a choice that would prove to be both prescient and ironic.

For of all of Ethel's children, David turned out to be the most like Georgeann: precocious, sensitive, troubled, extremely fragile.

Like David, Georgeann too had had a love-hate relationship with her mother, Big Ann, who had criticized and rejected her while doing her best to mold her into her own image. Said Little Georgeann, "My grandmother always harassed my mother, 'You've got to go to Elizabeth Arden's. You've got to do something about how you look. You're not pretty.' Stick that in a person's head long enough and they believe it." And sadly, both Georgeann and David shared a fatal flaw in the Skakel family genes: they had severely addictive personalities, more so than any of the other Skakels or Kennedys of their generation.

Now, in the early eighties, as the godson was sliding deeper into heroin, the godmother's descent into booze and pills had escalated to a critical point.

Georgeann's husband, George Terrien, himself an alcoholic, now spent most of his time living at the New York Athletic Club. Georgeann's children were off like Ethel's, dealing with their own problems. Georgeann, who had lost part of a lung to cancer in the early seventies, now lost half of her other lung.

"She was living in that mausoleum of a home and she was lonely and frightened and hurting and afraid," said her cousin Betty Skakel Medaille.

In Greenwich, Georgeann had become a prisoner of Sursum Corda, a recluse who didn't drive or fly. She hadn't gone much beyond the grounds of her home in years. Her closest companions were Jessamine Andrews, the cook, and Bernie Kavanaugh, the chauffeur, who spent hours polishing Georgeann's rare and rarely used black Austin Princess, the same Vandem Plas model the Queen Mother rode in. Georgeann's contact with the outside world was mostly by telephone; she spent long hours talking into the night—often incoherently—to her sister-in-law Virginia Skakel and to Betty Medaille.

"She ran the world from her phone," as Little Georgeann put it.

Ethel, like all of the Skakels, knew Georgeann was in serious trouble. But Ethel, struggling with her own problems, knew better than to stick her nose into Georgeann's business; her sister had always had little use for her opinions, she knew.

But at one point Ethel did break with tradition long enough to send Georgeann a lengthy letter, according to Betty Medaille.

"During one of our conversations she told me that she'd gotten a ten-page letter from Ethel who told her what she should do was to stop her drinking. Georgeann was furious and terribly hurt because Ethel had taken it upon herself to lecture her about a subject that Georgeann thought was none of Ethel's business. Georgeann had the feeling of being hit when she was down. She gave me the impression that she responded with five words, replete with invective."

Ethel never had any connection with Betty, particularly after the Michael Medaille murder case in the fifties. She was, however, aware of Georgeann's friendship with Virginia Skakel.

"It's wonderful that you're so close to my sister,"

Ethel once told Virginia. "You should call Georgeann more often." Later Virginia said, "That's about the only personal thing that I can remember that Ethel had ever said to me about poor Georgeann, and it's amazing that she said that. She knew I spoke with Georgeann every day. I think Ethel thought she really should have called Georgeann more. I think she felt guilty."

Virginia said that as Georgeann's alcoholism worsened, "no one" among her siblings except for Rushton made a move to help her. The reasons had to do with ancient childhood rivalries and adult envy. Ethel and her sisters were still jealous that Georgeann was the only sister who had benefited over the years from the many perks of Great Lakes Carbon because of her marriage to two company officials, John Dowdle and George Terrien. The acrimony also dated back to when they had been children and Georgeann, traditionally left in charge when Big Ann traveled, had often acted bossy and condescending to the younger children, something they never forgave or forgot.

Finally, in May 1982, when Georgeann was in Greenwich Hospital, her children made a last-ditch effort to save her.

"We decided we weren't going to let Mother die like a Bowery bum," Little Georgeann said.

They discreetly contacted the Freedom Institute in New York, a counseling facility for alcoholics and drug addicts, for help. The resulting intervention involved a heart-rending confrontation between the children, Georgeann, and counselors from the institute. Because the subject of her alcoholism had never been discussed so openly—and certainly never in front of strangers—Georgeann, lying in her hospital bed, was humiliated and angry. Institutionalization of any kind terrorized her; she still felt intense guilt about Alexandra, the retarded daughter she had been forced to lock away years earlier.

Through the Freedom Institute, Georgeann was placed in St. Mary's Rehabilitation Hospital in Minneapolis—her first and last such treatment. Ironically, St.

Mary's was also David Kennedy's last stop before he made his ill-fated trip to Palm Beach.

While Georgeann Terrien was at St. Mary's, George Terrien was forced to go into rehab himself, at the Betty Ford Clinic. He'd taken the cure several times before, but always returned to drinking. For years a functional alcoholic, George had been given a final ultimatum by the board of directors of Great Lakes Carbon, where he was a vice president: either sober up once and for all, or be fired.

After a month of treatment at St. Mary's, Georgeann came home in early June 1983, dry, but still angry; irate at her children for putting her there, for bringing her lifelong problem to the surface. And just like David, Georgeann quickly returned to her deadly habit.

Despite having agreed to go into rehab, George Terrien was fired by Great Lakes Carbon a few weeks after his release.

For the first time in their lives, Georgeann and her seven children found themselves without the Great Lakes Carbon perks they had been so accustomed to: the use of company cars, planes, parking spaces in Manhattan, telephone credit cards, secretaries, and a New York apartment decorated all in white by Rushton's daughter Julie Skakel-Kracke, an interior designer. George's ouster touched off a running feud between the Terriens and those members of the Skakel family who had given him the boot. Meanwhile, Georgeann's sisters—who never benefited from those perks in the first place, Ethel included—wore Cheshire grins. To mourn their fate, Georgeann's children placed a small bronze plaque on their favorite stool in Martin's, a popular Greenwich bar and Skakel hangout. The plaque read: CWP 1983. The initials stood for "Children Without Perks."

On August 25, 1983—three months after her treatment in Minneapolis—Georgeann Skakel Dowdle Terrien died at Sursum Corda at age sixty-five. Her obituary in the *Greenwich Time* said she had passed away "after a lengthy illness."

"My mother actually died of alcoholism," Little

Georgeann acknowledged later. "It took me a long time to be able to say that. If anybody asked, I'd say cancer."

Ethel came to Georgeann's funeral in Greenwich, and hugged Little Georgeann warmly, but there was no discussion about her sister's death or its cause.

Almost eight months to the day after Georgeann Skakel Terrien's death, David Kennedy overdosed in his hotel room.

Little Georgeann was in Palm Beach at the time but couldn't bear to go to the funeral. A couple of days later she talked to Ethel. "Everything's okay now," Ethel told her, "because I know David's with Bobby." She said nothing about her sister.

• • •

The tenuous bond that appeared to be holding Ethel and her siblings together in the early eighties was financial—the business created by their father more than six decades earlier. But Great Lakes Carbon, like some of George Skakel's middle-aged offspring, had fallen on difficult times. The problems involved poor family management and economic downswings in the steel and aluminum industries.

For some time now, Ethel and her two surviving sisters, the widowed Pat Cuffe in Ireland and the twice-divorced Ann McCooey in Greenwich, had been seeking to cash in some or all of their Great Lakes Carbon stock.

As Jim Skakel put it, "To the girls a pile of cash was more alluring than a pile of dusty coke."

Always in need of money, Ethel was clamoring the loudest. But longstanding agreements restricted the stockholders—the Skakels and the Gramms, the other founding family—from selling shares to outsiders, the only interested buyers. Thus, except for declining annual dividends, Ethel's net worth in Great Lakes Carbon was only a fluctuating and meaningless number on paper.

However, in 1983, around the time of Georgeann's death, Ethel received a windfall. Through the efforts of her brother Jim, Great Lakes Carbon implemented an employee stock-option plan. As a result, Ethel had a source to unload some of her shares, $5 million worth to be precise. For the first time in a long time, she was on easy street, at least financially.

At that point, all of the Gramms and all of the Skakels, with the exception of Rushton and George Terrien, who had inherited all of Georgeann's stock and was now the single largest Great Lakes stockholder, decided to sell the company outright.

"There just wasn't a lot of sentimentality left about Great Lakes Carbon, especially among the next generation, such as Ethel's kids," said Patrick Gramm, son of the cofounder.

But to their consternation, corporate America wasn't beating down the doors. The "For Sale" sign was out for nearly a year before Horsehead Industries, a holding company whose operations included New Jersey Zinc, inventors of the American process for making zinc oxide, expressed interest.

In a leveraged buyout in early 1985, Horsehead picked up Great Lakes Carbon for a song. Depending on who was telling the story, the sale price (never published because both seller and buyer were closely held) ranged from a low of $120 million to a high of $150 million in cash, before taxes.

Either way, the profit, which had to be split among many family members, was far less than the Skakels had anticipated, and they were left reeling.

"The word was that the Skakels weren't bright enough and weren't smart enough and all they knew was how to fight among themselves, so why not go for their jugular vein," said Little Georgeann later. "We got nailed."

Ethel, however, was happy with the way things had turned out. She was at least $7 million richer and could look forward to a more secure old age.

After the sale, George Terrien moved back to Sursum Corda from the New York Athletic Club, a far richer man than he was when he first made dinner for Ethel and Bobby in their little house in Charlottesville in the early fifties.

Like his wife, Georgeann, Terrien became reclusive,

drank more than ever, and doled out small amounts of money to the children, now in their thirties and forties, none of whom had been named in their mother's will. All of their attempts to contest it had been futile.

On August 25, 1991, Ethel's thirty-six-year-old nephew John Dowdle—the fourth of Georgeann's six children—was charged with breaking into Sursum Corda, where he had grown up, and beating his sixty-eight-year-old stepfather, George Terrien.

Terrien, who had been left with his hands tied, freed himself and was treated at Greenwich Hospital. Two days later, Dowdle was arrested in New York City and turned over to Greenwich police, who charged him with first-degree unlawful restraint, assault, third-degree burglary, and making threats. He was released on $25,000 bail, and the charges were eventually dismissed.

Little more than a year later, George Terrien died while awaiting a liver transplant so he could, as one embittered Skakel put it, "drink for another forty years."

Terrien had bequeathed the bulk of the estate he had inherited from Georgeann, some $14 million plus the proceeds from the sale of Sursum Corda, to Harvard and the University of Virginia Law School, the two schools that he and Bobby had attended together. The children got not a penny, except for the contents of the house. John Dowdle was left out of the will altogether. Terrien was buried next to his wife in St. Mary's Cemetery in Greenwich.

"Ethel was at the funeral and was shocked that George hadn't left anything substantial to us," said Little Georgeann. "She couldn't believe it."

112 ✱ Union Label

FLUSH WITH HER share of the proceeds from the sale of Great Lakes Carbon, Ethel, for the first time in years, no longer had to worry about her spending. Her financial nemesis, Steve Smith, suffering from the early stages of cancer, had finally gotten off her back and Ethel was free to buy three-thousand-dollar jackets from her favorite new designer, Emanuel Ungaro, without thinking twice.

For Ted's fifty-sixth birthday party, in February 1988, she arrived on a chariot dressed as Cleopatra. Earlier in the day, as preparations for the party were underway, she galloped into Ted's newly refinished kitchen on a horse, jumped the kitchen table, tore up some of the new floor tiles, and let out a whoop. "Don't you think this is just great?" she squealed. Ted didn't. To old friends who were present, Ethel hadn't changed much since her horseback rides through the big house on Lake Avenue almost a half-century before.

Two months after Ted's birthday bash, Ethel marked a major milestone—her own sixtieth—by throwing a glitzy party for some two hundred friends that brought back fond memories of Hickory Hill in the golden days of Camelot.

Guests had to pass through an entrance desk marked ETHEL AIR, where they were handed authentic boarding passes for airlines such as Pan Am, Eastern, and National that directed the "passengers" to their seats. Each table was named after a country or a city—places Bobby and Ethel had visited during his career, and each of the place cards were genuine airline luggage tags. The airline motif seemed to have nothing to do with the actual theme of the celebration, which was billed as a "Memorial Costume Party." The guests were required to dress in what they'd worn when they first met Ethel eons ago.

Three weeks later, after months of planning, Ethel celebrated a more solemn milestone—the twentieth anniversary of Bobby's assassination—with a moving candlelit "Mass of Remembrance and Rededication" at Arlington National Cemetery.

More than ten thousand people attended, many marching across Memorial Bridge from Washington. They sat or knelt on a great greensward near Bobby's grave, marked by a simple white cross and a stone bearing the words, *Make gentle the life of the world*. Not far away flickered the eternal flame near the grave of his brother John.

During the ceremony, Ethel, proud and solemn, her face now heavy and marked by lines of age, sat flanked on the left by Ted, his puffy eyes closed, and on the right by her once troubled son, Joe, now a U.S. Congressman from Massachusetts—the first of his generation to be elected to office. Around Ethel sat the nine other surviving members of her brood, ranging in age from nineteen to thirty-six, many with children of their own. *USA Today* that weekend called Ethel "a quiet inspiration for her children. . . ." While Ethel didn't speak at the Mass, she did tape a rare, brief interview with NBC's Tom Brokaw. She talked about the last campaign that had cost Bobby his life, and about the impact he had had on his children. In closing, she admitted she didn't much like interviews. "I'd rather have another baby," she joked.

The ceremony was, to all appearances, a memorial planned and organized by the widow and her family with loving care and devotion. Andy Williams was there to sing his Kennedy standards, "Ave Maria" and "Battle Hymn of the Republic," solo and with the National Children's Choir. Altar boys included John F. Kennedy, Jr., Christopher Lawford, and Rushton Skakel, Jr.

No expense, it seemed, was spared to honor the man who had, his brother Ted told the gathering, "a restless, morally awakened spirit . . . something we have missed these past twenty years." For each member of the throng who had come to Arlington in the gathering darkness there was a gift—a souvenir program printed on elegant cream paper stock, emblazoned with Aaron Shikler's 1975 oil painting of Bobby. The program, which included a white silk marker with tassel, symbolized the best of the Kennedys in the minds of those present at the public Mass.

Months earlier, Ted had approached his friend Gerald Macantee, international president of the powerful American Federation of State, County, and Municipal Employees (AFSCME), the largest union in the AFL-CIO. Ted mentioned the forthcoming memorial service and said he would welcome any help from the union. Over the years he had been a recipient of campaign contributions—as had untold other senators and congressmen—through AFSCME's political action committee.

Not long after, Sabina Parks, the union's art director, was summoned to the executive offices at AFSCME's headquarters a few blocks from the White House. Parks was instructed to cut into her already busy production schedule to design, lay out, and oversee production of the souvenir program that would be handed out at the memorial Mass. The union, she was told, had agreed to pick up the tab. She was told the job shouldn't take her very long, that it could all be done in-house for minimal cost. Parks knew better, but kept her mouth shut.

The first stumbling block Parks encountered was a difference of opinion between Ethel and her twenty-seven-year-old daughter Kerry, who had recently gotten her law degree from Boston College and was helping to run the Robert F. Kennedy Center for Human Rights in Boston. Kerry was helping to organize the event and was writing the Mass. Kerry, in Boston, and Ethel, at Hickory Hill, were arguing by phone over virtually every aspect of the project.

Recalled Parks: "In the middle of the night they

were fighting over which hymn was going to be sung at a particular time. There were battles over the text at three o'clock in the morning with Kerry on the phone in Boston and with me and Ethel's assistant, Caroline Croft, on the phone in my apartment in Washington. I had typesetters in Virginia waiting overnight for delivery. We went through five or six sets of galleys within a period of forty-eight hours. Ethel had final approval, Kerry had final approval, and a couple of the Kennedy hangers-on had final approval. There were even arguments over the string bookmark."

About a week before the Mass, Parks was told to go to Hickory Hill to get Ethel's final approval. Exhausted after weeks of haggling, she was driven out by the union president's chauffeur. Also along was Parks's assistant, a graphics designer from Guyana whose family had long idolized the Kennedys. "I thought it would be exciting for her to meet Ethel," Parks said.

Parks and her assistant arrived at the appointed hour and were welcomed into the house by one of Ethel's preppy assistants, who seated them in the living room and left.

"My first impression was one of shock," Parks said, "because the room was so dingy, particularly for someone who had so much money. The furniture was threadbare in places; the rugs were worn; the colors were awful sixties colors and were faded. It was dingy, it was threadbare, it was somewhat dirty. It was like a lower middle-class place, except for the fact that originally the stuff must have been fairly expensive."

They had arrived on the dot for the two-thirty meeting with Ethel and were still staring at each other at three o'clock. Thirsty, Parks had to ask someone for a ginger ale. After another fifteen minutes she went outside to tell the chauffeur, "I don't know what the story is, wait a little while longer." Back in the house, she sat for another fifteen minutes before finally telling another of Ethel's assistants, dressed in a plaid skirt and Peter Pan-type collar, that she was going to leave if Ethel didn't soon show.

"Miraculously, Mrs. Kennedy suddenly appeared—in a tennis outfit," Parks said. "I was very angry and she picked up on that. I told her we had been waiting more than an hour, that I had to get back to my office, and that I had the union president's driver waiting. Realizing I was pissed, she immediately started pouring on the charm—'Oh, this is so wonderful what you're doing; it's so beautiful'—which was just about enough to make me barf.

"Then she got on the phone and called Kerry while we're sitting in the living room to once again finalize the text. We had to go into layout and the program had to go to the printer and now she's again hassling back and forth with Kerry over the 'Mine Eyes Have Seen the Glory' issue. While she was talking, there were three or four of her little handmaidens standing around. Something came up and one of the girls said something to Ethel dealing with the context of the actual program and Ethel yelled at her, snapped back at her, and the girl burst into tears and ran out of the room.

"After Ethel got off the phone with Kerry she excused herself. We waited for her for another twenty minutes, but she never came back. Eventually we just got up and left."

In all, the union had spent almost twenty thousand dollars to design and print some fifteen thousand copies of the twentieth anniversary memorial program.

"When the bills came, they were very chagrined, very upset," Parks said later. "One thing I did do—I managed to get a credit line at the very end of the program that read, *Special thanks to the American Federation of State, County, and Municipal Employees, AFL-CIO, for producing this program—Gerald W. McEntee, International President; William Lucy, International Secretary-Treasurer,* along with the union label.

"Around headquarters," Parks said, "those on the pro side felt there was nothing wrong with doing Teddy a favor. Others questioned the high cost."

Not long after her final meeting with Ethel, Parks walked into her office and was greeted by a huge flower arrangement—almost funereal in size—with a thank you note.

But Ethel's gift didn't change Parks's mind about her experience.

"It was shocking to me that Kennedys never put up a penny of their own. My poor little assistant really had a major dose of reality on the Kennedy thing. She came from a country where the people have pictures of Martin Luther King and Jack and Robert Kennedy hanging on their walls. She was outraged over everything: how we were used and abused. She was also offended by the way they were treating this image, this memory of Bobby Kennedy."

Despite what had transpired, Sabina Parks attended Bobby's twentieth anniversary memorial Mass. Like the thousands of others there, she was moved by the ceremony, particularly the words of Ethel's son, the Congressman, who recalled a childhood in which, he said, he and his siblings had been taught to feel compassion for the poor and to challenge themselves to reach higher levels of achievement. "On behalf of my family," Joe told the gathering, many now weeping, "I want to thank all of you for still caring. Twenty years after his death, all of us in our family share with countless others those precious moments of his public life . . . and those moments seem especially clear as we stand here at his grave tonight. . . . His was a restless, morally awakened spirit, and it is something we have missed these past twenty years."

113 * Ethel, Cliff, and Norm

AT NINE O'CLOCK on the evening of Thursday, December 10, 1992, millions of couch potatoes flicked their remotes to NBC to watch another episode of the wildly popular "Cheers," a show about the lovable, hard-drinking habitués of a fictional Boston tavern.

Viewers saw the familiar wooden sign—*Cheers, Est. 1895*—with its old-fashioned icon of a friendly hand pointing down to the bar. Under the shot, viewers heard the voice of Sam Malone (Ted Danson), the recovering alcoholic bartender, ex–Boston Red Sox pitcher, and noted roue announcing, " 'Cheers' is filmed before a live studio audience."

The short opening scene—known as the teaser—showed ditzy postman Cliff Claven (John Ratzenberger) and the beer-bellied, slightly disheveled accountant Norm Peterson (George Wendt) emerging bleary-eyed from Cheers into the afternoon sunlight. Norm suddenly spots several people standing in front of the bar, one of them a somewhat rotund woman wearing a navy blue blazer jacket and a skirt, and sensible heels.

"Norm, Norm, it's the *Kennedys*," Cliff whispers excitedly in his Boston accent.

"Let's go tell the guys," says Norm.

"No, no, no, no, no," says Cliff. "I gotta camera with me. Here," he says, slipping a point-and-shoot to Norm. "Let's get a snapshot of them. I'll pretend I'm with them. I'll be nonchalant."

With that, Cliff walks behind the woman in the blue blazer, who is chatting away with her friends.

Suddenly, she sees the two gawkers.

"Oh, would you guys like a picshuh?" she asks, a Brahmin to Cliff's South Boston.

"Oh, that would be great," answers Norm. "Do you mind?"

"No, no," the woman responds chipperly.

"Thank you, thank you," Norm and Cliff chorus.

In an hysterical move, Norm then hands Cliff's camera to the woman, rushes to Cliff's side, and both smile as she snaps *their* picture.

"All right!" Norm exclaims.

Norm and Cliff slavishly thank the woman, who says, "Nice to see you. Bye."

As she and her companions walk off, Norm and Cliff

slap hands victoriously. The camera holds on them as their expression changes from joy to puzzlement, realizing what has just transpired.

Cut to an exterior shot of Cheers and the familiar theme: *You wanna be where everybody knows your name . . .*

But most viewers of "Cheers" would never have guessed the name of the woman in blue.

At sixty-five, Ethel Skakel Kennedy, matronly and corpulent, was virtually unrecognizable. To those at home she looked nothing like the vivacious, coltish blonde in trendy miniskirts—the Chief Counsel's wife, the Attorney General's wife, the Senator's wife, the Presidential candidate's wife—whose picture had graced the covers of magazines and the front pages of newspapers through the years; the woman who might have been First Lady.

Ethel's appearance on the show, which came at the spur of the moment, had received scant press coverage, even though the NBC media relations people had managed to get out a short press release: "KENNEDYS CAMEO ON CHEERS. Members of Massachusetts's Most Famous Family Visit Boston's Most Famous Tavern . . . Ethel, her son, Michael, and his wife, Vicki Gifford-Kennedy . . . make a cameo appearance in the opening scene of NBC's hit comedy series 'Cheers' this Thursday . . ."

For Ethel—who'd seen and done practically everything in her lifetime—getting a spot on her favorite TV show with her favorite characters, Cliff and Norm, was a dream come true.

Ethel's appearance came about because of her long friendship with John Pike, a former Boston TV station executive who was now head of Paramount Television, which coproduced the show with Charles-Burrows-Charles, the program's creators. At her behest, Pike had mentioned Ethel's interest in making an appearance to "Cheers" director and cocreator, Jim Burrows.

Burrows was thrilled.

In the past, there had been cameos by other famous

Massachusetts politicians—Tip O'Neill, for one—and for some time Burrows had tried to get Ted to make an appearance to no avail; the Senator, Burrows assumed, was sensitive about the issue of drinking, despite Burrows's pitch that the show was about people loving one another, not about alcoholism.

But now Burrows had another famous Kennedy *volunteering* to be on "Cheers." He was overjoyed.

"We try to use people who you would believe would be in a Boston bar," Burrows said. "Ethel certainly fit the mold."

At the appointed hour, Ethel showed up at the Boston location—the front of the Bull and Finch Tavern—which served as the model for the fictional Cheers sports bar.

"She came dressed appropriately and we fluffed her up a little," said Burrows, who directed the segment. "We made up the teaser as we went along. She made up the small talk and George [Wendt] and John [Ratzenberger] and Ethel knew the concept, so we did two or three takes—it took about twenty minutes—and we used the best one. Ethel loved it. She absolutely loved it."

For her time, Ethel received the Screen Actors Guild minimum, $466.

Burrows, who'd been in the business for years, was highly impressed with his new find.

"She played 'Ethel Kennedy,' which is really difficult—because it isn't easy for someone to play themselves; it's hard for someone to be themselves on screen. But Ethel did great. She's a fine actress."

How appropriate it seemed that one of the most famous of the Kennedy women, and *the* best known of the heavy-drinking Skakel clan, would make her network TV sitcom debut on a show about wacky barflys.

• • •

But Ethel had serious interests, too. By the early 1990s, through the auspices of the RFK Center for Human Rights in Boston, she had become increasingly involved in human-rights causes. This interest included a trip to

Namibia with her youngest, Rory, who was attending Brown University.

Mother and daughter had visited a sprawling campsite in Windhoek, where hundreds of poor Africans were given basic living needs, a mattress, food, and blankets. "I can't think of anything that has impressed me more," Ethel said at the time. In the town of Dobra, she was photographed holding a black child as she gave singing lessons to the natives.

In Nairobi, she presented a human-rights award to activist lawyer Gibson Kamau Kuria, who had been held in prison for nine months after he filed a lawsuit alleging that three of his clients had been tortured by Kenyan police. In a meeting with President Daniel Moi, Ethel demanded that Kuria be given back his passport, which had been confiscated.

Since 1983, when the first RFK Human Rights Award was presented, Ethel and the rest of the family had vowed to stay out of the organization's decision-making process. No pressure, they promised, would be placed on the judges whose decision it was to honor someone who had struck out against injustice and oppression at great personal risk. Ethel's only role was to help raise funds, arrange for the awards luncheon or dinner, make an occasional fact-finding trip such as the one to Africa, and be there to present the prize, a bust of Bobby and a check for thirty thousand dollars.

But in 1991, for the first time, a firestorm erupted privately within the Kennedy family over the committee's choice.

The judges—Rose Styron, Burke Marshall, Robert Bernstein, Drew Days, and Pat Derian—had selected Raji Sourain, a human-rights lawyer. Ethel and the children privately threw a fit when, upon reviewing Sourain's background, they discovered that he was a Palestinian from Gaza. In making their choice, the committee members had completely forgotten that Bobby's assassin, Sirhan Sirhan, had been a Palestinian. For Ethel, the anger she had felt in the wake of Los Angeles, an anger that had all but subsided after almost a quarter-century, suddenly come swirling back.

"For two months, various members of Ethel's family were telling me various reasons why it was not a good idea picking Mr. Sourain," said Rose Styron, a poet, noted human-rights activist, and longtime friend of Ethel's. "After all, Bobby was killed by a Palestinian. And this particular man, when he was a student, had belonged to a terrorist organization that had committed a lot of terrorist acts, and he had never renounced them.

"While Ethel never said anything directly to me, others in the family had both political and emotional reasons for not wanting Sourain. The fact is the judges never thought of it. But, in the bosom of the family, there were a lot of feelings about it. The first reaction was it would be politically bad to choose a Palestinian; the gut reaction surfaced later. It must have been there all the time, but we didn't understand it. The minute it was voiced, we all said, 'Oh, my God.' And that just shows how our heads were stuck in the human-rights end. We were being fair and honest and thinking about who was worthy of getting the award and not about the family's feelings. But we should have thought of everything."

A close family friend said he had never seen Ethel so livid as when she was told that a Palestinian had won. "How could those people [the judges], some of whom I've known and trusted for years, pick someone with that background? It's insane. It's disgusting. It's an insult to me and my children. They're all a bunch of killers," he quoted her as saying, then went on to explain, "It's the first time in all those years since Bobby was killed that I actually saw the hate Ethel felt for Sirhan. She had never voiced it or showed it—at least to me—until the judges chose that man for the award."

Rose Styron, however, felt Ethel had shown considerable restraint in the face of the controversy.

"She was discreet about our selection, at least with me," Styron said. "Kerry and Kathleen were particularly effective and very persuasive in letting their negative feelings be known. We were willing to do whatever the family wanted, including resign, so that they could do something else. But as a family they worked it out. I don't think it would have gotten resolved if Ethel hadn't said fine, whatever you want."

In the end, two awards were given: one to the Palestinian, the other to a Jew—Avigdor Feldman, who was the director of the Litigation Center for the Association of Civil Rights in Israel. Feldman had been originally nominated but was eventually ruled out by the judges in favor of Sourain. One of the key criteria for selection was that the person's life be at risk; Sourain's was, but Feldman's wasn't.

"But we added Feldman," Styron said, "because we thought it would make everyone [in the Kennedy family] feel better. But it made only half of them feel better. But the family all rose above it; they all got together and they did it; they had the ceremony and it was wonderful, and the Israeli was absolutely incredible.

"As for Ethel, she's got her head screwed on right, at least in anything I'm involved in."

Ethel became entangled in a very public and controversial human-rights issue in 1994, this one involving the Irish Republican Army and a highly publicized murder case.

Ethel's involvement came about because of her daughter Courtney, whose marriage to television executive Jeff Ruhe had fallen apart in the late 1980s. All efforts by Ethel to bring about a reconciliation had failed, and the two were quietly divorced. The fifth in Ethel's brood, Courtney was the first of Ethel and Bobby's children—the first of the entire new generation of Kennedys, for that matter—to have a marriage dissolve, but she would not be the last. The divorce had left Ethel devastated. Her views about the sanctity of marriage—ingrained years earlier by Big Ann, Rose Kennedy, and the Sacred Heart nuns—had never changed. "My wonderful mother would turn over in her grave if she knew her granddaughter had gotten a divorce," Ethel confided to a friend at the time. But Ethel was determined to see her daughter get back on track. Not long after Courtney's divorce, Ethel's son Joe, holding Congressional hearings to probe human-rights violations by the British in Northern Ireland, introduced his mother to a fascinating young man who had been one of the witnesses. His name was Paul Hill. He was thirty-five years old and had grown up in the poverty of Belfast's Catholic ghetto. He was bright and good looking. Ethel felt Hill would be a perfect match for Courtney—despite the fact that he was at the epicenter of a political earthquake.

Along with two other Irishmen and an Englishwoman, Hill had just been released on appeal from a British prison. On the basis of forced confessions, Hill and the others had been convicted for the October 1974 bombing of a pub that had left five dead and fifty injured in the town of Guildford, near London. Hill and his compatriots were dubbed the Guildford Four. When Ethel met Hill, a life sentence still hung over his head for another crime—the kidnapping and murder earlier in 1974 of a former British Army soldier, Brian Shaw. During the police interrogation into the bombing, Hill had also confessed to the Shaw murder, but later claimed the confession had been coerced, and he retracted it. After he was released from prison, he wrote *Stolen Years*, a book about his prison experiences.

Ethel believed Paul Hill's story that he had been framed, became his biggest supporter, and arranged for him to meet Courtney. The couple was soon spotted together in the Irish bars on Manhattan's East Side, where Courtney had an apartment. They quickly became an item, with their romance making the pages of *The National Enquirer*.

Like her aunt Pat Skakel Cuffe, who decades earlier had married an Irishman and settled near Dublin, Courtney tied the knot with Paul Hill in 1993 in a small, private ceremony attended by Ethel on a yacht in the Aegean Sea. As with Courtney, this was Hill's second marriage. The newlyweds took up residence for most of the year in Ireland. They got a place in County Clare and began frequenting Dublin's trendy nightspots such as Lily's Bordello, frequented by the likes of shaved-headed chanteuse Sinead O'Connor, and Neil Jordan, director of *The Crying Game,* a film about an IRA member's relationship with a transvestite hairdresser.

In 1994, the story of the Guildford Four became the subject of a highly acclaimed film, *In the Name of the Father*. It gave Hill's side of the story, infuriating many Britains who didn't believe his version of events and who were still seeking retaliation for the murders twenty years earlier. The film made Hill, with his rugged features and shoulder-length hair, into a celebrity, angering some factions even more.

But the issue exploded onto the front and editorial pages of newspapers around the world when, in early 1994, Ethel led a contingent of Kennedys to Belfast to display support—and the Kennedy clout—for Hill as he appealed his conviction in the death of the British soldier. With Ethel was a party of twenty, including Joe, Kathleen, Rory, and Kerry, who had merged with another powerful political family when she married New York Governor Mario Cuomo's son Andrew in 1990.

In an effort to influence public opinion, the British news media called the Kennedys' involvement "rubbish," while *The New York Times* op-ed page ran a commentary by Rose Styron that asked, "Why hasn't Britain freed Paul Hill?" The *Times* identified Styron as a writer and longtime member of Amnesty International U.S.A., but not as a pal of Ethel's.

When Ethel's contingent arrived in Belfast, Protestant politicians added fuel to the fire by claiming that it was costing taxpayers there about seventy-five thousand dollars a day to guard the Kennedys. One Ulster MP, Ken McGinnis, who claimed to have survived numerous attempts on his life by the IRA, asserted that Ethel and her family were "exposing police officers to assassination. They should have arranged their itinerary and accommodations in a better way."

One of those seated behind Ethel and her party in the three-judge Court of Appeals in Belfast was Maureen Shaw, widow of the murdered British soldier.

"The Kennedy visit is a joke," the outraged woman

declared. "Who are they to come over and try to make an impression? Kennedy is just a name. After all, they have had their scandals as well. . . . I want to see justice done. . . . He [Paul Hill] should be behind bars for the rest of his life."

Responding to questions from the press, Joe Kennedy declared: "We're here today to support my brother-in-law in his struggle for justice. . . . Given the history of my family, I also want to let the Shaw family know that we know what it's like to be a victim of political violence. But one wrongful act should not condemn an innocent man for the rest of his life." Standing proudly next to her son, Ethel brushed reporters' questions away and remained mum.

But back in the U.S. she told a family friend she was confident that her son-in-law would be vindicated.

"Paul's one of us now, a Kennedy. No one pushes Kennedys around."

Finally, on April 21, 1994, Paul Hill's fifteen-year nightmare ended when the appeals court overturned his conviction in the Shaw slaying. The judges said his confession was tainted by new evidence that British police intimidated him with an unloaded pistol after his arrest. The court noted that "a confession obtained by improper means must still be excluded even if the court may consider it to be true." In effect, the court emphasized that it was not ruling on Hill's guilt or innocence in its decision. Ethel was at her son-in-law's side when the verdict was announced.

Joyful over Courtney's marriage to Paul Hill, Ethel was still heartsick that her daughter's first marriage had ended in divorce. Friends said she felt ashamed. But Ethel was optimistic and believed divorce would never happen again to one of her children, that Courtney's situation was a fluke.

But then she discovered that Joe's marriage of almost a decade to Sheila Brewster Rauch, the mother of his twin sons, was on the rocks, and that he had become involved with Beth Kelly, a pretty one-time temp at his Citizens Energy Corporation in Boston. Beth had become, as Joe put it, the "heart and soul" of the business, eventually being named director of special projects.

When Joe won his first election to Congress in 1986, succeeding former House Speaker Tip O'Neill in Massachusetts's Eighth Congressional District, Beth followed him to Washington and became Joe's girl Friday. Of his initial meeting with her, Joe would say, "All I remember is she was someone who could really type and get all the grammar and punctuation right."

Ethel tried to be understanding but she was livid.

"When Ethel found out that Joe's marriage to Sheila was in trouble, she was furious," a family friend revealed. "She blamed the marriage's failure on him. She called him every name in the book. She said, 'Haven't we had enough scandal?' She compared him to his Uncle Ted. Ethel rarely spoke negatively about Ted [who remarried in 1993]. But in the heat of the moment there was no other analogy she could think of."

Joe's marriage had hit the skids in 1990 and Kelly's involvement with a friend of Joe's had fallen apart. As Joe and Beth explained it, they looked up one day and discovered they were in love. "We were both coming off heartbreaking experiences," Joe said. "It brought us closer together."

Besides Ethel, no one could have been more heartbroken about the breakup of the marriage than Joe's wife, Sheila. To make matters worse, while obtaining a civil divorce, Joe had petitioned the Vatican for an annulment so that he could marry Beth in the Catholic Church. Friends said it was Ethel who pushed for the annulment. Now that she had faced the issue of a second divorce in her family and had seemingly come away weathering the storm, she demanded from Joe that for her sake, his second marriage be in the Church.

But Sheila was irate and would hear none of it. Going up against Ethel and the rest of the Kennedys, she went public with her feelings, writing an angry letter to *Time*, which had published a story about Joe's petition under the headline TIL ANNULMENT DO US PART. The mention of Joe was part of a larger story about the ease of getting an annulment in the Catholic Church in the U.S. and how displeased the Vatican was about the situation. In her letter, written several weeks after Joe announced his engagement to Beth in August 1993, Sheila wrote that she intended to "continue to defend the bond that brought my children into the world . . . even though the odds of prevailing . . . are bleak. If our marriage were deemed never to have existed in the eyes of the Church, then our children [Matt and Joe] . . . would have been neither conceived in, nor born to, a sanctified union. . . . I find this contention . . . abhorent and contrary to the Church's teachings."

The Vatican shuffled its feet on Joe's petition, so he went ahead with the marriage without an annulment. In October 1993, he and Beth tied the knot in a civil ceremony at his home in Brighton, Massachusetts. Exiled Haitian President Jean-Bertrand Aristide gave a Scripture reading. Then the family—led by Ethel, and Ted, and his new wife, Vickie—sang "When Irish Eyes Are Smiling" as the couple walked up the aisle.

Not long before the ceremony, Joe had said, "[Beth and I] try to achieve a balance between our private and public lives. Sometimes I look at Bill and Hillary Clinton and I can't believe they don't need to spend more time together."

All of Joe's brothers and sisters had come to the wedding, including Bobby Jr. and his lawyer wife of twelve years, Emily, mother of his two children, Robert F. Kennedy 3d and Kathleen Alexandra Kennedy. Kathleen's middle name had been chosen by Ethel in honor of her sister Georgeann's retarded child. Ethel believed that Bobby and Emily had a happy marriage. At least it appeared that way. But they were having serious problems. In 1992, Ethel was rocked when Bobby told her that he and Emily had quietly gotten a formal separation. They had decided to live under the same roof, though, for the sake of the children. However, Bobby soon began appearing in public with another woman, a pretty New York architect named Mary Richardson. In late March

1994, Bobby, an environmental lawyer, flew down to the Dominican Republic and got a quickie divorce. Less than a month later, he married Mary, six years his junior, and pregnant. A Roman Catholic Mass had been performed by a New York Supreme Court justice, and the actual ceremony took place aboard a boat in the Hudson River.

There was another shock for Ethel, the diagnosis that her sister-in-law Jackie had cancer, and her sudden death at sixty-four in mid-May 1994.

All of it—the three divorces, the controversy over Paul Hill, Jackie's death—had knocked Ethel for a loop. By the spring of 1994, having celebrated her sixty-sixth birthday, she felt drained. For the first time in years, friends heard her long for Bobby's love, support, and security.

"Ethel just didn't know how to deal with the situation," said a longtime family confidant. "She once again felt in a state of turmoil. She was as confused about what was happening to her life, and to her family, as she had been in that period after the assassination in Los Angeles, and during that terrible time when the boys had gone wild.

"Now, at a point in her life when she should have been feeling content and secure, everything seemed to be falling apart around her. She seemed absolutely crushed. Between the joys and horrors she had endured all of those years with the Skakels and the Kennedys and her own large brood, Ethel felt she had been put through the wringer enough. She had no idea what the future held for her. So Ethel did what she always does in the face of adversity: she went to church and prayed."

Selected Bibliography

Barson, Michael. *Better Dead than Red*. New York: Hyperion, 1992.

Beale, Betty. *Power at Play*. Washington, D.C.: Regnery Gateway, 1993.

Block, Herbert. *Herblock: A Cartoonist's Life*. New York: Macmillan Publishing Co., 1993.

Brown, Joan Winmill. *No Longer Alone*. Old Tappan, N.J.: Fleming H. Revell Co., 1975.

Brown, Peter Harry, and Patte B. Barham. *Marilyn: The Last Take*. New York: E. P. Dutton, 1992.

Buck, Pearl S. *The Kennedy Women*. New York: Cowles Book Co., Inc., 1970.

Burke, Richard E., with William and Marilyn Hoffer. *The Senator: My Ten Years with Ted Kennedy*. New York: St. Martin's Press, 1992.

Cameron, Gail. *Rose*. New York: G. P. Putnam's Sons, 1971.

Clinch, Nancy Gager. *The Kennedy Neurosis*. New York: Grosset & Dunlap, 1973.

Cohn, Roy. *McCarthy*. New York: The New American Library, 1968.

Collier, Peter, and David Horowitz. *The Kennedys*. New York: Summit Books, 1984.

Damore, Leo. *Senatorial Privilege: The Chappaquiddick Coverup*. New York: Dell, Bantam, Doubleday Publishing Group, Inc., 1988.

David, Lester, and Irene David. *Bobby Kennedy: The Making of a Folk Hero*. New York: Dodd, Mead & Co., 1986.

David, Lester. *Good Ted, Bad Ted*. New York: Birch Lane Press, 1993.

Dickerson, Nancy. *Among Those Present*. New York: Random House, 1976.

Evans, Peter. *Ari*. New York: Summit Books, 1986.

Exener, Judith (as told to Ovid Demaris). *My Story*. New York: Grove Press, Inc., 1977.

Fay, Paul B., Jr. *The Pleasure of His Company*. New York: Harper and Row, 1966.

Felsenthal, Carol. *Power, Privilege and the Post*. New York: G. P. Putnam's Sons, 1993.

Gentry, Curt. *J. Edgar Hoover: The Man and the Secrets*. New York: W. W. Norton & Co., 1991.

Gifford, Frank, and Harry Waters. *The Whole Ten Yards*. New York: Random House, 1993.

Goodwin, Doris Kearns. *The Fitzgeralds and the Kennedys: An American Saga*. New York: Simon and Schuster, 1987.

Guthman, Edwin. *We Band of Brothers*. New York: Harper and Row, 1971.

Hamilton, Nigel. *JFK: Reckless Youth*. New York: Random House, 1992.

Heymann, C. David. *A Woman Named Jackie*. New York: Signet, 1990.

Hodgson, Godfrey, and Bruce Page. *An American Melodrama*. New York: The Viking Press, 1969.

Kelley, Kitty. *Jackie O!* New York: Ballantine Books, 1979.

Kennedy, Rose Fitzgerald. *Times to Remember*. New York: Doubleday & Co., Inc., 1974.

Koskoff, David E. *Joseph P. Kennedy*. Englewood Cliffs, N.J.: Prentice-Hall, Inc., 1974.

Laing, Margaret. *The Next Kennedy*. New York: Coward-McCann, Inc., 1968.

Lasky, Victor. *JFK: The Man and the Myth*. New York: Dell Publishing Co., Inc., 1977.

Lawford, Patricia Seaton, with Ted Schwarz. *The Peter Lawford Story*. New York: Carroll & Graf Publishers, Inc., 1988.

Lerner, Max. *Ted and the Kennedy Legend*. New York: St. Martin's Press, 1980.

Manchester, William. *The Death of a President*. New York: Harper and Row, 1967.

Martin, Ralph G. *A Hero for Our Times*. New York: Ballantine Books, 1983.

Newfield, Jack. *Robert Kennedy: A Memoir*. New York: E. P. Dutton, 1969.

Phillips, Cabell. *From the Crash to the Blitz*. New York: The New York Times Co., 1969.

Reeves, Richard. *President Kennedy: Profile of Power*. New York: Simon & Schuster, 1993.

Reeves, Thomas C. *A Question of Character*. New York: The Free Press, 1991.

Reeves, Thomas C. *The Life and Times of Joe McCarthy*. New York: Stein and Day, 1982.

Rogers, Warren. *When I Think of Bobby*. New York: HarperCollins Publishers, 1993.

Schlesinger, Arthur M., Jr. *Robert Kennedy and His Times*. Boston: Houghton Mifflin, 1978.

Slevin, Jonathan, and Maureen Spagnolo. *Kennedys: The Next Generation*. Washington, D.C.: National Press Books, 1990.

Spada, James. *Peter Lawford: The Man Who Kept the Secrets*. New York: Bantam Books, 1991.

Spoto, Donald. *Marilyn Monroe*. New York: HarperCollins Publishers, 1993.

Stein, Jean (interviewer). *American Journey: The Times of Robert Kennedy*. Edited by George Plimpton. New York: Harcourt Brace Jovanovich, Inc., 1970.

Summers, Anthony. *Goddess: The Secret Lives of Marilyn Monroe*. New York: Macmillan Publishing Co., 1985.

Summers, Anthony. *Official and Confidential: The Secret Life of J. Edgar Hoover*. New York: G. P. Putnam's Sons, 1993.

Thomas, Evan. *The Man to See*. New York: Simon & Schuster, 1991.

Wendt, Lloyd, and Herman Kogan. *Bosses in Lusty Chicago*. Bloomington: Indiana University Press, 1943.

Whalen, Richard J. *The Founding Father: The Story of Joseph P. Kennedy and the Family He Raised to Power*. New York: Signet Books, 1964.

Witcover, Jules. *85 Days: The Last Campaign of Robert Kennedy*. New York: G. P. Putnam's Sons, 1969.

Slevin, Jonathan and Maureen Spagnolo. *Kennedys: The Next Generation*. Washington D.C.: National Press Books, 1990.

Spada, James. *Peter Lawford: The Man Who Kept the Secrets*. New York: Bantam Books, 1991.

Spoto, Donald. *Marilyn Monroe*. New York: HarperCollins Publishers, 1993.

Stein, Jean (interviewer). *American Journey: The Times of Robert Kennedy*. Edited by George Plimpton. New York: Harcourt Brace Jovanovich, Inc., 1970.

Summers, Anthony. *Goddess: The Secret Lives of Marilyn Monroe*. New York: Macmillan Publishing Co., 1985.

Summers, Anthony. *Official and Confidential: The Secret Life of J. Edgar Hoover*. New York: G. P. Putnam's Sons, 1993.

Thomas, Evan. *The Man to See*. New York: Simon & Schuster, 1991.

Wendt, Lloyd, and Herman Kogan. *Bosses in Lusty Chicago*. Bloomington: Indiana University Press, 1943.

Whalen, Richard J. *The Founding Father: The Story of Joseph P. Kennedy and the Family He Raised to Power*. New York: Signet Books, 1964.

Witcover, Jules. *85 Days: The Last Campaign of Robert Kennedy*. New York: G. P. Putnam's Sons, 1969.

Notes and Sources

CHAPTER 1: YAZOO COUNTY, MISSISSIPPI

3 ETHEL SKAKEL KENNEDY'S ROOTS. The biographical information in this chapter is based on various family genealogies furnished to the author by Skakel family members, including but not limited to Bob Skakel, Betty Skakel Medaille, and Georgeann Dowdle. A descendant of the Jordan family, Harry Baker Jordan, supplied genealogical data for the Skakel family. A great deal of detail and color of certain places, times, and people—and for the genealogies—was based on tape-recorded and written reminiscences given to Bob Skakel and various family members by Margaret Skakel, sister of George Skakel, Ethel Skakel Kennedy's father.

4 YAZOO WAS A LIVELY. Harriet DeCell and JoAnne Prichard, *Yazoo: Its Legends and Legacies* (Yazoo City, Miss.: Yazoo Delta Press, 1976).

CHAPTER 2: ALCOHOL, BIGOTRY, AND RACISM

6 THE SKAKELS WERE THE KIND OF PROTESTANTS. Interviews, Betty Skakel Medaille.

7 THE FAMILY FORTUNES. From writings and taped recollections of Margaret Skakel.

7 IT WAS A PARODY IN CONTEMPT. Medaille, op. cit.

8 SHE USED TO TALK. Interviews, Bob Skakel.

8 A BIGOT. Interview, Doris MacConnal Skakel Green.

CHAPTER 3: BILLY "THE CLOCK" SKAKEL

8 COLORFUL DETAILS ABOUT THE LIFE OF BILLY "THE CLOCK" SKAKEL from Lloyd Wendt and Herman Kogan, *Bosses in Lusty Chicago: The Story of Bathhouse John and Hinky Dink* (Bloomington, London: Indiana University Press. Originally published as *Lords of the Levee*, Bobbs-Merrill Co., 1943).

9 SKAKEL WAS DEVOTED. Margaret Skakel writings. Bob Skakel, op. cit.; interviews, Jim Skakel.

CHAPTER 4: RANCH LIFE

10 A DOT ON THE MAP KNOWN AS TYNDALL. Maxine K. Schuurmans, *One Hundred Years of Tyndall: A Centennial History* (Tyndall, S.D.: B & H Publishing, 1979). Additional material on life in Tyndall from Evelyn Fuchs, librarian, Tyndall Public Library, and Joan Lee.

CHAPTER 5: DEATH FROM DRINKING

12 LIFE AT THE SKAKELS WAS HELLISH. Reminiscences of Margaret Skakel, Bob Skakel, op. cit., Betty Skakel Medaille, op cit.

14 I TOLD BOBBY THAT SOME SAY. Bob Skakel, op. cit.

CHAPTER 6: FINDING A WIFE

17 THE YEAR WAS 1913. Jim Skakel, op. cit.

18 NEVER BREAK ANOTHER MAN'S RICE BOWL. Medaille, op. cit.

18 LIVERPOOL IRISH. Jim Skakel, op. cit

18 DAD WAS ONLY ABOUT. Interviews, Rushton Skakel.

18 MANY OF THE DETAILS about Ann Brannack Skakel's early life in Chicago were given to author by Florence Ferguson Kumpfer. Kumpfer quotes are from interviews with author.

19 HOTEL WORKER, NIGHT WATCHMAN. Jim Skakel, op. cit.

CHAPTER 7: OFF TO WAR

21 IT WASN'T UNTIL FEBRUARY. U.S. Navy records.

22 SHE WENT BACK. Kumpfer, op. cit.

22 GEORGE DECIDED TO BECOME. Jim Skakel, op. cit.

22 ONE BITTER NIGHT. Ibid.

22 AFTER BOOT CAMP. Records, op. cit.

22 THE ONLY SUIT HE OWNED. Jim Skakel, op. cit.

23 GEORGE TOOK IT. Ibid.

23 AT THE COAL COMPANY. Ibid. Interviews, Patrick Gramm.

23 THEIR FIRST OFFICE. Rushton Skakel, op. cit.

24 GEORGE SKAKEL WAS A MAN. Patrick Gramm, op. cit.

24 WHEN MY FATHER. Jim Skakel, op. cit.

25 THE MONEY REALLY STARTED. Ibid. Gramm, op. cit.

25 AN ARTICLE ABOUT CARBON. Ibid.

CHAPTER 8: MINING MONEY

27 ANN WOULD JUMP BEHIND THE WHEEL. Kumpfer, op. cit.

28 IT BECAME AN ANNUAL EVENT. Interview, Liz Henebry.

29 BOASTING IN LETTERS. Letter, courtesy Bob Skakel, dated August 27, 1929.

29 BESIDES ENTERTAINING. Rushton Skakel, op. cit.

CHAPTER 9: BABY ETHEL

30 WITH EACH PREGNANCY. Interviews, Mary Begley.
30 BORN WITH A CLUB FOOT. Interviews, family members, friends.
31 A TELEPHONE BOOTH. Kumpfer, op cit.
31 LIKE A DUNGEON. Interview, Dodie Dwyer.
31–32 AT THE CORE. Gramm, op. cit.
32 IF ALL OF HIS KIDS. Jim Skakel, op. cit.
32 JIM WAS THE TRIAL. Rushton Skakel, op. cit.
33 ANN NEVER TOLD GEORGE. Kumpfer, op. cit.
34 I REMEMBER WE WERE TALKING. Doris MacConnal Skakel Green, op. cit.

CHAPTER 10: THE CRASH

35 OVER EASTER. Medaille, op. cit.
35 ASKED HIS BROTHER TO JOIN HIM. Ibid.
36 NOT LONG AFTER. Ibid.
36 GEORGE WROTE TO HIS MOTHER. August 27, 1929, op. cit.
37 UNLIKE OTHERS. Jim Skakel, op. cit.
37 GLUB, GLUB. Rushton Skakel, op. cit.
37 WHAT THE HELL IS THIS. Jim Skakel, op. cit.
39 JOE SOLARI, A SHREWD. Medaille, op. cit.
39 HE DIDN'T WANT. Jim Skakel, op. cit.

CHAPTER 11: DEPRESSION YEARS

43 SHROUDED IN HOPELESSNESS. Cabell Phillips, *The New York Times Chronicle of American Life: From the Crash to the Blitz, 1929–1939* (New York: New York Times Books, 1969).
44 YOU CAN'T QUOTE SILENCE. Jim Skakel, op. cit.
44 OLD MAN SKAKEL. Begley, op. cit.
45 GEORGE'S DAYS WERE FILLED. Rushton Skakel, op. cit.
45 SALES OFFICE IN MOST FOREIGN. Jim Skakel, op. cit.
45 THICKET OF REGULATIONS. Interviews, Jay Mayhew.

CHAPTER 12: MOVING EAST

46 BECAUSE SO MUCH BUSINESS. Gramm, op. cit.
47 A GREATER EMOTIONAL. Kumpfer, op. cit.
47 GENETIC HEART. Rushton Skakel, op. cit.
47 IN JUNE. Ibid.
48 SOMETHING OF A MASCULINE. Interviews, Martin McKneally.

CHAPTER 13: LARCHMONT LIVING

49 THE SKAKEL HOME HAD BECOME. Rushton Skakel, op. cit.
50 GEORGE EVEN TROTTED OUT. Ibid. Bob Skakel, op. cit.

51 JIMMY SKAKEL'S REPUTATION. Mary Begley, op. cit.
52 WHEN DR. HUME. McKneally, op. cit.

CHAPTER 14: THE TUTOR

54 FROM THE BEGINNING. McKneally, op. cit.
56 A REAL LITTLE DICK. Interview, source.
57 KEEP ETHEL REAL BUSY. McKneally, op. cit.

CHAPTER 15: LAKE AVENUE

61 I WAS WONDERING. Interviews, Anita "Pan" Jacob.
62 MEMBERSHIP IN THE FASHIONABLE. *Greenwich: An Illustrated History* (The Historical Society of the Town of Greenwich, 1990).
62 A LOT OF PEOPLE. Interview, Peggy Klipstein Larned.
62 WHEN ZALMON GILBERT SIMMONS. Rushton Skakel, op. cit.
62 THE FURNITURE WAS BIG. Interviews, Pat Grant Mudge.
63 THEY WERE A SPECK WILDER. Interview, Bobby Banks Kaufman.
64 ETHEL'S FAMILY WAS A BIT. Interviews, Priscilla "Pixie" Meek.
64 ROWDY IRISH MICKS. Interview, source.
64 MY PARENTS AND ETHEL'S JUST WOULDN'T. Interview, source.
64 THE SKAKELS WERE NOT. Jacob, op. cit.
65 THE WEALTHY DEPARTMENT STORE. Interview, source.
66 HE FANCIFULLY LISTED. Jim Skakel, op. cit.
66 I'M MISERABLE HERE. Jacob, op. cit.

CHAPTER 16: A WASP SCHOOL

68 ABOUT TEN OF US. Interview, source.
69 IT BOTHERED HER. Interviews, Anne Morningstar Huberth.

CHAPTER 17: BEARER OF THE CROSS

69 I WAS RIGHT. Interview, source.
69 NOW DEAR, WHO DID YOU. Interview, source.
70 PRYOR WAS A COLORFUL. Marilyn Bender and Selig Altschul, *The Chosen Instrument: Juan Trippe, the Rise and Fall of an American Entrepreneur* (New York: Simon and Schuster, 1982).
70 SHE'D SWEEP ME INTO. Interviews, Franny Pryor Haws.
70 BUT I COULDN'T SWALLOW. Huberth, op. cit.
70 EVERYTHING I KNEW ABOUT. Meek, op. cit.
71 SHE WAS ABSOLUTELY ADAMANT. Haws, op. cit.
71 THE SWIMMING POOL. Bob Skakel, op. cit.
72 BECAUSE HIS FATHER WAS. Ibid.
72 YOU'RE NOT GOING TO HEAVEN. Ibid.

73 DON'T WORRY YOUR COUSIN. Doris MacConnal Skakel Green, op. cit.
73 DORIS, IF YOU AND CURT. Ibid.
74 THE SKAKELS WERE OUR EARLIEST. Interviews, Brother Patrick Hart.
76 HE TOLD ME, "DON'T." Mayhew, op. cit.

CHAPTER 18: THE PEP GIRLS

78 ETHEL, WHO HAD. Jacob, op. cit.
79 BESIDES FRENCH, ETHEL HAD. Ibid.
80 SHE WAS ALWAYS A TOMBOY. Mudge, op. cit.
80 MISS ETHEL WILL BE. *Greenwich Time*, May 25, 1939.
81 SUCH EXCURSIONS BECAME. Jim Skakel, op. cit.
81 AT ELEVEN SHE PARTICIPATED. *New York World-Telegram*, July 13, 1940.

CHAPTER 19: NATIONAL VELVET

82 BIG ANN WASN'T AN OUTDOORSY. McKneally, op. cit.
82 SHE TOOK TO RIDING. Interview, Billy Steinkraus.
83 HORSE GURU. Larned, op. cit.
84 WE CAME BACK FROM DINNER. Huberth, op. cit.
85 SHE SHOCKED TEDDY WAHL'S. Interview, Bobbie Wahl.

CHAPTER 20: FAST CARS AND SMOKING GUNS

86 THOSE SKAKEL KIDS. Interview, Ken McDonnell.
86 THE SKAKEL KIDS WEREN'T. Jacob, op. cit.
89 SCARED AND BLEEDING. Interviews, sources and Jim Skakel.
89 THE SHOOTER IN WHAT. Mayhew, op. cit.

CHAPTER 21: SKAKELS AT WAR

91 DECEMBER 7, 1941. Jim Skakel, op. cit.
91 AROUND FIVE O'CLOCK. Interview, source.
92 EARLY IN THE WAR. Mayhew, op. cit.
92 ONE OF HIS RUBE GOLDBERG. Ibid.
92 ON THE HOME FRONT. Medaille, op. cit.
92 EARLY IN THE WAR. *The Greenwich Press*, July 30, 1942.
93 I HAD NO IDEA WHY. Rushton Skakel, op. cit.
94 HE TOO WAS QUICKLY. Jim Skakel, op. cit.
94 BACK AT HOME. Ibid.
95 GOD KNOWS WHAT THOSE. Interviews, Hope Larkin Johnston.
96 ONE DAY ON THE TRAIN. Interview, source.
96 THE SKAKELS WERE GREAT. Interview, Joe Busk.

CHAPTER 22: BALLS, TEAS, AND SPAGHETTI DINNERS

97 SHE WAS NEVER ABLE TO MAKE. Pixie Meek, op. cit.
98 SHE MIGHT HAVE BEEN A BEAUTIFUL. Interview, source.
99 SHE'D HAVE SPAGHETTI PARTIES. Interview, source.
100 IT WAS NO SECRET. Johnston, op. cit.
101 ONE OF GEORGE'S FAVORITE. Interview, Tom Hayes.
102 HE WAS NOT A SIMPLE, LOVABLE. Interview, Sam Robbins.

CHAPTER 23: ETHEL OF THE SACRED HEART

103 THEY WERE THE DESCENDANTS. V. V. Harrison, *Changing Habits: A Memoir of the Society of the Sacred Heart* (New York: Doubleday, 1988).
103 MAPLEHURST WAS A WORLD. Interview, Margot Gotte MacNiven.
103 A SELF-WILLED, SPONTANEOUS. Interview, Mother Elizabeth Farley.
104 JUST PLAIN ETHEL. Interview, source.
104 IT WAS A STRANGE. Interview, source.
104 SHE WAS EASILY THE MOST. Interviews, Louise Paul Wood.
104 HER FIRST NIGHT. Interview, Eleanor Conroy McGrath.
105 WE DIDN'T THINK SHE WOULD. Interview, Mother Marion Duffy.
105 IT WAS PRETTY SPARTAN. Interview, Alice Meadows Buetow.
106 SHE'D PUT STUFF IN THE BED. Interview, Mary Bayo Garofoli.
107 ONE FALL WEEKEND. Interviews, sources.
108 ETHEL WAS VERY PRIVATE. Interview, source.
108 JACKIE WAS VERY BORING. Jacob, op. cit.
108 FOR A WHILE. Ibid.
108 SPORTS WERE MORE IMPORTANT. Duffy, op. cit.
109 THE ORALS WERE HORRIBLE. Buetow, op. cit.
109 SHE COULD THINK ON HER FEET. Interview, Nancy Corcoran Harrington.
109 THE CHURCH AND THE SCHOOL. Huberth, op. cit.
109 WE WERE ENCOURAGED. Louise Wood Paul, op. cit.
109 ETHEL EMBRACED A LOT. Gotte, op. cit.
110 ETHEL WAS CERTAINLY NOT. Farley, op. cit.

CHAPTER 24: OFF TO COLLEGE

113 THE ANDREWS SISTERS. *Chronicle of the 20th Century* (Mount Kisco, N.Y.: Chronicle Publications, 1987).
114 THEY'RE PLASTERED. Interview, Sylvester Larkin.

114 HER FIRST GAG. Interview, source.
115 THE STUDENT BODY ADOPTED. Interview, Sister Mary Byles.
115 WE WERE ALL PRETTY MUCH. Interview, source.
115 SOMETIMES THE FAMILIES. Byles, op. cit.

CHAPTER 25: THE KENNEDY CLAN

A variety of books were used as source material for the writing of this chapter, most notably: Peter Collier and David Horowitz, *The Kennedys: An American Drama* (New York: Summit Books, 1984); Rose Fitzgerald Kennedy, *Times to Remember* (Garden City, N.Y.: Doubleday, 1974); Doris Kearns Goodwin, *The Fitzgeralds and the Kennedys: An American Saga* (New York: Simon and Schuster, 1987); Arthur M. Schlesinger, Jr., *Robert Kennedy and His Times* (New York: Ballantine Books, 1978).

122 VERY CHILDLIKE, VERY NAIVE. Interview, Jeanne Cassidy Duffy.

CHAPTER 26: ETHEL AND JEAN

123 MY MOUTH FELL OPEN. Interviews, Margaret Geoghegan Adams.
123 MY FATHER LOVES. Ibid.
124 ETHEL HAD A VERY MAGNETIC. Interviews, Kay Simonson Waterbury.
124 ETHEL WAS TOTALLY DIFFERENT. Interviews, Ann Marie O'Hagan Murphy.
124 THE TWO OF THEM MADE. Interviews, Abbyann Day Lynch.
124 GREAT FRIEND. *Times to Remember*, op. cit.
124 THERE WERE A BUNCH. Ibid.
125 AT MANHATTANVILLE. Adams, op. cit.
125 ETHEL AND JEAN JUST DIDN'T. Interview, Helen Quigley Williams.
126 A LOT OF GIRLS WANTED. Interview, source.
126 FRIENDS SAY SHE CHOSE. Interview, sources.
126 SHE APPEARED TO BE. Lynch, op. cit.
126 IN THE BEGINNING, ETHEL. Interview, source.
126 THERE WAS A LOT OF MANIPULATION. Interview, source.
126 ETHEL WAS A B-PLUS. Byles, op. cit.
127 I THOUGHT SHE WAS FUN. Interview, Ann Cooley Buckley.
127 KEPT THEIR ROOMS. Interview, Sister Mary McCarthy.

CHAPTER 27: RICH GIRLS

127 EACH CLASS HAS ITS. Interview, Nancy David Sweeney.
127 THE TWELVE APOSTLES. Interviews, sources.

128 COOK AN EGG. Interviews, sources.
128 ONE OF HER CLOSEST. Interviews, sources.
128 WE WERE VERY CLIQUEY. Interview, source.
128 THEIR GROUP THOUGHT. Interviews, Jeanne Cassidy Duffy.
128 ON THE WHOLE WE GIRLS. Adams, op. cit.
128 I KNEW JUNE. Lynch, op. cit.
129 SURPRISING THOSE WHO WERE. Interviews, sources.
129 MANHATTANVILLE GIRLS WERE SUPPOSED. Waterbury, op. cit.
130 ETHEL HAD TERRIFIC TASTE. Interviews, Courtney Murphy Benoist.
130 ONE SATURDAY ETHEL DECIDED. Murphy, op. cit.
130 IN THOSE DAYS WE WORE. Ibid.
131 COLLEGE RATE. Interview, source.
131 I REMEMBER US DASHING. Waterbury, op. cit.

CHAPTER 28: CHASING BOYS

132 NINETY-NINE PERCENT OF THEM. Byles, op. cit.
132 ETHEL WOULD NEVER. Interviews, sources.
132 ETHEL WAS ALWAYS LIKE A BUDDY. Interview, source.
132 BESIDES BOBBY THERE WAS. Waterbury, op. cit.
132 THE SON OF THE CHAIRMAN. Interview, Billy Steinkraus.
133 CRUSH IS NOT. Ibid.
133 ETHEL WAS A REAL. Ibid.
133 SHE ADORED THE FAST. Waterbury, op. cit.
134 MOST OF THE GIRLS. Adams, op. cit. Interviews, Bill Geoghegan, Dey Watts, Ross Traphagen.
135 HIS WIFE WOULD BE PROPOSITIONED. Interview, Traphagen.
135 SO STRONG-MINDED. Interview, source.

CHAPTER 29: BOBBY KENNEDY

See note, Chapter 24, for primary biographical sources for this chapter.

138 DON' SHOOT. Francis Trego Montgomery, *Billy Whiskers* (New York: Akron, Ohio: The Saalfield Publishing Co., 1917).
139 JEAN HAD RECRUITED. Interviews, sources.
139 BOBBY AND I WERE. Interviews, George Terrien.
139 VERY OUTGOING, FRIENDLY, VERY IRISH. Interview, source.

CHAPTER 30: MAN OF HER DREAMS

140 ETHEL CAME BACK TO MANHATTANVILLE. Adams, op. cit.
141 YOU'RE DEFINITELY NOT. Interview, source.

141 AT ONE TIME OR ANOTHER. Jim Skakel, op. cit.
142 I COULDN'T HAVE HANDLED IT. Rushton Skakel, op. cit.
142 ANN WAS ADAMANT. Haws, op. cit.
142 ETHEL'S BEDROOM AT HOME. Interviews, sources.
142 SOFT AND REFINED. Interviews, Pat Norton Mullins.
143 IT WAS ONLY A CASUAL. Benoist, op. cit.
143 WAS CRAZY. Murphy, op. cit.
143 SIMMERING SIBLING RIVALRY. Interviews, sources.
143 WE USED TO TEASE HER. Interview, Mamie Jenkins.
144 ETHEL WAS HEAD OVER. Murphy, op. cit.
144 AFTER EVERY WEEKEND. Waterbury, op. cit.
144 HAND-HOLDING WAS THE CLOSEST. Interviews, sources.
144 BOBBY WAS VERY HELPFUL. Waterbury, op. cit.

CHAPTER 31: WILD CHILD

145 SHE WROTE AND WROTE. Interview, source.
145 ETHEL WASN'T TOO KEEN. Benoist, op. cit.
145 ALTHOUGH ETHEL SKAKEL. *Greenwich Time,* September 5, 1946.
146 THE GREATEST IRISH CATHOLIC. Interview, source.
146 SHE KNEW HOW. Lynch, op. cit.
146 IT WAS THE FIRST TIME. Williams, op. cit.
147 FOR GOD'S SAKE. Murphy, op. cit.
147 HEY, KID, WHO TAUGHT. Interviews, Mary Adele Bernard Hill.
148 ETHEL GRABBED THE BOOK. Interview, source.
148 JEAN WAS BEHIND ETHEL. Interview, source.
148 EVERYONE WAS FURIOUS. Interviews, Tish Coakley O'Neil.
148 A NOTE WAS FOUND. Interviews, sources.
149 ETHEL HAD EIGHT. Interview, McCarthy.
149 IT WAS JUST AMAZING. Interview, Marie Haggerty Henelley.
149 DIPPED IN GOLD. *Changing Habits,* op. cit.
149 WHEN JIM SKAKEL. Interviews, sources.
149 I REALLY THOUGHT SHE MIGHT. *Changing Habits,* op. cit.
150 THE NUNS GAVE ETHEL. Buckley, op. cit.
150 WHILE HER CLASSMATES WERE. Interview, sources.
150 WE WENT TO A. Benoist, op. cit.
150 ETHEL WAS OTHERWISE. Interview, source.

CHAPTER 32: HOMECOMING QUEEN

150 ARE YOU GOIN'. Interview, sources.
150 THE SKAKEL FAMILY WAS. Interviews, Anne Heide Quigley.
150–51 THEY SEEMED CULTURALLY. Interview, source.

151 Mrs. Skakel ruled with. Simonson, op. cit.
151 I was convulsed. Mullins, op. cit.
151 I didn't enjoy. Interview, source.
151 Inebriated state of some. Interviews, sources.
152 Darts was a favorite. Interviews, sources.
152 He had the top down. Interview, source.
152 We had been playing. Interview, source.
152 Hurling both young men. Interviews, Don Tase, Mrs. Robert Judge, Jim Skakel, op. cit.
152 That accident was. Interview, source.

CHAPTER 33: BOBBY'S FLING

This chapter is based primarily on interviews with George Terrien and Joan Winmill Brown, and references in Winmill's book, *No Longer Alone* (Old Tappan, N.J.: Fleming H. Revell Co., 1971).

CHAPTER 34: DON'T LOOK BACK

159 At the senior prom. Interviews, sources.
159 An excited hoarse voice. *Manhattanville Yearbook.*
159 Ethel is remembered. Interviews, sources.
159 She just came flying into. Interview, source.

CHAPTER 35: ENGAGEMENT AND MARRIAGE

163 A bookish assistant. Interviews, sources.
163 Irish Republican Army. Interview, source.
163 Big Ann had numerous. Interviews, sources.
163 Pat was more or less. McKneally, op. cit.
163 More than seven hundred. *Greenwich Time,* October 10, 1949.
164 A number of her friends. Interviews, sources.
164 For Father James Keller. Interviews, sources.
164 Central Intelligence Agency. Interviews, sources.
164 This was one of the few. Interview, source.
165 Ethel told me. Interview, Mother Duffy.
165 I had misgivings. *Times to Remember,* op. cit.
165 I just sort of played. *Washington Evening Star,* March 24, 1957.
165 Big Ann saw herself. McKneally, op. cit.
165 Low life, Irish trash. Interview, source.
165 Ethel Skakel's engagement to. *Chicago Herald-American,* January 10, 1950.
166 The formal engagement notice. *Boston Sunday Post,* January 8, 1950.
166 She might have taken. Benoist, op. cit.
166 Guests never got a chance. Interview, source.

166 LOOK WHAT MRS. KENNEDY. Interviews, sources.
166 HE DELIVERED A HUGE TRAY. Benoist, op. cit.
167 PIXIE AND I WERE LOOKING. Jacob, op. cit.
167 SHORTLY AFTER THE ENGAGEMENT. Benoist, op. cit.
168 THE KENNEDY CLAN DECIDED. Medaille, op. cit.
168 JUST LOOK AT THEM. Benoist, op. cit.
169 A LOT OF THE BRIDESMAIDS. Interview, source.
169 I KNOW WHY THAT SON. *New York Journal-American*, June 21, 1950.
169 A SPECIAL TRAIN. *Boston Globe*, June 17, 1950.
170 DRUNK BY THE TIME. Interview, source.
170 SKAKEL TOSSED A FEW COINS. Terrien, op. cit.
170 GEORGE WOULD DO ANYTHING. Jim Skakel, op. cit.
171 YOU CAN'T DRINK AND TAKE. Terrien, op. cit.
171 JOHN DOWDLE HAD BEEN. Interviews, sources.
171–72 WE TOOK A GREAT DEAL. Begley, op. cit.

CHAPTER 36: CHARLOTTESVILLE

172 ETHEL AND BOBBY WERE FEARFUL. Terrien, op. cit.
173 EVERY MORNING BOBBY AND ETHEL. Ibid.
173 CAN YOU BELIEVE THIS. Interviews, sources.
173 I TOLD ETHEL. Interviews, Marie O'Hagan Murphy.
174 FROM THE START I. Interviews, Gerald Tremblay.
174 BOBBY WAS REALLY SLOPPY. Murphy, op. cit.
175 SHE WAS DESPERATELY. Interviews, Sue Drake.

CHAPTER 37: SETTLING IN

175 ETHEL DIDN'T CARE A WHIT. Terrien, op. cit.
176 CHEESE DREAMS. Ibid.
176 CONSISTED OF FOUR VEGETABLES. *McCall's*, February 1962.
176 ETHEL HAD A LOT. Interviews, Ellie Tremblay.
177 ETHEL NEVER DID ANYTHING. Murphy, op. cit.
178 SCRAPPY AND PUGNACIOUS. Ibid.
178 ETHEL DEAR. *Times to Remember*, op. cit.
178 I'LL BET I CAN. Interviews, Gerald Tremblay.
179 ONE AFTERNOON ETHEL'S BROTHER. Interview, source.
179 BOBBY'S SUCH A CHICKEN-SHIT. Interview, source.
180 VISITORS TO HER PRIVATE. Interviews, sources.
180 ETHEL ALWAYS HAD. Interview, source.

CHAPTER 38: PERFECT PARTNER

181 I'M TERRIBLY EMBARRASSED. Murphy, op. cit.
181 AN ELABORATE DINNER. Terrien, op. cit.
181 HOW COULD THAT SON. Ibid.
181 SHE WAS A BIMBO. Murphy, op. cit.

182 SOURCES FOR THE MCCARTHY-KENNEDY RELATIONSHIP INCLUDE: Nicholas von Hoffman, *Citizen Cohn* (New York: Doubleday, 1988); Roy Cohn, *McCarthy* (New York: NAL, 1968); Thomas C. Reeves, *The Life and Times of Joe McCarthy* (New York: Stein and Day, 1982); *Robert Kennedy and His Times,* op. cit.

183 YOUNG COMMIES ARE TRAINED. *Look,* March 12, 1949; Michael Barson, *Better Dead than Red!* (New York: Hyperion, 1992).

183 THE PEOPLE AT THE SCHOOL. Interviews, Alice Whitney Lorillard; Terrien, op. cit.; McKneally, op. cit.

184 I FOUND HIM RATHER TERRIFYING. Drake, op. cit.

184 LET ME SHOW YOU. Ibid.

184 BUT THE MANAGER OF THE. Tremblay, op. cit.

CHAPTER 39: FIRST STORK

185 A MONTH BEFORE. Terrien, Drake, op. cit.

185 SHE HAD QUIETLY PLEDGED. Interviews, sources.

185 JOE AND I BEGAN. *Times to Remember,* op. cit.

186 NEVER LOOKED FORWARD TO. Interviews, sources.

186 ANY FORM OF PHYSICAL. Interviews, sources.

186 ETHEL WAS SICK AND. Drake, op. cit.

186 THE WHOLE FAMILY. Interviews, Virginia Skakel.

186 AN INTEGRAL PART. *Times to Remember,* op. cit.

186 A DAY OR TWO AFTER. Interviews, Luella Hennessey. (All quotes with Hennessey in this chapter are from interviews with author.)

189 AT SUMMER'S END. Benoist, op. cit.

CHAPTER 40: ALEXANDRA AND JOE

191 BARELY SETTLED. *Times to Remember,* op. cit.

191 ETHEL WAS SCARED. McKneally, op. cit.

191 LOOK AT THE ONE I GOT. Ibid; Terrien, op. cit.

191 ATTEND THE REPUBLICAN NATIONAL. McKneally, op. cit.

191 SHE MADE HER HAND. Interview, source.

192 THE CHRISTENING. Begley, op. cit.

192 HER HANDS WERE TREMBLING. Interview, source.

193 ETHEL JUST DIDN'T WANT TO. Interview, source.

193 PLACED IN UVILLE. Terrien, op. cit.

193 PRIVATELY, ETHEL. Interview, source.

193 AUNT ETHEL TOLD ME. Interviews, Little Georgeann Dowdle.

194 ETHEL DIDN'T SAY MUCH. Hennessey, op. cit.

194 THE CLOSE MATCHING. *Times to Remember,* op. cit.

CHAPTER 41: FAMILY FEUD

195 THE WHOLE FAMILY'S VIEW. Begley, op. cit.
195 IN ALL THOSE YEARS. Virginia Skakel, op. cit.
195 IT WAS THE FIRST TIME. Interview, source.
196 JACK WAS AT THE HELM. William Buckley newspaper column, 1966.
196 BIG ANN HARBORED. Interview, sources.
196 BIG ANN HAD LITTLE OR NO. Interviews, John McCooey.
196 WHY DID I EVER LET HER. Terrien, op. cit.
197 IT CAN'T BE. I STILL HAVE. McCooey, op. cit.
197 ONE EVENING AT THE. Interview, source.
197 IF BOBBY CAN'T TREAT ETHEL. Interview, source.
197 MRS. KENNEDY CAME SPECIFICALLY TO. McCooey, op. cit.
198 AREN'T YOU MRS. SKAKEL. Virginia Skakel, op. cit.
199 BOBBY HAD REACHED. Interview, source.
199 BOBBY DIDN'T CARE. McKneally, op. cit.

CHAPTER 42: LAKE AVENUE AND THE FIFTIES

200 HE'S GOT A GREAT FAMILY. Virginia Skakel, op. cit.
201 WHEN YOUNG WOMEN CAME. Interview, source.
201 DRUNKER THAN A HOOT. Mayhew, op. cit.
201 MY OWN SON WON'T. Hayes, op. cit.
202 STRICT RULES GOVERNING. Virginia Skakel, op. cit.
203 IT WAS ABSOLUTELY UNREAL. Interview, source.
203 ONCE, ON AN ANTIQUING. Interviews, sources.
204 THE ROAD GANG. Begley, op. cit.
205 SHE USED TO BUY. Interview, source.
205 ONE CHRISTMAS BIG ANN. Virginia Skakel, op. cit.

CHAPTER 43: WASHINGTON BOUND

Sources for this chapter, for the most part, are listed above for page 183. Additional material from interviews, sources.

CHAPTER 44: FIRST HOME

208 GAVE ETHEL A RENT BUDGET. Interviews, sources.
208 ONE OF HER CUTBACKS. Begley, op. cit.
209 YOU'RE MARRIED TO. Jim Skakel, op. cit.
209 SHE WANTED A RETURN. Interview, source.
209 ONE OF HER FIRST. Interviews, Sarah Davis.
210 THEY WERE LIKE HAM AND EGGS. Interview, source.
210 MY FRIENDSHIP WITH. Interview, source.
210 MORE THAN A FEW OF. Interview, sources.
210 ETHEL HAD WHAT. Interview, source.
211 WHILE GETTING HER HAIR DONE. Interview, source.
211 AT JANSEN, FOR EXAMPLE. Christopher Ogden, *Life of*

the Party: The Biography of Pamela Digby Churchill Hayward Harriman (New York: Little, Brown and Co., 1994).
211 Among Sarah Davis's talents. Interview, source.
211 He really let her. Interview, source.
212 At Bergdorf's, Ethel hit. Interview, source.

CHAPTER 45: ETHEL AND JACKIE

212 Ethel began throwing. Interviews, sources.
213 The most gorgeous. Interviews, Anne Marie O'Hagan Murphy.
214 Jack was hardly paying attention. Interviews, sources.
214 Ethel came back. Murphy, op. cit.
215 She wasn't sexually attracted. C. David Heymann, *A Woman Named Jackie* (New York: New American Library, 1990).
215 Ethel made jokes. Interview, source.
215 With those clodhoppers. Kitty Kelley, *Jackie O!* (New York: Ballantine, 1989).
215–16 Ethel Kennedy has the mind-set. *A Woman Named Jackie,* op. cit.
216 Ethel and Jackie could never. Interview, source.
217 A notorious scavenger. *Times to Remember,* op. cit.
217 Louis Quinze sofa. *Jackie O!* op. cit.
217 If you walked. Begley, op. cit.

CHAPTER 46: MARRYING THEM OFF

219 A week after the. McCooey, op. cit.
219 A solid gold. Ibid.

CHAPTER 47: KENNEDY VS. COHN

220 Ethel couldn't have been. Interviews, sources.
221 A worthless rattle brain. Mayhew, op. cit.
222 When she'd get home. Hennessey, op. cit.
224 Ethel just loved. Interview, La Verne Duffy.

CHAPTER 48: A LAST GOOD-BYE

224 For months during. Mayhew, op. cit.; Jim Skakel, op. cit.; McCooey, op. cit.
225 My father needed. Rushton Skakel, op. cit.
226 As early as. Ibid.
226 A practical joker. Interviews, sources.
226 The Skakel planes also. Interviews, sources.
226 The Kennedys didn't have. Terrien, op. cit.
226 Bobby had deigned. Begley, op. cit.
227 This time out. Ibid.
228 We smelled gas. Hayes, op. cit.

CHAPTER 49: END OF AN ERA

228 A MAID ANSWERED. Interviews, sources.
229 AS SHE READ. Ibid.
229 HER BROTHER RUSHTON. Rushton Skakel, op. cit.
230 THE INNER CIRCLE. Begley, op. cit.; Terrien, op. cit.; McKneally, op. cit.
230 GEORGE HAD CALLED ETHEL. Begley, op. cit.
231 DEAR GOD, YOU SPEND. Ibid.
231 WHILE FLYING NORTH. Virginia Skakel, op. cit.
232 THERE WERE THREE WITNESSES. Jim Skakel, op. cit.
232 IT WAS A MIRACLE. Rushton Skakel, op. cit.
232 I THINK IT'S SOMETHING. Bob Skakel, op. cit.
232 THE CHURCH DECIDED TO WAIVE. McKneally, op. cit.
233 WHEN EVERYONE HAD LEFT. Interview, source.
233 THE HOUSE WAS CRAMMED. Medaille, op. cit.
233 THAT EVENING, ETHEL. Interview, sources.
233 SHE KNEW THEY WERE IN HEAVEN. Davis, op. cit.
234 JUST WHO WAS THIS GUEST. Medaille, op. cit.
235 AGAINST EVERYBODY'S WISHES. Little Georgeann, op. cit.
235 TREATED UNFAIRLY BY. Rushton Skakel, op. cit.
235 THEY WERE IN A CASH BIND. Hayes, op. cit.
236 BOBBY MADE AN EFFORT. McCooey, op. cit.

CHAPTER 50: HICKORY HILL

239 I LIKE TO SEE BOBBY IN ACTION. *Washington Star,* March 24, 1957.
239 SHE EVEN LOOKED AT ME. *Life,* October 11, 1961.
240 MORE KENNEDY THAN THOU. Interview, source.
240 I JUST CAN'T UNDERSTAND. *New York Daily News,* March 16, 1957.
240 ETHEL CLIPPED EVERY. Interview, source.
240 I'D NEVER BEEN TO. *Washington Evening Star,* op. cit.
240 WHY AREN'T YOU HOME. Evan Thomas, *The Man to See* (New York: Simon & Schuster, 1991).
240 FOR YEARS ETHEL WOULD HAVE. Ibid.
240–41 UNBEKNOWNST TO MOST. Terrien, op. cit.
241 AT NIGHT ETHEL HAD. *Newsweek,* April 1, 1957.
242 KENNEDY COMPOUND. *Times to Remember,* op. cit.
243 IF HE COULD HAVE. *New York Daily News,* March 16, 1957.
243 FUNCTIONAL, SMOOTH. *New York Journal-American,* November 28, 1961.
243 IT'S THE FIRST TIME. *Washington Evening Star,* November 13, 1958.
243 TYPICAL OF THE AMBIENCE. *Washington Post,* May 22, 1957.

CHAPTER 51: AN EMBARRASSMENT FOR BOBBY

245 THE GOLDEN COUPLE. Begley, op. cit.
245 A GUEST CRIPPLED. Interviews, sources.
245 ANOTHER TIME, AT A PARTY. Ibid.
245 PUBLISHED SOURCES FOR the incident and reaction are *Time, New York Herald Tribune, New York Post,* Associated Press.
246 ETHEL WAS ACTING. Terrien, op. cit.

CHAPTER 52: A TANGLED WEB

247 WANTS TO SHOW HIS FAMILY. Terrien, op. cit.
247 JOHN DOWDLE WAS AN. Rushton Skakel, op. cit.
248 I THOUGHT THAT DADDY. Little Georgeann Dowdle, op. cit.
248 YOUR DADDY'S IN HEAVEN. Ibid.
248 THAT BASTARD IS OUT. McKneally, op. cit.
249 BOBBY ORDERED ETHEL. Interviews, sources.
249 DESPITE WHAT THEY HAVE. Begley, op. cit.
249 BUT TERRIEN STEPPED IN. McKneally, op. cit.
249 I SAID BOOM. Rushton Skakel, op. cit.
249 I WAS KICKED OUT. Little Georgeann Dowdle, op. cit.
250 I TOLD ALL OF THEM. Terrien, op. cit.
250 ETHEL WAS QUITE BITTER. Jim Skakel, op. cit.
250 THIS IS JUST REVOLTING. Ibid.
250 MY GOD, GEORGE. Interview, source.
250 TERRIEN HAD INSISTED. Interview, sources; Terrien, op. cit.; McKneally, op. cit.; Jim Skakel, op. cit.
251 MOTHER SUDDENLY LOOKED AROUND. Little Georgeann Dowdle, op. cit.
251 WE ALWAYS HAD WALKERS. Ibid.
252 WATCH, THEY'LL ALL. Interview, source.

CHAPTER 53: A MURDER IN THE BRONX

252 A GOOD-FOR-NOTHING. Medaille, op. cit.
253 SHE HAD NOTHING. Ibid.
254 Details of the events leading up to the murder, the crime itself, and its aftermath are based on interviews with Medaille and newspaper accounts.
256 WHY DON'T YOU COME. Medaille, op. cit.
256 I WAS PRESENT. Terrien, op. cit.
257 ETHEL WAS AWARE. Medaille, op. cit.

CHAPTER 54: WINNING THE BIG ONE

258 WHAT'S UP THERE. *Washington Post,* December 17, 1960.
259 $150,000 LAWSUIT. *New York Daily News,* November 4, 1960.

260 BEFORE THE BUNTING. LBJ Library, Austin, Texas.
260 ETHEL RESPONDED ENTHUSIASTICALLY. Ibid.
260 THE SKAKELS AS USUAL. Jim Skakel, op. cit.; Rushton Skakel, op. cit.
260 ETHEL TOOK HER. Interviews, sources.
261 BOBBY WAS BROUGHT UP. Jim Skakel, op. cit.
261 IF YOU ANNOUNCE ME. *The Kennedys: An American Drama,* op. cit.

CHAPTER 55: A SEXY INAUGURATION

265 I CAN'T MAKE UP FOR. *The New York Times,* January 14, 1961.
265 HE ALSO ACKNOWLEDGED. Ibid., January 13–14, 1961.
266 I DON'T SEE ANYTHING. Ibid., January 22, 1961.
266 AMOS T. ACKERMAN. Ibid., May 8, 1961.
266 HER INAUGURAL DRESS. Interview, Mrs. Norman Paul.
266 THE PRETTY WIFE OF. *New York Journal-American,* January 10, 1961.
267 ETHEL ADORED GEORGE. Davis, op. cit.
267 HE TOLD ME AFTERWARD. Interviews, Bettan Olwaeus.
267 GEORGE WAS GIVING KIM. Jim Skakel, op. cit.
267 NONE OF THAT HERE. Ibid.
267 I HOPE YOU ARE GOING TO. Paul Fay, *The Pleasure of His Company* (New York: Harper and Row, 1966).
268 HOORAY FOR HOLLYWOOD. Interview, source.
268 MÉNAGE À TROIS. *A Woman Named Jackie,* op. cit.
268 SOMETIMES IT SEEMED. Interviews, Bill Whiteford.
268 THE MOST SINCERELY HAPPY. *New York Journal-American,* January 23, 1961.

CHAPTER 56: GLAMOUR GIRL

269 IN ONE INSTANCE. Interviews, Barbara Gamarekian.
269 SIMPLY BY BEING THE SISTER-IN-LAW. *New York Journal-American,* October 28, 1961.
269 IT WOULD BE EASY TO MAKE. *Life,* October 11, 1961.
269 A SECRET WEAPON; WHEN ETHEL HEARD. Ibid., June 9; August 18, 1961.
270 ETHEL, YOU DID FINE. *Washington Post,* October 25, 1961.
270 I DON'T KNOW WHETHER. *Life,* October 11, 1961.

CHAPTER 57: THE KNOCKOFF CLOSET

270 WHEN SWISS-BORN. Interview, Mrs. Norman Paul.
271 EXPLICIT INSTRUCTIONS. From Mrs. Paul's private correspondence.
271 MAYBE YOU CAN DO SOMETHING. Paul, op. cit.
272 FORTY THOUSAND DOLLARS A YEAR. *Jackie O!* op. cit.

272 PEOPLE SAID ETHEL. Paul, op. cit.
272 SHE HAD A VERY STRONG. Ibid.
272 MAKE COPIES OF THE LATEST. Private correspondence, op. cit.
272 BUT NO ONE ELSE. *Washington Post*, October 27, 1965.
273 WHEN I VISITED ETHEL. Paul, op. cit.
274 SEW HER FINGERS. Interview, source.
274 ETHEL TELEPHONED THE WHITE HOUSE. Paul, op. cit.
274 WHITE FUR SKI HAT. Private correspondence, op. cit.

CHAPTER 58: HANDMAIDENS

275 IT WAS FUN. Barbara Howar, *Laughing All the Way* (New York: Stein and Day, 1973).
275 BREEZY ETHEL KENNEDY. Ibid.
275 SOMETHING THAT REQUIRED TRUE. Ibid.
275 S.S. GIRLS. Interviews, Barbara Howar.
276 LIKE ETHEL, THEY WERE. Interviews, sources.
276 ASTRONAUT SCOTT CARPENTER'S. *Washington Post*, March 19, 1968.
276 SCURRY AROUND TO FIND. Ibid., October 25, 1961.
276 IT WAS A VERY EXCITING. Davis, op. cit.
276 IT WAS BIZARRE. Howar, op. cit.
277 DEAN WAS A WONDERFUL. Interview, source.
277 ONE OF THOSE WHO DESPERATELY. Interview, source.
277 ETHEL DIDN'T HAVE TIME. Ibid.
277 WHAT WAS INTERESTING WAS. Howar, op. cit.

CHAPTER 59: BAY OF PIGS

278 THE NIGHT BEFORE THE. *The Pleasure of His Company*, op. cit.
279 HIS FREQUENT COMPANION. Interviews, sources.
279 THE COUNTRY'S SUGAR PRODUCTION. Jim Skakel, op. cit.
279 THEY WERE POINTING TOMMY. Tase, op. cit.
280 USED TO TAKE 157 PEOPLE. Jim Skakel, op. cit.
280 AFTER THE BAY OF PIGS. United Press International, April 25, 1961.
280 WHEN BOBBY HEARD WHAT. Terrien, op. cit.
280 VERY FEW PEOPLE ARE THE. Correspondence, JFK Library.

CHAPTER 60: HICKORY HILL COMES TO JUSTICE

281 FOR A TIME, BOBBY WAS. *New York Journal-American*, August 25, 1961.
282 IT'S GOING TO GO OUT. Ibid., March 2, 1961.

282 YOU'RE GETTING OLD. *New York Herald Tribune*, January 28, 1962.
282 LATE ONE AFTERNOON. Ibid., April 11, 1961.
282 I JUST DON'T BELIEVE. *Life*, October 11, 1961.

CHAPTER 61: EVERYBODY INTO THE POOL

283 ETHEL WAS CHILDISH AND. Marion Schlesinger, conversation with author.
283 HER JOKES DIVERTED HIM. *Robert Kennedy and His Times*, op. cit.
284 I WAS DELIGHTED TO READ. Correspondence, JFK Library.
284 A SOURCE CLOSE TO. *The New York Times*, June 21, 1962.
285 LATER, LEE UDALL. *McCall's*, June 1974.
285 THEY WERE KIND OF. Tremblay, op. cit.
285 SHE WAS NOT THE. Interviews, Violet Marshall.
286 UNDER DURESS FROM MY. Ibid.
286 THOUGH ETHEL IS. Ibid.
286 I LIKE COMPETITION. *Life*, October 11, 1961.
286 NEVER, NEVER, EVER. Marshall, op. cit.
286 THAT'S ETHEL. Ibid.
286 I'LL NEVER IN MY. Ibid.

CHAPTER 62: A QUESTION OF ARSON AND ADULTERY

287 BOUGHT A BROWN WIG. *New York Journal-American*, February 28, 1962.
287–88 I WAS THERE TO GIVE ETHEL. Interview, Susie Wilson.
288 WITH INCREASING DREAD. George Terrien, op. cit.
288 PAT SKAKEL CAUSED. Interviews, sources.
288 HAD RECENTLY BANNED GEORGE. Little Georgeann Dowdle, op. cit.
289 WE WERE IN OUR. Begley, op. cit.
289 GEORGE TOLD ME PAT. Terrien, op. cit.
289 IT DESTROYED THOUSANDS. Jim Skakel, op. cit.
290 IN THE BUSHES I FOUND. Terrien, op. cit.
290 ETHEL MUST HAVE CALLED. Ibid.
291 SHE WAS VERY WILLFUL. Begley, op. cit.
291 IT LOOKED LIKE GERMANY. Jim Skakel, op. cit.
291 HE DIDN'T WANT. Terrien, op. cit.

CHAPTER 63: SEDUCING THE PRESS

292 BEN BRADLEE, THEN CHIEF. *Power, Privilege and the* Post, Carol Felsenthal (New York: G. P. Putnam's Sons, 1993).
292 SHE WAS VERY CAREFUL. Howar, op. cit.
293 IF A BOMB HAD EVER. Interview, Douglas Kiker.
293 HICKORY HILL WAS THE PLACE. Gamarekian, op. cit.

293 A LOT OF BIG-TIME. Kiker, op. cit.
294 THE KENNEDYS KNEW PERFECTLY. Interview, Sophie Burnham.
294 HORRIFIED AND SPEECHLESS. Ibid.
294 THERE WERE A LOT OF JOURNALISTS. Interview, Sander Vanocur.
294 SHE WAS A SUPER-GOOD. Interview, Richard Starnes.
295 I WAS ALWAYS EMBARRASSED. Interview, Roger Mudd.
296 A TERRIBLY GLAMOROUS. Interview, Polly Kraft.
296 WOULD YOU HELP ME CARRY. Wilson, op. cit.
296 I FELT I GOT SO MUCH. Ibid.
297 ETHEL HAD DECIDED. *Ladies Home Journal*, February 1978.

CHAPTER 64: ETHEL'S ENEMY LIST

297 ETHEL ONCE TOOK A POKE. Tremblay, op. cit.
298 WHEN ETHEL HITS YOU. Ibid.
298 NOT NOTICEABLY ADEPT. *The New York Times Magazine*, 1969.
298 UNUSUAL ELEVEN-PAGE. Interview, Susan Sheehan.
298 IMPULSES ARE ALL POSITIVE. *Boston Globe*, April 26, 1963.
300 OBVIOUSLY BURKE WROTE THE. Kraft, op. cit.
300 THERE WAS A VERY QUIET. Ibid.
301 YOU DIDN'T INVITE BEN. Interview, source.
301 NOT FORGOTTEN. *Washington Post*, January 31, 1974.
301 SEEING THE NAMES POLLY AND JOE. Interview, source.
301 MRS. KENNEDY TOLD THE. Interview, Ruth Darmstadt.
302 WE RESPONDED TO HER. Mudd, op. cit.
302 THE FIRST PERSON WHO DARED. Interview, source.
302 JUST DON'T PUT US. Interview, source.
302 KRAFT UNEXPECTEDLY. Kraft, op. cit.
302 ALL JOE AND I. Ibid.
303 THIS IS ROGER MARRIS? Mudd, op. cit.
303 I DON'T KNOW OF ANY. Ibid.
304 I HAD BEGUN TO SEE. Ibid.
304 IT WOULD BE A GOOD. Richard Burke, *The Senator: My Ten Years with Ted Kennedy* (New York: St. Martin's Press, 1992).
305 THAT SON OF A. Ibid.
305 SHE NEVER TOLD ME. Mudd, op. cit.

CHAPTER 65: WE LOVE ETHEL

306 IT'S SO SILLY. *Washington Evening Star*, March 3, 1962.
306 THE TRIP, WHICH COST. *Palm Beach Post*, March 22, 1962.
306 WHAT A CHARMING IDEA. *Newsweek*, March 5, 1962.
306 I JUST COULDN'T FIND THE BRAKES. *New York Daily News*, February 22, 1962

307 CRASH KENNEDY. George Dixon, "Washington Scene," King Features Syndicate.
307 ETHEL WANTED TO SWIM BACK. Wilson, op. cit.
307 AFTER ALL, BOBBY HAD TO. Associated Press, February 23, 1962.
308 WHAT'S MY SECRET. *Time*, February 16, 1962.
308 ETHEL'S EGO WAS BURSTING. Interview, source.

CHAPTER 66: THE MONROE AFFAIR

308 I WANT TO BE PLAYED. Interview, source.
308 PLANTED STORIES. *The New York Times*, September 23, 1961.
309 THE STORY LINE. Ibid.
309 ETHEL WAS VERY SUPPORTIVE. Interview, Budd Schulberg.
309 TALK ABOUT IT AROUND. Geoghegan, op. cit.
309 GOSSIP AND INNUENDOS. Schulberg, op. cit.
309 I THOUGHT IT WAS QUITE. Ibid.
309 THE TWO GOT INTO A HEATED. *Esquire*, March 1963.
310 Besides interviews, the author found several books invaluable in writing about the Monroe-Kennedy relationship. They include: Anthony Summers, *Goddess: The Secret Lives of Marilyn Monroe* (New York: Macmillan Publishing Co., 1985); Peter Harry Brown and Patte B. Barham, *Marilyn: The Last Take* (New York: E. P. Dutton, 1992); Donald Spoto, *Marilyn Monroe: The Biography* (New York: HarperCollins, 1993); James Spada, *The Man Who Kept the Secrets* (New York: Bantam Books, 1991); Patricia Seaton Lawford with Ted Schwarz, *The Peter Lawford Story* (New York: Carroll & Graf, 1988).
310 ETHEL WAS SO FURIOUS. Interview, source.
311 PETER HATED ETHEL. Interviews, Patricia Seaton Lawford.
312 BOB ASKED ME TO COME ALONG. *Goddess*, op. cit.
312 BOBBY WAS SOUNDING VERY MACHO. Terrien, op. cit.
313 GEORGE FELL OVER LAUGHING. Ibid.
315 AFTER BREAKING THROUGH THE. *Robert Kennedy and His Times*, op. cit.
315 HAD NEVER SEEN. Ibid.
316 ETHIE TOLD GEORGEANN. Terrien, op. cit.
316–17 TO FALL ALL OVER. Geoghegan, op. cit.
317 WILLIAMS HAD A MEETING WITH. *The Man to See*, op. cit.
317 ONE OF THE MORE. *Goddess*, op. cit.
318 WHAT ABOUT BOBBY AND ETHEL. *Marilyn: The Last Take*, op. cit.
319 MORE THOROUGHLY DOCUMENTED. *Newsweek*, October 14, 1986.

320 THERE'S NO DOUBT. Interview, source.
320 JUST LIKE JACK, BOBBY. Interview, source.
321 IN HIS OWN SUBTLE WAY. Interview, source.
321 SHE GOT PREGNANT. Interview, source.
321 BOBBY HAD DEVELOPED. *Goddess,* op. cit.
322 IT WAS A PRIVATE. Traphagen, op. cit.
322 BOBBY WAS SITTING. Betty Beale, *Power at Play* (Washington, D.C.: Regnery Gateway, 1993).
322 ETHEL ONCE TELEPHONED. Nancy Dickerson, *Among Those Present* (New York: Random House, 1976).
323 WHEN BOBBY SAW THE COPS. Kiker, op. cit.
323 I SPENT MUCH MORE TIME. Interviews, Polly Bussell.
323 THEY WERE THE CUTE. Interview, source.
323 RAY TAPPED ETHEL. Interview, Helen Downey.
324 A WASHINGTON JOURNALIST. Tremblay, op. cit.

CHAPTER 67: ETHEL, THE OMNIPOTENT

325 STAY IN TRIM WITH. *New York Journal-American,* January 29, 1962.
325 I SIMPLY LOVE DESSERTS. *New York Post,* April 29, 1962.
325 I TURNED THEM OVER ON. *This Week,* December 17, 1961.
326 ETHEL WOULD HAVE THE DRIVER. Interview, source.
326 PEOPLE WHO LIVED. Wilson, op. cit.
326 SUSIE, YOU'RE THE ONLY. Ibid.
327 ETHEL DID HER BEST. Davis, op. cit.
327 NATURAL-BORN CON MAN. *Robert Kennedy and His Times,* op. cit.
327 ETHEL WAS RESPONSIBLE FOR US. Interview, Gertrude Corbin.
328 AWFULLY UNFORTUNATE. *Newsweek,* March 18, 1963.
328 ETHEL THREW ONE FOR. *Boston Globe,* March 17, 1963.
328 AFTER THE PARTY GOT ROLLING. Jim Skakel, op. cit.
328 BOBBY RUSHED UP TO CLAIM. Rushton Skakel, op. cit.
329 ETHEL WAS SOMEONE WHO. Interview, Rose Styron.
329 I'M COMING TOO. Ibid.
330 ZEMO WAS HANDED A. *The New York Times,* December 30, 1966.
330 WE KNEW THIS WAS. *Boston Globe,* January 24, 1967.
331 AN ADMITTED HORSE THIEF. *Washington Post,* January 10, 1967.
331 I HAD A LITTLE TOO. *Boston Globe,* January 24, 1967.
332 TO GET TO THE FAYS'. Johnston, op. cit.
332 IT WAS THE FIRST FROST. Ibid.

CHAPTER 68: FAMILY AFFAIR

333 BILL AND ANN WERE DRAWN. Interviews, Bev Keith.
334 IT WAS ALMOST AS IF. Interview, source.

334 ANN ACKNOWLEDGED IT. Interviews, Royall O'Brien.
334 I KNEW THE BABY WASN'T. McCooey, op. cit.
334 ANN HAD THE BABY. Ibid.
334 ETHEL, FOR ONE, STOPPED. Interviews, sources.
335 BOBBY WAS CHANGING. McCooey, op. cit.
335 ANN WENT TO MEXICO. Ibid.
335 ALSO ENDED IN DIVORCE. Interview, Peter Ryan.
336 HE WAS CONCENTRATING ON SWEDES. Whiteford, op. cit.
336 GEORGE WAS TOTALLY AMORAL. Ibid.
336 GEORGE WAS CHARMING. Olwaeus, op. cit.
337 THAT KNIFE SLICED. Whiteford, op. cit.
338 ALL RIGHT, GEORGE. Ibid.
338 YOU KNOW, PAL. Ibid.
338 VERY UNHAPPY AND LONELY. Olwaeus, op. cit.
338 HE LOVED ETHEL A LOT. Ibid.
339 HAD GROWN APART AFTER. Virginia Skakel, op. cit.
340 I WAS IN MY NIGHTGOWN. Ibid.
340 I WENT OVER TO JIM. Ibid.

CHAPTER 69: LIFE AND DEATH

341 WE'RE ALL SIMPLY. *New York Journal-American,* April 18, 1963.
341 NUMEROUS COMPLICATIONS. *Boston Globe,* July 6, 1963.
342 SHE WASN'T FEELING WELL. *Washington Post,* January 24, 1963.
342 ETHEL WAS UNDER A LOT. Terrien, op. cit.
342 SHE WAS UNDER INCREDIBLE. Interview, Sam Meek.
342 SHE WAS ALWAYS JOYOUS. Davis, op. cit.
343 ETHEL DID EVERYTHING. Ibid.
343 HER PERSONAL INVOLVEMENT. Tremblay, op. cit.
344 WHOM ETHEL HAD BEGUN. Interview, Moura Chabor.
344 KID, WOULD YOU GET. Davis, op. cit.
344 ETHEL WAS ALWAYS VERY MUCH. Interview, source.
344 ETHEL LOST HER COOKIES. Ibid.
345 ETHEL'S KIDS. Davis, op. cit.
346 THEY CAN LEARN MORE. *Washington Post,* February 11, 1963.
347 HE LOOKS LIKE A PRETTY. *Life,* August 9, 1963.

CHAPTER 70: DALLAS

For the events surrounding the assassination of President Kennedy, the author's primary source was William Manchester's *The Death of a President* (New York: Harper Row, 1967). Newspaper and magazine stories were also used.

350 A MAID OR PERHAPS. Jean Stein and George Plimpton,

American Journey: The Times of Robert Kennedy (New York: Harcourt, Brace, Jovanovich, 1970).

350 DON'T YOU THINK CHIEF PARKER. Edwin Guthman, *We Band of Brothers: A Memoir of Robert F. Kennedy* (New York: Harper & Row, 1971).

353 ETHEL AND BOBBY WERE NEVER. Davis, op. cit.

353 HE'S IN HEAVEN. Terrien, op. cit.

CHAPTER 71: AFTER JACK

356 THE SKAKELS ARE PRETTY. Terrien, op. cit.

356 IT WAS WELL UNDERSTOOD. *Times to Remember,* op. cit.

356 BOBBY HAD CHOSEN TO. *The New York Times,* November 28, 1963.

356 SHE QUIETLY THANKED THEM. *Washington Post,* November 27, 1963.

357 SHE CAJOLED HIM TO. *New York Journal-American,* December 19, 1963.

357 YOU'RE NOT A TIGER. *New York Post,* December 21, 1963.

357 WITHOUT ETHEL, BOBBY. Interview, source.

357 YOUR BROTHER DIED. *Saturday Evening Post,* March 28, 1964.

358 IN LATE DECEMBER. *Palm Beach Post,* December 24, 1963.

358 IT REALLY WASN'T FOR. *Saturday Evening Post,* March 28, 1964.

359 COULD I HAVE THEM OUT. *Washington Evening Star,* March 1, 1964.

360 I THINK IT'S BEEN REALLY ROUGH. *Newsday,* November 11, 1964.

360 THEY STILL CAN'T QUITE. Correspondence, LBJ Library.

360 MAIN PILLAR OF STRENGTH. *Times to Remember,* op. cit.

360 I THINK HE IS THE MOST. *Jackie Oh!* op. cit.

361 HE'S SPENDING AN AWFUL LOT. *Washingtonian,* June 1983.

361 I KNOW ETHEL WAS VERY. Interview, source.

361 MARY DE GRACE, WHO WORKED. *A Woman Named Jackie,* op. cit.

361 TOGETHER IN A BANQUETTE. Interview, source.

361 BOBBY WAS GETTING A LOT. Interview, Stanley Tretick.

CHAPTER 72: TO THE SENATE

362 SOMEBODY UP THERE DOESN'T LIKE ME. *Robert Kennedy and His Times,* op. cit.

363 CURIOUSLY REGISTERED AS. United Press International, September 13, 1964.

363 NOT TOO ENTHUSIASTIC. *Washington Post,* August 26, 1964.

363 YOU COULD TURN ON. *McCall's,* August 1965.
364 JACKIE COULD HAVE HELPED. *New York Journal-American,* November 4, 1964.
364 AT CAMPAIGN STOPS. *The New York Times,* September 28, 1964.
364 I SHALL DEVOTE. Ibid., August 26, 1964.
364 A FALSE ISSUE. Ibid., September 11, 1964.
364 HE IS NO JOHNNY. *Washington Post,* August 26, 1964.
364 ETHEL PLEDGED THAT. *New York Journal-American,* August 25, 1964.
365 THE KENNEDYS' NEW YORK MANOR. *Newsday,* August 26, 1964.
365 SHE SURE DID ENJOY. Interview, source.
365 SHE TALKS ABOUT THE THINGS. *New York Post,* September 21, 1964.
365 I DELIVER THE SPEECH. *Washington Post,* October 2, 1964.
365 YOU'LL HELP HIM. *New York Journal-American,* September 11, 1964.
365–66 SHAME ON YOU. Ibid., September 27, 1964.
366 WHAT DO YOU INTEND. Ibid., October 20, 1964.
366 ETHEL, LET'S GO. *The New York Times,* October 11, 1964.
366 A SPIRIT WE CAN ALL. Ibid., November 1, 1964.
366 ETHEL SHOOK THE HANDS. *New York Journal-American,* October 29, 1964.
367 IN THIS CASE. *The New York Times,* October 7, 1964.
367 WELL, HERE WE ARE. *McCall's,* August 1965.
367 AND SHE HOSTED NINE. *New York World-Telegram,* October 27, 1964.
367 I LOVE THAT BOY. *McCall's,* op. cit.
368 WE MADE IT. Maria Riva, *Marlene Dietrich* (New York: Alfred A. Knopf, 1993).
369 I THINK THE ONLY THING. *Newsday,* November 4, 1964.
369 THANK YOU FOR MAKING. *New York World-Telegram,* November 4, 1964.
369 MY GOODNESS, WE NEVER. *Newsday,* op. cit.
370 CHILDREN ARE CHEAPER. *New York Times,* January 20, 1965.

CHAPTER 73: CAMELOT VS. THE GREAT SOCIETY

373 I HAVE ABSOLUTELY NO. *Washington Post,* January 5, 1965.
373 IT WAS WAR. Interview, source.
374 LOYALTY TO BOTH. *Laughing All the Way,* op. cit.
374 DON'T GET YOUR DRESS. Howar, op. cit.
374 SHE WAS EVEN NICER. Ibid.
374 LYNDON AND LADY BIRD. Interview, LaDonna Harris.

375 UNDERNEATH THAT CHEERFUL EXTERIOR. Interview, source.
375 LANDED ON FAY. *Robert Kennedy and His Times,* op. cit.
375 THE FAYS WERE OFF. Interview, source.
376 FROM THE MOMENT THEY. Harris, op. cit.
376 I JUST COULDN'T KEEP UP. Marcia Chellis, *The Joan Kennedy Story* (New York: Simon & Schuster, 1985).
376 OUT OF THE BLUE. Harris, op. cit.
376 JOAN SHOWED UP. Ibid.
377 ETHEL DESPISED WEAKNESS. Terrien, op. cit.
377 HAD A VERY CONDESCENDING. Interview, Richard Burke.
377 THERE WAS NO QUESTION. Interview, source.
377 STRIKINGLY BEAUTIFUL. *Times to Remember,* op. cit.
378 ETHEL TREATED JOAN. Gibson, op. cit.
378 WHETHER JOAN COULD HOLD UP. *The Senator: My Ten Years with Ted Kennedy,* op. cit.
378 IT COULD BE DANGEROUS. Ibid.
378 JOAN COULDN'T STAND IT. Interview, source.

CHAPTER 74: A PREMONITION

379 I REMEMBER GEORGEANN. Terrien, op. cit.
380 I STILL CAN'T SHAKE. Ibid.
380 NEVER AGAIN. *Washington Post.*
380 THAT DREAM I TOLD. Interview, source.
381 IT WAS THAT DREAM. Terrien, op. cit.
382 TAKE HEART. Correspondence, LBJ Library.
382 IT'S NO FUN. Ibid.
382 I BELIEVE IT WAS. Terrien, op. cit.

CHAPTER 75: KNACKY BABY

383 THE KENNEDYS HAD SHOPPED. *The New York Times,* June 18, 1965.
383 BY SPRING 1967. Ibid., March 1, 1967.
383–84 AT ONE EVENT. *Washington Post,* May 19, 1966.
384 BLACK MAIDS WITH LITTLE. Johnston, op. cit.
384 ETHEL'S SOCIAL LIFE. *Washington Post,* July 12, 1966.
384 WHEN SHE CAME BACK DOWN. Ibid., March 1, 1966.
384 IF I WORE THOSE. *New York World-Telegram,* March 7, 1966.
385 POOR ETHEL HAD TO. Interview, source.
385 WOMEN'S LIB WAS MAKING. Harris, op. cit.
385 AFTER HAVING READ. Executive file, LBJ Library.
386 I FELT IT WAS REALLY. Harris, op. cit

CHAPTER 76: DEATH WISH

387 MY DAD, WHO FOUND. Whiteford, op. cit.
388 THAT TERRIBLE GRIN. Interview, source.

389 THAT LUNATIC ALWAYS HAD. Interview, source.
389 LADY BIRD AND I. Correspondence, LBJ Library.
389 IT WAS QUITE A. Interview, source.
390 WITH INCREDIBLE GRACE. Davis, op. cit.
390 WHILE MY BROTHER GEORGE'S. Jim Skakel, op. cit.
390 A SKINNY GUINEA FLOP. Rushton Skakel, op. cit.
390 I WAS APPREHENSIVE. Bettan Olwaeus Whiteford, op. cit.
390–91 EIGHTEEN MONTHS AFTER. Stipulation Motion and Order, Civil Case #1–68–16, U.S. District Court, District of Idaho, December 23, 1970.
391 DOWN IN THE DEPTHS. Interview, source.

CHAPTER 77: THANKSGIVING RIDE

392 TO BE AROUND KICK. Little Georgeann Dowdle, op. cit.
393 HI, I'M OVER HERE. O'Brien, op. cit.
393 HOPEY WAS OUT. Ibid.
394 IT WAS HORRIBLE. Ibid.
394 HOPEY'S HAND HELD MY FINGER. Ibid.
395 IT WAS JUST SOMETHING. Ibid.
395 THAT'S THE REAL WAY. Ibid.
396 WE WERE NEVER INVITED. Ibid.
396 SHE CALLED ME AT. Little Georgeann Dowdle, op. cit.
397 PAT SKAKEL TRIED TO BE. O'Brien, op. cit.

CHAPTER 78: RECORD BREAKER

398 MY MOTHER SAID IF. *Washington Post,* March 25, 1967.
399 JUST KEEP EACH ONE. Ibid., April 13, 1967.
399 A FORM OF EXHIBITIONISM. Conversation, Marion Schlesinger.
399 SEX WAS NEVER IMPORTANT. Interview, source.
399 THERE WAS A LOT OF. Harris, op. cit.
401 MY ADVICE IS. *The New York Times,* May 8, 1967.
401 WE WERE OUT ON. Tremblay, op. cit.

CHAPTER 79: FINAL MEAL

402 I HAD A FEW DRINKS. Interview, Hilbert Heberling.
403 AFTER ABOUT TEN MINUTES. Ibid.
403 I PUT ONE AND ONE. Ibid.
403 DISTANCED HERSELF AS MUCH. Begley, op. cit.
404 MY SISTER WAS A. Conversation, Lawrence Corroon.
404 ETHEL WOULD NEVER HAVE. Interview, source.
404 RUSHTON SKAKEL EXPRESSED INTEREST. Rushton Skakel, op. cit.
404 BUT ETHEL HAD THIS. Terrien, op. cit.
405 ETHEL KENNEDY DISAPPEARED. *Washington Evening Star,* June 19, 1967.

405 THE INFAMOUS KENNEDY SWIMMING. *Washington Post,* June 19, 1967.

CHAPTER 80: HAT IN THE RING

409 HE HAS LOTS OF. *Washington Post,* March 18, 1968.
410 WITHOUT ANY QUESTION. *Chicago Tribune,* May 22, 1968.
410 THAT SHOWS YOU HOW. *Look,* June 25, 1968.
410 SHE'S A GREAT SUPPORTER. Ibid.
411 THE NOSTALGIC RHETORIC. *Washington Post,* March 17, 1968.
411 CHRIS, THIS IS YOUR. Ibid.
412 THE CROWDS, THE PRESS. Jim Skakel, op. cit.

CHAPTER 81: SAVE THE WHITE HOUSE

412 ETHEL THOUGHT SHE WAS. Interview, source.
412 NOT EVEN THOUGHT. *Women's Wear Daily,* April 17, 1968.
412 WE ALL LOVED HER. Interview, source.
414 THERE ARE ALWAYS PLENTY. *Washington Post,* March 18, 1968.
414 EVERY SPANISH COUPLE. Interview, source.
414 YOU WILL GET THE KIDS UP. Interviews, Bob Galland.
414 TWENTY-FOUR HOURS A DAY. Ibid.
415 SHE WASN'T THE EASIEST. Ibid.
415 YOU'RE TALKING TO YOUNG. Ibid.

CHAPTER 82: MORE BOMBSHELLS

For this and subsequent chapters dealing with Robert F. Kennedy's Presidential campaign and assassination, a valuable source was Jules Witcover's *85 Days: The Last Campaign of Robert Kennedy* (New York: G. P. Putnam's Sons, 1969).
416 LET'S OPEN SOME. *American Journey: The Times of Robert Kennedy,* op. cit.
416 WELL, HE NEVER DESERVED. Jack Newfield, *Robert Kennedy: A Memoir* (New York, E. P. Dutton, 1969).
417 WE EMBRACED. *American Journey,* op. cit.
418 APPRECIATE BOBBY FOR. *Women's Wear Daily,* April 17, 1968.
419 SHE MARCHED DOWN THE AISLE. Interview, Richard Harwood.

CHAPTER 83: "OLD MOMS"

420 ONE OF HER RULES. Galland, op. cit.
420 SHE'S HAD EIGHTEEN. *Washington Post,* April 28, 1968.
420–21 THERE WERE TIMES. Galland, op. cit.
421 IT WAS INCREDIBLE. Ibid.
423 THERE IS NO UPBRINGING. *D. C. Examiner,* May 24, 1968.

423 DAVID WAS CHIDED. Galland, op. cit.
424 IT MAY HAVE BEEN. Ibid.
424 WERE NOT HARD. *Los Angeles Times,* June 4, 1968.

CHAPTER 84: THE JACKIE PROBLEM

425 TOTALLY MISUNDERSTOOD. Peter Evans, *Ari: The Life and Times of Aristotle Onassis* (New York: Summit Books, 1986).
426 MAKING IT TOO. Fred Sparks, *The $20 Million Honeymoon* (New York: Bernard Geis Associates, 1970).
428 I NEVER BOUGHT. Tretick, op. cit.
429 I SAID TO MYSELF. Ibid.

CHAPTER 85: WINNING AND LOSING

429 ETHEL SEEMED TO SUDDENLY. Interview, source.
430 FURTHER INFORMATION WILL. *Cape Cod Standard-Times,* May 10, 1968.
430 WOULD SET BACK FOR. *Washington Post,* May 9, 1968.
430 I WISH THEIR PARENTS. *New York Daily News,* May 22, 1968.
430 BUT WHAT WOULD WE. *Look,* June 25, 1968.
431 WE TOOK OFF FROM. Tremblay, op. cit.

CHAPTER 86: CALIFORNIA SUNSHINE

432 ETHEL WANTS SIX. Galland, op. cit.
433 YOU WON'T BELIEVE IT. *Robert Kennedy: A Memoir,* op. cit.
433 HIS FACE LOOKED LIKE. Ibid.
433 WE HAD A MOTORCADE. Galland, op. cit.
434 WHY DON'T YOU TAKE. Ibid.
435 EVERYTHING'S FINE. Ibid.
435 MUMMY'S SO TIRED. Theodore H. White, *The Making of the President,* 1968 (New York: Atheneum, 1969).
435 AT THE BEVERLY HILLS. Galland, op. cit.
436 SHE AGREED, KISSING EACH. Ibid.

CHAPTER 87: THE LIGHT IS SNUFFED OUT

437 IT WAS IMPOSSIBLE TO. *American Journey,* op. cit.
438 I GOT THE IMPRESSION. *National Enquirer,* October 26, 1976.
438 THE SPEECH WAS OVER. Galland, op. cit.
439 ETHEL WAS SORT OF. Mudd, op. cit.
439 THERE WAS NO DOUBT. Galland, op. cit.
440 HE PROBABLY FOUND HIM. Ibid.
441 ETHEL LOOKED UP AT. *American Journey,* op. cit.
441 HOW IS SENATOR KENNEDY. *Boston Globe,* June 19, 1968.
443 WE GRIEVE AND PRAY. Correspondence, LBJ Library.

444 THERE WERE A COUPLE. Galland, op. cit.
444 I JUST WANT TO MAKE. Ibid.
444 AT HICKORY HILL. *The Kennedys: An American Drama*, op. cit.
445 ETHEL WANTED YOU. Davis, op. cit.
445 THEY DIDN'T APPRECIATE. Interview, Dan Stewart.
445 HE'S DEAD. I SAID 'DEAD?' Ibid.
446 GLENN HAD TOLD ME. Galland, op. cit.
448 IT SEEMED IMPOSSIBLE. *Times to Remember*, op. cit.
448 I HAD TO KEEP MOVING. Ibid.
448 ETHEL WAS THE MOST ADMIRABLE. Ibid.
449 DO YOU KNOW WHAT. *Robert Kennedy and His Times*, op. cit.
450 EVEN THOUGH JIM. Virginia Skakel, op. cit.
450 GINNY, COME DOWN TO. Ibid.
450 JIM HAD HEARD WHAT. Ibid.
450 THE POLICE CAME AND PICKED. Interview, Dr. Blake Watson.
451 I WAS IN BED. Corbin, op. cit.
452 WE HAD PLANS TO. *Washington Post*, June 6, 1968.
452 EVEN THOUGH BOBBY WAS. Davis, op. cit.
453 WE WERE IN INTENSIVE. Watson, op. cit.
453 MYSELF AND ANOTHER DETECTIVE. Stewart, op. cit.

CHAPTER 88: GOING HOME

458 AFTER WE GOT TEN. *American Journey*, op. cit.
458 IF BOBBY HAD BEEN. Interview, source.
459 PHYSICALLY SHE WAS FINE. Watson, op. cit.
459 ETHEL TRIED TO CHEER UP. Vanocur, op. cit.
459 EVERYONE WHO WAS ON. Ibid.
459 I'M SURE I WAS TOLD. Ibid.
459 THAT WAS THE END. *American Journey*, op. cit.
460 NO ONE ASKED ME. Mrs. Norman Paul, op. cit.
460 IT'S OVER. Galland, op. cit.

CHAPTER 89: BACK IN NEW YORK

463 ONCE ETHEL LEFT. Davis, op. cit.
463 SHE LOOKED INCREDIBLY GREAT. Ibid.
463 HEY, KID, HAVE YOU. Ibid.
463 SHE WAS SO STEADY. Ibid.
464 SOMETIMES YOU GO INTO. Watson, op. cit.
464 I'M SO GLAD. *Robert Kennedy and His Times*, op. cit.
464 OUR HEARTS ACHE. LBJ Library.
465 I NEVER HAD ANY. Watson, op. cit.
465 ETHEL SPENT THE EARLY-MORNING. Davis, op. cit.
465 ETHEL ALWAYS WANTED. Ibid.

466 THE BEDROOM IN THAT. Interview, source.
466 THERE ALWAYS WAS A. Interview, source.
466 SHE WAS JUST HORRIBLE. Interview, source.
467 THE DILLONS HAD CAVIAR. Interview, source.
467 SHE WAS TRYING TO GET DRESSED. Interview, source.
468 YOU JUST INSIST. *American Journey,* op. cit.
468 ABSOLUTELY NOT! *National Enquirer,* August 6, 1985.
469 I WON! I WON! *American Journey,* op. cit.
469 OH, IT WALKS. Ibid.
469 I NEVER WANT TO. Interview, source.

CHAPTER 90: THE FUNERAL

470 ETHEL SEEMED TO DAWDLE. Davis, op. cit.
470 THEY'RE NOT GOING ANYWHERE. Ibid.
471 ETHEL LOOKED JUST PERFECT. *American Journey,* op. cit.
471 IF THERE'S ONE THING. Ibid.
473 I REMEMBER THAT. Ibid.
473 SHE DID ME IN. *Washington Evening Star,* June 9, 1968.
473 JOSÉ, WHERE HAVE YOU. *American Journey,* op. cit.
473 HAVE YOU EVER BEEN. *The New York Times,* June 9, 1968.
474 IT WAS A NIGHTMARE. Galland, op. cit.
474–75 YOUNG DAVID, WHO HAD. *The Kennedys: An American Tragedy,* op. cit.
475 I HAD NEVER SEEN. Davis, op. cit.
476 I CAN SEE ETHEL NOW. Interview, source.

CHAPTER 91: LIFE RESUMES

477 SHE NEVER COLLAPSED. Terrien, op. cit.
477 IF SHE'S DOWNBEAT. *Boston Herald,* May 25, 1969.
477 HE WAS EVERYTHING TO. *Time,* April 25, 1969.
478 NO ONE I KNOW. *McCall's,* August 6, 1968.
478 ETHEL WAS NOTHING MORE. Interview, Burton Berinsky.
478 IT'S A CONSTANT PILGRIMAGE. *Redbook,* September 1969.
479 I APPRECIATE YOUR LETTER. LBJ Library.
480 IT WAS A PICNIC. Galland, op. cit.
480 IT WAS VERY DEPRESSING. Corbin, op. cit.
480 WE PRAY TO GOD. *The New York Times,* June 16, 1968.

CHAPTER 92: FIRST SUMMER

An invaluable source of anecdotal information about Ethel Kennedy's relationship with her children in the wake of the assassination was Collier and Horowitz, *The Kennedy's: An American Drama,* noted earlier.

483 WE DIDN'T HAVE ANY. Bill Thompson, interview.
483 SHE UNLOCKED THE DOOR. Ibid.

484 WITH LOTS OF EMPTY. Ibid.
484 AN INCREDIBLE MESS. Ibid.
484 I RAN DOWN. Ibid.
484 ETHEL'S HICKORY HILL. Galland, op. cit.
484 SHE WAS HAGGARD. Ibid.
485 IN THE MOMENTS. LBJ Library.
486 THERE WAS A LOT OF. Galland, op. cit.
486 FALLING TO THE COURT. *Time*, op. cit.
486 ANDY WAS THERE MORE THAN. Galland, op. cit.
487 ETHEL DIDN'T LIKE THE NOSE. Interview, source.

CHAPTER 93: MONEY MATTERS

489 HICKORY HILL WILL ALWAYS. *Washington Post*, August 17, 1968.
489 WHY SHOULD ETHEL GO. *Washington Evening Star*, August 16, 1968.
489 IN APRIL 1967. *Time*, April 25, 1969; *The New York Times*, September 28, 1968.

CHAPTER 94: NUMBER ELEVEN

491 A THANKSGIVING PRESENT. Interview, source.
492 ON THE EVENING OF FRIDAY. *Washington Post*, September 24, 1968.
492 SHE HAD VERY STRONG FAITH. Hennessey, op. cit.
492 SHE WOULD BE SO EXCITED. Ibid.
495 I SAID TO HER. Ibid.
495 TED STAYED. Ibid.
495 I THOUGHT IT WOULD BE. Ibid.
495 I NOW HAVE SIXTEEN. *Redbook*, September 1969.

CHAPTER 95: TWO FACES OF ETHEL

496 ETHEL WENT FROM. Terrien, op. cit.
496–97 SHE BECAME A LITTLE FIERCER. Interview, source.
497 I WOULD LIKE TO SEE HIM. Terrien, op. cit.
497 I GOT IT BECAUSE OF MY COOKING. Interview, source.
499 ETHEL HAS GREATER RESPONSIBILITY. *Times to Remember*, op. cit.
501 WE ALL FELT A LOT. *The Kennedys: An American Drama*, op. cit.
502 SPENT THE FOUR-DAY TRIP DRINKING. Ibid.
502 WHITTAKER THREATENED. Ibid.
502 WE'D SIT IN THE DARKNESS. Ibid.
502 WE DON'T ASK MUCH. *Washington Post*, June 8, 1969.

CHAPTER 96: CHAPPAQUIDDICK SUMMER

An invaluable source of chronological and anecdotal information for this chapter was Leo Damore's *Senatorial Privilege:*

The Chappaquiddick Coverup (New York: Dell, Bantam, Doubleday Publishing Group, Inc., 1988).

505 SHE WAS LIKE ETHEL. *Washington Post,* July 26, 1969.

507 ONE OF BOBBY'S MOST DEDICATED. *Times to Remember,* op. cit.

507 HE WAS SO UNLIKE HIMSELF. Ibid.

507 NOBODY SAID A WORD. *The Kennedys: An American Drama,* op. cit.

507 AT FIRST SHE DIDN'T. Interview, source.

508 IT WAS SUPPOSED TO BE. *Washington Post,* July 23, 1969.

510 ETHEL ALWAYS HAD THE PHILOSOPHY. Interview, source.

511 ETHEL FELT AS IF SHE. Terrien, op. cit.

511 FIRST IT WAS FATHER. Ibid.

511 TED WAS SUPPOSED TO BE. Ibid.

511 ETHEL TOOK A VERY DIM. Interview, source.

CHAPTER 97: LETTING GO

514–15 ALL OF HER LIFE. Interview, source.

515 I HAVE TWIN BUTLERS. Interviews, sources.

515 SHE DIDN'T APPROVE. Gibson, op. cit.

515 MRS. KENNEDY WASN'T SCRIMPING. Interviews, Noelle Fell. (All quotations attributed to Fell in the book are from interviews with the author, unless otherwise specified.)

518 ETHEL KENNEDY WITH ALL HER. *Washington Evening Star,* March 2, 1978.

519 THE HORSES AND THE JUMPS. Interview, source.

519 LEM TOLD ME THEY WERE. Tremblay, op. cit.

520 GERRY EXPLAINED TO ME. Interviews, Mrs. Magruder Dent.

520 I WAS SO SHOOK. Ibid.

520 IT WAS A VERY SAD. Ibid.

521 TWO OF THE KENNEDY. Ibid.

521 THERE WASN'T ANY. Ibid.

521 MRS. DENT, MAY I. Ibid.

522 ETHEL KNEW WHAT DRINKING. Interview, source.

522 POTENTIALLY LETHAL COMBINATION. Barbara Gibson, *The Kennedys* (New York: Thunders Mouth Press, 1993).

522 SHE SO FEARED BEING. Ibid.

523 I HAD A LITTLE BLUEY. Interview, source.

CHAPTER 98: LITTLE BROWN BAG

523 MERCHANTS BEGAN CALLING. Burke, op. cit.

524 IT GOT SO BAD. *Parade,* March 2, 1980; *USA Today,* December 30, 1986.

524 AT ONE POINT, ETHEL WANGLED. *Life of the Party,* op. cit.

525 ETHEL NEVER REALLY GAVE STEVE. Burke, op. cit.
525 FOR A WHILE IT SEEMED. Interview, source.
525 SEVERAL THOUSAND DOLLARS. Interview, Don Burns.
525 NOBODY HAD PUT OIL IN IT. Interview, Bobby Jones.
526 FORCED TO WAIT SIX MONTHS. Interview, source.
526 IT GOT SO I DIDN'T. Interview, source.
526 I WONDER WHEN WE'LL. Interview, source.
526 ON APPROVAL, HAVE A PARTY. Interview, Michael Lehman.
526 I'M MRS. ROBERT F. Interview, source.
526–27 SHE FELT VICTORIOUS. Fell, op. cit.
527 SHE BELIEVED THAT THE NAME. Interview, source.
527 WE'D GO TO A LOCAL. Burke, op. cit.
527 SHE THOUGHT I WAS SENDING. *A Woman Named Jackie,* op. cit.
527 THE WORST THING ETHEL. Gibson, op. cit.
528 SHE LOOKED QUITE NICE. Interviews, Jane Abraham. (All quotations in this book attributed to Jane Abraham are from interviews with the author.)
530 SHE ALWAYS EXPECTED. Interview, source.
531 OTHER INCIDENTS. Interviews, Diana McClellan, Steve Hammons.
531 SHE DEFINITELY HAD HER. Interview, Alice Dineen.
531 ONE DISTURBING INCIDENT. Interview, source.
532 WHEN BLOOMINGDALE'S EMPLOYEES. *Washington Post,* November 16, 1979.
532 SHE WOULD GO INTO. Interview, source.
533 SHE'D GO TO THE STORES. Gibson, op. cit.
534 ETHEL HAD RETURNED. Fell, op. cit.

CHAPTER 99: ETHEL AND ANDY

535 WE HINTED TO HER. Interview, source.
535 I WAS PLAYING GOLF. Interview, Pierre Cossette.
536 YOU SHOULD PAY ATTENTION. Ibid.
536 BRIEF, RATHER INTENSE. *The Peter Lawford Story,* op. cit.
536–37 PETER WAS DEFINITE. Interviews, Patricia Seaton Lawford.
537 THE CLOSENESS OF THE RELATIONSHIP. Maxine Cheshire, *Ladies Home Journal,* October 1971.
537 THIS IS WHAT YOU GET. Ibid.
537 THAT'S OKAY. Ibid.
537 IT'S THE SORT OF THING. Ibid.
537 WE COULD TALK. Ibid.
538 CLAUDINE HAD COME. *Who's Who in America, 1974–75.*
538 ANDY OFFERED THE KIND. Interview, source.

539 IF ANDY AND ETHEL. *Ladies Home Journal,* op. cit.
540 THE LAKES REGION TRADER. *Washington Post,* August 1, 1971.
540 TELLING PALS THAT HE BELIEVES. *Parade,* July 4, 1971.
540 WHAT IN THE NAME OF GOD. *Washington Post,* May 16, 1971.
541 CARY GRANT LIFTS THE LID. Ibid., June 6, 1971.
541 SHE THOUGHT IT WAS ALL. Terrien, op. cit.
541 ANDY AND I SEE SO MUCH. *Ladies Home Journal,* op. cit.
541 HE WAS ALWAYS QUITE AN. Interview, source.
542 ONE DAY IN THE MIDST. Cossette, op. cit.
543 SHE HAD ENORMOUS. Ibid.
543 OH, JOHN RAITT. Ibid.
544 WE USED TO HANG OUT. Ibid.

CHAPTER 100: DATING GAME

545 STOLEN ROGERS AWAY. Interviews, sources.
545–46 I SUPPOSE THE REASON ANN. Interviews, Coates Redmon.
546 WARREN WAS ATTRACTIVE. Interview, source.
546 EIGHTEEN MONTHS LATER. *Washington Evening Star,* January 29, 1972.
547 THE MAN TURNED OUT. *Washington Post,* December 18, 1969.
547 I TOOK ONLY ONE LOOK. Frank Gifford and Harry Waters, *The Whole Ten Yards* (New York: Random House, 1993).
548 IF HE WASN'T MARRIED. *Washington Star,* July 1, 1975.
548 MRS. KENNEDY WAS CRAZY ABOUT. Fell, op. cit.
548 SHE SET UP A TABLE. Interview, source.
548 FIRST LADY OF NEW YORK. *Washington Star,* December 21, 1976; *Washington Post,* April 20, 1977; Ibid., March 23, 1977.
548 SHE LIKED TO HEAR. Fell, op. cit.
548–49 ETHEL ARRIVED UNEXPECTEDLY. Gibson, op. cit.
549 MRS. KENNEDY HAD A FIT. Ibid.
549 I JUST THINK WE'VE. *Family Circle,* February 1976.
549 SCARY EMERITUS. *Washingtonian,* April 1992.
550 SHE HAD STARTED WEARING. *Washington Post,* May 13, 1973.
550 THERE WAS AN OLD LADY. Ibid., April 11, 1972.
550 PADDED BRAS. Fell, op. cit.
550 HER ARMS AND LEGS. Ibid.
550 YOU KNOW WHAT'LL HAPPEN. *Family Circle,* op. cit.
550 WHENEVER I SEE SOMEONE. *Washingtonian,* June 1983.
551 NO, I'M ETHEL. *Boston Globe,* July 4, 1974.
551 WE'D BE IN A CAR. Interview, source.

551 WE NICKNAMED HER. Jim Skakel, op. cit.
551 LIFE-SIZE PHOTOS. Fell, op. cit.
551 THERE WERE PICTURES. Howar, op. cit.
552 THE GHOST OF BOBBY. Interview, source.
552 THE WHOLE SKAKEL. Terrien, op. cit.

CHAPTER 101: ANGER AND FURY

552 DON'T WORRY, I CAN. Interview, source.
553 I'VE GOT ANOTHER. Interviews, Ruth Darmstadter.
553 COME ON UP. Ibid.
553 WELL? SHE ASKED. Ibid.
554 THE SECRETARY MERELY SHRUGGED. Ibid.
555 VISITING HICKORY HILL. Patricia Seaton Lawford, op. cit.
556 I NEVER HEARD HER USE. Fell, op. cit.
556 WHEN MRS. KENNEDY ASKED. Ibid.
557 IN NEARLY FIVE YEARS. *Boston Globe,* September 11, 1976.
557 SHE SAID SHE WASN'T. Fell, op. cit.
558 IT SEEMED TO HER THAT. Gibson, op. cit.
558 ETHEL ROUTINELY HAD. Interviews, sources.
558 I DON'T CARE WHAT YOUR METER. Fell, op. cit.
559 REALLY HAULED OFF. Ibid.
560 I COULD JUST SEE MYSELF. Darmstadter, op. cit.
560 YOU KNOW WHAT MOMMY. Ibid.
560 MRS. KENNEDY HAS FORGOTTEN. Ibid.
561 DON'T WORRY ABOUT IT. Ibid.

CHAPTER 102: STOMACH PAINS

562 STAY OUT OF ETHEL'S WAY. Darmstadter, op. cit.
562 MAGNETIC, STRONG, LOVABLE. Fell, op. cit.
562 WHEN YOU GO OUT TO. Redmon, op. cit.
563 THROW-UP DAY. Ibid.
564 WHAT THE HELL. Ibid.
564 ETHEL STORMED IN. Ibid.
564 WALKED INTO A WALL. Ibid.
565 SHE CAN BE VIOLENT. Ibid.
565 TOSSED ALL OF THE. Ibid.
566 WE HAD JUST COME. Fell, op. cit.
567 ETHEL'S LIFE WAS WONDERFUL. Interview, source.

CHAPTER 103: HORROR HILL

567 OUR TREASURE. Warren Rogers, *When I Think of Bobby* (New York: HarperCollins, 1993).
567 IF IT WASN'T. Ibid.
568 MAKE SURE THIS DOESN'T. Fell, op. cit.

568 EVERYONE WHO WONDERED. *When I Think of Bobby*, op. cit.
569 SHE HAD FELT THE SAME. Interviews, sources.
569 THE THING I MISS MOST. Fell, op. cit.
569 YOU KNOW THE REASON. Ibid.
569 ENA REALLY CALLED. Burke, op. cit.
570 I'M FED UP WITH HER. Fell, op. cit.
570 THERE WAS A PERIOD. Burke, op. cit.
571 I REMEMBER SENDING. Interview, source.
571 PAUL NASS, A YOUNG CHEF. *Washington Post*, October 12, 1979.
572 THERE WAS EVEN POOP. Interview, source.
573 THEY TRIED TO FEED IT. Fell, op. cit.
573 I REFUSE TO USE HERS. Ibid.
574 ONE OF THE MEN. Gibson, op. cit.
575 AT ONE EVENT AT. *Washington Post*, November 30, 1971.
575 DID MEET AND EXCHANGE. Ibid., December 2, 1971.
575 THEY WERE SAYING WHAT A MESS. Burke, op. cit.

CHAPTER 104: BAD BOYS

576 ETHEL HAD A KNACK. Lawford, op. cit.
577 I NEVER KNEW ETHEL. Interview, Joey Brode.
577 THEY GROW IT ALL THE TIME. Burke, op. cit.
578 IT WASN'T THE WORST MOMENT. *Boston Globe*, February 24, 1972.
578 AT THE HOME OF DIANE. *The Kennedys: An American Drama*, op. cit.
579 YOU REALIZE THE MISTRUST. *The New York Times*, February 14, 1973.
580 I WOULD HOPE YOU. *New York Daily News*, August 21, 1973.
580 IT WAS ALL MY FAULT. Ibid.
581 FOR ETHEL IT WAS ALL. Terrien, op. cit.
582 WE'D TALK AND HE'D SAY. *The Kennedys: An American Drama*, op. cit.

CHAPTER 105: ZANY PLAYGIRL

582 MY MOTHER'S NOT INVOLVED. Interviews, Nancie Alexander.
583 PLEASE HELP ME. *The New York Times*, March 28, 1972.
583 ETHEL FAKED THE INJURY. Interview, source.
583 WHEN SHE WAS NABBED. *Washington Post*, April 8, 1975.
584 HONESTLY, ETHEL. *Washington Star-News*, November 28, 1975.
585 ONE OF HER VICTIMS. Ibid., October 16, 1972.
585 AFTER PROMINENT WASHINGTON. *Washington Post*, November 1, 1973.

585 GEORGE PLIMPTON. Ibid., July 15, 1975.
585 NO, NO, NO. Interviews, Luciano Klosterman.
586 THIS IS ABSOLUTE INSANITY. Cossette, op. cit.

CHAPTER 106: MARTHA MOXLEY

587 SOMETHING HAD HAPPENED. Fell, op. cit.
587 DETAILS OF THE murder, the investigation, and the aftermath come from numerous author interviews, press reports, and an investigative article published in 1991 by the *Greenwich Time*.
589 WE LOVED GREENWICH. Interviews, Dorthy Moxley. (All subsequent quotes from Dorthy Moxley are from interviews with author.)
591 MARTHA WAS VERY. Joe Romanello, interview.
595 I FOUND MARTHA. Dorthy Moxley, op. cit.
595 WHY DON'T I GO. Ibid.
595 IT'S MARTHA, SHE'S DEAD. Ibid.
596 MY SISTER. Ibid.
596 MY WIFE TOLD ETHIE. Terrien, op. cit.
598 VERY DISORGANIZED. *Greenwich Time,* op. cit.
598–99 SINCE THE GOLF CLUB. Ibid.
599 RUSHTON SKAKEL WAS TOTALLY. Ibid.
599 WE WERE AFRAID. Ibid.
599 MAYBE IT WAS THE SKAKEL. Ibid.
600 JUST DON'T GET MY NAME. Jim Skakel, op. cit.
600 IN 1975 WE WERE. Romanello, op. cit.
600 WE WERE JUST VERY. Ibid.
603 GOLF CLUBS WERE LEFT. *The New York Times,* June 24, 1977.
603 SET THE FAMILY'S MIND. Moxley, op. cit.
604 MY SISTER AND. Interview, Buck Jolgren.
604 THIS, AFTER CAREFUL. *Greenwich Time,* op. cit.
604 RUMOR HAD IT. Interview, source.
605 I NEVER UNDERSTOOD. *Greenwich Time,* June 2, 1991.
605 TOO HOT AND HEAVY. *The New York Times,* op. cit.
606 NO NEED TO PROVE. Ibid.
606 IT JUST DIDN'T SEEM LIKE. Ibid.
606 TED KNEW ABOUT. Burke, op. cit.
607 TOMMY INTRODUCED US. Interview, Harvey Hamment.
608 ETHEL AND EUNICE ARE FREQUENTLY. Mim Udovitch, *Village Voice,* December 24, 1991.
609 WE HAD FRIENDS CALLING. Jolgren, op. cit.
609 HERE'S ANOTHER ONE. O'Brien, op. cit.
611 I WANT TO KNOW. *Greenwich Time,* July 7, 1991.
611 YOU SHOULD REALLY TALK. Moxley, op. cit.
611 YOU CAN'T. Ibid.
612 IT WAS CREATING A GREAT DEAL. Jim Murphy, interview.

CHAPTER 107: MORE SCANDAL

614 SHE ANGRILY DENOUNCED. Interviews, sources.
614 MIKE WOULDN'T DO EXNER. Howard, op. cit.
615 WHEN SHE SAW IT. *Chicago Tribune,* January 24, 1977.
615 DISTORTED HISTORY, AND LACKED. *New York Daily News,* April 18, 1983.
615 SHE WAS IN THERE TOOTH AND NAIL. Interview, source.

CHAPTER 108: DAVID'S DRUGS

616 ETHEL HAD VOTED REPUBLICAN. *Miami Herald,* January 24, 1977.
616 DEAR, MR. PRESIDENT. Correspondence, Jimmy Carter Library, Atlanta.
617 IT IS TOO EARLY. Ibid.
617 I KNOW YOU WILL. Ibid.
617 IT'S LIKE A BIG. Memo, Jimmy Carter Library.
618 SOME PRETTY QUICK ACTION. *Washington Post,* May 21, 1978.
618 I UNDERSTAND OUR NEIGHBOR. Ibid.
618 DAVID WAS MRS. KENNEDY'S. Fell, op. cit.
619 OH, MY GOD. Ibid.
620 THE WINDOW WAS BROKEN. Ibid.
620 I TOLD HER WHAT HAD HAPPENED. Ibid.
621 THERE'S NOTHING I CAN DO. Ibid.
622 MY UNCLE'S AS BAD AS I AM. Burke, op. cit.
623 RACHEL WANTED TO GET. *The Kennedys: An American Drama,* op. cit.
623 WE SMOKED JOINTS. *People,* September 24, 1979.
623 I'M A STONED-OUT JUNKIE. *People,* op. cit.
623 OUR OFFICE ISSUED. *The Senator: My Ten Years with Ted Kennedy,* op. cit.

CHAPTER 109: BOBBY'S DRUGS

624 A HEAVY DRUG USER. *The Kennedys: An American Drama,* op. cit.
625 EVERYONE KNEW LEM WAS QUEER. Terrien, op. cit.
626 ONE MORNING. Fell, op. cit.
626 IF YOU WANT TO COMPETE. *People,* April 12, 1982.
627 SHE'S INTERESTED IN KEEPING. *The New York Times,* April 5, 1982.
627 HE ALSO LOST HIS. Ibid., March 18, 1983.

CHAPTER 110: DAVID REDUX

630 I AGREED TO TAKE IT. Alexander, op. cit.
630 I TRIED TO MINISTER TO HIM. Ibid.
630 SHE'S OBLIVIOUS. Ibid.

630 I AM WHAT I AM. Ibid.
631 SHE'S JUST DOING HER. Ibid.
631 BECAUSE HE COULDN'T GET. Ibid.
631 AS FAR AS THE PROBLEMS. *Orlando* (Florida) *Sun-Sentinal,* April 26, 1984.
633 ABSOLUTELY INACCURATE. *The New York Times,* April 27, 1984.
633 I MET HOROWITZ. Interview, Paula Sculley.
633 I SAW HIM WHEN HE LEFT. Ibid.
634 LIKE A TRANSIENT. *Miami Herald,* April 26, 1984.
634 WAS IN BAD SHAPE. *Palm Beach Daily News,* May 19, 1985.
635 HE SOUNDED PERFECTLY. Sculley, op. cit.
635 MRS. KENNEDY SAID NO ONE. *Palm Beach Post,* April 26, 1984.
635 I HAD AN OMINOUS. *Palm Beach Daily News,* April 27, 1984.
635 SHE MADE A MOTHER'S SOUND. *Time,* May 7, 1984.
636 I DIDN'T KNOW HE WAS. Sculley, op. cit.
636 INVESTIGATORS WOULD ONCE AGAIN. *Palm Beach Daily News,* May 20, 1985.
637 ETHEL, I JUST WANTED YOU. Virginia Skakel, op. cit.

CHAPTER 111: END OF A DYNASTY

638 MY GRANDMOTHER ALWAYS. Little Georgeann Dowdle, op. cit.
639 SHE WAS LIVING IN THAT. Medaille, op. cit.
639 SHE RAN THE WORLD. Little Georgeann Dowdle, op. cit.
639 DURING ONE OF OUR. Medaille, op. cit.
639–40 IT'S WONDERFUL THAT YOU'RE. Virginia Skakel, op. cit.
640 WE DECIDED WE WEREN'T. Little Georgeann Dowdle, op. cit.
641 CHILDREN WITHOUT PERKS. Ibid.
641 MY MOTHER ACTUALLY DIED. Ibid.
642 EVERYTHING'S OKAY. Ibid.
642 TO THE GIRLS. Jim Skakel, op. cit.
643 THERE JUST WASN'T A LOT. Gramm, op. cit.
643 THE WORD WAS THAT. Little Georgeann Dowdle, op. cit.
644 DRINK FOR ANOTHER. Interview, source.
644 ETHEL WAS AT THE FUNERAL. Little Georgeann Dowdle, op. cit.

CHAPTER 112: UNION LABEL

645 DRESSED AS CLEOPATRA. *New York Daily News,* February 24, 1988.
645 SHE GALLOPED INTO TED'S. Interview, source.
645 ETHEL AIR. *New York Post,* April 18, 1988.

646 I'D RATHER HAVE ANOTHER BABY. *USA Today,* June 7, 1988.
647–48 IN THE MIDDLE OF THE NIGHT. Interview, Sabina Parks.
648 I THOUGHT IT WOULD BE EXCITING. Ibid.
648 MY FIRST IMPRESSION WAS. Ibid.
649 ALMOST TWENTY THOUSAND DOLLARS. Ibid.
649 WHEN THE BILLS CAME. Ibid.
650 IT WAS SHOCKING TO ME. Ibid.

CHAPTER 113: ETHEL, CLIFF, AND NORM

653 BURROWS HAD TRIED TO GET TED. Interview, Jim Burrows.
653 WE TRY TO USE PEOPLE. Ibid.
654 I CAN'T THINK OF ANYTHING. *Boston Globe,* August 28, 1988.
655 FOR TWO MONTHS. Styron, op. cit.
655 HOW COULD THOSE PEOPLE. Interview, source.
655 SHE WAS DISCREET. Styron, op. cit.
656 MY WONDERFUL MOTHER. Interview, source.
657 FREQUENTING DUBLIN'S TRENDY. *The New York Observer,* February 21, 1994.
659 PAUL'S ONE OF US NOW. Interview, source.
660 HEART AND SOUL. *Boston Globe,* July 28, 1993.
660 ALL I REMEMBER IS SHE. Ibid.
660 WHEN ETHEL FOUND OUT. Interview, source.
660 WE WERE BOTH COMING OFF. *Boston Globe,* op. cit.
661 CONTINUE TO DEFEND. *Time,* September 6, 1993.
661 TRY TO ACHIEVE A BALANCE. *Boston Globe,* op. cit.
661 KATHLEEN'S MIDDLE NAME. Interview, source.
662 ETHEL JUST DIDN'T KNOW. Interview, source.

Index